The way the objects and ingredients of our existence in the universe—the "everyday things" that surround us—are mixed and matched in our personal environment can create great beauty and joy in our lives or great dissonance and displeasure. It's really up to us.

Using the best of the ancient psychic and metaphysical tools at our disposal, we can know a tremendous amount about the power of everyday things as they relate to us as individuals. If we can exercise some amount of control over these things—specifically what they are and where they are in the physical context of our lives—that can help turn the tide for us from dissonance to beauty and displeasure to joy, shouldn't we do it?

This book provides three distinct lenses through which we may experience our sense of individual union with the material world around us. The mysterious and beautiful sciences of astrology, numerology, and the kabbala bring the vastness of our universe into our individual awareness. They are like three windows each looking at the same point in the universe—your birth date—each from a unique perspective. Study your numbers and birth dates and those of your loved ones and look around you—your eyes will widen and your hearts will open to the wonder of the simple, powerful associations before you. These associations—colors, shapes, textures, images, herbs, essences, sounds, planets, and more—provide insight and inspiration to surround ourselves with the material objects favorable to our spiritual harmony. Over time, it will become natural to use the power of everyday things to psychically enhance our existence here on earth.

—from the Introduction

The Hidden Power of Everyday Things

A COMPLETE PERSONOLOGY GUIDE TO YOUR LIFESTYLE FOR EACH DAY OF THE YEAR

Julie Gillentine, Alan Oken,
Jonathan Sharp, and Constance Stellas

WITH AN INTRODUCTION BY ALAN OKEN

POCKET BOOKS

New York   London   Toronto   Sydney   Singapore

An *Original* Publication of POCKET BOOKS

 POCKET BOOKS, a division of Simon & Schuster, Inc.
1230 Avenue of the Americas, New York, NY 10020

ISBN: 0-671-03620-3

First Pocket Books trade paperback printing November 2000

10 9 8 7 6 5 4 3 2 1

POCKET and colophon are registered trademarks of Simon & Schuster, Inc.

Book design by Helene Berinsky
Cover design by Tom McKeveny

Printed in the U.S.A.

C/K/✗

Acknowledgments

Alan Oken: I am lovingly indebted to my two grandsons, Tyler Daniel Oken and Connor David Oken, whose smiles of subtle wisdom encourage me in my life and work.

Julie Gillentine: I wish to express my deep appreciation to the stargazers and lore masters of antiquity, for keeping the flame of wisdom alight through ages of darkness and ignorance so those of us who seek will find; my admiration to Alan Oken for always holding to the highest standard of spiritual and professional astrology; my thanks to Philip Sedgwick for his pioneering work in deep space astrology; my special gratitude to my husband, Buz, and my family for believing in me.

Jonathan Sharp: My deep thanks to Caroline and Victoria Sharp for their support and patience and to Fr. A.G. who showed me the way.

Constance Stellas: I thank my astrologer and teacher, Leor Warner, for all his help, and my husband, Frank Guido, for all his love.

✳

In addition, we gratefully acknowledge the efforts of editor Ellen Mendlow and the amazing Kip Hakala, who know a thing or two about keeping a really big book moving. And thanks to Emily Bestler, who loves the magic of things as much as we do.

Contents

The
Hidden Power
of
Everyday Things

Introduction

Each individual life and the greater cosmic whole in which we live are intimately related. Every object in our universe is also part of that rhythmic, cosmic whole. We are all made of the same stuff, and each individual object we encounter or create on earth contains ingredients from that original universal source. The way these objects and the ingredients of our existence in the universe—the "things" that surround us—are mixed and matched in our environment can create great beauty and joy in our lives, or great dissonance and displeasure. It's really up to you.

Using the best of the ancient psychic and metaphysical tools at our disposal, we can know a tremendous amount about the power of things as they relate to us as individuals. If having some amount of control over these things—specifically, what they are and where they are in the physical context of our lives—can help turn the tides for us from dissonance to beauty and displeasure to joy, then shouldn't we do it?

The objects we surround ourselves with, if chosen to resonate with our particular planets, numbers, and stars, can enhance our lives and give us greater spiritual harmony. When a person surrounds himself or herself with objects, colors, minerals, or shapes that "speak" to him, it can bring a feeling of ease and comfort, even confidence. Ease and comfort in turn create a positive outlook, and a positive outlook naturally increases the joy of living and furthers creative solutions to everyday problems.

This book provides three distinct lenses through which we may experience our sense of individual union with the material world around us. The mysterious and beautiful sciences of astrology, numerology, and the kabbala bring the vastness of our universe into our individual awareness. They are like three windows looking at the same point in the universe—your birth date—but each from a unique perspective. Study your numbers and birth date and those of your loved ones and look around you—your eyes will widen and your hearts will open to the wonder of the simple, powerful associations before you. These associations—colors, shapes, textures, images, herbs, essences, sounds, planets, and more—provide insight and inspiration to surround ourselves with the material objects favorable to our spiritual harmony. Over time, it will become natural to seek to use the power of everyday things to psychically enhance our existence here on earth.

Astrology, numerology, and kabbala are all abstract systems of thought that arose from man's basic urge to succeed and flourish in an uncertain world. This book translates knowledge from what are essentially spiritual disciplines into material, everyday objects such as colors, minerals, shapes, or sounds. We have applied these disciplines to help you determine those everyday things that most resonate with you. The correspondences are based on lore, tradition, planetary relationships, and numerological and symbolic values compiled over the centuries and updated to encompass what we see around us today.

For example, everybody needs a bed or place to sleep but every individual will signify a preference for the kind of bed or the materials that the bedstead is made from. Mars rules metals. It would be logical to make the connection that Aries, a sign ruled by Mars, would prefer a wrought iron or brass bed, rather than a cherry wood bed. If you are not an Aries but find that you love your antique brass bed frame, this is not to say you won't have a perfectly good night's sleep in your metal bed. This is to say, however, that sleeping in a bed made of a material with which you have a stronger association may optimize your experience. Don't go discarding all the objects you own that are not in perfect sync

for you. But do be sensitive to the ways in which all of the objects that surround you affect you in the aggregate, and which could be working for you instead of against you or merely not at all. Be conscious of what you learn here as you work your way from day to day, editing your environment. You'll find you are not likely to do the overdramatic thing and, say, toss that brass bed out by the curb, but you may become more purposeful as all kinds of things come and go in your material world. And you certainly will become more purposeful as you share with others—for instance, if you knew that mirrors would be a source of strength and inspiration to someone you love, wouldn't you be sure there were mirrors aplenty?

Being aware of the associations for your sign, your numerology, and kabbala will bring insight and the accompanying growth and knowledge that can change your life. What you take from here may be just the beginning of an exploration of how everyday things work to focus, enhance, and empower our lives. Happy searching!

Astrology~The Cosmic Science

Astrology is based on the Law of Correspondences, which states, "As above, so below." As it is written in the heavens, so life manifests on earth. It also implies "as within so without," which can mean surrounding the self with those things that resonate within. After many thousands of years of observing both celestial movements and terrestrial events, astrologers have developed a system allowing them to penetrate the complex patterns of human psychology and behavior. Just as planetary cycles are astronomically predictable, so too are the directions of human activity.

Though a complex study to master, astrology is accessible to everyone on some level, as astrology's symbolic language is representative of the familiar objects, people, and situations that we encounter in our everyday lives. Each of us can look into ourselves and find that romantic Venusian aspect of our nature that seeks to magnetize, attract, and merge with the object of our hearts. Most of us know a friend born in April who charges headlong into life like a ram butting heads with a rival. Astrology endeavors to reveal the intimate and holistic relationship existing between the signs of the zodiac and the planets of the solar system with all expressions of life here on earth: mineral, vegetable, animal, and human.

Over time astrology has built up a number of associations based on the planets' rulership of the signs and the four elements: fire, earth, air, and water. Each of the planets had characteristics for the ancients that determined which parts of earthly existence they ruled. The Moon was considered feminine, nocturnal, cold, moist, and phlegmatic. Mercury is described as cold, dry, and changeable. Venus is considered feminine, cold, moist, nocturnal, and fortunate. The Sun is hot, dry, masculine, and fiery but more temperate than Mars. Mars was thought to be nocturnal, hot, dry, choleric, and fiery. Jupiter was considered diurnal, temperately hot, moist, and sanguine. And Saturn, the last planet known to the ancients, was diurnal, cold, dry, and melancholy. Astrologers then observed the natural world and derived rulerships for objects, animals, sounds, colors, etc.

This book considers the associations and rulerships of each sign and translates them into a message, suggestion, and description for each birthday.*

---

*The days given for the sun signs are approximate. Depending on the year, the sun may change signs sometime during the previous day indicated as the beginning of a sign. People born on either the first or last day indicated for a sign are "cuspal" by nature and should therefore read the indications of the previous or next sign respectively, as their personality will definitely have traits of both astrological designations. In general, you may wish to read the day before and the day following your birth date for additional guidance.

Each of the 366 astrological passages found in the body of this book describes personality traits, activities, professions, and everyday things associated with a specific day of the year and updates them for our contemporary world.

In trying to create harmony in your world, you can derive comfort and power from having things near you that resonate with your sign. Alternatively, if your birthday is extremely strong in one element, say fire for example, objects may be included from the earth element to temper and balance you.

There are characteristics associated with the twelve signs that give an inclusive envelope of identity to each of the astrological months and all people born within these perimeters. If you add the information contained in the following pages to what you find under your particular birth date, you will discover more about your individual place in the universe.

Aries the Ram

MARCH 21 TO APRIL 19

Motto: I am, therefore I am.

GENERAL CHARACTERISTICS: With the forthright courage and bravado of his ruling planet, Mars, the god of war, Aries is always preparing for or setting forth into life in search of new worlds to conquer. He is ever seeking to establish himself as a separate and complete individual, one with a unique and original prespective on life. Aries is especially good at inspiring others, for he is highly motivated, incredibly driven, and will not take no for an answer. If rebuffed, he just retreats long enough to marshal his forces and then forges on ahead once more. Aries is definitely a leader, even if he is only leading himself! The Ram is very direct in his approach to life. In fact, many people find him tactless and too confrontational. He has little patience with diplomacy and subtlety and is usually straightforward and direct in dealing with life's challenges.

Aries's greatest weakness is the tendency to be aware only of his own needs, desires, and objectives, assuming that what is correct for him is also right for everyone else. *Compromise* is not a popular word in Aries's vocabulary, which gives him a reputation for being pushy and egocentric. Yet his fiery nature warms and excites other people, giving hope and promise for the possibilities of tomorrow.

FINANCES: As in everything he does, Aries is impulsive, dynamic, courageous (often because he cannot see any possible impediments to his actions), and very self-projective. He is not afraid to take risks, nor is he averse to blazing a new trail or innovating a plan or project. He tends not to save money or invest with long-range profits in mind. His is a very immediate world, and he prefers an exciting high-risk venture that will return a potentially greater rate of return than following a safer (and boring!) course of action. Aries is usually a free and impulsive spender. You will not want to go to him for financial advice, but you certainly would like to be in his company, as he distributes his resources with gusto and pleasure.

RELATIONSHIPS: Aries is a passionate sign, someone who seeks an intensity of relationship that may not be matched by longevity. He is easily aroused and attracted, but his flames tend to burn fiercely only for a short time. The Ram is capable of a long-term commitment only if his partner is able to create situations that constantly stimulate. Although in time Aries can recognize the importance of having his fire properly contained, he cannot abide having those flames put out. Aries certainly lends direction, creativity, adventure, and sexual stimulation to any relationship. Sagittarius, Leo, and Aquarius are complementary signs for the Ram. He is also very charmed by Libra, but this is not the easiest sign for relationship, as the Scales and the Ram are complete opposites. Taurus and Virgo can add a needed dose of practicality and stability to Aries's life, but in order for this relationship to work, people of these signs must also posses some fire of adventure themselves. Capricorn and Cancer are probably the most challenging signs for the Ram.

Taurus the Bull

APRIL 20 TO MAY 20

Motto: I have, therefore I am.

GENERAL CHARACTERISTICS: Taurus is the embodiment of Mother Earth. Her feelings, like the richness of the earth's bounty, lie buried deep within her profound sensitivity. On the surface Taurus may seem tranquil and unmoving, but then, quite suddenly, the earth begins to tremble, and a great quake takes place. The usual placidity and supportive Taurean nature should not be taken for granted. Although she is loyal and steadfast, she should never be deceived or betrayed. The Bull may be slow to erupt, but when she does, you will not want to be in the path of Taurus's powerful charge.

Taurus may suffer from inertia. By nature, she does not like change, especially those changes brought about by others and thus not completely under her control. The Bull is usually exceedingly cautious, a trait that can lead either to an excellent sense of timing or a complete paralysis of action. Taurus is not usually good at initiating something new and original but is very gifted at sustaining and enriching those efforts previously begun by others. When she does have her own projects in mind, she never wavers from the path leading to their successful completion. Taurus must believe in the true value and real worth of something or someone before she gives her support.

FINANCES: Taurus tends to hold on and save her resources. She often believes that money is an end in itself, and may often place too much importance on economic security. So profoundly can she relate to having that not having is a very real source of fear in her life. Taurus loves luxury items, especially when someone else is paying for them! She is very connected to her senses and appreciates all of the finer things that abundant financial resources can bring. Basically, Taurus tends to be very conservative about money and, unlike Aries, tends to invest for the long term rather than take any chances. Real estate and fine art are two very good investment areas for the Bull.

RELATIONSHIPS: It may take quite a while to earn the love of a Taurus. But once this is accomplished, Taurus returns your efforts with loyal devotion, remaining steadfast through the most difficult of circumstances. Taurus is a child of Venus, goddess of love, and is thus very romantic. Once her heart is given, it is often with "forever" in mind. She will constantly ask for proof of affection both through special gifts and an abundance of physical affection. This is one of the most sexual of all the signs, as the Bull is earthy by temperament. Taurus goes well with Virgo, Capricorn, Pisces, and Cancer. She is attracted by Scorpio but finds people of this sign quite challenging. Deep friendships can be made with Aries and Libra. Relationships with Aquarius and Leo definitely have their rough spots.

Gemini the Twins

MAY 21 TO JUNE 21

Motto: I think, therefore I am.

GENERAL CHARACTERISTICS: Known as the "Child of the Zodiac," Gemini displays a youthful vitality, and an avid curiosity about life. This is an airy, communicative sign, one ruled by the fleet-footed messenger of the gods, the planet Mercury. Geminis are therefore always on the move, with a mind to match. These are people who are always alive with ideas and constantly express the need to relate, talk, and connect with others. Gemini tends to be very rational, analyzing life and separating thoughts and ideas into smaller pieces. Although this tendency can make for a highly intelligent, versatile, and quick-minded individual, it also contributes to Gemini's tendency to be dispersed, nervous, and mentally fatigued.

Gemini likes to travel about, hopping here and there in a never ending search for experiences of all kinds. Sometimes, the need for movement becomes more important than the purpose for the journey, and Gemini can lose direction. As Gemini matures, he becomes increasingly more discriminating and he clarifies the focus of his life orientation. Nevertheless, he will try to stay an adolescent as long as possible, for he loves the many faces and the many small adventures he meets along his versatile way.

FINANCES: As a rule, Geminis tend to be generous with their money and like to share. They have no problem adjusting to any set of circumstances, which is good, as their finances tend to fluctuate many times during their lives. While Taurus maintains a steady eye on her financial future and Aries may risk it all on the single throw of the dice, Gemini likes to play with money. In this respect, the more intellectual Gemini types tend to play the stock market and are often quite entrepreneurial, tending to be in several businesses or areas of investment at the same time.

RELATIONSHIPS: Gemini has a wide variety of interests and seeks a partner who is as (or even more!) intellectually stimulating as he or she is sexually attractive. Gemini needs a companion who is mobile, versatile, and nonpossessive. The sign of the Twins has a wide range of friendships and hates the feeling of being restricted and tied down. Gemini's partner has to be very patient, as this is not the most consistent of the zodiacal signs. Relationships with Gemini are very exciting, stimulating, and full of variety but tend to be devoid of true emotional intensity. Gemini gets on very well with Aquarius, Aries, and Libra but has difficulties with the more emotional signs: Scorpio, Pisces, and Cancer. He also does well with Leo and Sagittarius but is challenged by Virgo, Capricorn, and Taurus.

Cancer the Crab

JUNE 22 TO JULY 22

Motto: I feel, therefore I am.

GENERAL CHARACTERISTICS: This is the sign most closely associated with home, family, and especially one's mother. Almost all Cancers have an incredibly strong link to their past. If their earlier stages of life were healthy and strong, then it is likely that the Crab will grow up into an emotionally healthy and stable individual. If there were deep wounds in childhood, and the mother-child relationship was not particularly nurturing, Cancer will grow up into an emotionally needy individual. But once Cancer is healed of such painful experiences, she becomes a wonderful supplier of emotional strength and support for all and everyone.

Cancer is a born collector. She is quite nostalgic and sentimental and never forgets. Not only will she always remember a face, but she can also easily recall the smell of her grandmother's perfume, the taste of her sixteenth birthday cake, or the sound of her father's snoring. Her home is the center of her life, and her family and children are at the very core of her care and concerns. If you are a close friend you are considered a member of the family. But should you hurt or offend Cancer, you are considered the "enemy at the gate."

FINANCES: Cancer will always have a hot meal and a warm bed ready for a loved one. You need some clothes, the use of a car, a home to call your own for a while—no problem! But Cancer tends to hoard and is much more reticent to hand over coins. Cancer is concerned about primary security and is thus likely to be a bit tightfisted with financial resources. She favors conservative mutual funds or real estate as the most comfortable ways to invest. She also may live frugally but can be counted on to have a nest egg put away "just in case."

RELATIONSHIPS: Once Cancer gives her heart, her commitment tends to be total. Relationships are very private, personal, cozy, loving, gentle, and extremely intimate. Cancer has a deep inner world, one filled with incredible compassion and understanding, but to win the key to this secret place, you have to prove your trustworthiness. She may offer this to you easily enough (certainly quicker than either Taurus or Scorpio), but if betrayed, the personal treason will never be completely forgotten. Cancer tends to hold on to things, feelings, and people. As a lover, she is faithful and giving but can be quite irrational and moody. At these times, it is always best to let her alone until these feelings pass. Cancer knows what will make another person happy, just give her the time and space to offer them to you.

Leo the Lion

JULY 23 TO AUGUST 23

Motto: I will, therefore I am.

GENERAL CHARACTERISTICS: Much can be understood about the celestial lion when we know that this is the sign that rules the heart, that part of ourselves in which many of our highest virtues are said to reside. When at his best, Leo is the embodiment of honor, loyalty, faithfulness, and trust. Yet Leo has to take care about developing an exaggerated sense of self-importance. The heart is the center of the circulatory system, and it is also the center of life. Often Leo feels that he is the center of every life situation in which he finds himself. The immature lion cub thus can be quite egocentric and very demanding of attention. But the mature lion is quite different. His heart is boundless in its generosity and not continually fixated on the focus of his own needs and desires.

Leo is the sun's own sign and the sun never exhausts its fuel. The truly benevolent Leo is a person whose sun casts no shadows but burns brightly to bring light, heat, and warmth to everyone and everything around him. Self-centered Leo mistakes his friends for admirers, uses other people's creative energy to advance his own purposes, and gives very little of himself but his projected ego.

FINANCES: Leo likes to spend his money in ways in which it can be seen. He is prone to expensive cars, flashy clothes, jewelry, and home furnishings. If the lion is wealthy, he will tend to invest in art and artifacts. Generous with children and friends (but changeable as to their favorites), Leos tend to pick up checks at restaurants and buy special gifts for their loved ones. Leos need to know that even kings and queens need to save and conserve some of their income.

RELATIONSHIPS: Leo is the personification of the romantic: passionate, poetic, ardent, and adoring. He also expects his love to be returned with the same intensity, fervor, and devotion. All too often, Leo's love can be overwhelming and possessive. At first this can be rather flattering, but after a while, the lion needs to let up a bit so that the other person has a chance to breathe. Leo's pride is always at stake, and no matter how loudly he roars, his ego is delicate and fragile. Leo has to know that he is being appreciated and in return will be incredibly kind and generous. The lion's partner has to be very strong and somewhat independent or else the romance becomes too much of a Leo show. Lions do very well with Aries, Sagittarius, and Libra. They are challenged by Aquarius, Taurus, and Scorpio, can be good friends with Virgo and Pisces, and will also have to work at harmonizing their relationships with Cancer and Capricorn.

Virgo the Virgin

AUGUST 24 TO SEPTEMBER 23

Motto: I serve, therefore I am.

GENERAL CHARACTERISTICS: Virgo is a sign that gives a person many skills to cope successfully with life's challenges. It is almost as if Virgo comes into life with a special "toolbox," one that is filled with many different methods, techniques, and processes. Most Virgos are very hardworking, diligent people. Their job is very important to them, and in fact, they are always in search of a better position in life. Virgo has a very active mind, in fact she may have trouble relaxing in order to fall asleep. Like her Gemini astrological brothers and sisters, she is also ruled by Mercury, the mental planet. Her highly analytical mind gives her a critical attitude about life, and she can be too fault-finding both with herself and others. Virgo can just as easily find a hole in your logic as she can spot one in your sock! Yet the wise Virgo is more aware of abundance rather than lack, opportunity rather than restriction, how to create improvements rather than dissension.

Food, diet, and health are very important to Virgo. They can be extremely fussy about what and how they eat. This is only natural, as Virgo rules the digestive system. Virgo's stomach and intestines are very sensitive, and they should never eat when they are emotionally upset. Wise Virgo is discriminating about everything in life, but the immature Virgin can be among the most wasteful and self-indulgent of people.

FINANCES: Job and money, money and job! These can be the major topics of Virgo's conversation and concern. Although this is the sign that corresponds to harvest time and is thus naturally oriented to material surplus, many Virgos believe that they are closer to the abyss of lack than to the horn of plenty. What follows is an ancient secret truth that if mastered by Virgo will lead her to total financial security—"Energy follows thought." Virgo has to learn how to master her own mind so that she can program her own prosperity and not detract from it.

RELATIONSHIPS: Virgo does well with a partner who has a strong personal agenda and who means to get ahead in life. Virgo gets very irritated with lazy and shiftless people, and no matter how sexually attracted she may be, she will not stay in a relationship for too long with a person with little economic or social potential for success. Virgo can be very particular about the person she is with. She would prefer to go out with friends or even stay home and work on one of her numerous projects than go out with the wrong person. In marriage she tends to be faithful, supportive, and very much a friend. Virgo gets along well with Taurus, Capricorn, Cancer, and Scorpio. She makes good friends with Aries, Libra, Leo, and Aquarius but has her difficulties with Sagittarius, Pisces, and sometimes with Gemini and other Virgos.

Libra the Scales

SEPTEMBER 24 TO OCTOBER 23

Motto: I unite, therefore I am.

GENERAL CHARACTERISTICS: Libra is usually at work trying to balance the oppositional forces he feels all around him. Ruled by Venus, goddess of love, Libra is a sign that definitely searches for peace, quality, and justice in everything he does. Even though his orientation is an equitable one, he often finds himself in conflicting situations that require him to create resolutions. The wise Libra has an instinct for what is fair and is very useful as a mediator, judge, or a true friend arbitrating differences between others.

In his own life, he may find that there is a basic duality. One of his scales is usually tipped toward compromise while the other leans toward getting his own way. Libra has to beware of his tendency to put off or avoid what seems uncomfortable. He can be quite flighty and airy, denying personal responsibilities, preferring instead to create only temporary and superficial solutions. This is a sign that is quite socially aware, and many Libras are dedicated to issues of human rights.

FINANCES: As a sign of the goddess of beauty, Libras love luxuries and good living. Yet as the sign of balance, Libra tries to equalize his urge for the finer things of life with proper saving and economizing. Quite often, however, the scales tip back and forth, and Libra finds himself having to peri-odically tighten his belt due to previous bouts of unbalanced spending! Many Libras seek to invest their money in partnership ventures. This usually works out better for them if the partner is not the same person with whom they are sleeping. Money and love are, often not the best combination for this sign, although there are of course, exceptions. If they invest in the stock market, they will naturally gravitate to a balanced portfolio of stocks, bonds, and funds.

RELATIONSHIPS: This is the sign of unions, partnerships, and marriage. Libra is born with the urge to merge and will be quite romantically inclined at a very early age. He has a very difficult time being alone and may prefer to be in a difficult relationship rather than be in no relationship at all. Libras have the tendency to idealize their lovers, preferring to exaggerate the good and minimize what is difficult. As this is not a balanced attitude, such an orientation often leads to disappointment. When mature, Libras have an instinctive sense of give-and-take and are very fair and just in all their interpersonal contacts. They definitely are inclined to long-lasting relationships. Libras attempt to get along well with people of all signs but are especially good with Leo and Sagittarius.

Scorpio the Scorpion

OCTOBER 24 TO NOVEMBER 22

Motto: I desire, therefore I am.

GENERAL CHARACTERISTICS: Scorpio is the most intense sign of the zodiac and the most mysterious. She is very secretive by nature, a trusted friend, a fearsome enemy. She has the ability to penetrate into the core of another person's being and has piercing eyes for that purpose!

Scorpio is the sign most closely associated with two facets of life that are the most feared and the most fascinating: death and sex. Both of these areas of life are filled with the power of the unknown. They are also both incredibly transformative in nature. The negative Scorpio abuses sex, manipulating personal magnetism to gain power and control over others. The wise Scorpio uses sex as a healing tool, always seeing sexuality within the context of love and never confusing one with the other. Scorpio is the most regenerative of all the signs, for the Scorpion is a person who rises up after every crisis and perfects herself through her struggles of refinement.

FINANCES: Known as the sign of "other people's money," Scorpio does very well as an investment banker, financial counselor, stockbroker, or business agent. Positive Scorpio knows how to make money for other people and earns her own income as a result. She is an expert at recycling and making the most out of the least. Negative Scorpio is a constant borrower and, needless to say, never pays back what is owed. Until Scorpio realizes that true wealth lies in knowing how to circulate resources, she will be quite tightfisted and cheap.

RELATIONSHIPS: Scorpio is very sexually aware. Sometimes the sexual aspect of relationships totally dominates her common sense, and she may place herself in compromising situations because her passions have been stimulated to the point of obsession. Astrologers call Scorpio the sign of frozen fire, meaning that she contains an enormous amount of inner potency just waiting to be released. But ice is melted by the sun, symbol of love, not desire. Many Scorpios find that this frozen fire represents sexual repression as they struggle to release their sexuality in healthy and holistic ways. In general, Scorpios are faithful to the people they love but can be possessive and jealous in relationships. The most compatible signs for the Scorpion are Cancer, Pisces, and Capricorn. Scorpio also tends to get along very well with Virgo but is challenged by Taurus, Leo, Aquarius, and Aries. Relationships are also not the easiest with Gemini and Sagittarius, while contacts with Libra can be very romantic.

Sagittarius the Centaur

NOVEMBER 23 TO DECEMBER 20

Motto: I seek, therefore I am.

GENERAL CHARACTERISTICS: The Sagittarian is the true adventurer of the zodiac. He is highly charged with creative fire, eager for excitement and opportunities to widen his horizons. He is especially fond of travel and has a difficult time standing still. He carries a sign that says:

I SEE MY GOAL. I REACH MY GOAL.
AND THEN I SEEK ANOTHER.

Enterprising and resourceful, Sagittarius is constantly in search of fulfilling his dreams. The greatest challenges to the Centaur are the need to balance the real with the ideal, and to accept the current state of his life's responsibilities so that he may build a solid future.

Sagittarius is known as the "philosopher of the heavens." He is very keen to expand his knowledge and can be a perpetual student. His basic urge is to learn and then to teach what he knows. He gets in trouble when he imagines he has mastered a skill before he has really done so and makes this situation worse by trying to teach what he really does not thoroughly know. He has vision and can be quite prophetic in his way, but he often lacks the patience to perfect himself in the practical world. Nevertheless, this is the luckiest sign in the zodiac, and Sagittarius somehow manages not only to survive but also to prosper.

FINANCES: Ruled by fun-loving and expansive Jupiter, Sagittarius is not known for his ability to stay within the confines of a budget. Not one to care about such details as a price tag or a credit limit, Sagittarius will often spend beyond his means. This can lead to frequent financial difficulties, as his optimistic nature tells him that tomorrow will take care of today. Sometimes he is quite correct, but not always! Sagittarius likes to play games and is attracted to speculation and gambling, sometimes doing quite well at it. But he is a mutable sign, and his financial highs can just as easily become economic lows. He needs to learn from Libra and use balance and temperance in his financial dealings.

RELATIONSHIPS: An adventurer in love as in everything else, Sagittarius is called "the bachelor sign," as he has a very difficult time in committed relationships. He enjoys a sense of personal freedom and needs a partner who gives the Centaur plenty of room to roam. He is usually attracted to the "damsel in distress" and feels gratified when he is in a position in which he can help a person out of their emotional difficulties through loving him. He will stay with a partner who is independent by nature, passionately romantic, and who also possesses the urge to travel and explore life. The most compatible signs for the Centaur are Aries and Leo.

Sagittarius also makes excellent partnerships with Libra and Aquarius. Challenges come especially from Pisces, Gemini, and Virgo. Relationships with Taurus and Cancer are also not the easiest and require some work.

Capricorn the Mountain Goat

DECEMBER 21 TO JANUARY 20

Motto: I build, therefore I am.

GENERAL CHARACTERISTICS: The Mountain Goat is ever climbing upward toward the fulfillment of her goals. Capricorn is the sign of greatest ambition, but it is also the sign that experiences the deepest sense of social responsibility and personal limitation. Her early life may not have been the easiest, as she may have felt that the joys and freedom of childhood were somehow restricted and unavailable to her. It often takes Capricorn quite a while to feel that it is okay to express herself or to find the inner tools that allow such creative and emotional expression the right outlets.

Once she has built the pathway to her own success, however, there is no stopping her. In time Capricorn learns how to build upon her ideas, profit from every venture, and gain in a material or social sense from each of her experiences. She often makes friends of older people or those in superior positions who can be of help to her on her rise to the top of her particular mountain. Although she may have started in life with little stamina and almost no courage, she continually learns from her practical contacts in life what works and what does not. Eventually, she arrives victorious at some hard-won pinnacle, and her later years are often the best.

FINANCES: Financially conservative, Capricorn likes to invest her money in sure things and then watch her assets slowly but steadily grow. She has some very clear ideas about investment strategies and is not one to waste or dissipate resources. As a rule, Capricorns are status conscious and enjoy wearing designer clothes, staying in fine hotels, and eating in the best restaurants. She has worked hard to obtain what she has and is proud of her achievements. Capricorn is not ostentatious, however, preferring the tasteful over the blatantly showy.

RELATIONSHIPS: Capricorn is a very practical sign. Marriage and other forms of committed relationships are usually considered from several perspectives, not just the angle of physical or emotional attraction. Capricorn will definitely favor a person who is less attractive but ambitious and hardworking over someone who is beautiful but lazy. Some Capricorns find no difficulty at all in a relationship that is purely physical, as she can be cool in her heart and head but very passionate in terms of her body. Mountain Goats combine well with Taurus, Virgo, Scorpio, and Pisces. They have the most challenging relationships with Aries, Leo, Gemini, and Sagittarius. They make good friends with Libra and often find themselves involved in very important relationships with Cancer.

Aquarius the Water Bearer

JANUARY 21 TO FEBRUARY 19

Motto: I know, therefore I am.

GENERAL CHARACTERISTICS: This is the most unpredictable sign of the zodiac. Aquarians are called the "heavenly bohemians," as they seem to have their own rules and regulations about their conduct and absolutely reject anyone telling them what to do. Aquarius is a fixed, airy sign, meaning that these are people who are very cerebral by nature and quite firm in their opinions. Even though an Aquarian may completely disagree with what you believe, he is open-minded enough to support your right to believe as you do. But don't try to impose your system or code upon him. Aquarians will resist any attempt to have you change or influence the way they go about leading their lives.

There is a minority of Aquarians who are quite prejudiced, however, keeping only to their own group and rejecting every other system of belief as false and unimportant compared to the "real truth" they know to be right. But the majority of Water Bearers are social experimenters, futuristic defenders of the oppressed and downtrodden. Aquarians tend to be involved with technology and communication, as they hold within themselves an important sense of mission and want to be able to get their message out to as many people as possible.

FINANCES: Aquarius is very impulsive with his use of money. He enjoys spending money on friends and is very open, sometimes to his own detriment, to sharing resources. He tends to invest in the latest in the high-tech sector of the economy. He also invests in people, lending money to those whom he believes have great ideas but only need the backing to make their dream a reality. Aquarius is quite idealistic by nature and not the most discriminating when it comes to the practical use of financial resources. He does have one advantage—he is very much in tune with the changing trends of the times and can therefore do well in advertising, promotion, and public relations.

RELATIONSHIPS: Aquarius is the sign of friendship, and it is absolutely essential for the Water Bearer to feel that he and his lover are the best of friends. This is one sign that makes a point of remaining pals with his ex-spouse, ex-business partner, or ex-lover and cannot understand why other people have a hard time doing this. Perhaps this is easy for the Water Bearer, as he is not a particularly intense sign emotionally. His passion runs more to compassion and he is definitely neither jealous nor possessive by nature. He is a very loyal companion but he does not have to be so intensely personal in his intimate relationships as do Leo or Cancer, for example. Aquarius gets along with everyone but is especially good at relationships with Aries, Gemini, Sagittarius, and Libra. It is a bit tougher for him with Scorpio and Taurus.

Pisces the Fish

FEBRUARY 20 TO MARCH 20

Motto: I understand, therefore I am.

GENERAL CHARACTERISTICS: Pisces is the most compassionate and empathetic of all the signs. She is willing and able to hear other people's troubles, offering endless support and comfort. This same emotional openness can be her greatest challenge. The oceans have wide expanses with no boundaries and limitless depths. At times, the Fish can swim about in an endless sea of emotions with no shore in sight. She can absorb so much emotional energy from her environment that she becomes drained of vitality and has to withdraw into a self-imposed exile and solitude.

Pisces is the most mystical of the signs. She knows that there is an invisible world and often feels burdened by the restrictions and responsibilities of the practical reality in which she lives. Many Pisces try to relieve the pressures of everyday life through self-abusive addictions. These are the Fish who swim downstream. Other Pisces choose a path that brings them consciously into contact with their deep spiritual nature, working for charities and organizations of a distinctly humanitarian orientation. These are the Fish who swim upstream.

FINANCES: Generous and sensual by nature, Pisces loves to indulge in the pleasures of life. They are usually openly giving to their friends and partners, sometimes to the point where they leave little for themselves. Yet this is a very resourceful sign, and Fish can find numerous ways to support and sustain themselves. In fact, one of the names for Pisces is "the sign of hidden resources." Once she spots a treasure, be it in a garage sale, an auction, or the talents of another person, Pisces is very astute at bringing such riches to the surface. Pisces would do even better if she created and developed some sense of firm financial structure and a savings plan, but this might be asking a bit too much from a person who lives in the ocean.

RELATIONSHIPS: A deep-hearted romantic, Pisces is known to sacrifice everything for love. A relationship with Pisces is a deep emotional experience with a person of ever-shifting moods and feelings. At times it is positively amazing how the Fish can know the most subtle facet of our feelings. At other times, Pisces seems to disappear totally from sight, and you wonder who exactly is the person with whom you are sharing your life. The more you try to define the Fish, the more elusive she becomes. Yet this is a kind, thoughtful, and devoted individual who usually does her best to be supportive and nurturing. The Fish swim very comfortably with Cancer and Scorpio and often find happiness with Taurus and Capricorn. The most intense challenges come from Aries, Leo, Virgo, Gemini, Aquarius, and Sagittarius. Libra contacts can be very sweet, romantic, and idealistic.

Numerology
The Hidden Power of Numbers

We can compare numerology to ordinary mathematics in the same way we could compare psychology to physics. Traditionally, applied mathematics, like physics, serves to describe our material world, its nature, dimensions, form, and structure. Numerology and psychology speak to us about things that are less tangible. In the same way that psychology exposes the subtleties of our inner motivations and instincts, numerology reveals the hidden world contained within the power of the simplest of numbers.

The formation of the modern science of numerology has its origins with the ancient Greek scholar Pythagoras. He left home in 581 B.C. at the age sixteen to expand his understanding of life. He sailed forth from his native island of Samos and went to various centers of learning in Phoenicia, Babylon, and Egypt. After several decades of travels and study, he founded his own university on his home island in 545 B.C. Some of his most important work was accomplished in southern Italy, where he created the roots for the numerology to be found in the pages of this book.

The basic "alphabet" used in the science of numbers is very simple. It is composed of the numbers one through nine, the zero, and what we call the "Master Numbers" 11 and 22. Let's examine the deeper meanings of these numbers so that you will be able to see the hidden power in your telephone number, your address, and even your name. To do

this, we will first take a brief look at the significance of the above-mentioned numerological alphabet.

NUMBER ONE: This is the number of beginnings and represents the initial cause of all things. The number one gives impetus, drive, inspiration, and motivation to life. As such, it is the most projective and outgoing of all numerical energies. A strong presence of the number one in a name, telephone number, address, or any other important numbered identification card or document brings a definite degree of individuality and forthrightness.

A strong Number One is very much the individual, one who identifies strongly with who he is and what he does in life. When number one is strongly present in the life of an immature person, we have a highly egocentric individual, one who cares about himself and himself alone. But when the number describes a more emotionally developed man or woman, we have someone who is a pioneer, unafraid to explore what is new and different. This number represents leaders and highly motivated individuals.

NUMBER TWO: This is the number of duality and indicates the relationship between opposites. It points to the urge to balance and relate left and right, light and dark, male and female. Number Two could be said to be the "urge to merge" and carries within itself a strongly magnetic attractiveness. Number Two teaches us the reactions to our actions and brings a sense of social responsibility. It furthers the ability to bring out harmony in our interactions with others and expands our receptivity to other people's feelings.

A strong Number Two tends to be cooperative and sharing. This is an individual who much prefers to do things in pairs than to do things by herself. Number Two people like to contribute to the creation of a beautiful environment and are often musically or artistically inclined. This is a romantic number, one that fosters unions, marriages, and positive social interchanges.

NUMBER THREE: A call to expansion is the energy contained in this number. Three stimulates the development of our intellect, increases our communication skills, and serves to bring us in touch with all kinds of useful information. This is the "education number" and specifically applies to the way we learn to use words, numbers, tools, and mental skills. Computers, pens, calculators, paintbrushes, all come under the vibration of the Number Three.

A strong Number Three is very verbally expressive. This is an individual who likes to move his ideas out into the world through the written and spoken word. A busy and highly active person, the Number Three individual is always eager to learn and to teach what he has acquired along life's journey. A person weak in the Number Three is usually quiet and withdrawn, finding it difficult to communicate what he feels and thinks.

NUMBER FOUR: This is the number of Mother Earth, and represents the four natural elements: fire, earth, air, and water. Number Four indicates the practical use of these substances in the creation of all the forms of everyday life. Number Four is much more concerned with what is permanent than with what is transient. It represents social traditions, roots, and foundations. It is thus a rather conservative number, seeking to build upon what has already been established.

A strong Number Four type of person is con-

cerned with security, money, and finance. This is a hardworking individual, one who prefers a sure thing to taking any risks in the unknown. Dependable, loyal, and trustworthy, the Number Four individual seeks the predictable in life and much prefers long-term relationships to scattered flirtations. In return, the Number Four person offers solid friendship and faithful companionship.

NUMBER FIVE: As this is the middle of the numerals one through nine, Number Five indicates a turning point and an urge for expansion. Five takes the solidity and foundations established through Number Four and seeks to go beyond the boundaries of the status quo. It opens us to new patterns and stimulates the urge to experiment, travel, and open ourselves to additional modes of creative self-expression.

A strong Number Five person is one who avoids entrapment in the routine. The Number Five man or woman is curious, active, and ready to try anything that adds excitement to life. Fives make great adventurers and travelers and exemplify people who never take no for an answer. They are passionate in romance and eager to share their urge to grow with their partners. Future oriented and visionary by nature, they see today as a platform for tomorrow.

NUMBER SIX: This is the most harmonious and artistically creative of all the numbers. It takes all of the expanded experiences of Number Five and seeks to find a place in society where such understandings can be useful to many people. Number Six teaches us to communicate with compassion and wisdom. It is a number connected to a deep sense of social justice and brings into our consciousness the urge to serve others so that all people may lead happier and more fulfilling lives.

A strong Number Six is very connected to the sense of inner harmony. A supportive and caring domestic life is of utmost importance. Number Six people are sensitive to their immediate surroundings and will strive to make their homes as beautiful and peaceful as possible, not only for themselves and their immediate family, but also for anyone who enters their dwelling. They are often found working for community affairs and neighborhood improvement projects.

NUMBER SEVEN: This is traditionally called the "Philosopher's Number," as it is the prime component in so many mystical systems and occult formulas. Astrologers, for example, take the number of the signs of the zodiac (twelve) and multiply it by seven to arrive at the natural human life span of eighty-four years. The Bible tells us of the "Seven Thrones Before God" and the "Seven Days of Creation." It is through the Number Seven that we become introspective and contemplative as we seek to understand the many mysteries of life.

A strong Number Seven needs to spend a lot of time by himself. He is apt to take life more seriously than most other people, ever probing and searching for a deeper meaning of events. Sevens are often found working in laboratories and in those fields of endeavor requiring a great deal of research. These are not socially oriented people. They do not like to go to parties and large gatherings, preferring to read books and have intimate conversations with people they love and admire.

NUMBER EIGHT: This number brings us solidly back to earth. After all, eight is a double four and takes the practical lessons learned through the latter number and seeks to expand them. Eight is traditionally associated with great wealth and material abundance. If you place the numeral eight on its side, you have the symbol for infinity! Eight brings the urge for power and adds prestige and will. It is also a number associated with the many responsibilities that come with wealth and social position.

A strong Number Eight–type of person is good at selling and merchandising their goods and services. This is a person who wants to make it in the material world and through her drive and ambitious nature usually does. Eights like to dress for success and are known to wear the most expensive clothing and drive the best cars they can afford. They have no problem taking on positions of responsibility, much preferring to control than to be controlled.

NUMBER NINE: As this is the last of the prime numbers, Number Nine indicates completion. It is the number of synthesis and as such is filled with a great deal of comprehensive understanding. Nine brings freedom and liberation. Number Nine represents the link we have with the ebbs and flows of life. It thus adds detachment from personal cares and concerns, replacing them instead with an acceptance of life's cycles and patterns.

A strong Number Nine is usually generous, charitable, and patient. Number Nines are often involved with spiritual or religious interests and are concerned with other people's welfare. This is the number of true teachers, healers, and prophets. They carry an inner sense of joy that remains undiminished no matter what kinds of adverse experiences come into their lives. They serve to inspire and uplift others with their faith and kindness.

ZERO: This is not a number but more a representative of the "all and everything" of life. It is symbolic of the expression of the life force found in every facet and form of the world around us. Zero is Spirit and representative of creative potential. When an individual (1) merges with Spirit (0), he or she moves to the next level of life expression (10). Thus Zero brings increased possibilities to all of the numbers. It takes away nothing and adds everything.

The Master Numbers: Eleven and Twenty-two

When either of these two numbers appear in your personal year, name, date of birth, telephone number, or other key numbers, they indicate a great positive potential for increase and awareness. They add creative energy, strength, and expansiveness. Not everyone who finds either an eleven or a twenty-two in their lives will live up to these indications. These numbers indicate potential; it is up to us to actualize their indications into the reality of our lives.

NUMBER ELEVEN: This is the number of illumination and is especially connected to the faculty of intuition. It allows people to perceive immediately the inner meaning of life's events so that we are not fooled by the outer forms of either people or circumstances. People who are strongly affected by Number Eleven will seek to take their expanded vision and communicate it to as many people as possible. These are individuals who seek to change the way we live by bringing sometimes revolutionary ideas into the collective consciousness of society. The urge to act for the greatest good of the greatest number through group effort and mass communication are characteristics of this master number.

NUMBER TWENTY-TWO: Known in numerology as the number of the "Master Builder," Twenty-Two is associated with the urge to create great and encompassing social structures and political laws. This master number is intimately connected to the science of metaphysics, which in its true and accurate practice is the study of the relationship between the visible and the invisible. Twenty-Two combines the communicative and idealistic approach of Eleven and doubles it, thus adding even greater power, potential, and understanding. Just as Eleven could be called the "higher octave of two," Twenty-Two is the higher octave of four. As such, it takes all the material concerns and expertise of Number Four but to a much higher plane of manifestation. People who can live up to the potential of this number when found in their name or birth date are usually great political or spiritual leaders.

Your Personal Year

Throughout this book you will see the hidden power of everyday things associated with your date of birth, based on the cycle of one calendar year. You may also want to explore the power of numbers in two other classic ways: the number of your own "personal year" and the power of the number associated with your name. By understanding the hidden power of your personal year, you can bring to each and every year of your life greater understanding, joy, love, and abundance.

Here are a few simple steps that will allow you to find your personal year:

1. Take the number of your birth date (month and day) and add the current year. Let us say that you were born on May 5 and you wanted to find your personal year for 2001. Reduce all of these factors to numbers:

5 (May) 5 (day) 2001 (year).

2. Add all of these numbers together and get a total:

5+5+2+0+0+1 = 13

3. Unless this number is a Master Number—11 or 22—reduce this number to a single digit:

1+3 = 4

Thus the year 2001 would be a Four Personal Year for you.

Your Personal Year begins at your birthday and ends the day before your birthday on the following year. It does not matter even if you were born on December 31. Calculate your Personal Year as indicated above and the resultant number will be in effect from birthday to birthday.

Now consult the following list of meanings to determine what each year of your life holds as its hidden power for you:

ONE PERSONAL YEAR: This is a year for developing your individuality through expressing who you are in the world. The circumstances in your life at this time will underscore who you are and equally important—*who you are not*. Define your likes and dislikes, refine your talents and gifts, and get involved with new situations that support your growth as an individual.

TWO PERSONAL YEAR: This is a year for developing your personal relationships and creating greater creative cooperative freedom between yourself and others. The circumstances in your life at this time will tend to bring to you the understanding of the more subtle emotional and psychological patterns that condition your connection with those close to you. Advancement is made in the art of give-and-take as well as in all circumstances where sharing is important.

THREE PERSONAL YEAR: This is a year for the development of your mental abilities. The circumstances in your life at this time will support you in your studies, and increase your communication skills. The refinement of your talents and abilities can lead to opportunities for career advancement. You will find that you are spending more time out and about in social situations, meeting new people and experimenting with your life.

FOUR PERSONAL YEAR: This is a year for the development of your practical life interests. You may find that you have to work harder in order to advance yourself economically. This is not a year in which you necessarily encounter lack, but it is one in which your efforts at material gains should pay off. But efforts will have to be made! This can take the form of some deliberate exercise in self-discipline, so pleasure may have to take a backseat to consistency.

FIVE PERSONAL YEAR: This is a year of personal expansiveness. You will be very open to trying something different with all of the skills, talents, and abilities you have been refining and accumulating. This is a time when you tend to break free from routine and open yourself to adventure in all avenues of your life. New facets in existing relationships develop as well as the chance to develop an interesting rapport with someone completely different from your usual choice of companions.

SIX PERSONAL YEAR: This is a year for developing a greater sense of peace and harmony both within yourself and externally in your environment. Family and friends take on a great deal of

importance as you seek to expand your way of loving those close to you. One great advantage to a Six Personal Year is that you have the opportunity to create a more intimate connection between your talents and the creative outlets for these skills.

SEVEN PERSONAL YEAR: This is a year for renewed efforts at personal development. You will find the need to delve more deeply into yourself and explore the more philosophical side to your nature. This increased self-awareness serves to bring a wider comprehension about life in general. Those who are more analytical will follow the path of science and technology, while those of a more spiritual temperament will increase their vision quests through religion or metaphysics.

EIGHT PERSONAL YEAR: This is a year for the development and expansion of personal prosperity. This is a good year to use your various social and business contacts to garner support for your plans and projects. This is also a year in which you can reap the rewards from previous efforts at hard work. Financial challenges can come during an Eight Personal Year from previous laziness and a lack of personal responsibility.

NINE PERSONAL YEAR: This is a year of completion for you. During this time you have the chance to put the final touches on plans and projects and bring a sense of conclusion to your efforts. It is also a time to use your knowledge and experience to aid the people around you. Certain relationships may come to a complete end. Other friendships may see the close of a major stage in mutual growth so that these connections may burst forth fresh and new when your cycle begins again next year.

ELEVEN PERSONAL YEAR: This year has many of the qualities of a Two Personal Year but on a much larger scale. One-on-one relationships give way to group efforts. Your personal need to communicate is such that you wish to reach large numbers of people with your ideas and visions. You may also find that you are drawn to studies and interests that serve to increase your intuition and help you to release personal hang-ups that inhibit your growth.

TWENTY-TWO PERSONAL YEAR: This year has many of the qualities of a Four Personal Year, but your hard work involves group interests and is not done just for personal gain. This is a time in which you can reach a pinnacle of influence in the world around you. Personal responsibilities will grow, and you have to be ready to put a lot of self-interest behind you in order to expand into a new, more impersonal social role.

SUSAN HERMAN
13115 859415 = 5
32
(11) Name Number *11+5=16*
(= 7)

Another useful and interesting expression of numbers can be found by ascertaining the numerological significance of your name. This is done by exchanging the letters in your name for their numerical equivalents. Please take a look at the table below:

NORMA = 25 = (7)
5 69 41

1	2	3	4	5	6	7	8	9
A	B	C	D	E	F	G	H	I
J	K	L	M	N	O	P	Q	R
S	T	U	V	W	X	Y	Z	

whole name
(7)

Once you can determine your Name Number, you will have a profound understanding of the way you energetically express yourself. By changing the way you spell your name, by removing a middle name, or by giving yourself an entirely new name, you can affect the nature and direction of your life. Those of you who have already altered your name through marriage or other forms of personal choice might wish to compare the different numerological meanings in the various names you have used or nicknames you have been called at various stages in your life. The process is a very simple one and just calls for you to use the information in the table above.

1. Write out your entire given name (or any other name you wish to use for this exercise).

Do not include any numbers or abbreviations that may occur after your name, such as Jr., Sr., III, Ph.D., Esq., etc. It is only your full given name at birth that reveals your fundamental, initial life expression.

2. Place the numerological equivalent above each letter in your name. Here is my full name and its numbers:

1 3 1 5   3 8 1 9 3 5 1   6 2 5 5
A L A N   C H A R L E S   O K E N

3. Add the numbers in each of the names and reduce them to a single digit. Do not reduce any name that adds up to either an eleven or a twenty-two.

Alan = 1+3+1+5 = 10 = 1+0 = 1
Charles = 3+8+1+9+3+5+1 = 30 = 3+0 = 3
Oken = 6+2+5+5 = 18 = 1+8 = 9

4. Add these three final numbers and reduce to a single digit, but do not reduce them if they total either eleven or twenty-two.

1+3+9 = 13 = 4

The total Name Number of my full given name is a four.

I have never changed my name but used Alan C. Oken from the time I was a boy until about the age of twenty-one, when I began using Alan Oken and have used just this name ever since. Using the table above, I note that my name with just the middle initial comes out to be a four, while the name I feel most at home with, the name that feels most like "me" and the one I have been using for over thirty years comes out to be a one.

After you have determined your Name Number(s), please read the following descriptions and discover the hidden power and special significance of your name and the names of people close to you:

ONE NAME: You continually project yourself out into your environment in a highly individualistic

ROSE = 9+6+1+5 = 21 = 3
HERMON 32 = 5
959415

LOUIS
3+6+3+9+1 = 23 = 5

and dynamic manner. If there is something that interests you or that you enjoy doing, you do not hesitate to express yourself completely and enthusiastically. You also do not hide your displeasure or irritation if there is something that is going on around you that you do not like. A Number One Name indicates a person who is a natural born leader and one who may be counted upon to inspire and direct others.

The negative facets of a Number One Name are self-centeredness and egocentricity. There is a tendency to be so absorbed with your own thoughts and opinions that you can be close-minded and deaf to other people's concepts and ideas. You can be domineering, pushy, and controlling. Even if you are not trying to bend people to your will, you certainly are on your own track and resist any influence over your life other than your own.

TWO NAME: You have a caring disposition and tend to be sensitive to other people's feelings. You are a natural-born confidant, one who is usually available to listen sympathetically to the cares and needs of your friends and loved ones. Yours is a personality that expresses a "comfort zone," for you are definitely there when things are rough and uncertain. Relationships are important to you, and you are careful to maintain harmony with others in your immediate environment.

Every Name Number type has its opposite and more challenging tendencies. A Number Two Name can indicate a person who is too sensitive for his own good. You can be overly reactive to emotional shifts and changes in your surroundings and find that you have unpredictable mood swings. When taken to the extreme, a Number Two Name can be a person who is codependent, possessive, and excessively needy. Emotional detachment is then seen to be a major life lesson.

THREE NAME: This is a person who is very mentally alert and socially active. A communicative individual by nature, the Number Three Name always has something to say about every situation in life. You have an open and friendly disposition and can strike up a conversation with anyone. You have a list of special interests and are always seeking more information about the things that interest you. You have a fine sense of humor and find it easy to stimulate people's minds as well as their hearts.

The opposite side to a person with a Number Three Name is an interest in so many things that there is a danger of becoming a superficial dilettante. You may also talk too much, taking center stage all too often but without the power or informational content to hold other people's attention. When a Number Three Name individual is out of balance, there is the tendency to be so spaced out and detached that it is very difficult to feel at all connected.

FOUR NAME: You tend to be a very practical person, one who is diligent, honest, sensible, and hardworking. You like to have your life well organized and under control. The immediacy of your material needs is more important than any type of philosophical speculation. As a Number Four Name person, you have your feet on the ground and focus your attention on improving your financial state, keeping your property in good order, and making sure that your loved ones have the security they need for a happy life.

On the other hand, a Number Four Name person can be so overly concerned with money and its potential loss or lack that all the fun and spontaneity is taken out of life. One then tends to be very repressive, worrisome, and fearful of breaking away from routine. There can be so much attention placed on how things look or how to keep life circumstances safe that one becomes old before one's time and a terrible bore.

FIVE NAME: Your name gives you a personality that is refreshingly free of personal repression and denial. You have a need to expand your horizons, love to travel, and are basically a very open and adventurous person. It takes very little to make you smile, as you are optimistic and definitely tend to look on the bright side of life. You see possibilities where other people see limitations, and you see exits where others experience blocks. Courage and joy are two of your most admirable traits.

Two of the least admirable traits in a person with a Number Five Name are wastefulness and self-indulgence. You can be an escapist who would rather go off into a world of fanciful idealism than deal with the immediacy of your personal responsibilities. Some Number Five individuals may have a philosophy about life that many people find so "far-out" that it is difficult to relate to their concepts or lifestyle.

SIX NAME: This is the most artistic of the Name Numbers. There is a great need on the part of Number Six people to bring a sense of aesthetic harmony out into the world. This can be in the fields of music, writing, or art, all of which are natural vehicles for your creative self-expression. Socially responsible and emotionally dependable, the Number Six Name individuals are well respected and liked and admired for their caring, concern, and compassion.

Many Number Six people can use so much energy trying to be of help to others that they completely forget to take care of themselves. They can thus lose sight of the necessary boundaries between people and may easily feel taken advantage of or victimized by their own kindness and emotional vulnerability. They often have to learn the difference between social diplomacy and when the need to say no is required.

SEVEN NAME: This Name Number is associated with someone who is highly analytical, contemplative, and reflective. A Seven Name often describes an individual who is attracted to serious studies. Some Sevens are scientifically oriented, while others pursue psychology and the humanities. Whatever the subject, the interest will be profound and the orientation dedicated to uncovering the truth and hidden meaning of life.

The more negative side of a Number Seven is the tendency toward being a recluse. The mental side of life may be overly stressed while the emotional side is paid scant attention. This makes romantic and sentimental relationships challenging, although intellectual or spiritual friendships are often quite successful. Sometimes the mind is so overactive that the Number Seven person does not hear what other people are saying and is distant and aloof.

EIGHT NAME: Often associated with the most productive and worldly people, the Number Eight Name is very skilled at creating material comfort. You carry a certain sense of status in your personal conduct and certainly like to dress for success. You have an inner self-confidence and are very comfortable with taking on responsibility and assuming control. You get things done and are highly respected for your consistent effort and dependability. When your sympathies are aroused, you can be very charitable and giving.

Some Number Eight people are overly materialistic to the point of greed and selfishness. The more compassionate side to human relationships may thus be overlooked and neglected. Power and social status are very much at the top of this type of Number Eight's list of priorities. It comes as no wonder then that they are mistrusted by others and seen as quite manipulative and controlling.

NINE NAME: This Name Number is closely linked to the more metaphysical and philosophical among us. People look up to such individuals, as they are possessed of clear insight and a perceptive knowing about life. Number Nine individuals have an inner grace and strength that comes from this inclusive understanding, and they are very open to sharing what they see. Highly idealistic, romantic, and poetic, Number Nine people are usually refined and artistic.

You may find that your high idealism can create disappointment when your lofty aspirations are not being fulfilled. You often see more potential in a person or a situation than is practically possible to achieve. The Number Nine person can also feel drained of energy and vitality when their urge to be of help to others is greater than the individual's desire to be helped.

ELEVEN NAME: An intuitively gifted individual, the Number Eleven wants to make sure that his or her ideas are widely known by large numbers of people. Your concerns go beyond the personal considerations of everyday life. You are involved with issues and principles that pertain to the welfare of humanity in general. The Number Eleven Name person is dedicated to the creation of social change and usually has the communicative abilities necessary to achieve such goals.

Number Eleven people in general need a lot of fresh air and healthy food, as their metabolism tends to be quite high. The more negative side of the Number Eleven Name is the tendency toward impracticality. Number Eleven may have difficulty separating the real from the ideal, the visionary from the pragmatic. Sometimes the nervous system is very high-strung, so the individual experiences a consistent sense of anxiety that has no basis in fact or the surrounding circumstances of one's life.

TWENTY-TWO NAME: You are an extremely capable person with an ability to succeed at almost anything you intend to do. Your vision and perceptions are wider and deeper than most others in your environment and you find that in most social situations, you are automatically given the role of leader or advisor. Your general frame of reference is community orientated or even global, and you have a hard time dealing with petty and selfish people. You are charismatic by nature, and you will find that many people want to be close to you.

The fact of having this Master Number as your name signification is not an absolute guarantee of success in the world—but it certainly does help! You have to be careful about not manipulating other people through your abundant vitality and highly directed will. There is the tendency to assume a leading role without having first earned it. Nevertheless, your creative potential is enormous; use it wisely.

SUSAN = 1 + 3 + 1 + 1 + 5 = 11

NORMA = 5 + 6 + 9 + 4 + 1 = 25 = 7

HERMAN = 8 + 5 + 9 + 4 + 1 + 5 = 32 = 5

ROSE — 21 = 3

LOUIS — 23 = 5

DAVID — 22 = 4

4 1 4 9 4

SUSAN HERMAN = 16 = 7

LOUIS HERMAN = 10 = 1

ROSE HERMAN = 8

DAVID HERMAN = 9

The Kabbala
Sacred Pathway to Self-Knowing

The third tool we are using in *The Hidden Power of Everyday Things* is perhaps the most esoteric and mysterious of all: the ancient Hebrew kabbala. Legend has it that the kabbala is descended from revelations given directly to Abraham and Moses. What is known to us is that the oldest of the kabbalistic books, the *Sepher Yetzirah* (*The Book of Formation*), was penned by Rabbi Akiba around the year A.D. 120.

The kabbala is truly an extraordinary study. But perhaps "study" is not quite the right word for this doctrine that presents a cohesive key to unlocking some of the most profound metaphysical mysteries. The kabbala contains a great deal of the body of esoteric Judaic studies. It is therefore an integral part of Judaism. It is also a philosophy or system of thought that transcends religion, for it is open to all who can penetrate its depths, regardless of race, religion, or faith. The kabbala is the foundation upon which the entire science of the tarot is based. It is impossible to be a true reader of the tarot cards without having studied kabbala.

The word *kabbala* itself means "the secret or hidden tradition." It can also be interpreted as "the unwritten law," and according to early Hebrew rabbis, it was given out to humanity so that through its principles and theories, we might be able to learn more about ourselves through the unfolding of universal truth. Kabbala was an oral tradition long before it was written. It was then written in parts long before it was codified into a system revealed in books. The oldest of the three most important kabbalistic texts was written early in the second century A.D. The second of these books, the *Sepher ha Zohar* (*The Book of Splendor*), was written by a disciple of Rabbi Akiba, Simeon ben Joachai, sometime between A.D. 161 and 173. The *Zohar* was further expanded by Moses de Leon, a Spanish Jewish mystic, around the year A.D. 1305. The third of these foundation stones of the kabbala, known to us as *The Apocalypse,* is of an uncertain date and authorship. There are hundreds of more recent texts about the kabbala, including the English-language works of British scholars G. Mathers and Dion Fortune, respectively.

The theories and principles of kabbala and the kabbalists strongly influenced the intricacies of medieval alchemy and Christian esotericism. Its legacy and influence are also intimately interwoven within the fabric of modern hermeticism, Rosicrucianism, and Freemasonry. The kabbala is an essential element of what we call the "Ancient Wisdom Teachings," and as such it is the root of much that is revealed to us through modern numerology and astrology.

The kabbalists divided their sacred studies into five principal parts:

1. *Natural kabbala* is used solely to delve into the mysteries of nature, including the weather.

2. *Analogical kabbala* sets out to prove one of the most important of all esoteric laws, "The Law of Correspondences," which is also written "As Above, So Below." This facet of the kabbala reveals that there is only One Universe and that everything within it is related.

3. *Contemplative kabbala*, which aids the development of the higher mind through exercises that stimulate abstract reasoning and intuition.

4. *Astrological kabbala,* or that branch of this sacred science dedicated solely to astrology, including the spiritual significance of our planet, Earth.

5. *Magical kabbala,* which is dedicated to the study of healing through the use of talismans, amulets, and the invocation of holy words.

The pages of kabbalistic philosophy open to reveal a system that is at the same time amazingly simple and totally obscure. It is almost impossible to describe the kabbala, for to know it, you must enter its sanctuary, its "Holy of Holys." Once inside, you either become totally lost and get out as quickly as you can, or you find yourself surrounded by light and led to a precise path of self-knowing. The kabbala presents a revelation of the deepest truths through an intricate study of words, letters, and numbers. It uses the simplest keys—ten ciphers and twenty-two pathways of energy—to attempt the impossible: the understanding of "the Word made flesh," the nature and structure of Creation. Being dedicated to studying the kabbala also offers the student the promise of somehow, in some ineffable way, being able to touch the fingertip of the Creator. What I can present to you is merely a brief outline of the primary tenets of this ancient doorway. It is to be hoped that a reader may be further inspired to delve deeper into this study and learn more.

The previous, numerological section of this introduction mentioned that twenty-two is considered a "Master Number," containing enormous potency and power. There are also twenty-two cards in the Major Arcana of the tarot. The reason for this attribution is that twenty-two is the number of letters in the Hebrew alphabet, considered by kabbalists to represent the building blocks of the universe. The Hebrew alphabet is extraordinary in that each letter is also a number while at the same time having an intrinsic meaning, as is represented in the following table:

Hebrew	English	Number	Path	Meaning	Significance	Tarot Card
Aleph	A	1	1–2	Ox or Bull	Thinker	Fool
Beth	B, V	2	1–3	House	Foundation	Magician
Gimel	C, G, J	3	1–6	Camel	Travel	High Priestess
Daleth	D	4	2–3	Door	Opportunity	Empress
Heh	E, H	5	2–6	Window	Observer	Emperor
Vau	U, V, W	6	2–4	Nail	Choice	Hierophant
Zayin	Z	7	3–6	Sword	Conflict	Lovers
Cheth	Ch	8	3–5	Fence	Defense	Chariot
Teth	T	9	4–5	Serpent	Revenge	Strength

Hebrew	English	Number	Path	Meaning	Significance	Tarot Card
Yod	I, J, Y	10	4–6	Hand	Energy	Hermit
Kaph	K	20	4–7	Palm of hand	Wise	Wheel of Fortune
Lamed	L	30	5–6	Prod	Driven	Justice
Mem	M	40	5–8	Water	Caring	Hanged Man
Nun	N	50	6–7	Fish	Introspective	Death
Samekh	S	60	6–9	Prop	Supportive	Temperance
Ayin	O, Oo, Ou	70	6–8	Eye	Materialism	Devil
Peh	P, F	80	7–8	Mouth	Social	Tower
Tzaddi	X, Ts	90	7–9	Fishhook	Crafty	Star
Qoph	Q	100	7–10	Back of head	Emotional	Moon
Resh	R	200	8–9	Face	Rational	Sun
Shin	Sh	300	8–10	Tooth	Judgmental	Judgment
Tau	T, Th	400	9–10	End	Honest	Universe

The four elements used in astrology to describe the four primary types of people are also reflected by Hebrew letters with their corresponding numbers as follows:

Element	Letter	Number	Characteristics
Fire	Shin	300	energetic, impulsive, initiatory
Water	Mem	40	emotional, compassionate, caring
Air	Aleph	1	mental, rational, organized
Earth	Tau	400	material, physical, practical

The ancient kabbalists created their astrological system long before the discovery of Uranus, Neptune, and Pluto. They used what was called the "Seven Sacred Planets." The following two tables equate the planets and the signs of the zodiac with letters, numbers, and everyday things:

Planet	Letter	Number	Characteristics and Correspondences
Mercury	Beth	2	highly mobile, changeable, versatile
Moon	Gimel	3	the subconscious, the supernatural, formation
Venus	Daleth	4	love, romance, health issues
Jupiter	Kaph	20	luck, abundance, happiness
Mars	Peh	80	aggressive, determined, physical activity
Sun	Resh	200	creative, protective, paternal
Saturn	Tau	400	repressive, melancholic, traditional

Sign	Letter	Number	Characteristics and Correspondences
Aries	*Heh*	5	initiation, creative thought, radiance
Taurus	*Vau*	6	structure, unity, magnetism
Gemini	*Zayin*	7	division, duality, relativity
Cancer	*Cheth*	8	protection, boundaries, discipline
Leo	*Teth*	9	inner power, spine, brain
Virgo	*Yod*	10	evolution, destiny, solar system
Libra	*Lamed*	30	right action, balance, freedom

Sign	Letter	Number	Characteristics and Correspondences
Scorpio	*Nun*	50	emergence, rebirth, ascension
Sagittarius	*Samekh*	60	conquering materialism, dominion over illusion
Capricorn	*Ayin*	70	greed, avarice, jealousy
Aquarius	*Tzaddi*	90	wisdom, higher knowledge, individualism
Pisces	*Qoph*	100	compassion, intuition, spiritual aspiration

The most well-known feature of all of kabbala is the "Tree of Life," or the "Tree of the Sepheroth," as it is also known.

The Tree of Life is composed of ten globes (sepheroth) that are arranged into the three vertical columns illustrated on page 31. These ten are connected by a series of pathways or channels of energy that number twenty-two. The three columns are called Mercy (on the right), Severity (on the left), and Mildness (center). They are also known respectively as Wisdom (female), Strength (male), and Beauty (perfect union). This is the Hebrew trinity, for it is known throughout all branches of the Ancient Wisdom Teachings that all of manifestation is based on three. The twenty-two paths are the same as the letters and numbers of the Hebrew alphabet and their respective Tarot cards.

The name, number, and physical correspondence of the ten sepheroth are as follows:

Hebrew Name	English Name	Number	Parts of the Physical Body
Kether	the Crown	1	top of the head
Chochmah	wisdom	2	left brain, left side of head
Binah	understanding	3	right brain, right side of head
Chesed	mercy	4	left shoulder, left adrenal
Geburah	severity	5	right shoulder, right adrenal
Tiphareth	beauty	6	sternum, heart
Netzach	victory	7	left hand, arm, and kidney
Hod	glory	8	right hand, arm, and kidney
Yesod	foundation	9	sexual organs
Malkuth	kingdom	10	base of spine, lower body, and feet

When we combine the ten numbers that correspond to the sepheroth and the twenty-two letters of the energetic paths of life, we arrive at the thirty-two elements that are particular to the Tree of Life. These thirty-two correspond to the parts of our physical body, minerals, gemstones, plants, animals, the signs of the zodiac, the planets in the solar system—every and all things! Our kabbalist has made a profound study of all the intricacies and systems used in this incredibly complex system of universal relevance and determined the kabbalistic correspondences to your birth date and those everyday things that correspond to this most important day of your life.

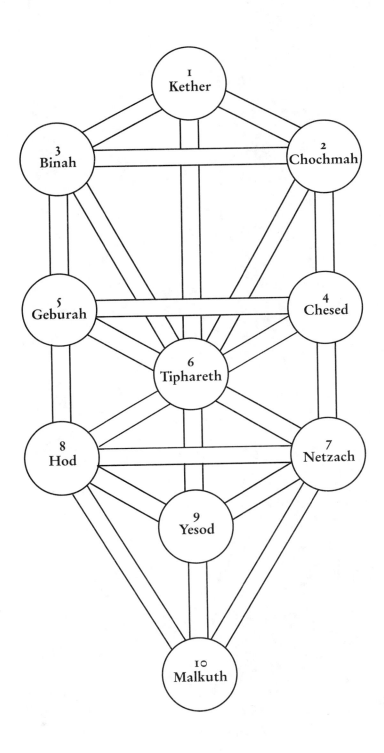

Sounds, Colors, Gems, Minerals, and Deep Space Objects

Astrology, numerology, and the system of kabbala provide powerful insights into our nature. A better understanding of ourselves leads the way to a more fulfilled life. In addition to these ancient ways of knowing, objects, images, and even distant stars and deep space objects can affect our lives, especially if we are open to their influence.

These sorts of items, associated with the days of the year, can act as tools to enhance your existing nature, to supplement a weakness, or to augment a missing quality in your personality. A fragrance may evoke an old memory. The right sound may bring out latent qualities. Certain colors or gems will bring out your best expression. Items in your home may serve to soften sharp edges, harmonize discordant emotions, or bring other elements into clear focus.

Does a certain object strengthen or subdue your nature? Does a particular sound or image draw you out or tone you down? As a wise person said, "If your only tool is a hammer, every problem looks like a nail." Explore, experiment, and watch the results.

OBJECTS/IMAGES: Associations of gems are drawn from their colors as well as the number of sides to the crystals and how they grow in the earth. Are they igneous rocks born of fire and violet eruptions, or sedimentary rocks deposited over eons by the action of the sea?

SHAPES/MATERIALS: Do you prefer round shapes or the precision of squares and rectangles? Do you like to be elevated, or do tunnels fascinate you? Not everyone is naturally conscious of the influence of shapes, textures, and materials on their physical and spiritual experience. Pay attention!

COLORS: Matadors wave a red flag before the bull to invite attack. Marketers have learned that red and yellow packages sell better than those of other colors. Blue calms and soothes. Pink creates a positive state of mind. Yellow activates the mind and enhances learning. Green blends with the colors of the earth and helps to harmonize our emotions, aid creativity, and promote healing. Use what you know of color—its personal associations and common truths, such as those noted above—to achieve the state you desire.

ASTROLOGICAL COLOR CHART		
Sign	*Color/Chromatic Scale*	*Musical Note*
Aries	red	C
Taurus	red/orange	C#
Gemini	orange	D
Cancer	orange/yellow	D#
Leo	yellow	E
Virgo	yellow/green	F
Libra	green	F#
Scorpio	green/blue	G
Sagittarius	blue	G#
Capricorn	blue/violet	A
Aquarius	violet	A#
Pisces	violet/red	B

NUMERICAL COLOR CHART		
Number	*Color*	*Action*
1	red	excites
2	orange	warms, instills confidence
3	yellow	stimulates mental processes
4	green	calms, promotes healing
5	blue	cools, soothes
6	indigo	grounds, steadies
7	violet	evokes spirituality

ANIMALS: Ancient Egyptian gods, Neters, each had an animal form representing its primary divine quality. Native Americans use animal totems in a similar manner. Each animal has a quality or characteristic that we admire: Eagles fly high and possess keen sight; bears are strong and protective of their young; serpents shed their skin and have long been associated with renewal; spiders spin webs, weaving beautiful structures to inhabit and trap their prey. Focus on the quality of an animal as a characteristic you wish to develop.

PLANTS, HERBS, EDIBLES: The popular expression, "You are what you eat" is a commonsense guide to working with plants, herbs and other things we ingest. Both ancient and modern medicine draw on the power of plants and herbs to heal, strengthen, or immunize our bodies. Chinese medicine, which draws on thousands of years of herbal lore, is a potent healing system.

ESSENCES: Odors are said to be our most potent and primal triggers, often evoking long-forgotten memories. And fragrance is a powerful mood-altering substance. Respect and take to heart the associated powers of the essences in your everyday surroundings.

SOUNDS/RHYTHMS: The rousing marches of John Philip Sousa stir feelings of pride and patriotism. We sing a lullaby to a sleepy child, literally to lull them to sleep. The driving beat of African drums reverberates in our bones. The haunting sound of bagpipes transports us to the Scottish Highlands and evokes images of brave warriors. Hymns touch our sense of the sacred and quicken our devotion. This is some of what we know of the physical effects of sound and rhythm—but what if we cultivated what we can learn from their innate associations?

MUSICAL NOTES: Sound creates form. Notes occur in cycles per second and resonate at a certain frequency. Notes correspond with numbers and colors through the musical chromatic scale; therefore, the associations of musical notes are powerful.

DEEP SPACE OBJECT: Contemplating the nature of a deep space object infuses us with a sense of the infinite, as every part of creation is alive and expressed according to its nature. Inhabitants of deep space are archetypes of energy, similar to the manner in which animals display characteristics. Knowing the deep space object that is significant to our day of birth can link us to a larger reality, moving our identification from earthbound awareness to light years in space.

Gaseous Nebula: An interstellar cloud of dust and gas, moving silently through space.

Protosolar Nebula: Motion and gravity cause a center to coalesce within the interstellar cloud, creating the possibility for star birth.

Stars: The center separates from the rest of the cloud and ignites. A star is born. Stars come in different sizes and colors, but all stars burn for the same reason: to convert the hydrogen at their cores to helium and release energy. Stages of stellar life might be described as potential, coalescence, ignition, radiance, swan song, exhaustion, and death, not unlike the stages of a human life. Stars fuel their lives with fire from within, casting life-giving radiance into the deep darkness of space. Most stars, like our own Sun, are main-sequence stars, steadily burning fuel in the middle era of their lives.

Open Clusters of Stars: Hot, young stars, such as the Pleiades or Hyades, burn brightly in the night sky and have spawned myth and legend for as long as humans have walked the earth.

Planetary Nebula: Actually a colorful ring of material jettisoned after the death of a star. Planetary nebulae were misnamed because early astronomers saw them as round and planet-shaped.

Nova: Gas from one star in a binary system enters and is consumed by its partner, fueling a brilliant stream of fiery gas visible in telescopes.

Supernova: The violent death of a super-massive star, which obliterates everything in its path for thirty light years, creating raw material for a new creation.

Pulsar: A highly compressed neutron star that is a remnant of a supernova explosion. Pulsars rotate rapidly and seem to pulse in space, releasing material as they spin.

Black Hole: Another remnant of a supernova explosion, black holes are matter so compressed, with gravity so extreme, that nothing can escape their attraction. They are identified by a stream of X-rays emerging from their cores as light is consumed.

Quasars: Quasi-stellar radio sources are believed to be the cores of young galaxies at the very edge of our universe. They are the brightest and most distant objects visible.

Globular Clusters: Astronomers believe globular clusters to be the most ancient objects in the universe, formed more than fourteen billion years ago. They are amalgams of vastly ancient stars, orbiting outside and above or below younger galaxies.

Galaxies: Groups of stars, galaxies come in three shapes: spiral, elliptical, and irregular. Stars gather together, ranging from small galaxies of only a few thousand stars to megametropolises of trillions of stars.

Galactic Center: The core of our own Milky Way, thought to be an enormous black hole.

Supergalactic Center: The colossal elliptical galaxy around which our own galaxy rotates. The center of our local group of galaxies, consisting of the Milky Way, Andromeda, and twenty-eight other small galaxies.

Deep Space Object	Key Word or Influence
gaseous nebula	potential
protosolar nebula	energy
stars	individuality
open clusters	development
planetary nebula	release
nova	sacrifice
supernova	blaze of glory
pulsar	signals
black hole	attraction
quasars	rebirth
globular clusters	experience
galactic center	higher self
supergalactic center	divine will

It is the hope and wish of the two astrologers, the numerologist, the kabbalist, and the team of editors of this book that as you unlock *The Hidden Power of Everyday Things,* you will also unlock the mystery and wonder of yourself.

Alan Oken
Santa Fe, New Mexico

January 1

YOUR SIGN
Capricorn

YOUR ELEMENT
Earth

YOUR RULERS
Saturn, Venus
10–11 degrees
Second Decanate, yang

The Astrological Interpretation

Although you are aware of the past, you are not afraid to make new inroads in life. You know that within you there is a tremendous wealth of possibilities. Yours is a path that seeks to explore and initiate new forms to your creative drives. Although you may sometimes experience life as a series of obstacles to be overcome, your powerful will allows you to surmount them. All you need is time and experience, so be patient with yourself. Take care that in your urge for success, you do not step on others. Those born this day have a profound love of nature and should follow the urge to walk among the beauty of natural surroundings. You may have a special attraction to mountains and will endeavor to climb to your own pinnacle of success.

This birthday signifies the diplomat born to hold positions of trust and handle secrets. January 1 may serve in government or within his/her immediate family circle; in either sphere, *serve* is the important word. At home you feel comfortable behind a large wooden desk. This is your command station and should have leather desk accessories such as a blotter, pencil holder, and in/out box. A finely crafted pen completes your home office. Convenience and style are the important qualities. You may have a fondness for old parchment paper and have antique documents hanging on your wall. At home your style is classical with plenty of thick carpets, which give a hushed quality. You prefer smaller rooms with doors linking the rooms together. Consider a bud vase with a single flower in each room or an arrangement of dried flowers.

Outdoors January 1 needs a garden with both light and shade. Handcrafted garden tools would be welcome; perhaps some are hand-me-downs from parents and grandparents. A rock garden with a lawn statue will also be very centering to you.

A Kabbalistic Interpretation

If you were born on this day, then you will know from experience that it is no good being a shy New Year baby. Anyone trying to celebrate a birthday surrounded by people desperately seeking to recover from the excesses of New Year's has to be fairly outgoing and maybe even a bit pushy. It's no surprise that those born on this day are partial to bright colors, with yellow likely to be a special favorite. To combat a certain lethargic tendency that you may feel on this day, carry a bloodstone or red jasper. In the home, invigorating incense or essential oils such as lemongrass can be used to create a sense of motivation.

You can increase the amount of air in your life by hanging wind chimes in your home, particularly if they are of a silvery color. People born this day have an unusually acute sense of smell and are quite sensitive to perfumes and scents. You may be attracted to fairly pungent odors and enjoy the natural aromas of warm earth or newly cut grass. When choosing potted plants for your home or apartment, base your selection on those whose fragrance attracts you along with their looks.

A Numerological Interpretation
YOUR MAGIC NUMBERS: 2 AND 1

The first day of the first month reduces to two, a number of duality, conjuring images of pillars or doorways. This day heralds the portal into the new year of the Julian calendar and confers energy for tireless pursuits. Visualize a large group of pheasants bursting from the perceived security of a country hedge; their flight is breathtaking. Begin the year with such courage and energy. Don't hide your light in the bushes. Take flight in your life. You can accomplish anything you desire. The first day of the year reduces to one and contributes the force of beginnings and initiative to this path. There can be a danger of mediocrity if you become trapped by a need for too much security. Collect rare coins, these symbols of timeless value are reminders of your worth. Midnight blue will soothe you at the end of the day. Garnet and moonstone will be grounding influences.

OBJECTS/IMAGES
terra-cotta pots, brick homes, ceramic dishes, distinctive eyeglasses

SHAPES/MATERIALS
amber glass bottles, graphite, mohair

COLORS
sage green, copper, light gray, blood red, tangerine

ANIMALS
donkey, llama, pheasant

PLANTS, HERBS, EDIBLES
nightshade, black tulips, comfrey

ESSENCE
cedarwood

SOUNDS/RHYTHMS
sound of a hammer on metal, rhythm of an arabesque, a long sigh

MUSICAL NOTES
C and C#

DEEP SPACE OBJECT
globular cluster

January 2

YOUR SIGN
Capricorn

YOUR ELEMENT
Earth

YOUR RULERS
Saturn, Venus
11–12 degrees
Second Decanate, yang

The Astrological Interpretation

You have a deep respect for knowledge and are ever seeking to increase your understanding of life. To you knowledge is power, and you very definitely want to achieve a place of honor and respect in the world. Education will therefore be a very important part of your life. You will definitely feel held back if you do not accomplish your academic goals. Get that extra training and put forth the additional effort, it will pay off for you in the long run. You are very goal oriented and always have an objective and a target. Although your ultimate achievement may take more time than you would like, you have the staying power to make it through. Older and wiser people may prove very helpful to you as you progress in life.

Some January 2 birthdays may fall on the fixed star Pelagus, which the ancients considered signified optimism and a religious tendency. Whatever path you choose to follow you have the ability to lead a crusade. You may have an exceptional memory. Your reasoning abilities help you throughout life, and you are curious about human nature. You may find your talents well used in government or managing groups of people. An image for you is a lecturer speaking without notes. To rest your brain from its labors consider having one room in your home where no work is allowed. A soft sofa with needlepoint pillows and botanical prints on the wall is an excellent environment for you. Wearing fabrics such as velour and cashmere will feel comforting. Colors for you are creamy white, slate gray, and brown.

Outdoors you may enjoy visiting grand old homes with extensive grounds and gardens. Tudor-style houses may appeal to you. Your own outdoor space could have touches of baronial splendor such as a patio of flagstones and chairs centered around an old tree. A statue of Cupid or a religious figure would be an interesting addition to your garden

A Kabbalistic Interpretation

Today is a lucky day to be born, whichever way you look at the date. The numerological significance of this date of fruition and abundance can be accentuated by using sumptuous decoration in your home. You may be particularly drawn to paintings in rich oils that appeal to you.

In terms of decoration, all things Indian may attract you. Don't be afraid to go all-out, as this style suits you. Even your taste buds favor the culinary flavors of the subcontinent, and you may particularly enjoy spicy food. The desire for spice in all things extends to your choice of air freshener or perfume. It would not be unusual to find the scent of patchouli oil wafting through your house.

You can be somewhat sharp in your dealings with others, particularly in the workplace. To combat this and grow in popularity find some blue stones (a sapphire is ideal if you can afford it) and place them in front of you on your desk.

A Numerological Interpretation
YOUR MAGIC NUMBERS: 2 AND 3

The second day of the first month reduces to three, the number of growth and unfoldment. This is a path of positive self-direction. It isn't necessary to understand everything before moving ahead. The first steps out of a perceived safe haven are tentative. You enjoy being an expert and have an innate ability to teach others. Weighing and balancing ideas is appropriate, but practical application is the key. Take care not to substitute "book learning" for actual experience. You feel at home in wide-open spaces that will inspire and strengthen you. Surround yourself with green and earth tones. Venture into open grassland. Listen to the calls of wild birds, and feel the wind on your face. The second day of the year reduces to two, adding the quality of reflection to the energy of this path. Emeralds will empower you.

OBJECTS/IMAGES
tweezers, tunnels, pottery

SHAPES/MATERIALS
plaster, quarried rock, sardonyx

COLORS
ebony, carrot, coral, amber

ANIMALS
fox, eland

PLANTS, HERBS, EDIBLES
umbrella pine, beechdrops, wood rush

ESSENCE
fir

SOUNDS/RHYTHMS
footsteps in a cathedral, largo tempo

MUSICAL NOTES
C# and D

DEEP SPACE OBJECTS
Sigma Sagittarius, Nunki

January 3

YOUR SIGN
Capricorn

YOUR ELEMENT
Earth

YOUR RULERS
Saturn, Venus, Mars
12–13 degrees
Second Decanate, yang

The Astrological Interpretation

You are gifted with an active intelligence, ever seeking to expand your horizons. Knowledge to you is more than a practical tool that may be used to accomplish your goals. You also have a very philosophical turn of mind and a curious and open attitude. This birth date gives a person the ability to probe deeply; you will never be satisfied with the superficialities of life. At times you may find that you are too serious and may sometimes want to cut yourself off from people and your environment. But this is a necessary facet of your nature, so respect yourself for your own depth and urge to search for meaning. You are developing many communication skills that will help you in your profession. An important aspect of this trait is proper communication with yourself, so take the time and make the space to cultivate your inner garden.

Although an earth sign, this birthday is influenced by the fire element. January 3 has high aspirations and may go on many adventures to satisfy her wanderlust. There is also a shrewdness to January 3 that may lose sight of the purpose of all her efforts and fall in love with power for its own sake. The living room, hopefully with a fireplace, is the center of the home. Your furniture should be classical and plush, as Saturn-ruled January 3 needs softness in life. Place some rock or minerals in the four corners of your home. This reminds you that no matter how high you fly you will always come back to earth. Consider decorating with brightly colored Turkish kilim rugs. One ancient text suggests that this birthday resonates with cities of the East, especially Constantinople, and a few reminders of that past will help you maintain continuity.

Outdoors, a charcoal barbecue or hibachi is the focal point for entertaining. If you can have an open fire with a tripod and brazier so much the better. Your garden is the place to work off steam. Celebrate your birthday with Christmas roses, whose blooms appear in the dead of winter.

A Kabbalistic Interpretation

If you were born this day you can be a veritable whirlwind—sometimes you move so fast you leave no time to see where you have been, never mind where you may be going. Good colors for you include deep plum and dark purple. Such colors resonate with your mental energy and help to soften your hectic pace.

Classical music is excellent for your concentration—in the morning, you could try listening to some appropriate classical themes, depending on your plans for the day.

You may be less than fastidious in your dress—you can often mix rather than match your outfits. Your day has a significance related to the hand, and you will probably be one of the few people who always knows where their gloves are. Gloves, rings, and bracelets of all kinds are excellent accessories for you, anything that emphasizes the hand and the wrist. You may even want to try a small tattoo, or for something less permanent try Mehndi, the Indian art of hennaing designs on the skin, wrist, or fingers.

A Numerological Interpretation

YOUR MAGIC NUMBERS: 4 AND 3

The third day of the first month reduces to four, a number signifying solidity and the four-square foundation of the physical plane. You possess a natural understanding of the fiery magic of light that underlies three-dimensional reality. Place your ear to the earth, and listen to her wisdom. Don't detach yourself from nature or your fellow human beings. This is a path of resource utilization. You learn mastery through expression of your aspirations. You enjoy elegant cutlery, fireplaces, and candles. A beautiful fire opal will put a sparkle in your eye. Bloodstone and red jasper will strengthen your resolve. The third day of the year reduces to three, providing a warm, creative streak to your personality. Drive a red sports car for fun and nurture your free spirit. Watch a sunrise to quicken your sense of magic.

OBJECTS/IMAGES
*paisley shawls,
a worn carpetbag,
a burgundy briefcase*

SHAPES/MATERIALS
zinc, wedges, jet

COLORS
*pewter gray, winter white,
cantaloupe, bittersweet*

ANIMALS
asp, griffin, rhinoceros

PLANTS, HERBS, EDIBLES
*goat cheese, sour candy,
sloes, chicory*

ESSENCES
cypress, classical perfumes

SOUNDS/RHYTHMS
*the sound of ice-coated
branches in the wind,
stately rhythms, rockabilly*

MUSICAL NOTES
D and D#

DEEP SPACE OBJECTS
*Zeta Sagittarius, Ascella,
the Arm of the Centaur*

January 4

YOUR SIGN
Capricorn

YOUR ELEMENT
Earth

YOUR RULERS
Saturn, Moon
13–14 degrees
Second Decanate, yang

The Astrological Interpretation

You are a very practical person, one who places a great deal of value upon your material and financial state. You have an aptitude to discern the difference between the petty and the important. This talent will be of great value to you, as a constant test of your advancement is knowing what to keep and what to release. This applies not only to information and skills but to personal relationships as well. An essential tool or partnership today may be a burden tomorrow. One of the most vital things you need to master is the ability to release yourself from mental and emotional clutter. Once this proficiency is achieved, you will find that you will always have the space in which to express yourself and move forward creatively.

Your birthday has a few special astrological goodies; it may fall on a critical degree or on the fixed star Manubrium. A critical degree signifies a personality that will react strongly to the highs and lows of life. The fixed star Manubrium was considered by the ancients to indicate a heroic, defiant character who might suffer blindness from explosions. January 4 is committed to building a foundation in life and has the mental acuity to accomplish it. In your home you may enjoy having copies of ancient bas-reliefs hanging on your walls. Consider having real granite or some kind of earthen tile on your kitchen counters or bathroom. January 4 likes real solid materials. A library with floor-to-ceiling bookshelves, and an old-fashioned pine swivel desk chair would be a perfect place for you to work.

In your garden have some rocks decorating your flower beds. Belgian block, pieces of mica schist, or granite would be good choices. Flowers for January 4 are perennials such as poppies, hostas, and chrysanthemums.

A Kabbalistic Interpretation

One of the many exciting and stimulating aspects of the use of occult kabbala is the way in which the most simple symbol or letter can generate an increasingly complex set of patterns. January 4 has a value of five in kabbalistic numerology. Five is the number of Mars, so anyone born on this day can benefit from surrounding themselves with heavy, preferably metallic, ornaments. These will enhance your self-confidence and sense of purpose.

Five is also the number of the letter *Heh*, which when spelled in full has a value of ten. Interestingly, ten is also the value of the Hebrew date for this day. Ten is associated with material gain, and as a result you should favor colors such as gold or silver in your decorating and even in your dress. You may want to collect ancient coins.

The heavy martial influence indicates a love of strong robust flavors. When entertaining, try spicy dishes, dark beer, and full-bodied red wines. Indeed if you are looking for a gift for someone born today, you could do a lot worse than to buy a special red wine.

A Numerological Interpretation
YOUR MAGIC NUMBERS: 5 AND 4

The fourth day of the first month reduces to five, a number implying change and movement. Many have said that change is the only constant in life. This path requires an innate understanding of the material world. You treasure and revere the work of human hands and suffer because while you desire things to endure, you experience them as sand castles that dissolve with the shifting tides. You tend to be acquisitive, but don't hold on too tight. Keep experimenting with your possessions and creations.

Enter the sacred silence of an inner sanctum, inhale the aroma of frankincense. Relish the architecture and grace of magnificent cathedrals or temples. Feel the reverberation of church bells in your bones. Play Beethoven's Fifth Symphony at maximum volume to make your spirit soar. The fourth day of the year reduces to four, adding some concrete order to the sense of constant change in your life. Topaz will give you a sense of timeless beauty. You love things with texture.

OBJECTS/IMAGES
night watchmen, stoneware, temples, tattoos

SHAPES/MATERIALS
waterfall shapes, zinc, sapphires, wool

COLORS
ecru, lemon, honey

ANIMALS
bighorn sheep, griffin

PLANTS, HERBS, EDIBLES
goatsbeard, rue, sour pickles, wintergreen

ESSENCE
tea tree

SOUNDS/RHYTHMS
bones cracking, syncopations

MUSICAL NOTES
E and D#

DEEP SPACE OBJECTS
Omicron Sagittarius, Manubrium

January 5

YOUR SIGN
Capricorn

YOUR ELEMENT
Earth

YOUR RULERS
Saturn, Venus
14–15 degrees
Second Decanate, yang

The Astrological Interpretation

This is a birth date that endows a person with a profound sense of responsibility. Yet this does not have to be a restriction to your happiness. You may achieve a great sense of joy out of harnessing resources for other people's benefit. In this respect, you may find you are drawn to a career in social service. Although you like predictability, you also require adventure, activity, and the opportunity for continuous growth. You hate feeling stagnant, especially when you are held in place by the fear of moving forward. As your career plays such an essential part of your life, look for a vocation that provides stability and potential while at the same time giving you the sense of adventure that is so important to you. In relationships, it should be the same—a stable and secure partner who is mature enough to support your individual aims.

There is a possibility of martyring yourself to your responsibilities. A rock of garnet crystals in your pocket that you can play with will remind you that life is too serious to take seriously. Keep toys like a yo-yo, Hula Hoop, Etch-a-Sketch, or a doll around and they will help you go through any difficulties life may hand you.

Decorate your home with simple, clear lines. An arch between rooms is pleasing. Your artistic nature may show in your love of ceramics and also your joy in photographs—both displaying them and taking them. Candles of pure beeswax encourage your playful side. For fashion, classical styles are for you; an understated tailored look will always feel right.

In your garden, work out your feelings about life. You will put a lot of effort into weeding it and keeping the earth fertile. Divide the garden spot into flowers, then herbs, then perhaps a few vegetables. Each area has its own needs.

A Kabbalistic Interpretation

The basic value of today's date is six, which equates to the Hebrew letter *Vau* and is associated with the element of air. The single best material for you is glass and lots of it. You will want to have a home with lots of windows that are as large as possible. Especially beneficial to your health is a large window on the south wall of your main living room. Hang crystals in your windows to catch the sun's rays in the late afternoon and early evening—the prism of brilliant colors should help you feel revitalized at the end of a long day

Try to avoid heavy fabrics wherever possible—anything fine and made from natural materials is far more in tune with January 5. Some pottery or ceramic decoration in your home, especially if it is decorated with some flashes of red, can offset a tendency to become too vague and disconnected from the rest of the world. Particularly suited are designs invoking the sun—the brighter the better.

A Numerological Interpretation
YOUR MAGIC NUMBERS: 6 AND 5

The fifth day of the first month reduces to six, a number that embodies harmony and beauty. You have the ability to see past surfaces and circumstances to the inner beauty of things. This day's path requires that you learn from even the most challenging experiences. A recognition of our partner's capacity enables us to share resources. Seize the richness in every encounter. Don't be fooled by appearances, and be kind to strangers. Some are really angels of which we are unaware. Make snow angels in freshly fallen snow. Inhale the cold, clean air and feel sunlight on your face in spite of the cold. Bite into a juicy apple. The fifth day of the year reduces to five, contributing a comfort with continual changes and modifications to your creations. Heliodor set in gold will cheer you.

OBJECTS/IMAGES
*an evergreen forest,
leather gloves,
antique wristwatches*

SHAPES/MATERIALS
*jet stone, pumice stone,
black amethyst glass, triangle*

COLORS
*blue violet, cream,
warm beige, indigo,
lime green*

ANIMALS
mole, bear

PLANTS, HERBS, EDIBLES
*flaxseed, hemlock, plantain,
quince trees, citric salt*

ESSENCES
*wisteria, the smell of
cut lumber, church incense*

SOUNDS/RHYTHMS
*ticktock of a clock, tolling bells,
early rock and roll*

MUSICAL NOTES
F and E

DEEP SPACE OBJECTS
Alpha Lyra, Vega

January 6

YOUR SIGN
Capricorn

YOUR ELEMENT
Earth

YOUR RULERS
Saturn, Venus
15–16 degrees
Second Decanate, yin

The Astrological Interpretation

Harmony is a key word expressing the essential meaning of this birth date. You require a peaceful balance between domestic and professional lives. Physical health and well-being are also essential elements to the harmony of your life. You tend to work very hard in order to achieve both your material and emotional goals. Such efforts can give rise to tension, but this can be beneficially transformed with the right diet and regular exercise. Self-respect and personal nourishment are essential elements for your success. Make sure that you are able to visit a park or wooded area on a regular basis. You may even be attracted to a profession or a hobby that is somehow connected with ecology and nature.

January 6 has a great talent for utilizing practical experience as a tool for self-development. Whatever experiences you attract in life will be food for your own imagination and philosophy of life. Horses and riding may be a hobby of yours. A home filled with books and dark wood furnishings is a comfortable environment for you. You may be quite handy with tools and want to create some furniture for yourself. Throughout your home have light-switch plates or drawer pulls that amuse you. It's a small touch, but they can help keep you in a good humor. Some area of your home could be dedicated to sports. Your patience is suited to practicing your putt or lifting a few weights at odd moments. Cherished possessions could be antique farming implements.

Outdoors, January 6 wants to indulge Venus, the ruler of your decanate. A small bridge over a brook would be a graceful addition to your garden. If there is no brook in your yard consider creating a rockery and a bridge to link the two garden areas. Flowers for you are wisteria, winter jasmine, and rock cress.

A Kabbalistic Interpretation

You like to be perceived by others as a good, solid, reliable individual and you have a tendency to reflect that in the way you dress. Because the energy of this day has strong associations with authority and even punishment, there is a real danger that people may see you as austere and stern. A good way to counter this impression is to adopt a relaxed style of dress with soft, even pastel colors.

Your genuine love of history is more than just an interest. It gives you a sense of stability and certainty in what often seems a chaotic world. You can work with those interests by using antique furnishings and objects to decorate your home. Military scenes and sculptures have particular appeal and value to you.

You may improve your emotional life by the judicious use of some very simple objects. If you have a bedside table or cabinet find some particularly attractive glasses, preferably with a deep bowl, and place two in a prominent position by your side of the bed—if you can find any with a hint of orange in them so much the better.

A Numerological Interpretation
YOUR MAGIC NUMBERS: 7 AND 6

The sixth day of the first month reduces to seven, a number that indicates rest and temporary cessation of effort. This is a path of self-discipline and liveliness of interest. The lessons involve cooperation and self-realization through working with others. Study the processes of commerce. There is a danger of being too mundane. Comprehend the harvest of what's been invested so far. Wear yellows and oranges for cheerfulness and mental clarity. Get out of the city; camp in the forest and ride horseback along a quiet trail. The sixth day of the year reduces to six, adding the element of beauty and symmetry to this path. Remember to smell the flowers.

OBJECTS/IMAGES
waterfalls, the river Styx, subways, temples

SHAPES/MATERIALS
well shapes, wrapping materials, teak, kyanite

COLORS
spinach green, apple green

ANIMAL
hoary marmot

PLANTS, HERBS, EDIBLES
blue vervain, balsamic vinegar, sweet potatoes, yew trees

ESSENCE
galbanum

SOUNDS/RHYTHMS
a raven's caws, melancholy melodies

MUSICAL NOTES
F# and F

DEEP SPACE OBJECTS
Alpha Sagittarius, Rukbat, the Knee

January 7

YOUR SIGN
Capricorn

YOUR ELEMENT
Earth

YOUR RULERS
*Saturn, Venus, Mars
16–17 degrees
Second Decanate, yin*

The Astrological Interpretation

This is a birth date that creates a profound awareness of what is right, proper, and correct, in terms of society's demands upon you. You may feel that your individual urges have had to be submerged into acceptance of what is expected of you. Now is the time to integrate into your life the joy of doing what makes you happiest. Find out what you truly love and create a space for it. You will feel less restricted if it is you who create your own boundaries. Open yourself to the realization that you have agreed whether consciously or unconsciously to the situations in your life. Now agree to something else! Agree to explore your own inner wealth of resources. Agree to open yourself to new experiences. Climb your own mountain.

January 7 is interested in separating what is essential from what is trivial. This does not mean that you perpetually wear a serious face. Your wit and intelligence can see the humor of humanity's striving. With Venus ruling your decanate, your style is understated and classic and you enjoy being in a well-appointed environment that doesn't feel cramped. Consider having some copies of archaeological artifacts such as Greek or Cycladic sculpture in your living room. Antique carved ivory or an old set of dominoes are objects you may enjoy. Sounds and privacy are very important to you. If you live in a city have a white noise machine or a collection of nature tapes.

Outdoors, January 7 takes solace in gardening and trees. Flowers such as bird-of-paradise might be interesting to you, and growing brown roses could be a delight. Pine and cypress trees are the best for January 7. If you feel bottled up go to your garden and shake the trees. They like the attention, and you'll feel better. Another adventure for January 7 is to find a beautiful secluded lake, pond, or beach and have a skinny dip. January 7 likes to get back to basics.

A Kabbalistic Interpretation

The value of this day is linked to the tarot card the Chariot, which suggests lots of wonderful goal-centered energy—with some potential to run off course or off the rails entirely. In addition this day holds powerful connections to the Death card, an indicator of major change. Something as simple as investing in a good solid table and some decent kitchenware should help you to slow down and appreciate the homely things in life.

By contrast, being full of energy at work can be great for your career. In the workplace you might want to have pictures of galloping horses or even a simple arrowhead design as the screen saver on your computer, to enhance and give direction to your activities.

While energy abounds, organization may be lacking in both your career and your love life. As a result you sometimes explode when you discover that your best laid plans have gone awry due to some small oversight. In order to assist your organizational skills you could get a bonsai oak tree and keep it in your office or home, or you could try hanging a rich yellow square of silk edged with black above your desk.

A Numerological Interpretation
YOUR MAGIC NUMBERS: 8 AND 7

The seventh day of the first month reduces to eight, a number signifying the ebb and flow in the cycles of life. Whether you relate to the annual cycles of the fields, from planting seeds to harvesting crops, or the life cycle of a product in manufacturing, know that nothing is fixed.

Sit alone and watch the ocean tides ebb and flow. Be a participant, not an observer. Immerse yourself in life. Swim naked in the moonlight. Drink deep from the well of experience. Do something with your hands. Work with clay. Form your own creation on a potter's wheel. Try carpentry, gardening, or sewing, but make something. Carnelian, peridot, and citrine will energize your imagination. The seventh day of the year reduces to seven, supporting your path by insisting on periods of rest between creations. Grow Easter lilies for inspiration.

OBJECTS/IMAGES
a blackboard and chalk, a secret drawer in a wooden desk

SHAPES/MATERIALS
jet stone, interlocking Greek key design

COLORS
taupe, hunter green, ivory, emerald green

ANIMALS
burrowing animals, cocker spaniel

PLANTS, HERBS, EDIBLES
shepherd's purse, fumitory, poppy seeds

ESSENCES
sandalwood, pine

SOUNDS/RHYTHMS
church bells, wind rattling panes of glass, the hokeypokey

MUSICAL NOTES
G and F#

DEEP SPACE OBJECTS
Gamma Aquila, Tarazed

January 8

YOUR SIGN
Capricorn

YOUR ELEMENT
Earth

YOUR RULERS
Saturn, Venus
17–18 degrees
Second Decanate, yin

The Astrological Interpretation

You are a person with a great deal of ambition and drive. To achieve your goals in life you must be aware of how to structure power and personal will. You will want to have friends in high places and will seek such a place of influence yourself. Money is important to you not just for what it can buy but also for the status and creative freedom that come with financial success. You like being in a position in which you can make things happen and take your responsibilities seriously. You have good powers of visualization and are quite insightful. You would do well to avoid envy and pride while doing what you can to help others attain their success in life. Your sense of isolation will lessen the more you make your abundant talents available to others freely and from the heart.

You are the type of person who wants to hone your interests and not bother with areas that you don't enjoy or feel you are not good at. Your concentration can lead you to be impatient or peevish with activities that are necessary but that you don't enjoy. At home, practice flexibility by doing a routine of stretches in the morning. Your home may be one of your interests and it may not be. Keep decor simple and elegant. January 8 enjoys luxury and might particularly like marble floors and bathtubs. An entry hall with a black-and-white marble floor design would be a noteworthy feature. Granite counters in the kitchen will keep you in touch with your earthy nature. Encourage your soft side with special cream for the elbows and hands. Pine salts and a good soak in your marble tub will chase your irritability away.

January 8 may love the outdoors and winter sports in particular. Practical parkas and all equipment necessary for the cold are items for January 8. In your own yard mosaic stepping stones could grace your garden. Plant goatsbeard and flowering quince. The one flower recalls your symbol and the other the beauty that lies within you.

A Kabbalistic Interpretation

For all their innate complexity, people born this day emanate a sense of calm and genuine understanding. Temperance and balance are the keys to this day, and you may wish to reflect those qualities in your home. Avoid any ornaments that are unusually large or small in comparison with your other decorations, as you may experience headaches when things are out of proportion. A fantastic color combination for you is blue and orange. Look for a pair of vases in these colors or even better, paint them yourself. Placed prominently in your living room, they can help you feel at ease with the arrangement of your home.

One of your complexities is that although you are a very balanced individual you have extremely high ideals, which you sometimes press too forcefully. If you have room on your desk at work, put an arrangement of white flowers in a white vase in a position where you can both see and smell them. The flowers should help temper your intensity.

A Numerological Interpretation
YOUR MAGIC NUMBERS: 9 AND 8

The eighth day of the first month reduces to nine, the number of completion. Being born on this day indicates a life path of teaching others and sharing what you learn and master. Extend an open hand to those who seek your counsel. You have been given the chance to exercise spiritual stewardship. Make things simple and practical. Your ease at mastering skills can look like magic to others. Yellow quartz, citrine, and amethyst will enhance your clarity. Colorful waving flags will make you smile.

Surround yourself with objects that imply vintage: wine, old books, grandfather clocks. Listen to the steady beat of an antique clock in the darkness. The eighth day of the year reduces to eight, adding the quality of rhythm and flux to your awareness.

OBJECTS/IMAGES
valleys, wallets, rocky waterfalls

SHAPES/MATERIALS
black stones, sulfur, chromite, small circles

COLORS
dry wine color, cobalt blue

ANIMALS
star-nosed mole, donkey

PLANTS, HERBS, EDIBLES
willow trees, sour cream, caperbush, rusty-back fern

ESSENCE
tea tree

SOUNDS/RHYTHMS
sound of digging, glockenspiel music, Elvis Presley's music

MUSICAL NOTES
G# and G

DEEP SPACE OBJECTS
Beta Lyra, Sheliak, The Tortoise

January 9

YOUR SIGN
Capricorn

YOUR ELEMENT
Earth

YOUR RULERS
Saturn, Venus
18–19 degrees
Second Decanate, yin

The Astrological Interpretation

Many people born this day have found that they were expected to assume adult responsibilities at a very early age. You seem to have been born with a sense of maturity well beyond your years. As you grow older, you will be able to recapture a childhood that might have been lost or injured due to early family circumstances. Do not be surprised if you grow "younger" as you mature. You are a person who has a deep sense of compassion for other people and their limitations. If you work to cultivate patience, you will find that you have an ability to help people move outside the boundaries of their limitations. In your career, there is a distinct talent for making the most out of the least and an understanding of how to structure whatever resources are around you for everyone's benefit.

The fixed star Deneb is located near some January 9 birthdays. In ancient times this star was believed to give the ability to command and be a successful warrior. You may be a solitary personality with great concentration skills. To balance your serious nature you should practice silliness. A clown dartboard on the bathroom door will give you a target for frustrations. Keep a set of pick up sticks, checkers, and a Monopoly game around. The child part of your personality is eager to play. When considering adult issues such as decorating, you enjoy a sense of importance and grandeur in your surroundings. Arches between rooms give you a sense of space, and wall fluting reminds you of ancient temples. The kitchen should include some earth-colored brick or tiles.

Outdoors, the rocks are as interesting to you as the flowers. Consider limestone in unusual shapes and petrified wood. Belgian block could border your garden. Flowers that January 9 would enjoy are pincushion flowers, phlox, and fringed iris.

A Kabbalistic Interpretation

You love excitement and should feel free to express it in your home. You like the idea of a jazzy home environment, but the influence of a certain conservative element to your nature may override your more expressive side. If this is true, you need to let go of that restraint. Surround yourself with as many colors as possible. Use lots of bright yellow initially and you should find that you are able to open up to even more color in your life.

Unusual designs have a strong appeal for you, especially if they have an eastern flavor—Oriental rugs and large vases will sit very well in your living space. The ambiance this creates matches your culinary habits, as you are likely to be a great lover of Asian and Indian cuisines.

In your dress you are always pulled together, but not to the point of standing out. You can add vitality to your image through the use of one brilliant piece of jewelry. Anything with a serpentine design is ideal for you. This could be a snake bracelet or simply an elegant jacket pin with a complex spiral pattern.

A Numerological Interpretation

YOUR MAGIC NUMBERS: 10 AND 9

The ninth day of the first month reduces to ten, indicating a drive for perfection that compels you to try, try again. You are eager to try new things and are often the first among your group to experience the latest fad. Savor the taste of unusual fruits like pomegranates, kiwi, or fresh dates. Decorate your bedroom in yellows and blues with rich, textured fabrics like velvet and tapestries and cuddle up in a plush robe at night and watch an art film. Containers, especially unique gift bags, will give you pleasure. Howlite, lapis, and topaz will complement your disposition. The ninth day of the year reduces to nine, supporting your innate need to see things through to the finish.

OBJECTS/IMAGES
wharves, wheelbarrow, watchmakers, and shawls

SHAPES/MATERIALS
titanite, sapphire, pebble sand, ravine shapes

COLORS
charcoal, deep purple

ANIMALS
raccoon, panda bear

PLANTS, HERBS, EDIBLES
currants, knotgrass, ground moss, and holly

ESSENCE
Moroccan cedar

SOUNDS/RHYTHMS
a carpenter's saw, the sound of musical notes blown on bottles

MUSICAL NOTES
A and G#

DEEP SPACE OBJECT
supernova

January 10

YOUR SIGN
Capricorn

———

YOUR ELEMENT
Earth

———

YOUR RULERS
Saturn, Venus
19–20 degrees
Second Decanate, yin

The Astrological Interpretation

Many Capricorns are loners and have a deep and often difficult sense of isolation. You, on the other hand, will find that your sense of creative fulfillment will come through your ability to participate in group activities. You will be at your best when you can contribute your very strong sense of individuality to some collective project. You may find that your natural abilities to structure and synthesize will often be called upon. You are very good at finding the hidden talents and resources in others and know how to blend these talents together to produce a more harmonious whole.

This birthday gives great strength of character. Capricorn in general rules the shoulders, and this particular birthday is fashioned to handle great responsibility. To help you shrug off your responsibilities on occasion, emphasize a comfortable bathroom with a Jacuzzi or hot tub. Roll those shoulders around as you soak and you won't feel overwhelmed by your activities. Tile and unique pottery may adorn your home. If you can manage a room of your own with windows facing north and east you'll have a "sanctum sanctorum" where you can recharge your batteries.

Music is a wonderful way for you to relax. Little Tibetan bells and mountain horns gently remind you of your reserves of strength. When it is time to laugh, seek clowns and clown images.

Outdoors, gardening is an artistic and relaxing activity. A secret cave or hideaway could be a special place for you. A garden that contains specially selected stones surrounded by moss is delightful. A slate step that doubles as a seat in the midst of the garden is a place to gather energy. A sundial completes the picture.

A Kabbalistic Interpretation

The styles and moods of the late 1960s would likely have suited you to a tee. As we live in an individualistic age, there is no reason you should stop yourself from bringing this model back—you can live in a house replete with bead curtains and lava lamps, if you wish. If the actual trappings of that era are not your style, you may wish to seek modern equivalents. It would not be at all unusual for someone born today to have a stack of crystals at home, or other characteristically New Age essentials. Your home should offer encouragement to explore as many unusual avenues of thought as your inquiring mind desires.

Despite a somewhat "flighty" nature it would not be surprising for you to own your own business, as this is a day particularly well favored for financial luck. You can boost that lucky streak with the use of circular furniture in your workplace, especially the tables where you close major deals and conduct important meetings. Carrying a small block of granite or another mundane mineral with you to the office will do wonders for you in the workplace, as it will add a much needed touch of gravitas to your presence.

A Numerological Interpretation
YOUR MAGIC NUMBERS: 2 AND 10

The tenth day of the first month reduces to two, a number representing receptivity. Two follows one and in a sense is dependent upon the first number for its identity. You have a strong sense of responsibility to your family, however you define them. You may choose a traditional grouping, or your family unit may be you and your dog. It is not so much your dwelling as the beings who inhabit it that are important. To you, the cacophony of blended voices of loved ones can sound like music.

The tenth day of the year reduces to ten and adds the influence of mastery and perfected cycles to your path. Jade, sodalite, and moss agate will ground and warm you. Take your dog on a sailboat. Listen to the rustle of the wind, and let the wet air caress your face.

OBJECTS/IMAGES
a mine shaft, an igloo

SHAPES/MATERIALS
smoky quartz crystal, lapis lazuli, carnelian, jet stone, decahedron, choir loft

COLORS:
variegated colors on the dark side, magenta, seal gray, tangerine, aubergine

ANIMALS
rabbit, owl, cuckoo

PLANTS, HERBS, EDIBLES
wolfsbane, cumin, goat cheese

ESSENCES
apple cider vinegar, gardenias

SOUNDS/RHYTHMS
music of the spheres, 6/8 time, vocal music

MUSICAL NOTES
C# and A

DEEP SPACE OBJECT
SS433, Anomalous Neutron Star

January 11

YOUR SIGN
Capricorn

YOUR ELEMENT
Earth

YOUR RULERS
Saturn, Venus, Mercury
20–21 degrees
Third Decanate, yang

The Astrological Interpretation

Although you are focused on your own goals and ambitions, you are aware that cooperation between yourself and your partners or coworkers is essential for everyone. You can use your abundant willpower and drive to stimulate the creative potential of the people around you. Your natural talents at blending and harmonizing people allow you to weave a wonderful tapestry of human enterprise. An intuitive person, your perceptive vision easily permits you to penetrate beyond the masks of others, encouraging and supporting them. People will naturally gravitate to you for advice, and you take the responsibility of their confidence very seriously. You may not start off in a leadership position but yours is the sign of Capricorn; while you may move slowly, your footing is sure. You never lose sight of your mountain peak and have a natural urge to take a lot of people with you as you reach for the top.

Through pragmatic creativity, January 11 becomes a focal point for group opportunities and self-development. Surround yourself with all the tools you need for work and play. If you love snowshoes then have the best you can buy. Your home should have some heavy heirloom furniture in mahogany or oak mixed with lighter, more modern pieces. A special grandfather clock or other large timepiece reminds you of one of the symbols for Capricorn, Father Time. Surround yourself with enough lamps, and consider full-spectrum lighting to ward off winter blues and boost your spirits.

The garden is a place where you can relax and create. Consider having a Zen rock garden, very spare with low-lying bushes. A part of your garden could be for winter plants, another for spring, and a free-for-all space for summer. January 11 needs to leave a little pocket of chaos in life if for no other reason than the fun of straightening it out.

A Kabbalistic Interpretation

All the possible values of this day point to an overriding concern with order, specifically moral order, a preoccupation that may well be reflected in your taste around the home. There is nothing wrong with living in a relatively spartan environment, but you could afford to lighten your home space by adding some pale-colored soft furnishings such as an ottoman or armchair upholstered in pastel fabric.

To reflect your desire for order in a constructive and positive way you might consider investing in some antique trunks or chests. These should ideally have brass metal fittings and be close to cubic in proportion.

Avoid drinking coffee whenever possible, even decaffeinated, as this will sharpen an already short temper. Instead try cool water-based drinks with a slight hint of fruit flavoring. You might consider buying some bottled water and leaving it in the south window of your house where the sun's rays will penetrate it at midday before drinking.

A Numerological Interpretation
YOUR MAGIC NUMBERS: 3 AND 2

The eleventh day of the first month reduces to three, the number of growth and unfoldment. Continually expressing the creative process is vital to your well-being. You must be able to see and touch the tangible results of your creativity. Witnessing each part of the process as a distinct aspect or stage is critical for you. Watch the process unfold in stages, and be aware of the unique aspects of larva, caterpillar, chrysalis, and butterfly. You seek to understand where you fit in the scheme of things. At your best, you can bring all the pieces of the puzzle together in one perfect unit. Collect stamps. Solve puzzles. Sacred music inspires and soothes you. Green quartz, malachite, and garnet will stabilize your emotions.

The eleventh day of the first month reduces to two, adding the element of repetition to the lessons of this path. Bake cookies, get your hands in dough, cut out imprints, and decorate the finished products.

OBJECTS/IMAGES
a tuxedo, a spiral staircase leading upward, work gloves

SHAPES/MATERIALS
all-weather fabric, ore, glue

COLORS
gray, winter white, dark green, peach, sunset orange

ANIMALS
Great Dane, goat

PLANTS, HERBS, EDIBLES
goutwort, comfrey

ESSENCE
cedar

SOUNDS/RHYTHMS
running feet, a grinding stone, a slow bell

MUSICAL NOTES
D and C#

DEEP SPACE OBJECTS
Gamma Lyra, Sulaphat

January 12

YOUR SIGN
Capricorn

YOUR ELEMENT
Earth

YOUR RULERS
Saturn, Mercury, Mars
21–22 degrees
Third Decanate, yin

The Astrological Interpretation

There is tremendous inner strength contained within this birth date. Your task is to unfold that power consciously. You are able to take up life's challenges and through the sheer force of your faith and will, overcome them and succeed. Many people born on this day have achieved a great deal of compassion and empathy for other people's shortcomings. The key here is to avoid getting stuck in the memory of one's own and other people's mistakes and errors. Avoid "injustice collecting" and putting the blame for life's problems on your parents, social environment, boss, husband, or wife. Great success can come to you only after you have properly processed both your own and other people's failures, and can march forward with the wealth of this experience in your heart.

January 12 has an unusual sense of mission in whatever you choose to do. Caution and bravery are two of your qualities. Many born on this day will be interested in helping people less fortunate. Communication may figure strongly in your activities. Beautiful stationery would be an old-fashioned way to fulfill this desire. In the modern world, an up-to-date computer system and printer ensures that you get your message out. At home, January 12 needs some repose from striving. Settle down in a modern leather chair that comfortably allows you to slouch. Look at picture books of gardens and exciting weather environments to slow and relax your mind. Saturn, your planet, rules minerals in general. Mineral clusters, bookends made of quartz, or geodes will keep you in contact with the riches of the earth.

Outdoors, January 12 enjoys gardening and creating an environment with a monumental feel. A colonnade alongside your garden would look great. Plant baby's breath, cypress trees, and black poppies. A splash of color indoors could be red poinsettias.

A Kabbalistic Interpretation

Neutral earthy colors are ideal for you, especially brown. Your affinity with low-key, sober tones is connected to the Hebrew letter *Cheth,* a letter that can reflect a somewhat defensive approach to life. In addition the value of your birthday in English refers to the tarot card the

Hanged Man, which is a card of self-sacrifice, suggesting an aversion to self-display.

While you feel most at home in the background, you do need to do something to promote your own interests and push yourself into other people's line of sight. Try wearing a pendant or carrying a piece of red jasper or something made with this stone and you will almost definitely find yourself feeling more confident and talkative.

You have a strong affinity for water, so you may want to take regular, soothing, meditative soaks in the tub. Doing this will give you some time to relax and go into yourself. Add some rosemary or rosemary-scented oil to the bathwater. Afterward treat your skin to some sandalwood-based massage oil. Ask your partner to give you a massage, if you like.

A Numerological Interpretation
YOUR MAGIC NUMBERS: 4 AND 3

The twelfth day of the first month reduces to four, the number of order and measurement. Born on this day, you have the capacity to adapt to situations, making the best of things and always learning from events. To use a cliché, you turn stumbling blocks into stepping-stones. If in the military, you would strive to advance to general.

The twelfth day of the year reduces to three, adding the quality of creative expression to your path. You do well when you follow your hunches, but you like to know the reasons for things, so you often second-guess your inner knowing. Listen to your inner voice. City skylines at night inspire you to achieve. Stand in the stillness of an early morning rain and drink in simple realities. Garnet, ruby, and fluorite are stones to harmonize your life force. Play with Tinkertoys, or Erector sets. Build a model airplane, or decorate a dollhouse.

OBJECTS/IMAGES
umbrellas, military medals, antique firearms

SHAPES/MATERIALS
silica, pottery materials, urn shapes

COLORS
burnished brown, crimson, tangerine

ANIMALS
ox, rhinoceros

PLANTS, HERBS, EDIBLES
prunes, spleenwort, shepherd's purse

ESSENCE
oakmoss

SOUNDS/RHYTHMS
a wooden xylophone, fife and drum corps

MUSICAL NOTES
D# and D

DEEP SPACE OBJECTS
Epsilon Capricorn, Castra

January 13

YOUR SIGN
Capricorn

YOUR ELEMENT
Earth

YOUR RULERS
Saturn, Mercury, Mars
22–23 degrees
Third Decanate, yin

The Astrological Interpretation

This birth date indicates persons who are very aware of their social responsibilities. You are one who works very hard to achieve your goals. Yet you do not seek the rewards that life has to offer just for purely egocentric aims. You know that to receive you have to give, and you enjoy the trust you feel in the ability of others to live up to their commitments. You certainly strive to live up to yours!

January 13 is serious and philosophically minded. You may be something of an antiquarian. Whatever is tried and true interests you. There is also elegance in your birthday and the ability to communicate clearly. In your home environment have some reminders from the Sumerian or Egyptian civilizations. A shower curtain with hieroglyphics would not be too silly. Your ability to pursue a goal is strong. An image for you is a Middle Eastern caravan. The camels cross the desert slowly but surely. Military medals may also feature in your home decor. These could be from family members or antiques you have collected. The medals remind you of bravery, which is a quality January 13 possesses in great measure. At home, use clear crystal wineglass-shaped glasses, even for orange juice or water. You will enjoy seeing the liquid's color reflected in the crystal. Creating an occasion from everyday events appeals to you.

Outdoors, January 13 enjoys gardening and may want to delve into agriculture. Plowing a piece of earth would be an interesting activity for you. No matter how rocky the terrain, January 13 will plough a straight furrow. In your garden, plant annuals and tulips for the spring. An outdoor sandbox is a good idea for both children and adults born on January 13.

A Kabbalistic Interpretation

You are very concerned with the accumulation of material goods. One way to remind yourself of the financial position to which you aspire is to carry a small gold charm with you in the shape of the part-goat, part-fish figure that represents Capricorn. Or you may want to keep an aquarium full of goldfish.

You need to be careful of pursuing your financial goals at the expense of other priorities in your life, especially your family. If you have children then carrying a small piece of aquamarine may help improve your relationships with them. If you put a photo of your partner on your desk in a frame that is a double circle and hinged rather like a large locket the effect can be very powerful.

Because of connections of this day with the letter *Nun*, kabbala indicates that you may not have the greenest of thumbs; however, you do need plants around you so that you can keep in touch with the organic aspects of Capricorn. Try some air plants, as these are both bright and long flowering and easy to take care of.

A Numerological Interpretation
YOUR MAGIC NUMBERS: 5 AND 4

The thirteenth day of the first month reduces to five, a number of uncertainty, transition, and mediation. You often feel isolated from other people. This path forces you to recognize yourself and gain a sense of identity through your achievements. You desire recognition and praise from others for your numerous accomplishments. In what ways do you see yourself reflected?

Look beneath the surface; probe the deeper meaning of praise. What are you seeking? Whom do you really wish to please? You enjoy soap operas, adventure or romance novels, and melodramatic plays. Take a walk in a snow-covered forest and drink deep of the fragrance of evergreen trees. Feel the feather-light touch of snowflakes on your face and experience deep peace. Sodalite and amber will augment your connection to the earth.

The thirteenth day of the year reduces to four, adding the stability and order of four to the unsettling influence of five. Your medals of valor should serve the common good rather than self. Discover a cure for cancer before you apply for a patent for personal glory. One choice yields universal goodwill, the other leads to desolation.

OBJECTS/IMAGES
a country parsonage, a cave, scarecrows

SHAPES/MATERIALS
asbestos, chalcedony, a skeleton

COLORS
creamy brown, flat black, saffron, grass green

ANIMAL
mole

PLANTS, HERBS, EDIBLES
barley, beech trees

ESSENCE
rosemary

SOUNDS/RHYTHMS
a clock's chime, traditional campfire songs

MUSICAL NOTES
E and D#

DEEP SPACE OBJECTS
Alpha Pavo, the Peacock Star

January 14

YOUR SIGN
Capricorn

YOUR ELEMENT
Earth

YOUR RULERS
Saturn, Mercury
23–24 degrees
Third Decanate, yin

The Astrological Interpretation

You seek a sense of personal security that goes beyond the material nature of things. You allow the outer experiences of your life to stimulate your deeper understanding of a more profound reality. This gives you a foundation of knowledge that serves you well, as you are often called upon as an advisor to your friends and associates. You have a tremendous need to explore your creative possibilities and endeavor to go beyond the temporary limitations of the moment. You use your talents and abilities to inspire the best in others. Although you well understand how others may feel restricted, you much prefer not to dwell on the negative, opening yourself instead to the many opportunities available in life.

Your birthday gives you a committed nature. Life is meaningless without some enduring allegiance to an idea, mission, family, or your native land. Your principles lead you forward, and you may gain recognition for work in medicine, theology, or statesmanship. Perhaps you sometimes feel like the rock of Gibraltar? Add softness to your life with angora wool, down pillows, a massage now and then, and a long soak in sulfur springs or a Jacuzzi. Decorate your home with light colors. An Oriental rug in blues and reds might be a prized possession. Both men and women should include in their wardrobes a few well-tailored suits. Consider charcoal wool with a small red streak.

Gardening is a hobby and a meditation for you. Create a rock garden on one side and a flower bed on the other. If your hot tub could overlook both, then you would be very content. Flowers for January 14 are Japanese plum, tuberose, and cape colony nerine

A Kabbalistic Interpretation

One of the tools used in occult or esoteric kabbala is gematria. Gematria is the process of analyzing a series of letters and comparing them to other sequences. This particular day has a value of 434 and is connected strongly to ideas of magic in general and specifically to the mysteries of womanhood. Whether male or female, to realize your full potential in this regard, keep plenty of blue in your wardrobe, especially really rich dark midnight blues. This is a color that you will feel most happy and empowered wearing.

For jewelry the influence of the Empress card in your day's value may incline you toward gold, but you will do better if you opt for silver or platinum, as this shade reflects your connection to the moon and its influence. The moon can be a fickle influence in life because of its association with some of our deepest emotional states. However, you have a very positive relationship to the lunar force and can enhance this further by opting for crescent-shaped jewelry and ornaments. Make sure that the crescent points upward.

A Numerological Interpretation
YOUR MAGIC NUMBERS: 6 AND 5

The fourteenth day of the first month reduces to six, the number of equilibrium. Your birth date indicates a path of striving for mental harmony. When you commit, you give yourself utterly. A quest for success in the marketplace, or yearning for financial security, will ultimately lead to awareness of the balance required between the aspects of your true nature. Your birth path is six, but the first month gives a sense of urgency, yielding a hunger for harmony.

The fourteenth day of the year reduces to five, which keeps things constantly moving in your life. A beautiful place to retreat from strife is essential to your well-being. Resist the urge to pile up beautiful possessions or escape into too many romance or adventure novels. Use that energy to volunteer for a charity. Stillness or soothing melodic music will enhance your serenity. Incorporate the healing influence of walks in nature. Trees, especially arbors and orchards will inspire you. Colors to strengthen you are indigo and orange. Gems to ground you are legrandite and azurite. Wear saltwater pearls to remind you of the ocean.

OBJECTS/IMAGES
a magnifying glass, dominoes, storehouses, tabernacles

SHAPES/MATERIALS
spade shapes, steel, faience pottery, amazonite

COLORS
auburn, lemon, lime

ANIMALS
gnu, teddy bear

PLANTS, HERBS, EDIBLES
tamarisk, sour grapes, balsamic vinegar, wolfsbane

ESSENCE
pine

SOUNDS/RHYTHMS
stamping rhythms, tom-toms

MUSICAL NOTES
F and E

DEEP SPACE OBJECT
the Aquila Nova

January 15

YOUR SIGN
Capricorn

YOUR ELEMENT
Earth

YOUR RULERS
Saturn, Mercury, Venus
24–25 degrees
Third Decanate, yin

The Astrological Interpretation

The harmony of your surroundings is very important to you. At home, you are likely to keep many beautiful objects, not so much as symbols of success, but because of the psychological and spiritual comfort their beauty brings. Harmony also extends into your human relationships. This birth date indicates a person who realizes that true success is not achieved alone. You can be very charming and helpful and will find that this attitude brings the support you need to reach your own targets in life. In this respect, you have good coordinating and organizational skills that you can use for the benefit of all concerned. You have a sense of tradition and history and may well enjoy visits to museums and art galleries as a way to relax and for personal inspiration.

This birthday gives an overwhelming sense of mission to a person. Whether the mission be home, career, or family, you want to pursue your vision with tenacity and clarity. Peaceful order should reign in the home, with plenty of sturdy furniture that supports the back and is comfortable. Leather upholstery in rich browns, grays or black, or burgundy is soothing and practical. You enjoy a cheerful bright kitchen area, decorated with yellows and cream colors and well stocked with herbal teas. Photographs of grandparents and other ancestors in old-fashioned frames give January 15 a sense of continuity. Capricorn is ruled by the god Kronos, and a handsome clock would be a welcome addition to the home. Images of pyramids are energizing. Rocks and minerals from travels are excellent ways to decorate throughout the home.

Outdoors a garden that is orderly and colorful cheers you on your way. White and amber chrysanthemums are flowers for contemplation and delight. A corner of the garden could have a little gazebo or resting place where you can go to unwind.

A Kabbalistic Interpretation

Hot Chocolate's famous track, "You Sexy Thing," could have been penned with you in mind, as people born on this day are often quite literally bursting with sexual energy. Red and black are both fantastic colors for you that reverberate with your sensual charm. You do need to find a source of calm in your life, and this may be achieved by the use of emerald green—possibly in an accessory such as a tie, scarf, or brooch. The use of this color can add some balance to your thoughts.

In your home green is an effective decorating motif, again to add some calm. You can use candles to decorate, and you may consider placing some in the west of your bedroom if you wish to energize your more emotional side.

At work you are likely to be a fairly important figure, however, you can be a little harsh at times. You might set a bowl of blue-colored water, perhaps with a lotus design cut into the glass, on your desk. This may gradually create a greater sense of peace and goodwill.

A Numerological Interpretation
YOUR MAGIC NUMBERS: 7 AND 6

The fifteenth day of the first month reduces to seven, a number of safety and security. Remember to rest after your labors and take pride in your results. Sleep in on your day off. Savor your coffee and morning paper. The fruits of labor shouldn't die on the vine but be shared with the larger community to nourish and strengthen everybody. Your own threads of contribution should become part of the tapestry of society. Take a moonlight stroll on a cold night, and stare at the dark sky. Center your ornate desk on an Oriental carpet in woven threads of yellow and indigo. The fifteenth day of the year reduces to six, adding the quality of beauty and symmetry to this path. Jasper and calcite will soothe your emotions. Listen to the haunting strains of a nocturne.

OBJECTS/IMAGES
tile, coves, sculpture in marble and metal, timepieces

SHAPES/MATERIALS
wool, quartz crystal, onyx, petrified wood, pewter

COLORS
dark brown, navy blue, indigo, gray, turquoise, royal purple

ANIMALS
goat, burrowing animals, camel

PLANTS, HERBS, EDIBLES
barley, beech trees, comfrey, flaxweed, horsetail, quince

ESSENCES
wintergreen, pine, English Leather

SOUNDS/RHYTHMS
Gregorian chant, minuets, classic blues, gentle drizzle

MUSICAL NOTES
F# and F

DEEP SPACE OBJECT
Spiral Galaxy

January 16

YOUR SIGN
Capricorn

YOUR ELEMENT
Earth

YOUR RULERS
Saturn, Mercury
25–26 degrees
Third Decanate, yang

The Astrological Interpretation

Yours is a birth date that inspires contemplation, philosophy, and a distinct need for quiet times and peaceful surroundings. Although you can handle the pressures of daily life and certainly live up to the responsibilities that you assume, your efficient and somewhat detached outer personality does not represent the sensitive person inside you. This precious part of yourself is revealed to very few—in fact you may often keep it hidden from yourself! Take long walks in nature, especially near the ocean or other bodies of water. Such experiences not only bring comfort but also stimulate your creative possibilities and potentials. Open yourself to the artist and poet that live inside you. Learning how to balance the real and the ideal, the artistic with the pragmatic, is an important lesson for you.

January 16 is able to master a variety of experiences in life. You proceed with your own élan and have a spontaneous wit that enables you to assert yourself with good grace. January 16 has a whimsical side to the personality that tempers Capricorn's famous sense of duty and responsibility. An image for you is a water sprite skimming over mud flats. At home you will enjoy decorating with horns of plenty or anything in the shape of a cornucopia. Choose colors reminiscent of the earth for your living room and emphasize the color of grapes for the bedroom. Your bedroom furniture should be dark wood and perhaps be an inherited piece. Carved newel posts add to a sense of importance and dignity. Have a white or natural crocheted bedspread and a stuffed goat in the middle of the pillows.

If you do not live near the sea consider nautical touches in your garden such as an old anchor, a figurehead from a ship's prow, or a large model sailboat that you use for a planter. Flowers for January 16 include large carnations and a tropical flower called jacobinia.

A Kabbalistic Interpretation

You are by nature a collector—the value of your day in Hebrew ties it to words associated with the collection and recording of data. A good career choice for you would be professional archivist. One of your planetary connections is Saturn. As the oldest of the planets, it can be connected to memory and tradition. A color associated with Saturn is a pinked gray, and you may wish to find objects or do some painting using that color.

Because Mars is another planetary connection with this day, seek out iron objects, especially those related to historical events. You are attracted to periods of crisis in history and need to offset the energy of the memorabilia of such times by the use of positive symbols. Lighten your mind-set with jewelry in a figure-eight pattern or some brightly colored costume jewelry.

Yellow, and especially a yellow gold, is an excellent color for you, as it accentuates the positive aspects of a traditionally forceful personality. You might have a wallet or gloves in this color. A steering wheel cover in this shade can help you drive confidently but without aggression.

A Numerological Interpretation

YOUR MAGIC NUMBERS: 8 AND 7

The sixteenth day of the first month reduces to eight, a number of constant motion. The energy of eight moves back and forth in a rhythm of flux and reflux, ebbing and flowing like the motion of the tides. Choose antique lamps with shades of yellow, lime green, and blue violet to warm your abode. Wear rings of beryl set in gold. It's easy for you to acquire treasures, but don't hold on too tight. Keep things in circulation, and share your gifts. When you choose to do something, nothing less than perfection and total integrity suit you.

You are an excellent student. Be spontaneous whenever you can. Climb to a mountaintop, and follow the path of a stream cascading down from alpine peaks. The sixteenth day of the year reduces to seven, adding the need to rest between cycles of activity. Calcite and epidote will enhance your charm.

OBJECTS/IMAGES
convents, Father Time, knees, pottery

SHAPES/MATERIALS
coal, galena, plank shapes, white onyx

COLORS
russet, sea foam, royal blue

ANIMALS
giraffe, caribou

PLANTS, HERBS, EDIBLES
henbane, ice

ESSENCE
patchouli

SOUND/RHYTHM
Ethel Merman singing "There's No Business Like Show Business"

MUSICAL NOTES
G# and G

DEEP SPACE OBJECT
CP1919, the first discovered pulsar

January 17

YOUR SIGN
CAPRICORN

YOUR ELEMENT
Earth

YOUR RULERS
Saturn, Mercury
26–27 degrees
Third Decanate, yang

The Astrological Interpretation

The symbolic climbing of a mountain is a theme for all Capricorns. But each degree of this sign climbs that mountain differently. You will find that you are well equipped to tackle your challenges of ascension if you include knowledge and special training in your equipment. You benefit from associations with older people, whose life experiences can be passed on for your support and growth. Study history and philosophy. Learn as much as you can about the cycles, achievements, and errors of humanity. A mountain must first rise out of the earth before you can reach its pinnacle. The more you are able to understand our common human foundations, the more successful and rewarding your own particular life path will be.

January 17 may fall on a critical degree, which means that you experience highs and lows in life more keenly than others. You have a strong and somewhat impatient nature—finding a way to blow off steam is advisable. Sports such as boxing, martial arts, and track are great outlets for you. At home decorate the wall flanking a flight of stairs with photos, awards, and commendations as your personal gallery of accomplishment. Part of your character enjoys being surrounded with softness. Mohair and angora wools are excellent materials for you. Clay vases and statues are good decorative objects. You may enjoy looking at pictures of the black and red clay vases that the ancient Greeks created. Try sculpting in clay as a hobby.

Outdoors, your yard should have a sculpted look with a mixture of rocks and flowers. Have a slate-lined garden walk. Flowers suitable for you are baby's breath and decorative purple cabbage. A nearby churchyard is a place to visit and muse.

A Kabbalistic Interpretation

Your Capricorn's connection to the earth is deep rooted, but it sometimes finds expression in an unhealthy concern with materialism rather than with the earth as a source of natural enjoyment. To offset this tendency, an orange ceramic bowl filled with colorful and aromatic fruits should be a permanent feature on your kitchen table. Make time to sit and smell them at least once a day.

The rapid pace of change in your life can creep up on you and take you by surprise. Carry a yellow stone, especially a small citrine, to assist in sharpening your mind. Then you can anticipate when the next change is coming. Because of a connection to the tarot card the Tower, you tend to feel many developments as initially unwelcome and even catastrophic disruptions to your sense of security. To counter these feelings, paint at least one room in your house in muted dark colors. Far from being oppressive, you should find this a soothing place to sit and collect your thoughts.

In your workplace or den consider keeping an executive toy consisting of ten metal balls. The number is the important thing; any ornament using patterns of ten will help you focus your mind and gain a sense of control.

A Numerological Interpretation

YOUR MAGIC NUMBERS: 9 AND 8

The seventeenth day of the first month reduces to nine, signifying the end of a cycle. Nine is a number of fulfillment, completion, and attainment. Being born on this day cloaks you in an aura of solitude. You will always feel somewhat alone, even in the midst of friends, family, and crowds. Yours is a path of self-sufficiency and personal self-mastery. Your sense of well-being comes from success in your chosen endeavors. Retreat to your mountain hideaway, build a fire, and listen to logs crackle. Smell the fragrance of burning wood. Wear a handwoven poncho of chartreuse, indigo, and gray. A carved walking stick will connect you to the earth.

The seventeenth day of the year reduces to eight, adding a natural sense of rhythm to the cycles you feel. Hang a painting of the snow-covered peaks of the Himalayas, and be comforted by their stillness and permanence. Amethyst and peridot will strengthen you.

OBJECTS/IMAGES
a granite fountain, ink, caverns

SHAPES/MATERIALS
mohair, cube shapes, gypsum

COLORS
burnt umber, cobalt blue, aquamarine

ANIMALS
stag, mountain goat

PLANTS, HERBS, EDIBLES
goat cheese, red iris, staghorn sumac, dried citron

ESSENCE
cypress

SOUNDS/RHYTHMS
clink of a mountain pickax, working songs

MUSICAL NOTES
A and G#

DEEP SPACE OBJECT
globular cluster

January 18

The Astrological Interpretation

Your birth date carries within it a very important quality—synthesis. This means that you are filled with a number of talents and resources and a high potential for further creative possibilities. Yet the attainment of an advanced degree of achievement requires that you build your own plateau for success. If you settle for the status quo, you will feel that your potential is not being realized. You have a lot of willpower but sometimes feel that your will is being thwarted by the outer circumstances of your life. Accept what is around you only as a launching pad for greater success in the world.

Your birthday gives you the desire to explore a wide variety of interests. Navigation, astronomy, and mathematics may be of particular interest to you. An image for you is brightly colored birds flying about. At home, have equipment from your travels around you. You may want to carry a compass or have a compass installed in your car. You like to know what direction you are going. Other decorative items could be woven cloth from a Native American tradition, or wall hangings from the East. Dark wood furniture and a lighted globe complete your home atmosphere. In the bedroom consider a sleigh bed. You can imagine you are traveling through the frozen north before you go off to dreamland.

Outdoors, January 18 would enjoy a weathervane and earthenware pots filled with flowers. A brick area in front of your garden would give you room for an outdoor table and chairs. Flowers for you should include ornamental kale, Jerusalem artichoke, and wall germanders.

A Kabbalistic Interpretation

People born on this day sometimes seem to effortlessly negotiate the trials of life without even a raised eyebrow or an angry word. This ability is in part explained by the dual connection between the tarot cards Temperance and the Star. This combination creates not only calm and understanding but also a sense of optimism and direction. You can increase your good fortune by incorporating star patterns, especially seven pointed stars, into your wardrobe. Try a star-shaped pin or a scarf with a star pattern. You may choose to dress somewhat conservatively at work. The use of gray and black can help you to be taken seriously, particularly at meetings.

The downside of all the serenity and luck you have is that it can sometimes allow you to stagnate when you have great potential to grow. At home you may wish to invest in as many different mugs as you can fit into a nice display in your kitchen. Elsewhere in the house you can place unusually shaped ornaments or plants such as cacti. This decorating scheme may be uncomfortable for you at first, but it has great benefits in making you challenge your sense of self.

A Numerological Interpretation

YOUR MAGIC NUMBERS: 10 AND 2

The eighteenth day of the first month reduces to ten, the number of perfection and dominion. Born on this day, you naturally gravitate to leadership roles. This is a path of achievement. You have a knack for utilizing and applying resources for the common good in a group. You can sense and identify diverse needs and assess their solutions. You are capable of embodying the positive attributes of a patriarch looking after the needs of the clan.

The eighteenth day of the year reduces to nine, adding a sense of completeness to your accomplishments. Visit a country estate, and view acres of cultivated land and manicured gardens. Inhale deeply of the fragrance of the earth. Wear a jaunty scarf woven in threads of purple, indigo, and blue. A moonstone pendant, set in silver, will calm your heart.

OBJECTS/IMAGES
archaeology, bricklayers, calendars, calm

SHAPES/MATERIALS
antimony, calcium, carbon, coin shapes

COLORS
flat black, indigo, burnt sienna

ANIMALS
koala bear, yellow-bellied marmot

PLANTS, HERBS, EDIBLES
buckthorn trees, flaxweed, fumitory, goatsbeard

ESSENCE
cajeput

SOUNDS/RHYTHMS
knocking sounds

MUSICAL NOTES
A and C#

DEEP SPACE OBJECT
supernova

January 19

YOUR SIGN
Capricorn

YOUR ELEMENT
Earth

YOUR RULERS
Saturn, Mercury
28–29 degrees
Third Decanate, yang

The Astrological Interpretation

You have a tremendous need to create something special out of your talents and resources. This can only be done when you feel free to use what is around you as the clay for the creation of your own masterworks. If you become too stuck in that clay, then you will be the one who is molded rather than being the artist who molds. The lesson here is very clear—learn how to objectify your surroundings and not just be a part of them. This requires special education and the use of your creative will to master a particular field of endeavor. If you do whatever it takes to perfect this special interest, then you will definitely be rewarded for your efforts.

You are a planner and a seeker interested in trying to match up the everyday world with patterns of universal truths. You may even have some talent for divination. The runes, tea leaves, or dowsing may serve as channels for your intuitions. January 19 also has leadership capabilities. At home, dark woods and serenely lit rooms are restful for you. An old carved trunk is an excellent decorative object. If the trunk is an heirloom, so much the better. Wall sconces in the shape of candelabra lend your home elegance. Art or collecting art may feature in your life. See if copies of paintings of Paul Cézanne (born January 19) appeal to you. A trip to the south of France where Cézanne was born might be a special adventure. In your kitchen keep strings of garlic, herbs, and peppers.

Outdoors January 19 wants a simple garden and enjoys walking in the woods. A copy of *The Thinker* by Rodin might be a wonderful addition to a corner of your yard. Gardens for you are creative and restorative. Go there to think among rue, yellow corydalis, and evergreen trees.

A Kabbalistic Interpretation

Unlike many born this month you tend to wear your heart visibly on your sleeve. When you are out with your partner you can ensure that this has its best effect by wearing a gold brooch studded with emeralds or some other precious green stone. In the workplace, where you might prefer to keep your emotions under control, keep a pale brown square of cloth or cardboard in your pocket or purse to give solidity to your demeanor.

You are quite willing to give your all to your job, provided you can genuinely believe in the product or service you are selling. People born today make excellent sales representatives, and you can aid your chances of success by always sitting in the south when conducting sales meetings.

At home a traditional look is best. The effect you want to create is one of opulence and especially warmth, so surround yourself with lots of heavy furniture, tapestries, and thick luxuriant rugs. An ideal feature for your house would be a large open fire or wood-burning stove, located in the south if possible.

A Numerological Interpretation
YOUR MAGIC NUMBERS: 2 AND 10

The nineteenth day of the first month reduces to two, signifying duality and polarity. You are always aware of contrasts and the opposing view of any position. You desire to know the secrets of the unseen world, and your native intuition probes the outer coverings, peering deep inside. Superstition can be a danger because you see significance in everything and can at times imagine a pattern that isn't there. The nineteenth day of the year reduces to ten, adding the sense of perfection to the pairs of opposites you perceive.

Waterfalls and fountains will soothe you. Walk through an herb garden in bloom, and breathe deeply of the fragrance. Observe a Zen tea ceremony and its fine porcelain tea sets. Hang wind chimes in your garden. Celestite, azurite, and tourmaline are gems to invigorate you. Wear silver bracelets and the color teal whenever you can. Enjoy teas from around the world. Mirrors will enlarge your perspective and enhance your sense of reflectivity.

OBJECTS/IMAGES
beards, coves, fences, a gardener's trowel

SHAPES/MATERIALS
asphalt, astringents, the shape of a clock's pendulum, ebony

COLORS
dark brown, bittersweet, dark purple

ANIMAL
dancing bear

PLANTS, HERBS, EDIBLES
belladonna, aconite (plant), spleenwort, baked potatoes

ESSENCE
opopanax

SOUNDS/RHYTHMS
bass notes, old-fashioned songs

MUSICAL NOTES
C# and A

DEEP SPACE OBJECTS
Alpha Vulcan and a dark nebula

January 20

YOUR SIGNS
Capricorn/Aquarius

YOUR ELEMENTS
Earth/Air

YOUR RULERS
Saturn, Mercury, Uranus
29 degrees Capricorn–
00 degrees Aquarius
Third Decanate, yin
First Decanate, yang

The Astrological Interpretation

Your birth date falls between the last degree of Capricorn and the first degree of the following sign, Aquarius. As a result, you will experience a pull between past and future, established and innovative, secure and experimental. Your task is to blend these tendencies into a harmony of creative self-expression. You have respect for what and who has come before you as well as a tremendous urge to communicate something new to the world. Work with committees and in small groups to achieve common aims and ideals. In your personal relationships, you seek the security of real commitment, yet you also need the freedom to be yourself. You will be happiest if you can bond with a partner who is also quite independent and inventive. Work at creating an original relationship, as you may feel somewhat restricted in a traditional partnership.

Depending on the year and time of your birth, January 20 is either the tail end of Capricorn or the beginning of Aquarius. A convenient image for Capricorns born on January 20 is the ancient silk route—timeless and tradition-oriented. Those just peeking into Aquarius should think of a space-age route: unknown and exciting. You tend to be a collector of ideas and objects. Antiques will feature in your environment. If you tend to Aquarius, these antiques could be scientific instruments, such as an antique medicine chest with apothecary bottles. Capricorn January 20 would love a collection of old coins. You need a space at home for contemplation and musing. A corner facing a large, old tree where you have a comfortable chair and a hassock or footrest is perfect for you.

Warm earth tones are the best palette for January 20 to wear; cashmere is a luxury that you can indulge in. Your more eccentric side might come out in silver jewelry in strong geometric designs.

Outdoors, you want as much raw nature as possible. If you are near the woods this is where you should walk to restore yourself. In more populated areas, a garden with a bench situated near a small circular pool is a place to dream.

A Kabbalistic Interpretation

In occultism, the first day of Aquarius is one of the four "Kerubic" signs, or signs that represent the elements in the Western mystery tradition. When we perform rituals invoking the powers of the universe it is in the West that we locate air—the ruling element of Aquarius. The value of today's date has the same value as the Hebrew word meaning "west." Whenever you are working on something important you should try to do it in the west of your home. You will also benefit if you place your prized possessions in the west.

Some elements of this day's value point toward an interest in facts rather than speculation. Keep a good collection of reference books in your family room or study. The bookcase may be quite plain or have a simple wavy abstract design carved on the sides. If you paint it, use yellow or yellow with a red border.

To encourage a clear flow of thought and an impetus to engage in some self-reflection, invest in some mirrors that are as attractive as they are useful. Avoid thick wooden frames—instead opt for lightweight metallic casings.

A Numerological Interpretation

YOUR MAGIC NUMBERS: 3 AND 2

The twentieth day of the first month reduces to three, the number of growth and unfoldment. You are driven to create and participate in an inner circle of peers, thereby ensuring security and predictability in the circumstances of your life. The lesson of this path is to use your gifts to capitalize on the resources for the good of all, not just your chosen circle. The Masonic orders are secret societies that do public services for hospitals and schools. In the role of architect, does one build a personal palace or design schools, hospitals, art galleries, and concert halls? The twentieth day of the year reduces to two, adding the sense of the continual repetition necessary to learn our lessons. The danger you face is selfishness. Create an inner sanctum in your home. Stained glass in shades of green, red, and indigo will uplift you. Study the Masonic orders and their rituals; this will stir a deep response. Jade, ruby, and tanzanite will enhance your sense of tranquillity.

OBJECTS/IMAGES
blindfolds, castles with parapets, a spaceship blasting off

SHAPES/MATERIALS
amber, leather bags, parallel lines

COLORS
mottled blue, shale gray, buttery yellow

ANIMALS
camel, unicorn

PLANTS, HERBS, EDIBLES
aspen trees, spinach, hops, cornflowers, holly trees

ESSENCES
balsam, rosemary

SOUNDS/RHYTHMS
the sound of arrows hitting bull's-eyes, the sound of sheeps' bells

---

MUSICAL NOTES
D and C#

DEEP SPACE OBJECT
Alpha Sagittarius

January 21

YOUR SIGN
Aquarius

YOUR ELEMENT
Air

YOUR RULER
Uranus
00–1 degree
First Decanate, yang

The Astrological Interpretation

Your birth date indicates a highly communicative person, one who enjoys being surrounded by friends. You love to discuss life and the creative possibilities that can occur when people work together to achieve their common goals and interests. You dislike being restricted by established codes of personal behavior and are very much an individual in your own right. Good at social organizing and planning, it is easy for you to find a common thread that enables people to join together for shared events. You come into conflict with others when you insist that what you see and how you see it is the one and only way to get things done. Learning how to be flexible without feeling that your personal will is being compromised is a very worthwhile personal goal to achieve.

The fixed star Albireo in the constellation of the Swan may fall on some early Aquarian birthdays. The ancients considered this a position of beauty and a lovable disposition. Exploration, design, the arts, and executive ability are all potentially part of your character. A modern home with classical touches characterizes you. In your wardrobe have designer clothing and then add your own flair such as a brilliantly colored scarf or a belt. A shepherd's crook is an image for you, as you wield your authority gently. The gemstones amethyst and aquamarine suit your temperament. Wear jewelry with these stones or carry a piece of the raw mineral.

Outdoors, January 21 has a connection to the land of his/her birth. If you live far away, you will want to maintain flowers, trees, or other reminders of your native soil. Winter heather and blue hydrangeas are two flowers you will enjoy no matter where you are.

A Kabbalistic Interpretation

You are the ultimate dreamer, and while very rewarding in many respects your idealism can get you into difficulty. Your day can be represented as the three letters *Shin Yod Gimel.* The central letter, *Yod,* corresponds to the sign of Virgo, while the full value of these three letters relates to one of the angles of the sign of Virgo. Virgo likes everything to be in order, which can help offset your dreaminess.

When you are away from work you can feel free to let your lunar nature shine. You may want to wear shimmering pale colors around the house, which can be mixed together in a shining rainbow effect rather than in blocks of color. Men can use a tie or handkerchief or even a scarf that is appropriately colored. Consider sitting and listening to some New Age ambient music. The effect of allowing your true self to emerge from the day's stresses will be extremely potent.

Although you like to escape from the real world on a regular basis you are a stickler for cleanliness. Opt for straight clean lines and minimal color in your decorating. Try burning an earthy incense such as dittany of Crete and you may find that you are far better organized and more focused in your work.

A Numerological Interpretation
YOUR MAGIC NUMBERS: 4 AND 3

The twenty-first day of the first month reduces to four. Four is a number of solidity and stability. A square or cube symbolizes strength and a firm foundation, a cornerstone. This is a path of coming to understand the principle of support. What is everlasting? Enduring friendships, breadth of vision, universal orientation, depth of character. The twenty-first day of the year reduces to three, contributing the principle of natural unfoldment to the orderly expression of your life.

Admire and collect antiques. Visit ancient monuments such as the pyramids in Egypt. Listen to the wind in ancestral redwood trees. Take a quiet walk through the grounds of an old adobe mission. Read the headstones in the cemetery. Enjoy a sip of vintage port from an old oak cask. Amethyst, rose quartz, or rhodonite set in white gold will deepen your sensitivity. Grow red poppies and purple irises.

OBJECTS/IMAGES
cyclones, marionettes, mansard roofs, wheels

SHAPES/MATERIALS
batik, hand-painted fabric, Indian mirror fabrics, spheres

COLORS
iridescent green, apricot, orange

ANIMAL
markhor

PLANTS, HERBS, EDIBLES
croton oil, exotic foods, crossandra, guzmania,

ESSENCE
patchouli

SOUNDS/RHYTHMS
ping of a triangle, electric xylophone

MUSICAL NOTES
D# and D

DEEP SPACE OBJECTS
Alpha Aquila, Altair, the Flying Eagle

January 22

YOUR SIGN
Aquarius

YOUR ELEMENT
Air

YOUR RULER
Uranus
1–2 degrees
First Decanate, yang

The Astrological Interpretation

You are striving to achieve a balance between your own orientation to life and the need to work within a group context. It is emotionally essential for you to establish solid friendships and successful relationships with coworkers. Yet you are sometimes torn by the feeling that your individuality will be lost if you do not vigorously stand up for yourself. It is necessary for you to develop a sense of inner security in your actions and activities that cannot be destroyed no matter what the social pressures surrounding you. Use your intuition and your heart to perceive other people's value and worth, and try not to let insecurity and ego get in the way of truth.

The fixed star Altair is located at one degree forty-seven minutes of Aquarius. The ancients called this degree the Flying Eagle and attributed boldness of action to it. You may begin life conservatively and later begin to explore your eccentricities. Have confidence that if you go your own way you will find satisfaction. January 22 wants to be surrounded by one-of-a-kind objects. Perhaps you have glasses made from soda bottles, or ceilings covered with glow-in-the-dark stars. Create your physical space with as much wit and whimsy as you can. A piece of lapis lazuli, uncut, can be a lucky amulet you carry. Eating exotic foods will keep your system tuned up and flexible. If there is an ethnic neighborhood near where you live, go and browse. Indian curries, Chinese vegetables, and Jamaican sauces stimulate your imagination and taste buds.

You may find that you frequently bring matters to a dramatic head that literally clears the air. The rhythm of an unexpected thunderstorm is an image for January 22—the still, heavy air before the storm, the release of tension, and fresh air afterward. Consider a sculpture garden for your yard. See if you can't create outdoor furniture with different sculptured shapes.

A Kabbalistic Interpretation

Living by the edge of a warm and fairly gentle stretch of ocean would be ideal for anyone born this day. If you are in the market for a new home, you might try to find a beach cabin style of house, the squarer the better. If you can't actually get to the sea on a regular basis, keep mementos of the ocean nearby: sand, collections of shells, images of the shore. Keep an aquarium and fill it with crustaceans and shellfish. Add an anemone for color.

The reduction of the value of this day gives us the Hebrew letter *Cheth,* which corresponds to the tarot card the Chariot. Tap the positive energies of this card by having a well-kept garage and ensuring that your car is always running at its best. The downside of *Cheth* is that the defensive energy associated with it can block good emotional communication. Counter this trend by drawing on the symbolism of other influences for this day. A collection of Pierrot or sad clown dolls in the bedroom can help loosen your emotional side.

A Numerological Interpretation

YOUR MAGIC NUMBERS: 5 AND 4

The twenty-second day of the first month reduces to five. Five is an unpredictable number of change, uncertainty, and transition. You can be temperamental and unpredictable like passing storm clouds, sunny one moment, dark and brooding the next. You resent control, and what can be predicted can be controlled. You revel in the unexpected. Sit in the darkness and experience the potentially devastating power of a thunderstorm and the cleansing clarity of the aftermath. Watch a rainbow at dawn. Hang a pair of antique swords over your mantel. Play the *1812 Overture* during breakfast. Go horseback riding in the country.

The twenty-second day of the year reduces to four, contributing the comforting sense of continuity and permanence to the pervasive change in your life. Wear an amethyst pendant for luck.

OBJECTS/IMAGES
face stickers, blue lamp shades, a disco ball

SHAPES/MATERIALS
ray shapes, sapphires, shellac

COLORS
bright blue, electric pink, golden yellow, russet

ANIMALS
electric eel, gnu

PLANTS, HERBS, EDIBLES
wood sage, blue vervain, wisteria

ESSENCE
spike lavender

SOUNDS/RHYTHMS
off beat, crystal water glass music

MUSICAL NOTES
E and F

DEEP SPACE OBJECTS
Beta Aquila, Alshain, Eagle

January 23

YOUR SIGN
Aquarius

YOUR ELEMENT
Air

YOUR RULER
Uranus
2–3 degrees
First Decanate, yang

The Astrological Interpretation

Your birth date indicates that you are a true Aquarian rebel! You have felt from early in your childhood that even though you can easily identify with all people, you do not easily fit into any established mode. It is very important for you to find the focus and form of your own creative self-expression. You have a natural love-hate relationship with organized groups. You need to acquire a deep knowledge of human behavior, as people really interest you and your friendships are of utmost importance. Yet you do not want to be identified with any organization or idea that is not essentially your own. You will be involved with many kinds of people from all sorts of ethnic and social backgrounds—the more different from the norm, the better. Eventually you will find that your group is composed of highly individualistic people just like yourself.

January 23 may be a rebellious romantic. The arts, law, and social welfare attract you. A thought for you is "no man is an island . . . he's a peninsula!" At home you may enjoy having an hourglass prominently displayed or an antique water clock. January 23 likes ingenious reminders of the past. Consider using bolts of diaphanous material in your decor. These could be used as drapes or hung under ceiling lamps to create a billowing cloud effect. If you use your creativity to express your romantic side you will feel less need to challenge authority.

Outdoors, old wooden steamer chairs are a perfect piece of furniture for you to lounge on and look up at the passing clouds. A series of birdhouses around your yard is a good touch. If you catch an indigo bunting or blue jay flying through the trees it is a lucky day.

A Kabbalistic Interpretation

Like most Aquarians you have a decidedly individualistic approach to life. But your sun sign is only a part of the story. The value of your day creates values that represent a balance of earth and air. An excess of either would not be good for your sense of well-being. People born on this day may feel particularly at home in their cellar, as they like to feel close to the earth. Be sure to add a skylight or some other means of allowing in natural light.

If you were born this day you may have an unusually strong love of the cold. While the rest of us are shivering you are eager to go for a nice long walk in the ice and snow. Make sure that you have plenty of ice in the freezer, and consider investing in an ice cream maker.

A definite must for you is a walk-in wardrobe with plenty of richly colored clothes. Ideal materials for you are velvet or fur, or if you prefer, fake fur with realistic patterns. You could hardly do better for yourself than to consider a feline companion. The more aloof the cat, the more you will love her.

A Numerological Interpretation
YOUR MAGIC NUMBERS: 6 AND 5

The twenty-third day of the first month reduces to six. Six is the number of balanced polarities. You are clear where and when you take a stand. You dislike rules, meaningless loyalties, and misplaced alliances. Search for the significance of where you would swear your fealty. Sometimes an oath is a worthy and noble act. Don't carry independence to extremes. This path carries the risk of rebellion for its own sake. Study the rules of engagement. Choose your battles; know your enemy and be certain before you get on the mat. Steel is forged in a furnace, and gold is metamorphosed from lead in the athanor of the alchemist.

The twenty-third day of the year reduces to five, contributing the awareness that you will live to fight another day. Study Tai Chi or another martial art. Amethyst and sapphire set in gold will cool your ardor. Observe the behavior of bull elk or rhino. Purple, orange, and blue are harmonious colors.

OBJECTS/IMAGES
torchère lamps, tornadoes, pinball machines, and grenades

SHAPES/MATERIALS
paisley, madras, lightning rod shapes, and lapis lazuli

COLORS
indigo, lime green, cream

ANIMAL
toucan

PLANTS, HERBS, EDIBLES
Virginian cowslip, Indigo bush, game meats, and feverfew

ESSENCE
lavender

SOUNDS/RHYTHMS
radio theme songs, electric bouzouki

MUSICAL NOTES
F and E

DEEP SPACE OBJECTS
Alpha Capricorn, Al Giedi, the Goat

January 24

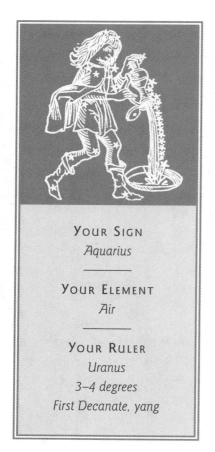

YOUR SIGN
Aquarius

YOUR ELEMENT
Air

YOUR RULER
Uranus
3–4 degrees
First Decanate, yang

The Astrological Interpretation

You have had to do a great deal to combat the pressure you feel to conform to the prevailing rules and regulations of society. Your life contains a distinct challenge—how to be yourself and still maintain harmonious relationships with those close to you. Your birth date is indicative of a person who seeks to create peaceful understanding between yourself and others. You have to be different from others, and yet you do not want to alienate the people who matter to you. There is a definite humanitarian urge within you. You certainly are aware of social oppression and will work to maintain both your own and other people's personal liberty. Your challenge is to create a clear sense of your individual responsibility to life. This allows you the freedom you require but permits you to contribute in a practical way to the welfare of society.

January 24 may be located near the constellation Corona Borealis which the ancients believed bestowed a clever and penetrating mind. Unusual ideas and therapies that can benefit yourself and others fascinate you. You may develop an alternative healing modality, which combines body therapies and mental imaging. An image for you is the White Magician. At home have a collection of tapes with music of the spheres. You may want to have your astrology chart interpreted musically. Your home should be completely modern and spare. If your climate is suitable consider having solar panels or using wind power as a source of energy. Meditation chimes are objects of beauty and inspiration for you.

Outdoors, January 24 would enjoy a garden of medicinal herbs as well as aromatic flowers for massage oils and aromatherapy. Cassia, foxglove, feverfew, and lavender are scents and oils with which to experiment.

A Kabbalistic Interpretation

Very often in life you find yourself torn between two equally attractive but opposite paths. To help ease such tensions, find an attractive painting of either a yin-yang symbol or a large hexagram in red and blue and hang this on a west-facing wall in your home. You can also purchase some sodalite, which is available from most pharmacies. When relaxing in a warm bath hold the sodalite and focus on the decision at hand while allowing your mind to become more rational and logical in its approach.

You need to ensure that you have an area in your home that is clearly your own, even when you are in a serious relationship. You can mark this space by investing in an antique chair—if you can find a rocking chair, so much the better.

One of the best investments you could make to encourage good family relationships is to buy some very large earthenware pots and place them outside your home. Ideally these pots should be filled with water not earth. If you want to put some plants in them, opt for water lilies or a similar plant. One of the values of this day corresponds to the Kamea, or magic square, of the planet Mars. By surrounding your home with water you are effectively dampening the volatile element in your personality.

A Numerological Interpretation
YOUR MAGIC NUMBERS: 7 AND 6

The twenty-fourth day of the first month reduces to seven. Seven is the number of victory and rest. Victory doesn't mean win-lose but successful accomplishment. Victory in this sense doesn't mean domination of another, but the sense of the biblical metaphor where the Creator rested on the seventh day. This path embodies satisfaction in accomplishment and renewal of the spirit for continued development. Rest is healing and ministers to the spirit.

The twenty-fourth day of the year reduces to six, the number of harmony of opposites and reconciliation of polarities. Topaz and halite are calming. Take a leisurely canoe trip on a gentle river. Spend a long weekend at a health spa or retreat. Have a relaxing massage while a soft melody plays in the background. Watch a cat napping to learn the art of relaxation. Yellow-orange and blue-violet are colors to harmonize your energies.

OBJECTS/IMAGES
laser beams, X rays, posters, light therapy

SHAPES/MATERIALS
flying buttresses, lead, sapphires, ray shapes

COLORS
phosphorescent radio dials, kelly green

ANIMALS
penguin, demoiselle crane

PLANTS, HERBS, EDIBLES
cypress trees, kava kava, table salt, blue chicory

ESSENCE
spikenard

SOUNDS/RHYTHMS
pentatonic scale, news broadcasts

MUSICAL NOTES
F# and F

DEEP SPACE OBJECTS
Beta Capricorn, Dabih, Lucky One of the Slaughterers

January 25

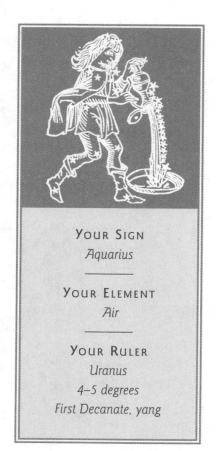

YOUR SIGN
Aquarius

YOUR ELEMENT
Air

YOUR RULER
Uranus
4–5 degrees
First Decanate, yang

The Astrological Interpretation

This birth date is especially geared to communicating with a wide variety of people. You will find that the Internet and E-mail services offer you many opportunities to gather information and exchange ideas. It is important for you to be in the know. You are less a conformist to fads than an originator of your own style. It is difficult for anyone to change your mind or course of action once you have set your sights on a given objective. Yet this intellectual stubbornness does not stop you from investigating, exploring, and studying those unusual fields of endeavor that stimulate your mind. Take care that you do not dissipate your energy by trying to cover too many bases at the same time.

January 25 has a highly tuned nervous system and is like a lightning rod for ideas. You may be scrupulously honest about what you know and what you don't. Idealistic in love, you are likely to have many platonic relationships. To support your nervous system try valerian tea. Sip your tea in a white cup with a distinct modern shape. You enjoy being around one-of-a-kind things. You can be partial to oriental designs; a Chinese robe in purple, gold, and blue would be a perfect at-home garment. Intricate puzzles and boxes within boxes fascinate you. Physical flexibility is important for January 25 to cultivate. Stretch your body frequently, and in your work area have articles that remind you of curved waves. The double helix is an image for you to think about.

Outdoors, January 25 likes an expansive environment with an artistic focus. A sculpture garden or rooftop with interesting shapes feeds your imagination. You may prefer cold weather; penguins are animals that intrigue and delight you.

A Kabbalistic Interpretation

Though in many ways people born this day can be charming and seem like quiet individuals, on the rare occasions when you are offended or hurt you will make absolutely certain that you get your revenge no matter how long it takes. A jade ring or pendant may help to grant a sense of perspective and objectivity when such situations arise.

You like to feel in tune with the natural ebb and flow of life, and as a result you may forget to make sufficient plans to direct yourself toward a specific goal. Try growing a yucca or cactus plant in your study or in whichever corner of your living room you like to sit and think. These plants emphasize the importance of clarity in personal growth.

Emotionally you feel things very deeply and can sometimes be oversensitive to comments or actions of others that are not actually meant to hurt you in any way. By regularly adding jasmine oil and some chips or crystals of amethyst to your bathwater you will find that you have a much better understanding of other people's intentions.

A Numerological Interpretation
YOUR MAGIC NUMBERS: 8 AND 7

The twenty-fifth day of the first month reduces to eight. Eight is the number that signifies the continual rhythm and repetition of cycles. We learn what is to come by observing what has gone before. You have great respect for history and tradition, but our ancestors have not always been wise. We can learn the lessons of our elders or repeat their mistakes. Tradition can be an inspiration or a trap.

Curl up on your antique sofa with an engaging historical novel filled with castles and crown jewels. Attend an event brimming with pageantry, pomp and circumstance. Wear royal purple for fun. An amethyst pendant set in gold will make you feel special. The twenty-fifth day of the year reduces to seven, adding a respite to the feeling of continual movement you experience.

OBJECTS/IMAGES
cyclones, clubhouses, gyroscopes

SHAPES/MATERIALS
chalcedony, lapis lazuli

COLORS
bright purple, azure, plum

ANIMALS
pheasant, quail

PLANTS, HERBS, EDIBLES
clover, niacin, hummingbird's tongue

ESSENCE
tarragon

SOUNDS/RHYTHMS
claps of cymbals, Indian ragas

MUSICAL NOTES
G and F#

DEEP SPACE OBJECT
globular cluster

January 26

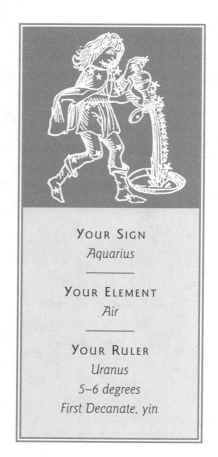

YOUR SIGN
Aquarius

———

YOUR ELEMENT
Air

———

YOUR RULER
Uranus
5–6 degrees
First Decanate, yin

The Astrological Interpretation

This is the birth date of a person who has a need to achieve a place in society. Many people born on this day find themselves drawn to the creation of personal wealth. You realize that in order to achieve this aspiration, you will need to align yourself with friends and associates who are involved with helping one another reach this goal. You have an inner engine that keeps on manufacturing innovative ways to be enterprising. Your job is to learn how to transform the ideal into the real. Once this is accomplished, you can be very successful indeed.

January 26 has an elusive and mysterious quality and a subtle mind. You can actually think and analyze thoughts at the same time. If you feel self-conscious, look at yourself in two mirrors placed directly opposite each other. No use watching yourself if you go on forever! Have a variety of ingenious toys to play with. Mechanical banks, toy trains, even a motorcycle might be engaging pastimes. Music attracts you, and you may particularly enjoy listening to J. S. Bach. Decorate your living space with charcoal and line drawings. Escher?? The best way to calm your mind is to sink back in a comfortable blue sofa and watch a mobile made of interesting shapes bob and weave in the breeze.

Outdoors, January 26 likes hilly terrain and space to putter. Outdoor lighting may be a place to display creativity. Japanese lanterns, recessed garden lights, or some gadget that you invent to highlight your outdoor space would all appeal to you. Having sliding glass doors between your home and yard is the best idea you could possibly have.

A Kabbalistic Interpretation

This day carries a great deal of force. You are likely to be attracted to images and objects of dynamism and action. Feel free to make liberal use of color throughout your home. Oranges, all shades of red, particularly crimson, and any bright tones of green are all suited to you and will highlight your active and vivacious personality. You might cover your walls with prints from various pop artists to create an atmosphere of verve and movement in your living space. In your wardrobe, on the other hand, you may want to offset your natural energy with quieter colors and emphasize a few carefully chosen accessories. These will have an added impact if they incorporate wheel designs or images of birds.

You like having a busy lifestyle, and unlike many people you have little need of a space where you can sit and fully unwind. You will need a lot of shelves to house your many gadgets and trinkets. Selecting brass or lead objects adds some stability and grounding to your life. In the garden, consider a Japanese minimalist approach with lots of white gravel and individual plants.

A Numerological Interpretation

YOUR MAGIC NUMBERS: 9 AND 8

The twenty-sixth day of the first month reduces to nine. Nine is the number signifying completion and the close of a cycle. This is a path of interpreting the drama of life for the sake of others. You have a tendency to overreact to events and create artificial high drama. Turn that quality to storytelling. Entertain others. You can be a great mimic, as your ear detects subtleties of expression in others. You are highly sensitive and feel other's pain. Sleep time is very important to your well-being. Your most important growth work occurs in your dreams. Read books of dream symbols. Drink plenty of pure water. Amethyst, malachite, and chrysocolla will balance your energies. Eight-pointed stars will calm you and draw you inward.

The twenty-sixth day of the year reduces to eight, contributing the sense of the continual rise and fall of the curtain on the stage of life. The show is never really over. Sleep in a four-poster bed with down comforters and purple-and-lime-green print sheets. Don't be ashamed to sleep with stuffed animals and teddy bears. Listen to lullabies as you drift off to sleep. Read about night-blooming flowers that open in the moonlight.

OBJECTS/IMAGES
a van with psychedelic colors, rodeos, guns

SHAPES/MATERIALS
uraninite, valve shapes, windmills

COLORS
dazzling white, ice blue, royal blue, turquoise

ANIMALS
penguin, laughing gull

PLANTS, HERBS, EDIBLES
popcorn, oxalis, silver bell

ESSENCE
lavendin

SOUNDS/RHYTHMS
wind chimes, cha-cha-cha

MUSICAL NOTES
G# and G

DEEP SPACE OBJECT
nova

January 27

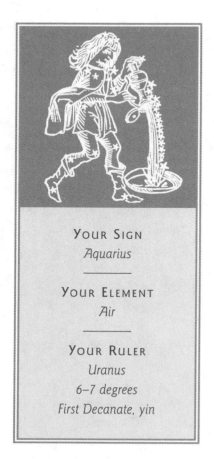

YOUR SIGN
Aquarius

YOUR ELEMENT
Air

YOUR RULER
Uranus
6–7 degrees
First Decanate, yin

The Astrological Interpretation

Your birth date indicates a person eager to uncover the mysterious and hidden facets of life. You are curious and tend to have a wide variety of friends with whom you can explore the many things that draw your attention, but you are close to only a few. You rebel at the thought of being just another name and number in society's collective computer. It is therefore of vital importance to you to create a firm sense of your own individuality. You need a partner who is independent and supportive of your desire to explore life on your own terms. This person has to be involved with his or her own path; as soon as you feel hemmed in or restricted by someone's emotional demands, you tend to flee. Compassion for other people's needs should be cultivated, even if you are not necessarily the one who can fulfill them.

January 27 approaches life with a childlike self-centeredness that can be charming and attractive. You have an excellent memory and intuition. You may not choose to develop your abilities, but they will steer you well in a pinch. Precision instruments interest you. An astrolabe could be a decorative item in your home. A compass, retractable tape measure, and a carpenter's level are all tools that come in handy. The spare decor of a Zen dojo appeals to you. Your home could feature tatami mats instead of rugs. If you have a large storage area you will probably fill it with equipment from past interests.

Outdoors, a small reflecting pool is a good addition to your yard. If the pool reflects outdoor lights at night, you will find the patterns hypnotic. In your garden the shapes of flower beds as well as the flowers are of interest to you. Think about using unique containers, such as Lucite boxes, as planters on a balcony or terrace. Fill them with lantana plants and petunias.

A Kabbalistic Interpretation

To enter the home of someone born on this day is like entering a church or other religious space, in that there is a sense of peace and tranquility throughout the whole house. People born today are lovers of serenity and should indulge that preference to the fullest. A recording of Gregorian chants is an excellent gift choice for January 27 birthdays—you will love it for its purity and seriousness. If you were born today you will gain a lot of pleasure and contentment if you populate your cabinets with a variety of religious symbols.

There is a strong association with the tarot card the Hanged Man in today's date. Since this is a card that emphasizes self-sacrifice, you should be encouraged to treat yourself. Though not public about your emotions, you are likely to be extremely passionate. This date is a very secretive day, and in order to feel more secure consider buying ornamental boxes, especially if they are decorated with green details or brass fittings. A lockable diary and a lockable drawer in which to keep it are an absolute must.

A Numerological Interpretation
YOUR MAGIC NUMBERS: 10 AND 9

The twenty-seventh day of the first month reduces to ten. Ten is the number of dominion and perfection. Ten closes the cycle before beginning anew. Cultivate resourcefulness. Create yourself in your own image. This path requires complete understanding of how our choices create our reality. Take care not to overstimulate. Retreat from electronic equipment and devices. They will affect your energy field. Keep an aquarium of blue-violet and fuschia-colored freshwater fish. Listen to the lilting sounds of a string quartet.

The twenty-seventh day of the year reduces to nine, which adds the sense of satisfied completion to the close of cycles in your life. Fluorite, clear quartz, and rhodochrosite are gems to stimulate you to begin again. Visualize a lake, smooth as glass, in the moonlight. Enjoy the earthy smell of night air.

OBJECTS/IMAGES
wish dolls, a dragon-spout-whistling teakettle, and news anchor people

---

SHAPES/MATERIALS
opals, ray shapes, electrical insulation, and muscovite (mineral)

COLORS
changeable colors, violet

ANIMALS
kiskadee flycatcher, golden warbler

PLANTS, HERBS, EDIBLES
bleeding heart, oyster plant, microwaved dishes, and spikenard

---

ESSENCE
yarrow

SOUNDS/RHYTHMS
music by Mozart

MUSICAL NOTES
A and G#

DEEP SPACE OBJECT
supernova

January 28

YOUR SIGN
Aquarius

YOUR ELEMENT
Air

YOUR RULERS
Uranus, Saturn
7–8 degrees
First Decanate, yin

The Astrological Interpretation

You have been known to surprise your many friends with quixotic and unpredictable behavior. As soon as someone thinks he really knows you, you come up with a new facet of your personality that causes him to think twice. In fact, you may do something completely spontaneously just to turn people's heads. You enjoy the company of unusual people and are inventive about how to create opportunities for social interaction. It is much easier for you to have a wide variety of associates and many social engagements than to be in a close relationship that requires a profound commitment of emotional intimacy. You would do well as a professional communicator and may have a natural talent for working in the field of computer technology.

January 28 emphasizes the ingenious aspects of the Aquarian nature. If you think of the Hubble deep-space telescope depicting a Uranian influence, you can appreciate the far-reaching vision of your sign. Your gifts may also include sudden impulses and insights. Try calming herbs like valerian and lady's slipper, as all this electrical energy is tough on the nervous system. Your home environment might include a collection of old radios or telephones. January 28 may also be fond of very cold water. Keep sparkling mineral water in the fridge, and drink it with ice. If you sip your water in a multicolored or striped glass it will be all the more pleasing.

You are interested in the humanitarian connection among people. A magnifying glass is an image for you. The glass distorts objects at a distance but clarifies and enlarges them for close inspection.

Outdoors the starry night is your natural habitat. Create constellations on your ceiling so you can learn to identify them. Meteors and comets may hold particular appeal. You may especially enjoy reading about the historical development of astrology.

A Kabbalistic Interpretation

The full value of the date in Hebrew has connections to ideas of totality and unity as well as enormous diversity. White, the color that contains all other colors, is perfect for you because it is simple while containing complexity.

A prism placed in a window that lets in the midday sun will produce a rainbow of colors that is wonderfully inspirational. You may want to give free play to your abundant artistic nature by investing in a watercolor set so that you can capture the patterns created by the prism.

As much as you love to express your artistic side, you are shrewd in the field of human interaction. A silver ring on your little finger will give you an extra edge when communicating with your staff and colleagues. To give yourself a boost of confidence when it comes to management, make sure your office has some touches of red and green—you could even try painting something yourself.

A Numerological Interpretation
YOUR MAGIC NUMBERS: 2 AND 10

The twenty-eighth day of the first month reduces to two, a number of receptivity and duplication. Two is the mirror image of one, a perfect reflection. Inherent in this day is the necessity to purify and clarify values. What is worth copying to perfection? Sometimes the figure in a wax museum can evoke the emotions about the character portrayed. You value thoroughbreds in every facet of life, whether they are racehorses or contractors. You might say that you strive to be a perfect ten. Don't pay excessive attention to outer forms. An old cliché affirms that "clothes don't make the man." But go ahead, dress up, and have a candlelight dinner in an elegant restaurant. Sip a bubbly flute of fine champagne.

Colors to soothe and inspire you are purples, blues, and sunset orange. Minerals to ground and strengthen you are celestite, azurite, and tourmaline. Surround yourself with statues and figurines, beautiful paintings, or sculptures and scented candles. Objects of art should be enjoyed. Visit your favorite museum or gallery. The twenty-eighth day of the year reduces to ten, adding the sense of a perfected process to this path.

OBJECTS/IMAGES
fiber optics, a pilot flying, compasses

SHAPES/MATERIALS
rhomboid, lucite

COLORS
azure blue, deep purple, orange

ANIMALS
snow goose, blue heron

PLANTS, HERBS, EDIBLES
celandine, aconite, cornflowers

ESSENCE
impatiens

SOUNDS/RHYTHMS
Morse code, ragtime

MUSICAL NOTES
C# and A

DEEP SPACE OBJECT
the Dumbbell Nebula

January 29

YOUR SIGN
Aquarius

YOUR ELEMENT
Air

YOUR RULER
Uranus
8–9 degrees
First Decanate, yin

The Astrological Interpretation

It is not enough for you to hold a vision in your mind or a dream in your heart. You have to act upon what you value and believe. Take the necessary time to get whatever training and education your aspirations require. Unless you are firm and clear in what you seek to achieve, you will not be able to convince others of your convictions. People who are born on this date are often gifted with a high intuitive sense. You may know what people are about to say before they even open their mouths. Although strongly attached to your own ideas, you are open to what other people have to say. You know that you cannot be changed in your direction, but you can find something of value in almost everyone you meet and incorporate what truth you perceive into your own life.

January 29 has many original ideas concerning the nature of existence. You have a particular talent for letting light into dark places. Your opposing sign's symbol, the lion, is a figure for you to think about. Yours is not a superstitious nature, just one aware that unseen forces often guide our lives. Charms you have collected in your travels are good objects to carry in your pocket. A copy of your own astrology chart could be an interesting decorative object in your home. A whimsical touch in your home could be signs or pictures from vaudeville theaters; January 29 has a dramatic sense of life and enjoys corny fun.

Outdoors your garden may be less than organized. Zinnias are flowers for you. Place some whirligigs or toy windmills in among your flowers. A small model of the Eiffel Tower is a pleasing shape for you and a reminder of foreign lands.

A Kabbalistic Interpretation

Because of this birthday's connection with all things natural and your innate ability to nurture and encourage growth in others, you would be very comfortable living on a farm. If you don't live in a rural setting you can make yourself feel at home with some pictures depicting traditional bucolic scenes.

People born on this day tend to be solid and reliable. The full value of this day corresponds to the energies of the negative aspects of Taurus. This may make a person taciturn, stubborn, and occasionally unenthusiastic. You can counter this energy by carrying an iron object in your pocket and wearing moonstone jewelry.

You are an excellent craftsperson and love to work with your hands. You can work well with clay or wood and prefer to make elegant objects with minimal decoration. While you may naturally like to make pots and other spherical pieces you could try some angular designs to add some fire and air energy to your life.

A Numerological Interpretation

YOUR MAGIC NUMBERS: 3 AND 2

The twenty-ninth day of the first month reduces to three. Three signifies creative self-expression. You excel at storytelling and re-creating an event in a dramatic and humorous way. The world's a stage, and you have the ability to transform images. Imagine you hold a flag with the embroidered image of a falcon. By waving the flag, you can make the falcon fly. Make the most of things. Be able to take a stand, but take care to choose your battles wisely. Many victories are empty, and broken hearts are not easily mended. There is a major difference between crossing swords and dueling to the death. Meditate on the difference between self-dedication and vindictive pride.

Fly a colored flag on your porch. Buy season tickets to the theater. The twenty-ninth day of the year reduces to two, adding the sense of repetition to the creative expression of this path. The antics of a toy French poodle will amuse you.

OBJECTS/IMAGES
a pen/flashlight, unicycles, and faith healers

SHAPES/MATERIALS
octagons, ball shapes, freshwater gray pebble pearls

COLORS
azure, streaked colors, carrot, bisque

ANIMALS
buffalo, unicorn

PLANTS, HERBS, EDIBLES
frankincense, table salt, locoweed

ESSENCE
cedar wood

SOUNDS/RHYTHMS
hiccoughs, vesper bells

MUSICAL NOTES
D and C#

DEEP SPACE OBJECT
Alpha Tucana

January 30

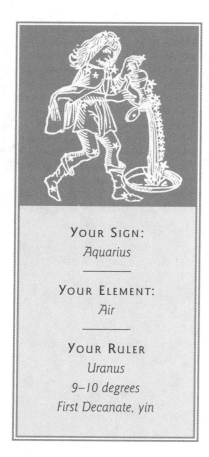

YOUR SIGN:
Aquarius

———

YOUR ELEMENT:
Air

———

YOUR RULER
Uranus
9–10 degrees
First Decanate, yin

The Astrological Interpretation

It is a simple matter for you to understand the common threads of human experience, no matter what language a person speaks or what the color of his or her skin may be. You are able to grasp the fact that we all belong to the same human family, and this understanding gives you a great advantage in your social relationships. You are good at organization and seem to have a sixth sense about knowing who should sit next to whom at a dinner party. The drawback to your intuition is that you may tend to see people as types not individuals. Although it is certainly not difficult to approach you, it can be difficult to be intimate with you. You do very well when you cover a large territory as your vision is more suited to the general than to the specific.

January 30 can fall on what astrologers call a "critical degree." This means your Aquarian nature may experience highs and lows, such as extremes in popularity. Your character gives you the ability to look at life and problems from an unusual angle. Look at your home, clothes, and office and throw out anything that doesn't appeal or have a special meaning for you. If you have been keeping important papers in a worn, gray folder, get a collection of purple or neon blue folders. A little change might herald bigger changes. Decorate at home with some pictures or pieces of ancient Greek art. Lavender is a scent you might find irresistible. Place sachets in your drawers and buy or make a silk lavender pillow to place over your eyes before you sleep. Keep changing the position of furniture and objects in your home to renew your energies.

Outdoors, you like a crisp wind blowing through your hair. A motorcycle might be the perfect way to zoom around. In your garden, think about placing some replicas of archaeological statues. January 30 is also technologically savvy and may design a lighting system to highlight areas of the garden or yard.

A Kabbalistic Interpretation

From your behavior in the office your work colleagues would generally assume you are a spartan individual, with little desire for creature comforts. They are often surprised the first time they visit you at home because there you feel free to let loose and show your softer side. To soften your image on the job, add some pastel colors to your office wardrobe. This will also help you lower your stress levels.

Despite your spartan work appearance, you love the sentimental and can derive great benefit from this aspect of your life. In fact you could fill your spare shelf space with cute figurines and especially cuddly toys.

One value of your day is thirty-one, which is the value of one of the kabbalistic names or aspects of God, relating to the compassionate aspect of the divine. It also connects with the Hanged Man card in the tarot. Compassion is a wonderful virtue, but it can sometimes lead to a lack of joie de vivre—you can circumvent this by bathing with an invigorating oil such as jasmine while burning a sky blue candle.

A Numerological Interpretation

YOUR MAGIC NUMBERS: 4 AND 3

The thirtieth day of the first month reduces to four. Four is the number of order and solidity. Your sense of stability must be sustained from within, not from the ephemeral approval of others. No matter how enthusiastic the applause, the true measure of your significance comes from you. External recognition is simply encouragement, not an end in itself. You can be cool in a crisis when everyone else is in a panic. Observe the behavior of sports fans. Today's darling can become tomorrow's forgotten hero. Enjoy jazz. Purple and red are colors to sustain you.

The thirtieth day of the year reduces to three, adding the influence of natural unfoldment to the innate order of the number four. Go to the World Series and enjoy a big tub of buttery popcorn. Watch the academy awards. Rhodochrosite and tourmaline will recharge your batteries.

OBJECTS/IMAGES
astronauts in space, blue votive candles

SHAPES/MATERIALS
wing shapes, sheer fabric with metallic threads

COLORS
periwinkle blue, jade, butterscotch

ANIMAL
glowworm

PLANTS, HERBS, EDIBLES
celandine, wood sage

ESSENCE
myrrh

SOUNDS/RHYTHMS
telegraph messages, folk rhythms

MUSICAL NOTES:
D# and D

DEEP SPACE OBJECT
Beta Mensa

January 31

YOUR SIGN
Aquarius

YOUR ELEMENT
Air

YOUR RULERS
Uranus, Mercury
10–11 degrees
Second Decanate, yin

The Astrological Interpretation

You are the recipient of sudden flashes of inspiration. These bolts of awareness awaken you to instantaneous understandings and an immediate resolution of problems you may have been contemplating for a long time. No matter how foggy or uncertain times may be, at some appropriate moment, you know you will receive the opening for which you have long been waiting. You may not have the means of implementing what you know in the day-to-day world in which you live. You are then left with the realization of your own responsibility—you must acquire the practical knowledge that like a lightning rod brings your inspiration safely down to earth.

January 31 is idealistic and mindful of contributing to social welfare and the common good. Your first ruling planet, Uranus, bears the name of the ancient Greek sky god. Your thoughts are ever upward. All zigzag shapes please you. At home decorate with lamps that have unusual shapes and reflect a variety of colors. A neon sign with your name or street address could be a unique touch. Invest in a good hairbrush; January 31 tends to have a lot of static electricity, and a brush will feel good and calm you. At home a retreat for you might be an attic with a skylight or high window. If you live in a city a high-rise building would suit you. Watch weather systems roll in; you may find your moods affected by different weather.

Outdoors, January 31 has a strong need to exercise. Physically your body is quite forceful, and with all the mental activity you are capable of, you need exercise to balance you. Running on a track or fast walking is just the thing. You may particularly like running in the cold weather. For your own garden consider planting climbing vines such as clematis.

A Kabbalistic Interpretation

You like a little bit of everything in your life, which makes you a fun person to know. When you entertain you make sure that the occasion is a veritable feast for the senses. You can be extravagant, mixing spices and flavors from a variety of cultures and cuisines. Your natural sense of balance, indicated by the association with the Temperance card in the tarot, will produce a gastronomic delight, no matter what the mix.

The value of your day is filled with symbols of balance and harmony. It is nearly always the case that when we accentuate our natural personality through the use of symbols and sympathetic objects we are happier and generally more content in the way our life develops. Ideal for you would be a brooch or tiepin in the shape of a traditional scale. Tradition says this should be made of tin, though you may prefer to find one in gold or silver.

Purple, which represents the balance of the two major creative forces of fire and water, is an ideal color for you. In your home, try white walls with a royal purple border, or you could look for purple glass or crystal vases.

A Numerological Interpretation
YOUR MAGIC NUMBERS: 5 AND 4

The thirty-first day of the first month reduces to five. Five is the number of mediation, halfway between one and ten. Five is in constant motion. Yours is a path of understanding what truly inspires you and becoming intimate with that realization. When your efforts benefit the community, you derive great joy. Yours is the birth path of fluctuating fire supported by the firm foundation of four to give permanence. Drink deeply from the well of your spiritual understanding of connectedness. If directed selfishly, your nature leads to self-obsession.

The thirty-first day of the year reduces to four, contributing the quality of solidity to the continuous change you experience in your life. Volunteer for the Red Cross. Keep a pair of lovebirds, and arrange purple, red, and orange flowers in a pottery vase. Wear a red robe and teal pajamas or nightgown. Laugh often and have one-on-one intimate conversations with your close friends. Calcite and zircon will ground your energies. Wear a copper bracelet when you can.

OBJECTS/IMAGES
bright blue ceramic birds, satellite dishes, inventions

SHAPES/MATERIALS
azurite, lead, obsidian

COLORS
tie-dyed colors, sunshine yellow, tangerine

ANIMALS
indigo bunting, willow ptarmigan

PLANTS, HERBS, EDIBLES
spring larkspur, microwave black popcorn, wandering Jew

ESSENCE
vetiver

SOUNDS/RHYTHMS
radio static, ondes martenot (early synthesizer)

MUSICAL NOTES
E and D#

DEEP SPACE OBJECTS
Epsilon Aquarius, Albali, the Swallower

February 1

YOUR SIGN
Aquarius

YOUR ELEMENT
Air

YOUR RULERS
Uranus, Saturn, Mercury
11–12 degrees
Second Decanate, yin

The Astrological Interpretation

You are a person whose varied interests stretch to the horizon. As you travel through life experimenting and experiencing, you will find it increasingly important to establish a sense of priorities. In your eyes all people have equal importance and should be treated impartially by the law and be able to walk on this planet free of prejudice. Although this is definitely true, you will find many complications in your life if you do not also see the truth and beauty in our differences. All your friends cannot be your *best* friend. Your life will give you many opportunities to express yourself creatively, and it is up to you to distinguish the A list from the B list. Once you have established this sense of structure, you will find it easier to organize your success in life.

In ancient times Aquarius was ruled by Saturn. When Uranus was discovered in 1781 astrologers designated it the new ruler of Aquarius. Some Aquarians hearken back to the rulership of Saturn and are more conservative; others blaze forward as pioneers willing to upset the old order to find something new. February 1 tends to look forward but can get into a tussle with himself as to which philosophy, the new or the old, will triumph. This internal conflict takes energy, so your home environment needs softness and comfort. This style will tend to be modern with a very-old fashioned bed with lots of comforters. Deep blues and purple pillows soothe your charged nervous system. A spiral stairway connecting floors or leading to a sleeping loft is a great way to increase your sense of space. Also you like the unlimited possibility of the upward spiral.

Outdoors you like a windswept environment. A garden is nice, but you probably won't spend much time tending it. A vista of space gets your imagination going. A windmill—life-size or a model—characterizes this sign's inventive and powerful character.

A Kabbalistic Interpretation

Ever since the 1960s hit song "Age of Aquarius," Aquarians have been misperceived as airheads with a flowery spirituality and an unhealthy penchant for bell-bottoms and ruffled shirts. While there are indeed many Aquarians who are drawn to the flower child aspects of New Age culture, people born February 1 are more likely to be attracted to the shadow side. Your flare for the dark and the unusual may be reflected in your choice of pet, which could be a scorpion or a collection of exotic spiders.

You are fairly materialistic for an Aquarian, and this is represented by today's correspondence to the Devil card in the tarot. You may want to choose some blue display cabinets to show off your beloved possessions. Oak cabinets and shelving will inject an element of benevolence and justice in your life

The most positive aspect of your interest in the dark and unusual is your energetic and enthusiastic nature. You can help yourself to use that infectious energy in a directed and goal-centered way by wearing anything with an orange-yellow hue to it and hanging very geometrical artwork in your work space.

A Numerological Interpretation
YOUR MAGIC NUMBERS: 3 AND 5

The first day of the second month reduces to three. Three is the number of multiplication. This is a path of experiencing creation's limitless levels of expression, like octaves on a piano, or a stairway to heaven. You are always in forward motion, looking ahead. The negative aspect is the desire to stay ahead of the Joneses instead of making constructive progress. Ponder snowflakes, a paradox of unity and diversity. Do snowflakes compete for the complexity of their hexagonal uniqueness, or is that expression inherent in the creative workings of the universe? If each snowflake is unique, how much so are humans? Play the piano. What is the significance of first violin in an orchestra?

Fluorite, tourmaline, and dioptase will aid your focus. The thirty-second day of the year reduces to five, adding comfort with change to your continual upward movement.

OBJECTS/IMAGES
model airplanes, kilim patterns, ankle bracelet

SHAPES/MATERIALS
spray paint, variegated wool, glitter eye shadow, star sapphire

COLORS
ice blue, salmon

ANIMALS
greyhound dog, blue jay

PLANTS, HERBS, EDIBLES
bird-of-paradise, cornflowers, quail

ESSENCE
smell of winter

SOUNDS/RHYTHMS
click of electric switches, wind rattling a window, electric guitar riffs

MUSICAL NOTES
D and E

DEEP SPACE OBJECTS
Theta Capricorn, Dorsum

February 2

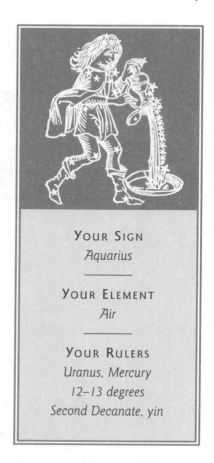

The Astrological Interpretation

You have an instinct about how people will behave under a given set of circumstances. You know how to characterize events and find that what may be a surprise to others is quite matter-of-fact to you. Although the future may stand clear in terms of other people's lives, your own future is not always so simple to define. You are an idealistic person and tend to be quite optimistic and even cavalier about life and its events. Be sure to acquire knowledge and technical methodologies that can anchor your mind in more earthly, practical ways. Once you have developed some concrete skills, you will find that your intuition has a firmer place to land and your inner insecurities will gradually give way to true creative power.

The fixed star Dorsum may be located on some February 2 birthdays. This position was considered by ancients to make one liable to bites from venomous creatures! Your strong assertiveness means a challenge in life could be to tame your headstrong attitude. If you or anyone in your family was in the military, then consider framing medals, discharge papers, or other insignias. Under Mercury's influence, you may have a love of communication gadgets. A walkie-talkie to keep track of family members would be efficient and fun. You can have a strong love of home but be too busy to spend a lot of time on domesticity. In your dining area keep a candle centerpiece and light the candle at mealtimes; this ritual is simple and can help center you.

Outdoors, February 2 is interested in weather and would enjoy some kind of instrument that tells the direction of the wind. Your garden area should be filled with unique and unusual flowers. Blue flowers such as harebell are ideal.

A Kabbalistic Interpretation

You are probably something of a gambler, liking to place the odd bet and also happier than most to take risks in your life. An appropriate good luck charm might be a miniature roulette wheel, all red or red and gold in color. Any wheel shapes are good for you, thanks to the kabbalistic associations of this day. In order to keep your work life running smoothly you could find a wheeled ornament to put on your desk.

Whether you are male or female it's likely that your home will have the atmosphere of a "bachelor pad." Colors are bold, rooms cluttered, and it probably wouldn't be described as scrupulously tidy. February 2 birthdays have a strong connection to physical activities and sports. An old print of a boxer in a heavy wooden frame can help this birthday feel more positive about the challenges in life.

There is a connection in today's value to the tarot card the Tower. The Tower card indicates that catastrophic upheaval needs to be taken seriously. You will never be someone who takes the safe route, but you could become more aware of the possible consequences of your actions. To facilitate this, use some narcissus oil in your bath and buy plain gray files and shelves to house papers of importance.

A Numerological Interpretation
YOUR MAGIC NUMBERS: 4 AND 6

The second day of the second month reduces to four. Four is the number of measurement and order. The English word *ruler*, used to indicate a measuring device as well as a monarch, stems from royalty's original role of ordering, measuring, and meting out reward and punishment. The number of this day also indicates the desire for balance and harmony. Your sense of order includes a striving for symmetry and serenity. You prefer things at peace and at rest, rather than in constant motion. You crave dependability. If you have a house full of antique clocks, they will all chime together. Steep a pot of English tea, and curl up on a comfy sofa that has lots of red, purple, and yellow pillows. Place an antique barometer on your bookshelf.

The thirty-third day of the year reduces to six, adding an appreciation of beauty and harmony. The beauty of ruby, halite, and diamond will soften the rough edges of life.

OBJECTS/IMAGES
trademarks, toboggans, the Hyde Park speaker's corner

SHAPES/MATERIALS
squiggle shapes, sapphires, neon lights

COLORS
metallic colors, peach

ANIMALS
tiger, zebra

PLANTS, HERBS, EDIBLES
wild madder, periwinkle, puffed cereals

ESSENCE
elemi

SOUNDS/RHYTHMS
eccentric rhythms, firecrackers

MUSICAL NOTES
D# and F

DEEP SPACE OBJECT
NGC 6905, planetary nebula

February 3

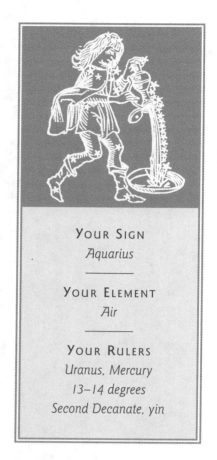

YOUR SIGN
Aquarius

YOUR ELEMENT
Air

YOUR RULERS
Uranus, Mercury
13–14 degrees
Second Decanate, yin

The Astrological Interpretation

You are a person who is very sensitive to any form of restriction. This is true not only relative to the laws and conventions that guide our society but also about your mind and the way you conceptualize reality. You have your own methods and techniques about your approach to life and guard your individuality fiercely. You have to be careful, however, that you do not flee from responsibilities or from the more earthbound people who also share this planet with you. Your true freedom of mind and spirit can only be earned and enjoyed by paying attention to where your feet are walking. A balance is therefore needed between the inner world of your ideals and the outer world of your activities.

As long as versatile February 3 feels mentally engaged it really doesn't matter which of their many talents they are using. Your home is a great focal point for your many projects, and you can stay indoors for hours and be quite content. A large round table with a wax candle in the middle serves as a mental and spiritual center. The circular or oval shape helps consolidate your many impulses and thoughts. Electronic appliances that make life easier are important to you. Much as you might want quiet you probably will have an active cell phone. Even in the shower you are thinking up interesting ways to live your life. Scented glycerin soaps in green and purple could be favorites.

Outdoors, you favor balconies or raised areas where you can watch the people traffic below. In the country try to have a view of the next house. An outdoor round table with an umbrella to shield you from the sun is the perfect addition to your yard. City dwellers will particularly enjoy sitting at an outdoor café, sipping a long tall cool beverage.

A Kabbalistic Interpretation

Fortune has a way of smiling on almost every aspect of your life. You can enhance your good luck by having pictures of sea life in your house—an old fishing boat or an oil painting of an angler would be ideal for this purpose.

You have a mystical side to your nature, and you may wish to encourage that side of your life. Even if you use it just decoratively, you could buy yourself a crystal ball—any large roughly spherical piece of crystal will work. If you position the crystal in the north of your home or workplace you will find yourself much more in control of the mundane aspects of your life and able to spend more time with your thoughts.

If you have no phobias or anxieties and you practice some form of meditative exercise on a regular basis, a cross can be a very powerful force for good in your life. If you want a symbol that will be of use to you in a number of situations then get yourself a triangle pendant. This will not only help balance you, but will also give you vitality and enthusiasm for life.

A Numerological Interpretation

YOUR MAGIC NUMBERS: 5 AND 7

The third day of the second month reduces to five. Five signifies uncertainty and change. This path contains the lesson of courtesy. Trains proceed on schedules and don't try to get through the tunnel at the same time. A train entering a tunnel provides a temporary cessation of light, a suspension of the pattern in motion, and an interlude of darkness. We always have a choice of how we interact with our fellows. Do we respond from generosity of spirit, or do we keep our goodwill and what we have to offer to ourselves? Decorate with yellow and orange marigolds.

The thirty-fourth day of the year reduces to seven, adding a desire for temporary cessation between your continuing projects. Peridot, malachite, and mimetite are gems compatible with your path. Take a trip on the Orient Express. The billowing smoke and piercing whistle will inspire you. Feel the power of the locomotive as the train pulls out of the station.

OBJECTS/IMAGES
ankle bracelet, static electricity, flocks of birds migrating

---

SHAPES/MATERIALS
textiles with metallic threads, ray shapes, pale blue aquamarine

---

COLORS
shocking pink, indigo, bright lavender, tawny yellow, moss green

---

ANIMALS
mynah bird, cockatoo, zebra

PLANTS, HERBS, EDIBLES
amaretto, turmeric

ESSENCE
myrrh

SOUNDS/RHYTHMS
electronic music, vibraphone music, echo chambers, train whistles

---

MUSICAL NOTES
E and F#

DEEP SPACE OBJECT
NGC 6811, open cluster of stars

February 4

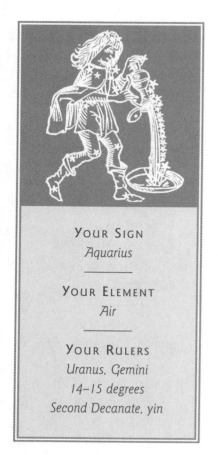

YOUR SIGN
Aquarius

YOUR ELEMENT
Air

YOUR RULERS
Uranus, Gemini
14–15 degrees
Second Decanate, yin

The Astrological Interpretation

Your birth date speaks about a person who has strong humanitarian instincts and a need to help the world. Although you can do your share in building a better planet, you cannot do it alone. You may find it somewhat difficult to join with others in a focus of communal intent. Although you are attracted by group endeavor, you are definitely not a "groupie." What is important is to have a way to maintain your own individuality while working within a more collective context. This requires that you perfect the definition of your own skills. Make sure that you always take the time and energy it costs to bring your own individual contribution to the next level.

February 4 is adventuresome and enterprising and may mingle with many different kinds of people. You enjoy not only actual traveling but also adventures of the mind. An image for you is a ship in full sail on a sunlit sea. When you come into port your home should reflect your cosmopolitan spirit. Fabrics from Bali, masks from Africa, photographs of the Himalayas, all will interest you, whether you have visited them or not. Keep your basic furnishings simple. Torchère lamps appeal to you. A large media center might also be a focal point for you. Making videos and playing and designing computer games are interesting activities that you have a talent for. With all that electrical energy, February 4 needs a way to cool down. Carry hematite or pieces of quartz as a regulator. In times of stress, whistle.

Outdoors February 4 likes windy hilltops and trees bending with the wind. A lookout tower would be a perfect structure for you. Furnish it with binoculars and scan the horizon.

A Kabbalistic Interpretation

Every permutation of the value in this day points to persons who are far too hard on themselves. You are likely to be well educated and have the capacity and drive to do well. You should focus on your intellectual side, but allow yourself the space to think and reflect without pressure. One simple step you can take to soften your tendency to self-criticism is to have a mirror with a white or aqua frame, which will help you feel far more tolerant of yourself. If you can, hang a picture of an Egyptian ibis in your study or wherever you do your thinking. Any sort of skyscape or moon images can help you pace your racing mind and ambition to a reasonable level.

While you are probably tempted to go for a sleek minimal look in your kitchen with lots of gleaming white and chrome surfaces, this can serve to accentuate the way you drive yourself too hard. Instead opt for a more traditional look; consider some exposed brick walls or exposed beams in the ceiling, and the kitchen will become a great place for you to recharge and feel good about yourself.

A Numerological Interpretation
YOUR MAGIC NUMBERS: 6 AND 8

The fourth day of the second month reduces to six. Six is the number of balanced polarity and harmony of opposites, the quintessential number of love. You yearn for that special someone to share your life. You enjoy sharing your favorite activity with a close friend or loved one. The romantic side of life is more appealing to you than the practical, and you seek to complement yourself with a perfect match. Your best friend should be your life partner. This path requires that you also see yourself in others or you will suffer a self-imposed blindness.

The thirty-fifth day of the year reduces to eight, adding a sense of rhythm to your experiences. A confidence in cycles supports your innate sense of symmetry. Amethyst, peridot, and fluorite will warm your heart. Copper and gold will aid your process. Canoe on a peaceful lake. Keep a pair of lovebirds. Watch *Romeo and Juliet* and cry. Vacation in an ivy-covered English cottage, with a lovingly tended garden with lots of purple flowers. Sing a romantic duet with your partner while walking hand in hand.

OBJECTS/IMAGES
batteries, ankle bracelets, hammocks, gamins

SHAPES/MATERIALS
amber, auras, checked patterns, jacinth, lapis lazuli

COLORS
electric blue, apple green, sea foam

ANIMAL
cassowary

PLANTS, HERBS, EDIBLES
mocha, clover

ESSENCE
tolu

SOUNDS/RHYTHMS
verbal voting, sound of a boomerang, Alice Cooper's music

MUSICAL NOTES
F and G

DEEP SPACE OBJECTS
Alpha Grus, Al Nair

February 5

YOUR SIGN
Aquarius

———

YOUR ELEMENT
Air

———

YOUR RULERS
Uranus, Mercury, Saturn
15–16 degrees
Second Decanate, yang

The Astrological Interpretation

You visit a modern art museum and find that no matter how unusual the shapes, how varied the styles, and how shocking the subject matter, you can identify with it all. Everything you see has a certain beauty, a definite message, a value to be noted and respected. One of the greatest artists in such a museum is the curator, whose organizational skill shapes the whole. You have such a broad spectrum of friends, experiences, skills, and interests that unless they are organized properly, your personal museum will wind up in total chaos. If your life is still a foggy morass of bits and pieces, then you know that the attainment of such organizational skills has to be your number one priority.

This birthday gives an unpredictable character and diversified talents. The nervous system is highly wired, and the home environment should offer stimulation as well as retreat. Consider beanbag furniture in bright blues and greens where you can change the shape of the chair or couch. A study area should feature a large desk, either wood or glass, from which you can command your world and your imagination. A crystal paperweight will encourage creative thoughts.

With the corulership of Mercury, you will be involved in communication. Fax, phone, and computer should all be up-to-date. Place a piece of amethyst on top of the computer. For feelings of depression a small trampoline will give you a little exercise break and keep your spirits buoyant. Outdoors, you seek a unique environment, perhaps a maze of pebbles in your backyard? A tent lit by a kerosene lamp will give you a sense of adventure and privacy. Pitch the tent up high so you can see nearby lights, but also look up at the stars. City dwellers will find inspiration on their rooftops.

A Kabbalistic Interpretation

You have been blessed with an extremely passionate nature. You should surround yourself with objects and images that call to mind great emotions. Whether you mount portraits of tragic heroes on your walls or listen to a Beethoven symphony give free reign to your emotions in a positive way.

The values attached to your date of birth correspond to various words and phrases associated with water, particularly boiling water. The image of boiling water represents the negative side of passion or the ability to get into a blazing rage. Settle the elemental mix of fire and water down with some earth energy. Stock your garden with mature fruit trees or decorate something in your living room using a pattern of yellow-green squares.

You can be something of a worrier and you need to make sure that this doesn't get out of hand. You should make sure that your kitchen is very brightly decorated. Invest in some colored saucepans and hang them on steel hooks. Consider burning frankincense or olibanum incense in the evenings.

A Numerological Interpretation

YOUR MAGIC NUMBERS: 7 AND 9

The fifth day of the seventh month reduces to seven. Seven is the ancient number implying a sworn oath of honor. It is the number of victory. Since we take nothing material with us when we die, what is it we strive to accomplish in life? We discern our individual talents and abilities, work to perfect them, and offer them up to society. Executives in a large corporation can be serving their own superficial ambition, or contributing to the whole through constructive self-realization. The idealistic work of the United Nations or Peace Corps is a concept that inspires you.

The thirty-sixth day of the year reduces to nine, and striving for attainment is amplified by a yearning for completion and fulfillment. Volunteer for international Scouting. Helping young people gain a sense of self-worth will be satisfying. Labordorite and chrysocolla deepen your desires. Display your plaques and awards. Wear green and blue to feel your best.

OBJECTS/IMAGES
telegraph machine, mobiles, a mountain refuge

SHAPES/MATERIALS
amber, textiles with metallic threads, zigzags

COLORS
checked patterns in blues-greens, azure

ANIMALS
red-winged blackbird, indigo bunting bird

PLANTS, HERBS, EDIBLES
puffballs, hydroponic vegetables, mixed floral bouquets

ESSENCE
sea salt

SOUNDS/RHYTHMS
air rustling leaves of paper, syncopation, jerky rhythms

MUSICAL NOTES
F# and G#

DEEP SPACE OBJECTS
Alpha Delphinus, Sualocin

February 6

YOUR SIGN
Aquarius

YOUR ELEMENT
Air

YOUR RULERS
Uranus, Venus
16–17 degrees
Second Decanate, yang

The Astrological Interpretation

Your birth date falls exactly in the middle of the sign Aquarius. This is one of the most "fixed" degrees of the zodiac, indicating that you are a determined person when it comes to achieving your plans and purposes. The more you feel the pressure to vary from your stated approach to life, the more you hold firm. Your general demeanor of openness and positive attitude toward others should not be misconstrued as a sign that you will bend to their wills. You are especially good at holding the central aim of group projects. You have a sense of what is correct for the whole, no matter what the differences in opinions may be of people around you.

Practicing flexibility will help your overall outlook. Yoga might be an excellent exercise for you. You have humanitarian concerns and may spend some time in your life working for a charitable organization. At home, support your energies with a roomy environment with lots of interesting shapes. Lamps that can be bent to change the direction of the light would suit you. Glow-in-the-dark stars arranged on the ceiling and walls will give you a thrill after dark. Your personal style may be quite casual with touches of eccentricity. Perhaps you favor a huge warm shawl in the winter rather than a coat, or a sarong in the summer. Men may be partial to cowboy boots. Whatever you decide you'll carry it off with panache.

Outdoors, you might want to have a small screened-in tower in the middle of your yard—this would be the place for you to retreat and meditate. Looking over a garden of blue flowers will aid your concentration. Consider bachelor's buttons, cornflowers, and Texas bluebonnet.

A Kabbalistic Interpretation

This day is intensely maternal, with all of its values expressing a tendency to care for others, especially youngsters. One definite consideration for people born today when considering how to use objects to enhance their life is to think about what children will do with them.

If you are typical of this day you probably have pictures of your little charges all over the house. You must make sure that you also have a good picture of yourself up there. Ideally this should be in an oval frame hung in the east of the house. This is one method by which you can encourage yourself to take time to consider your own needs.

Your home is important to you , affecting how you feel about everything else in your life—it is your oasis of safety and security in a world that often moves at a pace too hectic for your liking. You will already have very firm ideas about how your living space should look, but you could consider pine flooring throughout your house rather than carpet. The liberal use of Oriental throws with spiral patterns of blue or red will help prevent any scraped knees and bruises for your little ones.

A Numerological Interpretation
YOUR MAGIC NUMBERS: 8 AND 10

The sixth day of the second month reduces to eight. Eight is the number meaning rhythm. Give-and-take, cooperation and reciprocity, are essential to community. An ideal society is formed of fully functioning units, each prepared to perform their roles to support and protect one another. Society is a work in process. The thirty-seventh day of the year reduces to ten, adding a quality of vigilance, an impatient desire to see perfection. Stand back and observe. You could risk being honest to a fault.

This path demands that you learn diplomacy. Have a loyal watchdog and companion. Study the interaction among wolves in a pack. Volunteer for your local fire department. Brightly colored pansies will cheer you. Hornblende and fluorite are compatible gems.

OBJECTS/IMAGES
batteries, bicycles, and auras

SHAPES/MATERIALS
cannon balls, chalcopyrite, and spirals

COLORS
pink fluorescence, cerulean

ANIMALS
watchdog, buffalo

PLANTS, HERBS, EDIBLES
hybrid corn, Greek valerian, clover, and foreign foods

ESSENCE
cypress

SOUNDS/RHYTHMS
cherry bombs exploding, electronic keyboards

MUSICAL NOTES
G and A

DEEP SPACE OBJECT
pulsar

February 7

YOUR SIGN
Aquarius

YOUR ELEMENT
Air

YOUR RULERS
Uranus, Mercury
17–18 degrees
Second Decanate, yang

The Astrological Interpretation

You have many friends and associates with whom you share a wide range of interests. You are very supportive of people around you, encouraging them to express themselves with the same individualistic attitude that you yourself possess. The leaves on your tree are connected to their branches. Make sure that no matter how busy you are, no matter how many appointments and social engagements you may have, that you take the time to connect with your own roots. You will find that you can nourish your entire network of business and personal associates, loved ones, and friends by coming back to those roots. This can be done through a few quiet minutes alone when you are listening to the silence within you. It can also happen when you are involved in some sport or activity that supports your connection to yourself.

Another image for February 7 is the lightbulb. A bulb burns brightly, sometimes gives us a eureka experience, and then turns off. Share your epiphanies with friends. At home you might have a collection of Oriental parasols that serve as lamp shades for overhead lights. A carpetbag is a useful and romantic object for you. February 7 is a traveler and likes the feeling of picking up and going. Carry some colored crayons with you. While observing human nature you might want to make a few sketches.

Outdoors, February 7 likes a windy hill or niche high up on a roof where she can have a full panoramic view. The wind through your hair is a tonic. Running with a kite bobbing behind you is a wonderful activity for February 7. Have a friend fly one too and see how they entwine.

A Kabbalistic Interpretation

You have a certain affinity for the wild side of nature, and a real attraction to wolves. You get on well with all animals and will derive a great deal of personal benefit from your contact with them. If you are looking for a dog, then you should be looking at Alsatians rather than poodles, in keeping with your wild nature.

To counterbalance your wild streak, you have a very analytical mind. This aspect of your personality is useful in keeping your potential for aggression under control. If you need to lend more weight to the rational, analytical part of your mind then add a touch of orange to your outfit. This effect will be maximized if you include a complementary hint of yellow. A tiny dash of color is all that is needed to create the desired effect.

Shapes have a very real effect on the way we feel, think, and even how others perceive us. In France long stretches of highway are augmented with geometrical shapes meant to affect the way people drive. You might consider trying the same effect by placing a number of triangular objects in your office or work space. If you do this you will find that your tendency to worry about your decisions lessens and you are more confident and generally empowered.

A Numerological Interpretation

YOUR MAGIC NUMBERS: 9 AND 2

The seventh day of the second month reduces to nine. Nine is the number signifying attainment and the goal of an endeavor. Perhaps one day we'll measure love or kindness on some kind of instrument, and place genes in test tubes to assure we have enough brain surgeons or Picassos, but for now we must work without such manipulations. Life to you is a great laboratory of cause and effect, and you yearn to know its secret foundations. You wish to see beneath the surface, pulling away the masks and outer coverings to penetrate the deepest core reality. Contemplate the morality of experiments on living creatures to assess reactions to stimulation. Try direct perception of mysteries through meditation.

Use lots of glass containers in your lime green and blue kitchen. Hang a pictorial chart of herbs and spices over your work counter. Put a periodic chart of the elements on the wall of your study. Use a combined digital and analog clock. Light an antique oil lamp, smell the oil, and gaze into the flame. The thirty-eighth day of the year reduces to two, contributing the elements of contrast and comparison to your quest.

OBJECTS/IMAGES
*a wizard's hat,
a psychedelic-colored van*

SHAPES/MATERIALS
*spiky shapes, radio tubes,
uranium, clear quartz*

COLORS
*dazzling white,
glow-in-the-dark colors,
azure, deep orange*

ANIMALS
penguin, macaw bird

PLANTS, HERBS, EDIBLES
*spotted plantain, gooseberry,
kumquats*

ESSENCE
spikenard

SOUNDS/RHYTHMS
*electronic music, staccato,
a crow's call*

MUSICAL NOTES
G# and C#

DEEP SPACE OBJECT
supernova

February 8

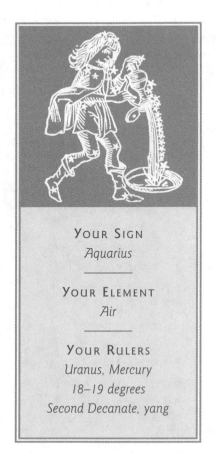

YOUR SIGN
Aquarius

YOUR ELEMENT
Air

YOUR RULERS
Uranus, Mercury
18–19 degrees
Second Decanate, yang

The Astrological Interpretation

You are a person who likes to interact with others and are quite communicative by nature. You can just as easily begin a conversation with a stranger in a market as you can pick up the phone to call one of your dozen or so best friends. You live in a world of creative possibilities—some you invent yourself, others beckon from the world around you. You easily find yourself doing many things at the same time, having many relationships simultaneously, and skimming across a wide surface. As a result, you may not have the energy you need to do the things you finally decide are important to your life. It is not that you lack will, it is more the right use of will that you have to determine.

February 8 combines unusual intelligence with talents that may be marked with sudden impulses and surprising inspiration. An image for you is the cartoon of a man having a "bright idea," with a lightbulb over his head. Electrical appliances interest you. You may want to get a shower radio so you can keep track of the news and weather. At home have an electric treadmill or NordicTrack for exercise. You may have some of your best ideas when you are exercising. Although you probably prefer writing on a computer, think about getting a special notebook with a metal cover for thoughts, inventions, and dreams. You might also sketch some of your ideas.

Outdoors, February 8 is partial to speed and thrills. A motorcycle may be a prize possession. A racing bike could be a safer alternative. Mountain plants and trees are important to February 8. Alpine asters and purple rock cress are two plants you might particularly enjoy.

A Kabbalistic Interpretation

The value of this date points to an excellent sense of humor and a general love of life. A large amount of fire energy around this date indicates you may enjoy practical jokes at home and at work.

You need to exercise your brain and engage yourself visually to avoid becoming bored and to keep your inner vision sharp. Invest in some hidden eye paintings—you can spend hours trying to see the image hidden within the patterns. Or try an old-fashioned lava lamp. The movement of the colored bubbles will keep you intrigued while the slowness of the display will help you to relax and wind down.

The classic colors of the Fool—a tarot card strongly associated with your day—are red and yellow. You should consider clothing or personal accessories in these colors, if you want to connect with the innocence and openness of this card. To bring out your best side carry a clear rose pink crystal, such as rose quartz.

A Numerological Interpretation
YOUR MAGIC NUMBERS: 10 AND 3

The eighth day of the second month reduces to ten. Ten is the number of dominion and mastery. Ten enjoys successful finishes. This date's bearers are not above generating a crisis just to enjoy the adrenaline and the thrill of solving the dilemma. We learn who we are and what we're made of when challenged to the limit. How deep is your concern? Would you return to a burning house to save a child? Put this energy to good use by becoming a paramedic.

Social responsibility is your issue—could I lift a car to release a trapped victim? Am I capable of heroism or only voyeurism? Amethyst and star sapphire set in silver will calm you. The thirty-ninth day of the year reduces to three, which adds a sense of the natural unfoldment of processes. Consider German shepherds who are trained to locate victims in earthquakes buried under rubble or Saint Bernards rescuing avalanche victims. Purples, blues, and blue-green are harmonious colors.

OBJECTS/IMAGES
air fresheners, go-carts, ankle socks, hobos

SHAPES/MATERIALS
asymmetrical shapes, half shapes, lapis lazuli

COLORS
pearlescent colors, navy blue, russet

ANIMAL
black bear

PLANTS, HERBS, EDIBLES
indigo shrub, snowberry, astragalus (herb), airplane food

ESSENCE
Tibetan cedarwood

SOUNDS/RHYTHMS
high-pitched electrical noises, wind rushing down a city street

MUSICAL NOTES
A and D

DEEP SPACE OBJECT
the Crescent Nebula

February 9

YOUR SIGN
Aquarius

YOUR ELEMENT
Air

YOUR RULERS
Uranus, Venus
19–20 degrees
Second Decanate, yang

The Astrological Interpretation

Most people have enough on their hands fighting only their own battles in life. Your birth date signifies a person who is willing to take up the cause of other people's struggles. Thus it is very common for people born on your day to be involved with community service projects of all kinds. It is important to you that each individual be free to live a healthy and productive life. You have your own sense of personal conduct and morality, one that does not necessarily conform to what other people expect of you. This does not mean that you are an eccentric, but it does mean that you find it necessary to live according to what you feel is right for yourself, no matter what other people may think.

Some February 9 birthdays may be located on the fixed star Nashira. The ancients believed that though Nashira signified a conflict with evil, it also signified ultimate success. Your birthday's talent is to press on after setbacks and to sustain yourself through your own energies. An image for you is a great tortoise who, with measured activity, always gets where he is going. In your home you may want slightly offbeat touches. A pair of bongo drums hanging on the wall or a miniature parachute covering a ceiling lamp all accord with your aesthetic. You will enjoy unique objets d'art and may want to collect Chinese snuff bottles or small netsuke statues. In the bedroom consider a metal headboard with scrolls and vines. An inflatable mattress for guests is the kind of useful object that February 9 loves.

Outdoors, you will enjoy a sloping lawn with metal lawn chairs and a clear space for a telescope. Stargazing or looking at the neighbors would be equally enjoyable. Unique rock shapes in your garden would be pleasing. Flowers for you are purple rock cress, dwarf campanula, and yellow corydalis.

A Kabbalistic Interpretation

Stepping into your home, if you have decorated it in keeping with your nature, could be like stepping back in time. You are a serious and dignified individual and you reflect the spirit of restrained good taste in your home. If you can only afford to invest in one really great piece of antique furniture, consider a really good antique clock made of solid polished wood with a brass pendulum. You should find the ticking of the clock and chiming of the hour reassuring and relaxing.

There is a danger that your sense of dignity may remove you from the grittier realities of life. While this may seem quite pleasing to you, it needs to be tempered. You could buy yourself a workbench and some power tools. Using them to make things will help you feel in control.

You may feel very deeply that you are more comfortable expressing your feelings through gifts or letters rather than by speaking directly to your partner. But if you cut a sprig of hawthorn and place it in your bath, then you will find that you can communicate without feelings of awkwardness.

A Numerological Interpretation

YOUR MAGIC NUMBERS: 2 AND 4

The ninth day of the second month reduces to two. Two is the number of receptivity. This day's path requires drawing wisdom and guidance from an inner source. Learn to recognize the subtle signs and messages that guide you. They may seem silly or superstitious to others, but learn to trust them. Communication with the unseen is another form of language. Follow your hunches. Pay attention to your dreams. Experience shows them to be inexplicably accurate. Study Native American medicine signs. The fortieth day of the year reduces to four, adding certainty to your intuitions and the interpretations of the signs you see. Rose quartz, Rhodochrosite, and Celestite set in white gold will enhance these communications.

Use special journals to record your impressions and thought processes. Collect the feathers you find and study the nature of the birds. Blues and reds will balance your emotions. Spend time outside. Listen to the calls of wild birds. Smell the fresh air. Quiet, unobtrusive spaces soothe your mind. Sleep beneath the feather softness of a down comforter. Carry on a conversation with your parrot.

OBJECTS/IMAGES
lava lamps, whirlpools, pulleys, quaint homes or shops

SHAPES/MATERIALS
uranium, whirling shapes, sodalite, jet stone

COLORS
electric blue, salmon, sand

ANIMALS
blue-faced booby, black-legged kittiwake

PLANTS, HERBS, EDIBLES
hollyhock, arnica, cassia, bastard box (plant)

ESSENCE
vetiver

SOUNDS/RHYTHMS
sound of a doorknocker, wind whistling through the trees

MUSICAL NOTES
C# and D#

DEEP SPACE OBJECTS
Gamma Capricorn, Nashira

February 10

YOUR SIGN
Aquarius

YOUR ELEMENT
Air

YOUR RULERS
Uranus, Venus
20–21 degrees
Third Decanate, yang

The Astrological Interpretation

Crises are not new to you. You have experienced many reversals that have required you to be firm and resilient. Your ability to come through such situations has left you with an inner strength and a quiet determination to succeed in life. Your birth date does not mean that you will always have to struggle. Once you have established a clear and definite sense of yourself, life will unfold with greater ease and your goals will be much simpler to achieve. You are involved with the refinement of personal choices that reveal the objectives in your life with greater clarity. You are not selfish in this knowledge but seek to aid other people with the understanding that comes from your personal experiences.

Your birthday combines attention to the unique and the aesthetic. You may have a particular fondness for electronic gadgets, but if they are not well designed you will pass them by. Your home could have sleek lines with old-fashioned touches such as inherited rugs that add color to your surroundings. A combination media/living room is the center of the home where you can entertain people and discuss ways to improve the world. Curtains that throw a lacy pattern of light on the room stimulate your mind. Consider using dimmer switches throughout your home so you can regulate the light to your satisfaction.

Accessories in clean geometric shapes suit you. A rectangular glass table resonates with your sense of refinement. You might enjoy tableware that has a unique design.

Outdoors, high places and mountaintops stimulate the imagination. Garden furniture set on a high spot in your yard would be a perfect setting for you to catch the view and gaze at the night sky. A garden of healing herbs planted according to the phases of the moon might be of particular interest to you.

A Kabbalistic Interpretation

You are both thoughtful and emotional in a selfless way, and although you may not be aware of it, you have a chance of significant spiritual development in your life. If you want to pursue your spiritual inclinations, consider hanging some Buddhist mandalas, especially in the west side of your home.

You have a strong connection to the energies of the earth, and while you will probably live in the city, you should favor natural materials in decorating your living space and adding personal touches to your office. In terms of color avoid anything too bright and gaudy, as this can cause irritability and tension for you and those around you. Opt for pale cream shades and light browns. Avoid pure white, as this is too stark for your sensitive nature.

A naturally private person, you are unlikely to parade your personal interests in front of colleagues. A stone such as jasper can be carried discreetly out of sight and resonates with energies suitable to your makeup. If you carry a red jasper flecked with green you will find yourself more energetic and optimistic about life.

A Numerological Interpretation
YOUR MAGIC NUMBERS: 3 AND 5

The tenth day of the second month reduces to three. Three is the number signifying growth and unfoldment. Disappointment can be our greatest teacher. An infant grows toward adulthood through constant trial and error, encountering numerous bumps and bruises along the way.

Don't dwell on failure. Sweep it away and try harder. How do we accept defeat? Do we discern a temporary setback, rise and try again, or sit in the middle of the road crying? Don't look for fulfillment outside yourself. Others have their own needs and paths. Learn that disappointments can drive us deeper in our search for meaning and challenge us to reach for true understanding of ourselves. Don't cry over spilled milk. Defeat is not final, just another opportunity to learn. The forty-first day of the year reduces to five, providing an innate grasp of the necessity of change and exploration. Watch toddlers taking their first tentative steps—the tears and the laughter. Take dance lessons. Play chess. Jasper and moss agate will strengthen your resolve. Greens and tangerine orange are stimulating colors.

OBJECTS/IMAGES
silhouettes, holographs, iridescent feathers

SHAPES/MATERIALS
obsidian, Australian opals, octagons, free-form sculpture

COLORS
periwinkle blue, indigo, opalescent white, golden yellow

ANIMALS
antelope, hoopoe bird

PLANTS, HERBS, EDIBLES
frankincense (plant), star of Bethlehem, cherry-filled chocolates, garam masala, bird-of-paradise

ESSENCE
chicory

SOUNDS/RHYTHMS
cha-cha, crunch of snow on very cold days, lyre

MUSICAL NOTES
D and E

DEEP SPACE OBJECT
quasar

February 11

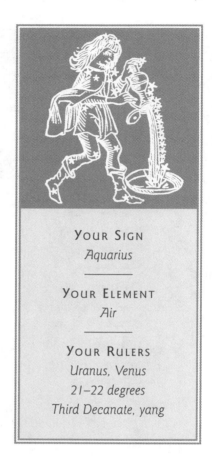

YOUR SIGN
Aquarius

———

YOUR ELEMENT
Air

———

YOUR RULERS
Uranus, Venus
21–22 degrees
Third Decanate, yang

The Astrological Interpretation

You are experimental by nature. You have always sought the different and unusual, both in the sphere of your activities and the network of friends and associates you cultivate. New people that enter your life are not considered strangers but opportunities for learning and sharing. You enjoy travel to distant and exotic places, relishing the chance to experience customs and cuisines different from those that are part of your usual surroundings. The only place that may have felt truly strange and foreign to you was your early home environment. Your earliest urges were to create a distinct sense of your personal identity, no matter what the cost. You still refuse to compromise where your individuality is concerned.

A key to your character is two concentric circles. February 11 is happiest when there is an easy exchange between the circle of themselves and of society. Aquarius's symbol, the water bearer, is offering the waters of knowledge to all people. You may find your contribution to society or your work involves new uses for technology. A sleekly designed media center with CD, DVD, and HDTV may be a part of your world. You can gain power from lightning imagery. Why not stencil bolts of lightning around your den or study work space? There is some resonance between February 11 and monasteries. Think about a book of monasteries or illuminated manuscripts for your living room table.

Personal style tends toward the eccentric. Geometric jewelry with bright colors may be just the right touch to declare your independence. Rainbow-colored fabric could be your personal fashion touch.

Outdoors, February 11 likes cold, crisp air that crackles with static electricity. You may enjoy plunging your face into cold water on a frosty morning. Binoculars, or a telescope, in your outdoor space feed your love of inquiry. Plus you may be able to spy on your neighbors and learn something new about humanity!

A Kabbalistic Interpretation

You probably have a greater love of, not to mention talent for, music than most of your friends and colleagues. As this day specifically relates to wind instruments, a piccolo or a set of panpipes in silver in your house are ideal. It doesn't matter whether you play these instruments; they represent the subtle voice of harmony and beauty that is so important to you.

One method of calculating the value of your date leads to a strong association with the planet Mars. Other influences suggest that this is not Mars in its capacity as warrior energy but as pioneering force and willingness to take risks. You may like to better your chances in a risky situation by eating a peppered steak or even a raw chili pepper beforehand. The ritual will attract the requisite Martian qualities into your psyche.

There's a good chance that you will have several children or will spend a lot of time with children. Growing pansies or snowdrops in your window box will enhance your already excellent rapport with younger people.

A Numerological Interpretation
YOUR MAGIC NUMBERS: 4 AND 6

The eleventh day of the second month reduces to four. Four is the number of measurement. There is a miraculous aspect to this day where everything needed seems to materialize or appear. This birth path indicates that everything you will ever need—any skill, talent, or connection—you have within yourself. Your life experiences will provide the opportunities for you to determine the necessary skill for the present task and hone and refine your methods.

If you only focus outwardly, you will desire to pile up luxuries. If you turn inwardly, you will develop your potential. Steel is forged in a furnace. Visit a steel mill. Gazing into a fire opal will stir your soul. Collect articles of hand-blown glass. Squeeze fresh orange juice. Have a spontaneous sunrise picnic in the woods on a rose-colored blanket. The forty-second day of the year reduces to six, adding the quality of love and harmony to your quest.

OBJECTS/IMAGES
airplanes, the Crusaders, bombs

SHAPES/MATERIALS
mood rings, original shapes, black pearls

COLORS
changeable colors, sunset orange, moss green

ANIMAL
buffalo

PLANTS, HERBS, EDIBLES
croton oil, allheal

ESSENCE
opopanax

SOUNDS/RHYTHMS
twitchy rhythms

MUSICAL NOTES
D# and F

DEEP SPACE OBJECTS
Alpha Equuleus, Kitalpha

February 12

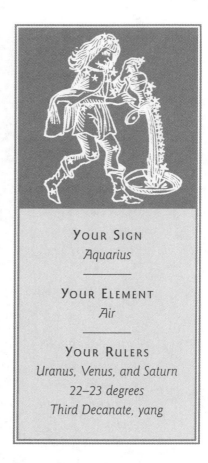

YOUR SIGN
Aquarius

YOUR ELEMENT
Air

YOUR RULERS
Uranus, Venus, and Saturn
22–23 degrees
Third Decanate, yang

The Astrological Interpretation

Your birth date takes the individualistic urge shared by many Aquarians one step further; you need to devote any personal achievements in self-development to causes and ideals that are larger than yourself. In order to do this, you will have to add one more quality to your list of accomplishments—self-discipline. You are not a person who easily takes orders or advice from anyone else. You tend to be very willful and stubborn when anyone tries to modify your nature. Yet you will not be able to concretize your many hopes and wishes unless you take on the responsibility of crafting your potential into some real skills that can be used to benefit your own and other people's welfare. Once this is accomplished, you can match your lofty aspirations with the creative potential within.

You are strong-minded and can use your gifts for benevolent activities or destructive ones. Sometimes the passion that injustice for certain groups excites in you leads you to be intolerant of others. Aquarius is a fixed sign, and all Aquarians need to temper their unique nature with flexibility. Imagine a Gumby doll—it can bend any which way and always smiles! At home, surround yourself with interesting electronic equipment. Gadgets that solve a problem creatively and stylishly are for you. Adjustable magnets on pressure points or any tender spot might be ideal for aches and pains. The space under the eaves of a roof is a hideaway for you. Being up high gives you a bird's-eye view of your own and humanities' struggles.

Outdoors, you may enjoy visits to botanical gardens housed in glass. A wheelbarrow filled with cornflowers and bluebells would be a suitably unique addition to your own outdoor environment, but it would be best to keep some uncultivated land around you. February 12 likes wilderness.

A Kabbalistic Interpretation

Today is a day of great force and enormous physical energy, but that energy can be wayward if not harnessed. You need to learn the lesson of the Chariot card, which refers to the potential for direction and victory, if one can only reign in the power at one's disposal and guide it.

Carry a piece of flint with you—a flint arrowhead would be wonderful. You will find it significantly easier to learn how to forge a path rather than charge around in circles.

Exercise is important for your spiritual as well as your physical well-being. You can use your physical activity to generate the air energy that may be lacking in your life. Regular use of an exercise bike or rowing machine can stimulate the air aspect of your personality.

While you have all the energy and motivation required to have a physically intimate relationship, you sometimes need more subtlety to keep a relationship moving along. Before a romantic evening, pour some essence of witch hazel into your bathwater, and you should find that you are irresistible.

A Numerological Interpretation
YOUR MAGIC NUMBERS: 5 AND 7

The twelfth day of the second month reduces to five. Five is the number of continuous change and motion. This day confers a never-ending quest to convert your aptitudes into excellences. An agile tightrope walker from a family of acrobats once took tentative first steps with a net below. Weave yourself from the threads of your abilities into a skillful tapestry of beauty. Go to the circus and watch the performing circus animals. Admire the Clydesdales and the dancing bears. Thrill to the high-wire acts, and listen to the applause of the spectators.

This path carries a danger of immature craving for attention. Wear red-orange to make a striking impression. The forty-third day of the year reduces to seven, adding a thirst for a peaceful retreat to your experience of constant movement. Wulfenite and calcite are gems to ground you. Tin and steel are metals to galvanize your strength. Rich, woven fabric and tapestries should decorate your home.

OBJECTS/IMAGES
flashlights, hydroelectric power, taxicabs

SHAPES/MATERIALS
triangles, holograms, black pearls

COLORS
tie-dyed colors, lemon

ANIMALS
koodoo, white-tailed deer

PLANTS, HERBS, EDIBLES
fortune cookies, dragonwort, spearmint

ESSENCE
spikenard

SOUNDS/RHYTHMS
double time, firecrackers

MUSICAL NOTES
E and F#

DEEP SPACE OBJECTS
Gamma Cygnus, Sador the Breast

February 13

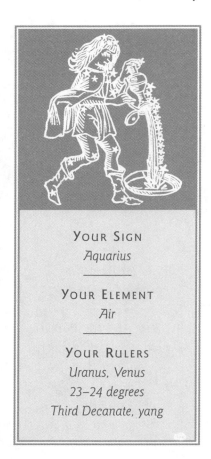

YOUR SIGN
Aquarius

YOUR ELEMENT
Air

YOUR RULERS
Uranus, Venus
23–24 degrees
Third Decanate, yang

The Astrological Interpretation

You are a hardworking individual who is dedicated to your beliefs and who will struggle with great determination to achieve your goals. You are a natural born teacher and take pleasure in passing on your experiences to others. You seem to know instinctively what other people are thinking. You also have a strong sense about the results of certain actions before a project has begun. These are very useful skills and ones that you can use to benefit those with whom you share your life.

You never like to take sides in interpersonal conflicts. You know that in order to be an effective helper and friend, you cannot get caught up in the frustrated desires and passions that were usually the cause of the difficulty in the first place. Sometimes this means that you have to be rather detached, giving the impression that you are cold and uncaring. This is the furthest from the truth!

February 13 is ever mindful of charity and the needs of humanity. Your benevolent ideas and ideals need to be expressed. Venus is your coruler; in between good works, put some attention to joy and pleasure. At home, unique and colorful telephones will give you a laugh. Think about placing unusual night-lights, perhaps of cartoon characters, around your home. Kids and you will get a kick out of them. Large clear quartz crystals, called generator crystals, will keep your energy tuned up. Aquarius rules circulation, and you may find an acupuncture tune-up every few months is an excellent way to keep yourself healthy.

The unexpected should rule your outdoor environment. How about a trapeze hookup in your yard? Or you might create a homemade acrobatic area for the neighborhood kids. Sculpting topiary animals or shapes could be an interesting outdoor hobby. If you live in a wintry climate, build snowmen and ice sculptures.

The Kabbalistic Interpretation

You tend to be somewhat obsessive about organization. You have probably already found a perfect place for this book on your shelf without disturbing your ordering system. A large piece of aquamarine somewhere in your living room can help you be a little less precious about the arrangement of your personal belongings.

If you are in the market for a new home, choose a house with large windows looking out on woods or natural landscape with a general atmosphere of light and space. This will appeal to your desire for purity and clarity in your life. The views from your windows may bolster an appreciation of the natural world.

No one could ever accuse you of being excessively adventurous in your life. If this suits you, look for a small velvet-lined box made of very old wood, which you can keep on your desk at work. If, on the other hand, you wish you could be more daring, try burning some olibanum in the morning when you are having your shower.

A Numerological Interpretation
YOUR MAGIC NUMBERS: 6 AND 8

The thirteenth day of the second month reduces to six. Six is the number of harmony and reciprocity. The conflict of polarity is surrendered for the beauty of balanced opposites. There is a quality of selflessness about this path. Inner peace is attained when there is balance in the conscious and unconscious aspects of yourself. Because ordinary pursuits no longer hold a glamour, there is a danger of dissatisfaction with the normal fruits of living. Don't withdraw too far. You must still function in the outer world. Teach at a community college, be a hospice volunteer, learn sign language. Shop at garage sales for fun. Wood opal and agate will energize your will. Yellow and purple will harmonize the sense of opposition you feel.

The forty-fourth day of the year reduces to eight, contributing the quality of reciprocity and the desire to enter the stream of life. Camp in the wilderness and sleep on a carpet of pine needles beneath evergreen trees. Listen to the silence.

OBJECTS/IMAGES
chandeliers, a curio cabinet, door knockers

SHAPES/MATERIALS
chalcolite, cyclone shapes, electrical wire

COLORS
changeable colors, neon white, chartreuse

ANIMAL
deer

PLANTS, HERBS, EDIBLES
red chestnut, lobelia, croton oil

ESSENCE
lemongrass

SOUNDS/RHYTHMS
double time, novelty songs

MUSICAL NOTES
F and G

DEEP SPACE OBJECT
Beta Equuleus

February 14

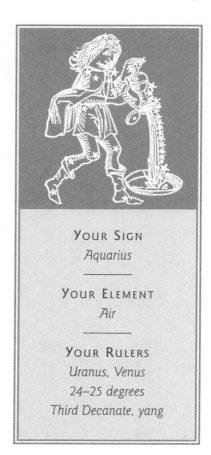

YOUR SIGN
Aquarius

YOUR ELEMENT
Air

YOUR RULERS
Uranus, Venus
24–25 degrees
Third Decanate, yang

The Astrological Interpretation

You are loyal and steadfast by nature and your friendships tends to last for many years. Yet you can run into trouble when your partner requires a deeper sense of emotional commitment than you are willing or able to offer. The more your beloved pulls you close, the more space you require to express yourself freely. Given freedom, you will do everything possible to fulfill the needs of your partner. But if you feel at all possessed or there are excessive expectations placed upon you, you will resist and rebel. It is important for you to be in a relationship with a person who is emotionally and mentally independent. You require the liberty to change your moods or even not express your feelings. You find no conflict in loving someone with whom you disagree politically. In fact, there is something you enjoy about the differences between you. Make sure that your partner feels the same way.

Though St. Valentine's Day falls within the realm of Aquarius, this sign rules love and compassion for all mankind rather than exclusively romantic love. February 14 basically wants to find the connections between personal love and societal well-being. An image for you is a red heart with strings tied around a globe. You are drawn to light: stage lights, photographic light, light of knowledge, and the bright light of invention. Your personality will find a variety of ways to shine. In your home you may collect lamps, especially lamps that cast colored light. Have as many windows as you can in your space so that you can watch the weather roll in. Although you may not want to live in a city permanently, living in a high-rise apartment building would be fascinating for observing the weather.

Outdoors, you would enjoy a miniature weather station. You could design a special sprinkler system to deliver the precise amount of water your plants need. Outdoor torchlights please you, and if you could create a small outdoor pavilion for summer shows, the light would attract your neighbors. Flowers for February 14 include dwarf campanula, rusty-back fern, and rose daphne.

A Kabbalistic Interpretation

Kabbalistically February 14 doesn't have a particularly romantic association. In fact its connection to the tarot card the Devil means that you tend to focus on the material side of life. To encourage greater riches to enter your life you might decorate your home with a few well-made corn dolls; you could even consider carrying one in your purse or briefcase.

St. Valentine was quite a tragic figure historically—he died a martyr's death in a hail of arrows. Although people born on this day should not anticipate such tragedy and high drama, they do tend to have fairly intense lives. In order to ensure that you have enough energy to maintain the relentlessly active lifestyle of this day you should grow sunflowers in a window box. These beautiful flowers will appeal to your taste and will also help you to see the attraction of a certain degree of simplicity in your life.

A Numerological Interpretation

YOUR MAGIC NUMBERS: 7 AND 9

The fourteenth day of the second month reduces to seven, the number of victory. Once a man watched a caterpillar struggle to emerge from a chrysalis. Feeling compassion, he pierced the shell to help the creature. But the butterfly was never able to fly because it didn't gain enough strength in its emerging wings from its struggle. Sometimes, what we perceive as handicaps are the means through which we attain our splendid uniqueness. The forty-fifth day of the year reduces to nine, implying attainment of what you set out to do.

Orthoclase and turquoise will heighten your resolve. Surround yourself with a comfortable cocoon to feel secure. Cuddle up in a feather bed and enjoy soothing, gentle melodies. Study the mystery of butterflies. Secretly observe the first flight of a baby bird. Listen to the hungry chirping of its nest mates. Greens and blues will calm and strengthen you.

OBJECTS/IMAGES
ankle socks, tops, video games, antiques

SHAPES/MATERIALS
amber, checked patterns, lodestones, jacinth

COLORS
fluorescence, sapphire blue

ANIMAL
cockatoo

PLANTS, HERBS, EDIBLES
green clover, purple prairie clover, mastiche, moonshine

ESSENCE
helicrysum

SOUNDS/RHYTHMS
radio jingles, electronic music

MUSICAL NOTES
F# and G#

DEEP SPACE OBJECT
nova

February 15

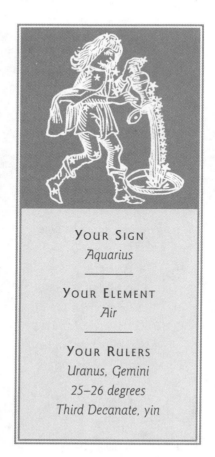

YOUR SIGN
Aquarius

YOUR ELEMENT
Air

YOUR RULERS
Uranus, Gemini
25–26 degrees
Third Decanate, yin

The Astrological Interpretation

We live in an increasingly technical age, in which our ability to use communication tools makes a huge difference to our level of success in the world. You have the innate ability to be a very effective communicator. This is true not only in the expression of your own ideas, but also in your ability to link other people's thoughts and opinions together for greater, collective harmony. You have a naturally friendly disposition and genuinely like people. You value your individual liberty and support other people's need to be themselves. It is easy for you to meet others and to be a vehicle to bring people together for mutually beneficial purposes. You tend to have many friends from diverse social groups and interests and derive a great deal of pleasure knowing that your communication skills are benefiting others.

February 15 has great theatrical flair and a dry wit. A tendency to act the part can overshadow your largely philanthropic nature. The image of the water bearer, Aquarius's symbol, is a good one for you. Have a large vase like an ancient Roman or Greek wine jug in your home. For everyday use, a pitcher of water will keep your mind and feelings synchronized. Electronic communications will help you keep in touch with family and friends—you can easily get hooked on the computer or Internet. Keep the media room separate from other living spaces. Keep a small round object, even a ball, on top of any electronic equipment. February 15 has a sensitive nervous system and needs round circles to center mind and heart.

Personally, you may feel that you don't have much in common with other people. The blue sky is over us all, and sapphire blue is the color for you. Outdoors, February 15 would enjoy a path of flagstones in the garden. An old-fashioned wooden pump in the middle of the garden reminds you of times when people would gather round the village pump for conversation, information, and, of course, water.

A Kabbalistic Interpretation

They say that clothes do not make the man; however, you might disagree with this viewpoint, as your clothing is the most powerful expression of your personality. In fact you may well work in design or in some other field that has connections to image and personal presentation. You should be reassured that if you think something looks good, then go with it, no matter how outrageous and challenging it appears.

An extremely independent person by nature, you need to make sure that you do not leave yourself feeling vulnerable and alone as a result of your nonconformity. If you can find some brass objects or brass-colored jewelry that uses square-based patterns, you will find it much easier to integrate yourself with others.

You can charge headlong into catastrophe without fully thinking through your plan or having a strategy to deal with an upcoming problem. Thanks to the positive influence of the letter *Kaph* in the value of this day, you usually emerge relatively unscathed. Wearing anything with a greenish gray hue will give you the courage to keep going until the crisis in question has resolved itself.

A Numerological Interpretation

YOUR MAGIC NUMBERS: 8 AND 10

The fifteenth day of the second month reduces to eight, the number representing rhythm and flow. Visualize the symbol for infinity, which looks like a number eight on its side. This illustrates the continual rhythm of movement throughout eternity. Analyze the significance of the patterns and cycles in your life. What pattern keeps repeating that you'd like to change? Take charge and change the next outcome. If you always plant lilacs, you'll never get roses. The forty-sixth day of the year reduces to ten. Ten adds the element of dominion, allowing you to pause at a still point between the tides. Buy a fountain for your home. Let the sound of the water soothe you. Azurite, sodalite, and lapis will empower you. Visit Niagara Falls, and watch the thunderous roar of the water.

OBJECTS/IMAGES
an antique telegraph machine, a pen with a digital clock, caricature drawings

SHAPES/MATERIALS
wavy lines, black pearls, fire opals

COLORS
mixed bright colors, purple, sea foam

ANIMALS
electric eel, firefly, indigo bunting bird

PLANTS, HERBS, EDIBLES
dragonwort, vervain, sourballs

ESSENCES
smell of shellac, unique fragrances from all over the world

SOUNDS/RHYTHMS
electric guitar, mariachi bands, wind whistling atop a mountain

MUSICAL NOTES
G and A

DEEP SPACE OBJECTS
Epsilon Cygnus, Gienah, the Wing

February 16

YOUR SIGN
Aquarius

YOUR ELEMENT
Air

YOUR RULERS
Uranus, Venus
26–27 degrees
Third Decanate, yin

The Astrological Interpretation

You may find yourself with certain artistic skills that have no traditional outlet. This means that you have to invent your own way of expressing yourself creatively. Your life often challenges the status quo, and it is up to you to establish your own way of doing things. You can derive support and inspiration from studying the lives of other people who have had to make their own way through life: inventors, explorers, philosophers, and trendsetters. It is important not to expect that everyone will appreciate the fact that you have to call your own shots and are unwilling to compromise. What you offer others is your unqualified support for living exactly as they wish to.

You are idealistic and concerned about not only your fellow man but also your own creativity. Your challenge will be to bend with changing circumstances without compromising your principles and vision. An image for you to think about is an ancient pottery dish filled with purple flowers. The traditional vessel holds something new and living. At home, decorate with a variety of flowers and plants. Growing a Norfolk Island pine tree will be a measure of time for you as well as a pleasing sight. Consider having a variety of old classical radios in your home. Some you may tinker with until they work and others you keep because the design is intrinsically beautiful or interesting to you. You may be attracted to a shortwave set and enjoy surfing the Internet.

Outdoors, February 16 would like old trees that have been on the property for years. Sequoia would be particularly pleasing. A public garden for February 16 might be more interesting than tending a personal one. Flowers that you enjoy are alpine asters, rock alyssum, and rose daphne.

A Kabbalistic Interpretation

Today's day has a very interesting series of values from a kabbalistic standpoint. Calculating the value of the day by relating it to the Hebrew name for the point of the zodiac in which it falls generates a value that is the same as the name for the ancient tribe of Judah. Your lucky animal is almost definitely the lion. If you are seeking financial luck then you can buy yourself some stone Chinese lions to place just before your front door.

Medieval history has a particularly strong appeal for you. Incorporate some of this imagery in your home. In your bedroom especially hang some traditional tapestries depicting courtly romances. If you opt for dark green–and–gold touches in this room you will find that your love life positively explodes, as these colors put you in an extremely romantic frame of mind.

In the workplace you can sometimes be slightly too demanding of yourself and others, leading to a certain amount of friction. In your case this usually results from not being able to see the forest for the trees in a particular project. If you keep a vase of fresh daisies on your desk or at your work station it should help you keep your eye on the larger picture.

A Numerological Interpretation
YOUR MAGIC NUMBERS: 9 AND 2

The sixteenth day of the second month reduces to nine, a number that connotes the end of a cycle. The message of this day is the meaning that underlies forms that are constantly changing. What lies beneath and behind the changing outer forms is an eternal, changeless reality.

Crocuses in the spring snow are beautiful images of the cycle of emergence. Collect pottery vessels, an art as ancient as humanity. The craft and shapes and purposes of the containers have been continuous through millennia. Amethyst, jasper, and chrysocolla will bring you peace. The forty-seventh day of the year reduces to two, which adds the quality of reflection. You enjoy anthropology and historical novels. Place violets in a pottery vase in your kitchen window. Placing flowers in a pottery jar is a timeless gesture. A gift of flowers means love and cheers the spirit. Enjoy the haunting strains of a Celtic harp.

OBJECTS/IMAGES
air-conditioning, somersaults, screws, questionnaires

SHAPES/MATERIALS
waterwheels, wavy shapes, azurite

COLORS
azure blue, blush

ANIMALS
mule deer, white ibis

PLANTS, HERBS, EDIBLES
lavender, rhubarb, wall germander, venison

ESSENCE
myrtle

SOUNDS/RHYTHMS
ventriloquism, minuets

MUSICAL NOTES
G# and C#

DEEP SPACE OBJECT
black hole

February 17

YOUR SIGN
Aquarius

———

YOUR ELEMENT
Air

———

YOUR RULERS
Uranus, Venus
27–28 degrees
Third Decanate, yin

The Astrological Interpretation

You never feel completely at ease or secure unless you know that the people around you are well taken care of. Your own self-interest is intimately linked with others; you could never be accused of being egocentric. The world is your family, and you will find that you are attracted to political and social causes geared for the welfare of humanity. You have a particular interest in nature and are genuinely concerned for the welfare of our planet. Although you easily accept people from all different backgrounds, you find yourself primarily attracted to and involved with others who share your political and social beliefs. You are much closer to such people than people from your own family background. You may consider such individuals your real brothers and sisters.

Your home is important to you, and you may want to furnish it in keeping with your ecological beliefs. Natural fibers, recycled materials, and energy-conscious solutions will please you. Venus is the ruler of your decanate, and you will want an aesthetic dimension to your ecological home. Pale blue is a good color for your home. Anything in an octagon shape is pleasing. Invest in some unique lamps. You may enjoy making lamps from discarded watercooler bottles or large ginger jars.

Outdoors, February 17 enjoys trees and vineyards. If you cannot grow grapes in your climate consider creating an arbor where you can sit and contemplate how you will improve the world.

A Kabbalistic Interpretation

People born today tend to be fairly intellectual and may have had parents who had high expectations for their success. You may find that you are an extremely capable person who lacks the self-confidence to push yourself forward. You can help overcome your shyness by using a violet-based bath oil or incense oil. Pour a few drops in your bath each night for at least a month. Burn some red candles and remember all the positive things that you have already achieved in life.

You have a particular love of all things creative, and your great favorite is literature. You are likely to be a real bookworm, but you may leave your growing collection of books strewn about the house.

You will get an enormous benefit beyond simply knowing where your books are if you invest in some brightly colored wooden bookcases.

The moon has a strong influence on today's birthday, encouraging imagination and emotional sensitivity as well as a certain degree of psychic ability. However there are times such as full moons or when the moon is very low in the sky when you can feel down and even tearful. Buying a moonstone and keeping it close to you at such times will help to keep you attuned to the positive and nurturing energies of the moon.

A Numerological Interpretation
YOUR MAGIC NUMBERS: 10 AND 3

The seventeenth day of the second month reduces to ten, signifying the perfection and enjoyment at the end of a cycle. This day endows an innate satisfaction in a job well done. You work hard, enjoying the effort, and derive pleasure from the completed task. The forty-eighth day of the year reduces to three. Three adds the influence of natural growth and unfoldment to your endeavors. You enjoy the process for its own sake. You love to be busy tackling jobs that give you joy. Build something you will keep. Have a vegetable garden and can your own produce. Fluorite, tourmaline, and amethyst will ground you to the earth. Build your own house, even cutting the trees for the lumber. Finish the basement. Enjoy projects you can do with your hands. Remodel an older home. Inhale the aroma of freshly cut wood. Run your hand across polished handmade furniture. Decorate with purples and greens.

OBJECTS/IMAGES
parking tickets, volcanoes, telephone booths

SHAPES/MATERIALS
feather boas, shellac, polonium, plaids

COLORS
electric pink, aubergine

ANIMALS
auk bird, chimera

PLANTS, HERBS, EDIBLES
carob, wild lupine, shooting star

ESSENCE
spikenard

SOUNDS/RHYTHMS
waltzes, sound of an auctioneer

MUSICAL NOTES
A and D

DEEP SPACE OBJECT
Veil Nebula

February 18

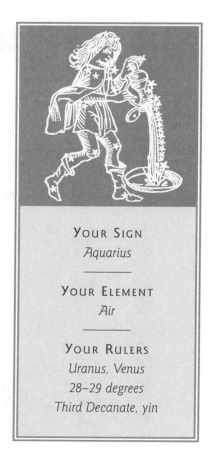

YOUR SIGN
Aquarius

YOUR ELEMENT
Air

YOUR RULERS
Uranus, Venus
28–29 degrees
Third Decanate, yin

The Astrological Interpretation

This birth date provides the opportunity for spiritual growth and creative development. You have within you great knowledge and understanding about human nature. You have a deep sense of compassion and a willingness to be of help to others. What is required of you is to find the form for your particular field of service. You can easily become bored with the ordinary and the usual, and your restlessness will take you far afield in search of new territory to explore. Your travels are not for sensual pleasure as much as they are for the chance they give you to reach into yourself and come up with your inner treasures. Your job is to develop the necessary discrimination that will help you choose your journeys and relationships wisely.

There is purity and clarity of purpose in your birthday. February 18's character and ideas are original and well suited for literature, drama, and music. You may be an innovator in whatever field you choose. An image for February 18 is a butterfly emerging from a chrysalis. The myriad possibilities of life fascinate you. At home, you will enjoy electronic equipment that makes life easier. Push-button drapes, lighting dimmer switches that allow you to regulate the amount of light, and easily sliding windows all appeal to your sense of invention. Sky blue is a color for you to use in decorating. Consider painting figures or scenes on your ceilings. Antique swords may figure in your decorating scheme, and a laurel wreath in the kitchen would be an appropriate reminder of your accomplishments. February 18 is ever in search of the new and original. Let your creativity blossom in your home.

Outdoors, February 18 would enjoy an interior courtyard garden and a location on a hill. You may want to keep a menagerie of talking birds and unusual animals. In your garden emphasize plants and flowers with blue blossoms.

A Kabbalistic Interpretation

You have a natural understanding of other people's emotional states and are good at helping them to articulate how they feel. This is very auspicious for anyone wishing to make a career in a people-oriented vocation—particularly counseling or psychiatry. In order to prevent other people's feelings from creeping negatively into your own psyche, drink plenty of mint tea and make sure that you have at least one piece of jewelry that is set with a sapphire.

One of the values of this day corresponds to the letters that represent the three elements of air, water, and fire. This combination suggests that people born today have a balanced outlook on life. The one missing element in this day is earth. It would be useful to place at least one ceramic bowl or vase in each room of your home to create a symbolic earthen vessel for the other elements.

You have a great love of life and manage to combine your ability to understand and listen to others with a developed sense of fun. You enjoy a wardrobe with plenty of bright colors, and all shades of green and yellow are good for you. You could also find something that has a rainbow motif or pattern to it.

A Numerological Interpretation
YOUR MAGIC NUMBERS: 2 AND 4

The eighteenth day of the second month reduces to two. You have a passion for learning and experience. You are always ready to discover something new and long to duplicate the excitement of your intellectual adventures. This is a mental quest above all, as your first love is the landscape of ideas. You'd like to know everything. Visit a large public library. Drink steaming coffee while you read. Caress the old leather covers of hardbound volumes.

Join the Noetic Society or Mensa. Share your ideas with others. Play three-dimensional chess to stretch your brain. Read science fiction. Visit the Exploratorium, a science fair, NASA. The forty-ninth day of the year reduces to four, contributing the quality of order to your quest. Have a robot, anything experimental. Sapphire, carnelian, and amethyst will ignite your metal processes.

OBJECTS/IMAGES
squalls, television sets, wheelbarrows, glittery makeup

SHAPES/MATERIALS
TNT, volcanic rock, propeller shapes

COLORS
dazzling white, saffron

ANIMAL
rhinoceros

PLANTS, HERBS, EDIBLES
rhubarb, castor bean, soapwort, blue hydrangeas

ESSENCE
sweet inula

SOUNDS/RHYTHMS
factory whistles, breaking glass

MUSICAL NOTES
C# and D#

DEEP SPACE OBJECT
spiral galaxy

February 19

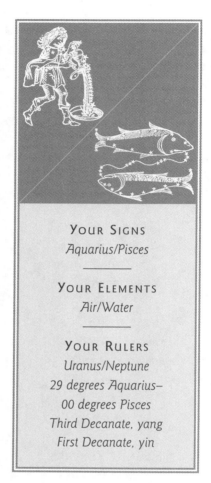

YOUR SIGNS
Aquarius/Pisces

YOUR ELEMENTS
Air/Water

YOUR RULERS
Uranus/Neptune
29 degrees Aquarius–
00 degrees Pisces
Third Decanate, yang
First Decanate, yin

The Astrological Interpretation

You are born on the cusp between Aries and Pisces. You have accumulated a great deal of knowledge about human nature through a mental or intellectual approach to life. Your birth date adds the quality of deep emotional factors and provides a training ground for the right use of feelings in your exchanges with others. You are broad in your tastes and interests and are open to all and everything. Although these attitudes are commendable and make you an unprejudiced person, they may not allow you to specify your own needs, wishes, and desires. You may need to wring out the sponge of feelings and relationships so that you can rid yourself of attachments and interests that no longer suit your state of mind. You must periodically create space in yourself so that you can fill it with the new and beautiful.

Some February 19 birthdays will lean toward the very beginning of Pisces. The watery nature of Pisces lends compassion to Aquarius's mental and conceptual abilities. Since water and air both pertain to your birthday try to create a home environment with lots of windows and light as well as a fountain or view of a body of water. Having a lap pool in your home would be an ultimate luxury. Amethyst is a stone for you. In addition to wearing it as jewelry, you might enjoy having a large piece of the raw crystal in your home. Your work will bring you in contact with many people, and you would be wise to have a routine to shake off all the vibrations you attract. Breathing exercises that emphasize exhaling are very good. Brushing off your body with your hands is another way of clearing your emotional space.

Outdoors, February 19 would be happy with a garden on some high ground and a pond or brook. Flowers for you could include lavender, lemon verbena, and bellflower.

A Kabbalistic Interpretation

If you were born today you are likely to have a very full and rich life. The values of this day point to someone who moves easily in society and is likely to have some status within the community. This suits you just fine, as you love to attend social events. When you go out, you should opt for a black dress or suit offset with small touches of midnight blue. If you are a man you will always look your most elegant in a black-and-blue pinstripe.

You will probably want for little in life and you are neither a mean nor self-seeking individual. This day has very strong associations with charitable behavior. To resonate with your generous nature grow some basil and rosemary in a window box.

As a child you were probably the first in your class to learn to swim, and you retain an affinity for water throughout your life. If you want to make your garden a place that you can deeply enjoy, then the most important element is not specific plants but a water fountain. Place it in the center of your garden and surround it with outdoor candles that can be lit each evening.

A Numerological Interpretation
YOUR MAGIC NUMBERS: 3 AND 5

The nineteenth day of the second month reduces to three, the number of creative expression. Yours is a path of conscious and joyous service to humanity. Life rewards you with the good fruits of your efforts. Like a flower that serves the world through its beauty or a fruit tree that offers its children as sustenance to others, you bloom according to your nature. We serve by who we are as much as by what we do. A loving smile ministers to a broken heart. Nature speaks to you when you enter in silence. You feel her voice more than you hear it.

The fiftieth day of the year reduces to five. Five adds the awareness that blooms are ephemeral. Yesterday's bud is today's blossom and tomorrow's faded bloom. What is the essence that continues to bloom again the following year? What is left of the rose when the petals fade? Stroll in a rose garden and inhale the intoxicating aroma of a thousand blooming roses of every color. Watch industrious honey bees gathering nectar. Touch the softness of rose petals. Greens, purples, and shades of orange will cheer your spirit. Green garnet, emerald, and amethyst will energize your emotions.

OBJECTS/IMAGES
butterflies, bubbles, gyroscopes, hallucinations

SHAPES/MATERIALS
crystal balls, morganite (pink beryl), celluloid

COLORS
iridescent colors/white, ivory

ANIMALS
unicorn, swordfish

PLANTS, HERBS, EDIBLES
woolly locoweed, large blazing star, gota kola

ESSENCES
Tibetan cedarwood, frankincense

SOUNDS/RHYTHMS
amplified tap dancing, synchronized swimming

MUSICAL NOTES
D and E

DEEP SPACE OBJECTS
Epsilon Pegasus, Enif, the Nose

February 20

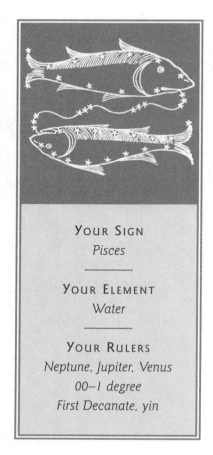

The Astrological Interpretation

You tend to be a very generous person, always willing to give of yourself. But where are your reserves? Although you know that the universe provides, you are a part of that universe and have to learn how to provide for yourself. You must respect your boundaries, and this requires that you learn how to create them. The difficulty can be in your ability to discern the differences between your individual feelings and the emotional pressures coming from the world around you. This is where solitude can play a vital role in your life. Take those moments that you need to be alone and use them wisely. You will be much more available for others when you insist that you are available for yourself.

February 20 is a placid, easygoing birthday until challenged; then you can display a firmness and formidable power. The trick will be to know when to let things drift and when to fight. Depending on your birth time, your birthday may fall on the degree of the fixed star, Fomalhaut. Fomalhaut was one of the royal stars of the Persians, called the Watcher of the South. At that time and location it inaugurated the winter solstice. February 20 retains a sense of that importance and likes to be surrounded with objects that confirm it. Royal purple is a good color for you. Decorate your home with chests of all sorts: jewelry, cedar, bridal. The idea of having a treasure chest that is beautiful in itself and contains interesting things is tantalizing to you.

Value the cautious part of your nature but don't fade into the background. Keep your personal power glowing with amethyst crystals and lavender bath salts. The ideal way to relax is a walk by the water, appreciating the industrious squirrels, and then soak in a hot tub.

A Kabbalistic Interpretation

One of the ways of calculating the value of this day generates a prime number, which always indicates something special and unique. If today is your birthday then you are probably used to being regarded as something of an eccentric by your friends and colleagues. As it is also a day with strong Cancer energy running through it, you may take these views to heart and find them upsetting. If you carry a piece of moss agate with you, it will be easier for you to see that these comments are meant in an affectionate way.

At home, you can relax and not worry about how different your taste might be from the norm. Some images of dragons on your walls would stand out and create a welcome sense of security and stability. Your day has a link with all shades of blue, but make sure that you have plenty of vibrant crimson and emerald green in your home to avoid quite literally getting the blues.

A Numerological Interpretation
YOUR MAGIC NUMBERS: 4 AND 6

The twentieth day of the second month reduces to four, the number of measuring, recording, and tabulation. This is a path of gaining awareness of how everything is related and somehow affects everything else. Study global economics and world trade. Success depends on the willingness of each member to do their part. Consider ice cubes—water as a solid—their geometry. The fifty-first day of the year reduces to six, which adds the desire for symmetry and beauty to your structures. Add the ingredient of love.

Citrine, wulfenite, and rose quartz will enhance your emotions. Visit a public market filled with a profusion of trading merchants, shouting children, brightly colored cloths, and a myriad of other sights and sounds. Let the smells of fresh produce and flowers fill your senses. Taste some ripe fruit or baked pastry. Each vendor comes with his or her own article. If the dairy farmer doesn't arrive, no one has milk or eggs. Enjoy the rich sensory bombardment. Can you see the pattern in the apparent chaos?

OBJECTS/IMAGES
bubbles floating in the sunshine, a geyser gushing, a footstool

SHAPES/MATERIALS
foam, chenille, parchment paper

COLORS
blue-green, azure, purple wine, sage green

ANIMALS
jellyfish, pig, crayfish

PLANTS, HERBS, EDIBLES
ambergris, coca plant, love potions

ESSENCE
smell of gasoline

SOUNDS/RHYTHMS
lutes strumming, minuets, drum roll

MUSICAL NOTES
D# and F

DEEP SPACE OBJECT
Nova in Cygnus

February 21

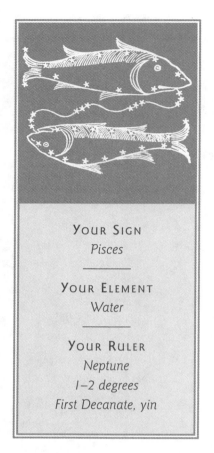

YOUR SIGN
Pisces

———

YOUR ELEMENT
Water

———

YOUR RULER
Neptune
1–2 degrees
First Decanate, yin

The Astrological Interpretation

Your birth date is particularly connected to the process whereby the oceans of the world wash away the sand castles, leaving a clean surface for future creativity. You should not attach too much to the forms of life, as these are eventually dissolved by greater forces. Look instead to eternal truths that are everlasting and sure. Armed with these, it will be easier for you to visit the many oceans of the world and build as many castles as you wish. People sense that you have a capacity to look deeply through the superficialities of the world and will come to you for advice and counsel. You are especially sensitive to people's pain and may need to take a rest occasionally from the external pressures you feel impinging upon your own feelings. Use your interest in art and music to help you relax, and pay attention to your own inner ocean, which calls to you.

Your birthday is a curious combination of ambition and laissez-faire. You can sometimes attract the good things of life simply by your undercurrent of passion and feelings. An image for you is a treasure chest floating on an open sea. You may particularly enjoy stringed instruments. In your home have a complete sound system that can be heard in all rooms. Old sheet music covers are perfect to frame and display. You might consider buying a player piano and old rolls that give a flavor of the original music. A multicolored rag rug would be a perfect touch in front of a fireplace. You need to be lazy every once in a while, and lying down on a rag rug in front of a fireplace would be the perfect way to zone out.

February 21 enjoys creating a beautiful outdoor space. In your flower bed have some pieces of petrified wood or driftwood from the beach. Wind chimes outdoors on a deck would be a pleasure. Flowers for you include rose acacia and miniature pomegranate.

A Kabbalistic Interpretation

In hermeticism certain sets of correspondences relate to a specific country or culture. It is likely that people born today will be attracted to Asian cultures. By wearing a jade amulet or pendant you can be in touch with the East while enhancing your fortune and understanding of the world around you.

You are a well-disciplined individual, and a sense of order and proportion is very important to you. An ideal office design for you would employ lots of black wood and have plenty of geometric abstract paintings. Whether male or female you may be interested in military history, although you are not at all violent by nature and find the consequences of war deeply disturbing. As you also appreciate fine craftsmanship a good present for you could be a pair of antique swords.

You may sometimes be guilty of putting too much pressure on yourself. You need to remember that you are not Atlas and the world will not fall apart or disintegrate if you take a day off from time to time. Put pale pink and blue bedclothes on the bed, run a bath with some jasmine oil, and let go.

A Numerological Interpretation
YOUR MAGIC NUMBERS: 7 AND 5

The twenty-first day of the second month reduces to five, the number of uncertainty, change, and adaptation. This day carries a note of wariness. The highest expression of a talent or quality is the result of developing judgment. It is the opposite of the old expression "Fools rush in where angels fear to tread."

The fifty-second day of the year reduces to seven, adding the element of assured victory when you apply good judgment and courageously step out. Topaz and heliodor will enhance your courage. Imagine castles with moats and drawbridges, and flying flags of yellow and green. Hear the closing of the iron gate, and feel yourself surrounded by thick stone walls. Wear a locket to symbolize faith. A fortress can keep you in as well as others out. Learn the significance of setting boundaries and conditions and knowing what's best for you. The downside is irrational fear and phobia.

OBJECTS/IMAGES
occult religions, miracles, false teeth, fables

SHAPES/MATERIALS
paraffin, rubber, all liquids, strontium

COLORS
burnt sienna, kelly green

ANIMAL
monarch butterfly

PLANTS, HERBS, EDIBLES
lotus, dwarfed plants, bonsai trees, opium poppies

ESSENCE
petitgrain

SOUNDS/RHYTHMS
Bach Transcriptions for Guitar
by Andrés Segovia

MUSICAL NOTES
F# and E

DEEP SPACE OBJECTS
Alpha Aquarius, Sadalmelik, Lucky One of the King

February 22

YOUR SIGN
Pisces

YOUR ELEMENT
Water

YOUR RULERS
Neptune, Venus
2–3 degrees
First Decanate, yin

The Astrological Interpretation

What is very particular about your birth date is the urge to be a healer of circumstances. You have a natural feeling for the good and the bad in life, the dark and the light, the high and the low. Sometimes you feel yourself being pulled apart as these oppositional forces play out their drama. Once you have stabilized this movement within yourself, you will be free to help people who are still suffering from their own inner divisions. Your deeply mystical side tells you there is an invisible world existing alongside the visible one. Some born this day will search for the hidden truths that can be found in the study of metaphysical and spiritual pursuits.

Your birthday gives you the gift of insightful original thinking. You may be drawn to public service, the arts, or business, and wherever you work you try to instill high ideals in those around you. Luminous clouds, floating like cotton candy in an azure sky, may evoke images of angels, birds, or butterflies. Still your mind, and sail away on their wings. You may find that you have an attraction to pearls, especially freshwater ones. At home, February 22 wants a well-decorated home with flower-patterned upholstery. Pale green is an excellent background color for you. Consider using scent in your home to freshen the air and to sweeten it. A room spray of eucalyptus will wake up your senses, and a spray of geranium essential oil will soothe and quiet you before sleep.

Outdoors, a pond or water source is centering to you. Large bodies of water may feel intimidating, so even a portable pool will do very nicely. Consider planting your garden in the shape of an S curve. Creating a variety of pathways with flagstone through the garden will make it a restful place where you can wander.

A Kabbalistic Interpretation

You are strongly drawn to rural settings and should make use of that inclination wherever possible in your home environment. Bake your own bread to lower stress. Relax to the sound of recorded birdsongs.

The Hebrew value of the day suggests a strong association with wood. Wood carries powerful earth energy and would be useful in grounding your sometimes fiery temperament. Necklaces and bracelets made from polished wood would be very effective at dispelling excess anger.

You will always look your best in green, particularly dark olive green. Not only will you look great but you will also find that you are able to communicate much more effectively with people. At times you can be reticent about your real feelings, but a silver ring worn on the little finger of your left hand will help you to open up in ways you normally find difficult or even impossible.

A Numerological Interpretation
YOUR MAGIC NUMBERS: 6 AND 8

The twenty-second day of the second month reduces to six, the number of love and beauty. No matter how lovely a situation is, if there is no movement, there is no growth. Once-living trees in a petrified forest are images of permanence, but also of inflexibility. Sometimes, things seem so beautiful as they are, we are reluctant to alter them. We can't keep our children young forever. What defines the quality of survival? Is a petrified forest still a grove of trees, or has it become something else? Walk in the magic of a redwood forest or an aspen grove. Scientists have discovered an aspen grove in Colorado that is actually a single entity whose roots are connected underground. What appeared to be a grove of many trees is actually a single being, the largest creature in the world. The cleansing action of a forest fire stimualtes the growth of the aspen, providing space and nutrients to promote growth. Without the purifying action of the fire, the aspen dies.

The fifty-third day of the year reduces to eight, which contributes the ability to see beauty in change itself. Grow bonsai trees. Plant a tree on Arbor Day. Wear a pendant of wood opal. Precious opal replaces organic wood. Dance a waltz in the forest under the stars.

OBJECTS/IMAGES
*a pedicure, jeweled sandals,
a light fog*

SHAPES/MATERIALS
wispy curls, gauze

COLORS
*lavender, creamy white,
mahogany, aquamarine*

ANIMALS
*little energetic dogs,
kissing gourami fish*

PLANTS, HERBS, EDIBLES
bogbean, yarrow, anchovies

ESSENCE
spikenard

SOUNDS/RHYTHMS
gourd rattles, jitterbug music

MUSICAL NOTES
F and G

DEEP SPACE OBJECT
*Alpha-Piscis Austrini
or Formalhaut,
Mouth of the Fish*

February 23

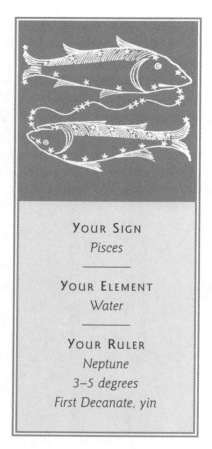

YOUR SIGN
Pisces

YOUR ELEMENT
Water

YOUR RULER
Neptune
3–5 degrees
First Decanate, yin

The Astrological Interpretation

This is a birth date that is particularly linked to beauty. You do not have to conform to prevailing trends, in fact, you much prefer to invent your own unusual mixtures and combinations of styles, colors, and fabrics. You are an adventurous and romantic person, but you also need and appreciate time spent alone. Socially, you seek to bring harmony into your surroundings and become upset if there are conflicts in your personal or professional relationships. This feeling worsens if you sense that you have been the cause of disharmony between people. Although it may be difficult for you to be always orderly, neat, and tidy, you appreciate structure and clarity. You aspire to precise emotional communication even though you sometimes enjoy the intensity of conflict. If this sounds a bit dualistic, it is. But then you are a Pisces, and this is a sign signified by two fish swimming in opposite directions.

Some February 23 birthdays will fall on a critical degree. This position gives you strong reactions to the highs and lows of life and many varied experiences. You have talents in the visual arts and music as well as crafts. Frequently you may not know how you are going to create something but your hands find the way. At home have touches of luxury such as silk Persian carpets or brocade fabrics on some of your chairs. Touches of lavender or purple are decorative accents for your home. Water imagery in the bathroom and kitchen is soothing to you. You may keep seashells on your windowsill and a bottle of colored sand in the bathroom.

Gardening may be a passion for you. Landscaping and placing flowers, rocks, fishponds, and a small gazebo would be an ongoing project for you. In addition to aquatic plants emphasize orchids and the shrub Carolina allspice.

A Kabbalistic Interpretation

You have an amazing temper when you are riled, and like a tiger, rather than lash out directly, you take your time and strike at just the right moment! You will inevitably be attracted to furniture and household ornaments that have an angular line and a point, such as tall metal candle spikes for your bedroom.

There are times in your life when you suddenly feel drained and can no longer maintain your usual bustling approach to the world. If you put a pale blue or aquamarine glass rose vase on a shelf in the south of your living room you will find it much easier to unwind and get the relaxation you crave. A tigereye stone in your pocket will help maintain sufficient drive when you really need it.

Some people might not share your ornate tastes but you are confident enough to ignore them—if you like gold-colored bath taps, why should anyone else pass comment! A wonderful addition to your kitchen might be a large picture of a bright golden sun with twelve rays coming out from its center. This will appeal to your love of big and bold decor while enhancing your positive "can do" approach in your career and your relationships.

A Numerological Interpretation
YOUR MAGIC NUMBERS: 7 AND 9

The twenty-third day of the second month reduces to seven, the number implying rest or temporary cessation. This day carries the energy of convergence, as if a multilaned super highway narrows to one lane. This date is the path of a cosmic air traffic controller for all the various influences, personalities, and challenges that meet at the crossroads in your life. You are capable of organizing these diverse travelers so that the highway of life has fewer traffic snarls.

Sapphire and beryl will energize you. Visit a busy airport and watch the jumbo jets take off and leave vapor trails across the sky. Remember the words of Robert Frost—"Two roads diverged in a wood, and I—/I took the one less traveled by,/And that has made all the difference." The fifty-fourth day of the year reduces to nine, which contributes the quality of successful completion, lending confidence to your endeavors. Wear greens and blues for good luck.

OBJECTS/IMAGES
roof gardens, raincoats, secret emotions, stockings

SHAPES/MATERIALS
Thai silk, platinum, petroleum, mineral springs

COLORS
purple, aqua, teal

ANIMALS
roseate spoonbill, little blue heron

PLANTS, HERBS, EDIBLES
waffles, chocolate, purple-fringed orchids, wild coffee

ESSENCE:
rose de mai

SOUNDS/RHYTHMS
cello music, rhapsodies

MUSICAL NOTES
F# and G#

DEEP SPACE OBJECTS
Alpha Cygnus, Deneb, the Tail

February 24

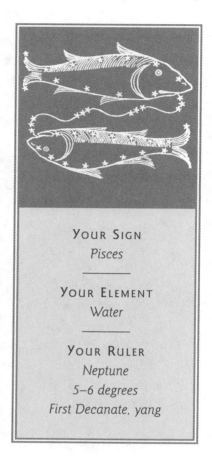

YOUR SIGN
Pisces

YOUR ELEMENT
Water

YOUR RULER
Neptune
5–6 degrees
First Decanate, yang

The Astrological Interpretation

This birth date indicates a compassionate, dedicated person with others' welfare always in mind. The more you reach out in your urge to be of service, the more the world around you will support your efforts. You do need a structure through which your contributions may be made. You have to know when enough is enough and when it is correct for you to withdraw, recuperate, and restore your life energies. The easiest and most pleasant way for you to regenerate is through the arts. You have an especial love of music, painting, and all things of beauty created by the human hand. It is important in your choice of intimate, personal relationships that you choose someone mature. What you do not need is to be in a relationship with someone who relies upon you for strength instead of looking within to his or her own inner resources.

Your imagination is strong and more comfortable living in the world of possibilities than actualities. The two Pisces fish exist both above and below the water, and you must rehearse and perfect the demands of life on earth. Education and training in a field where you can utilize your compassion is the answer. In your bathroom, create an underwater world. Have a big tub, dim lights, and a candle with a green shade, seashells, saltwater bath essences, and taped music of sea sounds. This is the room where you can recharge your imagination. In another part of your home, have the earth room, with a blond wood desk, a cluster of quartz or amethyst crystals, a ledger book or computer program to keep track of finances, pens and pencils, and colorful file folders. This is where you work to have the privilege of retreating.

Outdoors, you can have all the elements: earth, air, water, and fire. A garden with streamers tied to garden stakes that blow in the wind, a small brook or pool, and torchlights for outdoor entertaining combine all the elements. Special flowers for February 24 are fountain plant, dendrobium orchids, and water hyacinth.

A Kabbalistic Interpretation

One simple way of calculating a kabbalistic value for this day gives Yod Heh Vau Heh. This name of God, which is also known as the Tetragrammaton, represents all four of the elements, indicating a balanced individual. However, the Tetragrammaton may bring excessive severity in one's dealings with others. You can counter this judgmental aspect of your personality by taking a bath with some mallow leaves and flower heads.

Your home is always scrupulously clean and organized. Taken to exremes, this can make your home appear sterile and unfriendly. Satisfy your need for symmetry without sacrificing warmth by placing potted plants with heavy foliage in your space. The plants will encourage you to get in touch with your nurturing side thanks to the daily attention they need.

There is an excess of water in the overall value of this day. While you need to balance the water you also need to avoid too much fire, as this would only serve to make you irritable. Placing some dark green candles near each water source in your home will have a positive grounding effect.

A Numerological Interpretation
YOUR MAGIC NUMBERS: 8 AND 10

The twenty-fourth day of the second month reduces to eight, the number signifying reciprocity. What we give returns to us a hundredfold. This path requires understanding the mutual benefit of our interaction and sharing with family, friends, and companions. The fifty-fifth day of the year reduces to ten, adding the influence of the perfect embodiment of what you strive for.

Spinel, tanzanite, and sodalite are gems that will enhance your energy. Donate something to charity. Volunteer for the Humane Society. Attend a charity ball, wear a formal gown, and have a fabulous time for a cause you believe in. Dance in a ballroom to a big band or orchestra. Wear a corsage or boutonniere. Sip sparkling punch in your fuchsia silk gown or tuxedo with a turquoise cummerbund.

OBJECTS/IMAGES
schooners, seances, ice skates, sects

SHAPES/MATERIALS
washable silk, spire shapes, spongy shapes, petroleum

COLORS
burnt sienna, navy blue

ANIMALS
night heron, snowy egret

PLANTS, HERBS, EDIBLES
Virginia waterleaf, hooded pitcher plant, showy lady's slipper

ESSENCE
cassie

SOUNDS/RHYTHMS
harps, lyrical melodies

MUSICAL NOTES
G and A

DEEP SPACE OBJECTS
Gamma Aquarius, Sadachbia

February 25

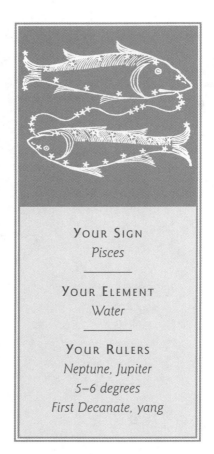

YOUR SIGN
Pisces

YOUR ELEMENT
Water

YOUR RULERS
Neptune, Jupiter
5–6 degrees
First Decanate, yang

The Astrological Interpretation

You accept other people for who they are and have no problem supporting their beliefs and philosophies. In your own unique and special way, you are a seeker of truth. You know that much in the world around you is made up of illusory glamour. At an early stage of life, you might be attracted to intensely emotional, romantic experiences. But as your life unfolds, you realize that there is something more to cherish than even the presence of the perfect partner. Your sensitivity to what lies beneath the surface of events is strong. You want to know what is really taking place in the world around you. Allow this part of your nature to flourish, as it will give a more profound significance to your work, relationships, and other life interests. Find your truth and stand on it as a source of inner strength as the outer circumstances of life ebb and flow and come and go.

You will find a way to incorporate your higher ideals in whatever path in life you follow. An image for you is an ancient pilgrim carrying a lamp to illuminate the spirit. Decorate your home with light-filled colors. You may have a fondness for impressionist paintings. A bowl of clear glass globes that catch the sunlight would be a perfect centerpiece for a dining room or coffee table. Raw amethyst crystal is a mineral for you and if possible a star sapphire. Consider burning incense in your bedroom. Sandalwood and jasmine might evoke visionary dreams.

Outdoors, February 25 wants a garden and a place to view the stars. Plant red-violet flowers such as chrysanthemums and phlox and consider creating a water lily pond. A telescope so you can see the stars will keep you confident in your path. Somewhere in your garden you might have a ship's anchor. February 25 needs a reminder that no matter how far you go you won't loose your moorings.

A Kabbalistic Interpretation

This day really is a day for lovers. The various values that can be calculated for the day all point toward an extremely sensual energy. The most important room in your life is the bedroom, and to make the most of this center of activity, decorate in a mixture of deepest purple, black, and midnight blue. A four-poster bed with drapes would be perfect. Failing that, make sure that your curtains are of a very heavy material and that you have no overhead lighting in the room.

A connection with the Moon card in tarot can be an indicator of deep-seated anxieties and problems with self-esteem. One possible remedy is to keep some water lilies in the house. Keep them in a ceramic vase that has a square rather than a circular shape.

You have a very quick wit and love of all sorts of secrets, riddles, and puzzles. This may mean that the ideal present for you is a complex three-dimensional jigsaw, while others born today might find this interest leads them to explore the secrets of unexplained phenomena.

A Numerological Interpretation

YOUR MAGIC NUMBERS: 9 AND 2

The twenty-fifth day of the second month reduces to nine, the number that embodies the pure, clear expression of the idea that began the cycle. Discipline is central along the path to success. The image of a precision dress military parade requires both individual effort and the rehearsal of the group to hold the idealized pattern together.

You have a flair for protocol. Take care not to expect special privileges based on status. The fifty-sixth day of the year reduces to two, which adds the quality of reflection and comparison to what has gone before. Is this year's parade superior to last year's? Aquamarine and rose quartz will strengthen your resolve. Attend an air show where top gun pilots perform aerial acrobatics. Let your spirit soar as the powerful military jets transcend the sound barrier. The steady rhythm of a marching band inspires you. Wear blue for strength.

OBJECTS/IMAGES
a witch's hat, whirlpools, mermaids

SHAPES/MATERIALS
tourmaline, trident shape, see-through material

COLORS
burnt umber, rust, royal blue

ANIMALS
starfish, seagull

PLANTS, HERBS, EDIBLES
sundew, tomatoes, yeast

ESSENCE
tea tree

SOUNDS/RHYTHMS
poetry, ritual music

MUSICAL NOTES
G# and C#

DEEP SPACE OBJECT
Beta Sculptor

February 26

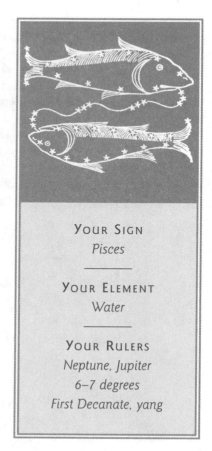

YOUR SIGN
Pisces

YOUR ELEMENT
Water

YOUR RULERS
Neptune, Jupiter
6–7 degrees
First Decanate, yang

The Astrological Interpretation

This birth date reveals a sensitive, generous, and charitable person. It is very difficult for you to turn away from the suffering caused by ignorance and inhumanity. Yet you are also a person with ambition and drive. How can you take your urge for success in the world and use any position you may achieve for the welfare of others? Integrating both your material and spiritual goals can be one of the major joys of your life. Once you believe in something, you want many others to know about it. You are magnetic and have the power to organize others but not by shouting and giving commands. Yours is a much more subtle path of gentle persuasion—you have the ability to bring out the best qualities of others.

You have reserves of devotion for whatever path of life you choose. You have the patience to pursue studies or projects that do not seem to have an immediate practical use. An image for February 26 is a private niche with a green shaded lamp, a book, and a missal or holy book. Have a room or corner at home that you can call your own. Your decor should feature cool blues and lavenders with bright spots of color. Fiesta ware might be something you would enjoy. A cowl scarf or hooded terry cloth bathrobe will have resonance for your devotions. Jewelry in a cross shape, whether the pieces are religious or not, will suit you. You may be fond of big, long books, both literature and romances. Stock your corner with them and go there to renew your energies.

Your outdoor environment should include water, a garden, and an oak tree. Jupiter, the coruler of Pisces, rules oak trees, a sturdy counterpoise to February 26's changeable and watery nature. Your garden may include whimsical touches such as Popsicle stick villages or miniature birch bark teepees that reflect your sense of humor and playfulness.

A Kabbalistic Interpretation

The energy of this day is bound up with the energies of the sun. If you live in a cold and rainy part of the country you might try to seek the sun to get the most happiness from life. Wear a rich yellow whenever it is important for you to succeed. Opt for gold jewelry rather than silver or any other material.

People on this day often come across as personifications of paradox, in that their tastes seem to embrace completely opposite extremes. The contrast tends to be between what William Blake called Innocence and Experience. People born today are very politically minded and cynically aware, yet they can be extremely innocent and childlike. An ideal gift for someone born today would be a train set or some other traditional toy.

Handicraft skills are very well aspected by this day's value. Try developing your skills by making your own jewelry and ornaments. It is likely that you will be interested in the culture of tribal groups and can use this interest as an inspiration for your own creations.

A Numerological Interpretation

YOUR MAGIC NUMBERS: 10 AND 3

The twenty-sixth day of the second month reduces to ten, the number of perfection and ultimate consequence. The process begun at the number one is complete. First cause has final effect.

We can never take freedom for granted. This path is one of defending and protecting higher ideals. Comprehend the importance of upholding standards like a nation's flag or the standard of a king when marching into battle. Why does the American flag never touch the ground during a ceremony? What does it mean to burn a country's flag? It isn't the cloth that has value. The flag is a symbol of high ideals. The fifty-seventh day of the year reduces to three, adding the influence of natural unfoldment that adds insight. Buddha said, "Be the light you desire in the world." Light a candle, don't curse the darkness. Azurite, tanzanite, and tigereye will fire your zeal. Indigo and orange are colors to both soothe and warm you. Visit the Vietnam Memorial or the Holocaust Museum. Listen to national anthems.

OBJECTS/IMAGES
*stained glass windows,
a snow globe with a mermaid*

SHAPES/MATERIALS
tin, marble, colored sea glass

COLORS
*sea green, dark purple,
apricot*

ANIMALS
ox, river whale

PLANTS, HERBS, EDIBLES
flax, coral tree, violets

ESSENCE
balsam

SOUNDS/RHYTHMS
*lute music,
the sound of a water pump*

MUSICAL NOTES
A and D

DEEP SPACE OBJECTS
*Delta Aquarius, Skat,
the Shinbone*

February 27

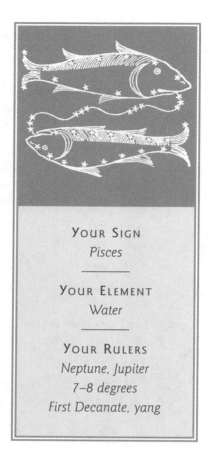

YOUR SIGN
Pisces

YOUR ELEMENT
Water

YOUR RULERS
Neptune, Jupiter
7–8 degrees
First Decanate, yang

The Astrological Interpretation

All Pisces people ebb and flow. You pull back into yourself to gather your forces and then, after a period of seeming stillness, rush forward like a huge wave and hit the shore! People will be surprised at your inner power—you seem like such a docile and gentle person most of the time. What they do not know is that you have a reserve of strength and a treasury of inner resources that emerges only after you have withdrawn into yourself to contact them. It is important for you to develop the right feeling for when you must withdraw and pull into yourself and how long you have to stay there, when to emerge, and with what degree of strength and level of intensity. You may enjoy dancing or learning a martial art as a way of refining your timing.

For retreat periods, a daybed or reclining couch with round pillows is the island where you can martial your forces. Staring at houseplants such as African violets or coleus will inspire you and keep your energies high. Have a variety of shoes around. You may learn something about human nature, as the saying "put yourself in my shoes" is quite literally true for you. When you are in a forward outer-directed mood, you could use a large date book in which to keep appointments, phone numbers, and addresses. Sometimes time escapes you, and organizing things is a way of combatting that tendency.

Outdoors, February 27 has a tender rapport with the environment. You may enjoy walking your pets or planting in the garden. Flowers for you are water hyacinth and a member of the orchid family, *Bletilla striata*. February 27 may also have a special delight in washing the car with a natural sponge. The water and sponge are both materials that resonate with your nature.

A Kabbalistic Interpretation

You tend to be a deeply rational person who views anything that cannot be proven by scientific evidence with considerable suspicion. If you really want to make someone born today feel special, rather than buying them an expensive piece of jewelry or a designer outfit, buy them the most up-to-date electronic gadget or a state-of-the-art computer. If today is your birthday and you receive such a gift, put it in the northeast corner of the room where you use it.

The Hebrew letter *Lamed*, which means "ox goad," is strongly associated with the value of this particular day. This letter can represent a tendency to drive yourself too hard. To ease the pressure that you sometimes pile on yourself consider installing a traditional Scandinavian sauna in your bathroom area.

Gadgets in general have tremendous appeal for you. Get them in black, as this is a color well suited to the value of this day. A splash of color around the house, especially some pretty pastel shades, will have a positive effect on your temperament. A fantastic gadget for you to have would be a good telescope. The pleasure you derive from gazing out at the stars and the planets will make the expense well worth it.

A Numerological Interpretation
YOUR MAGIC NUMBERS: 2 AND 4

The twenty-seventh day of the second month reduces to two, the number signifying the life force in many ancient traditions. The separation of one into two can look like opposition and antagonism. Two is the mirror in which one sees itelf. This path engenders an eagerness for self-expression. We are each called to a special charge, a unique working out of a mission and potential that only we can fulfill. Respond to your calling.

The fifty-eighth day of the year reduces to four, adding the quality of planning, surveying, gaining the lay of the land as we move ahead on the path of self-realization. Wulfenite, carnelian, and jasper are complementary gems. Visit Big Ben in London for fun. Surround yourself with beautiful clocks and mirrors and old-fashioned alarm clocks, which you wind to hear the bells clang.

OBJECTS/IMAGES
waterfalls, toupees, scarecrows, voodoo

SHAPES/MATERIALS
whirlpool shapes, trident shapes, aquamarine, amethyst

COLORS
turquoise, russet

ANIMALS
tropical fish, shark

PLANTS, HERBS, EDIBLES
yeast, whiskey, water arum

ESSENCE
carrot seed oil

SOUNDS/RHYTHMS
violins, all toe-tapping rhythms

MUSICAL NOTES
C# and D#

DEEP SPACE OBJECTS
Kappa Aquarius, Situl

February 28

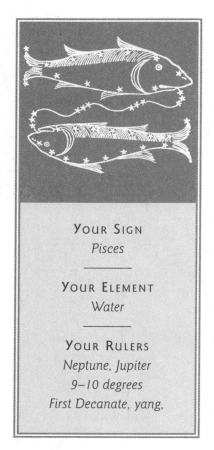

YOUR SIGN
Pisces

YOUR ELEMENT
Water

YOUR RULERS
Neptune, Jupiter
9–10 degrees
First Decanate, yang,

The Astrological Interpretation

You have great faith—faith in life, yourself, and in the process of unfoldment. You carry an optimistic belief that in the end, everything will work out just fine. Many people come to you for support, advice, and comfort. Cultivate knowledge, wisdom, and rational understanding to balance your faith and you will find that your creative powers increase. You are genuinely kind and considerate and are eager to be of service to others. Though it is hard to stand by and watch as people you care about bump into walls, it is important to realize when people need to find their own solutions to problems. Wait until you are called upon directly and in the meantime, develop and nurture yourself so that there is more of you to give.

Before the discovery of Neptune in 1846, Jupiter, the planet of priests and religious figures, ruled Pisces. You have a lusty appreciation for the sensual aspects of life and will not necessarily check into the convent or monastery, but fundamentally your search is for the sacred. A mortar and pestle is an object for you. Imagine you are a chemist trying to find the formula to bring out the best traits in yourself and others. As you grind spices or other concoctions you may reflect on all striving human beings. Care for your feet; they are your connection to the earth and need pampering. Soak them with scented lavender or rose petals in almond oil. Go to the ballet. Wear colorful socks; they will give your feet good vibes.

If you have a problem, imagine sitting on a cloud and looking down at the situation. You'll find your "cloud vision" gives you a new perspective. A garden planted in a circular shape is pleasing to you. February 28 goes into the depths to find sustenance. A well with a bucket that can draw water is a perfect object for your garden or outdoor environment.

A Kabbalistic Interpretation

This day connects to the image of stretching up toward God, especially the idea of Ra or the sun as God. This connection points to an environment full of living things all stretching up toward the sky. Your garden should be a symphony of aromas and colors, and indeed might be the high point of your home.

If at all possible seek a house on a hill or some other piece of raised ground. The higher the better, so an apartment on a top floor in a tall apartment building might work. An unusual home for you would be a former windmill or lighthouse. Whatever shape your house takes, help realize your true potential by using pale violet around the house; perhaps decorate with some violet-painted glass ornaments.

Animals are very important to you and will be a feature in your home and even more likely in your office. Horses are a common favorite among people born today. Certain energies of this day point to a tendency to gamble with an almost childlike optimism. This could prove disastrous at the racetrack, and consequently you should confine your appreciation of horses to activities that don't involve risking money.

A Numerological Interpretation

YOUR MAGIC NUMBERS: 3 AND 5

The twenty-eighth day of the second month reduces to three, the number of duplication and repetition. This day carries the path of striving for excellence through the competitions and struggles of everyday experience. Practice makes perfect. Implicit in practice is an upward movement of skill, progressing from beginner to professional.

The fifty-ninth day of the year reduces to five, adding the influence of adaptation to the process of developing talent and aptitude into skill. Do you have ten years of experience, or one year of experience repeated ten times? Remember when you learned to ride a bicycle or drive a car? Attend the winter Olympics. Marvel at the practiced magic of the pairs figure skaters. Watch their leaps, spins, and twirls and hear the sound of the blades digging into the ice as they stop. Sip a mug of hot chocolate. Wear an orange and yellow scarf and mittens.

OBJECTS/IMAGES
aquariums, boots

SHAPES/MATERIALS
gasoline, a boat neck collar

COLORS
deep violet, white, bittersweet

ANIMALS
puffin bird, brontosaurus

PLANTS, HERBS, EDIBLES
woundwort, borage, liqueur-filled chocolates

ESSENCE
clematis

SOUNDS/RHYTHMS
plink, plink, plink; calliope music

MUSICAL NOTES
D and E

DEEP SPACE OBJECT
NGC 7027, planetary nebula

February 29

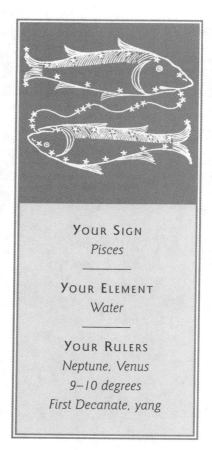

YOUR SIGN
Pisces

___

YOUR ELEMENT
Water

___

YOUR RULERS
Neptune, Venus
9–10 degrees
First Decanate, yang

The Astrological Interpretation

Astrology celebrates your birthday each year when the sun is between nine and ten degrees of Pisces. One of your natural gifts is your intuition. You are eager to share your insights and perceptions and find that your advice to people is usually correct. But sometimes, things need to be left broken for a while so that people can fix them for themselves. Life is filled with creative potentials; it is important for you to refine your ability to choose. This requires that you periodically release those situations and relationships that can go no further. It takes quite a bit of courage to say: "I must go and search a bit more." Yet when you take this step, what you meet a little way down the road is exactly what you have been looking for. Your birth date indicates a person who is developing a sense of faith in himself. In order to obtain this quality and the inner strength that comes with it, you will have to leave yourself open to the necessary tests.

Perhaps traditional religion does not appeal to you, but seeking how the sacred exists in daily life is important to you. Surround your home with geometric pieces like Arabic mosaics or Oriental rugs with a clear central medallion. You might have an interest in studying Sufi wisdom or seeing the whirling dervishes. These dervishes spin to blur the senses and achieve inner peace. Circular shapes will be significant to you. You might even want a round bed with your head placed to the north and feet to the south. A bowl of colored beads would also be a wonderful decorative object for your bedroom. A simple goldfish bowl completes the environment

Outdoors, you are true to the sign of Pisces. There should be some source of water nearby or in your yard. Plan on trips to the beach even in the winter. An outdoor ice rink is a great place for you to exercise in winter.

A Kabbalistic Interpretation

One way to represent this date is with the number eleven, which has a deep esoteric significance as a number representing things magical. There is a greater than usual chance that people born on this exceptional day will develop an interest in the mysterious and mystical aspects of life. A gift for you might be a pack of tarot cards, perhaps one with Hebrew letters and the appropriate astrological symbol on each card.

People born on this day have an excellent eye for detail and enjoy pastimes that require that quality. Thanks to certain other associations of this date you would do excellent work with a needle and thread and should seriously consider quilt making or some similar needlework-related craft.

Today's people have the courage and quite often the strength of a lion. You have a real feel for the spiritual side of life, and you are exceedingly tenacious and determined. Consider some ornaments or paintings that represent lions, tigers, and other feral beasts, as they will add to your self-confidence while livening up your home.

A Numerological Interpretation

YOUR MAGIC NUMBERS: 4 AND 6

The twenty-ninth day of the second month reduces to four, the number of reasoning. The Arabic numeral four is constructed of a triangle and a T square, tools of the surveyor. The focus of this day is keen observation. As if from the perspective of an aircraft, your path is to view the big picture and perceive the topography from above. You have the capacity for long-range planning and generating hypotheses.

The sixtieth day of the year reduces to six, adding the elements of balance and love to the distanced, abstract view. Display framed art maps in your study. Use a compass and a protractor to design things. Climb a mountain, not for the sake of getting to the top, but to enjoy the view. Take a ride in a glider and feel like an eagle soaring over the hilltops. Fly in a small plane or in a yellow, orange-and-green-striped hot-air balloon.

OBJECTS/IMAGES
*interlocking circles,
a cowl head covering,
a pilgrim walking with a staff*

SHAPES/MATERIALS
*enameled circle pins,
fleece-lined shoe pads*

COLORS
winter white, violet, mauve

ANIMAL
shark

PLANTS, HERBS, EDIBLES
purple loosestrife, mullein

ESSENCE
benzoin

SOUNDS/RHYTHMS
Irish jigs, clog dancing

MUSICAL NOTE
A#

DEEP SPACE OBJECT
supernova

March 1

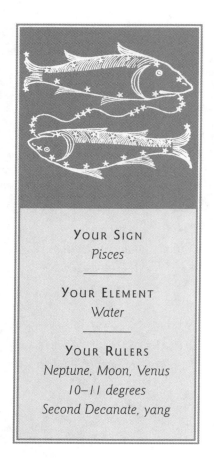

YOUR SIGN
Pisces

YOUR ELEMENT
Water

YOUR RULERS
Neptune, Moon, Venus
10–11 degrees
Second Decanate, yang

The Astrological Interpretation

You are a sympathetic listener and are very responsive to people and causes that need your aid, advice, and counsel. Although you demonstrate an open heart, it is necessary that you transform your sympathies into practical realities. You are an idealistic person, but your dreams can become solidified only by taking action. This means gaining the necessary training to participate in some group or organization that supports the causes in which you believe. In your personal relationships, you are very romantic. Sometimes, you prefer not to hear the truth or see the deeper realities concerning the people you love. But it is only by asking the correct questions and being prepared to hear the real answers that you will be in a position to help both yourself and the others involved in your life.

March 1 is a seeker of spiritual harmony and will roam the world in this quest. Keep a piece of rose quartz in your pocket to accompany you on the journey. Your clothing should be casual and comfortable, especially your shoes, as you are likely to do a lot of walking. At home, an aquarium full of goldfish will provide a focus for you to contact your spiritual center and find creative solutions to everyday problems. A basement hideaway is also a good place to renew your energy.

Outdoors you feel good in forests with a running brook or creek. Walking the dog is an excuse for some good thinking time. If your climate allows, think about having a fig tree in your backyard. The Buddha achieved enlightenment under a bodhi tree, and a fig might do it for you.

A Kabbalistic Interpretation

The predominant element for this day is air. The main color linked to air in the Western mystery tradition is yellow, but given the connection of this day to all kinds of organic growth, your best color is actually black with yellow highlights. That particular color combination represents the positive interaction of the energies of air with the material plane.

Daisies, snowdrops, and daffodils are all excellent for your garden. You could also consider growing a number of fruit trees. Your nature is wrapped up in the idea of fertility, growth, and plenty, so anything you plant should yield a fantastic crop of ripe, juicy fruit.

You have a very busy social life and enjoy the hustle and bustle of an active role in the world. Whereas many people tend to have a circle of friends who all have certain factors in common, you get along well with all sorts of people. An ideal piece of glassware for you to keep in a display cabinet would be a crystal punch bowl. You will have plenty of opportunity to use it, and it will enhance the sense of friendship and conviviality in your life.

A Numerological Interpretation

YOUR MAGIC NUMBERS: 4 AND 7

The first day of the third month reduces to four, a number meaning order, reason, and rulership. This day's path deals with issues of authority and the power of position. What exactly does a ruler govern, and what does the archetype mean to the individual? From where does the power of a figure such as the pope emanate? True illumination does not reside in a church or minister or priest. They can guide, but the light is within and must be sought. Are we dedicated to our spiritual unfoldment, according to our divine template? Or are we haphazard like the sorcerer's apprentice?

Traditions are important to you. Relish the pomp, circumstance, and pageantry of coronations and inaugurations. Indulge yourself in garments that remind you of vestments. The fragrance of candles and incense will inspire you. Rhodochrosite, jade, and adventurine will stabilize you. The sixty-first day of the year reduces to seven, which contributes the quality of victory and accomplishment to your endeavors.

OBJECTS/IMAGES
a clubhouse, moonlight on a pond, a small home altar, bath towels

SHAPES/MATERIALS
chrysolite, pumice stone, quartz crystal balls, squiggle shapes

COLORS
wine, sea blue, blue-violet, olive green

ANIMALS
small dogs, guppy

PLANTS, HERBS, EDIBLES
water ferns, chamomile tea, poppy seeds

ESSENCES
brine smell, smell of liqueurs

SOUNDS/RHYTHMS
church chimes, running water, the sound of ballet dancers' feet on a wood floor

MUSICAL NOTES
D# and F#

DEEP SPACE OBJECT
Alpha Hydrus

March 2

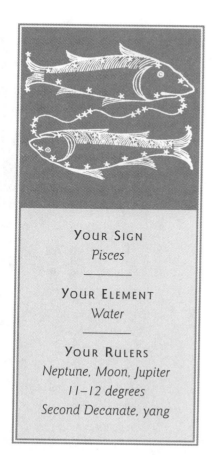

YOUR SIGN
Pisces

YOUR ELEMENT
Water

YOUR RULERS
Neptune, Moon, Jupiter
11–12 degrees
Second Decanate, yang

The Astrological Interpretation

The three human qualities that when correctly balanced and harmonized create a whole person are will, love, and intelligence. Your ability to love is unquestionable. You are a very compassionate person, eager to lend a hand to the less fortunate or misunderstood. You are also intelligent with a special interest in the arts, music, theater—anything that allows your beauty of spirit to flourish. The weakest of these three aspects for you is will. It is therefore of vital importance that you cultivate this quality. You are to use your will to direct the flow of your love and your intelligence so that you may make the most out of your talents and abilities. You may think that if you are too assertive you will anger or upset other people. If you define your needs clearly and stand up for what you really believe, this feeling will be eliminated and your self-esteem will rise.

You have a deep imagination and may be most comfortable living in imaginative realms. You may be a spiritual seeker or work where you show a great deal of compassion. Whatever you choose, give a thought to practical necessities and make friends with the element earth. To assist you in grounding your life carry quartz crystal. At home, you will enjoy being surrounded by blues, greens, and purples; add a few rich browns to the mix. Your kitchen may be the center of your home; taking care to eat properly is a great way to "feed" your dreams. A crystal ring where you can float flowers would be a perfect centerpiece for your dining room table. An image for you to meditate on is a gyroscope turning . . . no matter how many turns the gyroscope makes, it rests on the earth.

Outdoors you enjoy creating a colorful and orderly space in your garden. If your climate permits, consider growing orchids. They will inspire your imagination.

A Kabbalistic Interpretation

This is a day with very strong masculine energies. Although this date falls within the sign of Pisces the bold and courageous character of those born this day is decidedly Martian. Iron is extremely lucky for you, and if you find a bracelet in iron then you should wear it at all times. Red is a good color to focus on when you need to clinch an important deal.

One value of this date corresponds to the tarot card the Emperor. This card refers to material power and authority and is connected to the sign Aries, also ruled by the planet Mars. You like your home and office to have a strong sense of majesty and dignity. One piece of furniture you might acquire is a heavy wooden high-backed chair. This should be in a dark wood such as oak with lots of scrolling on the arms and the back.

It would be wrong to confuse authority and presence with a stodgy and staid approach to life. In fact the energies of this day point toward someone who is always willing and indeed eager to embrace change. This love of change is combined with a certain degree of intuition. You can enhance its effectiveness by growing some sage in a window box in your study and by regularly putting some drops of almond oil in your bathwater.

A Numerological Interpretation
YOUR MAGIC NUMBERS: 5 AND 8

The second day of the third month reduces to five, carrying the meaning of agency or process. The office of a president or king remains, though the individual wearing the mantle constantly changes. What is the origin of the power of personality and true character versus the empty machinations of a leader without integrity. What are the criteria or qualifications that we must meet along our spiritual path? Do we strive to exceed the highest expectations, or just go along with ordinary values?

The sixty-second day of the year reduces to eight, harmonizing the constant change inherent in this day. Forms change, principles endure. Strive for transcendent values rather than ordinary pleasures. National anthems stir your soul. Olympic sports, gold medals, tales about personal valor and those who overcome obstacles will inspire you. Display your diplomas, degrees, and certificates of recognition. Your pride of accomplishment is justified. Citrine and turquoise will calm and soothe you. Wear yellow to enhance your optimism.

OBJECTS/IMAGES
rosaries, galoshes, bayous

SHAPES/MATERIALS
aquamarine, beryl, cloud shapes

COLORS
blue-green, deep colors, gold, teal

ANIMALS
seal, faun

PLANTS, HERBS, EDIBLES
water arum, floating hearts, tea tree

ESSENCE
ambergris

SOUNDS/RHYTHMS
flutes, guitars strumming

MUSICAL NOTES
E and G

DEEP SPACE OBJECT
Rho Phoenix

March 3

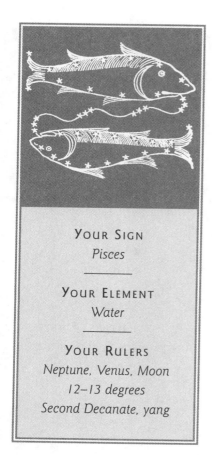

YOUR SIGN
Pisces

YOUR ELEMENT
Water

YOUR RULERS
Neptune, Venus, Moon
12–13 degrees
Second Decanate, yang

The Astrological Interpretation

Your sensitivity can be both an ally and a major stumbling block. When you open yourself to others, they can have no secrets from you, yet you may find that you have very little protection against the harsher realities of life. You can feel very vulnerable, with no shield against the onslaught of vibrations and sensations from your environment. Use your acute sensibilities to better advantage by cultivating your mind. You feel, but it is important to be able to define what you feel. You have faith, but it is essential to understand why you believe as you do. You are intuitive, but it is vital that your intellect be equally strong. Working to improve the clarity of your judgment and your powers of analysis will help you on your road to greater success in life.

Individuals born on March 3 may feel that they are meant to accomplish something on a large historical scale. This may be true or it may be a romantic, impressionable idea. Be careful what you absorb; dabbling with dark occult studies is not for you. Carry rose quartz with you to keep your spiritual energies high. Your personal color scheme may tend toward black, white, and violet. Make an effort to include some red. At home March 3 needs some inviolable space. Wherever you retreat have lots of pillows and think about getting a silk comforter cover. Your cocoon is where you recharge and take mental health holidays. Plan these into your life because your emotions get a workout.

Outdoors, you have a special affinity with water. A barometer is a good item to have, as you may be sensitive to slight changes in humidity and barometric pressure. In your backyard think about creating a design of circles within circles. This could be done with grass and flowers or grass and stones. Walking until you get to the center is the perfect way to still your feelings.

A Kabbalistic Interpretation

It is your natural curiosity that defines your personality. You have a great love of chat and gossip, and you enjoy your interactions with people. Invest in a good computer with Web access so that you can chat with a whole range of interesting and diverse people about all manner of subjects.

The value of this date has associations with global travel. You have a wonderful feel for the natural world. You can enhance your relationship to the world by representing the planet in the eastern corner of your living room. You might keep some historic maps or an antique polished wooden globe.

You are not likely to be a member of a gym or fitness club. You much prefer to get your exercise out in the open by going on long runs or bike rides in the country. As there is a very strong connection to the number three in this day, look for designs with triangular patterns. A pair of earrings or a necklace with a six-pointed star design would also be a valuable asset, as it will enable you to feel calm and focused in the face of difficult and chaotic situations.

A Numerological Interpretation
YOUR MAGIC NUMBERS: 6 AND 9

The third day of the third month reduces to six, the number of symmetry and beauty. This day carries the path of leading by example. A good example can be a priceless teacher. If we have a template, we can accelerate our learning. Whom do you admire? What examples do you choose to follow? What lessons does humanity learn from the great souls of history, or those whose behavior and consequences we choose not to repeat? Study choices that have changed the world for the better, including those of historical figures such as Gandhi, Mozart, Joan of Arc, Mother Teresa, Cleopatra, Cicero, Harriet Tubman, and Abraham Lincoln. What are the examples of their lives? Peridot and sodalite are gems that will ground and strengthen you. The sixty-third day of the year reduces to nine, providing the added element of complete, perfected expression of the seed idea.

OBJECTS/IMAGES
fog, gold filigree, shoe boutiques

SHAPES/MATERIALS
rubber, tin, the shape of curled ribbon

COLORS
red-violet, cream, black, apple green, royal blue

ANIMALS
jellyfish, angelfish, pink flamingo

PLANTS, HERBS, EDIBLES
caviar, water lilies, sea anemone

ESSENCES
sage sticks, church incense

SOUNDS/RHYTHMS
rhapsodies, footsteps on a wooden floor

MUSICAL NOTES
F and G#

DEEP SPACE OBJECT
NGC 7755, external galaxy

March 4

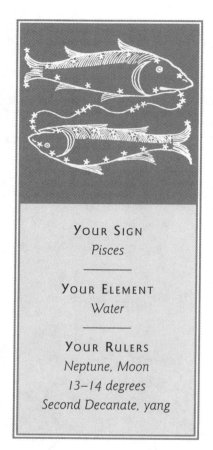

YOUR SIGN
Pisces

YOUR ELEMENT
Water

YOUR RULERS
Neptune, Moon
13–14 degrees
Second Decanate, yang

The Astrological Interpretation

You may have found that at a very early age you were attracted by religion, ritual, and the supremely beautiful. All of these interests serve to lift a person out of the ordinary and into the sublime. You seek to understand the unseen and to produce through your creative imagination and particular skills works that are in some way representative of the more subtle reality that is so much a part of your nature. You tend to see the best in people and may be quite disappointed when they do not live up to your expectations. You are open to what other people tell you, and are sincerely hurt when you discover any dishonesty in those close to you. It is hard for you to comprehend how people can be cruel, as you are so forgiving yourself. Strive to expand your contact with your philosophical, religious, or spiritual path so that your responses to the injustices of life are not taken so personally.

You are a hard worker and have a talent for representing yourself in the best light possible. You may have a tendency to lose or misplace everyday things like keys, glasses, or your wallet. Train yourself to put these items in one place and you will save time. At home, you might want to have light rooms and one dark room. The dark room should resemble a submarine on the ocean floor. Have dark woods and richly colored drapes and bedcovers. A lamp by your bed with a green shade gives a perfect underwater feel. In the light rooms, billowing opaque curtains and blond wood furniture would be pleasing. Scent is very evocative for March 4. Place potpourri in woodsy scents. A cabinet with crystal bowls would be an excellent decoration for you.

Outdoors March 4 likes a landscaped outdoors with flower beds and rock walls. A water lily pond would be a nice touch. You might find that having different levels to your garden is most pleasing to you. If you could build a waterfall it would be ideal. Flowers for you are cup-and-saucer plant, and dendrobium.

A Kabbalistic Interpretation

There is a connection in this day with the tarot card the Lovers, which represents difficult and often moral dilemmas. You are prone to being indecisive, and this is particularly true in emotional relationships, where you can be too willing to see good in people who really aren't right for you. Carrying a red crescent in your bag or pocket should help you to be more firm in decisions you need to make about your relationships.

Try to get yourself some opal jewelry in order to reflect your preoccupation with things of the mind rather than of the body. An opal will also have a strongly protective influence over your relationships. There are very spiritual associations with this day. You have a real sense of moral duty, which you sense as coming from somewhere outside of yourself. You may be haunted by a feeling that you will spend much of your life searching for a form of religious expression that you are comfortable with and that reflects your own deeply held inner belief system. Sometimes this search for your spiritual home can be quite disconcerting. At those times try burning some frankincense incense, mixed with dittany of Crete.

A Numerological Interpretation

YOUR MAGIC NUMBERS: 7 AND 10

The fourth day of the third month reduces to seven, a number of victory and temporary rest. The number seven also has ancient meanings of oaths and sworn compacts. This date implies what we collectively agree, albeit fleetingly, to what is in vogue. Make the most of what you have. Styles and fashions are ephemeral, but some people move gracefully from era to era with a timeless expression of style and taste. Represent your individual assets in the best possible light. Slaves to fashion lose all sense of individuality.

The sixty-fourth day of the year reduces to ten, contributing the quality of perfection, the ultimate perfection of a style or fashion. Malachite and azurite, colors of the earth, will ground you. Dress up and attend a fashion show or a new car expo, a display of the season's latest offerings, and contemplate the meaning of style.

OBJECTS/IMAGES
angels, bayous, psychic ability, riverbanks

SHAPES/MATERIALS
beryl, amethyst, aquamarine, meerschaum

COLORS
maroon, kelly green, navy

ANIMALS
gull, pig

PLANTS, HERBS, EDIBLES
beer, jelly, lobsters, rubber plants

ESSENCE
beech

SOUNDS/RHYTHMS
harps, lute

MUSICAL NOTES
F# and A

DEEP SPACE OBJECTS
Alpha Eridanus, Achernar, End of the River

March 5

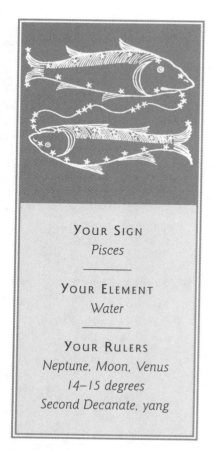

The Astrological Interpretation

You live in a world of enormous possibilities. It is easy for you to "go with the flow" and let things happen on their own; but to stop and give yourself clear and specific directions can be a difficult task. People want to be part of your life, as you do not judge others but offer compassion and friendship. Yet you may find that no matter how much support and admiration you receive, you are still far from reaching your own shores. Take up an activity that can serve as a tool for self-discipline. Pick something you like: a sport, a foreign language, a series of courses that may lead to a college degree. A good dancer is aware of the structure of the steps and the exercises it takes to be physically supple. Find your structure and stick to it.

The March 5 character is generous and often does not pay enough attention to the material world. Your home should feature rocks at the four directions to keep the energy balanced. The image of an arrow passing through a cloud will help keep you rooted. The bedroom is a place to retreat and recharge your batteries. If you give yourself permission to hide and zone out you will accomplish more in the long run. In the bedroom, think about a canopy bed with a light lavender canopy. The bed should be placed with your head north and feet south.

The bathroom is another area of renewal for March 5. A Jacuzzi or hot tub is good; a bathtub with plenty of aromatic oils does just as well. Pay attention to the full moons and head for the tub. For everyday use, a raw amethyst crystal in your pocket one day and clear quartz the next will keep you tuned up.

Outdoors, Pisces wants a space for parties and gatherings. A circular deck or patio is ideal. The garden should be round with a center statue or fountain. City dwellers can create a garden corner in their apartments with a small fountain.

A Kabbalistic Interpretation

March 5 is a day full of authoritative energy and associations with material power. If ever there was a day blessed for people wishing to become CEOs of large corporations, this is it. There is a powerful correspondence with the Emperor card in the tarot. This card is concerned with gaining and keeping earthly power. Keeping a nice healthy sunflower on your desk at work will add to your success and confidence, while a sprig of mint alongside ensures that you keep your confidence from metamorphosing into arrogance or aggression.

Another image of power for this day is its connection to the planet Mars. March 5's Martian energies are combined with those of the sun. The resulting overall effect is more of a vitality and a lust for life rather than any warlike or physically aggressive tendencies. The perfect indulgence for you is a convertible sports car, so that you can cruise along the freeway with the wind blowing through your hair.

A Numerological Interpretation
YOUR MAGIC NUMBERS: 8 AND 2

The fifth day of the third month reduces to eight, a number whose energies move back and forth like a pendulum. For every action there is an equal and opposite reaction. This law works with prefect precision and predictability, even if the original forces that set an event in motion are no longer apparent. Observe an assembly line, stamping out perfect replicas. As long as the machinery functions, there are continual, identical repetitions. The magic of this day is a paradox. You are capable of bringing excitement to everyday routines while understanding a larger reality.

The sixty-fifth day of the year reduces to two, adding awareness of polarized opposites within the process of duplication. Lapis and turquoise are minerals that will enhance your perception. Watch marching bands and military drills. The drums will evoke the awareness of the underlying rhythm of all life.

OBJECTS/IMAGES
clouds, monasteries, baby shoes, black stockings, toenail polish

SHAPES/MATERIALS
coral, rose quartz, moonstone, boiled wool, turquoise, carmine

COLORS
dusty lavender, white

ANIMALS
green-headed mallard, chameleon

PLANTS, HERBS, EDIBLES
opium, water-growing ferns, seaweed, creamy cheese

ESSENCE
oil of bergamot

SOUNDS/RHYTHMS
minuet, the Charleston, drizzle on a lake

MUSICAL NOTES
G and C#

DEEP SPACE OBJECTS
Alpha Phoenix, Ankaa

March 6

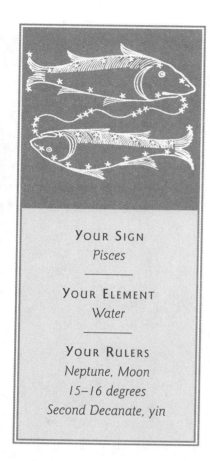

YOUR SIGN
Pisces

YOUR ELEMENT
Water

YOUR RULERS
Neptune, Moon
15–16 degrees
Second Decanate, yin

The Astrological Interpretation

This is a birth date that indicates a person with a magnetic personality. You may be shy and withdrawn at times, but as soon as you peek your head from outside your place of shelter, there are many others who will want you to participate in their lives. You can use your attractiveness and compassion by organizing events that have a common humanitarian purpose. You can benefit the lives of others by providing a unifying thread that can give form and focus to the creative activities of your friends or coworkers. Be inspirational and stand by your beliefs. Many people born on this day are quite poetic and artistic by nature. Do not suppress yourself and your innate talents. It doesn't matter what other people think about your work—just keep at it! You are not a judgmental person, so why be overly concerned about other people's judgment of you? Express yourself!

You may not understand the source of your imagination, but you should do what you can to develop your abilities. Your home and family are very important to you. Perhaps you want to share your artistic talents with everyone in your household. Consider a once-a-week painting festival. A bulletin board where you hone your poetic skills and leave essential household messages might also be a way of encouraging creativity. Lilac and lavender are colors for you. You will enjoy having a variety of "at home" robes or lounging wear that signify it is time to relax. Your kitchen could have wallpaper with fishing imagery or blue tiles as a border.

Outdoors, March 6 could construct an ingenious environment combining a grape arbor, fishpond, and gazebo. You are a romantic, and having places outside where you sit and dream would be a great addition to your life.

A Kabbalistic Interpretation

People born on this day generally love to play games. In the workplace your tendency to see the lighter side of even the most serious situations can sometimes prove a little awkward, especially if your boss hasn't got much of a sense of humor. One way to develop a sense of the important and serious at work is to buy a small leather pouch and fill it with some dried garlic, rue, and nettle.

If you are born on this day you have a tendency to leave things to chance, thereby causing some chaotic events in your life. This is alluded to by March 6's connection to the Tower card in the tarot. There is little you can do about this, particularly as you enjoy a certain amount of chaos in your life. You might enjoy objects that symbolize that chaos such as a clock that runs backward.

Your very strong intuitive feelings are usually focused around your close friends and family. Your gut instinct in family matters is so often right it is unfortunate that it is sometimes so hard to get people to pay attention to what you are saying. To combat this, keep some tulips, either cut in a vase or growing around the border of your garden. And you may want to eat food that is more spicy.

A Numerological Interpretation
YOUR MAGIC NUMBERS: 9 AND 3

The sixth day of the third month reduces to nine, the number of fulfillment and attainment. This day is a path of connecting with and entering into the flow of inspiration. Creative solutions to even the most daunting problems are always available to us. True inventiveness and ingenuity come from pulling ideas from the ocean of subconscious in which we reside. Employ not only linear thinking but also lateral. Always ask, how can this be improved? You love clever devices, gadgets, and stores that feature futuristic products. Patents, inventions, and Nobel Prize winners all fascinate you. Lapis and malachite, especially when worn together, will aid the focusing of your mind and stimulate your inventiveness. The sixty-sixth day of the year reduces to three, adding the influence of true creative self-expression, making the process easier.

OBJECTS/IMAGES
ecstasy, ferries, dance leotards

SHAPES/MATERIALS
the shape of stringed instruments, chlorine, cotton

COLORS
deep burgundy, sky blue, coral

ANIMALS
blue whale, jellyfish

PLANTS, HERBS, EDIBLES
Cuban cigars, bubblegum, hot cocoa, water hyacinths

ESSENCE
rosemary verbenone

SOUNDS/RHYTHMS
foot tapping, liquids bubbling

MUSICAL NOTES
G# and D

DEEP SPACE OBJECT
NGC 7217, spiral galaxy

March 7

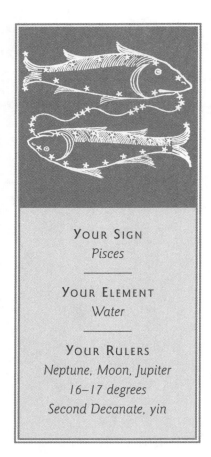

YOUR SIGN
Pisces

YOUR ELEMENT
Water

YOUR RULERS
Neptune, Moon, Jupiter
16–17 degrees
Second Decanate, yin

The Astrological Interpretation

It is important for you to know that your attitude toward life is unselfish, and it bothers you when you see other people behaving ego-centrically. You are a highly emotional person, romantic and totally supportive of the people you love. Give yourself to what you believe, but do not throw yourself away. Take care that you do not forget your own boundaries. You may find that you have an addictive personality. If so, then get addicted to what improves your life. Emotional and romantic excesses, blind devotion to a person or a religious belief, just will not work for you. You need to have the balance that comes with the development of your own skills and talents. You must risk being yourself and being accepted on your own terms. Find the thread that connects you to your own creative potential and never let go of it.

The fierceness underlying your tender soul emerges when protecting family; then the fish can become a tiger. Your feelings and intuition are extremely strong and can feel at times like a tidal wave. Calm the tides of your emotions with rose quartz. At home, black-and-white photos on your walls are perfect for decoration. You may also want to have or paint artwork with bold geometric designs in black, white, and primary colors. There is comfort for March 7 in rainy weather, but wear red rain gear. It will keep your spirits up. March 7 has dramatic ability and can enjoy costumes and masquerades. Consider listening to *Bolero* by Maurice Ravel.

Outdoors, March 7 wants a garden or outdoor space with a small bridge. The bridge doesn't have to go anywhere, but the experience of walking over it reminds you of the connection between the everyday world and the dream world. Also place some seashells in your garden. Reminders of the sea will always soothe you.

A Kabbalistic Interpretation

This day is directly connected to the tarot card the Hermit, which represents the wisdom of age. Pisces is the oldest sign in the zodiac, and as such, it relates to intelligence gained from experience. As a typical Piscean you feel a strong sense of duty to your family, but you need to make sure that you allow some space for yourself. If possible, find a small room in the house to claim as yours; if not, then a corner of a room. Mark your space with a large aquarium filled with small, brightly colored tropical fish.

You may often feel world weary and older than your years. While dark blue and dark green are probably the colors with which you feel most comfortable, you might want to find a space in your house where you can branch out a bit and play. You could decorate your bathroom in vivid energetic colors, even fluorescents. A young vital look in this room will energize you and keep at bay the cynicism that can creep up on you at times.

People born today spend a lot of time thinking and reading. Try reading in your personal corner while enjoying a cool drink. If you can find a nice tall glass decorated in pink and blue you will gain additional relaxation.

A Numerological Interpretation
YOUR MAGIC NUMBERS: 10 AND 4

The seventh day of the third month reduces to ten, a number signifying perfection. With every completed revolution of the wheel, the cycle begins anew. Artists and composers do not create just for their own sakes. Sharing their works is a celebration of beauty and an inspiration to others for future excellence. Nature is outrageous in her celebration of color and style. The sixty-seventh day of the year reduces to four, adding the awareness of stability and constancy. Carnelian and sodalite will add stability to your energy field. Travel to New Orleans for Mardi Gras. Buy a feathered mask or a new hat with an outrageous yellow-orange ostrich plume. Have a tank of brightly colored tropical fish in your study. Grow orchids or birds-of-paradise. Take part in an Easter parade. Splurge on a new outfit and strut your stuff. This is not an empty vanity but a striving toward fuller expression.

OBJECTS/IMAGES
a carnival barker, dew on morning glories, a perfume atomizer

SHAPES/MATERIALS
arc shapes, aquamarine, platinum

COLORS
iridescent shades, deep purple, indigo, amber

ANIMALS
bird, faun

PLANTS, HERBS, EDIBLES
Irish moss, purple loosestrife, conch

ESSENCE
clary sage

SOUNDS/RHYTHMS
rolling rhythms, sound of a lute

MUSICAL NOTES
A and D#

DEEP SPACE OBJECT
supernova

March 8

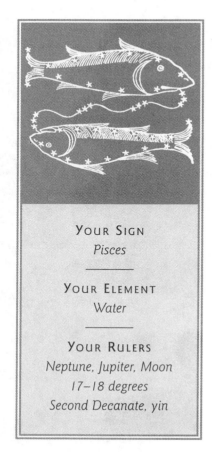

YOUR SIGN
Pisces

YOUR ELEMENT
Water

YOUR RULERS
Neptune, Jupiter, Moon
17–18 degrees
Second Decanate, yin

The Astrological Interpretation

Your birth date indicates a person who has collected a great deal of knowledge and insight about life. This makes you a natural-born teacher. You possess an inner fountain of resources that seems to spout riches whenever they are needed. You may not even know that you possess such insights or talents until they are called on by situations in your environment. Even if you do not have what is specifically required within your own "treasure chest," you are excellent at finding the right resource for what is needed. You are also a good matchmaker, instinctively knowing who to connect with whom. You have a love for the pleasures of life and are happy when surrounded by good food, interesting companions, and other sensual joys that make living on this planet more fun.

March 8 birthdays have a reputation for fairness and justice. You are very active and enjoy many sports. Consider pursuing placid sports, as your thrill-seeking side could prove problematic in more active endeavors. Furniture that is built in, such as a work area built into a kitchen corner, will help you maintain order. Have a cabinet that easily shutters off a computer or other work-oriented machines. You don't mind hard work but want home to be a retreat; seeing business tools could jar you out of your relaxation. Include some chenille fabrics or other soft blends in your personal wardrobe. Colors in the deep blue, brown, and purple family appeal to you. As befits your water sign, a source of spring water or purified water in your home will ensure that you are drinking the best.

Outdoors, March 8 devotes considerable time to a garden. A wire wall where vines such as morning glories, virgin's bower, and clematis can easily grow could be the entry to your garden space. Leave some room for sports and a pool and your outdoor environment would be complete.

A Kabbalistic Interpretation

You are not someone who rushes headlong into new challenges. You do enjoy variety, but you prefer that variety to evolve gradually in nonthreatening ways. Since you are a sensual individual, you can explore your enjoyment of comfortable change through food. Invest in the best pans you can afford and always keep a well-stocked collection of fresh herbs in your kitchen.

You love rich colors and have a penchant for fine material. Allow yourself to indulge this preference for luxury at home and you will find you can let go of stress from a hard day's work quickly and easily. Good objects for you are luxurious velvets in rich earth tones, or russet-colored leather armchairs.

There are times when it is necessary to move quickly in order to achieve your goals. At such times, you will need to combat your tendency to be too laid back. If you have shelves or bookcases in your office try putting an antique lamp on a south-facing wall. At home you should invest in some ornaments that depict lots of movement, a galloping horse would be a very good image for your living room.

A Numerological Interpretation
YOUR MAGIC NUMBERS: 2 AND 5

The eighth day of the third month reduces to two, a number of receptivity and dependence. Inherent in this day's path is the kind of confidence that acrobats or trapeze artists embody as they fly and spin through the air, knowing their partner will catch them. This type of performance brings an intensification of focus to consciousness. The element of risk and excitement hones perception to a fine point.

The sixty-eighth day of the year reduces to five, which adds the aspect of intuition and surety of knowledge from the unseen. Jasper and agate will complement your energies. Go to the circus and watch feats of derring-do amid smells of cotton candy and the music of the circus organ. Try skydiving or bungee jumping to stretch your limits. Ride in a rainbow-colored hot-air balloon at sunrise.

OBJECTS/IMAGES
mermaids, rainbows, lather, harbors

SHAPES/MATERIALS
frosted glass, meerschaum, jade, rubber

COLORS
maroon, poppy red, gold

ANIMALS
gull, angelfish

PLANTS, HERBS, EDIBLES
fragrant water lily, sardines, oolong tea, coffee ice cream

ESSENCE
galbanol oil

SOUNDS/RHYTHMS
minuets, lutes

MUSICAL NOTES
C# and E

DEEP SPACE OBJECT
Cygnus 2, 1876 Nova

March 9

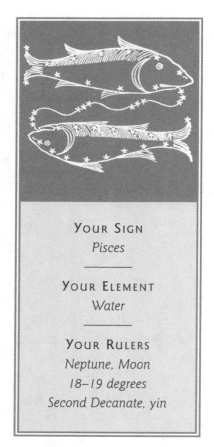

YOUR SIGN
Pisces

YOUR ELEMENT
Water

YOUR RULERS
Neptune, Moon
18–19 degrees
Second Decanate, yin

The Astrological Interpretation

You tend to act from behind the scenes and are often the unifying force within your group. Do not be too concerned if people do not understand your actions and motivations. You have a knack for getting the support in life that you need; all you have to do is to make these needs known to the people around you. At times you avoid doing this, as you have a reluctance to reveal your true nature and intent. You may then wonder why everyone around you seems to be getting ahead and you are left somewhere in an obscure position. You are a much more sensitive person than most, and you care what happens to the people around you. Although you want to get ahead, you do not want this to be at others' expense. These are beautiful qualities, and you will gain in the long run by sticking to them.

Compassion for others is part of your makeup; your challenge is to show the same compassion for yourself. Without this ingredient you can be contentious and live by empty rules. You may collect things from your past around you that clog up your energy. Throwing things away that you do not need or that carry unhappy associations is a liberating activity. March 9 enjoys luxury. Consider buying a few good pieces of furniture, such as a dining room set that pleases you, and you can add other pieces over time. Pale sea green is a restful color for you, and you may want to have wall-to-wall carpeting in sea green. To help protect your sensitivities and ground yourself, find a mineral called bornite and keep a piece in your pocket. Bornite is not a gemstone but a metamorphic rock with beautiful colors.

Outdoors, March 9 likes to create a peaceful and aquatic landscape. A garden curving around a circular-shaped pool is ideal. Place urn-shaped planters with light pink geraniums and bleeding heart around the pool, and plant marigold, china asters, and snapdragons in the garden.

A Kabbalistic Interpretation

One way of calculating today's value gives 225. The number 225 is the square of fifteen, which gives it a strong connection to the sephira Geburah or the Tree of Life. As this relates to people born today, you will likely be extremely physical, with a fierce temper. People born today can invest in a punching bag to release frustration. In addition carrying some blue-laced agate will help you stay calm.

You have traveling in your blood, but it is not so much seeing new places as the act of traveling that really appeals. A good pair of hiking boots is a must for your wardrobe, and if you really want to get the most out of your journeys, make sure your laces are dark gray.

You are in many ways a person whose emotions stay hidden from view yet run very deep. It is unlikely that you will ever be someone who wears your heart on your sleeve, but if you try keeping some roses on your bedside table you may find it easier to express your feelings when it is really important.

A Numerological Interpretation

YOUR MAGIC NUMBERS: 3 AND 6

The ninth day of the third month reduces to three, a number of growth and development. This day carries the experience of aligning with the natural bounty of life, living like the biblical lilies of the field, or Adam and Eve in the Garden of Eden. There is a sense of the importance of discerning your destiny and following your path to the end. You can learn to see teachers in all the people and experiences in life. What are the positive aspects of Peter Pan or Robin Hood?

The sixty-ninth day of the year reduces to six, adding the crucial element of balance, reciprocity, and complementary activities. Travel to a Las Vegas casino and try your hand for small stakes at a roulette wheel or a slot machine. Smile as three identical images appear, and coins tumble out of the machine. Life really isn't a gamble, but enjoying the serendipity of seeming coincidences is part of the fun. Carnelian and amber will bring you luck.

OBJECTS/IMAGES
horseback riding, ferries, charlatans, bubbles

SHAPES/MATERIALS
pearls, ivory, footprints

COLORS
lavender, tangerine, moss green

ANIMALS
Jack Russell terrier, laughing gull

PLANTS, HERBS, EDIBLES
lobsters, jelly, chocolate ice cream, kelp

ESSENCE
carrot seed

SOUNDS/RHYTHMS
bubbling water, guitars

MUSICAL NOTES
D and F

DEEP SPACE OBJECT
Beta Phoenix

March 10

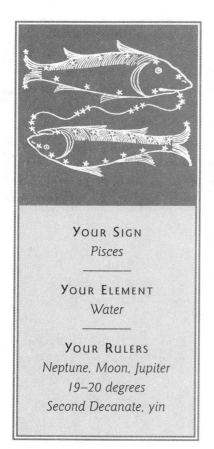

YOUR SIGN
Pisces

YOUR ELEMENT
Water

YOUR RULERS
Neptune, Moon, Jupiter
19–20 degrees
Second Decanate, yin

The Astrological Interpretation

You have a sense of tradition and history, and in your studies you may be drawn to the past. The development of art or architecture, archaeology, or anthropology may call to you. You are basically a sentimental person, one whose memory is always triggered by that special song or favorite dish. You may wish to travel to parts of the globe that are less technologically developed than the United States or other Western countries. You like a simple life, one in which a walk in nature is a daily event and the quiet of a rural and less hectic existence is readily available. Such situations are still possible, but they are found within your own silence. Take the time each day to respect your need for solitude and stillness. You may find this silence in a spiritually stimulating book or the romantic meanderings of certain novels. Many born on this day will be attracted to meditation, Tai Chi, or yoga.

A well-set table in a warm home brings a feeling of completion and sharing. A small sunporch with plants and prisms that catch the light give an encircled feel to the space. A back room or basement where you can listen to old waltzes and recharge your batteries is great for March 10. Watercolors in swirling patterns or seascapes are perfect wall hangings for this imaginative sign. The bedroom is your cocoon, and a brass bed gives you a feeling of solidity as you dream.

Comfortable shoes are essential for you. You may have a pair of pale pink or lavender ballet shoes hanging on your wall as a decoration. They could remind you that there is no better way to relax than to dance or move to music.

Create an oasis in the city with a small pool or musical garden fountain in the park or a stroll beside a meandering stream. At work keep a glass of water on your desk; it is calming, and handy if you get thirsty.

A Kabbalistic Interpretation

Change is the order of this day, although because of connections to values that represent the essential changelessness of the universe, you are not someone who is very comfortable with change. Wearing a mother-of-pearl necklace or carrying a mother-of-pearl object in your pocket will enhance your ability to embrace and adapt to swiftly moving circumstances.

While most of us look forward to the summer and a chance to catch a tan on the beach, you may prefer winter. If you are not fortunate enough to live in an area with a serious winter season, have a reminder, such as pictures of snow-capped mountain scenery, in your living room.

You are well known as a hard worker; people born on this day tend to be very trusted employees. However, you are very good at hiding your light under a bushel and need to learn to make your talents and achievements visible to those around you. This obviously takes a degree of confidence, so try keeping something in orange or crimson near you at all times. You could even keep a bowl of citrus fruit in the office.

A Numerological Interpretation

YOUR MAGIC NUMBERS: 4 AND 7

The tenth day of the third month reduces to four, signifying order. There is something solid, stable, and predictable about four, an assurance of all being right with the world, like the knowledge that the sun will rise each morning. This day's path requires your belief that no matter how many changes you experience in your life, you always know there is a reality behind appearances that never alters.

The seventieth day of the year reduces to seven, which provides the quality of victory and rest after labor. Don't take common blessings for granted. If you live in a city, spend a weekend in the country. Listen to the farm animals who wake before dawn each day. Milk a cow; smell the warm milk as it splatters against the bottom of the bucket. Have fresh eggs, milk, butter, and apple juice.

OBJECTS/IMAGES
ice skates, cut crystal glassware, hot-air balloons

SHAPES/MATERIALS
brushed velvet, white coral, beaded fabric, veils, peridot

COLORS
red-violet, pearly white, sea green, honey, grass green

ANIMALS
banded purple butterfly, jellyfish, angelfish

PLANTS, HERBS, EDIBLES
spider plants, succulent plants, tarragon, sour ball candies, pink cotton candy

ESSENCES
ambergris, star anise, clematis

SOUNDS/RHYTHMS
surf, 3/4 time, slowly trotting horses

MUSICAL NOTES
D# and F#

DEEP SPACE OBJECT
Gamma Pisces

March 11

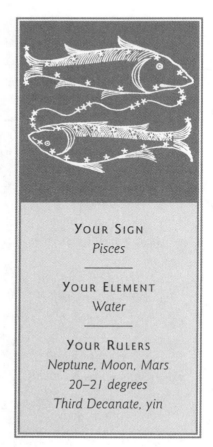

YOUR SIGN
Pisces

YOUR ELEMENT
Water

YOUR RULERS
Neptune, Moon, Mars
20–21 degrees
Third Decanate, yin

The Astrological Interpretation

Yours is a birth date that endows a person with intuition and a profound urge for spiritual or philosophical awareness. You have an internal calling that often pulls at you, making it difficult to concentrate your full attention on the demands of your outer life. At the very least, you know that there is more to life to explore. You have an avid need to be in contact with men and women of like minds and interests. You want to know that you are not alone in your need to grow and develop. You may find the Internet to be a helpful tool in your search. It is important for you to balance your ideals and aspirations with practical work and consistent efforts. Otherwise, your "otherworldliness" will distract you and keep you from paying attention to the responsibilities at hand. Your sensitivity needs to be well grounded so that you can bring your personal vision and truth down to earth.

You were born to balance your emotions and intellect. Like the two Piscean fish, sometimes mind and feelings swim in opposite directions. A lighthouse with a clear beam shining through a fog is an excellent image for you. Surround yourself with curved furniture. A Victorian round hassock in burgundy velvet is a pleasing shape for you. Clear quartz is the mineral for you to keep with you, as it will help keep feelings in synch. Another object of power for you is a crescent moon painting or sculpture. Pillows, boxes, and other objects in the shape of the crescent moon would be a wonderful addition to your home.

Your outdoor space should combine luxury with nature. Comfortable outdoor chairs and an umbrella table for summer meals create an extra room in your home during the good weather. A statue of an angel blowing a trumpet may remind you that you have a message to communicate.

A Kabbalistic Interpretation

You absolutely love life and automatically spread this feeling to those who come in contact with you. At home, surround yourself with living things, as you love to feel their positive energy. Fill your living room with plenty of brightly colored potted plants.

In kabbalistic terms the value of this day is connected to the planet Jupiter in its most beneficial aspect. You might find that you win lotteries and prizes more often than the average person. Carrying a small square made of tin in your pocket or handbag can add to your good fortunes.

The influence of the planet Jupiter along with other benevolent aspects of this day are strong indicators of a great love of children and the importance you place on being able to look after others. To satisfy your protective nurturing instincts you might have a pet. A border collie may be suited to your temperament, as they are wonderfully faithful and intelligent animals

A Numerological Interpretation

YOUR MAGIC NUMBERS: 5 AND 8

The eleventh day of the third month reduces to five, the number that embodies the principle of change and adaptation. Five is the means or agency of accomplishment. Nothing in life acts or exists in a vacuum, and this date is a path of integrating the seemingly diverse and unrelated threads of your life into a pattern and design that is yours alone. What are your talents? Where is your contribution to the whole?

The seventy-first day of the year reduces to eight, which provides the quality of natural rhythm, give-and-take, to the pervasiveness of change. Enter a talent show. Take ballroom dancing lessons or enroll in a martial arts class. Send yourself a dozen yellow roses. Amazonite and heliodor will stimulate your creativity. Undertake a journey of self-discovery with no holds barred.

OBJECTS/IMAGES
yachts, wizards

SHAPES/MATERIALS
waves, rubber, tourmaline

COLORS
white, translucent colors, violet, turquoise

ANIMALS
waterbirds

PLANTS, HERBS, EDIBLES
yeast, whiskey, trout lily

ESSENCE
rose water

SOUNDS/RHYTHMS
cello music, circle folk dances

MUSICAL NOTES
A# and E

DEEP SPACE OBJECT
quasar

March 12

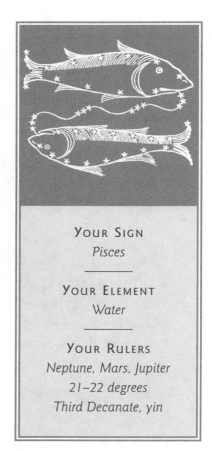

YOUR SIGN
Pisces

YOUR ELEMENT
Water

YOUR RULERS
Neptune, Mars, Jupiter
21–22 degrees
Third Decanate, yin

The Astrological Interpretation

Your birth date is especially connected to the planet Jupiter. You have the urge to expand your creative possibilities through travel and higher knowledge. You may also feel a sense of mission in life and will spend a great deal of time trying to understand what that mission is. Those who understand and support you in your search become your teachers and close friends. These are the people who deserve your loyalty, respect, and help in return. Take care that you do not lose yourself in relationships that do not encourage your true nature. If your particular field of work fulfills you in a spiritual sense, then you are definitely on the right track. If there is a duality between what you do and who you are, you will lose energy and real opportunity for success.

March 12 blends assertiveness with acute sensitivity. Sometimes you run and hide and other times you must put yourself forward. Imagine a stream of water that flows around, under, and over a red rock. The rock never impedes the water's flow. Carry a piece of amethyst or clear crystal. An old-fashioned vanity table is a romantic object for March 12 women. Men might be inclined to a dressing area with double sinks and a wooden valet. Choose toiletry articles with an eye for beauty as well as utility. Silver-plated brushes and hand mirrors are in tune with your aesthetic. Keep a volume of poetry handy so you can read a few passages during odd moments. The rhythm of words or melody always soothes you.

Outdoors you enjoy a water park with lots of rides, slides, and motion. In your own yard you may construct a wading pond, install a pool, or live near a creek. The water is your element, and you may feel disoriented if you are too far from it.

A Kabbalistic Interpretation

There is a great deal of sexual energy attached to this birthday. Indeed March 12 birthdays can be driven by sexual attraction above other considerations. If you were born today you will recognize yourself as someone who is interested in power. That doesn't necessarily mean you want vast amounts of power for yourself, but you are fascinated by the concept. If you want to feel really at home in your living room, buy some antique maps and some small statuettes in white marble or similar material to enjoy while relaxing in the evening. These will do wonders for your self-esteem. If you want to cheer up someone born on this date buy them some red or violet tulips.

This day also has values auspicious for farmers. There is a good chance you live in a city or suburb and thereby completely lack any knowledge of or inclination for farming, so instead find a related hobby, such as growing your own vegetables or keeping a Vietnamese potbellied pig.

A Numerological Interpretation
YOUR MAGIC NUMBERS: 6 AND 9

The twelfth day of the third month reduces to six, the number of balanced polarities and the harmony of opposites. This date embodies the path of a spiritual mandate. There is a sense of rightness, as if you have been to the mountaintop with Moses and received your personal commandments. Born on this day, you are cautioned not to let rightness become self-righteousness. You can only be responsible for your path and choices. Others have to make their own. Strive for the highest of which you are capable.

Lapis, howlite, and peridot will intensify your resolve. Play Beethoven's Ninth Symphony at maximum volume. The seventy-second day of the year reduces to nine, which contributes the energy of finality and completion. Climb to the top of a hill and watch the sun rise over a mountain peak. Listen to the cry of an eagle. Imagine that you could undertake a pilgrimage to Tibet and spend a month in a hermit's cave. How might that change your life?

OBJECTS/IMAGES
a sieve, houseboats, Poseidon

SHAPES/MATERIALS
bezoar (semiprecious stone), coral, peridot

COLORS
mauve, fuchsia, azure

ANIMALS
octopus, carp fish

PLANTS, HERBS, EDIBLES
plume poppy, cloudberry, fish, love-in-a-mist

ESSENCE
tea tree oil

SOUNDS/RHYTHMS
humming, ballet music from a pas de deux

MUSICAL NOTES
B and G#

DEEP SPACE OBJECTS
Alpha Pegasus, Markeb, the Saddle

March 13

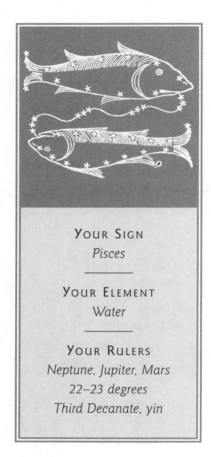

YOUR SIGN
Pisces

YOUR ELEMENT
Water

YOUR RULERS
Neptune, Jupiter, Mars
22–23 degrees
Third Decanate, yin

The Astrological Interpretation

Certain key words characterize this birth date: formation, structure, purposefulness, dedication. You are a person with a number of talents and abilities. Sometimes you lose sight of your goal as you get pulled in various directions at the same time. What is important is a distinct sense of self-discipline so that you are able to concentrate your energies where and when they are needed. You have to know when to eliminate those activities and relationships that no longer serve your highest good. This will require time alone and a place of quiet for the introspection that you need.

The fixed star Markab may be located on some March 13 birthdays. This star in the constellation of Pegasus was thought to bring honors but expose the native to danger from fire. With Mars ruling your decanate, March 13 does have a fiery but not dangerous nature. Your fire manifests itself in far-reaching and perhaps revolutionary ideas. You can easily imagine life on other planets and may be interested in reading science fiction. Closer to home, March 13 should pay attention to what is necessary to sustain your life on earth and what is necessary for the imagination. A purple notebook would be a perfect repository for your thoughts and dreams. In the bathroom, have seashell-shaped soaps and perhaps a special pillow for long, comfortable soaks in the tub. Bath salts with lavender are an evocative scent for you. Placing African violets in the bathroom would also be a nice touch.

Outdoors, March 13 should have access to a telescope so you can investigate if there is life on Mars. In your yard you might want to construct a box hedge maze or simply draw a series of circles on the ground that you follow to the center. Make the maze big enough to allow time for you to walk. This is a very good meditation for March 13. The other environment that is a guaranteed tonic is the beach.

A Kabbalistic Interpretation

To call you dynamic would be a serious understatement. You literally never stop and sometimes even need to force yourself to slow down enough to get some much needed sleep. For this reason it is important to have a bedroom painted in colors that relax you and encourage you to drift off—for the values of this day an ideal color scheme would be pale blue mixed with pale green and cream.

You have a very strong attraction to water, and in particular you are drawn to the sea. If you can relocate so that you live near a dramatic ocean with rocky beaches then you will probably never want to move again. If at all possible you should try your hand at deep-sea fishing.

Many people talk about having a personal lucky number. Yours is undoubtedly twelve, a portentous number in occult terms. You could cultivate good fortune by using patterns that involve groups of twelve in your office layout. At home, buy four candle spikes or candelabra, each with three candleholders, and put one at each corner of the main room in the house.

A Numerological Interpretation

YOUR MAGIC NUMBERS: 7 AND 10

The thirteenth day of the third month reduces to seven, the number of victory and rest—a temporary cessation of activity. In this period of stillness, this date carries an extreme sensitivity. You are usually aware of signals, influences, and messages from unseen realms. You may have seen fairies as a child, had invisible playmates, or had dreams of deceased relatives that troubled your parents. Don't tinker with crystal balls or psychic games.

The seventy-third day of the year reduces to ten, adding the influence of certainty that we begin each cycle at a new level. Emerald and sodalite will keep you grounded. You have to know exactly what you want in order to receive it. Place the order, and put yourself in a position to receive. What is your desire? What is your preparation?

OBJECTS/IMAGES
the Sirens, pennants, periscope

SHAPES/MATERIALS
a sieve or colander, peridot, moonstones

COLORS
white, purple, chartreuse, indigo

ANIMALS
space creatures, the Loch Ness monster

PLANTS, HERBS, EDIBLES
passionflower, rockrose

ESSENCE
rosewood

SOUNDS/RHYTHMS
cello music, dance of the seven veils

MUSICAL NOTES
F# and A

DEEP SPACE OBJECTS
Mu Pegasus, Sadalbari, Good Luck of the Excelling One

March 14

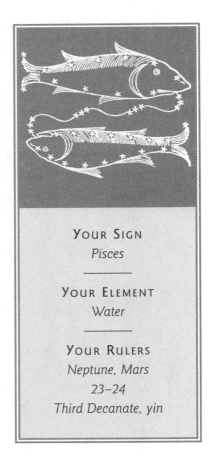

YOUR SIGN
Pisces

YOUR ELEMENT
Water

YOUR RULERS
Neptune, Mars
23–24
Third Decanate, yin

The Astrological Interpretation

Although this birth date gives you a great many talents and a profound urge for creative self-expression, you may easily find yourself burdened by too many activities and interests, people and things. You may find that you have too many interests and not enough time to pursue the training and education that you know is right for your life. Thus it is important for you to say good-by to those mental activities that waste your energy and concentrate on what will give you the right foundation to accomplish your true aspirations. This cleansing may also take physical form, by your eliminating eating and drinking habits not in your best interest. Purging is also periodically needed on the emotional level, requiring you to remove yourself from harmful relationships and to rid yourself of emotional patterns that do not support you.

March 14 has a magnetic personality that can draw on unknown sources for inspiration. Temper your imaginative wanderings with careful attention to everyday matters. The reflection of light through colored glass is pleasing to you; blue glass may attract you in particular. Your feet are a sensitive area of your body, and you may want to wear heavy boots to keep them warm and protected. Consider silk sock liners in the cold months. At home, you need more than a corner of space to call your own. A room with a cot or daybed so you can take solo naps is the way to regain your energies. Have a snug purple comforter and thick drapes, so you can burrow and snooze. You may enjoy the peace of total darkness.

Outdoors the environment is your laboratory for play and research. Experiment with hybrid plants or test the soil for its mineral content. Build a swing chair that looks out on your garden. Primroses, butterfly bush, and tulips may be among your favorites.

A Kabbalistic Interpretation

People born on this day are usually of an unrelentingly scientific and rational nature. It's very unlikely that anyone born this day will be reading this book except perhaps to point out to a friend how inaccurate it is.

If you are born March 14 you are likely to be very passionate about your garden. On the whole you like your garden to be orderly; you will rarely leave a plant untrimmed or untended. As you tend to be fairly ambitious, you could plant a thick hedge of hawthorn around the perimeter of your garden as a means to enhance success.

As fastidious as you are in the garden and in your home, you are probably less concerned with your own appearance, and while you are always neat and clean you may not be aware of color. A good color combination is a mixture of orange and gold. These are bold colors that might be difficult to pull off together, but if you are looking for a way to sharpen your clarity of thought you should definitely give this combination a try.

A Numerological Interpretation
YOUR MAGIC NUMBERS: 8 AND 2

The fourteenth day of the third month reduces to eight, a number that embodies the cyclic nature of reality. You have an innate rhythm, just like the seasons of the year, moving from planting to harvest. You possess a unique capacity for cultivation, as if you can coax an exquisite desert flower from parched and barren sand. You have a knack for attracting just what you need, just when you need it, often amazing your friends.

The seventy-fourth day of the year reduces to two, adding the fluid realm of the collective unconscious to the repertoire you can easily draw upon when manifesting beauty in your life. Take a cruise and find an uninhabited island. Imagine how you would transform your deserted island into a tropical paradise through your own ingenuity. Feel the sand in your toes, taste the salt air, hear the cry of the gulls, and conceive the possibilities. Aquamarine and amber will fire your imagination.

OBJECTS/IMAGES
footrests, pedicures, sandals, seclusion

SHAPES/MATERIALS
amethyst, surf shapes, tear shapes, tourmaline

COLORS
turquoise, teal, carmine

ANIMALS
eel, octopus

PLANTS, HERBS, EDIBLES
stanhopea oculata, (orchid), purple-fringed orchid, calla lily, tuna fish

ESSENCE
tea rose

SOUNDS/RHYTHMS
mariachi band

MUSICAL NOTES
G and C#

DEEP SPACE OBJECTS
Eta Pegasus, Matar, Fortunate Rain

March 15

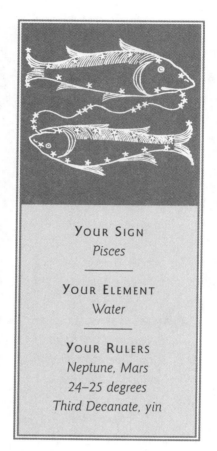

YOUR SIGN
Pisces

YOUR ELEMENT
Water

YOUR RULERS
Neptune, Mars
24–25 degrees
Third Decanate, yin

The Astrological Interpretation

Your life is deeply connected to your relationships, and you are capable of achieving a beautiful sense of intimacy with those you love. You do have to be careful of projecting your own imagination and fears onto others. Although you wish the best for your loved ones, you do them and yourself a disservice by allowing what disturbs you to bother them. Focus on your own individuality and support others to do the same. Though you are a very inclusive and accepting person, you can also be very intolerant of people when they do not do things the way you want them to. There is no single way of handling life's many situations. You will receive much more love from others by allowing people to be themselves. This does not mean that you should not offer your help, aid, and advice. It does mean that you should work to become detached from the results.

Water finds its own level, and March 15 will sometimes flow toward goals like a rushing river and other times like a spent trickle. Too much languishing on the sofa can cause you to drift. To enliven your environment and keep your focus have some furniture that is upright and functional. Have a ticking clock in a few rooms. Clear quartz is a wonderful regulator for your energies. Take crystals into the bathtub with you.

Your kitchen should have a central table where everyone meets. A lazy Susan for condiments, sugar bowl, etc., is a subliminal reminder of life going round and round. Cooking is an excellent art for you. Work with different spices, especially cayenne pepper, to spice up your life. You may be sports minded and like martial arts. A space in your yard where you could place a mat and practice would be ideal for you. Have a row of hedges between you and your neighbors; yours is a sensual birthday, and you might just want to romp au naturel.

A Kabbalistic Interpretation

You are more of a dreamer and idealist than a strictly rational thinker. You can help develop this character trait by bathing while burning a lavender-scented candle. For those times when your thoughts become muddled, consider sleeping with a piece of aquamarine under your pillow, and you will awaken with a much clearer view of things.

As this day is associated with the tarot card the Star, you might want to let some light into your house by installing a skylight. This will be particularly beneficial in the evening, when your room will be lit up by the silvery light of the night sky. An ideal ornament for your bedroom is a wind chime or mobile made with silver or metallic blue stars.

You tend to have a fairly strict moral code. You are unlikely to be puritanical, and you rarely impose your views on colleagues or friends, but you do set yourself very high standards. It is important that you not drive yourself too hard. To slow down, you should buy a lovely piece of jewelry or an accessory such as a rich emerald green-colored scarf.

A Numerological Interpretation
YOUR MAGIC NUMBERS: 9 AND 3

The fifteenth day of the third month reduces to nine, a number representing attainment and fulfillment. Nine completes a cycle and demands an accounting of performance. At the end of every cycle, there is an evaluation, a judgment, the purpose of which is to improve the next cycle. Should the same pattern be repeated or should the mold be reformed? Through evaluation and improvement we grow and unfold to a higher level.

The seventy-fifth day of the year reduces to three, adding the principle of growth, unfoldment, and the instinctive awareness that one and one will endlessly equal two until another element is added to the equation. You will accept nothing short of perfection from those in whom you place your trust. Study how prenatal care affects the newborn infant. Stare into a candle flame in the darkness. Walk in virgin snow. Toss a pebble into a pristine mountain stream. Sodalite and green quartz will harmonize your emotions.

OBJECTS/IMAGES
clouds, purple toenail polish, a silk sleep mask

SHAPES/MATERIALS
fisherman's cable-knit sweater, cotton turtlenecks, peridot

COLORS
red-violet, white, sea green, cobalt blue, coral

ANIMALS
loon, sea horse, catfish

PLANTS, HERBS, EDIBLES
mimosa trees, Spanish moss, tiger balm

ESSENCES
violets, clematis

SOUNDS/RHYTHMS
New Age wave music, 6/8 time, clog dance music

MUSICAL NOTES
G# and D

DEEP SPACE OBJECT
black hole

March 16

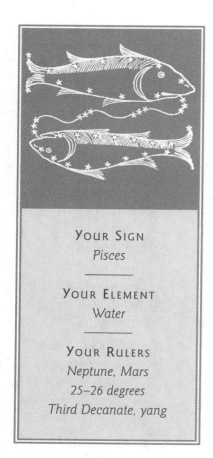

The Astrological Interpretation

Your birth date endows you with the ability to visualize the world of possibilities. People will find you to be a storehouse of information, and your natural generosity allows you to give freely of your insights to those who come to you. It is important for you to be discriminating, however, as many people neither want nor will hear what you say. You should therefore only give when there is honest need, and you should support only those people who are ready to accept the treasures you have to share with them. You also need to know how to refill and recoup the energy that you proffer so willingly. Such personal restoration comes from doing those activities that you love. This birth date is especially connected to the water. If you have the opportunity to take long, solitary walks along the beach or if you can spend time near a lake or river, then by all means do so. At the very least, enjoy the total privacy of a deep soak in your own bathtub!

March 16 has the ability to tentatively explore life until he connects with an experience or project that resonates with his/her deepest sensibilities. The process may be frustrating for those around you, but it is the way you go about things and must be honored. In your home keep music on in the background and notice how your mood changes depending on the music playing. Mirrors are important to you, and you may want to have a variety of stationary ones as well as hand mirrors. Your symbol, the two fish tied together, is a perfect motif for decoration. Shower curtains with swimming fish, dishes with glazed fish designs, and an aquarium are all good reminders of your imaginative duality. The new moon is an important time for you. Make a wish every new moon and see if it comes true!

Outdoors, March 16 enjoys water and flowers. Have a collection of brightly colored watering cans for your garden. A trellis in the middle of your garden would be a place to sit and search for your next "connection." Flowers for March 16 include orchids, arum lily, and clustered bellflower.

A Kabbalistic Interpretation

If you were born today you will have a lot of experience to offer others in practical areas. One of the values of this day connects to the earthy aspects of Pisces, so an ideal gift would be tools for working in the home such as a new power drill or a workbench.

This day is well aspected for traveling. The one thing you love most about your travels is being able to share them with others. Invest in a really good camera and some photo albums, perhaps buff colored and edged with gray. These albums will help keep the memories of your trips fresh in your mind.

A Numerological Interpretation

YOUR MAGIC NUMBERS: 10 AND 4

The sixteenth day of the third month reduces to ten, representing the completion of a process and readiness to begin again. The most positive expression of this day's energy is learning from experience and moving ahead, regardless of how painful the lessons seem to be. This is neither a blind leap into the void, nor a frozen tentativeness, but rather a steady, step-by-step progression into the future. Place an hourglass where you can see the sand flow through. Azurite and calcite will strengthen your resolve.

The seventy-sixth day of the year reduces to four, adding the significance of the implicit order underlying all outward reality. You know in your heart that if you reach out your hand, then the touch of guidance will reach back. The risk of this day is reluctance. What would happen if a baby bird clung to the nest, refusing to risk flight? Step outside on a dark night and glimpse the silver sliver of the new moon, containing the promise of her fullness. What if the moon could hold back her march? Cease resisting.

OBJECTS/IMAGES
nets, nomads, pajamas, mythology

SHAPES/MATERIALS
oil, paint, geyser shapes, imitation fur

COLORS
iridescent purple, deep purple, apricot

ANIMALS
double-crested cormorant, red-throated loon

PLANTS, HERBS, EDIBLES
lady's slipper, moth orchid, water mosses

ESSENCE
melissa

SOUNDS/RHYTHMS
oud (Middle Eastern instrument), German lieder

MUSICAL NOTES
A and D#

DEEP SPACE OBJECT
NGC 6946, spiral galaxy

March 17

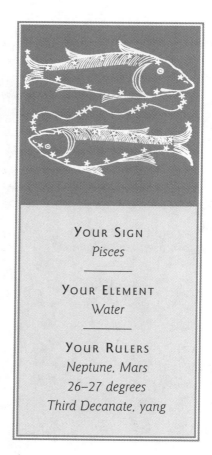

YOUR SIGN
Pisces

YOUR ELEMENT
Water

YOUR RULERS
Neptune, Mars
26–27 degrees
Third Decanate, yang

The Astrological Interpretation

Your inner self is like a horn of plenty, filled with all the bounty of nature. You have worked a long time to realize your own inner richness, and this is something you should honor and cherish. You have a great urge to nurture others and be helpful to as many people as possible. Yet it is impossible to be all things to all people. Even with your own great, personal storehouse of energy, you may find that certain individuals can zap and sap you! Beware of these "psychic vampires," as no matter how much you give them, they will always want more. It is important for you to learn how to create a relationship with yourself with clear structures and boundaries. You can be too idealistic and too caring, and this does not work if people do not honestly care about themselves.

Many astrological sources indicate this birthday is on an "occult" degree, which gives contact with the spirit world. If you do feel connected to astral planes it does not mean you can neglect the earthly. You must take special care to fortify yourself and learn to "translate" from one level to another. Avoid obsession! To help you keep your many talents and skills operating smoothly meditate on the color yellow. You may need, in moderation, food with a sweet flavor. At home images of the full moon would be good decorative touches. In your bedroom sanctuary, you may prefer dark colors and furniture that is very ornate. Incorporate the shape of the pentagram or five-rayed star in your decor.

A water lily pond either indoors or in your yard would be a source of pleasure and interest for you. Erect a tentlike structure outdoors with billowing material and you can pretend you are a prince or princess in the Arabian Nights. Fantasy is a way of renewing yourself and enjoying what the earth has to offer.

A Kabbalistic Interpretation

This day has the same value as the Hebrew letter *Mem*, meaning "water." Because of other values within this date, avoid anything like an ornamental fountain or a major water fixture. Try instead to find a house near a brook or stream or cut an appropriately meandering channel yourself. At work it is also desirable for you to be near water, so consider placing a small aquarium or a fish bowl in your office.

This is a day with particularly nurturing, even maternal, qualities, so children are likely to be important to you. Even if you don't have children you should have some attractive toys in your house such as an antique rocking horse. Warm and generous as March 17 is, you are also deeply emotional. You have a breadth of wisdom that informs your emotional reactions and prevents hypersensitivity. Home for you needs to be a place that vibrates and echoes your feelings of positive energy and love. Focus on very pale colors with a touch of reddish brown here and there. Try placing some lily-of-the-valley plants in lilac-colored pots, as these have a wonderfully relaxing and nurturing air to them.

A Numerological Interpretation

YOUR MAGIC NUMBERS: 2 AND 5

The seventeenth day of the third month reduces to two, a number that means reflection. The image of a blank canvas, full of unlimited potential, carries the promise of a finished painting. You must seize the creative process to participate. Make the first broad brush strokes across the linen landscape in bold colors with sharp angles. The seventy-seventh day of the year reduces to five, adding the influence of constant change. Process is a great blessing, and culmination does not cancel or invalidate an experience, rather it creates a new threshold.

Build your own miniature Zen garden. Shift the elements and designs and experiment with the result. Take a hay ride in autumn under a harvest moon. See the moonlight shimmer on the empty rows of harvested crops, and sip a mug of hot cider.

OBJECTS/IMAGES
aquariums, sandals, a fisherman's lamp

SHAPES/MATERIALS
ballet tutus and tights, beryl, mazes

COLORS
lilac, brick red, lemon

ANIMALS
chameleon, red-throated loon

PLANTS, HERBS, EDIBLES
absinthe, canned fish, blue curls, donuts

ESSENCE
star anise

SOUNDS/RHYTHMS
Balinese rain drum, Gregorian chant

MUSICAL NOTES
C# and E

DEEP SPACE OBJECTS
Pi Cygnus, Aselfafage, Horse's Hoof

March 18

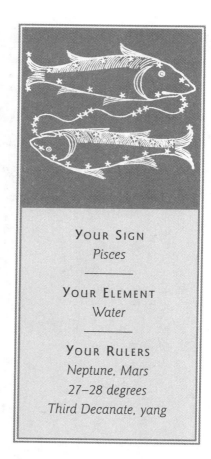

YOUR SIGN
Pisces

———

YOUR ELEMENT
Water

———

YOUR RULERS
Neptune, Mars
27–28 degrees
Third Decanate, yang

The Astrological Interpretation

You have the ability to express your creative urges with a powerful discharge of energy. Once a creative project, whether work or relationship, is over, it is important not to remain beyond the point of productivity. It is your job to sense when this creative culmination occurs and then how to leave the situation with grace and ease. When you have successfully withdrawn into yourself, take the time to rest and wait for the next creative urge to come upon you. Do not rush yourself. Your greatest strength is in your understanding of your own cyclic movements. You will enjoy music and dance, as these two activities are based on a structured beat, one that you profoundly appreciate.

March 18 may have an easy faith in life and its rhythms. You are a wisdom seeker and interested in nature as well. You have the ability to share your knowledge with others both casually and socially. No matter how deeply you study you can take simple satisfaction from everyday pleasures, tempering any tendency toward moodiness. A symbol for you is a red triangle with an open circle in the center. At home, decorate with woodcuts in a variety of colors and colored glass. You may particularly enjoy amethyst-colored depression glass. March 18 may go through many different collecting periods. The main criteria are beauty and color. In the bedroom, a bed high off the ground gives you a feeling of safety. A bedstead of metal in curved shapes would suit you. Consider having a fountain in your bedroom. The sound of water is a soothing way to sleep.

Outdoors, your garden should feature night-blooming plants that you visit at the time of the full moon. It will be a special pleasure to gaze at your fertile garden under the moonbeams. Flowers for March 18 could include elephant's ear and fragrant water lily

A Kabbalistic Interpretation

In today's cynical world you are scrupulously honest, and you look for honesty and truth in your potential partners. You are also likely to be something of an aesthete. As Keats once wrote: "'Beauty is truth, truth beauty,'—that is all ye know on earth, and all ye need to know." An excellent gift for you would be a beautifully bound volume of poetry, especially if it was a collection of the great Romantic poets such as Keats, Shelley, and Wordsworth.

People born today have something of a split personality when it comes to the workplace. While at home you may recline with a fine wine and a good book, at the office the energy of the Strength card from the tarot takes over. This streak of dominant energy can be a good quality in a manager, so carry a piece of tigereye with you to enhance this faculty. Alternately, a piece of angelica will help you to be more compassionate.

In the evenings you love to luxuriate. If you really want to feel pampered and looked after, then ask your partner to give you a massage using some coconut-based massage oil.

A Numerological Interpretation

YOUR MAGIC NUMBERS: 3 AND 6

The eighteenth day of the third month reduces to three. Yours is the gift of enjoying simple pleasures. You have the capacity to see beauty and derive joy from ordinary life—sunsets, rainbows, sparkling raindrops dangling from flower petals after a spring rain. You are as enriched by birdsong as others might be from a full orchestra. Yours is the path of rejoicing in the gift of an ordinary day, transforming a simple transaction into a touching memory because of your warmth and efficiency.

This day's magic renders the soul cognizant that every act is potentially sacred. Diamond and emerald are the gems that remind you of the priceless potential of ordinary things. The seventy-eighth day of the year reduces to six, the number of beauty as manifested in the infinite exquisiteness of six-sided snowflakes. Build a snow sculpture. Bake bread, and savor the texture and aroma.

OBJECTS/IMAGES
long-lens camera, chakras, disguises, docks

SHAPES/MATERIALS
acetone, amethyst, aquamarine, trident shapes

COLORS
mauve, orange, chartreuse

ANIMALS
orca, whooping crane

PLANTS, HERBS, EDIBLES
electrolytes, cappuccino foam, kelp, cymbidium (orchid variety)

ESSENCE
nutmeg

SOUNDS/RHYTHMS
viola da gamba, pipe organs

MUSICAL NOTES
D and F

DEEP SPACE OBJECTS
Beta Pegasus, Scheat, Upper Arm

March 19

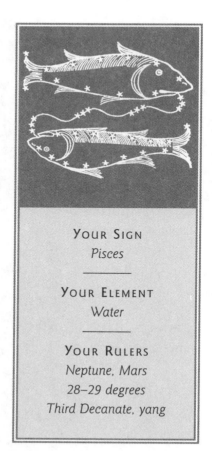

The Astrological Interpretation

You are born in the last degree of the zodiac, a point of supreme culmination. All the activities of the past are synthesized at this point, giving you a sense of connection to everything and everyone. You can thus be a friend to all people, as your comprehension of life is expansive and totally inclusive. Your individual task is to blend all of the characteristics and tendencies. You will need to establish a clear focal point for personal expression. This can be very challenging, as with all your possibilities, it may not be the simplest thing for you to create one primary avenue for your professional outlets. The key to your success is to choose a career that allows you a great variety of activities and is at the same time clearly defined in terms of personal responsibilities. You would be very good as a coordinator of various departments and facets of a company, as you have an inborn familiarity with the "all and everything" of life.

There are two fixed stars located near your degree, Scheat and Piscium. These positions may incline a person to take a fatalistic view toward life and to swim whichever way the current takes him rather than constructing a solid raft and navigating clearly. Your home may be filled with equipment from your various interests and abilities. Have an annual purge of whatever is no longer needed or interesting to you. Mirrors may figure prominently in your home. You aren't overly vain but do enjoy watching sun, moon, and electric light reflected in a mirror. Hang prisms wherever they will catch the light. An old clock may be a prized possession of yours. If the clock has chimes make sure the melody pleases you.

Outdoors, March 19 will enjoy a garden with some water. If there is no pond nearby, a sprinkler or sprinkler system would suffice. Plant flower beds in a circle with a garden statue or globe in the center. Flowers that are particularly pleasing to you are water mosses, umbrella grass, and water lilies.

A Kabbalistic Interpretation

The Fool card from the tarot has strong connections to the value of this day. A special quality of the Fool is the ability to take a half-full rather than a half-empty view of life. Good colors for this day are anything that is bright and cheerful. However, if you are attending a serious meeting you may need to dress down more than most to meet the solemnity of the occasion.

Many people find comfort in things that remind them of stability and solidity. People born this day, in contrast, have a strong attraction to those elements in life that remind them of the transient and temporary nature of things. For this reason you might enjoy keeping a butterfly collection, as the delicate and ephemeral nature of these creatures reflects the transience of life.

All forms of creativity are well aspected in the kabbalistic values of this day. Even if you are not professionally expert at playing an instrument, make sure that you play something simply for the joy of it. An unusual instrument, especially a mandolin or a set of bagpipes, would be a fantastic addition to the household of people born today.

A Numerological Interpretation

YOUR MAGIC NUMBERS: 4 AND 7

The nineteenth day of the third month reduces to four, the number that represents order and stability. Nature remains constant beneath outward changes. We gain control and mastery over circumstances through endless repetitions whereby we become familiar with nuance. When we obtain the same result through multiple trials, we can fashion some useful application through an internalization of principle. Fire opal and jasper will stir your creativity.

Observe light shining through a prism, refracting into the colors of the rainbow. Jewel tone clothing will enhance your charm. The seventy-ninth day of the year reduces to ten, adding the quality of surety of victory to the countless facets of experiences. Practice makes perfect. Go early to the symphony and listen to the orchestra tuning. Contemplate each instrument as a solo component compared with the full orchestral sound.

OBJECTS/IMAGES
beaches, asylums, angels, rain ponchos

SHAPES/MATERIALS
fishnet, flask shapes, pearls, paraffin

COLORS
hunter green, beige, spinach green

ANIMALS
faun, lobster

PLANTS, HERBS, EDIBLES
ale, lady's slipper orchid, hindu lotus, a clambake

ESSENCE
rosewood

SOUNDS/RHYTHMS
splashes, mysterious sounds in the night

MUSICAL NOTES
D# and F#

DEEP SPACE OBJECT
NGC 253, spiral galaxy

March 20

The Astrological Interpretation

You are born near the very first degree of the zodiac, a time of intense initiation of creative activity. You are on the cusp between Pisces, the most universal of the twelve signs of the zodiac, and Aries, the most individually focused. You have a powerful, fiery urge within you to declare to all the world: "I am here! I am myself! I AM!" But the acorn must be planted in fertile soil in order to grow, and you must learn how to temper the fiery and often undisciplined sense of yourself so that you may successfully cooperate with others in shaping your world. The pull of the ocean of Pisces is strong, and water puts out fire. You may find that instead of consistently projecting yourself into life with a firm statement of your own being, you retreat back into yourself, afraid to be too strongly self-assertive, as the path before you remains a huge unknown. You have the great sensitivity and inclusivity of the Pisces experience behind you, and now you must create your own way, shape, and form on earth.

The perfect environment to accommodate both parts of your nature is a campsite with a fire. Your Aries can break through the brush, build the fire, and set things up, and your Pisces side can relax by the stream and look up at the stars. If you hate camping, consider a screened-in porch or solarium. Stained glass reflecting colors soothes both sides of your nature.

Your home should feature pictures of the goals toward which you are working. If you are saving for a car, put a picture of it on the door so you see it as you leave the house. Visualizing is essential for you to gather together your energies and bring your dreams and wishes into reality. Consider having a silhouette picture or a sculptured bust of yourself made. It is positive for you to remind yourself of who you are and who you are trying to become. For fun keep a variety of hats in different styles and colors. They will give you a new image.

A Kabbalistic Interpretation

The kabbalistic value of March 20 reflects characteristics that are typically associated with Aries. Those born this day are extremely adventurous. An ideal gift for this birthday is a week of bungee jumping or water-skiing lessons. In decorating their homes people born this day tend to reflect their nature through the use of bold and frequently clashing colors.

Your drive to enjoy success in life is admirable. There is, however, some danger of placing career achievement too far ahead of family and friends. To boost your confidence about your level of success, place some cornflowers on your desk. Consider keeping a pressed rose in your pocket to remind you of loved ones.

You are likely to be creative with your hands and may even consider exhibiting and selling the wares you make. The energies of this day are particularly well suited to work in ceramics; you should get a great deal of satisfaction from using a potter's wheel.

A Numerological Interpretation
YOUR MAGIC NUMBERS: 6 AND 3

The twentieth day of the fourth month reduces to six, the number of balance, symmetry, and the beauty inherent in harmonized opposites. This day's path calls forth the ability to see how things fit together in life and the intrinsic rightness of Divine order in the grand scheme of things. There is a complementary relationship between the individual and the universe when one is truly oneself.

The eightieth day of the year reduces to three, adding the influence of natural unfoldment to your sense of how things fit together. Emerald and citrine are complementary gems. Visit a duck pond surrounded by weeping willow trees. Watch baby ducks follow their mother in a perfect row. Listen to their eager quacks as they move across the water. Collect brightly painted carved statues of ducks or other animals to cheer you.

OBJECTS/IMAGES
an old-fashioned still, crystal decanters, a blacksmith's forge

SHAPES/MATERIALS
carved wood, octagons, red coral

COLORS
red-purple, persimmon, carnation pink, sunshine yellow, turquoise

ANIMALS
lamb, hermit crab

PLANTS, HERBS, EDIBLES
miso soup, champagne, aloes

ESSENCES
horseradish, the smell of green tea

SOUNDS/RHYTHMS
chimes, the sound of synchronized swimming

MUSICAL NOTES
F and G#

DEEP SPACE OBJECT
quasar 2344

March 21

YOUR SIGN
Aries

———

YOUR ELEMENT
Fire

———

YOUR RULER
Mars
00–1 degree
First Decanate, yang

The Astrological Interpretation

The symbolic meaning of your birth date is connected to the image of a young sea otter, peeping above the water to see what surrounds him on the horizon. So much in life is new to you! Some people may interpret this facet of your personality as naïveté, but no matter how old you may be, you will not be jaded by life. You contain within yourself a passionate impulse to explore the most interesting possibilities your environment has to offer. Yes, there is the fear that you may not succeed and, like an adolescent, you take a number of tentative steps toward self-expression. But your urge to be *you* is greater than your fear of the process of becoming. No matter what setbacks you may encounter, you will always find the courage to move forward. It is therefore easy for you to pick yourself up, wipe the dust off, and get on with life!

March 21 is the first complete day of Aries after the spring equinox and the beginning of the sign of Aries. Your birthday may also be located on a critical degree, which means you may have strong reactions to both the highs and lows of life. Your energy and zeal for life may be stronger than your judgment. At home keep your energies vibrant with touches of red. Some kind of slow exercise routine in the morning will help you synch up mind and body. Rhythm, either singing, snapping your fingers, or drumming is a very good way of controlling your energy without dampening your enthusiasm. Quartz crystal will also help modulate your energies. In case the quartz isn't working, try a rabbit's foot.

Outdoors, chopping wood and building a log cabin would fit your personality. You enjoy being active and creating things that you can see. Flowers for March 21 are the early spring visitors: forsythia, crocuses, and daffodils.

A Kabbalistic Interpretation

The vernal equinox, the traditional first day of the year, represents new life that comes with the beginning of spring. As the first day of the first sign of the year, this day connects to the tarot card the Magician, a card that points toward a tremendous individualism within a person. One gift for someone born today might be a portrait done in an unusual expressionistic style.

People born on this day usually have a love of things connected to nature and will enjoy tending a well-stocked garden. Make yours a riot of color throughout the year. It is particularly important for someone born on the birth of spring to keep plants that blooms in the bleakest parts of winter. These offset the potential for depression while you wait for the warmth of spring.

The inside of your home should be bright and full of color to reflect your optimism and love of all things vital and vibrant. Though born on the day of new life blooming, you can be something of a traditionalist. Your favorite meal should involve plenty of home baking and be cooked on a traditional stove.

A Numerological Interpretation
YOUR MAGIC NUMBERS: 6 AND 9

The twenty-first day of the third month reduces to six, a number signifying beauty and the harmony of balanced opposites as the geometric form of six indicates. Two equilateral triangles interlaced is the emblem of love, the Star of David. This day is a path of self-realization and the ability to recognize and seize potential. Your quest is one of recognition and understanding of the interconnectedness of head and heart.

The eighty-first day reduces to nine, which contributes the quality of aspiration fulfilled. Enjoy fresh lilies, fragrant six-petaled flowers are emblems of resurrection. See yourself in others, and watch the principle of opposites attracting and complementing. Peridot and opal are balms for your soul.

OBJECTS/IMAGES
pocketknife, lighters, wrenches, scissors

SHAPES/MATERIALS
mahogany, flame shapes, ruby, magnets

COLORS
yellow-orange, forest green

ANIMAL
condor

PLANTS, HERBS, EDIBLES
geraniums, pimentos, jalapeño salsa, cockscomb

ESSENCE
coriander

SOUNDS/RHYTHMS
Mussorgsky's Night on Bald Mountain

MUSICAL NOTES
F and G#

DEEP SPACE OBJECT
pulsar

March 22

YOUR SIGN
Aries

YOUR ELEMENT
Fire

YOUR RULERS
Mars, Sun
I degree
First Decanate, yang

The Astrological Interpretation

Your birth date reveals a person who is very mindful of obtaining the right tools to succeed in life. You know that you have to have a marketable skill, not just because this is a basic requirement to achieve a place in society, but because you also contain within you a fiery seed of creativity that needs to be expressed. Your task is to develop the right form for the special talents you possess. You know that you have that "special something" but must be very self-disciplined to give it life. You also have to be consistent, as you often begin things with great relish and then abandon what you started. If these projects involve others, you run the risk of letting your responsibilities fall into other people's hands. Take the time to think things through and avoid the impulsive rush toward whatever momentarily attracts you.

March 22 coming right after the spring equinox holds all the potential for growth and new life promised each spring. Energy for this birthday is stronger than judgment, and a life challenge will be to balance action and thought. March 22 has an attraction for articles reminiscent of the military. Army fatigues, boots, and a camouflage hat are all "fashion statements." Treat your home and wardrobe as a laboratory of humor: whatever makes you laugh belongs there. A statue of a ram's head or a painting that includes a flock of sheep will remind you of Aries's symbol. March 22 may have great skill with precision instruments. A good set of knives with fancy hilts should be part of your kitchen. An antique sword over the fireplace will remind you to temper your power. To calm and settle your energy carry a piece of malachite.

Outdoors, you may enjoy a shooting range or some form of sport that tests dexterity. Tending a green lawn in the spring is an excellent activity for you. Plant forsythia and crocuses so nature can celebrate your birthday. You might also find a profitable hobby in growing varieties of chili peppers.

A Kabbalistic Interpretation

The Russian mystic Georgii Ivanovitch Gurdjieff was very fond of the idea of hard work as a spur to insight. One of the aspects of this day is a genuine enjoyment of physically hard work. There is little you like better than to spend a day up to your elbows in grease and engine oil. You may enjoy building your own car from a kit or working on a major remodeling of a house.

You are a very thoughtful individual, and you do a lot of your thinking when you are working. All types of unexplained mysteries fascinate you. You may wish to buy books about unexplained and strange phenomena, or read up on the more esoteric aspects of cosmology and physics.

Like many Aries people you have a positive outlook on life and firmly believe that you will succeed. There is some tendency to gamble associated with this day, which is not such a good idea for someone who never thinks he is going to lose. If you carry a piece of petrified wood near your money you may find it easier to resist the temptation.

A Numerological Interpretation

YOUR MAGIC NUMBERS: 7 AND 10

The twenty-second day of the third month reduces to seven, a number meaning victory. The meaning of this day carries the release of unrestrained self-expression of the personality. No fear. Who you are shines, and you can radiate your charisma to a group. The response of others gives you feedback on your performance. The risk of this day is your becoming a channel-surfing couch potato. The eighty-second day of the year reduces to ten, adding perfect expression to the delivery.

Fluorite and pyrite harmonize your emotions. Attend improvisational theater. Try out for a role in community theater. Join Toastmasters. Don't sit on the sidelines, get into the arena. Involvement is the key to your success.

OBJECTS/IMAGES
a coffee mug, children tending a campfire, rams' horns

SHAPES/MATERIALS
all metals, garnets

COLORS
scarlet, fire engine red, ochre, grass green, deep purple

ANIMALS
glowworm, hart

PLANTS, HERBS, EDIBLES
salad burnet, arrow head, capers

ESSENCE
coriander

SOUNDS/RHYTHMS
a steel drum

MUSICAL NOTES
F# and A

DEEP SPACE OBJECTS
Beta Cetus, Deneb Kaitos, Tail of the Whale

March 23

YOUR SIGN
Aries

YOUR ELEMENT
Fire

YOUR RULER
Mars
2–3 degrees
First Decanate, yang

The Astrological Interpretation

You have an inner courage and fortitude that emerges when you are challenged. But you do not have to wait for life to put obstacles in your path before you take action. You have an eagerness to prove yourself and a tremendous urge to travel and explore the greater possibilities in the world. Make sure that you are in a career with plenty of room for advancement and opportunities for originality and inventiveness. You need to get out, move about, and experience life. You do not wish to be inhibited by people in social positions above you. You definitely like to—have to—run your own railroad, preferring to lay down your own tracks as you race through life. You rely a great deal on your own resources and feel very awkward when you do not have the necessary tools or techniques to accomplish a particular goal. How you go about cultivating the additional skills you require will be an important part of your life story.

You have the strength for combat but have learned to use your energies in more productive ways. Humor may be your most effective weapon. Cartoons, practical jokes, quips, and pranks are your arsenal. At home you may collect humor books or write a few yourself. Keep your decor simple with plenty of wood furniture. Candelabras in verdigris or wrought iron are excellent decorative touches for you. You would prefer a gas range in the kitchen rather than electric or using a microwave. Cooking simple, tasty casseroles may be another way for you to express your delight in human fellowship.

Outdoors, have room for sports and games. Two trees with a net for volleyball or badminton would fill up your yard nicely. Flowers such as ageratum, rock cress, and begonia along the borders of your yard would be just the right amount of garden for you.

A Kabbalistic Interpretation

People born this day are bursting with energy. You should seriously consider taking up a martial art such as karate or jujitsu to channel your intensity. Find some dedicated space in your house or yard to practice this activity on a regular basis.

Your propensity for physically combative sport is paired with a deeply aesthetic side to your nature. You may be drawn to the majestic and romantic aspects of art and wish to decorate your house with some high-quality prints of old masters or American landscape artists.

A connection with the tarot card the Empress means that you have a love of the good things in life and your home will reflect this love of opulence. Good colors for decorating are gold and green. Put a large bowl of fresh fruit in a prominent place in your kitchen. Soft fruits such as peaches, mangos, and apricots are likely to be favorites.

A Numerological Interpretation
YOUR MAGIC NUMBERS: 8 AND 2

The twenty-third day of the third month reduces to eight, the number meaning that opposite forms of expression stem from a single cause or source. The flags of the United Nations, like colors and musical notes, create a symphony of peoples and cultures. Each provides a colored brush to be spread across the canvas to create a complete landscape.

The eighty-third day of the year reduces to two, adding the element of reflection, which aids in the mirroring experience that our cultural traditions can provide. Celebrate traditions, your own and others, in dance, song, food, and clothing. Ponder the significance of the Riverdance phenomenon, creating immense pride in Ireland and enthusiastic response around the world. What is the difference between pride and arrogance? Patriotism can be a positive attribute, but wanton imperialism is unjustified. Carnelian set in gold will warm your heart.

OBJECTS/IMAGES
top hat, armor, contests, bootleggers

SHAPES/MATERIALS
adrenaline, almandine, brimstone, bloodstones

COLORS
reddish brown, teal, russet

ANIMALS
firebug, falcon

PLANTS, HERBS, EDIBLES
topiary plants, rhubarb, caperbush, bryony

ESSENCE
pimento

SOUND/RHYTHM
conga drum

MUSICAL NOTES
G and C#

DEEP SPACE OBJECT
pulsar

March 24

YOUR SIGN
Aries

YOUR ELEMENT
Fire

YOUR RULER
Mars
3–4 degrees
First Decanate, yang

The Astrological Interpretation

A great many of your lessons in life are focused in the area of relationships. It takes many people working harmoniously together to accomplish the majority of life's objectives. You can sometimes be too rash and headstrong and may not recognize the need for compromise or the wisdom and help that is being offered by the person standing (or sleeping) next to you. You are aware of justice and its abuse and cannot stand by impassively when you see people being taken advantage of. Friends and associates will admire your courageous and no-nonsense approach to life. You want immediate results and are not afraid to take the necessary action to get them. But sometimes it is important not to act but to merely observe. It will be up to you to learn how to perceive this vital difference.

March 24 has a pleasure-loving nature and is eager to forge ahead with whatever projects interest you. Even if you do not attain everything you want you can see the positive side of experience. A challenge will be to avoid self-indulgence and vanity. You may be interested in collecting miniature soldiers and re-creating historic battles. Women may be interested in collecting marbles or metal buttons. Decorate your home with casual decor. Wooden benches with pillows covered in brightly woven blankets or hand-loomed materials with reds, purples, and orange will be of interest to you. You may enjoy having a Grecian-style robe to relax in. Keep houseplants such as flamingo flower and slipperwort.

Outdoors, a jungle gym and swing set would be pleasing as well as a garden with all different kinds of plants and colors. Just for fun think about placing bells on garden stakes. You will enjoy hearing them as the wind rushes through.

A Kabbalistic Interpretation

If you are born today, you are among the most romantic. Your life tends to revolve around your emotional affairs—so it is important to spend some energy keeping your career in shape. One way you can help to ensure that your life stays on an even keel is to keep a single pink rose on the eastern side of your desk at work. This will be reassuring to you and allow you to concentrate on the job at hand. When you are at home you can encourage a sense of emotional fulfillment and contentment by purchasing some tall pale blue vases and placing them in the corners of your bedroom.

Although you love a feeling of togetherness it is important that you have a room you can genuinely call your own. A heavy square wooden desk is an excellent investment for you. Its solidity will help to ground you and assist you in approaching problems in a pragmatic way. The rest of your solitary room should be almost bare; any other ornaments or features should be metallic and on a small scale.

A Numerological Interpretation
YOUR MAGIC NUMBERS: 9 AND 3

The twenty-fourth day of the third month reduces to nine, the number of successful outcomes. Implicit at the meeting of two young lovers is their idealizing the outcome of the encounter. Dangerous liaisons, versus home and family, are potentials. Without a sense of responsibility, a potentially damaging stream of consequences is set in motion. Follow your bliss, but don't avoid responsibility. Learn the difference between self-indulgence and healthy satisfaction. Observe the exploratory play of an infant, motivated only by curiosity and an intrinsically human desire to master her surroundings. At that stage, there is no social conscience, no brooding sense of responsibility.

Lapis and agate are stones that will make you smile. The eighty-fourth day of the year reduces to three, contributing the quality of unfoldment, development, and natural expression. Read romance novels and *Romeo and Juliet*. Enjoy a candlelight tryst with your significant other.

OBJECTS/IMAGES
physical therapy, brick ovens, a walking stick, hairdressers

SHAPES/MATERIALS
red rocks, shape of eaves, hemp, pediments

COLORS
vermilion, royal blue, tangerine

ANIMALS
English sheepdog, Tasmanian wolf

PLANTS, HERBS, EDIBLES
red clover tea, dock, globe thistle, allium karataviense

ESSENCE
sweet basil

SOUNDS/RHYTHMS
a drum major's commands, marimba music

MUSICAL NOTES
G# and D

DEEP SPACE OBJECT
NGC 157, spiral galaxy

March 25

YOUR SIGN
Aries

YOUR ELEMENT
Fire

YOUR RULERS
Mars, Sun
4–5 degrees
First Decanate, yang

The Astrological Interpretation

Your birth date indicates a person who wants to step outside the boundaries of what you have been given by your family and society. You need to move ahead, incorporating what you have inherited and making a life for yourself that is filled with new and greater creative opportunities. You may feel that you are surrounded by social circumstances that inhibit your drive and stifle your personal call to action. This may force you at times to break through the walls of your environment and current life situation. This courage is admirable, yet it is also important to be aware of the effects of your actions; you are not alone on this planet. Make sure that you do not so entangle yourself in commitments of mutual responsibility that in liberating yourself, you bring havoc to others.

Your progress in life comes from giving all your abilities flight. An image for March 25 is a triangle with wings. The color red-orange is a power color for you. Consider having some large pieces of furniture made of wood and metal. A sculptured bust of you or family members would be a great addition to your home. On museum trips examine busts of historical people. Character and physical form interest you. An iron or old-fashioned brass bed is an excellent object to support your fire nature. Burning candles is a meditative activity for you. Whenever you are agitated light one and let your thoughts wander.

Outdoors, March 25 wants trees and rocks. The coast of Maine or of the Mediterranean is the type of terrain that you enjoy. A visit to Mount Rushmore will inspire you. Closer to home, have some holly bushes in your yard and decorate with holly during the holiday season.

A Kabbalistic Interpretation

The energy of the Fortune card from the tarot combined with a slightly rebellious streak implies an essentially itinerant nature. You like to travel and may actually choose a lifestyle that means living out of a backpack or suitcase. When looking for your next valise, try to find one that has either triangle or circular designs on it and you will be unlikely to allow others to dictate your goals to you.

Your overwhelming need to explore extends beyond the physical realm and into the spiritual. Through your travels you can gain a philosophy and wisdom about the world that will benefit many people. Eastern ideas and belief systems are particularly attractive to you, and an artifact such as a reclining Buddha or a hanuman statue would make an excellent gift.

The full kabbalistic value of this date has the same value as words suggesting behavior that doesn't exactly fall within the law. The rebellious streak you possess needs to be tempered, or you could find yourself in some unwelcome hot water. Keeping a healthy ivy plant in your living space is a reminder to hold your nonconformity within the bounds of social acceptability.

A Numerological Interpretation
YOUR MAGIC NUMBERS: 10 AND 4

The twenty-fifth day of the third month reduces to ten, the number signifying the end of a cycle and the embodiment of seed ideas begun in number one. Time to start over. If we hold our intention pure and clear throughout the creative process, we will achieve the perfect result we imagined at the outset. Each new cycle affirms us to do better, refining our skills. We look up toward higher expression with purity of intention. Sodalite, amber, and turquoise will strengthen you.

The eighty-fifth day of the year reduces to four, adding the underlying certainty of permanence behind change. Contemplate the principle of order at work, meditate on the athanor of the alchemist. Experiment with a chemistry set. Sit in the darkness in front of a fire and watch the dance of the colored flames—creative transformation or destructive combinations.

OBJECTS/IMAGES
green pastures, the pioneers, a lighter

SHAPES/MATERIALS
felt, carbon, isosceles triangles

COLORS
carmine red, scarlet, indigo, amber

ANIMALS
fox, gnat

PLANTS, HERBS, EDIBLES
holy thistle, bistort, broom brush tea tree

ESSENCE
pepper

SOUNDS/RHYTHMS
Swiss long, brass horns

MUSICAL NOTES
A and D#

DEEP SPACE OBJECT
quasar

March 26

YOUR SIGN
Aries

———

YOUR ELEMENT
Fire

———

YOUR RULERS
Mars, Sun
5–6 degrees
First Decanate, yin

The Astrological Interpretation

Your need to experiment with life will take you far. Your sense of your own individuality has to be proven again, and again, and you will work very hard to create a foundation that supports your urge "to be." You seek both emotional and financial security and are a person with deep-seated ambitions. In order to achieve your goals, you have to work at harmony and cooperation. Drive and perceptive insights you have in abundance; patience and compassion may, however, be somewhat weaker in March 26's character. It will be a good exercise for you to do something for others without expectation of reward. This will open you up to a wider range of human experience and help you to become more wholistic and integrated in your approach to life and to relationships.

Your talents lie in initiating projects, yet your native restlessness may mitigate bringing things to conclusion. An image for you is a person on a horse standing at the edge of a cliff and looking into a valley where people are at work. You are a hard worker but feel your destiny is higher and sharper than regular life. Sharp edges and acute angles are shapes for you. You might enjoy Arts and Crafts movement furniture or Stickley pieces. Reds are usually Aries colors, but for March 26, green, symbolic of birth and anger in the Chinese classification of elements, is more appropriate. Plant life and animals in your home are advisable, and you may have an innate understanding of botany and zoology. Geraniums, green clove, and cactus could be favorite indoor plants

Outdoors March 26 wants to mark off property lines with box hedges. Your garden should include impatiens and hollyhock. Try taking a ride in a hot-air balloon. The rhythm of farming is a tonic for your hair-trigger temper and restlessness. You might think of taking a farming vacation if you don't live in the country.

A Kabbalistic Interpretation

Although situated in the first period of Aries, this date has an energy that is more water-based than fiery. People born on this day are therefore unusually emotionally sensitive for Aries individuals. You may want to counter your sensitivity and the accompanying melancholy by placing some brass figurines or other ornaments around the house. The figures will encourage positive emotions, while the metallic aspect will appeal to the more resilient aspects of your personality.

You have a real love of animals, and your home could be a veritable menagerie. The value of this day suggests a decidedly charitable and philanthropic nature. Someone born this day may find themselves rescuing dogs or cats from the pound, as you like the idea of saving those in need.

As much as you like to protect those who are weaker and less fortunate than yourself you also have a need to feel protected and tend to look for a very strong individual in your relationships. To ensure that you have a choice of partners you should throw leaves of witch hazel into your bath water.

A Numerological Interpretation
YOUR MAGIC NUMBERS: 2 AND 5

The twenty-sixth day of the third month reduces to two, the number of duplication and relationship. This is a path of self-direction. Light a fire in your belly as fuel for your experiences and accomplishments. Become your own internal combustion engine. Carnelian and citrine will fire your aspirations. Play with dominoes; experience the chain reaction that ensues once the first domino falls. Laugh at the madcap genius of Rube Goldberg, a name synonymous with creative contraptions. Don't surrender to your frustrations. Study quantum physics, contemplate how the material universe is an illusion and yet responds to the conscious aspirations of the human mind. The eighty-sixth day of the year reduces to five, adding the influence of continual repetition and replication.

OBJECTS/IMAGES
brick kilns, carved wood statues, darts

SHAPES/MATERIALS
brightly colored squares, steel, carbuncles

COLORS
spring green, flame yellow

ANIMALS
boxer dog, kangaroo

PLANTS, HERBS, EDIBLES
basil, arugula, briars

ESSENCE
juniper

SOUNDS/RHYTHMS
sound of a punching bag, the box step

MUSICAL NOTES
C# and E

DEEP SPACE OBJECT
NGC 246, planetary nebula

March 27

YOUR SIGN
Aries

YOUR ELEMENT
Fire

YOUR RULERS
Mars, Sun
6–7 degrees
First Decanate, yin

The Astrological Interpretation

You are a person who thrives in a challenging environment. You are not afraid to say yes to a plan that you know little about, and you often find that "on the job training" is all the experience you need to master a task. You are a fighter by nature. The wise warrior, however, knows which battles are worth the effort and which are best left behind. You would do well to cultivate this wisdom and use your fiery energies to conquer only objectives that are close to your heart. Many things reach out and appeal to you. Many people stimulate your intense desires. It is vital that you stay in close contact with what is true to your own nature.

March 27 is adept at compartmentalizing and shifting focus according to the demands of the moment. The challenge is to keep life interesting when times are idle. Keep a few round objects close at hand in your home. Tossing a ball or juggling is a good way to keep focused. You may spend a lot of time on the telephone and would benefit from a shoulder cradle rest or a headset so your hands can be free. When it is time to relax put away all electronics and sit down on a brown brushed cotton or corduroy sofa. Closing your eyes for ten minutes will rejuvenate you. In your windows you may want small pieces of colored glass or prisms. Try to have a southern exposure somewhere in your home. The sun fuels your fiery nature.

Outdoors, March 27 may be more fond of forest and wide open spaces than gardens. Some ancient texts ascribe interests in forestry and lumber to your birthday. If you don't feel inclined to live in the woods, visit the forest and hike from time to time. Pine and hawthorn trees are all under the rulership of your planet, Mars. If you happen to be in the Andes region, investigate the cinchona tree from which quinine is derived.

A Kabbalistic Interpretation

You have supreme confidence in your physical attractiveness. While your positive self-image is admirable, it could cross over from confidence to vanity. A mirror with images of daisies around the edge may encourage you to feel more humble.

Hard work is no stranger to you. You are an excellent employee, and the effort you put in at work means that you are likely to find yourself in a senior management position or even running your own company. The influence of the Hebrew letter *Lamed* can sometimes mean that you drive yourself too hard. You need to make sure you get some relief from stress even during working hours. Consider hanging a picture opposite your desk depicting a pastoral landscape or a stream.

You like to party as much as you like to work. Even if your socializing has an ulterior motive or agenda, you always go with the intention of enjoying yourself. The best food for you to serve when you are entertaining is a variety of seafood. When dressing for success, include a deep russet color in your clothes.

A Numerological Interpretation
YOUR MAGIC NUMBERS: 3 AND 6

The twenty-seventh day of the third month reduces to three, a number signifying growth, unfoldment, and expression. This date endows you with an innate facility to move within the different aspects of yourself. At your best, you can express conscious and subconscious awareness simultaneously. Cultivate precision in separating what is important from what is superficial, like honing a scalpel to razor sharpness. Watch someone riding a bicycle on a high wire. Peridot and carnelian will aid your focus.

The eighty-seventh day of the year reduces to six, the number of balanced polarities and harmonious opposites, adding additional poise to the balance you feel between aspects of yourself. Enjoy objects that measure and balance. Ride a teeter-totter with a friend at a playground. Try twirling a Hula Hoop. Hang a multiple time zone clock at your workplace.

OBJECTS/IMAGES
scalpels, brick kilns, hats

SHAPES/MATERIALS
firestone, obelisk shapes, magnetite, and malachite

COLORS
flaming red, coral, lime green

ANIMALS
Bengal tiger, wolf

PLANTS, HERBS, EDIBLES
arnica, Indian paintbrush, and wormwood (herb)

ESSENCE
zdravets (geranium oil)

SOUNDS/RHYTHMS
shivarees, shouts

MUSICAL NOTES
D and F

DEEP SPACE OBJECT
Alpha Reticulum

March 28

YOUR SIGN
Aries

YOUR ELEMENT
Fire

YOUR RULERS
Mars, Sun
7–8 degrees
First Decanate, yin

The Astrological Interpretation

The symbology of this birth date reveals a highly individualistic person, one who is very psychically sensitive. You are very perceptive about other people's feelings and may be overly influenced by them in your decision-making processes. The advantage you have is that you can offer understanding and emotional support to people who need this from you. The challenge that comes with this gift is that you allow impulse to rule reason when making decisions directing your life, and emotionality may reign over clear and precise judgment. You would do well to cultivate your mind. The universe will follow your lead if it knows where to go. This means that you need to deepen your sense of structure, order, and form. Take courses and perfect your skills. This will enhance your professional life and will aid your creative focus and self-discipline.

Some March 28 birthdays are near the fixed star Algenib, which is a white star at the top of the wing of Pegasus. Pegasus, the winged horse, carried Zeus's thunder and lightning, and your potential to be impulsive and rash resonates with this fiery image. Value the amount of energy you have to ignite the potential in your life but know when you are burning your bridges. A fleecy sheepskin in your home or as part of a coat will remind you of Aries's softer side. You may want to have a hat rack by the front door so you can express your mood by wearing different hats. Red Depression glassware may be a perfect collectible for March 28. Just for fun have a few kazoos around. If you feel like blowing your top, toot out a few tunes and you'll see things more clearly.

Outdoors, March 28 usually has many projects going. You may enjoy welding and creating metal sculptures to decorate your yard. An herb garden with chives, garlic, onions, and rhubarb could be a specialty. Keep some space outdoors for a jungle gym. You could get your best ideas hanging upside down.

A Kabbalistic Interpretation

If there is one thing you hate it is clutter. You like your life to have a definite sense of clarity and direction, and you prefer surroundings that reflect this aspect of your personality. Your minimalist environment may seem cold to others, but it is a style that keeps you secure and comfortable.

Your love affair with all that is minimalist and modern is offset by an equal attraction to the wild. Your bookcase may have some volumes about safaris, and you rarely miss a wildlife documentary. Add some African mats and rugs to your floors.

You may also have a taste for extreme weather. You could spend hours watching the Weather Channel's coverage of hurricanes and blizzards, and you love a good lightning storm. Most will be satisfied to witness the storm from the safety of their home, yet this day does generate more than its fair share of storm chasers. The ideal present for such a person is a video camcorder, particularly one with night-vision features.

A Numerological Interpretation
YOUR MAGIC NUMBERS: 4 AND 7

The twenty-eighth day of the year reduces to four, the number of order and measurement. This day generates a need for constant excitement. On the positive side, this keeps you in readiness for whatever experiences may come. You have a flair for sensing potential in any situation. On the downside, you could risk becoming an adrenaline junkie if you succumb to overstimulation. Study the relationship between stimulus and response; remember the lesson of Pavlov's dogs.

The eighty-eighth day of the year reduces to seven, the number of peace, safety, and security, soothing and relaxing your tendency to overstimulate. Jade and ruby will cool your energies. Take a friend to an amusement park. Ride the roller coaster and stroll down the arcade. Visit Disney World, and don't forget to watch the fireworks display.

OBJECTS/IMAGES
fire bellows, a whistle, a gladiator

SHAPES/MATERIALS
a spear shape, sardonyx

COLORS
saffron, fire engine red, orange sherbert, pine

ANIMALS
woodpecker, wild mustang

PLANTS, HERBS, EDIBLES
geraniums, scarlet sage

ESSENCE
holly

SOUNDS/RHYTHMS
glockenspiel, martial drums

MUSICAL NOTES
D# and F#

DEEP SPACE OBJECT
Alpha Lacerta

March 29

YOUR SIGN
Aries

YOUR ELEMENT
Fire

YOUR RULERS
Mars, Sun
8–9 degrees
First Decanate, yin

The Astrological Interpretation

You hold within you some powerful ideas that you seek to share with others. You have the daring to be innovative and the courage to move forward in order to manifest your thoughts in practical realms. You need to work with other like-minded individuals, each playing his or her part in a shared project. You are a natural-born initiator but may not have the patience, or the desire, to be the absolute leader. The important thing is to be clear in the presentation of your concepts and to maintain the directed energy that gives life to what you seek to create. If you dance off in too many areas of interest at once, you will accomplish nothing. You will gain more respect and openness from your partners and coworkers if you set an example of efficiency yourself.

The fixed star Algenib is located on some March 29 birthdays. Said to denote courage and aggressiveness, Algenib is associated with soldiers, sailors, and gunsmiths. March 29 has a particular talent for seeing far-reaching implications for personal activities. An image for you is from film: the close-up and the long shot. Both perspectives are your allies in life. Becoming a skilled marksman is an activity for you; however, it's best to confine shooting to a range or gallery. A crystal ball could be a decorative item whether or not you use it for "seeing." The smooth contours help you keep perspective. At home a collection of blooming cacti reminds March 29 that even prickly natures blossom.

Outdoors an old-fashioned oven made of red bricks will inspire your cooking. If you have a garden consider planting monochromatically each year—all red flowers one year, then all yellow, and all white the next. A basketball hoop in your yard is also a good way to focus the mind and have some fun.

A Kabbalistic Interpretation

This date has the same value as the number of paths in the Tree of Life. The Tree of Life is a diagram that represents an entire mystical system and can be seen as a symbolic map of the whole of Western occultism. Having a correspondence to this vast source of esoteric knowledge suggests someone with a natural feel for balancing the various elements of life. Such a person may have an interest in feng shui and may appreciate books and practitioners of this ancient art.

The influence of the Hermit tarot card compounds the intellectual dimension of people born today. You like nothing better than to spend hours in your favorite old chair with a pile of books. Certain influences on this date suggest an attraction to different cultures, so a tape of European classical music, South American panpipes, or Chinese string instruments are ideal accompaniments to your reading.

You will want to watch your health and may even keep a strict vegetarian diet. You prefer to maintain your fitness through organic methods rather than extreme physical exertion: meditative walking and yoga are good options. Treat yourself to a week at a health farm or a natural spa.

A Numerological Interpretation
YOUR MAGIC NUMBERS: 5 AND 8

The twenty-ninth day of the third month reduces to five, the number of change and adaptation. You have keen insight into how the larger cycles of the world are indicators and predictors of the changing cycles within your own experience. This capacity gives you an uncanny ability to see unfolding patterns and describe them as if you are seeing pictures in a crystal ball.

The eighty-ninth day of the year reduces to eight, which adds the comforting awareness that there is a pattern to change, and that everything is cyclical. Topaz and turquoise warm your heart. Try your hand at playing the stock market on your computer. Spend a day at a racetrack and bet small sums to test your predictions. Stare into a crystal ball to see what happens. Predict the weather for fun.

OBJECTS/IMAGES
pipes for smoking, metal hair clips, camouflage pants/shirts

SHAPES/MATERIALS
whetstone, red sand, wood carved in the shape of a pineapple

COLORS
orange, lemon, aquamarine

ANIMALS
mongoose, guard dog

PLANTS, HERBS, EDIBLES
thistles, wake-robin, tobacco

ESSENCE
pepper

SOUNDS/RHYTHMS
piano concerti, percussion solos

MUSICAL NOTES
E and G

DEEP SPACE OBJECTS
Gamma Pegasus, Algenib, Side of the Wing

March 30

YOUR SIGN
Aries

___

YOUR ELEMENT
Fire

___

YOUR RULER
Mars
9–10 degrees
First Decanate, yin

The Astrological Interpretation

As an Aries born on this particular day, your native pioneering spirit is connected to the urge for reformation and renewal. Your initiating drive manifests at its best when you can find new uses for an old idea or object, reshaping and refurbishing it until it glistens with new possibilities. You can do the same thing with people. You have an instinct for seeing the best in people, even if they are temporarily blind to their own talents. You are ruled by Mars, a planet symbolic of swords, lances, and other sharp instruments. You can probe beneath the surface, bringing to life what is dormant. You must use the point of your blades to penetrate wisely so that just enough pressure is evoked to stimulate and arouse but not irritate and annoy.

March 30 may be involved with discovering new forms for old symbols. The Mars energy of this birthday gives a triumphant feel to even the smallest accomplishments. Why not celebrate both? A large glass ball or a globe is an image for you. The globe could be of the earth or a star globe of the constellations. At home a print of fellow Aries Vincent van Gogh's work, especially *The Starry Night,* may be inspiring. Consider having decorative wrought iron somewhere in your home. Toys are important for March 30; a train set or a collection of snow globes are small objects that will bring you joy. Metal belt buckles are a way for you to express individuality. Military emblems or intricate metal designs may appeal.

Outdoors, March 30 will enjoy a weather vane on the roof. If you live in the country consider an antique metal bridle post outside your home. The natural environment you most enjoy is hilly ground with a collection of trees facing east. When sitting on a slight hill, facing east, you will find you get your best ideas.

A Kabbalistic Interpretation

More than anything you need to believe in yourself—keep working on your creative dreams. People born today have a wonderful eye for detail. If you are a friend or partner of someone born this day, go out today and buy them a set of oil paints—they'll love you for it!

One of the challenges for someone with your artistic intelligence is that you may get depressed observing the degree of materialism around you and the way most people never seem to take the time to sit and observe the world. You may find it difficult to find work that suits your creative spirit. If you do not have a job that allows you to express your creativity, you can alleviate this by decorating your work area with patterns based on triangle shapes colored in red and gold. This should help you to focus your energies on the work that needs to be done each day.

You have a varied taste in food and drink and are prepared to try anything at least once. Try drinking an infusion of burdock—this has a unique but delicious taste and will also do wonders for easing any sadness when you feel down.

A Numerological Interpretation
YOUR MAGIC NUMBERS: 6 AND 9

The thirtieth day of the third month reduces to six, lending this day the significance of integration of divergent perspectives. You have a gift for discerning the significance of and interplay among the various and multiple events of everyday experience. Therefore you can capitalize on every aspect of your heritage and experience. This attribute is a teaching tool for others who observe you, because you are able to interpret events and circumstances.

The ninetieth day of the year reduces to nine, adding the quality of completion of process, fueling your understanding of cause and effect. Green quartz and lapis will mobilize your energies. Learn sign language, and volunteer at a school for hearing impaired.

OBJECTS/IMAGES
red glasses, key rings

SHAPES/MATERIALS
crossed spears, lodestone

COLORS
vermilion, willow green, cobalt

ANIMAL
sheepdog

PLANTS, HERBS, EDIBLES
bistort, bog myrtle, burnt garlic

ESSENCE
juniper

SOUNDS/RHYTHMS
a drum roll

MUSICAL NOTES
F and G#

DEEP SPACE OBJECTS
Mu Draconis, Errai, the Shepherd

March 31

YOUR SIGN
Aries

YOUR ELEMENT
Fire

YOUR RULERS
Mars, Sun
10–11 degrees
Second Decanate, yin

The Astrological Interpretation

One of the most important gifts of a leader is his or her ability to take up a flag that everyone seeks to follow. Once you embody a cause and communicate it to others, the effects of your beliefs are very convincing. You stimulate and inspire other people. This is a huge responsibility. Once you pick up the gauntlet, you must not stop until you have finished the battle. To do otherwise would betray the people who have placed their faith in your hands and perhaps their money in your pocket! It is not enough to be incredibly self-inspired by your initial vision and the conquest of the first step along the path. Develop good relationships with coworkers, taking their thoughts and needs into consideration. You will need them more than they need you.

Your first project is managing your own energy so your dynamism may be accompanied by real substance. An image for you is the children's game Simon Says. The more engaged the followers are, the more eagerly they will follow your lead. At home, you may have a particular fondness for metalware. A simple example may be a highly practical and well-designed metal dish drain. A set of andirons and a scrolled screen for your fireplace would also be pleasing. In the bedroom, March 31 indulges the "lamb" side of Aries. Soft cotton or flannel sheets in pale yellow are relaxing. You would also enjoy a matching robe of similar material.

Outdoors, have a telescope to take in the view and keep your eye on the stars. Your own garden may feature flowers such as scarlet gilia and pasqueflowers. A metal Victorian carriage lantern would be a perfect object for your sense of history and design.

A Kabbalistic Interpretation

People born today make exceptionally popular and efficient managers as well as wonderful parents. The kabbalistic values of this date are almost all connected with protective paternal behavior. This includes a direct connection to the God name associated with the most fatherly sephirat on the Tree of Life—Chesed. An oak sapling or a young oak tree for the garden—or perhaps a bonsai oak for your desk—can symbolize the most positive aspects of this behavior.

In the tarot, your birthday is most resonant with the Justice card. People are happy to take their disputes to you to be settled, as you have a reputation for being scrupulously fair and unbiased. To recharge your batteries from this sometimes draining activity, have a cup of mint tea and take a bath while burning some sandalwood-scented candles.

You are an excellent romantic partner but must work far harder than most to make sure your relationships work. You are intensely loyal and will stick by your partner no matter what. If today is your birthday and you want to encourage the same kind of loyalty in others, give your partner a piece of jewelry that is set with sapphires.

A Numerological Interpretation
YOUR MAGIC NUMBERS: 7 AND 10

The thirty-first day of the third month reduces to seven, the number of peace and rest. God rested on the seventh day. The last day of March is imbued with a sense of scales having momentarily come into perfect balance, experiencing a temporary equilibrium before the next weighing exercise. This path carries a sense of the in-between, the silent spaces between thoughts that are gateways to the infinite.

The ninety-first day of the year reduces to ten, amplifying the sense that something is finished and should be appreciated before starting again. Black opal will fire your imagination. Place a small legal or pharmaceutical scale on your desk, and experiment weighing different items. Hang a papyrus of the Egyptian goddess of truth and justice, Ma'at, over your desk. Use an ink pen carved from an ostrich plume.

OBJECTS/IMAGES
a policeman's whistle, carving set, cowboy hat

SHAPES/MATERIALS
all metals, bismuth, flax, diamonds

COLORS
crimson, pea green, navy blue

ANIMALS
wolverine, elk

PLANTS, HERBS, EDIBLES
capsicum, garlic, scarlet avens, crocus

ESSENCE
vetiver

SOUNDS/RHYTHMS
well-tempered clavier, the Tijuana Brass

MUSICAL NOTES
F# and A

DEEP SPACE OBJECT
NGC 7261, galactic cluster

April 1

YOUR SIGN
Aries

YOUR ELEMENT
Fire

YOUR RULERS
Mars, Sun
11–12 degrees
Second Decanate, yin

The Astrological Interpretation

Aries is a sign of beginnings. You easily endow a plan or project with a tremendous burst of initial energy, but then enthusiasm may wane and you are off in search of another adventure. You share this trait with your brother and sister rams. But your particular birth date offers the symbol for "preparation." It is up to you to gather the necessary tools and supplies for your specific life battles and conquests. You will find that at any given point in your life, knowledge, love, or willpower will need to be perfected—and they will alternate in cycles. If it is knowledge that you require at the moment, obtain it through right study. If it is love, work at more open communication with the person who is currently touching your heart. If it is willpower, take on a task or responsibility that needs a great deal of self-discipline and don't give up until it is done.

This birthday has a profound impulse toward freedom and a will to go about life in its own way. The goal is to get as much fun out of life and explore new horizons—both physically and mentally. Your living space will reflect this sign's individuality. Lawn furniture in your living room? April 1 likes the outdoors, and being reminded of long summer days in the midst of winter pleases your sense of whimsy. A magnifying glass is handy to keep around, as you like to see clearly. Glass tables and hardwood floors keep your home environment light. Country landscapes should hang on the walls, and a few clusters of quartz crystals will keep your energy flowing consistently.

Outdoors you like to be high on a hill to catch the sunrise and watch flocks of birds as they migrate. A bench situated under a wide spreading chestnut tree is an ideal outdoor setting for your pet projects. Perhaps there is a place for croquet? April 1 loves to compete, and knocking wooden balls through hoops satisfies the urge to play.

A Kabbalistic Interpretation

Thanks to the association of this day with the Hierophant card from the tarot, you are likely to find yourself dwelling on spiritual issues and concepts. Your religious interests are wide ranging and fairly eclectic. As circle shapes are lucky for you, an authentic dream catcher would be an ideal object for you to hang over your bed.

As your friends and colleagues are aware already, you are an exceedingly generous individual. It is most likely that this characteristic manifests itself through your willingness to listen to other people and spend time with them when they need company. As with many unselfish individuals you may tend to neglect your own needs. If you carry a sprig of basil in your pocket at all times your financial needs should, at least, be taken care of.

Born this day, you are unusually passive for an Aries character. A clever use of color, such as always wearing a touch of red, along with the addition of a flint paperweight on your desk, should grant you more confidence to take the initiative about things.

A Numerological Interpretation
YOUR MAGIC NUMBERS: 5 AND 2

The first day of the fourth month reduces to five, the number of agency and process, the principle of order that proceeds from the abstract law of the number four. This day carries the path of developing an ample but impersonal ego. Inauguration ceremonies inspire you. Volunteer for a political campaign. Run for president of whatever group you belong to. Get feedback on how you affect people. You can unknowingly leave singed eyebrows in your wake. Do something fun. All work and no play makes for dullness. Strive for impersonal expression of the life force. Fire agate and red jasper will heighten your resolve. The ninety-second day of the year reduces to two, adding the quality of dependence on a higher order for inspiration.

OBJECTS/IMAGES
a baseball cap, red lipstick, wrought iron candlesticks,

SHAPES/MATERIALS
the square, Indian cotton, Corinthian columns

COLORS
spring green, scarlet red, red violet, coppery yellow

ANIMALS
wild goose, rooster, bighorn sheep

PLANTS, HERBS, EDIBLES
garlic, red peppers, holly, nettles

ESSENCES
the smell of a just lit match, patchouli, raspberry essence

SOUNDS/RHYTHMS
bongo drums and Australian didjerdu

MUSICAL NOTES
E and C#

DEEP SPACE OBJECTS
Alpha Cepheus, Alderamin

April 2

YOUR SIGN
Aries

YOUR ELEMENT
Fire

YOUR RULERS
Mars, Sun
12–13 degrees
Second Decanate, yin

The Astrological Interpretation

Many people born this day are infused with a great degree of strength, which leads them up the ladder until they reach a fine plateau of success. But this is not enough. Your nature requires that you challenge life and be challenged in return. But what equipment have you brought with you for your journey of self-exploration? You will find that your crises come about when you try to use methods from the past on the new situations confronting you. You have to continue to acquire more education or the knowledge you employ in your tasks will be naive and useless. It is necessary to find a special teacher or definite teaching that can take you to the next step of your development. Do not let pride or impatience stand in your way. Approach life with courage but also have a good dose of humility.

Ancient astrologers considered that degrees close to April 2 designated skill in medicine. Whether or not you pursue a medical career, you bring intuition and energy to your life and work. Patience is not one of your strong suits, and you may feel that life moves too slowly for you. Keep your energies buoyant with physical exercise and mental stimulation. Golf may be an excellent way for you to relax. Other interesting sports are fencing, mountain climbing, or martial arts. At home keep open spaces; have furniture such as canvas director's chairs that can be easily moved. A meditation image for you is an inverted blue triangle embedded in gold. Hang on to this image and it will help you discern what is on the path of your true calling and what is not.

Outdoors you may enjoy having a toolshed or workroom area in the garage. Male or female, you have mechanical ability and should have whatever tools necessary for the job. In your yard a decorative iron fence would appeal to you. You might also have scrolled wrought iron around a garden plot filled with red and yellow flowers.

A Kabbalistic Interpretation

You may often find yourself confronted with choices between two options of seemingly equal merit. It is wonderful to have so many choices in life and such a range of interests, but the downside of this path is that you can find it hard to make decisions about dilemmas, whether they are important or trivial. One way you can remove that constant decision-making struggle is to take the decision away. Flipping a gold medallion or other coin is a technique you can use whenever you feel stuck at a crossroads.

Possibly as a result of being unable to say no to the many possibilities that come your way, people born today tend to have a host of somewhat unusual hobbies. Collecting insects, either as specimens or as pets, is an ideal avocation for someone celebrating a birthday today. A locust or a stag beetle is an excellent insect to look for.

This is an excellent day for you to be born if you want to attract a lot of partners. If you have met someone born today and want to be certain of keeping them, buy some civet perfume and they will be unable to resist you.

A Numerological Interpretation
YOUR MAGIC NUMBERS: 6 AND 3

The second day of the fourth month reduces to six, the number of balanced polarities. You seem a contradiction to your family and friends. You are capable of an enigmatic, carefree indifference that causes some to label you eccentric. But your homing instincts are keen and your course true, no matter how haphazard it may appear to others. You are driven by a burning desire for freedom.

The ninety-third day of the year reduces to three, contributing the essence of pure expression to your boundless exuberance. Listen to soaring melodies, which will lift your spirits. Lift your own voice in song and transcend the moment. Study the patterns and behavior of migratory fowl and homing pigeons. Red and green jasper will connect you to the earth.

OBJECTS/IMAGES
engravings, freckles, jackknives, scalpels

SHAPES/MATERIALS
garnets, red hematite, shape of a battle shield

COLORS
fire engine red, moss green, carrot

ANIMALS
eagle, falcon

PLANTS, HERBS, EDIBLES
jack-in-the-pulpit, wild coffee, red morning glory

ESSENCE
pimento

SOUNDS/RHYTHMS
bongo drums, a siren

MUSICAL NOTES
F and D

DEEP SPACE OBJECT
Van Maanan's Star

April 3

YOUR SIGN
Aries

YOUR ELEMENT
Fire

YOUR RULERS
Mars, Sun
13–14 degrees
Second Decanate, yin

The Astrological Interpretation

Your sense of your individuality is strong but there is a need for a complement in a partner. You require a partner who is not merely emotionally and physically compatible but also mentally alive and able to keep up with the rapidity and potency of your mind. If your lover is too docile, you will reject him or her as not being stimulating enough. If your lover is too strong willed and independent, you will feel that your needs are not being recognized and supported. No matter how agreeable and cooperative, your partner also wants to be accepted by you. You therefore have to be very clear to leave a space within yourself where you can identify, embrace, and nurture your partner's needs.

April 3, in the constellation of Aries, is located near the fixed star Alpheratz, which is described as a double, purple-hued, white star. It attracts a great deal of attention because of its brilliance. April 3 people have a light about them that is bound to lead them to unique, trailblazing opportunities. The great question is how to use all this energy creatively? Stock your pantry with nutritious food because your fire needs stoking. Also keep the furniture in your home simple so you have plenty of room to jump on a minitrampoline, do stretches, or use a NordicTrack. A personal gym is a wonderful luxury. A powerful shape for you is a bright blue triangle. On the few occasions when you are relaxing in the bathtub have some effervescent bath salts. The bubbles will keep you entertained and encourage a good soak.

Outdoors, plan on wide open spaces so that you have room to maneuver. A hopscotch court painted on the driveway would be a nice reminder of childhood. Either your home or yard should face southeast. If you are ever doing a creative project consider moving your workspace with the sun's rays.

A Kabbalistic Interpretation

People born on April 3 have little time for relaxation and much prefer activities that get the adrenaline flowing. You may tend to treat each task as an absolute urgent priority. While this is a good trait in a crisis, over the long haul it can prove unhealthy for you. Meditation can help, but you may not slow down long enough to give it a try. A mixture of lavender and heather in a tall thin glass vase may remind you to take things a little easier.

You are likely to be interested in rock climbing or other rigorous outdoor activities. Your home should reflect your taste for adventure—you might consider photographing and framing some of your exploits and decorating your living room with the results.

The one thing that mitigates your ceaseless activity is your passion for music. Make this your meditation. You love gadgets of all kinds, so you can go all out and get yourself a state-of-the-art sound system. If you have enough space in your home, reserve a whole room for your listening pleasure. Put nothing in this room that can disrupt the experience. To really enhance your listening, burn some cedar wood incense while you enjoy your favorites.

A Numerological Interpretation
YOUR MAGIC NUMBERS: 7 AND 4

The third day of the fourth month reduces to seven, a number that means victory. Creation is accomplished, and there is a pause to step back and admire the handiwork. This day's path is paradoxical. If you approach your goals with anything less than a purity of intention, your efforts will be nullified. You have a characteristic impulsiveness that causes you to charge forward into circumstances and think about them afterward. Look before your leap. Endeavor to lengthen your fuse.

The ninety-fourth day of the year reduces to four, adding the quality of reason to mitigate your tendency to be impetuous. Moonstone and turquoise will calm your ardor.

OBJECTS/IMAGES
a snow globe with a mountain scene, an ornate letter opener, a painting of the sun

SHAPES/MATERIALS
light topaz, hardwoods, bricks

COLORS
flaming red, yellow, orange, emerald green

ANIMALS
serpent, mountain lion, sheep

PLANTS, HERBS, EDIBLES
fuchsia, wild anemones, barbecued ribs

ESSENCE
black pepper

SOUNDS/RHYTHMS
sound of squabbles, timpani, gongs

MUSICAL NOTES
F# and D#

DEEP SPACE OBJECTS
Alpha Andromeda, Alpheratz, Head of the Woman in Chains

April 4

YOUR SIGN
Aries

YOUR ELEMENT
Fire

YOUR RULERS
Mars, Sun
14–15 degrees
Second Decanate, yin

The Astrological Interpretation

What brings peace and harmony into your life? It would be wise for you to stop for a few minutes each day to contemplate the answer to this important question. You are an individual who tends to move outward into life, opening up pathways to a constant series of adventures. You feel that you have an inner mission, even if that goal is the attainment of some degree of material success. You can be so self-stimulating that it may be difficult for you to find any degree of natural relaxation and repose. If you do not concentrate some of your energy on stillness, you will find yourself constantly irritated by the concept of what you do not possess and what you have not achieved. In order not to burn yourself out, it is vital that you acquire the ability to pull back and listen to life. Look to the arts, the simplicity of nature, and the wonder of a child for the inspiration to awaken your own inner and outer balance.

Although April 4 is a fire birthday you may have a great attraction to the water and to swimming. Sports in general suit you. Golfing, sailing, and volleyball are a few possibilities. If you are not a sports person try ballroom dancing. Moving in time to music or rhythm is enjoyable and a good way to calm yourself. At home, April 4 will enjoy a rustic touch. Wooden beams and plain plank tables and chairs are simple clear lines that you enjoy. Keep succulents and cacti as houseplants. The desert plants remind you of the sun and the succulents of water. Diamonds are a gemstone that you may have an affinity for. Both men and women will enjoy the sparkling colors more than the status or value.

Outdoors April 4 is happy on a landscaped area with curves and rolling hills. A polo field might be attractive, and the speed of polo attracts you. Speed car racing, riding dirt bikes, or swinging from a tree all create the motion you crave.

A Kabbalistic Interpretation

If you had been born in an earlier time you would undoubtedly have been a warrior. Although there are few opportunities for freelance warriors these days, you can reflect your nature by adding a military touch to your home—a copy of a medieval shield, a samurai suit of armor, or a pair of dueling swords would be a very appealing addition to your house.

Like many people born under the sign of Aries you have a strong desire for wealth and position. The kabbalistic values of this day mark you out as someone who is swift to spot a gap in the market or a promotional opportunity well before the competition. You can help your ambitions along by keeping a leather pouch with some dried deadly nightshade in a drawer in your office. It is important to note that this plant is extremely dangerous and should never be absorbed into the body—so handle it with extreme care.

A Numerological Interpretation
YOUR MAGIC NUMBERS: 8 AND 5

The fourth day of the fourth month reduces to eight, the number of infinite back-and-forth movement of all the energy in the universe. The number eight on its side is the lemniscate, symbol of eternity, which moves like a serpent coiling back and forth upon itself. As you engage your subjective side, the significance of events in your life will be revealed to you. Pay attention, and you will gain a deeper understanding. The ninety-fifth day of the year reduces to five, the number of change, which enhances your awareness of life's constant flux.

Amber, topaz, and malachite are complementary gems for your personality. Listen to the music of a sitar and ponder the mystery of the Indian snake charmer and the sinuous movement of the snake. The cobra is deaf; the snake is charmed not by the sound but by the movement of the hands. The horn charms the audience, not the serpent.

OBJECTS/IMAGES
daggers, cadets, carpenters, freckles

SHAPES/MATERIALS
mahogany wood, brimstone, cinnabar, pointed shapes

COLORS
crimson, teal, butter yellow

ANIMALS
lamb, wasp

PLANTS, HERBS, EDIBLES
geraniums, horseradish, basil, chewing tobacco, cumin

ESSENCE
coriander

SOUNDS/RHYTHMS
drums, Elmer Bernstein's score to The Ten Commandments

MUSICAL NOTES
G and E

DEEP SPACE OBJECT
Pi Fornax

April 5

YOUR SIGN
Aries

YOUR ELEMENT
Fire

YOUR RULERS
Mars, Sun
15–16 degrees
Second Decanate, yang

The Astrological Interpretation

You are like a general seeking to lead an army of one—yourself. Once your battle plan is conceived, there is no turning back. You must move forward to attempt the conquest of your objectives. Your natural martial energy is great for opening the necessary doors or breaking down defensive walls so that your creative ideas may take root and flourish. If it is a love interest that you are pursuing, you will make your intentions clearly known. In all you do, the old statement that "the loss of a single battle does not mean the end of the war" holds true. You have persistence and fortitude and will definitely continue the fight.

This birthday has a natural beat to which you can tune in to guide your life. Dancing is an extension of your native exuberance. Decorate with mirrors. You will enjoy the reflected light and catching a glimpse of yourself as you parade by. Prisms hanging in the windows are a way to bring color and light into your environment. The bedroom and work area can be smaller, but you would love to have a big central living room where you can have friends over.

Your personal style includes comfortable clothes that do not require lots of care. Cherry tones and sunny colors are good for both sexes. With Mars as ruler, you may be partial to military styles and insignias. Perhaps a painting or bust of an ancient Samurai warrior will help direct your energy toward your goals.

Working in the yard under the sun is a good way to slow your pace. The golf course is a peaceful place, even if you don't play, and doing yoga exercises in the open air will go a long way to calming your formidable energy. There is an ancient connection between farming and April 5.

A Kabbalistic Interpretation

People born this day may well have some characteristics in common with their astrological sign's symbol, the goat. You have a tendency to take life head on and full steam ahead. You may not be inclined to take the time to organize your life as you charge straight for your goal, but it really is a necessity. You can encourage yourself to plan ahead by purchasing a small square of steel and keeping it in your desk drawer.

Certain elements related to this day suggest that you are a bit fussy at times and are usually conservative in your dress and your attitudes. This can manifest itself in some positive ways, as you have a strong moral stance on most issues. In a relativistic world this dose of moral clarity can be refreshing. You can afford to lighten up somewhat and could try wearing something silver next time you go to a party. You should find it helps you to let go and enjoy yourself.

You have a strong interest in history and in particular are likely to be attracted to the prehistory of our own species. You could make a serious study of human evolution. You might want to acquire a primate or human skull for a study or library.

A Numerological Interpretation
YOUR MAGIC NUMBERS: 9 AND 6

The fifth day of the fourth month reduces to nine, a number signifying the end of a cycle. You carry the drive for attainment, and this day's energy imbues you with diligence. You derive satisfaction from excellence in the expression of basic skills. The crafts of your culture give you a sense of pride. Hang handwoven Navajo blankets or tapestries on your walls. Savor the richness of the wool, the colors of the dyes. Run your hand across the knobby texture. Watch honeybees in the hive or birds building a nest. Produce something with your hands. Bake a pie or cookies from scratch. Azurite and malachite will build your endurance. The ninety-sixth day of the year reduces to six, contributing the influence of balance and equilibration.

OBJECTS/IMAGES
a fireman's helmet, a flashlight pen, a cast iron incense burner

SHAPES/MATERIALS
lava rocks, amethyst, arc shapes

COLORS
yellow-orange, magenta, ochre, royal blue, lime green

ANIMALS
tiger, mastiff dog, woodpecker

PLANTS, HERBS, EDIBLES
ginger, ginger flowers, red cyclamen, pepper

ESSENCES
charcoal burning, violet

SOUNDS/RHYTHMS
sound of armies charging, tap dancing, timpani

MUSICAL NOTES
G# and F

DEEP SPACE OBJECT
Nu Fornax

April 6

YOUR SIGN
Aries

YOUR ELEMENT
Fire

YOUR RULERS
Mars, Sun
16–17 degrees
Second Decanate, yang

The Astrological Interpretation

When it comes to achieving your goals, you work with amazing speed and directness of action. It takes very little to galvanize you into action when the object of your desires is in front of you, but sometimes you may use more force than is necessary. The symbolic meaning of your birth date does not ask you to diminish your power, but to be more conscious of its direction and level of intensity. It is important for you to know how to modulate your "frequency" so that you do not waste your energy or destroy what you wish to create. You may need much less force and much more subtlety when it comes to relationships. Other people are more sensitive than you give them credit for, and you do not need to take out all of your guns, tanks, and artillery to win over the man or woman of your choice. Try a little tenderness.

April 6 enjoys speculating on the intangible and secret aspects of life. Philosophy, the occult, and innovative scientific and engineering research may all be areas for your exuberant energy. You are a romantic and can express your softer side with your heart's desire. Magic tricks might be an interesting hobby for you. At home decorate with touches of red, it will signify heart energy as well as courage. A stone for you is rhodochrosite. Keep candles wherever you read or do quiet work; they will increase your concentration. Houseplants such as peperomia and sword ferns will help balance your ardor. In the kitchen keep lots of spices at hand.

Outdoors, April 6 loves natural beauty. Exercising outdoors is preferable to the gym, and running in sight of spring flowers such as forsythia and crocuses is a special pleasure. Perhaps a jungle gym in your backyard will provide you with a venue for accomplishing many feats.

A Kabbalistic Interpretation

You love comforts and luxuries of all kinds. Indeed you love your comforts almost as much as you love your family, yet the joy you find in material objects does not make you selfish in any way. The best color for this day is a bright yellow-orange, as it reflects the association of this date with solar energy. A possible kitchen decoration would be a large plaque bearing a stylized image of the sun.

You tend to be exceptionally lucky in life. In spite of your natural good fortune you may tend to be superstitious and could easily have a rabbit's foot or other charm hanging in your car. An ornamental horseshoe or a cast-iron four-leaf clover for your desk is a great gift.

Sensitivity is not exactly your strong suit, and your taste in music matches your personality—loud, brash, and full of positive energy and enthusiasm for life. You would definitely derive pleasure from investing in a drum kit. Play this when you are alone during the day.

A Numerological Interpretation
YOUR MAGIC NUMBERS: 10 AND 7

The sixth day of the fourth month reduces to ten, the number signifying dominion. Intrinsic to this day is a kinship with the elements and forces of nature. Einstein once said, "I believe the universe is friendly." You are invigorated by the dance of life, eternally acting out and celebrating the endless facets of existence and expression.

Place bright red poppies on your dining table. Build a sunset fire on the beach and see the sky ignite into a blaze of color. Wiggle your toes in the sand, listen to the surf, and watch children dance in the fading light, joyfully closing a perfect day. The ninety-seventh day of the year reduces to seven, adding the quality of celebration at harvest and rest after labor. Emerald and sodalite will soothe you.

OBJECTS/IMAGES
hat pins, pistols, alchemical signs

SHAPES/MATERIALS
flax, almandine, crude oils, malachite

COLORS
orange, navy blue, kelly green

ANIMALS
panther, wasp

PLANTS, HERBS, EDIBLES
pine sap, crimson pitcher plant, Peruvian bark, retsina wine

ESSENCE
vervain

SOUNDS/RHYTHMS
sound of an argument, timpani

MUSICAL NOTES
A and F#

DEEP SPACE OBJECT
Delta Cepheus

April 7

YOUR SIGN
Aries

YOUR ELEMENT
Fire

YOUR RULERS
Mars, Sun
16–17 degrees
Second Decanate, yang

The Astrological Interpretation

This is an Aries birth date that requires the individual to acquire inner repose and emotional balance. You are full of fiery energy and possess a real eagerness for life. You seek to project yourself endlessly forward into the many adventures and enterprises that call to you. Sometimes you are like a child in a huge toy shop—everything shines and glistens with potential fun and excitement! Yet it is important to realize that you have to pay for every toy that you take out of its box. It is therefore critical to think a few steps ahead. Do I really need it? What will happen when I take it home? Will I still want to play with my new toy in the weeks and months ahead? These words are not meant to dampen your genuine enthusiasm, they are just to remind you of the consequences that come with your actions. Your success in life will come when you begin to think in terms of complete cycles and not just initiating actions.

April 7 has an unusual combination of dynamic physical energy and metaphysical interests. The balance April 7 seeks is between supporting artistic or spiritual visions and the demands of making a living. Martial arts are a perfect activity for you, as they combine the physical and spiritual. Learn a few magic tricks. You can amuse yourself and your friends. At home, decorative ironworks such as a fireplace set and andirons are perfect for your Mars nature. Keep a box of long, scented matches for lighting your fire. In the bedroom your yang energy needs calming. Try a paisley comforter or sheets that blend earth tones with a touch of crimson. Carrying a magnet may also keep your energy flowing and your mind clear.

Your outdoor space could include room for sports and a shady glen. April 7 likes to be industrious outdoors and doesn't care to loll around. Trees that are particularly well suited to you are red birch and prickly pear. If you have a garden, wear a special straw hat with streamers—it will signify playtime to you.

A Kabbalistic Interpretation

One of the possible values for this day is eleven, a number that symbolizes magic itself in Western occultism. Other influences in this day point to an interest in religious truths, so someone born April 7 will likely seek a path involving spiritual pursuits. You might be inspired in your interests by a painting or symbol from pre-Christian religions such as a reproduction of Egyptian hieroglyphics.

There are connections in this day to the Hebrew spelling of the name Eve. You share Eve's insatiable curiosity about the world. This can lead to some wonderful surprises, but it also carries the potential for taking some ill-advised risks. A turquoise carried in your pocket or worn as a necklace may grant some protection when you find yourself in the difficult circumstances that arise from your natural curiosity.

You have a thoughtful and agile mind that rarely relaxes. To avoid headaches or melancholy that may result from your mind's ceaseless activity, meditate in a clarifying bath with some essence of citrus poured in the bathwater.

A Numerological Interpretation

YOUR MAGIC NUMBERS: 2 AND 8

The seventh day of the fourth month reduces to two, a number meaning duplication. This day carries the energy and the ability for you to meet your emotional needs by looking only within yourself. You can be totally self-sustaining and may choose to affiliate only with someone who appears to be identical to you to the exclusion of all others. Self-sufficiency is a strength, but not when carried to the extreme of isolation.

The ninety-eighth day of the year reduces to eight, contributing the influence of reciprocity to aid you in opening up to others. Involve yourself in some civic, social, or volunteer organization. Observe a soloist in a choir or orchestra. Throw a patchwork quilt of diverse fabrics on your bed. Have a bowl of potpourri on your credenza. Make a stew of many blended ingredients.

OBJECTS/IMAGES
a blacksmith's forge, wood carvings, knives

SHAPES/MATERIALS
acute angles, cinnabar

COLORS
discordant hues, holly berry red, crimson, turquoise

ANIMALS
rooster, wild pony

PLANTS, HERBS, EDIBLE
barberry, aloes, Red Hots

ESSENCES
the smell of coffee, juniper

SOUNDS/RHYTHMS
drums, tap dance rhythm, bagpipes

MUSICAL NOTES
C# and G

DEEP SPACE OBJECT
Lambda Andromeda

April 8

YOUR SIGN
Aries

YOUR ELEMENT
Fire

YOUR RULERS
Mars, Sun
17–18 degrees
Second Decanate, yang

The Astrological Interpretation

Your birth date suggests that you will move further in life through the use of mental agility than by force of will. People do not like to be manipulated. They do admire creative initiative and cultivated intelligence. Learn how to mold and structure your ideas and concepts and hold them within yourself until they are clear and distinct. Then when you release them, your ideas will speak for themselves and you will not need to use the force of your personality to get the cooperation that you need. You have intuitive insight into life and know how to guide people through their confusion and uncertainty in order to reach their goals. The important thing is not to be too attached to results. Offer your advice and counsel and then leave it to the other person to follow through (or not) on what you say.

Your romantic passions run high, and combining love and physical passion is important to you. Try to negotiate a peace settlement between your need for battle and your desire for relationship. At home, April 8 will enjoy furniture that is low to the ground and very casual. Scattered pillows or even an indoor-outdoor hammock might appeal to you. Dance could be the best outlet for your creative and physical energies. A studio or space in your home with room to move would be a great luxury. Put music on while you are cleaning up or doing the dishes and dance around. You don't really need formal training but you do need physical release. You might also benefit from carrying a piece of rose quartz or wearing some rose quartz jewelry.

Outdoors, April 8 likes space to move. Ascending a climbing wall, whether at the gym or at home, could be a very interesting exercise for you. Hang some ropes from chestnut trees and play Tarzan. You'll enjoy the drama as well as the sensation.

A Kabbalistic Interpretation

People born today are the soul of generosity. You only need ask an April 8 native for help and you will see heaven and earth moved on your behalf. Although others are appreciative of this altruistic approach to life, if this is your birthday, you will need to act selfishly from time to time in order to have a fulfilling life. If you wish to encourage some-one born this day to consider his or her own wishes, buy a rich indigo brooch or tiepin and suggest your friend wear it every day.

The connection of the tarot card the Sun to this day indicates that you have a natural affinity for and understanding of young people. No matter how old you become, there will always be a touch of the child about you. Children sense this and tend to gravitate to you. You also may well enjoy traditional board games.

If you were born on this day you like to keep your house nice and bright, with plenty of light streaming in through the windows. Find some stained glass panels or ornaments to hang in the windows so that the light splits into a rainbow of color reflected on the walls of your rooms.

A Numerological Interpretation
YOUR MAGIC NUMBERS: 3 AND 9

The eighth day of the fourth month reduces to three, signifying growth and unfoldment, the initial outward expression of the principles of one and two. This day endows you with the tendency to ponder over past events and choices. You strive to reconcile and reorient your inner reality with your outer reality, and then make the necessary adjustments to assure that your outer reality is the adjusted expression of that shift. You yearn to see significance.

The ninety-ninth day of the year reduces to nine, adding the quality of clear, pure working out of the original seed idea. Allow time for reflection, but get into the action. Don't succumb to analysis paralysis. Be spontaneous for the sake of the experience. Hang paintings of pastoral scenes where they will inspire your sense of continuity. All forms of agate will be soothing and healing. Visit the country and watch animals at pasture.

OBJECTS/IMAGES
axes, gauntlets, diamond cutters, furnaces

SHAPES/MATERIALS
diamonds, a Maltese cross, red hematite

COLORS
khaki, coral, sky blue

ANIMAL
rooster

PLANTS, HERBS, EDIBLES
watercress, cuckoopint (herb), hollyhocks, pepperoni

ESSENCE
geranium

SOUNDS/RHYTHMS
overtures, male flamenco dancing

MUSICAL NOTES
D and G#

DEEP SPACE OBJECT
NGC 615, spiral galaxy

April 9

YOUR SIGN
Aries

YOUR ELEMENT
Fire

YOUR RULERS
Mars, Sun
18–19 degrees
Second Decanate, yang

The Astrological Interpretation

You are very romantic by nature and have a great need to be in the right relationship. No doubt you have experimented a great deal. Sometimes you are too forceful in overcoming other people's resistance to your attentions. You win the battle but then lose interest in the prize. Your birth date reveals that you have to learn the difference between desire and love. The heart allows the two to be combined, and you can indeed be sexual with the person you love. But you have made the mistake in the past of creating romantic illusions around the object of your desires. You may need at times to consider your real needs. Are you trying to provide the love for the both of you? Is your partner capable of sustaining your fiery disposition, adding the fuel that nurtures your flames? Can you in return offer consistency, steadfastness, and abiding loyalty? Make sure you use your head as well as your body and incorporate compassion into your passion.

April 9 is interested in life's far-reaching potentials. You have a great deal of dynamic force and can assert your imagination in a variety of fields. The theater interests you as well as music and politics. In your home have a centrally placed carpet that you like. It could be Persian or Oriental or have some other brightly colored design. The image is a magic carpet that can take you on flights of fancy. Elsewhere in your home, April 9 is more practical and likes to have brightly colored dishes and tableware. A set of Depression red glasses and plates may be prized possessions. In your kitchen consider hanging garlands of dried peppers and garlic. You may want to keep your walls white and have accents of color. If you have any military heirlooms in your family, display them.

Outdoors, April 9 likes to have a panoramic view. The east is a good direction for you, and a house on the corner feels right. Cast-iron garden furniture complements a garden of red and gold flowers such as marigolds, chives, and celosia.

A Kabbalistic Interpretation

You may be greatly concerned with matters of physical health. As knowledge is power, get your hands on a good medical encyclopedia and a book about integrated medicine. A rose quartz placed under the pillow at night will help alleviate excessive medical fears.

People born today are generally quite brave individuals. You probably have no difficulty speaking out at social injustice and may be critical of many established institutions. The rebel within you does need to learn to wait for the best time to speak out. If you keep a small pot with sage and rue on the south side of your desk you will find it easier to pick your battles and keep your cool when necessary.

People born on this date can make excellent chefs, as this date favors the culinary arts. Experiment with new recipes and varied ingredients from all over the world. An ideal gift for you is a big barbecue and an enormous range of spices.

A Numerological Interpretation

YOUR MAGIC NUMBERS: 4 AND 1

The ninth day of the fourth month reduces to four, the number of order, measurement, and gaining the lay of the land. This day engenders a visionary scope to your logical mind. This is a path similar to the bicycle mechanics who achieved historic flight. Stretch your imagination, and indulge your flights of fancy. This will enrich your everyday endeavors. Enjoy a fantasy painting of mythological Pegasus. Read the *Arabian Nights*. Sail away on a magic carpet in your imagination. Smell exotic spices and campfires. Grow a night-blooming cactus. Citrine and tigereye will open your mind. The one hundredth day of the year reduces to one, adding the quality of originality and singleness of purpose to the breadth of your perspective.

OBJECTS/IMAGES
stakes, shields, ovens, and carved incense burners

SHAPES/MATERIALS
sandstone, granite pegmatite, rubies, spiky shapes

COLORS
crimson red, tangerine, scarlet

ANIMAL
wolverine

PLANTS, HERBS, EDIBLES
sarsaparilla, savin, plantain, prickly pear

ESSENCE
mastic

SOUNDS/RHYTHMS
musical scale of G, shouts, grand opera

MUSICAL NOTES
D# and C

DEEP SPACE OBJECT
quasar

April 10

YOUR SIGN
Aries

YOUR ELEMENT
Fire

YOUR RULERS
Mars, Sun
19–20 degrees
Second Decanate, yang

The Astrological Interpretation

Your birth date indicates a highly individualistic person; you are very much your own boss. It is much easier for you to be in competition with others than to be cooperative. You like to take the initiative, hate to wait on lines, and are always looking for shortcuts. It is important to realize that there are much larger and more inclusive cycles at work than the urgency to fulfill our particular needs. You are admired by your friends and associates for your courage and the direct way you express yourself. Yet you are sometimes resisted because of an aggressive attitude that does not take other people into consideration. It is your responsibility to turn this around and use your will intelligently. It is when the "I am" in you realizes the "we are" of life that you will have great success.

Your abundant fiery energy spills out into the world. This birthday offers the challenge of sharing your abilities as well as nurturing others. The home is a place to breeze through; give yourself enough space and remove clutter. The kitchen should have a gas stove and a barbecue unit if you have room. Metal sculpture is a welcome decorative touch; choose angular shapes and burnished metals. This birthday traditionally has a connection with mining; hanging an old miner's lamp on the wall may keep you in touch with the earth and slow your formidable energy.

If your space is very sunny have curtains or venetian blinds, which can moderate the sun. Too much light will interfere with your rest. Keep the bedroom cool, with light blankets on the bed. Paisley patterns are calming.

Outdoors, you like to look up at the mountains from a village or town. In your own garden create a small hill with red flowers. A metal wind chime keeps your energy high. A bird feeder where cardinals can gather will be a delight.

A Kabbalistic Interpretation

People born today have a fascination for what might be called the dark side, although this interest is mostly restricted to its fictional aspects. At the cinema you are happiest watching the latest horror movie, and your idea of a perfect evening at home may be curling up with a special friend and a collection of Vincent Price films. A fantastic present for you could be some framed classic horror movie posters.

Laid-back is a good way to describe you. You are an unusually tolerant person, and your natural openness promotes an interest in all forms of culture and lifestyles. You can reflect these passions in your home by including design touches with global inspirations, from pillars on either side of your front door to batik-printed tablecloths for your kitchen table.

Be sure to engage in some kind of brisk activity every day. You may find an affinity for activities that take you outdoors. Learn to rollerblade. Do Tai Chi in the park. Get yourself a terrier and go for a run in the woods.

A Numerological Interpretation
YOUR MAGIC NUMBERS: 5 AND 2

The tenth day of the fourth month reduces to five, a number that is characterized by mediation and versatility. This day imbues you with a generosity of spirit and a desire to be the means of nourishing the needs of others. You feel moved to share with other forms of life because you posses an intrinsic sense of how you are nourished and supported by Life.

The 101st day of the year reduces to two, contributing both the influence of receptivity and the understanding of the reciprocity of all living things. Keep bird feeders and watch the seasonal changes. Memorize birdsongs and colors. Imagine the moment when a bird is fearless enough to eat from your hand. What an act of faith and a response to your openheartedness. Place a statue of Saint Francis in your garden. Plant daffodils. Ruby, topaz, and moonstone will minister to your sensitivity.

OBJECTS/IMAGES
fire swallowers, stopwatch, bubbling champagne

SHAPES/MATERIALS
spears, pillbox hats, garnets, hibachi grills, cast iron

COLORS
scarlet, pink gold, sunflower yellow, sunshine yellow, russet

---

ANIMALS
golden retriever, bighorn sheep, sunfish

PLANTS, HERBS, EDIBLES
poppy, coxcombs, capsicum, chili peppers

ESSENCE
burning sage

SOUNDS/RHYTHMS
firecrackers exploding, beguine, macarena

MUSICAL NOTES
E and C#

DEEP SPACE OBJECT
Xi Cetus

April 11

YOUR SIGN
Aries

YOUR ELEMENT
Fire

YOUR RULERS
Mars, Jupiter
20–21 degrees
Third Decanate, yang

The Astrological Interpretation

Your sense of your own individual creative potency can mature to a very inclusive state and create a very fulfilling life. You can be in groups without having to be the leader. People respect you because you are always respectful of others. You do not easily compromise, but you are eager to facilitate collective decisions in which everyone may emerge a winner. That is the nature of human relationships. Your success will only be limited when you lose sight of or have not fully developed the more positive side of your nature. You will then misinterpret the good of others for your own good, family needs for personal needs, group direction for individual goals. Once you learn how to stand on the right side of this line, you will go very far.

The topaz-yellow fixed star Baten Kaitos, or the Whale's Belly, is very close to some April 11 birthdays. In ancient times, this fixed star ruled accidents and shipwrecks (rescued). Perhaps the ancient astrologers noticed the strength of energy with which April 11 attacks life. You may never have an accident but you are a fearless fighter. Consider exerting your energies in activities that require a sprinter's rhythm. Short bursts of energy are more effective for you than long sustained activity. To keep your energy percolating keep ginseng around. Your kitchen should have gas burners, and you may find that a gas barbecue is your favorite way to cook. Surround your bed with lots of pillows, dark reds, and earth tones. You may prefer a bed high off the floor. A backpack is an essential item to remind you of intrepid adventures that await.

Outdoors, focus on a sports arena rather than a beautiful garden. April 11 wants to be where the action is, and physical activity is a great way to exert yourself. If your taste runs to more meditative sports consider aikido or yoga, but try to practice outdoors. You need air and space.

A Kabbalistic Interpretation

Privacy is important to you. Think of locating in a quiet suburban area or, ideally, out in the country, as heavily populated or built up areas can make you feel claustrophobic. Make sure to put a hedge around your yard or property. A row of hawthorn bushes bestows good fortune on its owners.

As an individual you are driven by instinct more than logic. You have a strong inclination to unbridled passion romantically, and you tend to fall in lust with your partners as much as you fall in love with them. Though this is good for passionate romances, you may find this works against you when you wish to establish a more serious relationship. Because you may find more than one person you are strongly attracted to, you could risk losing someone who is genuinely important to you emotionally. If you are in a serious relationship then you should keep a water lily on your desk at work and also burn some frankincense candles or essential oils each evening when you get home.

A Numerological Interpretation

YOUR MAGIC NUMBERS: 6 AND 3

The eleventh day of the fourth month reduces to six, a number of balanced polarities and harmony of opposites. This path asks for the quality of living your life out loud for all the world to see and learn from. You exude self-confidence and feel capable of resolving and harmonizing conflicts within yourself and would-be opponents. You like to do things in style with an audience.

The 102nd day of the year reduces to three, which adds the energy of unfolding self-expression. Try Toastmasters, a debate team, or a martial arts class. Watch political debates and practice defending both sides of the issue. Jasper and agate will strengthen you.

OBJECTS/IMAGES
*an old-fashioned coffeepot,
a tennis racket*

SHAPES/MATERIALS
sharp angles, bouclé material

COLORS
*carmine red, chartreuse,
salmon*

ANIMALS
kite, fox

PLANTS, HERBS, EDIBLES
*hyacinth,
broom brush tea tree*

ESSENCE
pimento

SOUNDS/RHYTHMS
*laughter, crackling fire,
clog dancing*

MUSICAL NOTES
F and D

DEEP SPACE OBJECT
Eta Andromeda

April 12

The Astrological Interpretation

Your birth date gives you the opportunity to join opposing sides of your personality, the masculine and feminine within yourself, and emerge as a conscious, whole person. Aries is basically an assertive and self-motivated sign, and you will have the tendency to always push yourself forward. Yet your opposite sign, Libra, indicates balance, harmony, and cooperation. Your personal goals should include incorporating Libra's qualities into your personality. Once you have fused both sides of this astrological coin, an incredibly diplomatic and brave person will come to life, one who calls forth the recognition of coworkers and loved ones. Your indomitable spirit rises to the call of justice whenever you see people around you being abused. You combine sympathy with right action, understanding with courage, individual action with inclusivity of purpose.

In your birthday fiery Aries nature is magnified by Jupiter's expansiveness. An image for you is an ancient Greek coin. On one side is Ares, god of war, and on the other Aphrodite, goddess of love. At home, a brightly colored beanbag chair is the perfect place to flop and relax. You don't stand on ceremony and prefer a casual style. Wrought iron candlesticks with red candles are excellent objects for you. Balance the pointed candlestick shape with a carved round wooden box. If you have room in your home for musical gatherings, do not hesitate to hold them. If not, go out dancing and sing along. Your energy is strong; expressing it artistically creates good balance.

Outdoors, April 12th wants a garden that is stimulating. Have a rose arbor as an entryway to your outdoor space and fill the garden with bright reds and yellows. You may have a particular fondness for tulips.

A Kabbalistic Interpretation

The kabbalistic values of this date indicate someone whose favorite phrase might be "a place for everything and everything in its place." You find it frustrating when things in your house are not just so, yet your birthday indicates you may not find it easy to keep your own papers in order. You might really appreciate a filing cabinet of some kind—if you can find one with a greenish yellow border it might even improve your organizational skills. And you may wish to treat yourself to the services of a professional organizer to help you get started.

The influence of the Hebrew letter *Kaph* on this birthday means that you are handy. You will no doubt be first in line on the weekend at the local hardware store or Home Depot. Pursue woodworking if you can, as the smell of freshly cut wood may relax you and impart feelings of security.

That feeling of security is very important to you. Anything you cannot directly control can become an issue and may even interrupt your sleep. Meditate on a piece of topaz or jasper and carry one of these minerals with you at all times, to help allay your anxieties.

A Numerological Interpretation
YOUR MAGIC NUMBERS: 7 AND 4

The twelfth day of the fourth month reduces to seven, the number of victory and accomplishment. This date confers a path of seeing endless possibilities for your life, as if you are looking through an infinite number of open doors. You are called upon to clarify and crystallize your heart's desires. Walk through the open doors in your life without hesitation and learn what those experiences have to teach you. Live in a house with lots of doors and windows. Keep containers with numerous cubbyholes and tiny drawers for secret treasures. Fire opal set in silver will fire your passion. The 103rd day of the year reduces to four, adding the quality of order to your world and the ability to survey and choose the doorways you enter.

OBJECTS/IMAGES
*tiger prints,
spear-shaped curtain rods,
kohl eye makeup*

SHAPES/MATERIALS
*cinnabar, jacinth,
a coiled spring*

COLORS
*hot pink, scarlet, jade green,
ivory*

ANIMALS
*a woolly stuffed lamb,
thorny devil*

PLANTS, HERBS, EDIBLES
*scarlet banskia rose,
flaxseed, garlic*

ESSENCE
pimento

SOUNDS/RHYTHMS
drums, the Charleston

MUSICAL NOTES
F# and D#

DEEP SPACE OBJECTS
*Theta Eridanus, Acamar,
End of the Stream*

April 13

YOUR SIGN
Aries

YOUR ELEMENT
Fire

YOUR RULERS
Mars, Sun, Jupiter
22–23 degrees
Third Decanate, yang

The Astrological Interpretation

Your birth date occurs in that part of Aries that is also influenced by the sign Sagittarius. You will find that you are very eager to travel and explore life to its fullest. Your present horizon may seem too small for the inner abundance of your creative energies. You tend therefore to push yourself and your environment to the limits.

Make sure that you continue to educate yourself throughout your life, garnering those mental tools that can help you guide the more passionate and emotional sides of your nature. You may have already discovered that for every step you seek to advance yourself, you have to acquire the right information. Your willingness to take on the challenges that come with advancement both professionally and in the subtle sphere of human dynamics is not enough to succeed. You do have the right attitude, but you must also develop the patient self-discipline that allows you to master the skills and techniques that come with the job.

With your fiery nature, April 13 should cultivate consistency. Your energy is like champagne: bubble, bubble, then flat. If you moderate your involvement then you won't leave too many pots simmering. Keep a corked bottle of champagne around as a reminder! Your home should have plenty of windows and net curtains that allow light through. Your color scheme could be monochromatic, such as white or beige, with flashes of reds and yellow. Include in your furniture some large pieces—an armoire or over-size desk. On the dining room table or in a prominent spot have a horn of plenty. You may change the contents seasonally, but a cornucopia bursting with produce is a symbol of the richness of your life.

Outdoors April 13 loves daffodils and forsythia, the two harbingers of spring. Have a clear space in your yard or go to a park where you can lie on the ground and gaze at the sky.

A Kabbalistic Interpretation

You have an acute sense of smell, which you employ to its fullest extent. You have a great love of good perfume and aromas and often appreciate receiving perfume and scented bath products as gifts. Treat yourself to an aromatherapy massage or buy yourself an aromatherapy kit.

One of the kabbalistic values that can be ascribed to this day is twenty-five, which is the magic number of the planet Mars. Since Mars is also the ruling planet of your star sign you may want to temper the influence of this angry planet. Emphasize blue in your wardrobe and keep a blue bowl of water on the south side of your desk. Avoid too much spicy food.

Law-related careers are ideal for April 13 people. You have a keen sense of justice and are happy to be the means by which it is handed down. You may become a lawyer, and if you are you will be most comfortable as a criminal prosecutor, or you may work as a detective or law enforcement officer. Any kind of law enforcement memorabilia is interesting to people born this day.

A Numerological Interpretation

YOUR MAGIC NUMBERS: 8 AND 5

The thirteenth day of the fourth month reduces to eight, a number characterized by rhythm and vibration. Eight carries the implicit understanding that opposite forms of expression stem from a single cause. You sense the essentials in life and feel disdain for superficiality. You value privacy and do not easily share the secrets of your soul. You do not easily extend yourself to others, but when you do your sense of responsibility is complete.

The 104th day of the year reduces to five, contributing the influence of constant, changing activity. Fine silk scarves in teal or yellow will cheer you. Turquoise and citrine will energize your mind. Visit a beekeeper and observe the industrious honeybees at work. Watch the dance of the seven veils, which dramatizes the unveiling of Isis.

OBJECTS/IMAGES
a carpenter's saw, etchings, fire-eaters, a comet with a long tail coming toward Earth

SHAPES/MATERIALS
red jasper, carved wood, pointed lines

COLORS
brilliant red, reddish brown, teal, tawny yellow

ANIMALS
game cock, porcupine

PLANTS, HERBS, EDIBLES
basil, barberry, carbonated drinks

ESSENCE
coriander

SOUNDS/RHYTHMS
drums, The 1812 Overture

MUSICAL NOTES
G and E

DEEP SPACE OBJECTS
Xi Cepheus, Kurhah, White Spot in the Face of a Horse

April 14

YOUR SIGN
Aries

YOUR ELEMENT
Fire

YOUR RULERS
Mars, Jupiter
23–24 degrees
Third Decanate, yang

The Astrological Interpretation

By nature you are a creative visionary; your mind is like a motion picture projector constantly revealing the images of your aspirations. Life for you is a stage, a theater filled with possibilities. You enjoy being the director of your own play and making sudden unscripted changes in your cast and story. Although this makes you a very exciting person to be with, others may find your volatile changes quite difficult to handle. You have the charisma to evoke enthusiastic responses out of your audience but may lose them if you shift scenes too quickly. Then you may find yourself feeling abandoned and deserted. It is important for you to realize that you have a responsibility to others: if you are going to lead them, you have to stick with the plot. Slow down and train yourself to think things through to the end. Never lose your spontaneity or drive, but add to them a more carefully considered course of action.

Your birthday combines inspiration and hope. You have strong beliefs and ideals and may even be dictatorial in expressing them; however, even if someone is on the opposition you will give that person hope for all endeavors. Your home may be a center for like-minded people. A collection of rockers on the porch could be the place to discuss projects. You feel better when there is a lot of space around you. Have a variety of colored balls to play with at odd moments. Billiards and croquet would be good diversions for you, but also keep some small colored balls in a bowl so you can juggle, squeeze, and bounce them. Another object for April 14 is a set of good mechanical pencils. Diagramming what you want to say is good strategy.

Outdoors April 14 wants a setting with grace and size. A small garden house with a curved dome is a perfect adjunct to your space. Evergreen and oak trees may be of more interest to you than a flower garden.

A Kabbalistic Interpretation

Lycanthropy, or the possibility that people turn into wolves at the time of the full moon, was once a prevalent belief in many cultures. Though you stop short of turning into a beast, you are definitely affected by the energies of the moon. On the positive side, you are extremely intuitive and tend to have very evocative dreams. However you can become anxious, irritable, and sometimes depressed by lunar energy. Carrying a moonstone will keep you in touch with the moon's positive influences.

Gardening is a chance to express your creative urges. Your garden is as much a work of art as of nature, and you will go to great lengths to maintain a sense of balance and proportion even down to ensuring harmony of color and aroma. An excellent gift for you would be a selection of new rosebushes.

Inside your home you like to feel that you are surrounded by attractive things. What in some people seems an excessive taste for luxury is in your case considerably more subtle and understated. Visitors will probably only notice after spending some time in your house that all the materials are of a particularly fine quality. To enhance the quality of quiet elegance, consider hanging some muslin drapes at your windows to soften the brightness of the sun.

A Numerological Interpretation

YOUR MAGIC NUMBERS: 9 AND 6

The fourteenth day of the fourth month reduces to nine, the number of completion and attainment. This day engenders enthusiasm and generosity. Your own generous spirit seems to magically attract good fortune into your own life, as if you live poised beneath a cornucopia. You love giving and receiving presents. Use colorful wrapping paper, bright bows, and ribbons of reds, blues, and greens. Send yourself flowers.

Ruby, sapphire, and peridot will inspire you. The 105th day of the year reduces to six, which brings in the quality of complementary activities, balance, and loving openness to your generosity.

OBJECTS/IMAGES
left ear, mechanical engineers, etchings, and helmets

SHAPES/MATERIALS
electroplating, blade shapes, carnelian, and red hematite

COLORS
burnt orange, peacock blue

ANIMAL
Plymouth Rock rooster

PLANTS, HERBS, EDIBLES
cock of the rock, English daisies, dove's-foot, flax seed

ESSENCE
pimento

SOUNDS/RHYTHMS
conga drum

MUSICAL NOTES
G# and F

DEEP SPACE OBJECT
pulsar

April 15

YOUR SIGN
Aries

YOUR ELEMENT
Fire

YOUR RULERS
Mars, Jupiter
24–25 degrees
Third Decanate, yang

The Astrological Interpretation

The symbol for your birth date is a fiery cornucopia. Your mind is filled with a treasure house of ideas and creative potentials that you are eager to see manifest. Yet without a clear sense of structured direction, all the fruits of your basket will fall into a jumbled heap of chaos. The key word for you is *discrimination*. You have to begin to assess the true value and worth of your many thoughts and concepts, eliminating those that are weak and impractical. This requires mental discipline and the ability to think through each of your many projects to its proper conclusion. To get the attention of others, you will have to give, combining your energies, time, and resources with theirs. Avoid obsession and cultivate detachment. You know that you have a side to your personality that is as quick to turn on to something (or someone!) as it is to turn cool once the initial enthusiasm has worn off.

This birthday gives independence and the confidence to march to the beat of a different drummer. The popping sound of a champagne cork should celebrate each of your accomplishments. Carbonated apple cider will do just as well if you don't drink. At home April 15 will appreciate well-designed, functional furniture. Have some large pillows on the floor, next to a fireplace. You may have an affinity for literature and like to prop yourself up on the pillows and read by the fire. April 15 doesn't spend much time languishing in bed, so a futon that easily converts into a couch may be all the bedroom you need.

A noted seer mentions that northeast from your place of birth will be a fortunate location for you. Why not build your house, with plenty of light and geometric design, facing north and east?

Outdoors, April 15 would enjoy a corral or fenced-in grassy area. Horses may appeal. A bridle is a symbol that denotes the strength and passion of a beautiful animal, but it must be curbed in order to be productive.

A Kabbalistic Interpretation

On a weekend, you are likely to be found painting the town a million shades of red. No matter what point of life you are at, you still have the capacity to see the world like a wide-eyed teenager. Perhaps consider buying yourself a motorbike so that you can really be a wild child when the weekend comes.

Confidence is a virtue, but be aware that your faith in your own good judgment and expertise in all matters can make you seem extremely opinionated. Cultivate a practice of creating silence before you speak. Try drinking an infusion of mint and nettle tea.

Your ambition really knows no limits, and it is your intention to reach the very pinnacle of your chosen profession. There is no reason why you shouldn't achieve this, as you are prepared to work very long and very hard in order to achieve your goal. If you want to give your energies a boost, invest in a ring of white gold with a thin border of yellow gold around the edge.

A Numerological Interpretation

YOUR MAGIC NUMBERS: 10 AND 7

The fifteenth day of the fourth month reduces to ten, yielding the influence of perfect completion of a cycle of expression, a feeling of mastery or dominion between cycles. Born on this day, you are imminently resourceful and have a flair for seeing potentials and alternatives in every situation, and then adjusting circumstances for the perfect outcome for that moment. You also possess the ability to really know yourself, inwardly and outwardly. You love things with dials and gauges, lots of options for settings. Curl up with your remote in a high-tech recliner, and surf your satellite for the perfect, stimulating program for the moment.

The 106th day of the year reduces to seven, adding the quality of victorious achievement, enabling you to savor the cycles of accomplishment. Sodalite and jade will focus your mind.

OBJECTS/IMAGES
*fireman's helmet,
a blacksmith's anvil,
a wrought-iron chandelier*

SHAPES/MATERIALS
*an exploding star, malachite,
acute angles*

COLORS
*carmine, orange, magenta,
indigo, emerald green*

ANIMALS
*fire beetle, yellow jacket,
German shepherd*

PLANTS, HERBS, EDIBLES
*cardamom, fire thorn,
kava kava*

ESSENCES
*geranium, sharp smells,
sandalwood incense*

SOUNDS/RHYTHMS
*rap music,
trumpet processionals,
sound of firecrackers*

MUSICAL NOTES
A and F#

DEEP SPACE OBJECT
quasar

April 16

YOUR SIGN
Aries

YOUR ELEMENT
Fire

YOUR RULERS
Mars, Jupiter
25–26 degrees
Third Decanate, yin

The Astrological Interpretation

Your birth date indicates a person who does not allow past mistakes or failures to inhibit attempts at future victories and successes. This does not mean that you should put the past behind you. It is only through extracting the essential meaning of past difficulties that you are able to achieve the desired results of newly envisioned goals. One way to avoid the repetition of old patterns in relationships is to work to see a person as he or she really is. This means you should not project your romantic or professional aspirations on them. What you will see if you continue to emotionally assert yourself is a mirror of such projections. You can give a person a renewed sense of personal direction. You can add support and vitality to their lives, but you can not and should not try to save them from themselves.

April 16 is a daring birthday with energy and many abilities. Your special talent for visualization can be used in athletics, music, writing, inventing, or business. Getting a physical feel for something is the way to approach all learning. At home, have a set of stretches or warm-ups that you do. While you are working, take a break and bounce a ball up and down to clear your mind. Red is the color of inspiration for you, but you may want to use it sparingly, as it will increase your restlessness. Carved wood decorative objects are perfect for your home. You may especially like reddish-tinged teak or fruitwoods. Whittling would be an excellent hobby for both men and women born on April 16.

Outdoors, April 16 wants trees and mountains. Consider building a platform in a big old chestnut tree where you can get some perspective. Climbing trees may be an excellent way for you to relax. Your garden will be neither tame nor manicured. A profusion of reds, yellows, and oranges will energize you; consider trumpet vine, hibiscus, and globe thistle.

A Kabbalistic Interpretation

Today is a very creative day; most people born today will enjoy some form of artistic expression. This may be nothing more than some enthusiastic shower singing, but if you try your hand at one of the plastic arts you may surprise yourself. One of the kabbalistic values of this day has the same value as a Hebrew word meaning "clay," so try your hand at a traditional potter's wheel.

You have a very deep connection to your childhood and you may associate that period of your life with a sense of joy and fun. If you have pictures and other memorabilia from that time, you will want to collate them in a scrapbook or photo album so you can have your memories all in one place.

From time to time you like to be off by yourself for a while—usually just to sit and contemplate. You should feel free to indulge yourself in this activity, as this quiet time is your time to consolidate and lay the groundwork for creativity. If you always need to feel that you are "doing" something, then consider investing in a fishing rod and bait. Fly-fishing is particularly ideal.

A Numerological Interpretation
YOUR MAGIC NUMBERS: 2 AND 8

The sixteenth day of the fourth month reduces to two, a number signifying duplication and replication. Born on this day, you are driven to try everything and are generally successful at what you put your mind to. Someone born on this day probably caused the origination of the expression "too many irons in the fire." You love gadgets and clever pieces of gear. Cultivate discernment about when to say no. Learn when enough is enough.

The 107th day of the year reduces to eight, adding instinctive awareness of the cyclical nature of your endeavors. Visit an authentic blacksmith shop. Watch sparks fly from the hammer and anvil. Carnelian set in gold expresses your true nature. Wear hand-knit sweaters of red-orange, blue and yellows.

OBJECTS/IMAGES
trances, welding, hats, firemen

SHAPES/MATERIALS
edge shapes, skull shapes, spinel, diamonds

COLORS
mustard, burgundy, sea foam

ANIMALS
elk, red wolf

PLANTS, HERB, EDIBLES
great yellow gentian, curly dock, Indian paintbrush, pepper relish

ESSENCE
juniper

SOUNDS/RHYTHMS
"Moon River" by Henry Mancini

MUSICAL NOTES
C# and G

DEEP SPACE OBJECT
M31, the great galaxy in Andromeda

April 17

YOUR SIGN
Aries

YOUR ELEMENT
Fire

YOUR RULERS
Mars, Jupiter
26–27 degrees
Third Decanate, yin

The Astrological Interpretation

You are a person with tremendous vitality and a "never-say-die" spirit. Barriers and barricades, fences and walls, are no match for your relentless charge. If you find that your head gets banged once in a while, well that comes with the territory. You just heal your wounds and get on with life. You do need to realize that no matter how easily you recuperate, some battles are just not necessary to fight. Your birth date indicates that your enthusiasm and courage instill you with optimism. Positive as you are, you still should not promise more than you can deliver. You are asked by the circumstances of your life to find practical ways of handling situations. Your idealism is inspirational, but getting involved firsthand will strengthen you and lead to even greater success.

April 17 is astrologically a crowded birthday. Some April 17 birthdays fall on a critical degree, others on the fixed star Al Pherg, and others on the fixed star Vertex. Interpretations of these positions vary; suffice it to say that your life will resonate with intensity and energy. You are an explorer and may write about both your physical and mental journeys. An image for you is the indefatigable Sherlock Holmes. Consider wearing a Holmes-style overcoat and deerstalker hat. At home keep a variety of red and plaid scarves for wintertime and hot oranges and pinks for summer. Men may prefer tamer colors, but a touch of red is essential. A pedometer to keep track of your mileage when you walk could interest you. A hardware store is a meditative place . . . so many possibilities! Go there if you ever feel stuck on a creative or personal problem; you'll find out how to "fix" whatever is bothering you.

Outdoors, April 17 likes hilly ground with interesting twists and turns. If there is a sheep farm nearby, visit it. Hikes uphill in sturdy boots are invigorating. Another possible vacation spot is a nudist camp or beach. April 17 wouldn't mind a bit feeling the sun all over.

A Kabbalistic Interpretation

You have a strong imagination and love to float into the stratosphere. You may have a hard time keeping yourself focused on the grainy reality of the day-to-day; since the worlds you can create with your imagination are so much more exciting, you much prefer to dream. Your imagination is a tremendous gift but may not be something your boss appreciates about you. Wearing something amber-colored or keeping a piece of amber on your desk will help your concentration at work.

According to the kabbalistic values of this day, working with animals could be a job that actually holds your interest. Working in a zoo or nature preserve is ideal, as you have a love of the more exotic side of nature. A snake or a small lizard would make a wonderful pet for you.

Because of your association with air, you like to live with your windows open wide all the time. In the winter months, one way to get more air energy into your home is to buy some jasmine essential oil and an oil burner—you will find the resulting scent deeply invigorating.

A Numerological Interpretation
YOUR MAGIC NUMBERS: 3 AND 9

The seventeenth day of the fourth month reduces to three, a number that means growth and development. This day's path has the quality of self-determination. You strive to create your own destiny rather than feel like a victim of circumstance. You have the capacity to step back, review events, and rework your plan to achieve better results the next time. If you fall down, you get up. You don't sit in the road feeling sorry for yourself.

The 108th day of the year reduces to nine, providing the influence of goal achievement to your striving and regrouping. Agate and citrine will cheer you. Computer games stimulate your mind. Play chess, or take a gourmet cooking class for fun.

OBJECTS/IMAGES
acrobats, anvils, fireplaces, a ginger jar

SHAPES/MATERIALS
geometric angles, pointed shapes, garnets

COLORS
ruddy, ginger, cobalt blue

ANIMALS
stinging insects, lamb

PLANTS, HERBS, EDIBLES
allheal, catnip, cranberries, cardinal flower

ESSENCE
reunion basil

SOUNDS/RHYTHMS
sound of keys turning in locks, marching songs

MUSICAL NOTES
D and G#

DEEP SPACE OBJECT
NGC, spiral galaxy

April 18

YOUR SIGN
Aries

YOUR ELEMENT
Fire

YOUR RULERS
Mars, Jupiter
27–28 degrees
Third Decanate, yin

The Astrological Interpretation

Your birth date indicates that you have a very mental nature and as such it is important for you to cultivate the higher mind. This is the part of your nature that is aware of itself as the thinker—it is not your thoughts and it is certainly not your emotions. In order to do this, you would do well to study some philosophical or spiritual discipline that can increase your awareness of this part of yourself. If you are already on such a path, then make sure that no matter what the temptations or obstacles, you stick to this facet of your personal evolution. It is important for you to identify and use the "silent mind," that inner voice within you that does not speak in words but impresses its awareness through your intuition. This voice is encouraged by contemplation and meditation.

Your birthday may enjoy the vitality of argument and pugnacity. You have a strong power drive and enjoy competition. Winning is the ultimate objective, but a good contest also pleases you. Your arena of activity may be physical or mental. Your fiery nature does need discipline and may benefit from a sport or meditation system that includes movement. Kendo or kickboxing might be just the activity for you. At home, emphasize nature in your surroundings, with houseplants such as calathea and minerals such as raw amethyst. You need their steadying influence. In the bedroom consider having a metal bed frame and lots of soft pillows. A large year-round comforter that will provide some softness is for you.

Outdoors, April 18 might enjoy growing spectacular vegetables or large flowers. You have a talent for horticulture. If your yard does not have room for "farming" consider an herb garden with basil, ginger, and garlic.

A Kabbalistic Interpretation

The tarot card the Fool has very close associations with this day. Today's fool is very close to the traditional sense of the word—a joker and prankster, rather than a spiritual tyro. People born today love to play practical jokes, especially ones that they have constructed themselves. A gift idea for someone born this day might be a collection of movie makeup effects.

Your favorite dish is likely to be a well-done peppered steak—the larger the better. You may be prone to circulatory problems and therefore should probably learn to curb your carnivorous tendencies. One possible compromise might be to take up eating vegetable dishes that are very heavily spiced. You are likely to enjoy the flavor of food liberally marinated in cayenne or chili peppers.

A Numerological Interpretation
YOUR MAGIC NUMBERS: 4 AND 10

The eighteenth day of the fourth month reduces to four, the number of abstract reason. This day embodies the quest for spiritual independence. Your inner knowing tells you that superficial and ephemeral pleasures cannot be your guide for sustaining values. What gives meaning and motivation to your life must be by reason of your highest aspirations. What does perceived failure teach us? What are the lessons of van Gogh's life?

The 109th day of the year reduces to ten, adding an instinctive sense of the outcome of a situation once events are set in motion. Collect articles of quality and timeless value. Amber and azurite are gems to soothe you.

OBJECTS/IMAGES
hockey sticks, jackknives, fingernail polish, padlocks

SHAPES/MATERIALS
gun powder, jasper, mahogany, malachite

COLORS
cherry red, tangerine, indigo

ANIMALS
Mexican crow, gaming cock

PLANTS, HERBS, EDIBLES
wild ginger, wild pine, Maltese cross, hollyhocks

ESSENCE
geranium

SOUNDS/RHYTHMS
drumsticks, bass drum

MUSICAL NOTES
D# and A

DEEP SPACE OBJECTS
Alpha Pisces, Alrisha, the Knot

April 19

YOUR SIGNS
Aries/Taurus

YOUR ELEMENT
Fire/Earth

YOUR RULERS
Mars, Sun, Moon
29 degrees Aries–
00 degrees Taurus
Third Decanate, yin
First Decanate, yang

The Astrological Interpretation

You are born on the cusp between two signs: Aries the Ram and Taurus the Bull. These two-horned creatures symbolize the relationship between thoughts and the concrete manifestation of these ideas into the forms of life. Your birth date is represented by a very old and wise saying: "thoughts are things." It is thus very important for you to be able to merge these two pairs of horns so that you emerge with a one-pointed focus that allows you to manifest your dreams and aspirations in practical terms on earth. Your destiny involves fusion, integration, alignment, and union. You have the intense fiery will of the Ram but need to cultivate a correct assessment of how you can infuse your will into the physical world around you. Sometimes you may feel restricted by material circumstances and find that your inner freedom is overly bound by earthly responsibilities. This is only natural, as you are moving from a fiery and unfettered existence of ideas into one in which these concepts take root in reality. You are the seed; now you must plant yourself in the ground.

Taurean persistence adds weight and tenacity to Aries enthusiasm and spark. By focusing your energy you have a powerful combination of elements. Hearing is an important sense for April 19. You may want to keep music around you as well as sing yourself. The sound of a mixed choir may be particularly appealing. At home, April 19 wants room and comfort. Square wooden furniture with oversize pillows would be a good combination for April 19. Sumerian art (which includes rams' heads and bulls' heads) resonates with both Aries and Taurus. Consider having a book with photos or some museum reproductions. Your personal style will be sporty and casual. April 19 may give the impression that he or she is always between games.

Outdoors, April 19 will enjoy a garden filled with pink and yellow flowers. Poppies, evening primrose, and tulips are all good choices. A playing area for football, volleyball, and basketball would be great, and a barbecue will make your yard complete.

A Kabbalistic Interpretation

If you are a friend or a partner of someone born this day, then you know that your friend is an extremely practical individual with no time for pie-in-the-sky mysticism like kabbala. It would be surprising to find anyone born this day reading this book with serious intentions of improving their lives. People born today have a great love of anything that is solidly material. A good hobby might be remote-control models.

Work is of prime importance, and the value of this day indicates that you sometimes have difficulty knowing when to stop and go home for a rest. You are likely to be the boss at work, and the influence of the Emperor tarot card on this day can make you a somewhat stern individual to work for. If you carry a pouch of wormwood or valerian in your pocket you will be able to see the lighter side of life. Putting an orange-and-purple-colored lava lamp on your desk could also help.

A Numerological Interpretation

YOUR MAGIC NUMBERS: 5 AND 2

The nineteenth day of the fourth month reduces to five, the number signifying the means or agency by which something is accomplished. This day's path carries the possibility of being a spiritual inspiration to others through your capacity to give voice to eternal realities. When at your best, your example shines like a beacon to those around you.

The 110th day of the year reduces to two, adding the symbolism of perfect reflection of the divine to your aspirations. Listen to sacred music or enjoy a children's choir; their voices can lift the spirit like a choir of angels. Amber set in silver will quiet your spirit. Grow birds-of-paradise in your garden.

OBJECTS/IMAGES
corner buildings facing east, doorways, necklaces, wrought iron

SHAPES/MATERIALS
chimney shapes, brimstone, diamonds, almandine

COLORS
muted red, apricot, chestnut

ANIMALS
elk, bighorn sheep

PLANTS, HERBS, EDIBLES
wild coffee, charcoal-broiled meats, jalapeño peppers

ESSENCE
cumin

SOUNDS/RHYTHMS
The William Tell Overture, *pianos*

MUSICAL NOTES
E and C#

DEEP SPACE OBJECTS
Beta Andromeda, Mirach, Girdle

April 20

The Astrological Interpretation

Your birth date occurs at the first degree of the sign Taurus. You also have the fiery creative potency of Aries within you and you seek to take this potential and make it real. It is very important for you to express your self-worth, and to do this you have to find the right form to ground your talents and abilities. Once your career and life objectives are in place, you are a most determined individual. You hold your ground no matter what the odds—the more opposition that confronts you, the stronger you become. You love nature and take great pleasure in woods, fields, mountains, and parks. Loyalty and steadfastness grace your life.

Some April 20 birthdays are influenced by the fixed star Mirach. This star was said to bestow great beauty and aesthetic appreciation. Whether you lean more toward Taurus or Aries, April 20 is an industrious birthday with a great deal of energy and many changes of your life's course. Your talent is finding new applications for old principles. Consider fixing up an old home and removing all the room divisions to create a large open space. Although you love flowers, why not place bouquets of ribbons throughout your home? An exercise room or place where you can stretch and unwind is a great asset. Have music available for dancing and aerobic activities, and mirrors so you can admire your progress.

Outdoors, April 20 will find peace walking in a park or backyard. If there is a duck pond nearby, skip stones over the water and renew your energies. Your own garden should have familiar flowers like geraniums and zinnias. City dwellers will enjoy tending window boxes. An antique wheelbarrow may figure strongly in your interior or exterior environment. You might use it to cart earth to the garden, but you also might use it to hold your art supplies so that you can wheel to the best spot to paint or sketch.

A Kabbalistic Interpretation

This day has a strong connection to the High Priestess card from the tarot. This card is related to hidden or occult wisdom, suggesting someone with a high degree of intuition. To people who are not intuitive, this may sound like a wonderful gift. However, it can be confusing and sometimes worrying to experience other people's feelings. To derive the most benefit from your gift, invest in a set of well-painted tarot cards. Your ability to use and control your emotional insight will improve with training and practice.

Because of your consistently evenhanded attitude, you tend to be very popular at work as well as in your family. You may find yourself mediating other people's quarrels. Afterward, take time to sit down in your favorite chair and play some classical music to alleviate the stress this activity can create.

You may enjoy thumbing through design magazines before deciding exactly what to do in your own house. Pay attention to what greets your other senses as much as what meets the eye. Make sure that each room contains at least one vase of freshly cut aromatic flowers.

A Numerological Interpretation

YOUR MAGIC NUMBERS: 6 AND 3

The twentieth day of the fourth month reduces to six, the number of balance, symmetry, and the beauty inherent in harmonized opposites. This day's path calls forth the ability to see how things fit together in life and the intrinsic rightness of Divine order in the grand scheme of things. When one is truly oneself there is a complementary relationship between an individual and the universe.

The 111th day of the year reduces to three, adding the influence of natural unfoldment to your sense of how things fit together. Emerald and citrine are complementary gems. Visit a duck pond surrounded by weeping willow trees. Watch baby ducks follow their mother in a perfect row. Collect brightly painted carved statues of ducks or other animals to cheer you.

OBJECTS/IMAGES
*a pair of tongs,
chimneys on the horizon,
fine drafting/drawing tools*

SHAPES/MATERIALS
*wrought iron, a wedge shape,
sisal*

COLORS
*carmine red,
black trimmed with red,
violet, lime green, coral*

ANIMALS
sheep, mastiff, fox

PLANTS, HERBS, EDIBLES
*cayenne pepper, ferns,
bittersweet*

ESSENCES
pungent scents, sarsaparilla

SOUNDS/RHYTHMS
*shouts, stomp dances,
rock and roll*

MUSICAL NOTES
F# and D#

DEEP SPACE OBJECTS
*Omicron Cetus, Mira
(Latin for "Wonderful")*

April 21

YOUR SIGN
Taurus

YOUR ELEMENT
Earth

YOUR RULERS
Venus, Moon
00–1 degree
First Decanate, yin

The Astrological Interpretation

Your birth date indicates a person who is learning to develop willpower. You have a natural resistance to people telling you what to do and how to do it. Even if you are not sure yourself, you need to know that there is no unwanted, external force in control of your life. Many people will call you stubborn and unmoveable—and they may be right! But you will think of yourself as just expressing your own individuality, one that refuses to be compromised into agreeing to situations you oppose. You have a natural beauty that often needs no cosmetics or artificial enhancers. In fact, you could be called the personification of the "natural" man or woman—no bother, no fuss, you like to be just you. You take things as they come and are usually in no rush to get anywhere. You know and trust that if you just stay true to yourself, everything will eventually fall into the right place.

You are willing to work hard and have a great respect for the forms of life. You have artistic talents both in drama and the visual arts. Material well-being is important to you. Keep a piggy bank around that makes you laugh. If you start to feel anxious about money you can feel good about your savings. At home you like to have space with little nooks and crannies that have a personality all their own. Vases with silk flowers are perfect decorative touches. In the bedroom consider having a four-poster bed with a white bedspread and a variety of round colored silk pillows. A decorative doll or teddy bear in the center would be a homey touch.

Nature is an important part of your life. Wherever you live you will enjoy taking breaks or vacations in wilderness areas. The heath or plains may particularly appeal. In your own garden, cowslips, all lilies, and pansies appeal.

A Kabbalistic Interpretation

This day's values indicate a wellspring of enormous vigor and vitality. From the minute you leap out of bed, you probably spend your days in a state of constant activity. This active state extends to the endless workings of your mind and thoughts as much as to any physical activity you engage in during the day. Though you may often feel like you could stay in this highly dynamic energetic state forever, yours is the energy of a sprinter. It is healthier to engage your dynamic energies in short bursts. Wear a dark shade of blue fairly often and burn some mallow oil in the evening to achieve a quiet calm.

Energetic though you may be, you are not a brash person. You are, in fact, deeply romantic and given to expansive declarations of undying love when the mood takes you. In terms of romance the kabbalistic values of this day suggest that you are something of a traditionalist. If you want to seduce someone born on this day, rent some old black-and-white movies and invite them over to see them—followed by a romantic candlelit dinner.

A Numerological Interpretation
YOUR MAGIC NUMBERS: 7 AND 4

The twenty-first day of the fourth month reduces to seven, the number of victory. There is a quality to this day similar to the irrepressible spring shoot forcing its way upward through a concrete highway. When you call on your faith in yourself and your higher power, there is no limit to what you can accomplish. Your source of strength comes from deep inside yourself.

The 112th day of the year reduces to four, which contributes the influence of stability and predictability to your innate resourcefulness. Plant crocuses in the fall and watch their amazing emergence in the spring snow. Surround yourself with tulips, daffodils, or other fresh flowers to remind you of life's tenacity. Emerald and amber will fire your imagination.

OBJECTS/IMAGES
clown costumes, carpets, golfers, flavors

SHAPES/MATERIALS
lapis lazuli, emeralds, ring shapes, taffeta

COLORS
peach, forest green, cream

ANIMAL
Hereford cow

PLANTS, HERBS, EDIBLES
black cherry soda, filet mignon, nasturtiums, bearberry

ESSENCE
melissa

SOUNDS/RHYTHMS
bullfighting music, a cattle drive

MUSICAL NOTES
F# and D#

DEEP SPACE OBJECTS
Tau Eridanus, Angetenar

April 22

YOUR SIGN
Taurus

YOUR ELEMENT
Earth

YOUR RULERS
Venus, Moon
1–2 degrees
First Decanate, yin

The Astrological Interpretation

Money and financial security mean a great deal to you, but you are not very ambitious by nature. Your approach to your goals is more tortoise than hare. You know if you move steadily, you will achieve your objectives. You tend to take things in your stride and make few demands on life. You much prefer to say yes rather than no but are resistant to people who try to force your decisions before you are ready to make them. You are sensitive to other people's needs, and if they will just allow you to take your time about things, you will give others what they want from you. You must do everything in your own way, one thing at a time. People have to learn how to be patient with you, and if they do, then they will be amply rewarded in return.

Your considerable talents encourage you to make an impact on your world, whether in everyday affairs or historical events. Ancient writers have stated that April 22 gives talents in plotting and strategy. You may enjoy having a blackboard in your home so that you can try out your game plan before you commit to it. Keep your work area and living area separate, but even if you have an office elsewhere, keep a work desk at home. You are personally and professionally interested in transformation and need space to sketch out your plans. Have an elegant desk set with places for paper clips, paper, etc.

A bay window with a window seat is a place to relax your mind and hum. Taurus rules the throat, and humming will keep the energy circulating. The kitchen is a focus for April 22, as you will probably enjoy entertaining and cooking. Clay ovenware and ceramic ovenproof pots give just the right earthy touch to your kitchen.

Outdoors, April 22 wants room to pace. A yard or a park will do equally well. The essential ingredient is having enough room to go in a straight line and then following it back again. Rows of box hedges might outline your space. Flowers such as day lilies, daisies, and larkspur are well suited for April 22.

A Kabbalistic Interpretation

The kabbalistic values of this day point us in the direction of the sephira Hod on the Tree of Life. This sephira is associated with rational thought and all things intellectual and logical. You may find that there is never enough time to spend on the intellectual pursuits that really appeal to you. If you keep your books in an antique pine bookcase, bordered with deep orange, you will find that you are able to spend more time reading and thinking.

Your passion for intellectual pursuits is equal to your sensual passion, which makes you a wonderful romantic partner. Put a cast-iron bedstead in your bedroom to take advantage of Mars's influence.

One of the kabbalistic values of this day has the same value as the Hebrew word meaning "journey." People born today should seriously consider taking up hiking as an activity, as this will help you focus on your life's journey. A pair of olive green walking boots will make the miles fly by.

A Numerological Interpretation

YOUR MAGIC NUMBERS: 8 AND 5

The twenty-second day of the fourth month reduces to eight, the number that means rhythm. The energy of eight vibrates and moves in waves like the response of a pond to a thrown pebble. This date endows you with an inward mobilization. Used constructively, you can throw off your conflicts and stresses in the way that the thunder and lightning of an electrical storm create a catharsis in nature. The morning after has a crystal clarity, enabling you to see the road ahead.

The 113th day of the year reduces to five, supporting your path through the innate understanding of continuous transition. Experience a thunderstorm from a safe haven. Thrill to the lightning and thunder, smell the ozone in the air. Dance in puddles when the rain stops. Turquoise and citrine will invigorate you.

OBJECTS/IMAGES
a bullfighter, earmuffs, a singer

SHAPES/MATERIALS
ring shapes, flax, leather wallets

COLORS
pale blue, yellow, green, aquamarine, lemon yellow

ANIMALS
bulldog, Holstein cow

PLANTS, HERBS, EDIBLES
plantain, goldenrod, steak

ESSENCE
benzoin

SOUNDS/RHYTHMS
children's nursery rhymes, beautiful singing

MUSICAL NOTES
G and E

DEEP SPACE OBJECTS
Gamma Aries, Mesarthim, Minister

April 23

YOUR SIGN
Taurus

YOUR ELEMENT
Earth

YOUR RULERS
Venus, Moon
2–3 degrees
First Decanate, yin

The Astrological Interpretation

You love to be surrounded by beauty and are a sensual person by nature. You are at home in art museums, boutiques, greenhouses, and concert halls. You also have strong desires and find that it is important for you not only to visit beautiful places but also to live in one. You appreciate the finer things and want the best that life has to offer. But in order to accumulate and attract such objects into your life, you will have to learn how best to work with other people. You are not always the most communicative nor the most cooperative of individuals. What is important for you is to use your strong will, determination, and drive for the collective well being of others and not just for personal gains. Doing so will bring you much more of the abundance you seek.

The fixed star Sheratan, a pearly white star on the Ram's North Horn, may be located on some April 23 birthdays. This position was thought to indicate plotting, scheming, tact, and planning. You may make use of all these as you pursue artistic, military, or business ventures. You prefer to go your own way and basically want a carefree life. You may enjoy collecting baskets from different countries and using them to keep art supplies or ingredients. Mount a blackboard in the kitchen so you can write down the scheme of the day and make sure your whole family is up to speed on the day's events. Your bedroom should be an area exclusively for repose. Hang flowing drapes and landscape paintings with soft colors. You may want to have matching comforter, dust ruffle, and pillow sham sets that you change with the seasons.

Outdoors your environment should be a place where you can tinker with your car, build models, garden, tend the compost heap, walk the dog, or feed the chickens. You might want to grow grapes or have some fruit trees in your yard. Flowers such as myrtle, day lilies, and martagon lily all accord with your nature.

Kabbalistic Interpretation

People born on April 23 tend to be deeply ethical people who see life as a series of moral obligations to different groups of people. You may appear on first acquaintance to be somewhat joyless and dour, but this is far from the truth. You do have the potential, in always considering your obligations to others, to forget yourself. Take up something absurd like juggling or clowning as a way of putting the fun back in your life. You will find you are more joyful and it will break the cycle of considering only your duty to others.

You are a house-proud individual, and you derive pleasure from arranging everything to your liking. You are very fond of paired objects in your ornament displays, which may be partly due to the influence of Gemini the twins in the kabbala of this day. To add a sense of peace to your environment, buy a pair of ornate crystal glasses and place them in the west corner of your living room.

After a hot summer, you are likely to feel most at home during the bracing winds and changing scenery of autumn. If you want to make your bedroom a place where you can feel really cozy, paint the walls in various shades of brown and russet in a marbling effect.

A Numerological Interpretation

YOUR MAGIC NUMBERS: 9 AND 6

The twenty-third day of the fourth month reduces to nine, the number of completion and attainment. This day's path contains the promise of fulfillment as we enter into cooperation with the natural universe. This partnership is embodied in the beautiful outcome of a well-tended garden. When faith is wedded to hope, the outcome can be miraculous.

The 114th day of the year reduces to six, contributing the influence of beauty and harmony to your intrinsic sense of the order of things. Jade and turquoise are gems to harmonize your moods. Enjoy the gentle beauty of Japanese art. Grow ornamental trees such as bonsai. Walk in a fruit orchard in the spring, and inhale the intoxicating fragrance of their blossoms. Keep a bowl of ripe fruit in your house.

OBJECTS/IMAGES
futons, mittens, necklaces, and pillows

SHAPES/MATERIALS
opaque stones, emerald, moss agate, carnelian

COLORS
baby blue, cobalt blue, moss green

ANIMAL
barnyard cat

PLANTS, HERBS, EDIBLES
Cornish moneywort (plant), mugwort, marshmallow, molasses

ESSENCE
jonquil

SOUNDS/RHYTHMS
"Pretty Woman" by Roy Orbison

MUSICAL NOTES
G# and F

DEEP SPACE OBJECTS
Beta Aries, Sheratan, Two Horns

April 24

YOUR SIGN
Taurus

YOUR ELEMENT
Earth

YOUR RULERS
Venus, Moon
3–4 degrees
First Decanate, yin

The Astrological Interpretation

This birth date reveals a person who can be quite possessive. What is yours is yours, whether it is an object, an idea, or a person. Although this gives rise to a strong sense of individuality, it does make it difficult to release and let go. The important thing is to measure abundance through quality and not quantity. You will find that the increases you seek in the material world and the intensity you search for in relationships will come to you based on your own sense of self-worth. As you continue to honor yourself, you will be honored by others. As you allow self-love to grow within you, that love will attract its natural complement. As you share your possessions, you will become a magnet to which life's riches become increasingly attracted.

The sense of touch will be important in whatever work you choose. You may have musical and singing ability, and even if you do not sing professionally humming along to the radio is a good idea. There can be a measure of strife and discontentment with this birthday. Rest content in your abilities and the feel of your life. At home, have a number of fine leather goods such as wallets, gloves, and leather skirts or pants. You may want to indulge in manicures to keep your "sensors" beautiful. Have a solitary space in your home where you can practice yoga or sit and meditate. Meditation cushions in pale turquoise, green, and lavender may soothe your thoughts.

Outdoors, April 24 loves flowers and would like a warm climate. Plan a garden with a fence and trellis leading to a half-circle gate. Grow trumpet vine, morning glories, or jasmine. In your garden vary the color of flowers year to year. You may want to start with yellow, then white, and if you are feeling a little low, go for reds.

A Kabbalistic Interpretation

People who celebrate their birthday today are born gamblers, as indicated by the relationship to the Fortune tarot card. Other influences suggest that while you may be a gambler you choose rational methods. You may be attracted to the stock market, and a perfect day for you might be researching and trading some high-risk, high-yield investments on-line. You also like to indulge in some traditional betting, and love a day at the races. To increase your chances of winning, keep a basil leaf in your jacket pocket whenever you place a bet.

People born on this day tend to be deeply religious. Your spiritual nature finds you attracted to traditional religious ceremony with lots of ritual and structure. A wonderful gift for you could be some stained glass ornaments or windowpanes. Placed in the east of the house, these can have benefits for your health and well-being.

Whether male or female there is a certain roguish attractiveness about you. You are as cautious in your relationships as you are with your bets! If you want to tempt an April 24 individual into your life there is no better way than through her stomach. Try an old-fashioned fish fry, as April 24 loves seafood.

A Numerical Interpretation
YOUR MAGIC NUMBERS: 10 AND 7

The twenty-fourth day of the fourth month reduces to ten, the number of embodiment and ultimate outcome. This day's path contains the promise of the end of the rainbow. The journey to the legendary pot of gold is one of applying our best efforts and engaging our faith. Prayers are answered and abundance is manifested through a covenant with the universe.

The 115th day reduces to seven, contributing the quality of security and peace after victory. Grow a garden full of multicolored snap dragons. Stand outside during a rainstorm when you can see a rainbow. Smell the rain-soaked air, and watch sunlit raindrops fall from the roof. Fluorite will inspire your faith. Keep an empty pot by your front door in case the fairies visit.

OBJECTS/IMAGES
rings, nose rings, earrings, psychometry

SHAPES/MATERIALS
coin shapes, copper, pink coral

COLORS
cream yellow, deep purple, emerald green

ANIMALS
cattle, Texas longhorn

PLANTS, HERBS, EDIBLES
French beans, rose moss, daisies, wheat groats

ESSENCE
lily of the valley

SOUNDS/RHYTHMS
solfège vocalises, songs by Barbra Streisand

MUSICAL NOTES
A and F#

DEEP SPACE OBJECTS
Beta Cassiopeia, Caph Hand

April 25

YOUR SIGN
Taurus

YOUR ELEMENT
Earth

YOUR RULERS
Venus, Moon
4–5 degrees
First Decanate, yin

The Astrological Interpretation

Your gifts to yourself and others come through your ability to sustain and maintain the truth in all life circumstances. You have an ability to see the real value in people and are not easily fooled by affected airs and pretense. You prefer natural fabrics to man-made, whole and organic foods to packaged and prepared ones, down-to-earth friends to high-and-mighty ones. Your Taurus Sun allows you to pierce directly with a "Bull's Eye" into the heart of any matter. You succeed by your straightforwardness and willingness to be of help to others so that they may also come to accept life in clear and succinct terms.

April 25 is rich in heart wealth, naturally appealing, and likely to attract a good deal of affection. Venus rules artistic endeavors, so you may find you have a talent for illustrating your feelings in concrete form through drama, music, poetry, or inventions. The key for you is to treasure the links between people rather than hoarding material objects. Your sense of touch is highly developed. Flannel nightwear gives a comfy feeling, and you may like the sensual feel of silk or soft cotton underwear. The throat is a vulnerable area for Taurus; wear turtleneck sweaters in pale turquoise or green. Your favorite place may be a room in the middle of your home with dim light and low ceilings. If you have such a retreat, furnish it with round shapes and light blue carpeting. A mural on the wall of a country cottage and a woodsman chopping or stacking wood completes the decor.

Outdoors, April 25 likes daisies and a wheat field. You may want to stay on a farm for a time or visit one frequently. The gentle rhythm of nature suits you and can calm you if you occasionally see red and blow your top.

A Kabbalistic Interpretation

For most, idealism tends to fall by the wayside, but April 25 natives tend to hold on to theirs. Visionaries, prophets, and mystics may well be born on this day. Idealism is an admirable quality, but you may need to temper its effects once in a while. To lessen the influence of your lofty ideals, take a piece of fool's gold and make a point of spending ten minutes looking at it each night for a month.

Privacy is supremely important to you. You like to find your moments of solitude in natural surroundings. For many people this will mean spending time in their garden, but for you it is important to have a closed space where you can sit and feel completely alone. Seek a quiet grove of trees in the woods. Build a summerhouse that will allow you enclosed seclusion while still enjoying the open air.

Rather than having grass lawns consider using water as the base of your garden Try a pond or even a genuine water garden. Create a rock garden with little rivulets of water running over and among the stones.

A Numerological Interpretation
YOUR MAGIC NUMBERS: 2 AND 8

The twenty-fifth day of the fourth month reduces to two, a number representing the life force itself in ancient symbolism. This path carries the lesson of internalizing what is enduring in life and what is transient. A constant reevaluation is required, and it may seem at times that you experience losses. Your task is to embrace what endures: love, respect, compassion. The only things that are truly permanent are the intangibles. All forms eventually dissolve. Search for substance. Amber and celestite will harmonize your mental processes.

The 116th day of the year reduces to eight, amplifying your understanding of the impermanence of forms and the enduring nature of love. Place a bowl of seashells in your kitchen window. Spend time at the ocean, listen to the voice of the sea lapping against the shore. Hear the whisper of the wind. The tides ever change, but the ocean remains.

OBJECTS/IMAGES
toys, landscapes, teapots

SHAPES/MATERIALS
chamois cloth, taffeta, tassels

COLORS
turquoise, carmine, teal

ANIMAL
ox

PLANTS, HERBS, EDIBLES
magnolia, nasturtium, butterscotch

ESSENCE
helichrysum

SOUNDS/RHYTHMS
pipe organs, operatic arias

MUSICAL NOTES
C# and G

DEEP SPACE OBJECTS
Beta Cepheus, Alfirk, Flock of Sheep

April 26

YOUR SIGN
Taurus

YOUR ELEMENT
Earth

YOUR RULERS
Venus, Moon
5–6 degrees
First Decanate, yang

The Astrological Interpretation

Your birth date is deeply connected to the planet Venus, goddess of love. You tend to be very romantic by nature, and your personal and intimate relationships are thus very important to you. You have a great "urge to merge" and have a natural magnetism that draws many people to you. You are a very good and loyal friend and are quite generous with both yourself and your possessions. People can confide in you and know that you would never betray them. Physical love is important to you, and it would be very difficult for you to be in a relationship in which the sexual dynamics were lacking. You definitely enjoy long, sensual evenings and are much more receptive to being in intimate surroundings than out in large crowds. When your heart is engaged, you are a most healing individual, adding nourishment and kindness to your lovemaking.

April 26 has a diplomatic nature and an intellect capable of understanding a variety of disciplines. Your great gift is the ability to visualize information and concepts concretely. Surround your home with reminders of the natural world such as mineral geodes, uncut rose quartz, and agates. You might make a collage or piece of sculpture with pieces of bark, wood, and pressed flowers. Sounds are very stimulating to April 26. Have a door chime and telephone ring that is melodious. You may want to wear earplugs if you live in a noisy environment. Copper is an excellent metal for April 26 to wear or have in your home. Copper cookware could inspire you to create culinary delights.

Outdoors April 26 wants to mark off property lines with box hedges. Your garden should include impatiens and hollyhocks. You may be interested in hot-air balloons and should try to take a ride in one. The rhythm of farming is a tonic for your hair-trigger temper and restlessness. You might think of a farming vacation if you don't live in the country.

A Kabbalistic Interpretation

April 26 is full of energies that encourage an environmentally conscious approach to life. April 26 birthdays are often among early stumpers for environmental reform and first in line at the local recycling plant. You may want to do more than recycle and begin generating your own self-sustaining garden. The act of growing and tending your own food is not only a wonderful way to contribute to the environment but will also lead to unexpected and deeply rewarding changes in your own psyche.

The letter *Teth*, meaning "serpent," is associated with the kabbalistic value of this day. You are a deeply and profoundly spiritual individual. If you do not already have a regular meditation and yoga practice, it's time to begin. You may have a special affinity for kundalini yoga, a form of yoga practice that is best learned from an established practictioner with long experience. The purpose of this form is to awaken the serpent power residing in the energy center, or chakra, at the base of our spines.

A Numerological Interpretation
YOUR MAGIC NUMBERS: 3 AND 9

The twenty-sixth day of the fourth month reduces to three, the number of growth, development, and the unfoldment of the principles of one and two. This day's path involves the conquest of obstacles and challenges that come our way and through which we learn. If we come to a river on a journey, we can attempt to ford the current, go around, or build a bridge across, thereby easing the crossing for ourselves and all those who come after.

The 117th day of the year reduces to nine, which adds the quality of perfected outcome to your endeavors. Sapphire and citrine will stimulate your focus. Visit Niagara Falls and watch the rushing, pounding water pour over the falls as it has done for ages. Study bridges of all kinds. Plant climbing roses or wisteria and watch their progress as they climb.

OBJECTS/IMAGES
*brick kilns,
carved wood statues, darts*

SHAPES/MATERIALS
*brightly colored squares,
steel, carbuncles*

COLORS
*spring green, carrot,
cobalt blue*

ANIMALS
boxer dog, kangaroo

PLANTS, HERBS, EDIBLES
basil, arugula, briars

ESSENCE
juniper

SOUNDS/RHYTHMS
*sound of a punching bag,
the box step*

MUSICAL NOTES
D and G#

DEEP SPACE OBJECTS
*Alpha Triangulum,
Caput Trianguli,
Head of the Triangle*

April 27

YOUR SIGN
Taurus

YOUR ELEMENT
Earth

YOUR RULERS
Venus, Moon
6–7 degrees
First Decanate, yang

The Astrological Interpretation

A very resourceful person, you trust in what you have and in your own ability to take care of yourself and the people you love. It is important for you to know that you have a little extra money in the bank, some additional food stored away in your pantry, and that spare blanket or two in the closet in case the weather becomes really cold or some unexpected guests arrive. Although this practical side of your nature is to be admired, you have to take care not to place all of your faith in the material side of life. Your birth date indicates that you are a very earthy person, but even the earth quakes from time to time. Our real strength and power reside in our beliefs, those immutable inner values that see us through the tough times that come into everyone's life.

April 27 is a subtle degree, and you may have great bodily strength and health. Your sensual appetites lead you: channel your energies into the healing arts, both for yourself and for others. Massage is a great activity for you, and you might consider a deep muscle therapy. At home, you want some luxury. A candy dish half full of mints will help sate your sweet tooth. Flowing curtains that look like silk or organza are perfect, and all your furniture should be a soft "sink into the cushions" style. For the higher mind consider having some meditation music or a set of temple bells that you ring to clear your mind. April 27 is sensitive to music, and humming will be the best way to keep calm.

Outdoors April 27 is fond of flowers and farming. If you could keep a cow in your backyard you would keep in touch with your earth nature! If this is not practical how about a cardboard or metal cut-out cow grazing in your garden? Flowers that you may particularly enjoy are jonquils, shasta daisies, and English daisies.

A Kabbalistic Interpretation

The full kabbalistic value of this day generates a large prime number, pointing to a strong individuality. You have an interest in religion, although you tend to be skeptical about religious practices. Your interest is more intellectual than spiritual, and a great present for you would be books or images relating to extreme cults within major religions or religions of indigenous peoples.

You have a definite presence about you that is recognized both by your friends and your work colleagues. You are likely to climb the corporate ladder with ease. If you are planning a serious relationship with someone born this day it is important to realize that this person is likely to be the dominant individual in the relationship. If that suits you, purchase a solid wooden chair with red or purple upholstering for her to sit on.

The energy of this day carries a fascination with death. Understanding mortality is important, but be aware of a potential for morbid thoughts. Make sure that you use plenty of parsley and garlic in your cooking to liven your mood.

A Numerological Interpretation
YOUR MAGIC NUMBERS: 4 AND 10

The twenty-seventh day of the fourth month reduces to four, the number of order, measurement, and classification. The number four is equated with mercy on the kabbalistic Tree of Life. This day's path is inherently paradoxical. Your quest for the higher things and joys of life are sometimes played out through an endless search for personal gratification. You will mercifully learn through these experiences. Ultimately, the unfulfilling nature of the search will lead you to the deeper things you really desire.

The 118th day of the year equals ten, which supports your path with the energy of final self-mastery. Celebrate News Year's Eve at Times Square. Travel to New Orleans for Mardi Gras. Rent an outrageous yellow-orange and indigo costume, complete with feathered mask, party horns, and drums. Citrine and adventurine will give you strength.

OBJECTS/IMAGES
a mechanical bank, cabinetmakers, cash registers

SHAPES/MATERIALS
bowl shapes, dotted Swiss material, moss agate, alabaster

COLORS
pastel yellow, saffron, navy blue

ANIMALS
the minotaur, brush rabbit

PLANTS, HERBS, EDIBLES
pinto beans, oxeye daisy

ESSENCE
ylang-ylang

SOUNDS/RHYTHMS
balladeers and crooners

MUSICAL NOTES
D# and A

DEEP SPACE OBJECTS
Alpha Aries, Hamal, Lamb

April 28

The Astrological Interpretation

An extremely appealing quality of your personality is your ability to hold firm under fire, to see the goodness in the most challenging event, and to give comfort to others in times of stress. You are adept at seeing how something material can evoke an emotional state. This is one of the reasons why you can give a gift at just the right time or supply a special treat that you know is someone's favorite. You should never be overly concerned about your own finances. There is a definite difference between what a person desires and what he really needs. Your birth date embodies an ancient astrological dictum: "a child of Venus will never want for anything." Just as you endeavor to supply others with the requirements for their well-being, life will take care of yours.

April 28 combines the famous Taurean stubbornness with lunar resourcefulness and artistic abilities. The moon is exalted in Taurus. You can dig in your heels or imagine creative solutions to life's problems and ways of fulfilling your desires. You might investigate the ancient Minoan civilization on Crete. Their religion was based on goddess worship, and bulls' horns were a sacred symbol. The palace at Knossos was painted a unique shade of red; this may be a power color for you. Practice flexibility by moving familiar objects to different spaces. At home, keep houseplants in each room. During the winter, lilies are a pick-me-up. If you are up late, sit in a comfortable chair; sip a glass of water and bask in the moonlight.

Your outdoor space should resemble a farm. If you live in the country, outdoor pets and some cows will keep you in tune with your earthy nature. If you live in the city or suburbs, visit agriculture areas. The smell of newly mown hay is perfume for you. Imagine a variety of uses for a sleigh. Your magic is sufficient to come up with ideas even if there is no snow.

A Kabbalistic Interpretation

This day points to an abiding interest in language—not so much in speaking a different tongue but in learning about the development and internal structures of language itself. You might be a linguist or semanticist, study etymology, or be an aficionado of wordplay and puns. You might appreciate a framed print of some ancient script such as Coptic or ogham or even hieroglyphics to hang in your living room.

You probably have an interest in music, and like language, you love it for the semantic interplay of harmony and structure. Attend classical concerts. Favorite composers are likely to be dramatic figures such as Wagner or Beethoven. Listen to a great recording of *Der Ring des Nibelungen*, and try all nine of Beethoven's symphonies.

April 28 birthdays love sports, though they may not apply themselves to this endeavor as much as they do to music and language. Pictures of sporting heroes or a childhood baseball glove would make good decorations for the family room or den.

A Numerological Interpretation

YOUR MAGIC NUMBERS: 5 AND 2

The twenty-eighth day of the fourth month reduces to five, the number of adaptation and versatility. Yours is a path of transcending the obvious and devising clever means of solving problems. Your quest is to overturn a blind acceptance that a problem can't be solved. Change the context. Shift the paradigm. If there's no snow for the sleigh, use wheels instead. Float the sleigh across a lake. There is always a novel way to view a situation to alter the perspective.

The 119th day of the year reduces to two, adding the influence of receptivity to subconscious impressions that enhance your process. Imagine Santa Claus in downtown Los Angeles in a sleigh with wheels, pulled by a red convertible. Velcro and sticky notes sprang from lateral ways of thinking. Surround yourself with yellow and blue. Solve three-dimensional jigsaw puzzles. Read science fiction. Topaz and sapphire will stimulate your creativity.

OBJECTS/IMAGES
tatting, towels

SHAPES/MATERIALS
neckties, satin

COLORS
tints of blue, apricot, lemon, crimson

ANIMALS
stock dove, calf

PLANTS, HERBS, EDIBLES
vanilla, grapes on the vine, yams

ESSENCE
ylang-ylang

SOUNDS/RHYTHMS
wine being poured, trombone music

MUSICAL NOTES
E and C#

DEEP SPACE OBJECTS
Alpha Cassiopeia, Schedar, Breast

April 29

YOUR SIGN
Taurus

YOUR ELEMENT
Earth

YOUR RULERS
Venus, Moon
8–9 degrees
First Decanate, yang

The Astrological Interpretation

You have the ability to radiate a loving personality to all those with whom you come in contact. You know love on several levels. You are very capable of showing personal, intimate sexual love to the object of your heart. You are also present in a more impersonal way by offering love, loyalty, and cooperation to friends, coworkers, and associates. But there is another quality of love you have that is available to comparatively few people. This is "transpersonal love"—which is unconditional and asks for no rewards. Transpersonal love endows you with a soothing and healing quality, helping you to calm people who are in great distress with a detached compassion that lifts up and makes whole. Apply this part of your nature to yourself and you will find that even in your darkest times, you are in contact with your own inner light.

You are most interested in exchanging good feelings rather than possessions. If you notice that you are holding on to material things, concentrate on developing your heart and love nature. You'll enjoy life more and clean up any accumulated clutter. Objects that might help you in your emotional housecleaning would be heart shapes or drawing round circles when doodling. The color light pink is good for you. During the winter consider sleeping on red flannel sheets. Pictures of Ireland, the Emerald Isle, may be very pleasant for you to look at . . . a visit would be even better.

Outdoors, your home could be in a valley or overlooking one. A garden in steps set in a hillside would be particularly appealing. Myrtle trees and soft mosses resonate with your gentleness. Taurus rules all lilies, and you may particularly enjoy tiger lilies.

A Kabbalistic Interpretation

One of the main tarot cards associated with this day is the Lovers, a card that represents the need to make choices. April 29 birthdays can find it quite difficult to make the decision needed to move forward when confronted with a major opportunity or crossroads. Burn some cedar incense in your bedroom each evening to ease your decision-making process.

You can be witty and amusing, and your wit can have a sharp edge to it. You have a knack for making these acerbic comments without being aggressive, so you rarely cause offense. A collection of works by Oscar Wilde is a great gift idea for April 29 birthdays.

With your wit and humor you might be an excellent writer. You probably have a number of half-finished projects and manuscripts in a drawer somewhere. Keep some thyme growing in a yellow-and-red window box on the window ledge of your workroom or study if you want to increase your chances of maintaining a commitment to a project.

A Numerological Interpretation
YOUR MAGIC NUMBERS: 6 AND 3

The twenty-ninth day of the fourth month reduces to six, the number of beauty, symmetry, and harmony of opposites. This day's path contains the lesson that gifts, talents, and possessions are enhanced as they are shared. As we realize our potentials, joy and satisfaction are attained through sharing. Reciprocity is key to self-renewal with this path. Give freely of what you have been given, and strive to turn your abilities into expertise.

The 120th day reduces to three, which adds the trinity of creative expression. Decorate your home for all the holidays. Have an open house and share the seasonal festivities. Remember people's birthdays with cards and presents wrapped in yellows and greens. Peridot and amber will stimulate your generosity.

OBJECTS/IMAGES
scarabs, elves, frescoes

SHAPES/MATERIALS
mink, rose quartz, spinach jade

COLORS
pale peach, lime green, tangerine

ANIMALS
songbirds, hare

PLANTS, HERBS, EDIBLES
pulsatilla, elder, and dried apricots

ESSENCE
clove

SOUNDS/RHYTHMS
sonatas, songs

MUSICAL NOTES
F and D

DEEP SPACE OBJECTS
Gamma Cetus, Kaffaljidhma, Head of the Sea Monster

April 30

YOUR SIGN
Taurus

YOUR ELEMENT
Earth

YOUR RULERS
Venus, Moon
9–10 degrees
First Decanate, yang

The Astrological Interpretation

You have a special connection to natural beauty. You are at your most calm and are able to contact your inner strength when you are taking a walk in a forest or visiting a flower garden. Even if you live in a huge city, you will find that keeping plants or growing kitchen herbs will bring you a great deal of personal satisfaction. Be in touch with nature and you will be in touch with your real self. Your success in life is based on your personal values. As you define and refine what is important to you, you will see that your true direction will unfold with amazing clarity. Your own life requires regular "weeding" so that you may properly eliminate those ideas, desires, and people that stifle your growth. Nurture what and who is good for you and put the rest in the compost heap.

Some April 30 birthdays fall on a critical degree, which can bring extremes of experience into life. Your placid, patient nature is the key to weathering ups and downs. Your talents include singing and service to worthwhile projects. In fact, singing is the best tension reliever for you. You don't have to go public: singing in the shower counts. With both Venus and the moon ruling your birthday, you like luxury and softness. An angora or cashmere sweater may bring a great deal of pleasure. Earrings and cuff links are ornaments for April 30. Agate, sapphire, and jade are all good stones. Your sense of smell may be keenly developed, and floral scents such as tuberose and hyacinth create a sense of luxury for you.

You feel very relaxed in nature. An image for the daytime is a large waterwheel grinding corn. City dwellers should take frequent trips to public gardens. Keep mindful of the change of seasons. A nighttime image for you is a tiny new moon sliver in a very dark sky. This is the new moon to make a wish on.

A Kabbalistic Interpretation

This day's birthday tends to have enormous passion that is expressed quite freely. Having a relationship with someone born today can be akin to taking a box of fireworks to bed with you and lighting a match—every so often it is going to go off with a bang. If you were born today and you want to encourage an increased level of passion and potential for explosive bedroom activity, give your partner an emerald and ruby ring to wear on his index finger.

While you have a very loyal attitude to your partner, you do like travel and change in your life. You may find it difficult to settle down and may opt for a career that involves regular relocation. In your home you might use a lot of gray and pink marbling and keep a number of framed maps on your walls.

It is the element of fire in your life that gives you your driving passion and love of travel. Fire is important to you in both a literal and symbolic sense. Look for a house with a working fireplace or light your home with candles in the evening.

A Numerological Interpretation

YOUR MAGIC NUMBERS: 7 AND 4

The thirtieth day of the fourth month reduces to seven, the number of victory and sworn oaths. This day's path endows you with a keen sense of the pain and need of human beings less fortunate than you. Through Red Cross, Save the Children, or other similar organizations you can attain an awareness of the intrinsic universality of the human condition, and this erases the illusion of separateness. In a sense, your soul has sworn an oath of service and dedication that will bring you deep fulfillment.

The 121st day of the year reduces to four, adding the quality of stability and order to your efforts. Volunteer for a civic organization. Agate and opal will strengthen your ardor. Enjoy the special camaraderie of other volunteers—the smiles, laughs, and generosity of open hearts.

OBJECTS/IMAGES
*a matador's cape,
a piano-shaped music box*

SHAPES/MATERIALS
burnished copper, a scroll

COLORS
*turquoise, lavender,
forest green, amber*

ANIMAL
bulldog

PLANTS, HERBS, EDIBLES
silverweed, slippery elm, cake

ESSENCE
violet

SOUNDS/RHYTHMS
quiet, fusion rhythms

MUSICAL NOTES
F# and D#

DEEP SPACE OBJECTS
Eta Cassiopeia, Achird

May 1

YOUR SIGN
Taurus

YOUR ELEMENT
Earth

YOUR RULERS
Venus, Moon, Mercury
10–11 degrees
Second Decanate, yang

The Astrological Interpretation

You are fond of jewelry, clothes, and adornments and like to make a good impression on others. You receive a deep sense of emotional satisfaction when you feel that new gold bracelet on your arm or those extra bills in your wallet. Yet you do not want to be possessed by your possessions. You could spend the entire day thinking and dreaming about owning a new car and miss out on the creative opportunities life is offering you to buy it. Cultivate the richness of your own abilities and potential. Make the effort to obtain the additional training and put in the extra hours that a promotion in your field requires. You are the kind of person who knows how to relax and enjoy life. But it is absolutely necessary that you balance your desires with the practical efforts it takes to achieve them.

May 1 traditionally is celebrated as May Day—the coming of flowers and fertility in the harvest. The Maypole with its ribbons and flowers on top is an excellent symbol for the spiritual path of this birthday—to bring forth flowers of creativity in tangible form. Venus, the ruler of your sign, governs all artistic pursuits. Bring your famous steadfastness to creative projects and your life will flower. A garden with many different kinds of flowers is, of course, ideal. Concentrate on daisies, larkspur, and hawthorn. Sprinkling the flowers with a hose or watering can will calm the mind. Continue the festivities indoors with floral wallpaper and miscellaneous ribbons to add color throughout your home.

Mercury, which reigns over communication, is one of May 1's rulers. An antique pen and good quality paper are two items to treasure. For more technologically minded people, have a good computer and communication center. Remember to place a mineral on top of your computer: turquoise ore or malachite would be good to remind you of the earth and its bounty.

A Kabbalistic Interpretation

People born today are living representations of the true significance of May Day, a celebration of fertility and the vital regenerative energies of the earth. If your family and regular guests or visitors are open-minded consider getting a traditional phallic fetish to hang on the south side of your living room. If this is a little too direct for you, you can connect with the regenerative energies of this day at a wooden desk inlaid with a daisy pattern at the borders.

One of the most important elements in your life is to feel a sense of harmony in your environment. This desire to resonate harmoniously and peacefully extends to your relationships with both people as well as places and is suggested by the tarot card Temperance. However it is important that you not allow your desire for harmony to cause you to become a doormat for those around you. Keeping a piece of red jasper or a bloodstone with you at all times can counteract that potential.

A Numerological Interpretation

YOUR MAGIC NUMBERS: 6 AND 5

The first day of the fifth month reduces to six, the number of harmony and balance. Six brings total opposites into perfect equilibrium. This path calls for you to pour yourself into life with nothing less than total dedication. This is a path of stewardship; you are like a spiritual gardener. You must care for the charges in your life, whatever or whoever they are. Fill your home with potted plants such as African violets and miniature lemon trees, and care for them as tender charges worthy of your love. Volunteer at a day care center or children's hospital, and be sure to bring brightly colored balloons or flowers. Peridot and citrine are reminders of nature's bounty.

The 122nd day of the year reduces to five, adding a comfort with the constancy of change you experience in life. Since you like to keep things in balance, five aids your tolerance. Lime green will lift your spirits.

OBJECTS/IMAGES
spurting fountains of water, corsages, pressed flower collages

SHAPES/MATERIALS
satin, angora wool

COLORS
cream yellow, emerald green, turquoise, olive green, saffron

ANIMALS
calf, fluffy dogs

PLANTS, HERBS, EDIBLES
sorrel, beef tongue, nasturtiums

ESSENCES
lilies, gardenia

SOUNDS/RHYTHMS
circle dance rhythms, waltz time, the lowing of cows

MUSICAL NOTES
F and E

DEEP SPACE OBJECT
nova

May 2

YOUR SIGN
Taurus

YOUR ELEMENT
Earth

YOUR RULERS
Venus, Mercury, Moon
11–12 degrees
Second Decanate, yang

The Astrological Interpretation

You are by nature a gentle and supportive person. Yet your sense of individuality is also quite strong. You are challenged in your social exchanges when you feel that giving to others deprives you of your personal integrity. Being placed in positions where you have to be more cooperative than you care to be requires that you dig deeply into your own foundations and find what is really important to you. With enough discrimination, you will find that your center can never be taken away or compromised. The rest is superficial and you can give and share freely.

You can be quite strong-minded if you have to compete, but life feels good when you are with like-minded people and do not have to assert yourself. Your home and socializing are very important to you. You are attracted to quiet places of beauty, books that open your heart, music that calms your spirit, and intimate dinners with loved ones. Consider a combination family room–kitchen for entertaining. A central cooking island with copper cookware hanging above creates a warm hearth where you can socialize and prepare dinner. You may want to decorate your kitchen with dried herbs, wreaths of peppers, dried fruit, and dried flowers. A private nook might include your favorite music and a piano. Singing is a good activity for all Taureans. Even if you claim you are tone deaf, hum while you are in the shower. Your wardrobe could emphasize turquoise, and you might enjoy having a variety of colored scarves to protect your throat.

Outdoors, a garden with many different kinds of flowers is a place to create and be with friends. Orange flowers such as wood lily and orange hawkweed may give you a special thrill. If butterflies rest on these flowers then consider it a lucky day.

A Kabbalistic Interpretation

Emotional issues are the driving concern in your life. In order of priority, you tend to put career goals and financial concerns behind the state of your relationships. While many people would feel frustrated when their self-directed goals are put on hold, you are someone who derives equal pleasure from the enjoyment and achievements of those close to you. As someone who gives so much to others it is good to find some time in the day for yourself. Water is your element, so treat yourself often to a nice long bath. Put some matte red candles by the tub and pour some sandalwood essence in your bathwater. Around your home use pastel colors, especially lavender and violet, to lighten the spirit.

Balance is a key factor in your life, especially in your garden. To encourage the well-being of your family, plant at least one apple tree in your garden. Try to represent all the different elements by having many trees, shrubs, a rock garden, and at least one water feature, whether a pond, brook, or pool. A white fountain edged with gold is ideal. To really get the most out of the water energy position your fountain in the west.

A Numerological Interpretation
YOUR MAGIC NUMBERS: 7 AND 6

The second day of the fifth month reduces to seven, the number of rest after labor. Seven generates the need for cessation after a period of activity. This path contains the necessity of deliberate, conscious choice. Visit your favorite mall, or go window-shopping somewhere exotic like Rodeo Drive in Beverly Hills. This pattern requires skill in ascertaining in advance whether your choices are in alignment with your deepest desires. Cultivate your power of visualization so you can see outcomes before they materialize. Remember to incorporate all your senses into your mental pictures, making them rich in sensory detail.

The 123rd day of the year reduces to six, which adds an appreciation for beauty in the periods of rest between accomplishments. This helps you to stand back and admire your work. Wear purple to enhance your self esteem. Tourmaline wands will open your inner vision.

OBJECTS/IMAGES
a hoe, ear clips, Victorian valentines

SHAPES/MATERIALS
emerald, horn shapes, ramie cotton

COLORS
cream white, blue wash, pine, moss green

ANIMALS
cattle, cowbird

PLANTS, HERBS, EDIBLES
shortbread cookies, chocolate-covered cherries, curry

ESSENCE
vetivert oil

SOUNDS/RHYTHMS
country western music, circle dances, songs by Bing Crosby

MUSICAL NOTES
F# and F

DEEP SPACE OBJECTS
Alpha Cetus, Nekkar, Nostrils

May 3

YOUR SIGN
Taurus

YOUR ELEMENT
Earth

YOUR RULERS
Venus, Mercury, Moon
12–13 degrees
Second Decanate, yang

The Astrological Interpretation

You are a person whose methods of accomplishing your tasks are often slower than others'. Yet you are also more thorough and responsible for getting the job done right. You are a good observer of people and can see when someone is likely to make an error, especially through faulty judgment or the mishandling of financial resources. Continue to go at your own pace and find your own level of success. Slow and steady growth is much more comfortable to you than the promise of wealth achieved by taking great risks.

Though you enjoy putting forth effort to achieve, you rarely seem strained or tense. Taurus rules the throat, and May 3 in particular may have singing talent. Try it, if only in the shower. Keep your throat protected. A pale blue silk or soft wool scarf is excellent protection from the cold in the winter months. A lucky rabbit's foot is a talisman for May 3. At home, comfort should rule. An open kitchen and family room would be a great place to lounge and entertain. Maybe you'll sing or whistle while doing the dishes! Butterflies should be included somewhere in your home. Perhaps embroidered on guest towels or on the bathroom wallpaper. May 3 also would benefit from potpourri, but let the scent be sweet though not overpowering. Vanilla is a good scent.

Outdoors, May 3 should have a summer lilac (buddleia) or butterfly bush in the garden. As you stroll outside, seeing the butterflies drinking nectar from this bush offers a feeling of abundance and peace. If your outdoor space is small, leave some room for a garden or a few flowerpots. City dwellers will enjoy pots on their balconies or window boxes of daisies.

A Kabbalistic Interpretation

The energy of the day is outstandingly forceful. People born today are immediately recognizable as potential leaders and figures of authority. The best colors for you to wear when you want to emphasize this aspect of your nature are red and a greenish yellow. You might wear a ring in these colors on your third finger.

You are also imbued with an almost tangible erotic energy that can be easily sensed by others across the proverbial "crowded room." People born this day are sensitive to perfume far more than any visual stimulus. A good way to attract a May 3 baby is to wear a heavy musk-based scent.

The planet Jupiter has quite a strong pull on this date. The energy of this planet makes for benevolent and innately cheerful individuals who are blessed with immense charm and a hugely amiable personality. If you want to enhance the effect of Jupiter, wear a brooch or tie pin with a four-pointed star design on it made out of tin.

A Numerological Interpretation

YOUR MAGIC NUMBERS: 8 AND 7

The third day of the fifth month reduces to eight, the number of ebbing and flowing equal and opposite energies. This is a path of utilizing your energies in practical ways and finding constructive applications in even the most mundane circumstances. You are asked to capitalize on whatever resources you find available. Rather than merely watching the river flow by, this path suggests you build a dam to harness the energy. Watch beavers in their energetic and industrious construction projects. Teal is a color to bring out your best qualities. Have a tabletop fountain or an indoor rock garden. Build a small lily pond in your yard.

The 124th day of the year reduces to seven, contributing the influence of a rest period between the ever moving cycles in your life. Chrysocolla and amazonite will help you gather the forces of your mental energies.

OBJECTS/IMAGES
Minoan double ax, bonnets, a cravat

SHAPES/MATERIALS
silk embroidery thread, jade rings, plump round shapes

COLORS
light yellow, cream yellow, pastel orange, aquamarine

ANIMALS
bulldog, Irish setter, milk cow

PLANTS, HERBS, EDIBLES
black cherries, squash, daffodils

ESSENCES
lily, vanilla, strawberry scent

SOUNDS/RHYTHMS
march rhythms, singing, country western music

MUSICAL NOTES
G and F#

DEEP SPACE OBJECTS
Gamma Andromeda, Almach, the Badger

May 4

YOUR SIGN
Taurus

YOUR ELEMENT
Earth

YOUR RULERS
Venus, Moon, Mercury
13–14 degrees
Second Decanate, yang

The Astrological Interpretation

You are born at the exact middle of the sign Taurus. This is known by astrologers as the most fixed degree of the zodiac. You are capable of holding your ground and sticking to your opinions no matter who or what stands in your way. Your values are based on what has proven to work in the past. Some people will say that you are too conservative and traditional. Yet you know that your nature allows you to be a pillar of responsibility and that you offer a place of peace in the center of a storm. In this respect, your home is very important to you. You like to fill it with comfortable furniture, flowers, and warm hospitality. You tend to make very few abrupt changes in your environment and lifestyle, but what you have will last a lifetime.

Your birthday may fall close to the fixed star Almach, which will incline you to artistic ability or Menkar, which could incline you to injury from wild beasts. Your birthday has magnetic energy. You have the ability to persuade people and use your energies as a healer. You are responsive to scent and may want to include some aroma atomizers in your home. Sweet smells such as vanilla and Peruvian balsam attract you. Massage is an excellent way to keep flexible. Consider creating your own massage oils with scents you enjoy. In the kitchen your artistic and healing abilities come together. Putting up preserves and making your own healthful fruit concoctions could interest you.

Outdoors a myrtle tree with some low wooden benches would be a perfect place for you to sit and dream. Yellow tulips, jonquils, and daylilies are all good flowers for you.

A Kabbalistic Interpretation

The Hermit card from the tarot is a powerful force in the energies of this day. The Hermit points to a great deal of wisdom and a courage in attempting to penetrate the unknown. The Hermit also refers to a need for solitude in your life. If you can afford to, have a small cabin in the woods where you can go and spend a few days when you need to be alone. Or invest in a stout pair of hiking boots in a neutral shade and go off for long walks on a regular basis.

You are someone who is secure in who you are, and relatively untroubled by the minor neuroses and paranoias that seem to mark out the culture of the early twenty-first century. This may be a result of the amount of time you spend in your own company. A positive effect of this is that you are an exceedingly adaptable individual. Change does not hold the same fears for you as it does for many others. At times you can almost be too adaptable, and a vase of sunflowers on your desk or an outfit with a vertically striped pattern will ensure that you maintain your ground when you really need to.

Although you enjoy your own company, you are also happy in the company of animals. The kabbalistic values of this day point to a special affinity for smaller animals. A small rodent like a hamster would be a fantastic pet.

A Numerological Interpretation

YOUR MAGIC NUMBERS: 9 AND 8

The fourth day of the fifth month reduces to nine, the number of completion and successful attainment. This day's path is one of self-discovery and self-sufficiency. This pattern requires that your own sense of who you are emerges into full awareness and expression. Take a trip to the beach. Walk along the water's edge, searching for shells. Spread out a lime-green-and-yellow-striped towel, and play in the sand, recapturing the sense of freedom you felt as a child. Build a sand castle, then watch the waves melt the sand as your creation is reclaimed by the ocean.

The 125th day of the year reduces to eight, adding the influence of easy movement into the next cycle of manifestation. Aquamarine is a gem that will increase the serenity you feel with the shifting tides. Collect seashells. Place your ear to a conch shell, and thrill to the voice of the ocean.

OBJECTS/IMAGES
checkbooks, fragrances, garlands, mattresses

SHAPES/MATERIALS
moss agate, alabaster, bronze, emeralds

COLORS
aqua, turquoise

ANIMALS
the minotaur, tabby cat

PLANTS, HERBS, EDIBLES
thyme, ground ivy, sycamore trees, primrose, cudweed

ESSENCE
styrax

SOUNDS/RHYTHMS
matador music, "The Toreador Song" from Bizet's Carmen

MUSICAL NOTES
G# and G

DEEP SPACE OBJECT
Alpha Horologium

May 5

YOUR SIGN
Taurus

YOUR ELEMENT
Earth

YOUR RULERS
Venus, Mercury
14–15 degrees
Second Decanate, yang

The Astrological Interpretation

People know that they can depend on you for solid advice and consistent friendship. You are firm and steady in your approach to life, at ease with the established and traditional. You enjoy history, especially art history, and take great pleasure in viewing (and if possible, owning!) antique furniture and jewelry. At times, however, this attachment to the past may make it difficult for you to move forward, both in terms of relationships and creative ideas. You will have to overcome your own reluctance to change. What you value most is inside you, just waiting to come out and be developed, but it will take will to push yourself ahead. If you find yourself periodically blocked, it is your responsibility to search for the knowledge and friendships to enhance and expand your life.

You are very connected to the earth. City dwellers should keep landscape paintings around and as many natural materials in your house and clothing as possible. To renew yourself find a natural stream with clear, ice cold water, surrounded with moss, shrubs, and briars. Your garden should be full of roses, eglantine, and grasses.

You are a sophisticated person and like to be surrounded by elegant objects. For men a white silk muffler or ascot is a good touch; women might seek a turquoise silk cloche hat that always feels good. A one-story home with a circular feel to the space gives you room to roam. Sectional sofas that wind around in an egg shape are pleasing to the eye.

May 5 is a builder and needs a retreat space. A large cherry wood desk with a lamp shaded by green glass (like an old-fashioned banker's lamp) would be the place to redesign your personal world and perhaps parts of society in general.

A Kabbalistic Interpretation

This day has definite associations with family and inherited values and attitudes. A copy of their family tree or a traditional coat of arms would make a wonderful present for someone born this day.

Because of your overriding interest in things historical, some people might expect you to be somewhat stuffy and dull. Yet you are often the life and soul of the party. Unfortunately, you sometimes are too much inclined to be the biggest party animal around and allow yourself to overindulge. The next time you go out for a night on the town, take a small piece of angelica with you, as this may help you to moderate your behavior.

Personal space is extremely important to people born this day, although they may not realize it themselves. Without a calming space in the house, you may well overload yourself with stress. Excellent colors for you in such a space are russet, tawny brown, and olive green. If you could find a sofa or chenille or knitted throw cover in these colors you will have a wonderful place where you can sit and relax.

A Numerological Interpretation
YOUR MAGIC NUMBERS: 10 AND 9

The fifth day of the fifth month reduces to ten, the number of perfection and dominion. This day's path carries the requirement of enjoying to the fullest the roles you choose to play on the stage of life. You are innately aware that the world is a vast arena. Enjoy all the experiences of your life as theater and high drama. Choose your props, pay attention to lighting, staging, and costumes. Involve yourself in community theater for fun. Wear a feathered purple hat and yellow scarves that make you laugh, and turn heads on the street.

Ten also reduces to one, urging you always to the next level of experience. Amber is a gem to anchor your sense of bringing antiquity into the present moment. The 126th day of the year reduces to nine, adding a sense of fulfillment and completion. You know when it is time for the curtain to come down.

OBJECTS/IMAGES
beaded velvet bags, turtleneck sweaters, button earrings

SHAPES/MATERIALS
curved soapstone, petrified wood, emeralds

COLORS
saffron, orange, Aegean blue, navy blue

ANIMALS
Guernsey cow, angora cat, possum

PLANTS, HERBS, EDIBLES
cherries in brandy, coltsfoot, wheat fields

ESSENCES
bitter almonds, cardamom, kumquat

SOUNDS/RHYTHMS
early jazz, mambo

MUSICAL NOTES
A and G#

DEEP SPACE OBJECT
NGC 1407 elliptical galaxy

May 6

YOUR SIGN
Taurus

YOUR ELEMENT
Earth

YOUR RULERS
Venus, Moon, Mercury
15–16 degrees
Second Decanate, yin

The Astrological Interpretation

You prefer to go through life tending to your own affairs. You are very happy at the dinner table, and food is definitely the way to your heart. You are giving and supportive and enjoy sharing the pleasures of life with friends and loved ones. But you can become quite irritated when you feel that your kindness is misinterpreted for weakness. When your sense of boundaries is crossed, your Taurus nature will definitely see a red cape in front of you and charge without warning.

May 6 is a birthday of considerable power and ability. You like big thoughts and big projects, and a large home would be pleasing to you. In the bedroom be sure to have a bed big enough for all occupants. A reclining couch with a turquoise throw or lap robe would be a welcome addition to your boudoir. Men will particularly enjoy a high dresser with enough drawer space for sweaters and shirts. Venus is the ruler of May 6 and both men and women will be fond of stylish clothing. A few special antiques or decorative objects would be cherished possessions. A jade Chinese incense burner is a possibility or a carved statue of the Hindu goddess Kali. You will enjoy objects that are beautiful and are significant symbols.

Outdoors, May 6 would love acres of flowers and trees with a pavilion where you could have tea or cocktails. A visit to such a garden would be a treat. In your own yard, emphasize a wall trellis with morning glories or trumpet vine. Choose flowering fruit trees and orange lilies, amaryllis, lemon daylily, and regal lily for your garden.

A Kabbalistic Interpretation

This date is unusually spiritual for an astrological sign so deeply rooted in the element earth. If you were born on this day you probably have little time for organized religion. You are fiercely individual in almost every aspect of your life, and your spiritual life is no different. Take up a spiritual exercise regime such as hatha yoga. Because you are a visual person, you could also buy yourself some beautifully cut crystals to focus on while meditating.

No one could accuse people born this day of being dull. Your extreme intelligence comes across within a few minutes of meeting you. The positive solar energy that permeates this day is mixed with a mercurial part that loves all kinds of brainteasers. An ideal present for today's birthday would be a selection of traditional block puzzles, especially an antique Chinese puzzle box.

You have a strong libido. If you want to really enhance your smoldering appeal, then the colors to opt for are midnight blue and purple. In addition you will put yourself in an exceptionally sensual frame of mind if you dab a little sandalwood oil behind your ears.

A Numerological Interpretation
YOUR MAGIC NUMBERS: 2 AND 10

The sixth day of the fifth month reduces to two, a number connoting polarity and the division of unity into opposite forms of expression. Whatever the situation, you are able to see its diametric opposite. This path endows you with persistence and determination. When you have a vision of how things can be better, you are driven to share your ideal and will stop at nothing to accomplish it. You have a tendency to share your zeal whether others wish to listen or not. Learn to listen to the visions of others.

Don't forget to smell the flowers along your perceived superhighway. Study ants pushing articles heavier than their body weight, and watch as they create amazing colonies. Orange and blue sapphire are gems to inspire you and bring a sparkle to your eyes. Wear blue to calm your emotions and stabilize the conflicting thoughts within you. To maintain perspective, volunteer in a retirement home or hospice group. The 127th day of the year reduces to ten, adding the element of completed processes and embodiment of seed ideas.

OBJECTS/IMAGES
vases, towels, treasure chests, rouge

SHAPES/MATERIALS
womb shapes, washable silk, white stones

COLORS
rosy peach, indigo, amber

ANIMAL
kangaroo

PLANTS, HERBS, EDIBLES
rose vervain, dessert wines, wood sorrel, watermelon vines

ESSENCE
peppermint

SOUNDS/RHYTHMS
songs, poetic verses

MUSICAL NOTES
A and C#

DEEP SPACE OBJECTS
Delta Cassiopeia, -Ruckback, the Knee

May 7

YOUR SIGN
Taurus

YOUR ELEMENT
Earth

YOUR RULERS
Venus, Mercury, Moon
16–17 degrees
Second Decanate, yin

The Astrological Interpretation

Your home is very important to you. You love what is beautiful and have a strong need to collect possessions that bring you a sense of security and comfort. You are very happy in a bed covered with soft, down-filled quilts, sitting leisurely in overly stuffed armchairs, and wearing comfortable, natural fiber clothing. In fact, resting and taking it easy are two of your favorite pastimes. You tend to take your time about everything, and that includes love. You are not a gambler in romance, for when you give your heart, you expect your relationship to last a lifetime. Loyalty and faithfulness are critical in your attitude toward friends and lovers and you expect the same in return.

You may be involved with music or simply sing in the shower. In any case it is a good idea for you to keep a melody or musical tone in your head. You may experience a dichotomy between your desire for artistic pursuits and your concern for a secure living. Try to walk the middle way so you can have both aspects in your life. At home keep a pantry stocked with staple foods and a few delicacies like maple sugar candy or preserved cherries. An emerald ring could be a prized possession. As you collect treasured objects, consider an ornate musical jewelry box. You will please both your eyes and ears.

Outdoors, a small cottage in the country would be a perfect retreat. If you have room in your yard, have some torches lining an outdoor entertainment area. The torches might remind you that inspiration can motivate security. A Walkman or portable CD player so you can hear your favorite music as you walk or exercise is also a good idea. Consider listening to Tchaikovsky or Johannes Brahms, both born on May 7.

A Kabbalistic Interpretation

People born on this day are generally among the most generous and kind people one could meet. Unfortunately, it is all too easy for your generous, compassionate nature to be taken for granted. An ideal gift for May 7 is an oak sapling or something for the home with a distinctive oak leaf pattern on it, as this particular tree represents all that is commendable about the individuals born on this date: strength, rootedness, caring.

There is a very strong connection in this day to the Hebrew letter *Mem*. Kabbalistically, the letter *Mem* reflects the element of water, which relates to our deep emotional side. Keeping a pair of grayish pink glass vases containing a single lavender rose in the west side of your bedroom will help your house feel like your emotional home.

The full kabbalistic value of this date hints at a tendency toward melancholy. Combined with the primarily emotional nature of this day's personality there is a danger that you could spend an excessive amount of time feeling pretty mournful. One simple approach to combat this tendency is to hang some cheery posters in your home, especially pop art–style posters. In addition, make sure that all your doors have cast iron fittings.

A Numerological Interpretation
YOUR MAGIC NUMBERS: 3 AND 2

The seventh day of the fifth month reduces to three, a number representing growth, multiplication, and unfoldment. This day's path requires that you gain discernment between what you need and what you truly desire at the deepest level of your soul. Are you consuming all of your life's energies tending to practical necessities, leaving nothing for the true desires of your heart? Resolve to make time for whatever brings you joy and a sense of fulfillment.

What made you happiest as a child? Re-create that feeling. Jump rope, play hopscotch or softball. Keep a bowl of juicy oranges on your table. Hang a still life of brightly colored fruit in your kitchen. Wear a pendant of adventurine for inspiration. The 128th day of the year reduces to two, adding the quality of reflection and repetition to the unfolding journey of discovery in your life.

OBJECTS/IMAGES
a treasure chest,
a cash register, angels singing

SHAPES/MATERIALS
emeralds, nose rings, suede

COLORS
pastels, yellow,
burnt sienna, orange

ANIMALS
piglet, Hereford cow

PLANTS, HERBS, EDIBLES
gourds, thyme, chutney

ESSENCE
benzoin

SOUNDS/RHYTHMS
lush swelling music,
symphony orchestras,
folk melodies

MUSICAL NOTES
D and C#

DEEP SPACE OBJECT
NGC 957, galactic cluster

May 8

YOUR SIGN
Taurus

YOUR ELEMENT
Earth

YOUR RULERS
Venus, Moon, Mercury
17–18 degrees
Second Decanate, yin

The Astrological Interpretation

The opportunity for change is your best friend. Although you prefer to anchor and secure what is yours, you should do this with the view that you are creating foundations for growth. You are constantly refining yourself, so let go of anything or anyone that holds you back from living out your inner truth. You like to travel and explore the world, and you enjoy taking certain comforts and luxuries with you. New luggage in which to put your fine (but practical) clothing is a welcomed gift so that when you arrive at that nice hotel, you can feel that you fit right in. You enjoy the beach as much for water sports as you do for relaxing on the sand, taking in the sun, and reading your favorite magazines.

You can shrug off annoyances rather than react to them, but you can also read a room and know others' moods and dispositions. Your home should be a safe zone . . . no bad vibes allowed. Bolster your environment with the color yellow and furniture with plump pillows. An afghan throw on the sofa or a hassock invites you and your guests to lie down and relax. Tapes and CDs are also a perfect way to regulate your home atmosphere. In India there are certain ragas (melodies) that accompany different times of the day. You may want to investigate this system or create one of your own. At night think of having a tape of water sounds to lull you to sleep. In the morning, wake up to singing birds (natural or on tape).

Outdoors, May 8 will enjoy a garden and may set up an easel to paint there. A copse of trees in a circular shape could define your garden. Then in the interior circle plant grape hyacinths, Persian buttercups, tulips, or pansies.

A Kabbalistic Interpretation

People born on this day are unusually perceptive and often quite profound. Rather than applying their gifts in an intellectual field, those born today are generally involved in the arts. The values of this date point to a definite association with motion, and a great gift would be some form of kinetic sculpture.

You are always definite in your opinion of others. Indeed you set yourself and others extremely high moral standards. This facet of your personality is indicated by the association of this day with the tarot card Judgment. On the whole you are quite perceptive in your judgments of others, but in order to soften the potential for coming across as harsh at work you might consider keeping a small pouch of sage and mallow on your desktop.

Summer is by far your favorite time of the year. It's not just the heat that appeals to you, but you also love the whole smell of summertime. If you want to stay upbeat over the winter months, use a perfume that has a scent based in summer flowers. When the summer does come, invest in a good chaise longue in which to lie and dream up your next creative project. Ideally this should have a greenish blue pattern with an orange border around its edge.

A Numerological Interpretation
YOUR MAGIC NUMBERS: 4 AND 3

The eighth day of the fifth month reduces to four, the number of order, measurement, and classification. There is a quality to this path that drives you to determine what everyone in your life needs, and then provide it for them. This urge stems from a deeper, more universal desire to further advance the ends of humanity itself. Find a form of service and widen your focus. Feed the hungry as a volunteer at a homeless shelter or soup kitchen. Teach English as a second language in an inner-city school. Plant flower bulbs or wildflower seeds along the highway. Have orange lilies in your own garden.

Break some mental molds and personality templates just for fun. Add new ingredients to your recipes to see what happens. Brilliant shades of blue connect you to your soul. Amazonite widens your horizons and scope of vision. The 129th day of the year reduces to three, contributing the quality of creative genius to your endeavors of manifestation.

OBJECTS/IMAGES
leather bags, bonds, wall-to-wall carpeting

SHAPES/MATERIALS
gourd shapes, coral, bornite, shantung silk

COLORS
pale turquoise, sunset orange

ANIMAL
hog

PLANTS, HERBS, EDIBLES
yellow flag, sneezeweed, thyme, sweet wines

ESSENCE
sweet inula

SOUNDS/RHYTHMS
yodeling, spirituals

MUSICAL NOTES
D# and D

DEEP SPACE OBJECT
NGC 581, open cluster

May 9

The Astrological Interpretation

Animals, birds, and butterflies fill you with delight and joy. You are a lover of nature and feel very comfortable in a home filled with living things. You will get a great deal of satisfaction working in a garden or greenhouse, or keeping an assortment of flowering house plants. In business, you would be most successful providing products and services that enrich and benefit other people's lives. Make sure you bring some life into your office by keeping growing plants nearby. If that is not possible, a small bowl of fresh fruit or a vase in which to place a bloom or two brings energy and upliftment to your eyes.

Your birthday has great ideals and a desire to remake the world. This revolutionary potential could be in politics, the arts, or religion. If you are not working on the new order, May 9 can fall into a pleasant indolence. Finding the balance between these two poles will be your life's challenge. Old maps might be of decorative interest to you. If you are able, create a special reading room with green shaded lamps in your home; it will be a restful and imaginative place for you. Your bedroom should be free of any work items. Consider having a canopy bed or a bed that can be closed off from the rest of the room. You enjoy the feeling of going into your own private dreamworld. Sweet scents such as jasmine and vanilla contribute to a feeling of luxury. For quick energy, try a whiff of lavender.

Outdoors, May 9 may grow vegetables and donate them to the homeless. If you live in a city consider working in a soup kitchen. Perhaps you might want to share your yard with others and create a community garden. Plant potatoes, eggplant, and pumpkins. Daffodils, narcissus, and columbines are all flowers that harmonize with your energy.

A Kabbalistic Interpretation

If you have a date with someone born on this day then you shouldn't expect to be home before dawn! This is a day overflowing with erotic energy. A present for someone born today could be a photography book of black-and-white nudes, a subscription to *Yellow Silk*, or some tastefully erotic art to hang in their bedroom.

Another common factor of individuals born today is an overriding need to be in control of every aspect of their lives. This desire is an empowering aspect of your character and can be encouraged by keeping some iron objects near you. In your kitchen especially you should keep some decorative cast-iron kitchenware on display. It is likely in the workplace, however, that you will have a position of some responsibility, and you have to be careful not to let your desire for control make you too domineering.

Your interest in adventure and exploration of all sorts is strong. A vacation or trip exploring some remote part of the world might be a fantastic adventure. For many though, the interest is restricted to reading about the exploits of other famous explorers. Sitting down with some of your favorite books detailing great adventures and explorations will develop your confidence and increase your own sense of power.

A Numerological Interpretation
YOUR MAGIC NUMBERS: 5 AND 4

The ninth day of the fifth month reduces to five, the number of means, agency, and adaptation. This day's path is one of devising original and creative ways to accomplish your desires. You have an intrinsic understanding that the world is shaped by a succession of choices and consequences. This path requires constantly reevaluating outcomes and implementing alternative choices to see the result at the finale of the next cycle. Paint with watercolors, and experiment with extravagant hues to see the results. Try unlikely mixtures of tone and texture, and display your creations on your walls and refrigerator. Study the cultivation of flowers and plants so that you can make hybrids.

A vase of daisies in your kitchen window will make you smile, and brighten the day. Citrine and yellow jasper will enhance your creativity. The 130th day of the year reduces to four, which adds the calming influence of solidity and security to your sense of the ever-shifting panorama of reality.

OBJECTS/IMAGES
creamy soaps, safes, and painter's palette

SHAPES/MATERIALS
armenian (stone), polished substances, patterns, and ovals

COLORS
pale rose, butter yellow

ANIMALS
cow, collared peccary

PLANTS, HERBS, EDIBLES
tansy, mango tea, silverweed, and black snakeroot

ESSENCES
cabbage rose

SOUNDS/RHYTHMS
musical scale of A, rhymed couplets

MUSICAL NOTES
E and D#

DEEP SPACE OBJECTS
Delta Aries, Botein, the Belly

May 10

YOUR SIGN
Taurus

YOUR ELEMENT
Earth

YOUR RULERS
Venus, Moon, Mercury
19–20 degrees
Second Decanate, yin

The Astrological Interpretation

Avoid creating physical clutter in your environment and emotional clutter in your heart. You are a very magnetic person who will attract many others into your life. Your responsibility is to choose who will occupy that special space beside you. It should be kept open most of the time so that when the right person does come along, you will have a space ready to nurture this special relationship. The same can be said for your home. It is better for you to have fewer and better possessions than an abundance of material goods just to fill up the space. Quality and not quantity should very definitely be your code.

This birthday gently insists on living life on self-created terms. You have great flair for fashion and strive for a blend between the unique and the classical. Indulge your color sense and see what you come up with. Perhaps violet with an orange accent or turquoise and darker green. Your home should be comfortable. The bedroom may feel like a luxurious casbah where you retreat and dream about all the beautiful things you might make or buy, but the emotional center of your house will be a big kitchen. Copper cookware gives you a feeling of mastery and importance. Although it is good to share food and well-cooked meals with friends and lovers, watch that you don't consume too much cream, sugar, and butter.

Outdoors a garden with wooden lawn furniture is a tranquil place to connect to the earth. The garden should be riotous with ample room to spread. Growing vegetables is as pleasant as growing flowers. Violets may find a special place in your heart. With Mercury coruling your birthday you have an inquisitive mind and are apt to have many magazine subscriptions. A comfortable reading chair is a must, and a window that faces a bird feeder gives you a sense of well-being.

A Kabbalistic Interpretation

Your favorite song ought to be "We're in the Money," as your main pursuit in life is that of wealth. In your view money is a very good thing and you completely agree that you can never have too much of a good thing! If you want to increase your chances of generating wealth, keep some goldfish in your home, and if you can find a gold colored statuette of a Cretan bull you should place it in the north side of your house.

People born on this date also have a very artistic side to their nature. This can cause a certain amount of inner conflict, as you have to try to reconcile the materialistic and the artistic aspects of your life. Hanging a "yin/yang" symbol over your bed may help to encourage a reconciliation of your creative and business urges. One way of combining the two would be to collect art. You will appreciate the objects as an investment and as things of beauty.

A Numerological Interpretation
YOUR MAGIC NUMBERS: 6 AND 5

The tenth day of the fifth month reduces to six, the number of balance and equilibrium. Yours is a path of striving for poise and balance in the face of crisis or challenge. This day's pattern asks that you immerse yourself in life and participate fully in your experiences. The paradox of this day is utter involvement combined with dispassionate observation of your process. Enjoy movies where you can sense the distinctions among story, actor, and observer. What constitutes reality versus illusion in the experiences of life?

Display black-and-white photos of famous actors and roles. Watch old movies on late-night TV. Dress up like a clown, and visit a children's hospital. Snowflake obsidian is a gem that will ground your sense of identity. The 131st day of the year reduces to five, generating the added element of constant activity and change, making it difficult for you to pause and dispassionately analyze your life as a soap opera.

OBJECTS/IMAGES
coral, wooden cabinets, carpets, doll collections, rich earth, shoes

SHAPES/MATERIALS
rectangles, squares, bright colored silks and tafettas, translucent gems

COLORS
milky sky, aqua, pastel pink, burnt sienna, almond color, spring green

ANIMALS
swan, a little bird feeding on grapes, calf

PLANTS, HERBS, EDIBLES
beans, columbine, larkspur, mosses, white daffodils

ESSENCES
almond essence, lily of the valley, sesame oil

SOUNDS/RHYTHMS
crickets at night, swing beat, the rhumba

MUSICAL NOTES
F and E

DEEP SPACE OBJECT
Persei Nova

May 11

YOUR SIGN
Taurus

YOUR ELEMENT
Earth

YOUR RULERS
Venus, Saturn
20–21 degrees
Third Decanate, yin

The Astrological Interpretation

Friends and family know that they can depend on the solidity and consistency of your personality. You are not one to bend in the wind, follow the latest fad, or change your opinion because others think you are wrong. You have a deep, inner sense of what is right and proper and will not change to suit others.

Your voice is a special gift. You may love to sing and have real vocal talent. But your true offering is a voice that soothes and calms people. You have a way not so much with words as with tones. There is healing and peace in the sound of your voice, and you are particularly good at comforting children or friends in distress.

May 11 sometimes falls on what astrologers call a "critical degree," so experiences, both positive and negative, can be intense. You have a crafty streak, which can lead you to protect your own interests or even to meddle. Keep your thoughts and plans aboveboard. An image for you is the crow of Aesop's fable, who patiently puts pebbles in a pitcher so the water would rise to a level where he could drink.

At home keep all corners well lit. You may be particularly fond of candelabras or candle-shaped wall sconces. The kitchen is the hearth of the home, and a round table perhaps in addition to a center cooking counter keeps everyone in the house focused. A copper or brass chandelier over the table graces this central area.

Outdoors, May 11 wants blankets of flowers: daffodils on a hillside or bluebells in a valley. Excess is pleasing. Nature is the best place to shake off mental preoccupation and renew your contact with the earth. You should have a large flag on a flagstaff outside. You might want to design a personal banner.

A Kabbalistic Interpretation

You have an exceptionally strong character, and whenever possible you like to be in charge. For your home you should acquire an antique wooden high-backed chair. A piece of furniture like this will do wonders for your sense of position and place. It will act as a great boost for you if you ever come home feeling disempowered from your day at work.

A strong connection of this day's values with the Tower card from the tarot indicates a stormy personality type. You often feel you need to let off steam in order to avoid harboring resentments of those around you. One good way to deal with the potential buildup and avert the harm it might cause is to wear more blue, as this is a calming, peaceful color.

You may find that lady luck is somewhat fickle with you. Unexpected bad luck is balanced by an unusual level of good fortune coming completely out of the blue. If you want to maximize the positive aspects of this part of your life, keep a basil plant in the northern part of your garden, or if you have no garden, a window box will do.

A Numerological Interpretation
YOUR MAGIC NUMBERS: 7 AND 6

The eleventh day of the fifth month reduces to seven, the number that means victory and temporary rest after a period of activity or creation. The nature of this path demands that you hone your faculty of discernment to a fine point. Involve yourself in activities that sharpen your attention like a scalpel, easily cutting away the nonessential. Read books that challenge your mental status quo. Buy broccoli florets and dried cranberries at the supermarket. Take care not to become automatic in your responses. Know why you respond as you do. Don't miss this pleasure: take a deep breath and pause.

Emerald is a gem that will enhance your appreciation of nature. Solve puzzles and word games to exercise your mental muscles. Play chess. The 132nd day of the year reduces to six, contributing an important need for balance. Listen to the whisper of your inner voice when it speaks to you of rest.

OBJECTS/IMAGES
an ascot, choker necklaces

SHAPES/MATERIALS
cashmere, emerald ring

COLORS
yellow, sky blue, grass green, chartreuse

ANIMALS
weasel, wren

PLANTS, HERBS, EDIBLES
sage, coltsfoot, petits fours

ESSENCE
narcissus

SOUNDS/RHYTHMS
the swish of a matador's cape, jazz

MUSICAL NOTES
F# and F

DEEP SPACE OBJECT
NGC 40 planetary nebula

May 12

YOUR SIGN
Taurus

———

YOUR ELEMENT
Earth

———

YOUR RULERS
Venus, Saturn, Moon
21–22 degrees
Third Decanate, yin

The Astrological Interpretation

Establishing your self-worth is the core of your life. You may try to do this through the acquisition of beautiful clothing and fine objects. You may work hard to achieve a powerful and secure place in your work environment. But your deepest value has to do with your inner reserve of strength, your compassion for others, and your ability to support people with less stamina than you possess. You will test yourself and sometimes add a great deal of pressure to your life by attempting to surpass your limits. This you can do through sports, levels of production at work, or by putting up with someone's behavior that is contrary to your own. *More* may be one of your favorite words, but sometimes *no more* is the wiser course.

For some people born on May 12, your birthday falls on a critical degree. This usually brings highs and lows in life, and part of your challenge is to plow through all extreme experiences and remain true to yourself. You have a strong aesthetic sense and enjoy stylish simplicity. You may prefer soft cotton white sheets, for example, to any of the many colors and prints available. Decorate at home with copies of classical bas-reliefs or wall hangings. Pastoral landscapes of cows and oxen grazing remind you of a more peaceful and agrarian time. Scent is important to you. Potpourri in light fruit scents or orange with cloves would be good additions to your home. Choose natural scents, as anything artificially perfumed may be offensive.

Outdoors, you enjoy a circular garden with a round table in the center where you can have tea or cocktails. Raising doves might be a fulfilling activity for you. Good flowers for your garden are primrose and rudbeckia.

A Kabbalistic Interpretation

The value seventeen in the straightforward value of this day indicates that you are an optimistic person. The protective energies of the Star card in the tarot surround you in life, so you have good reasons to feel positive. You are protective by nature, especially toward your family. You enjoy having everybody—kids, sisters, brothers, parents, aunts, uncles—sitting together. A big round table in the kitchen would be a great focal point for such gatherings.

The predominance of the number two in the various ways of calculating the values for this date show that you always see both sides of every situation. This day is also connected with the energy of the sun, which is a very strong and determined force and may counterbalance any indecisiveness that the influence of two can cause. In order to enhance the effect of this solar energy, try wearing a touch of orange or yellow whenever you have a big decision to make. In addition, keep some pictures of sunsets or other skyscapes around your home. Not only do these pictures appeal to your romantic and idealistic side, but they also will help you to keep your own personal horizons as broad as those in your artwork.

A Numerological Interpretation

YOUR MAGIC NUMBERS: 8 AND 7

The twelfth day of the fifth month reduces to eight, the number of rhythm and vibration. This day's path is one of learning to consciously cooperate with your sense of the Divine. Inherent in this walk is gaining a sense of mission or purpose about life, which will endow you with strength and freedom from doubt. Go sailing at night, and learn to navigate by the stars like ancient mariners and modern astronauts. Guidance is always available, but we must place ourselves in a receptive mode to receive the information. Have a decorative crystal ball on a round table with an indigo cloth, to remind you to ask. Stare into tea leaves, and imagine you can read the signs. Display an antique sextant, compass, and astrolabe in your study. Build a model ship. Watch reruns of *Mission: Impossible*. Sodalite will aid your focus of concentration. The 133rd day of the year reduces to seven, adding both the need and ability for rest between your ebbing and flowing cycles of attainment.

OBJECTS/IMAGES
thick Turkish towels, wallets, wooden wardrobes

SHAPES/MATERIALS
velvet pillows, sugar, oval shapes

COLORS
alabaster white, teal, emerald green

ANIMAL
rabbit

PLANTS, HERBS, EDIBLES
taffy, throatwort, bonbons

ESSENCE
ylang-ylang

SOUNDS/RHYTHMS
brass music, koto music (Japanese stringed instrument)

MUSICAL NOTES
G and F#

DEEP SPACE OBJECTS
Gamma Eridanus, Zaurak, the Boat

May 13

YOUR SIGN
Taurus

YOUR ELEMENT
Earth

YOUR RULERS
Venus, Saturn, Moon
22–23 degrees
Third Decanate, yin

The Astrological Interpretation

This birth date speaks of a person who does not avoid taking action when circumstances require it. Although you are usually patient and understanding, it is hard for you to take abuse sitting down. This applies not only to your life, but it also pertains to your defense of people who are oppressed and mishandled by society. You would do well in any occupation that involves social services or humanitarian causes. Peace of mind comes to you when you know you have done the right job and acted in accordance with your conscience. Then you can relax and pursue some of your favorite pleasures. These involve the joys of the senses: good food, films, music, and making love top the list.

May 13 may have distinct physical traits that set you apart (tall, short, extrastrong, etc.). May 13 is big-hearted and is subject to feeling taken advantage of. Use Saturn, the planet of boundaries and discipline, to make wise choices. An image for you is a jewelry shop filled with glittering gems and beautiful possibilities. You may want certain jewels, such as emeralds, green jade, and tigereye, but more importantly, the jewelry shop represents each sparkling achievement of your life. At home, you are comfortable in the kitchen and particularly enjoy well-designed cutlery. A set of woven baskets such as farmers use for gathering fruit would make beautiful and useful decorations. A honey pot on the kitchen table holds the right condiment for you.

Outdoors you want forests and fields. Your own yard could have ash and alder trees and some rich grass. If there are nasturtiums in the garden and bees gathering nectar, you will feel content with the fullness of nature.

A Kabbalistic Interpretation

One method of calculating a value for this day generates a value of eight. The number eight in Hebrew is the letter *Cheth* meaning "fence" or "wall." This suggests that you may have a somewhat defensive personality. Because of other associations in the values of this day it is likely that you are somewhat anxious by nature, especially in company. If you keep a little piece of ribbon agate in your purse or pocket on social occasions you will find that you can talk much more freely in social situations.

The number twenty-six has influence this date. It is the value of one of the kabbalistic names of God. Even if you are not a member of any organized religion, you have a strong sense of moral values. At times your sense of right and wrong makes you appear a little stern to others, but wearing some silver jewelry will soften your approach considerably.

The full value of this day has the same value as a phrase meaning "the wonder of the world." Following a gematrial approach, you are likely interested in things that have inspired man's wonder. A great gift for your birthday would be a picture or model of one of the great wonders such as the Great Pyramid.

A Numerological Interpretation
YOUR MAGIC NUMBERS: 9 AND 8

The thirteenth day of the fifth month reduces to nine, the number of completion, attainment, and fulfillment. Yours is a path of understanding the meaning of the pearl of great price. What constitutes true worth and value? Contemplate the process and motivation of the transformation from common mineral to priceless diamond. Enjoy life's luxuries with a sense of detachment. Preserve only what endures.

Don't succumb to the temptation to hoard your treasures. Mythical dragons pile up vast treasures in their lairs, expending all their energy amassing and defending. Collect statues of miniature dragons to remind you of your detachment. Emerald and sapphire are gems to inspire your imagination. Shades of green will enhance your sense of security. The 134th day of the year reduces to eight, adding the assurance that all things ebb and flow through successive cycles. No matter how seductive the outer form, it eventually decays.

OBJECTS/IMAGES
satin pillows, a soft muffler, earrings

SHAPES/MATERIALS
plump shapes, flannel, vicuña

COLORS
pale peach, turquoise

ANIMALS
teddy bear, fluffy dogs

PLANTS, HERBS, EDIBLES
uva-ursi, cowslip, plums

ESSENCE
jasmine

SOUNDS/RHYTHMS
sonnets, romantic music

MUSICAL NOTES
G# and G

DEEP SPACE OBJECTS
Epsilon Casseiopeia, Segin

May 14

YOUR SIGN
Taurus

YOUR ELEMENT
Earth

YOUR RULERS
Venus, Moon, Saturn
23–24 degrees
Third Decanate, yin

The Astrological Interpretation

The symbol associated with your birth date is a large amusement park filled with all the delights and freedom of childhood. On a practical level, you like to earn money and anchor your personal security, yet you are open to indulging yourself in innocent pleasures. Perhaps this comes as the reward you give yourself after the day's work is done. You are not a workaholic, just a responsible person taking care of the everyday necessities of life. People admire the way you can be diligent and accomplish your goals and then leave your work at the office and enjoy your time at play. You would do well working with young people as a teacher, counselor, coach, or guide. The theater and dancing are also activities that have a definite appeal to you.

You have social skills and can easily get along with all sorts of people. Sometimes your self-discipline may need shoring up, but your basic understanding of how a person interacts with society is positive and will grace your life. At home keep a special set of silk underwear (for both men and women) or pajamas to wear when you want to relax and revitalize yourself. Colors that would be positive for you are pink, light turquoise, or apricot. You like the feel of good fabric and should take care that none of your furniture is rough or uncomfortable. Plump pillows are perfect additions to your living room and your bed. You may have a soft spot for art and enjoy abstract paintings as well as landscapes. A verdant landscape with peaceful cows grazing could usher your imagination to a simpler time.

May 14 may enjoy a public park more than a personal garden. You love nature and flowers but enjoy sharing them with the community. A home bordering a park would be the perfect combination for you.

A Kabbalistic Interpretation

The tarot card of the Hermit is important to this day. It represents those who are wise and who wish to learn more about the world we inhabit. This often indicates a preference for solitude as a life's path. It is likely that you will prefer understated colors and designs in your home. Ideal for your temperament is dark wood furniture. The

Hebrew letter *Kaph,* meaning "palm," is prominent in this day, as is an association with metals. People born this day should take up craft work as a hobby, especially metalwork. Gold-, silver-, or copper-smithing is ideal, but any workable metal would do. In premodern times this was thought to be a great day for a sword smith to be born, but today it is probably better to stick to less lethal objects!

You are a charitable person by nature, and you will probably involve yourself in some form of volunteer work. The concept of mercy and charity, which equates with a human form of divine mercy, is associated with the sephira Chesed on the Tree of Life. The color of sephira Chesed is a rich blue. In order to optimize your charitable efforts, wear an outfit or at least a tie of that color.

A Numerological Interpretation
YOUR MAGIC NUMBERS: 10 AND 9

The fourteenth day of the fifth month reduces to ten, the number that closes the cycle and carries the urge to begin again. This is a path of self-discipline and personal prowess. This pattern requires that you gain command over the forces of your personality and harness these energies into an authoritative expression of skill and mastery. Ancient Egyptians and Mayas understood that conquest of an enemy meant the internalization and application of their genius and power, not annihilation.

Display art of indigenous cultures. Gather a medicine bundle, and study shamanic practices. Listen to a recording of the haunting sound of an Australian didgeridoo, an instrument carved from a hollow log. Wear sodalite and turquoise to clarify your mental processes. The 135th day of the year reduces to nine, contributing the influence of fulfillment and attainment of your goals, supporting your sense of confidence.

OBJECTS/IMAGES
amusement parks, ballrooms, bonnets, cabinets

SHAPES/MATERIALS
accordion shapes, ticker tape, dollar signs, alabaster

COLORS
aqua blue, navy blue

ANIMAL
okapi

PLANTS, HERBS, EDIBLES
Delicious apples, apricot preserves, artichokes, alder trees

ESSENCE
cananga

SOUNDS/RHYTHMS
ballet music, baritones

MUSICAL NOTES
A and G#

DEEP SPACE OBJECT
red supergiant star

May 15

YOUR SIGN
Taurus

YOUR ELEMENT
Earth

YOUR RULERS
Venus, Saturn, Moon
24–25 degrees
Third Decanate, yin

The Astrological Interpretation

Even though you are a very romantic person, you keep your passion deep inside yourself. When you are attracted to someone, you know it, but you can be shy about expressing it. You have to dig deep into the earth in order to turn over the hard surface to find the rich, inner soil. You know your own emotional vulnerability and do not want to risk exposing yourself. You are the type of person who has to court and be courted. You like the dance and rhythm of romance and have a natural sense of the timing for intimacy. Your heart is won over through small and very personal gifts, while a quiet walk in the woods with an attentive partner means more to you than a fancy dinner with important people.

You are a tenacious defender of the public good. Your energies flow when you feel you are contributing to people's practical welfare. Sometimes you can neglect your own needs and dissipate your strength by trusting too much in others. To help you nourish yourself keep a blue or turquoise scarf around your throat. Royal bee jelly, a Chinese tonic, will also support your energy. At home keep the pantry well stocked with nutritious food. Your kitchen is the hearth of your home; consider having earthen cookware and some red bricks near the stove. Massage is an excellent way to regroup. The smell of vanilla is cozy and comforting.

Outdoors, you like public parks that combine playgrounds and paths through the woods. In your own backyard a garden of asters will be a delight. You like to have everything in working order and a toolshed where you can store your garden things and make a fix-it shop. It is the place to come to restore yourself and play.

A Kabbalistic Interpretation

One possible value of this date relates to the tarot card Judgment. As it also connects with the Hebrew letter *Ayin,* there is a strong possibility that you have a tendency to make judgments about people rather too quickly and, at times, a little harshly. In order to ensure a good level of balance in your dealings with others you should consider keeping a piece of clear quartz crystal on your desk at work.

The influence of the letter *Ayin* also suggests that you are someone with enormous energy and enthusiasm for life. You should consider some form of vigorous exercise after work like squash or a strenuous aerobic workout. You will find it boosts and maintains your natural vigor. You tend to be fairly lucky by nature. If you want to encourage your luck wear a circular piece of jewelry such as a small medallion around your neck. A very good color for this piece, and indeed for anything you wear when you need to be lucky, is golden yellow with a touch of crimson.

A Numerological Interpretation
YOUR MAGIC NUMBERS: 2 AND 10

The fifteenth day of the fifth month reduces to two, the number of duplication, reflection, and receptivity. This path carries the lesson of learning your niche and personal contribution to the larger society. How does the contribution of the individual support and enrich the community? Community exists through a division of labor and skills where each agrees to offer their talents so that the full spectrum of offerings is available to the collective. Spend time at a public park. Watch ball games, walk the hiking trails cleared for citizens to use. Enjoy the cultivated gardens or duck ponds, and savor the seasonal blooms.

Amber and citrine are gems that will harmonize your moods. Green will connect you to the rhythms of the earth. The 136th day of the year reduces to ten, contributing the quality of perfect embodiment of each cycle. This adds a sense of perfect endings and the call to new beginnings, supporting the ability to move from replication to synthesis.

OBJECTS/IMAGES
*surveyor's equipment,
a bull's-eye target, wallets*

SHAPES/MATERIALS
alabaster, half circle, emeralds

COLORS
*yellow, pale turquoise,
red-orange carmine, indigo*

ANIMALS
*bull, Holstein cow,
nightingale*

PLANTS, HERBS, EDIBLES
*columbine, daisies, wheat,
fenugreek*

ESSENCES
nectarine, apple blossom

SOUNDS/RHYTHMS
*sound of digging in the earth,
samba rhythm*

MUSICAL NOTES
C# and A

DEEP SPACE OBJECT
Alpha Caelum

May 16

YOUR SIGN
Taurus

YOUR ELEMENT
Earth

YOUR RULERS
Venus, Moon, Saturn
25–26 degrees
Third Decanate, yang

The Astrological Interpretation

If you take some time by yourself, you will see that life is trying to teach you an important lesson, one that requires you to adjust to other people's needs and soften your resistance to change. You do not have to compromise what is important to you, but you do have to learn what is truly meaningful. If you let the little challenges upset you, you will not recognize the major events when they happen. A quiet visit to a museum will calm and strengthen you and help you to establish a sense of balance and harmony. You like to be surrounded by lovely objects and will find that resting quietly while listening to gentle music can do much to restore your spirits and regenerate your vitality.

The fixed star Algol will be located near or on some May 16 birthdays. This star is said to be a violent position; however, it is rarely true that a single planet in this position destines a person to violence. The assets of this birthday are great strength and constancy. You have musical ability and an innate sense of poetry whether or not you pursue the arts. At home decorate your dining room with a candelabra. As a cook you have a special skill in creativly preparing leftovers. Somehow the raw material of whatever is in the refrigerator inspires you. Stimulate your imagination with different colors and textures; your sense of luxury is soothed by ribbons, satins, silks, and beads. Wrapping scarves around lampshades to create a different color effect is an easy way to change your atmosphere.

Outdoors, May 16 would enjoy a wooden chair swing facing a garden. Swinging on the chair, reading a good book, drinking a glass of iced tea and listening to music on a summer's day is a perfect mind vacation. Flowers in your garden could be freesia, peonies, Madonna lilies, and tulips.

A Kabbalistic Interpretation

You have a deep and abiding interest in the spiritual side of life. An association with the "anima mundi," or spirit of the world, represented in today's kabbalistic value suggests a desire to understand the whole range of responses we have to the idea of religion. A great way for you to decorate your study or den would be to use a wide variety of traditional religious images from a host of different cultures.

The letter *Qoph,* associated with the moon, has a powerful effect on this day. You may find that your moods are affected either by the full or the new moon. A great way for you to relax at night would be to stretch out on a rug, put some poignant music on the stereo, and burn some frankincense oil.

The moon also brings an association with water, traditionally the element of the emotions. You are extremely sensitive when it comes to relationships and tend to need a lot of affection. Have a body of water near you and your home. A small wading pool would be ideal, but even an attractive glass bowl full of water will provide some positive energy for you.

A Numerological Interpretation
YOUR MAGIC NUMBER: 3 AND 2

The sixteenth day of the fifth month reduces to three, the number of growth, unfoldment, and the outworking of the principles of one and two. This is a path of understanding your relationship with, and contribution to, the reality in which you find yourself. The universe is not an accident, and neither is your life. Every choice and action contributes to your future, as past thoughts and behavior have determined where you find yourself at the present moment. Pay attention to your choices, even those that seem to be of little consequence.

Place a spread of red-violet on your bed to inspire memorable dreams. Sing love songs to your beloved, and go to the opera. Watch the fiery magic of flamenco dancers. Rose quartz will open your heart, and labradorite will focus your mind. The 137th day of the year reduces to two, adding the quality of reflection, duplication, and repetition. This allows you to replicate your successful experiences and be aware of those you choose not to repeat.

OBJECTS/IMAGES
storerooms, wallets, shares of stock, marquetry

SHAPES/MATERIALS
spinach jade, opaque white stones, onyx, horn shapes

COLORS
red-orange, salmon

ANIMALS
mink, sable

PLANTS, HERBS, EDIBLES
pumpkin pie, larkspur, soapwort, sea holly

ESSENCES
myrtle, all pleasant odors

SOUNDS/RHYTHMS
passwords, piano concerti

MUSICAL NOTES
D and C#

DEEP SPACE OBJECTS
Kappa Perseus, Misam, wrist of Pleiades

May 17

YOUR SIGN
Taurus

YOUR ELEMENT
Earth

YOUR RULERS
Venus, Saturn
26–27 degrees
Third Decanate, yang

The Astrological Interpretation

You are a born lover, and you will spend a great deal of time working through the dynamics of intimate relationships. Yet love occurs on several levels: personal, impersonal, and transpersonal. When you discover the wealth of impersonal love, your life will change dramatically. This is love that is given freely without any emotional contracts. It is the kind of caring that is supportive of people who have nothing to do with your individual desires or needs. Some born on this date will experience transpersonal love. When this happens, you will be able to use your magnetism to bring healing and wholeness into other people's lives. You will be attracted to a profession that is service oriented and find that the spiritual life calls out strongly to you.

Your birthday has a thrifty, patient, and industrious reputation. May 17 combines common sense with a love of beauty and artistic expression. You may feel tightfisted about money, even though you have enough for your needs and some luxury. A chin-up bar in a doorway at home is good exercise and a way of practicing flexibility. A print of a medieval alchemical laboratory may be an interesting decorating touch for your home. If you are interested in occult studies, assiduously avoid any study or involvement with black magic. Your home could emphasize circular shapes; a curved bay window facing trees would be beautiful and comforting. Carpets over hardwood floors fit your aesthetic sense. You would enjoy small Oriental rugs or Native American designs.

Outdoors May 17 loves flowers. Your garden should be designed around a circular image with some centerpiece such as a statue, gazebo, or a pink flamingo. Flowers that you may particularly enjoy include daffodils, daisies, and nasturtiums.

A Kabbalistic Interpretation

Everybody enjoys your company because you always have a witty comment or a humorous anecdote to share. Your birthday is associated with the Fool from the tarot, but other associations present in this day mean that your wit can have a sharp edge, which you may want to take care to soften. While you may not be much of a reader, a collection of after-dinner speeches or amusing short stories would be an ideal gift for you at Christmas.

One of the values of this day can be related to the Hebrew letter *Aleph* which means "oxen." As a Taurean, any association with bulls is immediately significant. Images of bulls or oxen or for that matter a painting of buffalo on the American plains would be ideal for the walls of your home or apartment.

You are unusually fond of good food. Because of the strong influence of the Fool card over this day, what you most love is the sort of food you probably ate as a kid. While you no doubt enjoy a sophisticated meal, you are just as likely to thrill at the taste of a well-made macaroni and cheese, a peanut butter and banana sandwich, or a big bowl of Jell-o or ice cream!

A Numerological Interpretation
YOUR MAGIC NUMBERS: 4 AND 3

The seventeenth day of the fifth month reduces to four, the number of abstract reason and the ordering principle of the universe. This day's path is a quest to anchor your soul in eternal and inner realities that lie behind and beneath the outer forms of manifestation. Four anchors matter in geometric forms. You have a dislike for things that are superficial. You strive to maximize your own talents and master what you set your mind to. Don't judge inner worth by outer appearance. Study weaving, carving, or bead work. Collect cultural crafts and handiwork that inspire you. Hang a handwoven tapestry on your wall in shades of orange, blue, and purple. Jasper and agate are stones to soothe you and maintain your balance. The 138th day of the year reduces to three, adding the quality of trinity and natural unfoldment to the orderly processes of your life.

OBJECTS/IMAGES
tiled floors, gargling, checkbooks, and dolls

SHAPES/MATERIALS
coral, citrine, and basin shapes

COLORS
lemon chiffon, ginger

ANIMALS
bull, prairies warbler

PLANTS, HERBS, EDIBLES
pinto beans, wheat sprouts, coltsfoot, and yellow lady's slipper

ESSENCE
tuberose

SOUNDS/RHYTHMS
vocalizing, bassoon music

MUSICAL NOTES
D# and D

DEEP SPACE OBJECT
Running Dog nebula

May 18

YOUR SIGN
Taurus

————

YOUR ELEMENT
Earth

————

YOUR RULERS
Venus, Moon, Saturn
27–28 degrees
Third Decanate, yang

The Astrological Interpretation

You are born on the day when the sun conjuncts a group of stars called the Pleiades, located in your sign, Taurus. The Pleiades are commonly known as the Seven Weeping Sisters. But why do they cry? Sometimes it is because of loss: the loss of a lover or a treasured object or a lost opportunity for advancement. You are very sensitive to such circumstances and may have a difficult time releasing objects and people whose time has come. Yet with every removal, life gives us another opportunity to create a place for a more suitable lover, a more valuable possession, and a better job. It is then that the "Sisters" weep for joy! Your birth date gives you many opportunities to gain from loss and improve upon past mistakes. It is a very fortunate day if you approach life from the perspective that your glass is always half full and not half empty.

May 18 has a dependable nature and is fond of building something in life. Sometimes the allure of glamour attracts you; usually this path is neither satisfying nor productive. Learning which ideas and projects can be implemented and which are impractical will be part of your challenge. Indulge your sense of luxury and dreaminess at home with beautiful fabrics, such as brocade, and comfortable decor. You may enjoy books with color photos of jewelry designs and gems. You would enjoy owning a few exquisite pieces of jewelry. Emeralds, diamonds, and light green jade may specially appeal. A large armchair, positioned next to a lamp with a side table for a cup of tea, is your retreat area. Sit in your chair and dream up your next scheme.

Outdoors, May 18 could create a garden space with a curved trellis and a gate opening onto the garden. Wooden benches hidden among the daffodils and daisies add to your comfort. Flowers to plant in your garden are grape hyacinth, poet's narcissus, and Persian buttercups.

A Kabbalistic Interpretation

The numbers thirty-one and five are very important in determining the kabbalistic significance of this date. One of the effects of these numbers is that they suggest someone of considerable personal authority. You almost certainly like the idea of shouldering responsibility, and you do it well. You can encourage this in yourself by growing sage and laurel in your garden or window box.

A sense of "fatherhood" is also strong on this day. This does not mean literal fatherhood but rather the range of emotions and attitudes we tend to associate with the concept of fatherhood. Keep some clear rose-colored glasses on display in a wall-mounted bookcase, or find a stone elephant and place it in your hallway. The softening symbolism of the rose and elephant will help keep in check any potential for all that paternalism and authority to turn domineering.

The energy of the sun is very positive for you, especially when it is at its strongest. Whenever possible you should try to arrange your important meetings for midday, and if you cannot always achieve this, keep a picture of some sunflowers on your desk or in your wallet.

A Numerological Interpretation
YOUR MAGIC NUMBERS: 5 AND 4

The eighteenth day of the fifth month reduces to five, the number of agency, and the means whereby circumstances are brought about and adaptation occurs. This day's path engenders a search for fulfillment of your dreams and a requirement that you not lose heart. This quest demands courage of spirit so you don't give up and settle for less than your heart's desire. No loss or disappointment is final. If one wish isn't granted, wish for something bigger and better. Throw pennies in a wishing well. Go outside at midnight, and wish upon a star.

Keep a yellow-colored journal of your deepest and highest desires. Plant golden tulips, irises, and daffodils. Have fresh flowers in your home in winter. Topaz will fire your imagination. The 139th day of the year reduces to four, adding a sense of order and stability to the structures and process you experience.

OBJECTS/IMAGES
well-maintained lawns, laziness, museums, paint

SHAPES/MATERIALS
macramé lapis lazuli, matelassé cotton

COLORS
nectarine color, saffron

ANIMALS
ox, bobwhite

PLANTS, HERBS, EDIBLES
plantain, plum brandy, yellow-fringed orchid

ESSENCE
rose

SOUNDS/RHYTHMS
paeans, bouzouki music

MUSICAL NOTES
E and D#

DEEP SPACE OBJECT
Eta Taurus, Alcyone, Brightest Star in Pleiades

May 19

YOUR SIGN
Taurus

YOUR ELEMENT
Earth

YOUR RULERS
Venus, Moon, and Saturn
28–29 degrees
Third Decanate, yang

The Astrological Interpretation

This birth date carries the possibility to create variation and new circumstances in life. Although you like to feel secure in what you have and who you are, you are always in the process of seeking out better alternatives for the circumstances at hand. You tend to be more future oriented than stuck in the past and are eager to go out into life to prove yourself. You would be most happy with a permanent job that has a lot of room for growth. You want security but you do not want to be tied to a desk or a title for the rest of your life. You require a firm salary but would be more content with the opportunity to earn commissions or be involved with a profit-sharing scheme. You are a basically optimistic person who enjoys the company of cheerful friends and amusing environments.

May 19 has strong artistic and organizational abilities. There may be a conflict in your nature regarding pursuing your artistic goals and your organizational talents. One does not necessarily cancel out the other. Your will is strong, and you can find a suitable combination of your dreams and practical reality. At home, May 19 may thrive in creative clutter. A variety of different styled chairs, some with piles of papers and music on them, will please your artistic sense. You may like embroidered hand towels in your bathroom and a few old-fashioned touches such as dresser runners and lace doilies. Your personal style should emphasize turtlenecks to protect your throat area. May 19 men should wear a hat as well as a scarf. May 19 may be very attuned to different scents. The smell of leather rubbed with saddle soap is invigorating, while scented bath salts such as jasmine and rose are relaxing.

Outdoors, May 19 wants a garden with small-blossomed flowers such as lily of the valley, crocus, hyacinth, and spring gentian. A brick walkway such as those found in American colonial gardens may appeal to you. A wooden picnic table in your backyard or a nearby park could be your headquarters for the summer months. Having meals with friends in natural surroundings is peaceful and nurturing for you.

A Kabbalistic Interpretation

Although you were born in the sign of Taurus, the first of the Earth signs, this particular day is equally split between Air and Earth. This combination of elements can at times cause you to feel somewhat lethargic and interfere with your ability to make clear decisions. Burn a mixture of dittany of Crete and frankincense to offset this tendency. Introducing some cinnamon to your diet will act as a great energizer.

The kabbalistic value of this day connects it to Saturn. This planet is extraordinarily complex and is in fact the cornerstone of Western occultism. For you it suggests a tendency to melancholy, which can be combated effectively by keeping a charm or square of tin in your pocket.

A positive influence of this planet is the love of nature that it generates. In your garden, plant as many trees as possible. If you have an apartment then get some bonsai trees. Particularly appropriate for you are willow and yew trees, or anything with pale yellow flowers or leaves.

A Numerological Interpretation
YOUR MAGIC NUMBERS: 6 AND 5

The nineteenth day of the fifth month reduces to six, the number of balanced polarities and the harmony of opposites. This day's path engenders a strong desire to work and serve in combination with others, exercising your own gifts in an optimum division of labor. You thrive on the exchange of ideas, love generating solutions within a group or team, and enjoy examining the alternatives. Stretch yourself, moving your limits to test your capabilities. Play charades. Go on an old-fashioned scavenger hunt.

Have lots of green, flowering house plants to remind you of nature's diversity. Olivine and adventurine will stimulate your capabilities. Wear buttery yellow for optimism and mental clarity. Indigo will deepen your resolve. The 140th day of the year reduces to five, enhancing your path with an innate sense of the constant, shifting parade of forms, and the versatility and adaptability to thrive.

OBJECTS/IMAGES
picnics, pantomimes, lipstick, jesters

SHAPES/MATERIALS
perfume, pillow shapes, doupioni silk, emeralds

COLORS
pomegranate, lime green, gold

ANIMALS
nightingale, a sacred cow

PLANTS, HERBS, EDIBLES
natal lily, elder (herb), gumdrops

ESSENCES
benzoin

SOUNDS/RHYTHMS
sopranos, sonatas

MUSICAL NOTES
F and E

DEEP SPACE OBJECTS
Omicron Eridanus, Beid, the Egg

May 20

YOUR SIGN
Taurus

YOUR ELEMENT
Earth

YOUR RULERS
Venus, Saturn
28–29 degrees
Third Decanate, yin

The Astrological Interpretation

You were born at the end of Taurus and close to Gemini. Your personality combines the influence of Venus and Mercury. The Venusian side is the stronger and attracts you to intimate relationships, romance, and all things luxurious. You enjoy a warm home, a full stomach, and a passionate partner. Mercury's call to you is a bit more subtle. His is the gift of an adventurous spirit, which can be in conflict with your deep need for financial security and predictability. You want to know that your actions will yield definite, profitable results. Yet you have a tremendous need for spontaneity and variety. Although these two influences may be somewhat unsettling at times, you certainly do not have a boring life.

This birthday is close to the fixed star Alcyone, the brightest of the Pleiades. The ancients believed this position encouraged a strong loving nature and dramatic abilities. You like to "strut your stuff" in bright colors and fashions that say "Hey, I'm here." Peacock feathers are a perfect accessory or object in your home. Meditating on the center of the peacock feather will draw energies together and help maintain your balance. It is important for you to be watchful. You can become so involved with your present occupation that you are careless and invite needless accidents. Carry a piece of agate with you.

At home, have a barbecue and place to entertain. A deck facing some woods is a great place to cook up your next project. The natural environment most suited to you is formal gardens bordered by woods. Visit historical gardens and bask in their order and color. If you feel dreary in an urban environment, then looking at a picture book of beautiful gardens will be a real pick-me-up.

A Kabbalistic Interpretation

The number twenty-five in this day indicates an enormously passionate individual. You have very strong beliefs and are more than willing to defend them fiercely. This is commendable as long as you don't get too overheated. One way to maintain a calm demeanor is to have a room you can retreat to that is decorated using white gray and pink marble or marble-style painting.

You have a taste for excitement and a passion that may express itself as a taste for loud and driving rock music. If you are particularly enamored of raucous rhythms, you should pursue your interests full out and invest in the best stereo system you can afford. Make sure you have plenty of room to leap around. Occasional bursts of intense activity are good for you.

Because of the split between earth and air energies in your personality, you are good at keeping home and work, in separate mental compartments. As a result of this separation you may miss the fact that there is a place for emotion at work, just as there is at home. Try keeping a vase of roses on the west side of your desk. This should help you to use your heart as well as your head at work.

A Numerological Interpretation
YOUR MAGIC NUMBERS: 7 AND 6

The twentieth day of the fifth month reduces to seven, the number of victory and rest after labors. This day's path is one of enjoying and demonstrating the potential manifestations of form. Don't confuse outer beauty with the inner, eternal reality. Certainly the Creator lavished beauty, color, and abundance upon the physical world. Study and admire some of nature's amazing and colorful forms. A male peacock in full display is a daunting panorama of color and seeming excess. Tropical birds and fish are a riot of brilliant color. Go to Mardi Gras, and wear a feathered mask of green, purple, and yellow. Fluorite and watermelon tourmaline will enlarge your sense of nature's palette. Wear mauve, lilac, and lemon to soften your cynicism.

The 141st day of the year reduces to six, adding the awareness and need for everything to feel balanced in your life. You yearn for beauty and harmony; express your inner beauty first.

OBJECTS/IMAGES
*an incense burner,
a copper whisk bowl,
a "peacock" garden chair*

SHAPES/MATERIALS
*moss agate, soft jersey cloth,
puff ball*

COLORS
*turquoise, pale peach,
pale yellow, pea green*

ANIMALS
*piglet, cattle,
barnyard cat*

PLANTS, HERBS, EDIBLES
*donuts, fenugreek, cyclamen
plants*

ESSENCES
camphor, sweet smells

SOUNDS/RHYTHMS
*the sound of a bull fighter's
cape unfurling, 2/4 time,
early ragtime*

MUSICAL NOTES
F# and F

DEEP SPACE OBJECT
Atlas in the Pleiades

May 21

YOUR SIGNS
Taurus/Gemini

YOUR ELEMENTS
Air/Earth

YOUR RULERS
Venus, Mercury
29 degrees Taurus–
00 degrees Gemini
Third Decanate, yin
First Decanate, yang

The Astrological Interpretation

May 21 is a cusp birthday. Your fundamental life urge is experimental by nature, especially in terms of communication. You seek to connect with everything and everyone. It is natural for you to try to be in many places at the same time, and in this respect, you have to learn how to prioritize your many activities. If not, you will find that you become too dispersed and do not have the energy you need for the things that you really want to do. You will enjoy reading magazines rather than books, short stories rather than novels, articles rather than essays. You have an inner need for balance and will work hard at trying to integrate all of your interests and personal contacts into a network of connections that work for you. The key to your success comes from finding a strong focus for all of your many interests.

Your birthday straddles the end of Taurus and the beginning of Gemini. It is a combination of Earth and Air and can have the best of both elements. Earth stills Gemini's darting mind and Air enlivens Taurean steadfastness. Your home should nestle into a hillside where you have a view but feel protected from the elements. Inside, a rocking chair, luxurious rugs and wall hangings appeal to you. Ceiling fans might be a nice touch. Abstract paintings with pastel colors, black, and white interest you, and if your finances allow it you could be a serious art collector.

Outdoors your garden would look beautiful with a gate in the middle of a trellised fence. Plant morning glories and trumpet vine on the trellis, and have flower beds of sweet pea, grape hyacinths, and freesia.

A Kabbalistic Interpretation

The most simple method of calculating a value for this day produces a number that has the same value as the Hebrew word *YHVH,* the name for God. The particular kabbalistic associations of this name suggest someone who feels extremely protective toward family and friends. There is also a strong need to communicate effectively, and an antique writing desk would be an excellent object for you.

A correspondence to the tarot card the Empress indicates that you have a very social personality. People will enjoy your outgoing nature, as you are capable of generating a real sense of warmth among your acquaintances. In order to enhance this ability, wear a piece of silver jewelry when you are likely to meet new friends.

Your greatest weakness is that you sometimes see only the good side of others and may be disappointed by those who are not as well intentioned as they seem. Keep a piece of iron pyrite on your desk at work. Otherwise known as fool's gold, the symbolism of this mineral will help you focus on the healthy skepticism you need to see beyond immediate appearances.

A Numerological Interpretation
YOUR MAGIC NUMBERS: 8 AND 7

The twenty-first day of the fifth month reduces to eight, the number of rhythm, vibration, and the ebb and flow of cycles. This day's path requires that you become attuned and alert to every potential opportunity, and see the unfolding stream of consequence that flows from each choice. You are filled with an intense and childlike curiosity, and this drives you to examine every facet of your experiences. At your best, you have an innate poise and perspective that allow you to make optimum decisions for your welfare.

Gaze into a clear lake where you can see the bottom. Snorkel or scuba, and gain the perspective of the ocean beneath the surface; it is another world entirely. Blue-green will still and clear your mind. Turquoise and hematite will ground your energies. The 142nd day of the year reduces to seven, contributing a need to pause between efforts, evaluate your work, and determine if you have honored your commitments and seized every opportunity.

OBJECTS/IMAGES
an artist's easel, colored pencils, pennants flapping in the wind, elves

SHAPES/MATERIALS
lace, profile silhouettes, jasper, chrysolite

COLORS
pale blue, sea foam green

ANIMAL
guinea pig

PLANTS, HERBS, EDIBLES
anise, dandelion wine, colt's foot leaves, dropwort

ESSENCE
peppermint

SOUNDS/RHYTHMS
song duets

MUSICAL NOTES
G and F#

DEEP SPACE OBJECT
Alpha Perseus, Algenib, the Side

May 22

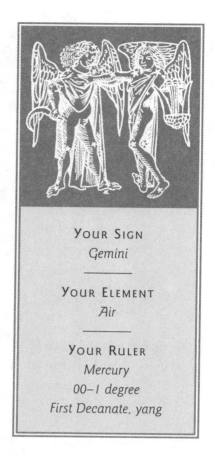

YOUR SIGN
Gemini

YOUR ELEMENT
Air

YOUR RULER
Mercury
00–1 degree
First Decanate, yang

The Astrological Interpretation

May 22 can include some Taurus influence as well as Gemini. Your birth date describes a very busy individual. Life is full of possibilities, and you wish to explore them all! Yet you must develop a sense of discrimination and mental focus. If you do not, you will find that you are pulled in too many directions at once. Be patient with your mental processes and learn how to control them. You can achieve very positive results by working with your hands. You enjoy giving gifts to friends, especially those you make yourself. Paper, wood, clay, and yarn are raw materials that lend themselves easily to your creative ideas and projects.

This birthday is close to the fixed star Alcyone, one of the brightest of the Pleiades. The ancients believed that Alcyone was the point on which Atlas rested while he supported the universe on his shoulders. May 22 is also associated with dramatic and literary ability. If you tend toward Taurus, emphasize drama; if you tend toward Gemini, emphasize writing and communication. To straddle your many abilities, remain flexible and always carry a small notebook to record changes in plans and feelings. A reclining couch may be where you get your best ideas. Silk scarves of pale green, blue, turquoise, and mauve will give you a sensual feeling. Wear them, hang them on a convenient doorknob, or drape them over a hat rack. When you travel, bring some of your colors with you so that anyplace can feel like home.

Outdoors, both signs agree on flowers. Yellow flowers are particularly pleasing, and any trees you have should be luxuriant. Pear trees may be particularly appealing. An image for this cusp birthday is a glass-bottomed boat moored in still water. Secure in your boat you can see everything under the sea.

A Kabbalistic Interpretation

One of the values of this day has the same value as the Hebrew word for *purity.* The kabbalistic system of gematria states that all words or phrases with the same value are in some way connected. Because of other influences this day, the idea of purity is strongly associated with pure or unspoiled countryside. Invest in a small cabin in an area of great natural beauty. If this is not possible, be sure to fill your home with plenty of wilderness images.

You have the knack of helping people to feel eager to work, and you love to organize. This characteristic extends beyond your work life, and into your home. You like a home environment that is ship-shape and efficient. Particularly important to you is your kitchen. You should make sure it is well designed with lots of convenient working space and storage areas. Invest in a good set of knives and professional cookware. You don't want a lot of gadgets, but what you do have should work well and fulfill many purposes.

A Numerological Interpretation
YOUR MAGIC NUMBERS: 9 AND 8

The twenty-second day of the fifth month reduces to nine, the number of completion and fulfillment. This day's path is one of expressing the bounty of nature in her myriad forms through generous expression in your own life. This path calls for a natural enjoyment of worldly goods without attachment or selfishness. You love to give and attend lavish parties and enjoy expensive gifts because you are in touch with nature's own seeming prodigality. This is the extravagant display of a tropical rain forest. Your path requires the sense of living in a Garden of Eden and sharing the bounty with all you meet. The mystery of receiving the gifts of the Earth is in the magic of believing, like the archetype of Santa Claus.

Tourmaline will still your mind. Bright, jewel-tone colors will cheer you. Dress up like Santa or the Easter bunny, and give presents to needy children. The 143rd day of the year reduces to eight, the number of rhythm and vibration. The continual back and forth flow of the energies of life seems natural to you. Live where you can enjoy the seasons.

OBJECTS/IMAGES
a purse with a hidden pocket, an ancient scroll, feather earrings, a draftsman's table

SHAPES/MATERIALS
treble and bass clefs, beryl

COLORS
pale blue, pale green, royal blue, turquoise

ANIMAL
cowbird

PLANTS, HERBS, EDIBLES
knotted figwort, heather, buttercups

ESSENCE
oakmoss

SOUNDS/RHYTHMS
Richard Wagner's "Pilgrim's Chorus," cowbells echoing on the breeze

MUSICAL NOTES
G# and G

DEEP SPACE OBJECT
planetary nebula

May 23

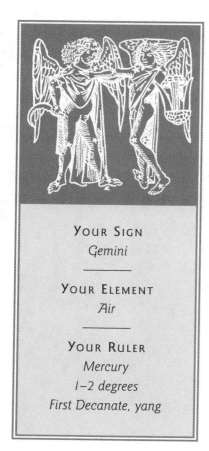

YOUR SIGN
Gemini

YOUR ELEMENT
Air

YOUR RULER
Mercury
1–2 degrees
First Decanate, yang

The Astrological Interpretation

You are a bright and intelligent person, one with an urge to expand your knowledge. But what is more important than what you know is how you use it. You have the tendency to rush along in at least two directions at once, hoping that somehow you will catch up to yourself. Work toward a more steady and direct line of approach to things and be aware when you feel instinctively pulled in a direction that is not well thought out beforehand. Remember to breathe and pause a moment before taking action. You love the outdoors, driving, riding a bike and ice skating—you just can't do them all at the same time!

Your birthday is considered a point of spiritual illumination. Whatever you pursue in life you will do with a great deal of precision. Your communication skills are well developed and you may enjoy studying foreign languages. At home keep the radio or music on in the background for company. Decor that suggests the outside may appeal to you. Adirondack furniture or bent willow wood would agree with your nature. In the bedroom have a bed that combines light wood and metal. A metal abacus might be an interesting decorative object.

Outdoors, you can carry your Adirondack or bent willow furniture to the porch and sip lemonade. You enjoy sitting where you can see the road and who is coming or going. Have flower bushes such as hydrangeas or barberry flanking your front stairs.

A Kabbalistic Interpretation

The letter *Kaph* and the sephira Hod are very important to this date. Kaph means "palm," and the sephira Hod is mainly associated with the mind, together suggesting that you enjoy mental manipulation. A great way for you to increase your mental prowess is to spend your evenings doing puzzles or logical teasers.

Another way of calculating the value for this day gives the equivalent of the Hebrew word *joy*. This connection indicates that you know how to live life fully. The specific details of this day point to a sensual side to your nature. You might like to buy some patchouli oil and encourage your partner to massage you with it. The supreme joy you should not neglect is chocolate!

Your pleasure-seeking nature means you are not shy in company. Your mercurial streak grants you great joy in expressing yourself and sharing that expression with others. You can be quite mischievous at times; practical jokes and wordplay are also sources of joy for you. If you want a fantastic evening, bring some new friends to the nearest karaoke bar and express yourselves.

A Numerological Interpretation
YOUR MAGIC NUMBERS: 10 AND 9

The twenty-third day of the fifth month reduces to ten, the number signifying dominion and perfection. Ten also implies a new beginning. This day's path carries the energy of understanding the positive qualities of wealth or social position. This is a walk of manifesting to the fullest degree the ultimate expression of your capabilities. This pattern is exemplified by the creation of such an enduring monument of beauty as the Taj Mahal. The danger of this path is selfishness or false pride, but at your best you are capable of transforming a diamond in the rough into an exquisite and priceless jewel. You can see what is possible and facilitate the luxurious expression of potential.

Diamonds are reminders of the potential value and worth to be cultivated from ordinary things. Blue is your color. Wear a star sapphire for luck and inspiration. The 144th day of the year reduces to nine, which adds a sense of completion and finality, and makes you conscious of achieving goals. Remember to set your sights higher for the next round.

OBJECTS/IMAGES
a tightrope walker, costume jewelry, megaphones, double Herma (ancient Greek sculpture)

SHAPES/MATERIALS
firestone, slate, thatched roofs, topaz

COLORS
blue-gray wash, indigo, azure

ANIMALS
fox, monkey

PLANTS, HERBS, EDIBLES
honeysuckle, olive spurge, savory, savoy cabbage

ESSENCE
bay

SOUNDS/RHYTHMS
jokes, simultaneous translations

MUSICAL NOTES
A and G#

DEEP SPACE OBJECTS
Xi Perseus, Menkib, the Shoulder

May 24

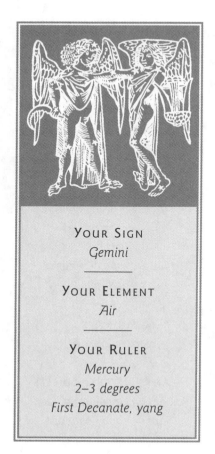

YOUR SIGN
Gemini

YOUR ELEMENT
Air

YOUR RULER
Mercury
2–3 degrees
First Decanate, yang

The Astrological Interpretation

There is a part of you that will never grow up. This characteristic gives you a playfulness and a sense of awe about life and its many mysteries. Your idea of a good time is going to see the latest film, eating at the newest restaurant, having a small party with a group of fascinating friends, buying a new outfit to wear, and doing all of this (and more!) in the space of one day. People find you amusing, as you have a great sense of humor and are quick to smile. You are thought of as witty, charming, versatile, and easy to get to know. You tend to be a busy person, one who has a hard time sitting still. Although your natural restlessness opens you to many experiences in life, it also makes it hard for you to take it easy and relax.

May 24 has a special talent for observation and communication. Your birthday may fall on a critical degree, which means that experiences, both highs and lows, affect you keenly. Your mind is accurate and poetic—an unusual combination. Words and self-expression are important to you. You may have a fondness for collecting dictionaries to see the etymologies of words. Foreign languages and a rhyming dictionary also interest you. You have a restless character and want to roam. Keep a notepad with you and see how your jottings add up. At home, keep versatile luggage so you can easily hit the road. If you are not fond of travel, your peregrinations will be new ideas and a restless pursuit of knowledge.

Outdoors, May 24 needs a place to walk and catch the breeze. A maze of hedges or a path on flat ground would be a perfect way to orient your mind. Flowers such as corydalis and crocuses interest you, but a walk in the woods and stumbling on a variety of wildflowers is more intriguing.

A Kabbalistic Interpretation

A connection with the energies of the planet Mercury is contained in this date's kabbalistic influences, with most of the effect on your quicksilver personality. This day has an association with the tarot card the Magician, suggesting an interest in the art of illusion. Visit a local magic shop or buy a book on illusions and card tricks; you will likely find yourself absorbed and intrigued.

Another key influence on this day is the letter *Ayin*, which means "eye." In the kabbalistic Western Mystery Tradition, *Ayin* is associated with the sign Capricorn. The symbolism of the mountain goat indicates a robust and athletic person, especially in terms of endurance. Consider taking up hiking or rock climbing, as this pursuit will increase your mental endurance as well as your physical strength.

The energy of the goat makes it likely that you are a lusty character by nature and quite probably those around you find you physically attractive. Wear a gray or black outfit with silver jewelry whenever you really want to increase your chances of finding a date.

A Numerological Interpretation
YOUR MAGIC NUMBERS: 2 AND 10

The twenty-fourth day of the fifth month reduces to two, the number of reflection, duplication, and receptivity. This day's path carries a pattern of responsiveness to the stimulation of the subjective side of reality. Immerse yourself in the magical landscape of your imagination, and share your fantastic visions with others. You love the cyclic rituals of the year and enjoy participating in the symbols. Hang mistletoe in a doorway, color eggs in the spring, and bake holiday cookies in festive shapes and colors. Send valentines, and watch fireworks on the Fourth of July.

Create your own rituals and traditions through the application of your wildest dreams. Carnelian and tourmaline will warm your heart. The 145th day of the year reduces to ten, adding the element of successful outcomes, engendering optimism to your receptivity. Always expect the best.

OBJECTS/IMAGES
couriers, dissertations, milestones, fingernail polish

SHAPES/MATERIALS
air, tartan plaids, lattice patterns, Judaica (stone)

COLORS
flat blue, rust, dark blue

ANIMALS
Pomeranian dog, hound dogs

PLANTS, HERBS, EDIBLES
twinleaf, aniseed, grass-of-Parnassus, butterfly weed

ESSENCE
fennel

SOUNDS/RHYTHMS
Bob Dylan's "Blowin' in the Wind"

MUSICAL NOTES
C# and A

DEEP SPACE OBJECTS
Gamma Tau, Prima Hyadum

May 25

YOUR SIGN
Gemini

YOUR ELEMENT
Air

YOUR RULER
Mercury
3–4 degrees
First Decanate, yang

The Astrological Interpretation

This is the birth date of a person who is sensitive to restriction. Although this tendency gives you an abundance of opportunities to explore, it makes it difficult for you to sustain lasting commitments. You should think carefully about the responsibilities you assume in life. Marriage can be successful if your spouse is open to your need to have many outside interests. It is wise for you to choose a partner who is independent by nature and who likes to spend time with his or her friends and personal pursuits. You appreciate children and make a very good parent, as you like to play games and enjoy being physically active.

Your varied interests may lead you to philosophy, writing, music, and healing. Your challenge will be to focus rather than scatter your energy. An image for you is a Corinthian column. The Corinthian style is ornate and delicate yet strong enough to support a building. Decorate your home with lacy paper cutouts or silhouette mobiles. An image for the two sides of the Gemini personality is Janus, the Roman god of the door and gate. Janus's face looks both ways to protect all those who enter your door. A mask or picture of Janus would be a wonderful decoration over your entryway or over a gate going into the garden. In the bedroom, a canopy bed with light gauzy fabric gives you a light airy feeling. Music is important to you and you may consider having a special stereo system in the bedroom.

Outdoors May 25 wants a place to walk and gather thoughts. A swing hanging from two hickory trees is an ideal place to let your mind wander. The sound of evening chimes echoing through the air gives you a harmonious feeling.

A Kabbalistic Interpretation

You may find yourself pulled in a number of incompatible directions in life. Most often yours is a tension between career and emotional attachments. It can be very difficult at times for you to decide whether it is going to be a late night at the office or at the movies with your partner. By keeping a piece of clear rock crystal on your desk you should become much more decisive and focused.

The influence of the Hebrew letter *Lamed* is strong this day. The meaning of this letter is "ox goad," implying that you drive yourself too hard and make excessive demands on yourself. You can trust your work ethic and give yourself the time you deserve to relax. A good way for you to do this would be to run yourself a nice large bath and drop in some sandalwood oil.

One possible value of this date is associated with the name of the sephira Kether. This sephira is the highest on the kabbalistic Tree of Life. This correspondence describes a person with very lofty ideals. A great source of inspiration for you would be to read some biographies of well-known pioneering figures from history. Their stories will resonate with your own life and values and show that some hardships along the way were necessary.

A Numerological Interpretation
YOUR MAGIC NUMBERS: 3 AND 2

The twenty-fifth day of the fifth month reduces to three, the number of multiplication and creative expression. This day's path is one of uniting with your deepest passions. This pattern offers the opportunity to leave your mark on everything you touch by responding to what stirs you deeply. Purple and orange will anchor your emotions. Jasper and agate will ground you. Amethyst will open your heart. Read magazines from the alternative press. Be a passionate recycler. Examine the issues of society that cry out for change, and find a way to get involved. Study the American Revolution. Write articles on social conscience. Volunteer for Greenpeace.

The 146th day of the year reduces to two, the number of mirroring, duplication, and replication. This adds the ability to reflect on your accomplishments, discerning what is of value and should be retained, versus what should be discarded.

OBJECTS/IMAGES
dictionaries, couriers

SHAPES/MATERIALS
polka dots, pearls

COLORS
slate blue, silver, caramel

ANIMALS
kea, locust

PLANTS, HERBS, EDIBLES
trefoil, starwort

ESSENCE
Peruvian balsam

SOUNDS/RHYTHMS
sound of propellers whirring, the two-step

MUSICAL NOTES
D and C#

DEEP SPACE OBJECTS
NGC 1499, the California Nebula

May 26

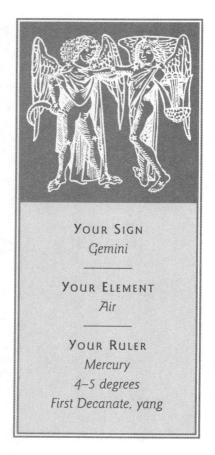

YOUR SIGN
Gemini

YOUR ELEMENT
Air

YOUR RULER
Mercury
4–5 degrees
First Decanate, yang

The Astrological Interpretation

Unlike many of your Gemini brothers and sisters, you are not satisfied with knowledge for its own sake. You are a practical person who seeks to benefit financially and socially from the things you learn. It is easy for you to make friends and gain the cooperation of coworkers, as you are a talented conversationalist and enjoy sharing ideas and insights. You are good at bringing people together and are a natural-born agent and coordinator. Your work must allow you plenty of room for movement, as sitting behind a desk all day is definitely against your nature. Your telephone, fax machine, and computer are always near at hand.

Some May 26 birthdays will fall on a critical degree, which means that experiences in life, both highs and lows, will be strongly felt. Your versatility and dexterity will attract attention in your life. Your basic attitude toward life is breezy, and chance may play a large role in your philosophy. Display magazines, newsletters, and almanacs in your home. You frequently dip into a magazine or newsletter as a mental refresher. Fountain pens may interest you, and you like to collect rare or unusual ones. Include some Chinese calligraphy in your home. The pictograms for Thought, Fortune, and Wind are particularly appropriate. Monograms on your towels, sheets, and men's shirts are a personal touch you would enjoy. Your home should be located on slightly elevated ground with a northeast view. Have as many windows as possible and consider rolled rattan curtains to give your living space a warm-weather feel.

Outdoors you enjoy a low-maintenance garden with defined paths and nooks with benches. Yarrow flowers are particularly well suited to you and have been used medicinally since ancient times. A swing set or swing attached to a tree is a relaxing spot for May 26.

A Kabbalistic Interpretation

The values associated with this day indicate a strong connection to religious concerns. Not only does the basic value of this day add up to thirty-one, the same value as one of the kabbalistic names of God, but twenty-six is also the value of another God name. The month number five is the number of the tarot card the Hierophant, a card associated with traditional religion and religious structures. All these godly connections indicate the potential for a strongly spiritually driven personality. If you are not already interested in a range of spiritual issues, then try dipping into a variety of religious books. You may surprise yourself with your interest.

Those who know you recognize that you have a strong and robust character. You are not afraid to speak your mind or stand your ground when challenged. This is partly due to your connection with the tarot card Strength. If you want to keep that strength in mind or even increase your confidence keep a little figurine of a lion on your desk or wear an item of jewelry that incorporates a lion image in its design.

A Numerological Interpretation
YOUR MAGIC NUMBERS: 4 AND 3

The twenty-sixth day of the fifth month reduces to four, the number of order, reason, and gaining the lay of the land. This day's path is one of probing the heights as well as the depths of possibilities that are open to you. It requires a willingness to risk present security for the sake of what you might achieve. Take a leap of faith. This is a path of digging for treasure, or diving for gold doubloons from a sunken Spanish galleon. Play the stock market for fun, and exercise your speculative muscles. Learn to dowse for water and proudly display your dowsing rod on the wall. Tigereye and zircon will expand your horizons. Wear an orange scarf for courage. The 147th day of the year reduces to three, adding the influence of growth and development, which enhances your sense of receiving dividends on your investments.

OBJECTS/IMAGES
pairs, seeing your breath on a cold morning, a manicure kit

SHAPES/MATERIALS
mercury, parallel lines, aquamarine,

COLORS
gunmetal gray, tangerine

ANIMALS
bobwhite, starling

PLANTS, HERBS, EDIBLES
woodbine, puff pastry, tansy (herb)

ESSENCE
camphor

SOUNDS/RHYTHMS
fast scales, the sound of a pen on parchment

MUSICAL NOTES
D# and D

DEEP SPACE OBJECTS
NGC 1792 spiral galaxy

May 27

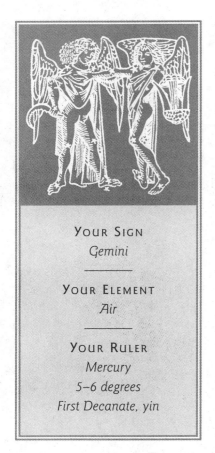

YOUR SIGN
Gemini

———

YOUR ELEMENT
Air

———

YOUR RULER
Mercury
5–6 degrees
First Decanate, yin

The Astrological Interpretation

Your birth date reveals a person who prefers breadth over depth, the many over the few, the general over the specific. You like to accumulate skills and information in the same way that a stamp or coin collector gathers his many examples. Friends think that you are a walking encyclopedia, as you often amaze them with your knowledge of unusual facts. Trivial Pursuit and Scrabble are definitely games at which you excel. Formal education may have been challenging, as you prefer to go about learning in your own way. You have a natural adaptability for what attracts you, but you are repelled by studies and situations that force you to use your mind against your will.

May 27 has an excellent intellect and may be very gifted in communication and languages. You have an urge to challenge the existing order of things and with little fanfare blaze your own trail. Travel is important, and you may have a collection of foreign dictionaries and word phrase books that you take with you. A decorative object for your home could be a poster of all the major linguistic groups. Physical activity and dance are good for you. For those who are not serious athletes, keep a minitrampoline at home and bounce on it every day. It will keep you fit and in good spirits. The decor of your home should be breezy. Think of the way air currents pass in a summer home and try to re-create that feeling. Cut crystal is a decorative object in keeping with your love of clarity.

Outdoors, May 27 would enjoy a practice range for golf as well as a garden. Ecology and proper use of land are important to you. Flowers that go well with your birthday are winter jasmine and hyacinths.

A Kabbalistic Interpretation

While not everyone born today will have a highly developed intellect, all of you tend to have a very wise outlook on life. Those around you will probably have noticed as you were growing up that you had a wisdom beyond your years. This aspect of your character should be nurtured, and you can help to do this by planting some sage in a window box.

The number seven appears often in the various values that can be computed for this day. The kabbala sees the number seven as having great virtue, and its repeated presence in this day suggests that you should be successful in most areas of life. If you plant a monkey puzzle tree in the south side of your garden you will increase your chances of achieving your ambitions in life.

Other influences in this day suggest that you are a lover of all things dramatic. In order to feel at your most positive at home you should make sure that you decorate at least one room of the house in very bold striking colors. This will be a good place for you to sit when you are feeling tired, and it will help to revitalize you and put a smile back on your face.

A Numerological Interpretation
YOUR MAGIC NUMBERS: 5 AND 4

The twenty-seventh day of the fifth month reduces to five, a number of adaptation and versatility. This day's path is one of entering fully into relationship with other human beings. The pattern carries the paradoxical awareness that the more you interrelate and assimilate the experiences of others, the more you become yourself. Wear chrysoberyl to harmonize with others; this gem almost always occurs as a twin crystal. Yellow will increase your self-reliance. Keep a vase of black-eyed susans on your dining table. Draw fresh water deep from the earth, and quench your thirst. Water partakes of the energies and memories of the earth herself and yet nourishes you as an individual. The 148th day of the year reduces to four, which adds the supporting influence of solidity and a firm sense of foundation and predictability.

OBJECTS/IMAGES
talking dolls or action figures, desks, glass icicles

SHAPES/MATERIALS
the shape of highway networks, schist (mineral), beryl

COLORS
muted yellow, butterscotch

ANIMALS
cerulean warbler, razorbill bird

PLANTS, HERBS, EDIBLES
southernwood, azaleas, alphabet soup

ESSENCE
eucalyptus

SOUNDS/RHYTHMS
flapping of wings, drums played with brushes

MUSICAL NOTES
E and D#

DEEP SPACE OBJECT
Epsilon Taurus

May 28

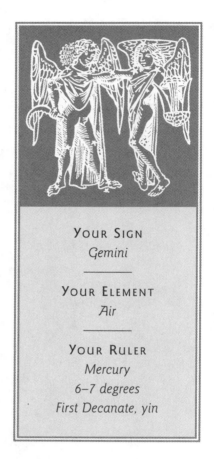

YOUR SIGN
Gemini

YOUR ELEMENT
Air

YOUR RULER
Mercury
6–7 degrees
First Decanate, yin

The Astrological Interpretation

You are not one to go along with what other people think just to preserve social harmony. Sometimes you can be argumentative just for the sake of being different and not necessarily because you are right. This is a tendency you should watch, as it may alienate people who are close to you. You are respected for your intelligence and logic, but you might do well to cultivate diplomacy in their use. In your intimate relationships, you need a companion whose mind can constantly stimulate your own. Yet the emotional content of relationship is also important and you may find that this is where many of your lessons are learned. You will enjoy journals and magazines of specialized interest; science and technology are areas that especially appeal to you.

Some of your thoughts and literary creations are dazzling. Your skill is based on the ability to easily think yourself into characters' minds and imaginative situations. The ancient god Hermes or Mercury in Roman mythology was the messenger god; but he was also considered a trickster. The darting quality of your mind may lead to mischief if words are not checked. Spend some time each day silent. A good reminder of silence is a double-terminated quartz crystal. At home an upright metal chair near a window is the "focus corner," where you can corral thoughts and create. Scents are stimulating to you. Cedar and melissa wafting in the breeze promote clarity.

Outdoors, you like a slight incline and a view. Wind chimes on a patio or deck could carry a message from Hermes to keep breathing deeply. A view of a peaceful valley with a lake on which swans float below a tall mountain is the perfect place for you to relax.

A Kabbalistic Interpretation

You are affected more than most by the kabbalistic energies in this day, which reflect aspects of the Gemini personality. Specifically, the energy of this day indicates that you are often of two minds about your emotional direction in life. A pair of rose-colored vases positioned on each side of your bed can help you to see your real emotional desires more clearly.

The tarot card Fortune affecting this day is connected to the idea of travel. You should make sure you take every opportunity to see more of the world. When you are planning your holidays consider a touring vacation or even a cruise rather than choosing a single destination.

When we look at the full value of the Hebrew version of this day we find that its value is made up of the three letters *Qoph, Kaph,* and *Daleth.* These letters mean "head," "hand," and "doorway," respectively. When looking at all the other aspects of this day it suggests that you can open the doorway to opportunity by using your superior intellect. Focus your formidable powers of concentration by wearing a topaz stone on a chain around your neck.

A Numerological Interpretation
YOUR MAGIC NUMBERS: 6 AND 5

The twenty-eighth day of the fifth month reduces to six, the number of balanced polarities and the harmony of opposites. This day's path carries within it the lesson of positive and constructive self-assertiveness. This pattern's dynamic teaches a refusal to accept a lesser reality when a greater outcome is possible. Your drive for a greater creative outlet moves you forward to an outcome of beauty and love, and moves the race forward as well. Study the lives of great artists, scientists, and inventors, and how their individual contributions influenced others. Visit art galleries often to inspire you. Display your favorite creations and the art objects you've collected.

Lime green and tangerine are colors that will stimulate your creativity. Snowflake obsidian is a gem to inspire you and engender a feeling of harmony. The 149th day of the year reduces to five, which contributes an acute facility for adaptation, which is critical to the process of this day.

OBJECTS/IMAGES
*airmail stationery,
a travel atlas*

SHAPES/MATERIALS
mirror images, tissue paper

COLORS
*gray mixed with sky color,
pea green, pale yellow*

ANIMALS
bookworm, crane

PLANTS, HERBS, EDIBLES
balloon flower, mulberry

ESSENCE
carrot seed

SOUNDS/RHYTHMS
*whispering, the sound of
a train departing*

MUSICAL NOTES
F and E

DEEP SPACE OBJECTS
*Alpha Taurus,
Aldebaran, the Follower*

May 29

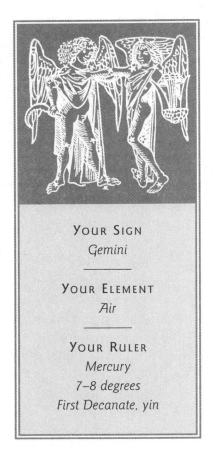

YOUR SIGN
Gemini

YOUR ELEMENT
Air

YOUR RULER
Mercury
7–8 degrees
First Decanate, yin

The Astrological Interpretation

Yours is a birth date that speaks about achieving a harmonious relationship between the real and the ideal. Many of your concepts are original and creative. Yet if you leave things hanging in the air, your understandings and perceptions can do very little practical good. It would be wise for you to cultivate the acquaintance of pragmatic friends and associates, as this will be a good balance to your intellectual nature. You would gain a great deal from working with the earth. Gardening, sculpting with clay, even cooking are all pastimes that can bring benefit to your life.

May 29 people have two distinct sides: a charming politic personality and one that is touchy, rash, and ready for a quarrel. Your Gemini dualism can be balanced by reminding yourself that you have a right to act in your own interest. An image for you is two masks tied together by a green ribbon: the truth lies with the one person within the mask. You have commercial skills, and even if you are not in business you may enjoy having a large ledger book where you enter income and receipts. You usually have a great sense of humor and may be known for playing pranks. Maintain your own good mood by putting humorous quotations on the fridge or have a blackboard with the quip of the day. Consider E-mailing your friends and associates your witticisms.

An image for your outdoor space is the Hanging Gardens of Babylon, as you enjoy an interesting structure as much as you do flowers and plants. Puffball bushes could be part of your environment. See if you can attract a tiger swallowtail butterfly to your yard. If not consider an outdoor mobile of butterflies.

A Kabbalistic Interpretation

The tarot card most associated with this day is the Chariot, indicating a tendency to live life in the fast lane, especially where work is concerned. You need to remember to take time to quite literally smell the roses. Keep a vase of fresh blooms on your desk, especially if they have a pale lemon color. Not only will they relax you, but their presence will also help you to keep your work pattern organized.

The letter *Lamed* is prominent this day in a very positive context, suggesting a highly defined sense of justice and fairness. This valuable quality will be much appreciated by those around you, as you are often called on to mediate when problems arise. Wearing something in a very pale green will serve to enhance this particular quality.

One of the values of this day corresponds to ideas of poverty and exclusion from society. This does not mean that you are likely to become destitute. Rather, it suggests that you have a great compassion for the dispossessed and disadvantaged in your community. If you are not already active, you should try some form of community volunteer work, and if you are looking for something to read choose Dickens or Steinbeck.

A Numerological Interpretation
YOUR MAGIC NUMBERS: 7 AND 6

The twenty-ninth day of the fifth month reduces to seven, the number of victory and accomplishment. This day's path requires the self-discipline of a great athlete or musician, and confers all the benefits of attaining that place in the scheme of things. The universe always responds to our efforts and attainments by bestowing victories. There is the sense of impeccable readiness, alertness, and preparation inherent in your nature. Contemplate a skilled warrior ready for battle, or a concert pianist the moment before a critical performance. Study Tai Chi for discipline and relaxation. Fluorite and citrine will aid you in focusing your energies. Wear orange for strength and purple for celebration.

The 150th day of the year reduces to six, adding the element of beauty and equilibrium, much needed on this path of continual emergence from crisis. Strive for balance.

OBJECTS/IMAGES
*rattan trunks,
a thatched cottage,
a dual-faced wristwatch*

SHAPES/MATERIALS
*two Ionic columns,
pale tourmaline,
coccolite (mineral)*

COLORS
silver, grass green, lime

ANIMALS
chameleon, chimpanzee

PLANTS, HERBS, EDIBLES
*caraway seeds, corn,
feather star (comatula)*

ESSENCE
lemon eucalyptus

SOUNDS/RHYTHMS
the shuffle, choral rounds

MUSICAL NOTES
F# and F

DEEP SPACE OBJECTS
NGC 1851 globular cluster

May 30

YOUR SIGN
Gemini

YOUR ELEMENT
Air

YOUR RULER
Mercury
8–9 degrees
First Decanate, yin

The Astrological Interpretation

This birth date indicates a person who has developed a close integration between thought and action. It is easy for you to coordinate mind and body, ideas and matter. You would make a good teacher, as the examples you give to students solidify concepts readily. You tend to have a number of close platonic relationships, and you treat your friends as if they were brothers and sisters. Whenever possible, you try to develop the relationships you have with your actual siblings into close and trusted friendships. You like to exercise and will enjoy jogging, tennis, golf, and most other one-on-one sports and outdoor activities.

An image for you is the labyrinth: depending on which way you go, there are many possibilities for discovery. At home, you may keep a variety of musical instruments, even if you don't play. A music box is also a wonderful idea. Your desk area should be ready for action. Consider a metal desk or a glass topped table. Transparent objects and a variety of pens and pencils are pleasing to you. Try a fountain pen or calligraphic pen for everyday use. On the wall of either your living space or work area, hang a quiver of arrows. This is a symbol of the quality of mind that always seeks its target.

Your outdoor space should be playful and intriguing. A garden with a path dividing the space into two areas might be particularly fun. Try a path of slate steps with a wicker bench at the end of it. May 30 enjoys the fresh air of early morning. Sleep with your window slightly open and consider some early-morning walks. The northeast is a powerful direction for you.

A Kabbalistic Interpretation

You are a great people watcher and may have a job or career that involves the observation of other individuals, such as counselor, private detective, or security guard. When picking artwork for your home, consider some contemporary photo art of street life. You might enjoy photography by great observers of ordinary people like Jacob Riis, Dorothea Lange, or Walker Evans.

The Hanged Man from the tarot deck is connected to this day, and its influence indicates that you are deeply altruistic. Selflessness is a wonderful and rare quality, but make sure that you are not neglecting your own needs in your enthusiasm to help those around you. Some touches of red, especially deep crimson, in your bedroom will ensure that you give some consideration to yourself.

Communication is another of your strong suits; you love to have a good chat. The influence of Jupiter suggests that you prefer social conversation to serious debate. You enjoy the spoken word as a means of relaxation and should try buying some books on tape as an alternative to reading.

A Numerological Interpretation

YOUR MAGIC NUMBERS: 8 AND 7

The thirtieth day of the fifth month reduces to eight, the number of rhythm and vibration. This day's path is a bit like the fictional adventures of a cartoon superhero. This pattern is one of calm in a crisis and the ability to emerge unscathed from what appears to be a life-threatening situation. Imagine a semitrailer rig careening down a steep incline and stopping at the last moment.

Your intrinsic awareness of the single origin of opposite forms of expression causes you to ultimately master seemingly impossible circumstances. Watch circus acts that perform without a net, or the cliff divers of Acapulco. Try skydiving or bungee jumping. Spinel, a gem whose name means thorn, will remind you of the danger of seizing the stem of a beautiful rose in a blind gesture of acquisitiveness. Wear blue-green for heightened awareness of potential dangers. The 151st day of the year reduces to seven, adding the energy of victory, success, and the need for a well-deserved period of rest between saving people in distress. Remember to refuel your tank.

OBJECTS/IMAGES
a papyrus scroll, musical notes

SHAPES/MATERIALS
striped stones, black and white silhouettes

COLORS
silver gray, teal, kelly green

ANIMALS
moth, swallow

PLANTS, HERBS, EDIBLES
cinquefoil, viper's bugloss, cotton candy

ESSENCE
clary sage

SOUNDS/RHYTHMS
choral odes, geese flying overhead, the scratching of a pen on paper

MUSICAL NOTES
G and F#

DEEP SPACE OBJECT
quasar

May 31

YOUR SIGN
Gemini

———

YOUR ELEMENT
Air

———

YOUR RULER
Mercury
9–10 degrees
First Decanate, yin

The Astrological Interpretation

Your favorite store is the travel agency! You have a naturally adventurous spirit and a need to prove yourself in the world. It is easy for you to travel light, as you know whatever you need on the road can be found by asking and inquiring. Your friends enjoy traveling with you and are delighted as you reveal the many facets of your personality. No one is a stranger to you, and you can always adapt yourself to your surroundings, finding something of interest in everyone you meet and everyplace you go.

May 31 has a finely tuned nervous system. You can easily throw yourself out of balance by a frantic involvement with too many projects. An image for you is a hang glider that rides the air currents gracefully and easily rather than plunging headlong into a downdraft. At home have some books of poetry and verse handy. They will help still your mind. A double terminated quartz crystal could be helpful for you. The double terminated crystals facilitate energy flow. A notepad that you carry with you may also be a way of organizing your many thoughts. Use old-fashioned handwriting to make notes rather than a computer or typewriter. The very act of writing pleases you.

Outdoors May 31 wants a garden with a profusion of flowers that attract butterflies. Possibilities are hyacinth, grape hyacinth, and lily of the valley. Chiming garden bells would be a charming and soothing addition to your outdoor environment.

A Kabbalistic Interpretation

Today is above all a day for thinkers. You are an introspective person and enjoy the chance for peace and quiet. Most often you tend to think of your close family, as you have a deep bond with all of your relatives. Create a photo album and ask your relatives to write something that could be included next to their pictures.

The presence of the Death card from the tarot in the value of this date means you are likely to experience a great deal of change in your life. Other aspects indicate that the main upheavals will relate to your location, and you may find that you move often. Other influences on this day make you an extremely adaptable person who may well enjoy all the variety. By keeping some thyme growing in a window box you can help to ensure a sense of some stability.

This day generates a value that is equivalent to the Hebrew word meaning "belly." It is likely that you are something of a gastronome. Some aspects indicate that food with something of a bite has a particular appeal. You are particularly likely to seek comfort in food when you are down. Next time you feel like diving into the ice cream try a lemon sorbet and add some real lemon juice.

A Numerological Interpretation
YOUR MAGIC NUMBERS: 9 AND 8

The thirty-first day of the fifth month reduces to nine, the number of completion and successful attainment. The last day of May carries the energy of finishing whatever you begin. This path requires a focus of energies and mental concentration. Born on this day, there is a risk of fragmentation and dissolution through an intoxication with diversity and stimulation. Complete a one-thousand-piece jigsaw puzzle by yourself. Write an article or a book, even if it is small. Keep a journal, and have the discipline to record something every day.

Stare into a candle flame for focus. Learn to walk with a book or pottery vessel on your head. Concentrate and bring your attention to a single point. Try walking a tightrope that is only two feet off the ground. Tourmaline and sapphire will strengthen your resolve. The 152nd day of the year reduces to eight, adding the quality of rhythm and vibration to your quest, preventing you from remaining too long with one thing.

OBJECTS/IMAGES
a printing press, telephones, voice-activated computers

SHAPES/MATERIALS
quicksilver, talc, blue aquamarine

COLORS
sage green, aquamarine

ANIMALS
flying squirrel, jackrabbit

PLANTS, HERBS, EDIBLES
canterbury bell (flower), coltsfoot, rice cakes

ESSENCE
melissa

SOUNDS/RHYTHMS
blank verse, chimes

MUSICAL NOTES
G# and G

DEEP SPACE OBJECT
supernova

June 1

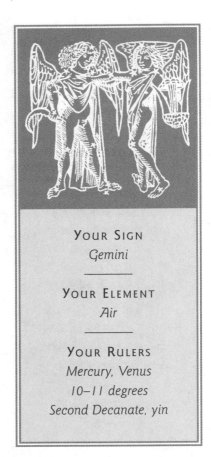

YOUR SIGN
Gemini

YOUR ELEMENT
Air

YOUR RULERS
Mercury, Venus
10–11 degrees
Second Decanate, yin

The Astrological Interpretation

You have an active and creative mind that pushes you forward in life. Yet not all of your many thoughts are worth following. It is your responsibility to prioritize so that you can make the most of your intelligence. The circumstances surrounding your early years have affected you deeply. Although it is wise to learn from your experiences, take care not to bring your past continually into the present. Open yourself to the new and put the old in its proper place in your heart. You would do well to keep a diary or a journal so that you may observe yourself and the way your mind works over time.

This exuberant birthday is interested in getting involved in as many experiences as life has to offer. The challenge is to focus your energy and not scatter it to the winds. Watch that you don't hold your breath when tense; humming a nursery rhyme or catchy melody will insure that you maintain an even flow. At home, divide your space into sections so you know which project is taking place where. Consider wicker furniture; it is light and portable. Also try a portable desk with writing tools so you can take your writing projects with you. A lucky agate stone will help keep you grounded. A retreat for you is a cupola or high balcony where you have an unobstructed view. Sit there and still your mind with deep breaths to focus your energy.

Outdoors, a weather vane tells you how the air is flowing. Your garden should feature tall flowers that wave in the wind as well as gourd vegetables like pumpkins or squash. You have an effortless green thumb, so be prepared for extraordinary growth.

A Kabbalistic Interpretation

This is a day for complete individuals. While many of us are to some extent governed by others, you are yourself without concession. Yet even you will be tempted sometimes to compromise and change an aspect of yourself to please another. Keep a figurine of an eagle on your desk or attached to a key chain and you will find that you are always centered in yourself.

While you have a strong personality, you are not overwhelming in your dealings with others. This day is connected to the tarot card Temperance, suggesting a calm and conciliatory approach to those around you. You may want to encourage this particular trait. Try installing a pond or perhaps two fish tanks inside your home, one each in the north and south.

One of the values of this day corresponds to the Hebrew phrase meaning "secret wisdom." This refers directly to the kabbala itself as a source of wisdom. In more general terms this phrase suggests you may have some latent psychic ability or an untapped interest in the unknown. Try buying a pack of tarot cards or other psychic deck and see how they speak to you.

A Numerological Interpretation
YOUR MAGIC NUMBERS: 7 AND 9

The first day of the sixth month reduces to seven, the number of victory, rest, and satisfaction. This day's path is a continual refining of selfhood through experimentation and self-analysis. You derive great satisfaction from trying different approaches, jobs, relationships, and styles. You love to weigh and balance options and continually reevaluate and refine the resources you find within yourself. Take care not to become too introspective or preoccupied with security. Watch game shows for fun and relaxation. Have a tarot reading. Just for the experience, stretch your limits of intuition and security at a race course. Ride a raft down a white-water river. Surround yourself with tones of green and blue. Malachite, lapis, and turquoise will settle your mind.

The 153rd day of the year reduces to nine, contributing the element of goal orientation and completion. Finish one thing at a time before moving on, and be sure to take a well-deserved rest in between.

OBJECTS/IMAGES
a quill pen, antique manuscripts, an ancient scribe in the marketplace, an outdoor thermometer

SHAPES/MATERIALS
gauze fabric, rippling lines, chrysoprase

COLORS
soft gray, muted green, dusty rose, emerald green, royal blue

ANIMALS
hound, parakeet, monarch butterfly

PLANTS, HERBS, EDIBLES
breath mints, parsley, pomegranate trees

ESSENCES
whiffs of a freshly baked pie, nail polish remover

SOUNDS/RHYTHMS
Gregorian chant, flute chamber music, wind whistling in the trees

MUSICAL NOTES
F# and G#

DEEP SPACE OBJECT
external galaxy

June 2

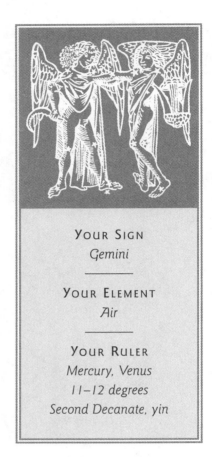

YOUR SIGN
Gemini

YOUR ELEMENT
Air

YOUR RULER
Mercury, Venus
11–12 degrees
Second Decanate, yin

The Astrological Interpretation

You tend to have a restless disposition. Many ideas, people, and possible adventures jump out at you simultaneously and you can find yourself trying to accomplish too many things with too little deep motivation. One way to give yourself the discipline and discernment you need is through music. Take up an instrument so that your mind can direct your hands to creative activity. You like to dance and have a natural sense of rhythm. If playing an instrument is too foreign to you, find a type of musical expression such as baroque or jazz, and study its structure. You will find that music is very logical and ordered, two qualities that are good for you to develop further.

You may waver between a self-conscious awareness of others' reactions to you and a need to express yourself. The key is to speak from your heart rather than retreating into sarcasm or unnecessary carping. A special room in your house where you can be alone, verbally let off steam, and talk out your problems would be a good way to manage your high-strung nature. Your communication skills are strong and you enjoy having newspapers and magazines from around the world. Consider decorating your home with calligraphy written in different languages and alphabets. Chinese or Japanese calligraphy might particularly appeal. For your wardrobe, two-toned materials and reversible jackets appeal to your dual nature. Try eating a black-and-white cookie from time to time!

Outdoors June 2 is very comfortable in a café setting. Your own home should include some bird feeders and a birdbath. Watching the birds splash focuses your active mind.

A Kabbalistic Interpretation

The element of chance is very important to this day. You will probably find that many of the most important changes in your life result in some way from luck and good fortune rather than from careful planning. You can increase your good fortune by wearing jewelry with some kind of tree motif or even a tie with a similar pattern.

Nobody could ever accuse you of being a plain Jane or John. You should always make the most of your appearance because when you look good, you feel even better. The Devil card from the tarot has an influence over this day, which adds to your natural sensuality. If you want to get yourself in the mood for love, play some smooth 1960s soul music.

Your life tends to be extremely busy, and you are very happy with that. You get a definite buzz out of a certain level of pressure in your daily life. However, there are times when you do need to let thing go and relax. A drop of lavender oil in your bathwater will do wonders to balance the stress of your days.

A Numerological Interpretation
YOUR MAGIC NUMBERS: 8 AND 10

The second day of the sixth month reduces to eight, the number of involution and evolution, the back and forth movement of the tides of the universe. All of creation moves in cycles, and this awareness is intrinsic to your path. This day's pattern is one of exercising the muscles of your individuality beyond the limits of your capabilities. Your path requires that you assert yourself and proclaim your views to build a sense of character. This is not rebellion for its own sake but experimenting with thought and behavior in order to grow and to expand the horizons of what you believe you can accomplish.

Navigate a Sunfish on the ocean. Try surfing or parasailing. Read a forbidden book. Wear the colors of the ocean to keep your spirit moving and your thoughts fluid. Serpentine and amazonite will strengthen your sense of self. The 154th day of the year reduces to ten and one, which adds the sense of mastery and pleasure to your achievements. This helps integrate the experience and keeps you moving on toward the next pinnacle.

OBJECTS/IMAGES
toothpicks, a footpath, storytelling

SHAPES/MATERIALS
twins, scrolls of paper, keyboard shapes, crystals

COLORS
matte gray, teal, magenta

ANIMALS
butterfly, shrew

PLANTS, HERBS, EDIBLES
wild blue phlox, tawny cotton grass, coltsfoot

ESSENCE
eucalyptus

SOUNDS/RHYTHMS
jump rope rhymes, sustained tones

MUSICAL NOTES
G and A

DEEP SPACE OBJECT
Gamma Camelopardalis

June 3

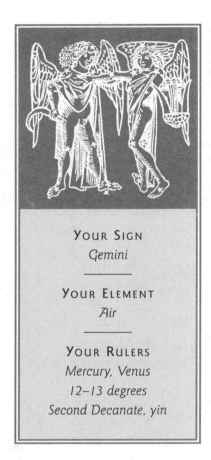

YOUR SIGN
Gemini

———

YOUR ELEMENT
Air

———

YOUR RULERS
Mercury, Venus
12–13 degrees
Second Decanate, yin

The Astrological Interpretation

Your birth date contains possibilities for inventive and original forms of communication. You have special interests you want to share with others and get a real sense of fulfillment from inspiring your friends and associates with your ideas. Create a Web site, local newsletter, or other communications tool to share your opinions and the causes in which you believe. The resulting interchange of ideas will expand your intellectual perimeters and open you to additional creative possibilities. It will also give other people a chance to learn from what you have to offer. If you are a student, join the staff of the school newspaper. If you are a professional, contribute to the company's annual report or other information journals.

High ambition and restlessness characterize June 3. Your nervous system is sensitive, so surround yourself with cooling colors like pale green and blue. A metal mobile hung in your entryway stimulates the imagination and gives you focus each time you cross the threshold. Consider French doors or clear glass bricks between rooms to create as much light and space as possible. If you have musical inclinations get a piano. Even if you just "fool around," the symmetry of the black and white keys and the tones will give you pleasure. There is mechanical skill in this birthday; you may want to channel your building energies into sculptures with blocks or metal shapes. Filigree work and intricate jewelry intrigue your mind and please your aesthetic.

The laurel tree and the flower mountain laurel have resonance for you. Your outdoor space can be crowded or spare but you enjoy being high up where there is constant wind moving. A weather vane on top of your home or garage will keep you oriented. Keep a bird feeder that attracts the very smallest birds.

A Kabbalistic Interpretation

In the Western Mystery Tradition the tarot card of the Hermit has a number of deeply significant associations. At one level it represents the individual seeking out the hidden truths in the universe. For you it indicates that you are capable of quite profound insights. When you are feeling thoughtful, find yourself an armchair covered with a green and yellow pattern to sit in and contemplate matters.

The Tower affects this day in its role as a representative of the energy of Mars. This martial energy can give you the edge when you need it to clinch a deal or bring a plan to fruition. By adding some red peppers to your diet you can enhance the effect of its influence.

You are certainly an ambitious person, and a correspondence between the value of this day and the Hebrew word meaning "kings" indicates that you intend to go far. In its original context this word "kings" refers to a type of angel, so some images of angels around your home can assist you in your efforts.

A Numerological Interpretation

YOUR MAGIC NUMBERS: 9 AND 2

The third day of the sixth month reduces to nine, the number of fulfillment, completion, and attainment. This day's path is one of maximizing your talents to their fullest expression. The pattern asks you to hone and refine your skills so that others are encouraged to do likewise. The energy of this day promises gratification and peak experiences if you make the effort. As you advance to higher levels of expression, you will glimpse the ever unfolding vista that awaits.

Diamond, most prized of minerals, is a symbol of the brilliance that can be achieved through getting at the heart of an object. Also required is the subsequent toil and craft of humans. What begins as a rock becomes a luminous jewel. Wear a blue diamond pendant or ring. Royal blue will intensify your aspiration. Whatever your gifts, develop and share them. Sing in a choir or quartet. Play in a band. Paint, and display your masterpieces. The 155th day of the year reduces to two, adding the influence of duplication and replication to your quest. Always look into the mirror and ask yourself what you learned.

OBJECTS/IMAGES
curtains blowing in the breeze, music paper, quill pen

SHAPES/MATERIALS
wainscoting, agate, chalcedony, tall pipe shapes

COLORS
stripes of white and light blue, pale green, China blue, rust

---

ANIMALS
monkey, gypsy moth

PLANTS, HERBS, EDIBLES
elecampane, tansy, woodbine

ESSENCES
smell of ink, light citrus scents,

SOUNDS/RHYTHMS
recorder music, whistling, quick tempi

MUSICAL NOTES
G# and C#

DEEP SPACE OBJECTS
Beta Eridanus, Kursa, Seat of the Central One

June 4

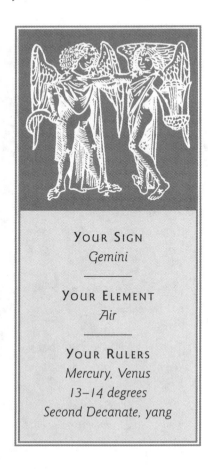

YOUR SIGN
Gemini

—

YOUR ELEMENT
Air

—

YOUR RULERS
Mercury, Venus
13–14 degrees
Second Decanate, yang

The Astrological Interpretation

You are very tuned in to the new, the fresh, and the different. You are sensitive to the interpersonal difficulties people are having at your workplace and in other social settings. As a natural go-between, take up the challenge and work to open up dialogues among the differing factions in your environment. You are an excellent mediator and have a facility for seeing all sides of a situation, coming up with those plans and possibilities that can serve to resolve conflicting opinions. Many people born on your birthday are very technically oriented. You will enjoy reading and hearing about the latest scientific discoveries and the newest upgrades in software and computers.

You have a restless character. You may be fond of short trips just for a change of scenery. You are also eager for new mental experiences to keep your mind entertained. Mental telepathy and nonverbal means of communication interest you. Tools of communication—such as telephones, faxes, Internet—also appeal. Try to find machines that are well designed and colorful as well as useful. In your home display any diplomas, certificates of merit, honors, etc., that you may have achieved. Caned chairs appeal to you. You may want to have a headboard for your bed made from caning. Rice paper on your bedroom walls would be a good decorative touch.

Outdoors, hang wind chimes from your roof. If you have a pet, a small doghouse in your yard would be pleasing. Flowers such as satin flower and Japanese spirea, and the herb vervain resonate with your restless nature.

A Kabbalistic Interpretation

One meaning of the value of this day is to "sweep away." You are a person who prefers to move on when things go wrong in life, rather than look backward. In the context of other energies in this day "sweep away" also indicates that at a practical level you like to have a neat and tidy living space. To really enjoy your home stick to a minimalist style of decoration. Keep an eye on any mounting clutter and clear "things" out on a regular basis.

You are protected by an influence represented by the tarot card the Star. As life goes on, you might notice that you manage to avoid many of the pitfalls and problems most of us suffer in life. Very often you will escape by the narrowest of margins, but almost inevitably you will escape. The protective effect of this card can be ensured by wearing a pendant with a seven-pointed star.

Another word that corresponds to the value of this day is the Hebrew word for *oak*. The key characteristic of oak is that it gives strength and endurance. Consider investing in a little bonsai oak tree to keep on your office desk, so that this influence remains with you at all times.

A Numerological Interpretation
YOUR MAGIC NUMBERS: 10 AND 3

The fourth day of the sixth month reduces to ten, the number of embodiment and perfection. The cycle ends and must begin again, preferably at a new level. This day's energies endow you with a heightened faculty of intuition. You have the capacity to sense and glean information from unseen and miraculous sources. The responsibility of this path is to utilize this talent to increase the awareness of the interconnectedness of all things. Personally, you can access these clues and hints to further your career or standing. You can advance the fellowship of the race.

Lie on your back in the desert and commune with the stars. Probe their ancient messages and meanings and invite their energies into your soul. Share your perceptions, and write or speak about your insights. Explore the landscape of your subconscious in your dreams. Apache flame agate will expand the horizons of your mind. Orange sapphire will heighten your awareness. The 156th day of the year reduces to three, contributing the element of creative self-expression to this path, supporting your efforts at communication.

OBJECTS/IMAGES
pens, monocles, names, costume jewelry

SHAPES/MATERIALS
scroll shapes, ink, mercury, whirlwind shapes

COLORS
yellow, wine, apricot

ANIMALS
flying squirrel, warbler

PLANTS, HERBS, EDIBLES
birch beer, trefoil, valerian, starwort

ESSENCE
tarragon

SOUNDS/RHYTHMS
soliloquies, sermons

MUSICAL NOTES
A and D

DEEP SPACE OBJECT
Iota Auriga

June 5

YOUR SIGN
Gemini

YOUR ELEMENT
Air

YOUR RULERS
Mercury, Venus
14–15 degrees
Second Decanate, yin

The Astrological Interpretation

You are extremely sensitive and respond strongly to emotional or physical pollution. You like cleanliness in the world around you and clarity in your communications with friends and lovers. It is vital for you to make sure that disagreements are resolved with as much understanding as possible. Words are things to you and you do not toss them about carelessly. You know that once something comes out of your mouth, it can never be retracted. It is easy for you to forgive and get on with life, for you have an easygoing nature. But that doesn't make you a pushover, nor does it prevent you from saying what you believe is correct.

You like a lot of variety and different stimuli in your environment. You could be very happy with two homes or apartments so you could change environments at will. Your home space should feature many telephones in different styles, as all communication devices are friendly to you. A good flow of air is essential; light curtains insure a steady stream of air. In the summer, even if you have air-conditioning, keep a fan going. When you need to calm the mind and refocus when restless, sitting in a corner with bookcases and a wooden chair will focus you. Personal objects that keep you happy are feathery decorations and jewelry.

Outdoors, you find solace in walking by a rapid inland stream or small river. Fly-fishing could be a good activity for the sports-minded. A tree house facing southwest is a great retreat and a place to share secrets with a friend.

A Kabbalistic Interpretation

Your heart is where your home is. You like nothing more than to be in the bosom of your family surrounded by your loved ones. However, you are also aware of your own independence, and it is important for you to have your own space. This might be as simple as a personal chair, but ideally you should find a space where you can close out the world and relax.

You are strongly influenced by the energy of the moon in your daily life. This influence can encourage your more creative side. To add to the moon's effect carry a moonstone in your pocket. But the moon can also encourage anxiety; counter this by wearing a ring or other jewelry with a ruby or other rich red stone set into it.

One of the values of this day corresponds to the value of the name Balaam in Hebrew. Like Balaam, who couldn't see the angel of God in the road, you can sometimes be blind to important matters that are directly before you. One way to improve matters is to introduce some rosemary into your cooking; its pungent flavor will help keep you mentally on the ball.

A Numerological Interpretation

YOUR MAGIC NUMBERS: 2 AND 4

The fifth day of the sixth month reduces to two, the number of opposite forms of expression and duality. This day's path carries the energy of continual dialogue with another aspect of yourself for the purpose of self-knowledge through reflection and mirroring. The pattern requires a constant and vigilant interchange with a broad range of potentials of existence, examining a myriad of possibilities of force within form.

Strive for synthesis. Learn another language, and travel to a foreign country where you can converse with the natives in their own tongue. Eat at ethnic restaurants. Observe sessions at the United Nations. What are the threads that tie humanity together, and what are the forces that are capable of ripping the fabric of community asunder?

Orange is a color that will lift your spirits and generate optimism. Rhodochrosite will still the rushing currents in your mind. The 157th day of the year reduces to four, adding the qualities of order, reason, and classification, supporting your path with the capacity to engage your logical mind.

OBJECTS/IMAGES
bookstores, catalogs, Cadillacs with pointy fins, EPCOT Center at Disney World

---

SHAPES/MATERIALS
twin Doric columns, swivel windows, sheer fabric, helix shapes

---

COLORS
crystal blue, pale yellow, geranium red, butterscotch

ANIMALS
carrier pigeon, copper butterfly, parrot

PLANTS, HERBS, EDIBLES
dog grass, sweet woodruff, azaleas, caraway seeds

ESSENCE
jasmine

SOUNDS/RHYTHMS
Middle Eastern music, whistling wind, rap music in different languages

---

MUSICAL NOTES
C# and D#

DEEP SPACE OBJECTS
Beta Orion, Rigel (foot)

June 6

YOUR SIGN
Gemini

YOUR ELEMENT
Air

YOUR RULERS
Mercury, Venus
15–16 degrees
Second Decanate, yang

The Astrological Interpretation

You know how to seize upon opportunities for growth and development and never cease to find new ways of applying what you know. Although you are filled with facts and figures, you also enjoy browsing through museums and art galleries, attending concerts and plays, and enriching your life through intellectual and aesthetic pursuits. Clothing is important to you; you may change your outfit several times a day, depending on your mood and the nature of your social events. You like to be quite active and find that you have a wide variety of friends with whom you enjoy the many pleasures of life. It may take a while to choose a life partner. You tend to avoid set schedules and established routines.

June 6 has tremendous verbal energy and dexterity. Your words can be powerful and you will want to choose them carefully. At home calm the number of ideas in your head by whistling. An attic retreat with windows and a view of the whole neighborhood is a place for you to be quiet and refocus your energies. June 6 may particularly enjoy pets and animals. A parakeet is a companion with whom you could try out your ideas before they burst forth. All communication tools such as computers, fax, telephones, etc., should be kept up to date. It would also be a good idea for you to designate one day of silence for yourself and turn off all media, phones, etc.

Outdoors, June 6 may enjoy a home with a slate roof. A garden area with seed-bearing plants is a good focus for you. Tawny cotton grass, baneberry, and pokeweed are all wildflowers that disseminate seeds. Up in the eaves of your slate roof give a thought to how ideas and spoken words are seeds that you plant, for you may grow either flowers or weeds.

A Kabbalistic Interpretation

A connection to the tarot card the Hanged Man shows that you are on the whole a selfless individual. You give of your time to others, but more out of a sense of duty than because you get any great satisfaction out of it. Try keeping a tigereye gem with you and you will find that you feel less guilty about suiting yourself from time to time.

Another significant influence this day is the Sun card. This card indicates that you work well with youngsters, perhaps as a teacher. Hang a wind chime decorated with sun patterns in your living room. and it will help you to maximize this positive energy

Connections among Hebrew letters that can be derived from the value of this day point to a highly imaginative personality. The connections also suggest that travel is an excellent way to fire up your imagination. You might want to consider taking up walking as a hobby or organizing a camping trip for you and some of your friends. Organize a teaching expedition and take some young folks with you.

A Numerological Interpretation

YOUR MAGIC NUMBERS: 3 AND 5

The sixth day of the sixth month reduces to three, the number signifying development and growth and the outworking of the influences set in motion in one and two. You have an innate understanding of the unfoldment of the potentials of creative expression. This day's pattern calls for an awareness of the right of every individual to have a potentially different voice and personality. There exists a profound social conscience and desire within you to remake the world according to your highest ideals. You carry the determination that everyone should have the chance to express their potential. Volunteer for a cause you feel passionate about. Don't be an armchair activist.

Citrine and topaz will energize your mental faculties. Yellow is a color that will clarify your mind and increase your positive outlook. The 158th day of the year reduces to five, contributing the quality of versatility and adaptation to your mental processes, making it easier for you to be flexible.

OBJECTS/IMAGES
wit, whistles, shopkeepers, yearbooks

SHAPES/MATERIALS
graphite, ink, stone tablet shapes, stick figure drawings

COLORS
yellow, apricot, gold

ANIMALS
buff-bellied hummingbird, bluejay

PLANTS, HERBS, EDIBLES
feather bells, white sweet clover, winter savory

ESSENCE
the smell of new tennis balls

SOUNDS/RHYTHMS
sermons, rhyming slang

MUSICAL NOTES
D and E

DEEP SPACE OBJECTS
Zeta Auriga, Hoedus, the Kids

June 7

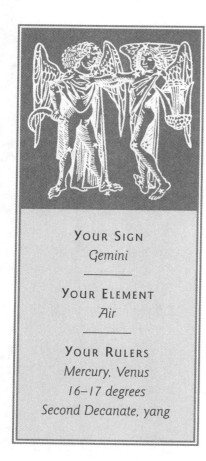

YOUR SIGN
Gemini

YOUR ELEMENT
Air

YOUR RULERS
Mercury, Venus
16–17 degrees
Second Decanate, yang

The Astrological Interpretation

Sometimes your thoughts and opinions differ so widely from those of friends and coworkers that you wonder how you arrived in your present environment. This independence of mind is your best friend, allowing you to be yourself no matter what pressures exist to the contrary. Your mind is a world that is yours alone, one into which you can retreat in order to find support and strength. You will be attracted to your lovers much more from a mental than a physical perspective.

June 7 is located near the fixed star Rigel. The ancients deemed it a favorable position for honors, the military, and ecclesiastical concerns. Those June 7 birthdays that fall on a critical degree of Gemini will experience highs and lows keenly. Your strong mental capabilities mean you can easily pass into a world of fantasy and imagination. When you feel you are in a mental whirl, carry an earthy stone such as mica, smoky quartz, or jasper to keep you grounded. At home your environment should be visually stimulating but not overly so. Colored mobiles or a chandelier with some crystal prisms are preferable to two or three television sets. A magazine rack with nature magazines is a good way to rest your mind. Hummingbirds and grasshoppers may particularly appeal to you.

Outdoors, you like a changing landscape. A walk that has light and shade, a house and open country, a brook and a small hill, will please your dual nature. In your garage, have many different ladders. They are good for fixing the roof and for sitting and thinking. Atop a ladder, watch the birds and butterflies come and go.

A Kabbalistic Interpretation

The value of this day has the same value as a phrase from the book of Exodus meaning "the staff of God." You are comfortable in positions of power, and having a staff as a symbol reminds you that you are more than capable of bearing heavy responsibility. A vase of daisies on your desk will balance this and help to keep in sight the simple things in life.

If you were an animal you would probably be a fiery feline! You are enormously territorial. Though being vigorously protective of your home and family can be positive, the same traits are not so easy to incorporate in environments like a busy office. Wear something violet to work, as this will make you more amenable to others when they encroach on your space.

The tarot card Judgment is important this day. Given your territorial nature you can seem quite severe with people. However the Judgment card indicates a fair and balanced person when it comes to settling arguments and conflicts. Your sense of balance extends to your taste as well as your attitude. To feel most comfortable in your home try to create a feeling of symmetry. A good idea is to buy ornaments in pairs when possible.

A Numerological Interpretation
YOUR MAGIC NUMBERS: 4 AND 6

The seventh day of the sixth month reduces to four, the number of abstract reason. Four is the ordering principle, which measures, classifies, and arranges the aspects of experience. You love learning new things and comparing and categorizing the information according to your wide-ranging knowledge. This day's path endows you with the capacity to internalize the experiences of all humanity through your imagination. This tendency must be cultivated in such a way that you develop your own individuality as a distinct counterpoint to the lives of your human family across the globe. Join a fraternal organization. Collect black-and-white photographs from around the globe.

Storage areas with lots of slots and cubbyholes fascinate you. Moonstone will enhance your visions. Wear lime green to stimulate your mind and widen your mental landscape. The 159th day of the year reduces to six, adding the element of bringing polarities into equilibrium. Don't stray too far to one end or the other of the continuum. Strive for balance.

OBJECTS/IMAGES
bicycle built for two, library steps, a metal newspaper rack

SHAPES/MATERIALS
straw, mirror images, parchment paper

COLORS
muted shades, monochromatic, tawny, spring green

ANIMALS
Rhesus monkey, swallow

PLANTS, HERBS, EDIBLES
caraway, cinquefoil, spareribs

ESSENCES
myrtle, sage

SOUNDS/RHYTHMS
the sound of a printing press, jazz riffs, a piccolo

MUSICAL NOTES
D# and F

DEEP SPACE OBJECTS
Beta Lepus, Nihal, the Hare

June 8

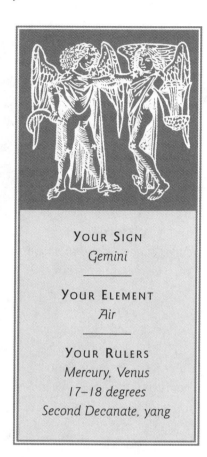

YOUR SIGN
Gemini

YOUR ELEMENT
Air

YOUR RULERS
Mercury, Venus
17–18 degrees
Second Decanate, yang

The Astrological Interpretation

The form that Gemini's duality takes in your life has to do with the integration of your mind with your emotions. Sometimes you are overly logical and the feeling nature is lacking. At other times, you are overly reactive emotionally in dealing with life situations. Work at not attaching yourself to either the mind or the emotions. Just watch and see which of your buttons is being pushed and stay aware of your reactions. There is a reason you are being pushed from one side of yourself to the other. Once you have properly blended the two, you will have true wisdom, something far richer than either logic or emotions when taken individually.

Some June 8 birthdays fall on a critical degree, meaning you experience life's ups and downs intensely. Calming the profusion of ideas and theories you can think simultaneously will be a challenge for you. One wall of your home should be pale yellow. If you set up a chair with a pair of library steps in a corner facing that wall you will have a creative rest space. Your taste leans toward modern, straight, clean lines with lots of windows and light. A ranch house with sliding glass doors could be the ideal home for you. With Venus coruling your birthday, June 8 is interested in creating a beautiful space at home and at work. Investigate the work of Frank Lloyd Wright. Lamps that have a touch of Prairie Style simplicity will please you.

Outdoors, June 8 needs a simple space to unwind. A triangular design in your yard may be of interest to you. Whenever life seems too busy, lie down on the grass with your head at the apex of the triangle and your feet and arms stretched out toward the base and sides respectively. This is a perfect way to focus yourself.

A Kabbalistic Interpretation

You are one of those rare individuals who always points other people toward wonderful new opportunities. As an excellent facilitator of other people's success you are a good person to know. By wearing some jewelry or a tie with an upward-pointing yellow triangle you will find that you start to help your own progress.

You are excellent at getting projects completed. The influence of the World card from the tarot indicates that you are one of life's finishers. It is also important to develop new ideas, and this is one area of life where you tend to have a block. Try growing a mixture of vervain and hawthorn in a window box to inspire your creative initiative and ideas.

You are likely to have a very close relationship to nature. Environmental concerns are of interest to you and you probably try to recycle as much as possible. When decorating your home you should take into account your environmental interests and opt for a range of natural fibers and recyclable products.

A Numerological Interpretation

YOUR MAGIC NUMBERS: 5 AND 7

The eighth day of the sixth month reduces to five, the number carrying the energy of change, process, and the means to an end. This day's path is one of specialization as the mechanism of refinement of a particular aspect of your personality's expression. This pattern can result in a highly developed mental nature. Learn another language and converse with a native. Program a computer. Read the classics of literature in their original languages. Join Mensa or a professional organization. Buy a new set of encyclopedias and read them cover to cover. Join a group that aligns with your specific interests or avocation. The risk of this pattern is a sort of intellectual superiority or exclusiveness. Enjoy the mental realm, but remember the mind is a tool, not the master. Tigereye and star sapphire will sharpen your inner vision. The 160th day of the year reduces to seven, contributing the awareness of a resting period and the need to pause, reflect, and still the teeming activity in your brain.

OBJECTS/IMAGES
butterfly stickpins/barrettes, paths, computer graphics, letters

SHAPES/MATERIALS
matched columns, the shape of musical notes, colorless beryl

COLORS
soft gray, lemon, kelly green

ANIMALS
orangutan, pika

PLANTS, HERBS, EDIBLES
blue vervain, dodder vine, spun sugar mouthwash

ESSENCE
white birch

SOUNDS/RHYTHMS
rustle of pages, a mockingbird's song, Robert Schumann's music

MUSICAL NOTES
E and F#

DEEP SPACE OBJECTS
Gamma Orion, Bellatrix (female warrior)

June 9

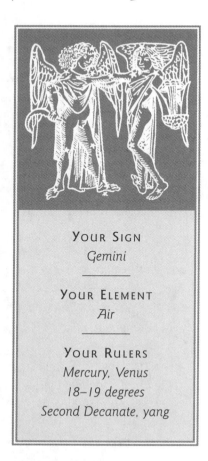

YOUR SIGN
Gemini

YOUR ELEMENT
Air

YOUR RULERS
Mercury, Venus
18–19 degrees
Second Decanate, yang

The Astrological Interpretation

Your birth date reveals a person who has learned how to integrate work with pleasure in order to achieve a balanced life. You realize that part of you has to fulfill social, financial, and familial responsibilities. You also know that there is a part that does not feel satisfied without at least some portion of the day devoted to pure fun. Yours is a permissive nature, one that allows other people their own foolishness and allows you to express your own urges to jump up and down and spin around when the mood suits you. You like to dress up and go out. You enjoy a restaurant's atmosphere and looking at the other people more than the food, the actors more than the play, the party more than the reason for celebrating. It is in these settings that you find the freedom that lets you go to work each day.

June 9 is a birthday of ardor and enthusiasm. Your challenge is to maintain flexibility without scattering your energies. Collecting old and rare books may interest you. Decorate your home with scroll shapes. These could be the capitals of Ionic columns, a wooden paper towel holder, or an ancient papyrus document that you frame. Word games and puzzles could also feature in your home. In the bedroom, a library bed with bookshelves set in the headboard would house your books and writing materials. You may want to jot down your dreams, as you may learn from their images.

Outdoors, June 9 likes a garden or yard with some pinwheels, whirligigs, or other toys that move with the breeze. Having a sound system where you can hear music outdoors would be a pleasure especially in the spring. Flowering shrubs for June 9 are flowering ash, flowering dogwood, and snowdrop tree.

A Kabbalistic Interpretation

The word *Suph*, meaning "limit," can be derived from one of the values of this day and points to your need for well-defined structures. Clear boundaries are important to you. We all like to know where we stand with our friends and our careers. However, one of the most fulfilling aspects of life is the willingness to see where the current takes us. If you decorate at least one room of your home in strong vibrant colors you will find that you can loosen up a great deal and enjoy the flow of life.

There is a connection this day to mechanical expertise and transportation. You could buy yourself a simple kit car. Even if you have never attempted anything technical before in your life, you will probably find that you get a great deal of satisfaction from building it.

Another word that corresponds to the value of this day is the Hebrew word for "life." In the wider analysis of the date this relates to all forms of animal life. Visit nature preserves near you, or the zoo, if you live in the city. If you don't have at least one pet you should think about getting one. If you are unable to have a pet then some animal figurines will brighten up your home and your life.

A Numerological Interpretation
YOUR MAGIC NUMBERS: 6 AND 8

The ninth day of the sixth month reduces to six, the number of equilibrium, symmetry, and complementary activities. This is a path of harmonizing opposing views and energies. This pattern requires connecting with and applying lessons of past experience, your own and those of the culture. At your best, you can draw upon prior experiences and lessons of history to chart your course from the present forward. Hike in the wilderness, mark your trail, and navigate by the stars.

Follow Forest Service maps through the national forest. Collect prints of ancient maps and display them in your study. Have a telescope on your balcony, and learn the stellar landscape. Fluorite and tourmaline will anchor you to the energies of the earth. The 161st day of the year reduces to eight, adding the influence of rhythmic flow, supporting this path's access to exactly what you need when you need it.

OBJECTS/IMAGES
wainscoting, typesetters, roads, telephones, novels

SHAPES/MATERIALS
pipe shapes, striped stones, quicksilver, pairs

COLORS
violet, lime, teal

ANIMALS
swallow, squirrel monkey

PLANTS, HERBS, EDIBLES
vervain, filbert trees, walnuts

ESSENCE
coumarin

SOUNDS/RHYTHMS
gossip, "It's De-lovely" by Cole Porter

MUSICAL NOTES
F and G

DEEP SPACE OBJECTS
Alpha Lepus, Arneb

June 10

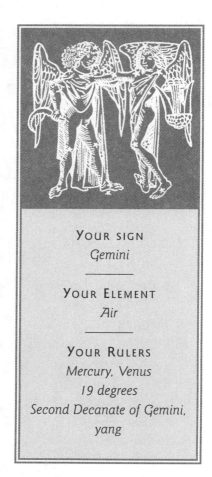

YOUR SIGN
Gemini

YOUR ELEMENT
Air

YOUR RULERS
*Mercury, Venus
19 degrees
Second Decanate of Gemini,
yang*

The Astrological Interpretation

You are very inquisitive and will search for answers to your questions until you either find them or learn that they can never be found. You do not like to be left in the dark. You like amusements that challenge your mental resources and may enjoy table, card, and video games with your friends. Many people born this day are attracted to more evolved and complex patterns and structures. Those with a metaphysical orientation will find themselves leaning toward numerology, astrology, and tarot cards, while others will be interested in mathematics, physics, and computer technology. Because of the strong mental emphasis, it may not be so easy for you to be emotionally intimate. You often try to explain or rationalize your feelings instead of experiencing them. Enjoy your wonderful mind, but do not forget your heart.

A library or at least a book corner in the home will be an enlivening environment for you. Keep books well dusted, as knowledge for you is a living force, not something to store away. A stylish desk where you can center your studies, thoughts, and writing activities is an investment worth putting some real time and consideration into. Your home environment should be airy with plenty of open windows and gauzy curtains. You might be partial to both hand and ceiling fans. Music and singing are important, and a karaoke set up would be a fine way to blow off steam.

The outdoor area should require minimal care. A rock garden with flowers that do not require a lot of weeding is ideal. Your preferred way to spend time outdoors is with a collection of white plastic furniture with ingenious shapes. You may not like the sun much and prefer a high view with a walnut tree for shade.

A Kabbalistic Interpretation

The Tower card from the tarot looms large in this day's analysis. This card represents catastrophic change, and on this day it indicates issues with authority figures controlling your life decisions. This relates mainly to your early life and may indicate a rebellious adolescence. Carrying a bloodstone will help you to maintain a healthy edge of personal freedom well into middle age.

This is a day that is governed by the element of air. While it means you are an excellent abstract thinker, the predominance of air can lead to emotional anxiety at times. If you feel the need for greater emotional stability in your life have some decorative elements in orange and navy blue. Try putting favorite photographs in picture frames in these color around your house.

The most positive aspect of the strong air energy around you is your brilliantly active mind. You will want to read as widely as possible on every conceivable subject. To get the most out of your personal time alone with your books, snuggle up in a yellow painted chair facing east.

A Numerological Interpretation
YOUR MAGIC NUMBERS: 7 AND 9

The tenth day of the sixth month reduces to seven, the number of victory and successful attainment. This day's path involves ascertaining your role of fullest contribution to the collective and thereby placing yourself in a position to receive the maximum in return. Imagine a cosmic cafeteria, where each individual contributes an item, and their offering entitles them to choose as they wish from the other selections. Know what you can best contribute, and also know what you really need.

Malachite and jasper will strengthen your focus and powers of choice. Window-shop at a twenty-four hour hypermart or an enormous department store. Observe the operation of an assembly line in a manufacturing plant and see how all the parts come together to make the finished product. Surround yourself with green to keep the creative juices flowing. The 162nd day of the year reduces to nine, which contributes a sense of attainment to your efforts, and fires your idealism.

OBJECT/IMAGES
vellum paper, quill pens, bookcases, nail polish, a high mountain path

SHAPES/MATERIALS
double-terminated crystals, pairs of mirrors, chintzes

COLORS
slate, gray-blue sky, pale yellow, pale apricot, silver, grass green, sky blue

ANIMALS
ladybug, swallow, squirrel

PLANTS, HERBS, EDIBLES
lungwort, yarrow, licorice, litchi nuts, parsley

ESSENCES
gardenia, anise

SOUNDS/RHYTHMS
fluttering leaves, all quick tempos, harmonic

MUSICAL NOTES
F# and G#

DEEP SPACE OBJECTS
Delta Orion, Mintaka, the Belt

June 11

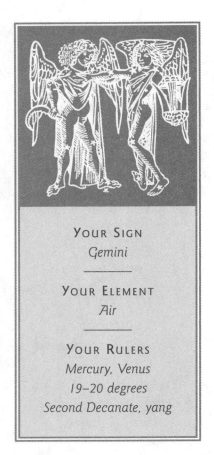

YOUR SIGN
Gemini

___

YOUR ELEMENT
Air

___

YOUR RULERS
Mercury, Venus
19–20 degrees
Second Decanate, yang

The Astrological Interpretation

This birth date contains potential for the development of real intuition. Intuition is a gift that allows you to go beyond logic and reason into a profound atunement with life. Your mind works so quickly you sometimes know how a situation is going to work out before it begins. You frequently know what another person will say before he or she says it. Intuition gives you a sense of oneness, permitting you to feel like you are connected to all people and not just your particular family or social group. If you are not in an artistic profession such as poetry, music, or theater, you may want to develop that side of your nature.

This birthday brings talents and impatience with those who lack intelligence and talent. Keep centered on your own abilities and don't obsess. Keep a glass of water on your desk to smooth out your feelings. Going to sleep with the sound of a fountain or even a tape of a babbling brook will help you relax. Your home should include windows with a variety of exposures. If you could have windows at all four compass points, it would be ideal. If not, consider a morning meditation of bowing to each direction. This is good for locating yourself and centering. Hang prisms and pieces of colored glass where they will catch the sun. An image for you is a red tree covered with golden fruit.

Outdoors, you like slight hills with a bench or small gazebo at the top so you can catch the view. The gazebo would be the perfect place to do the centering meditation to each of the four directions. A garden is nice for Gemini but more important is a landscape for you to paint, or birds and bees that inspire music.

A Kabbalistic Interpretation

People born on June 11 are thought to be under a star of protection. The protective influence of the kabbalistic path of Tzaddi is enhanced by a relationship with the Hebrew letter *Zayin*. The letter *Zayin* means "sword" and indicates that you have a courageous character and can look after yourself very well. As a leisure activity you might try some martial arts such as tae kwan do or karate. In planetary terms this day falls under the influence of Mars. The red planet has a positive influence in this case, especially in the realm of your working life and career aspirations. In order to get the most from this planet's energy keep some iron ornaments in the house. A pair of tall iron candlesticks with bright red candles would do very well.

One word that equates to the full value of this date is the Hebrew word for *glutton*. In certain cases this association might actually mean you are inclined to overindulge gastronomically. However, other tempering influences in this day indicate that your interest is more likely to be in the quality rather than the quantity of a meal. Treat your taste buds once in a while at your town's best restaurant. The flavors will inspire you.

A Numerological Interpretation
YOUR MAGIC NUMBERS: 8 AND 10

The eleventh day of the sixth month reduces to eight, the number of evolution. As the energies of nature move back and forth in a rhythmic ebb and flow, consciousness evolves from one cycle of expression to the next. This day's path is one of understanding and working toward a universal social stewardship. You are capable of great courage and willingness to grapple with complex social issues. Shades of blue and green are harmonious for you.

Work in organizations that deal with world hunger or the environment. Watch all the versions of *Star Trek*, and imagine Earth as a member of a galactic federation of planets. Go to a *Star Trek* convention for fun. Join the World Health Organization or CARE. Green quartz and tanzanite will amplify your courage and vision. The 163rd day of the year reduces to ten, contributing the influence of a completed process and readiness to begin again, supporting your path with faith.

OBJECTS/IMAGES
a perfume atomizer, a scroll

SHAPES/MATERIALS
*gentle fine curves,
mirror images*

COLORS
*slate, champagne, turquoise,
midnight blue*

ANIMALS
hamster, parakeet

PLANTS, HERBS, EDIBLES
heather, skullcap, linseed tea

ESSENCE
lily of the valley

SOUNDS/RHYTHMS
*medieval recorder music,
fan dance*

MUSICAL NOTES
G#, C#

DEEP SPACE OBJECTS
*Epsilon Orion, Alnilam,
String of Pearls*

June 12

YOUR SIGN
Gemini

YOUR ELEMENT
Air

YOUR RULERS
Mercury, Uranus
20–21 degrees
Third Decanate, yang

The Astrological Interpretation

An optimistic and upbeat person, you are always ready with a witty word, a smile, and an abundance of ideas for a good time. You like being with people and have a wide network of friends. Although your home is important, you enjoy leaving for frequent short trips and journeys. Even if you are not traveling out of town, you will spend many evenings and free afternoons away from home. You are easily bored and like to fill your spare time with visits to loved ones, giving yourself many opportunities to catch up on the latest films, concerts, and shows. You enjoy connecting with people, going to intimate dinner parties, and making life as pleasant as possible.

You are mentally quick and supercharged. You think more than you feel and may get caught up in your own imaginative web and inflate minor problems into full-blown windstorms. To calm the winds, blow out your tension as if you were blowing out a candle. Then you will be sure to take a good deep breath as you inhale. At home, chintz patterns on your furniture are pleasing. Lamps with parchment paper shades give a soft light to your environment. Try decorating with framed autographs or letters of people you admire. Weather patterns intrigue you, and a barometer on the wall near a door will be a good guide for you. Your own moods may be sensitive to changes in air pressure.

Outdoors, June 12 should have a garden with flowers that attract butterflies. A nearby track where you can run is an asset. Just for fun and to express your individuality consider putting up signs in and around your home. A personal traffic light would suit your sense of humor and order.

A Kabbalistic Interpretation

The design of your home is exceptionally important to you. You are more likely than most to have an active hand in its structural design. Indeed you would enjoy the prospect of extensive renovation of the right property. One feature that you should definitely have on any property you own is a walled garden, perhaps made of stone.

The presence of the gematrical equivalent of the Hebrew name for Jehovah tells us that you are a highly moral individual. Other factors indicate that your morality particularly applies to emotional relationships. Honesty in your partner is more important to you than any other quality they may possess. You also have a highly romantic, sensitive side. When you feel like an afternoon of indulgence sit down with a good romantic novel or old weepy film.

It may well be that you have an interest in making music yourself. If this is the case then you would do well to try some kind of percussion instrument, a good-size drum kit or an African drum would do nicely.

A Numerological Interpretation
YOUR MAGIC NUMBERS: 9 AND 2

The twelfth day of the sixth month reduces to nine, a number signifying fulfillment, and the culmination of the seed idea begun in number one. This day's path embodies the energy of joy in community. The pattern engenders a need to be among your human brothers and sisters, and requires that you enter into the shared experiences of life without reservation.

Your personal sense of completion is gained through optimum involvement in your community. Throw a big block party. Take square dancing lessons for fun. Organize a large potluck supper in your neighborhood. Spread red-and-white-check cloths on the tables. Have ethnic music, hold hands, and dance in an enormous circle. Rhodonite and rose quartz will open your heart. The 164th day of the year reduces to two, adding the quality of receptivity and comfort with interdependence.

OBJECTS/IMAGES
caducei, keyboards, an abacus

SHAPES/MATERIALS
quicksilver, crystal, natural pairs

COLORS
pale violet, azure, bittersweet

ANIMALS
gray and white kittens, magnolia warbler

PLANTS, HERBS, EDIBLES
wild celery, yarrow, madder

ESSENCE
balsam of tolu

SOUNDS/RHYTHMS
typewriters tapping, bird calls

MUSICAL NOTES
G# and C#

DEEP SPACE OBJECTS
Zeta Orion, Alnitak, the Girdle

June 13

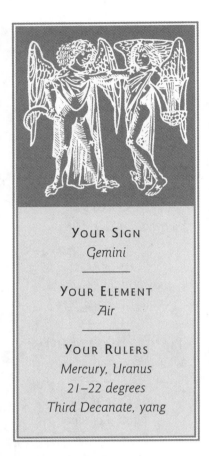

The Astrological Interpretation

It is hard for you to understand why so many people get so attached to the difficulties of life that they find themselves paralyzed. You prefer the freedom of an ice skater, gliding over a smooth surface, whirling and twirling with the music. Sometimes you find yourself in the same tight and burdensome situations you seek to avoid. You are then forced to put on a heavy mantle of responsibility, though you prefer the sheerest of silk. You have to learn to accept life's natural cycles. Sometimes these allow you to be a carefree child, but others force you to become an adult. As you integrate these two sides of yourself, you will have greater success in life.

The fixed star Alnilan is located on some June 13 birthdays. Alnilan is a bright white star in the center of Orion's Belt. The ancients considered this position to give fleeting public honors. Your nature is gregarious, and you have a talent for plunging into experience without reservations. An image for you is a barn dance where everyone participates with genuine human fellowship and fun. At home consider having wicker furniture both indoors and out. Books of poetry and old songs are decorative as well as delightful to read. You may be fond of folk music and particularly enjoy Irish tunes. Consider painting a sunrise on one of your walls. Each day's new potentials excite your mind.

Outdoors, June 13 likes a hilly terrain and slim trees that bend in the wind. A bird feeder could be a focus for your garden. Urban dwellers enjoy going to the park and feeding birds or ducks. If you have space in your home build a small gazebo with open latticework. This is the place for you to sit and dream.

A Kabbalistic Interpretation

We all have conflicts we have to deal with in life. In your case there is a conflict between a real desire to create change in the world and a tendency to avoid big decisions. The problem you have with leaps of faith is indicated by the tarot card the Lovers. You can encourage more decisiveness by wearing something with a red triangle pattern. The triangle should point upward.

In general, you tend to be ruled by your heart. In the structure of this date the letter *Nun*, which is connected to your emotions, rules the letter *Qoph*, which means "head." If you want to create the best environment for successful relationships you should make sure that you use a lot of light mauve around your home.

The value of this day has the same value as the Hebrew word meaning "riddle." It is likely that you have a love of language and will be attracted to the more amusing aspects of literature, especially limericks and nonsense verse. Try passing the time with intriguing word puzzles.

A Numerological Interpretation

YOUR MAGIC NUMBERS: 10 AND 3

The thirteenth day of the sixth month reduces to ten, the number of embodiment and perfect expression. This day's path is one of isolating and separating a facet of your potential and taking it to the ultimate limit of its expression. This is a pattern of specialization. You are asked to elevate a possibility to its highest expression. Nest bound and dependent upon its parents for survival, a baby eagle nevertheless holds the blueprint for the majestic bird of prey that will soar abroad over mountain peaks.

Choose wisely, since you will go to the limit with whatever you select. You are able to compare and contrast the evidence and influences to aid your selection process. Adventurine is a gem that will help focus your mind. The 165th day of the year reduces to three, contributing the element of creative self-expression to your soul's quest for adventure, conquest, and self-mastery.

OBJECTS/IMAGES
bookends, a fan, venetian blinds

SHAPES/MATERIALS
blue aquamarine, mirror images, helium

COLORS
gray-violet, yellow, heliotrope, salmon

ANIMALS
canary, piping plover (bird)

PLANTS, HERBS, EDIBLES
oswego tea, coralline, calamint

ESSENCE
myrtle

SOUNDS/RHYTHMS
songs in foreign languages, Celtic harp

MUSICAL NOTES
A and D

DEEP SPACE OBJECT
Alpha Mensa

June 14

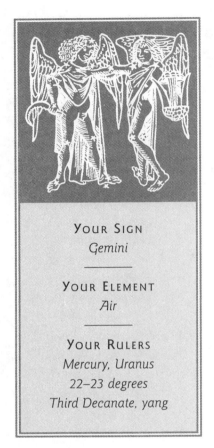

YOUR SIGN
Gemini

___

YOUR ELEMENT
Air

___

YOUR RULERS
Mercury, Uranus
22–23 degrees
Third Decanate, yang

The Astrological Interpretation

Your mind is alive with electricity and creative potential. You can create an entire universe within yourself in a matter of seconds. This gives you a tremendous sense of expansive potential. Yet others are doing the same, and you sometimes find that your worlds collide and you feel blocked and confined. Take the time to learn how to be more objective with your mental process. Slow down and carefully look around you. If you try to take more than one step at a time, you are likely to trip over your own feet. You have a definite affinity for air travel, automobiles, and trains as you like to get to your destinations in life as quickly as possible.

Your birthday gives you an impish sense of fun and adventure. The fixed star Alnilam in the constellation Orion will be located near some June 14 birthdays. This star was said to bestow fleeting public honors. You are interested in discovering all the avenues of self-expression that will entertain you and prevent boredom. Your challenge will be to sustain your interests rather than yielding to constant excitement. Guessing games and games of chance interest you. Enter contests whenever you can. At home you may have a stack of information books with little-known facts that you can call up at a moment's notice. Trivial Pursuit was designed for your elastic mind. You also enjoy swift motion. Rollerblades or ice skates may be your preferred mode of travel. In your home choose diaphanous materials that move with the breeze and let in light.

June 14 enjoys a garden to scoot around in. Flowers might catch your attention for a moment but in general nature is the backdrop for your activities. Have a yard swing or hammock and shrubs that require no maintenance. Manna ash and calico bush are good possibilities.

A Kabbalistic Interpretation

It's not likely that you are reading this entry expecting to see something that accurately describes your personality. As a rationalist you may simply be looking up this date for amusement's sake. Given your love of all things logical a great present for you would be some new software for your computer or an up-to-the-minute graphic calculator.

Your concern with the intellectual side of life is heightened by the influence of the Hermit card from the tarot. The Sun card from the tarot suggests that a great sense of joy and optimism prevail at the same time. Keeping some decorative images of the sun in your home will help you to lighten your generally serious approach to your day-to-day life.

Conversation is a strong point for you. The letter *Peh*, which means "mouth" in Hebrew, is exceptionally strong in the value of this day. Although you are an excellent talker, you often have so much to contribute that you find it difficult to stop and listen. Sleeping with an amethyst under your pillow will help you to sit back and hear other people.

A Numerological Interpretation
YOUR MAGIC NUMBERS: 2 AND 4

The fourteenth day of the sixth month reduces to two, the number meaning polarity and replication. This day's path carries the energy of a search for never-ending adventure and fun in the experiences of your life. This is a quintessential pattern of self-discovery and of building upon your successes and advancing to greater achievements. Don't surrender to static self-satisfaction. Go ice skating in the moonlight, or even at an indoor rink. Drink hot chocolate. Play games that challenge and stretch your abilities. Try something new that you've always wanted to experience.

Citrine and agate lift your spirits. Wear bright, warm colors to stimulate your sense of fun. Try out big hats and funny sunglasses. The 166th day of the year reduces to four, contributing the aspect of stability and order to your creations. You sense a reality that never changes behind the outer movement in your life.

OBJECTS/IMAGES
mail carriers, opera glasses, carrier pigeons, quill pens

SHAPES/MATERIALS
envelopes, shape of ancient tablets, graphite, aquamarine

COLORS
orange, ginger, taffy

ANIMALS
marsh rabbit, rufous hummingbird

PLANTS, HERBS, EDIBLES
endive, hay, hound's-tongue (plant), May apples

ESSENCE
eucalyptus

SOUNDS/RHYTHMS
ocarina, kazoo

MUSICAL NOTES
C# and D#

DEEP SPACE OBJECTS
Beta Columba, Wezu, Weight

June 15

YOUR SIGN
Gemini

YOUR ELEMENT
Air

YOUR RULERS
Mercury, Uranus,
23–24 degrees
Third Decanate, yang

The Astrological Interpretation

The meaning of your birth date can be symbolized by the image of a butterfly collector catching beautiful specimens for display. You tend to catch not only butterflies in your net but also grasshoppers, termites, bees, and even the occasional praying mantis. You have to learn how to be selective and discriminating in your life choices. So many things appeal to your curiosity, you may find yourself chasing a multitude of desires and winding up empty. Tune in to the deeper part of yourself and find out where your life path really leads. This can take time and periods of trial and error. It's okay to capture the odd bug or two before you discover what it is you really want.

To support you in your mental and physical travels and adventures invest in luggage with rollers. A vest with lots of pockets is a handy place to keep all your essentials. Air quality is important to you, so consider an air purifier or ion machine to keep the atmosphere at home electrically charged and clean. Your retreat corner is a pair of bookshelves angled so there is room for a comfortable chair between them. If you can hide from view and look out the window so much the better. Practice turning off the phone from time to time. Gemini gets so buzzed from talking and socializing that you can scatter your energies.

Outdoors, in the yard or garden, you will enjoy displaying articles from your travels. A totem pole from the northwest could stand alongside a bamboo wind chime from the South Seas. A slightly hilly yard with white outdoor furniture or a small screened-in gazebo suits you. Set up a badminton court. Time on the tennis courts is also good. City dwellers will enjoy visiting high buildings and feeling the wind.

A Kabbalistic Interpretation

You have an expansive nature and are regarded by your friends as an unusually generous individual. You enjoy the act of giving as much as or more than you enjoy indulging your own wants and desires. You like your home to reflect the atmosphere of warmth and generosity that you create around yourself. Keep a large earthenware bowl full of fruit on your kitchen table to share with others and remind yourself of largess and plenty.

There is a heavy lunar influence this day, which has a healthy impact on your self-image. Your creative side is important to you and the energy of the moon helps you to realize your latent artistic ability. Keep a pearl-bordered mirror in your bedroom and make a point of looking in it each morning—it will inspire your imagination.

The full value of your birthday is eight hundred and two. Kabbalistically this indicates that you have the ability to understand the intimate connections of all material things to the world of the spirit. Keeping a black cube on your bedside table may help you to achieve some profound insights.

A Numerological Interpretation
YOUR MAGIC NUMBERS: 3 AND 5

The fifteenth day of the sixth month reduces to three, the number of creative expression and unfoldment. This day's path entails the cultivation of a constructive pride in your efforts and achievements. You have the capacity to transform an unruly patch of land into an exquisitely beautiful garden. Yellow and orange flowers will complement your spirit. This pattern evokes your soul's sense of what is truly beautiful and endows you with the ability to enhance whatever you find. Rainbow jasper will intensify your imagination.

Win trophies and blue ribbons by entering your plants or recipes in contests at the county fair. Trim your ornamental shrubs into geometric shapes. Create your own topiary. The 167th day of the year reduces to five, adding the ability to be versatile and flexible. This supports the required changes of perspective this path requires.

OBJECTS/IMAGES
roller skates, a roller coaster, a compass

SHAPES/MATERIALS
figure eights, boat neck tops, stones with mica stripes

COLORS
tissue paper blue, silver gray, sandy yellow

ANIMALS
sparrow, ladybug, chimpanzee

PLANTS, HERBS, EDIBLES
echinacea, menthol, loquat syrup

ESSENCES
eucalyptus, gardenia

SOUNDS/RHYTHMS
a whistle, the swish of a long gown, jump rope rhymes

MUSICAL NOTES
D and E

DEEP SPACE OBJECT
quasar

June 16

Your Sign
Gemini

Your Element
Air

Your Rulers
Mercury, Uranus
24–25 degrees
Third Decanate, yang

The Astrological Interpretation

You were strongly conditioned by your early education and your relationships with your brothers and sisters. Most of your ideas come from this youthful conditioning, but life is asking you to expand your horizons. You can prepare yourself for these expansive voyages through reading, watching documentaries, and taking guided, group trips during your vacations. Education will always be your friend. Prepare your intellect with knowledge and then test what you have learned through the practical experiences of life. On the way, you will meet people who will want to support and aid you. You are a very friendly and open person whose basic nature is kind and helpful. The travel industry, publishing, and other forms of the media are natural doors that should easily open for you.

June 16 has a very strong mind and ability to study and think abstractly. Your concentration is a great talent and your communication with people offers sudden insights and depths. You may be interested in ancient learning and find research with old texts fascinating. At home surround yourself with books. A hurricane lamp, either electric or with a candle, is just the sort of old-fashioned image to stir your imagination. You might enjoy having a variety of desks designated for different purposes. Copies of original documents will be cherished possessions for you. On your walls consider hanging pictures of hot air balloons. The buoyancy and color are good metaphors for the quality of your mind.

Outdoors, June 16 would enjoy a screened-in porch facing the garden. Slate flagstones lining your driveway or front walk also appeals to you. If you find some copies of antique sculpture place them in your garden. Flowers for June 16 include bouncing bet, feather bells, and the shrub *Eupatorium sordidium.*

A Kabbalistic Interpretation

It is difficult to avoid having a great time in your company. You have a fantastic sense of humor and are always the life and soul of the party. The tarot card the Fool in the context of other values for this day manifests itself through your love of practical jokes. Good colors for you when you are in a playful mood are red and yellow.

There is also a strong influence from the number six this day. The number six in the kabbalistic system represents the sun, as well as the relationship of the individual to the divine. You would love to live by the sea in a sun-drenched resort. If you can't relocate, then you should try to retreat to a seaside haven often, and for your home try buying a wall-size decorative print of the sun.

Travel is very well aspected for you. If you don't already have an interest in geography explore some books about various cultures and locations. When you take a vacation go somewhere exotic and off the beaten path. You'll want to take the time to explore all the local fauna, flora, and customs.

A Numerological Interpretation
YOUR MAGIC NUMBERS: 4 AND 6

The sixteenth day of the sixth month reduces to four, representing the ordering principle of the universe. You want a place for everything and everything in its place. However, the soul's journey on this day's path requires a shift in perspective from the individual to the universal. This pattern requires learning to perceive the larger and more long term needs of the planet over the momentary needs of the individual. Hang a poster of the earth viewed from space over your mantel. Use solar energy. Study the effects of global warming and the potential impact of the hole in the ozone layer. Volunteer to search for alternatives to fossil fuels. Smoky quartz crystals will amplify your energy levels. Decorate with blue and green to remind you of the forests and oceans. The 168th day of the year reduces to six, adding the quest for beauty and harmony to all you experience. The order in the universe can also be beautiful.

OBJECTS/IMAGES
news, notes, briefcases, bookbinders

SHAPES/MATERIALS
rag paper, quartz crystal, butterfly shapes, mixed color stones

COLORS
crystal blue, taffy, lime green

ANIMALS
piping plover, parrot

PLANTS, HERB, EDIBLES
barley, paperflower, clematis, sesame seeds

ESSENCE
artemisia

SOUNDS/RHYTHMS
echoes, testimony

MUSICAL NOTES
D# and F

DEEP SPACE OBJECTS
Alpha Ursa Minor, Polaris

June 17

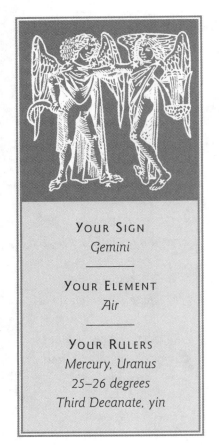

YOUR SIGN
Gemini

YOUR ELEMENT
Air

YOUR RULERS
Mercury, Uranus
25–26 degrees
Third Decanate, yin

The Astrological Interpretation

As with all Geminis, there are two sides to your nature. Your more positive aspect allows you to understand how to circulate energy properly. You do this well enough in your personal relationships, as you are a generous and supportive person. You like the freedom to explore the many ideas that circulate in your busy mind. One of the main lessons in your life concerns the commercial world. You would do well to study the handling of money and finances, as you have the tendency to spend freely, without giving thought to the consequences. This can lead to debt and restrict your natural fluidity. It is important for you to learn how to structure resources so that freedom is something solid you can enjoy for the rest of your life.

June 17 has a refined and artistic nature. Decorate with furniture and objects that are unusual and stylish, as you like splendor in your surroundings. You may particularly enjoy unique mirrors and furniture with angular shapes. Highly designed items such as a special mint julep swizzle stick, a 1950s-era orange juice squeezer, or a Pez dispenser may tickle your fancy. Wallpaper or prints of hot air balloons suit your adventuresome nature; taking a ride in a balloon could be a high point of your life. Even in the age of the Internet, you enjoy a shortwave radio hookup. Your personal style could include jewelry of crystal or clear glass in unusual shapes.

Outdoors, June 17 enjoys a view and a hill that catches the breeze. A tree house for yourself and your children is a perfect retreat or lookout. Stock the tree house with a telescope and enough provisions for overnight.

A Kabbalistic Interpretation

The value created by today's month and day together is twenty-three, equivalent to the Hebrew word meaning "joy." This suggests that you approach the world from an optimistic frame of mind. In order to reflect your own joie de vivre back to you, fill your world with the exuberance of nature by creating a garden ablaze with colorful flowers and shrubs.

Your innately cheerful experience of life is confirmed by the benefit of having fate on your side. This is a decidedly lucky day, and you are someone who often encounters chance opportunities that become life-transforming events. You can increase your chances of finding good fortune by buying some lead figurines, especially in pairs, and keeping them in your living room.

The tarot card Justice has a strong influence on this day, indicating an extremely fair and reasonable person. You particularly have the capacity to be evenhanded when it comes to emotional conflicts. Your wise, even-tempered nature can be enhanced by obtaining a pale blue crystal goblet or vase and placing it in the west of your bedroom.

A Numerological Interpretation

YOUR MAGIC NUMBERS: 5 AND 7

The seventeenth day of the sixth month reduces to five, the number of adaptation, transition, and versatility. This day's path is one of self-realization through movement out of a perceived comfort zone or place of security. This pattern calls for faith in your own gifts and potential. Strive for spontaneity in your responses, this will move you toward new experiences. Gaze into a crystal ball and imagine the impossible. Have your palm read by a gypsy. Listen to the music of the Gypsy Kings as you sail along the highway.

How do you expend your energy resources? Are you endlessly repeating the same old behaviors or moving into bold, new horizons? Clear quartz crystals will enhance your communication with other dimensions. Wear purple to awaken your wild side. The 169th day of the year reduces to seven, adding the influence of rest or temporary cessation after each cycle of expression. Take some time to integrate your new adventures.

OBJECTS/IMAGES
handwriting, hermaphrodites, Escher prints, mailboxes

SHAPES/MATERIALS
turquoise, metal filigree, parallel lines

COLORS
blue gray, sunshine yellow, jade green

ANIMALS
terrier dogs, black-billed magpie

PLANTS, HERBS, EDIBLES
monkey flower, elfwort, horehound, popcorn, laurel

ESSENCE
Spanish marjoram

SOUNDS/RHYTHMS
fan dance, tenor sax, "Ave Maria" by Charles Gounod

MUSICAL NOTES
E and F#

DEEP SPACE OBJECTS
Alpha Orion, Betelgeuse, House of the Twins

June 18

YOUR SIGN
Gemini

———

YOUR ELEMENT
Air

———

YOUR RULERS
Mercury, Uranus
26–27 degrees
Third Decanate, yin

The Astrological Interpretation

You are an excellent mimic. It is easy for you to blend into any social setting, which makes travel and adjusting to new situations quite simple and natural for you. You enjoy clothing and costumes, languages and accents, and friends from different countries. Your real test is in creating a unique style of your own. It is so easy for you to "borrow" from others, but unless you can assemble these parts into a whole of your own making, you will feel that there are too many spaces within you and not enough solid ground. The orientation to personal wholeness is your path in life and constitutes a wonderful adventure.

Some June 18 birthdays will be located near or on the fixed star Polaris in Ursa Minor (the Little Bear). This star is famously known as the North Star, representing a fixed point that can guide navigation. June 18 has so many ideas and creativity that an anchor or guide will be a welcome stillness in life. There is a possibility that the sheer profusion of ideas can bring about melancholy. Push away pessimism with music and physical activity. At home or at work June 18 would enjoy a Ping-Pong table or skittles to burn off nervous energy. Keep quartz crystal clusters that have been hand-mined in your home; carrying a piece of quartz is a quick way to center yourself. You might change the furniture arrangement frequently; a new physical setup is the quickest way to get your energy moving in a new direction.

Outdoors, June 18 would enjoy a separate, screened-in, hexagonal garden building or gazebo. This "fun house" would be the place to calm your mind, practice music, or just daydream. Your garden could surround the little house and should have delicate flowers such as yarrow, meadowsweet, and woodbine.

A Kabbalistic Interpretation

This day's primary energies give you the ability to take on considerable responsibility. Jupiter in its fatherly, controlling aspects is important this day. Using some square-shaped patterns in decorating your office will enhance and motivate you further as you take command of your latest projects.

The full Hebrew value of this day has the same number as the phrase "faithful friend." People who know you appreciate your loyalty and endurance. You always manage to make time for the important people in your life. Very often you find yourself acting as a strong shoulder to cry on. Try drinking an infusion of burdock from time to time, as this will help you to handle the emotional stresses of other people's issues and concerns.

The letter *Mem*, meaning "water," also plays an important role in your path. The element of water is particularly important to provide you with a sense of security and contentment in your home. If you have the space in your garden, install or build an ornamental pond, or if not, keep some water lilies in your home.

A Numerological Interpretation

YOUR MAGIC NUMBERS: 6 AND 8

The eighteenth day of the sixth month reduces to six, the number of balanced polarities and the harmony of opposites. Six is a path of striving for harmony through the reconciliation of apparent strife and antagonism. This day's path calls for making the most of every situation. The pattern requires understanding that neither the joys nor sorrows of life are permanent. All extremes of the human condition are ultimately reconciled if our attitude is one of learning the lesson encoded in experience. Cultivate resourcefulness and the ability to see something good in everything.

Fluorite and tourmaline are gems that will stabilize and calm your emotions. Go on a photo safari. Study the symbiosis of living creatures in the circle of life. The end of one life allows the continuance of another. Watch programs about animals in the wild. Surround yourself with shades of green to bring you peace of mind. The 170th day of the year reduces to eight, contributing the intuitive understanding that opposite forms of expression and emotion stem from a single cause.

OBJECTS/IMAGES
authors, beekeepers, delicate instruments, cars

SHAPES/MATERIALS
turquoise, aquamarine, white beryl, intersecting lines

COLORS
celadon, sea foam

ANIMALS
swallow, lark bunting

PLANTS, HERBS, EDIBLES
hare's foot, horehound, morning honeysuckle, chewing gum

ESSENCE
jasmine

SOUNDS/RHYTHMS
harmonica, piccolo

MUSICAL NOTES
F and G

DEEP SPACE OBJECTS
Beta Auriga, Menkalinan, shoulder of the Charioteer

June 19

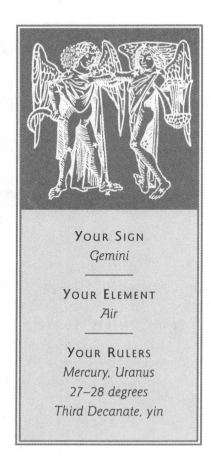

YOUR SIGN
Gemini

YOUR ELEMENT
Air

YOUR RULERS
Mercury, Uranus
27–28 degrees
Third Decanate, yin

The Astrological Interpretation

There is a natural progression in life that allows a person to gradually assimilate what he has learned into patterns and processes that work for success. It is time to clarify goals, focus will, and make your commitments clear. What you do not want to do is to see your accomplishments unravel. Advance your possibilities through higher education in a specific direction. If you are undecided, follow the wise advice: "Go where there is the most love." In other words, do what you love to do the most, as this has the greatest creative potential for you.

The fixed star Betelgeuse, in the constellation of Orion, may be located on some June 19 birthdays. June 19 people have a strong commitment to "delivering the message," by making their views and positions known. You have artistic abilities and may through mimicry be able to participate in life experiences that are beyond your personal experience. An image for you is a ventriloquist who can project her voice anywhere and imitate a variety of characters. The military nature of June 19 may lead you to adopt a "uniform." Epaulets, shoulder pads, and pea jackets are all possibilities. For formal occasions, women may wear an off-the-shoulder dress and men a diagonal sash. Antiques appeal to you, especially any object used for communication. Antique fountain pens, old Morse code instruments, and copies of telegrams are excellent decorative objects.

Outdoors, June 19 enjoys a house built on multiple levels with a wide park and silver birch or hickory trees. Rattan lawn chairs on top of a hill looking into a valley would be the place to rest from your campaigns. While sitting in your chair you might enjoy reading the classic *A Message to Garcia* by Elbert Hubbard, who was born June 19.

A Kabbalistic Interpretation

The value of this day reduces to twenty-five, the magical number of the planet Mars. More than any other aspect of the planet you are affected by its pioneering spirit. You are the person to have around when new ideas are needed. You would probably enjoy reading about the discoveries of historical explorers. Create some adventures for yourself to try.

The word *snake* has a direct connection to the values of your birthday. In modern terms this could refer to any type of lizard or reptile. Consider making a study of reptiles. Meditate on their qualities. Keep a snake or lizard as a pet, and you will learn a lot about yourself and your strengths.

The most important quality you look for in others is honesty, largely due to an association of this day with the Egyptian god Thoth. Thoth is credited with inventing writing and speaking the truth. Thoth is sometimes represented as a baboon, and so you may want to keep images of baboons or mandrills in your home. Go to the zoo and listen to baboons chatter. Or buy a coffee table book on these creatures and keep it on display.

A Numerological Interpretation
YOUR MAGIC NUMBERS: 7 AND 9

The nineteenth day of the sixth month reduces to seven, the number of success and victory. This day's path is one of uniting with the harbingers and heralds of unfolding consciousness. The pattern evokes an aspiration toward higher forms of expression. At your best, you strive for achievements beyond what seem possible, and as a result, you achieve them. This is exemplified by the one-handed catch at the wall in the bottom of the ninth inning, or the miraculous feats performed during Olympic competition.

Listen to birdsong in the early morning hours and learn how to distinguish the voices and personalities of the wild birds in your region. Pearls will remind you of the sacrifices often required to create a beautiful result. Blue-green is a color to deepen your resolve. The 171st day of the year reduces to nine, adding the awareness of completion and the certain knowledge that no form lasts forever.

OBJECTS/IMAGES
detour signs, cab drivers, information booths, felt tip pens, navy blue bell-bottoms

SHAPES/MATERIALS
pyrite, papyrus, rice paper, the shape of a collarbone

COLORS
silver, kelly green, bright blue

ANIMALS
black-billed magpie, mockingbird

PLANTS, HERBS, EDIBLES
meadowsweet, Indian pipes, echinacea, phyllo dough

ESSENCE
orris

SOUNDS/RHYTHMS
military salutes, reading aloud

MUSICAL NOTES
F# and G#

DEEP SPACE OBJECT
NGC 2129, open cluster of stars

June 20

YOUR SIGN
Gemini

YOUR ELEMENT
Air

YOUR RULERS
Mercury, Uranus
28–29 degrees
Third Decanate, yin

The Astrological Interpretation

You have spent a great deal of time gathering experiences and accumulating knowledge. You now want to use all of your physical, emotional, and mental possessions to decorate a home. There is a lingering restlessness and urge to rebel against the security you are seeking, and you are not quite sure if what you have found is enough for you. Your wedding ring or commitment to your partner and your career is wonderful on the one hand, but they still contain a sense of limitation on the other. "How much more time do I give this situation?" is a question that frequently comes up for you. Read the biographies of very successful people to learn about their struggles and crises. It would also serve you to anchor your spiritual beliefs so that you may incorporate what you have into a larger, more inclusive concept of reality.

With Uranus, the planet of revolution and sudden change, ruling June 20, you should expect the unexpected. Do whatever you do in your own way and you will feel harmonious. Around the house wear a Japanese kimono with butterflies painted or embroidered on it. Communication is important to you, and a phone in every room would not be indulgent. To calm your active mind watch a mobile floating in the wind or have some wind chimes in your garden or on the porch.

Outdoors listen for the first mockingbird of spring. His call resonates with you. Vocal development, either singing or articulate speech, is a wonderful attribute for you. Your garden may have a series of flagstones where you can perch and chant, recite poetry, or sing. All verbal expression strengthens you. In the cold months, wear a scarf of pale blue around your throat.

A Kabbalistic Interpretation

The simple value of this date generates the number twenty-six, the value of the God name Jehovah. Interestingly it is made up of the tarot cards Judgment and the Lovers. While you have authority, you will tend to think carefully before acting harshly toward anyone. Try drinking nettle tea—it has a very interesting flavor and will help you make accurate judgments of others.

You are very likely to be fascinated by the world of the unknown. One of the values of your day is equivalent to the Hebrew word for *occult*—it may be that you find yourself drawn into a serious exploration of mystical matters. As a first introduction, get yourself a set of richly illustrated tarot cards. See how they speak to you.

You have an unusually calm personality and look for harmony in your life wherever possible. Many of your friends will be quietly impressed with the way you always seem completely unflappable. You also like to create in your own personal space a feeling of balance. Use complementary colors in your decorating and in the objects you use, and you will always feel balanced throughout your home.

A Numerological Interpretation
YOUR MAGIC NUMBERS: 8 AND 10

The twentieth day of the sixth month reduces to eight, a number signifying rhythm, flow, and the fluid cycles of life. This day's path is a walk of realizing and expressing the true nature of attractiveness. Purely physical beauty is a quality as ephemeral as the blooms on a rosebush. This pattern requires invoking inner beauty and the timeless qualities of charm, grace, and poise. Even the gilded lily fades, but the beauty of a luminous soul is eternal. Amazonite will anchor your connection to the enduring support of the earth. Keep a journal of your most beautiful memories and describe them in rich, sensory detail. Write poetry, and capture your most profound thoughts. Listen to ballads and love songs to inspire you. The 172nd day of the year reduces to ten, contributing the element of mastery and perfection, supporting your path with an intrinsically long-range view. Only the intangibles survive.

OBJECTS/IMAGES
a scarf trailing in the wind, optical illusions, a portable tape recorder

---

SHAPES/MATERIALS
free-flowing rayon, double-terminated quartz crystals

COLORS
aqua, cloud gray, white, turquoise, orchid

ANIMALS
monkey, penguin

PLANTS, HERBS, EDIBLES
birch trees, madder plant, broccoli rab

ESSENCES
rosemary, smell of fingernail polish

SOUNDS/RHYTHMS
patter songs, fingers tapping on a table, limericks

MUSICAL NOTES
G and A

DEEP SPACE OBJECTS
Delta Ursa Minor, Yildun, surpassing star

June 21

YOUR SIGNS
Gemini/Cancer

YOUR ELEMENTS
Air/Water

YOUR RULERS
Mercury/Moon
29 degrees Gemini-
00 degrees Cancer
Third Decanate, yang
First Decanate, yin
Summer solstice

The Astrological Interpretation

Your birth date coincides with two auspicious events: the cusp between the signs Gemini and Cancer, and the summer solstice. The first of these means that you are oriented to establishing a firm foundation for your life and profession. You will seek out a committed relationship in which the security of home and family are achievable. You will also want a career with lots of upward mobility and creative potential. The second of these events means that you are born on the longest day of the year. The sun shines brightly and provides you with enthusiasm and energy for life. You will enjoy the outdoors, and have an affinity with the ocean. If possible, you will want to live in a community with access to water, as you find a great deal of peace and inner stimulation by taking long walks along the beach.

You have a special ability to communicate feelings. This could be in your profession or within your circle of family and friends. At home keep these two elements in mind. Mobiles in the bathroom would be an imaginative decorative touch. Silvery moon objects also appeal. Cancer is ruled by the moon, and Gemini likes silvery gray colors. Etchings and photographs in silver frames are also objects that would appeal to you. Quartz crystal clusters in your home or carrying a piece of quartz suit both air and water.

Outdoors, June 21 should have a screened-in sunporch looking out to a garden. A pond in the center that catches the noontime sun could be your personal sundial. Flowers for you are aquatics, moonwort, azaleas, and Japanese bitter orange.

A Kabbalistic Interpretation

The energies of this day indicate a very athletic individual, and you may even excel in a particular sport. The physical energy you have is mainly provided by the sign Aries. This vitality makes you particularly well suited to all forms of contact sports. You may like to try your hand at judo or jujitsu.

The combined influence of the Moon card and the Death card from the tarot means that you are likely to be subject to a great deal of change in your life. The Moon card's influence indicates that much of that change will be related to your emotions, your beliefs, and your values. A moonstone or a pendant of a nine-pointed star will help you deal with the emotional challenges life presents in a positive way.

One meaning of the full value of this date is "suffocate." You dislike enclosed spaces and need plenty of light and air in your home environment. If possible you should live in a property with lots of large windows. If possible, try to have a window that opens to the east. An ideal situation would be to find a house with a wraparound porch where you can sit in the evenings and enjoy a cool breeze.

A Numerological Interpretation
YOUR MAGIC NUMBERS: 9 AND 2

The twenty-first day of the sixth month reduces to nine, the number of culmination and completion. Nine engenders a need for fulfillment and attainment and endows you with ambition. This day's path is one of adapting to circumstances, even if it means changing your mind, in order to achieve the goal of your endeavor. You understand the concept of losing a battle to win the war. Water is imminently adaptable, conforming to whatever form it inhabits and changing form at different temperatures. You are similar; you haven't really changed your essential nature, just adapted to circumstances.

Blue chalcedony will keep your mental processes agile. Be around water to calm and steady your emotional nature. Learn to scuba. Enjoy the changing phases of the moon. Indigo and purple are colors to inspire your sense of magic. The 173rd day of the year reduces to two, contributing the quality of mirroring and reflection to aid you in your quest. Look into a still pond and see your reflection.

OBJECTS/IMAGES
tickets, schooners, cupboards, crystal chandeliers

SHAPES/MATERIALS
Calvatia (stone), moonstone, crescent shapes, pearls

COLORS
white, mulberry blue

ANIMALS
pollywog, hen

PLANTS, HERBS, EDIBLES
cucumber sandwiches, willow trees, narcissus, whipped cream

ESSENCE
jasmine

SOUND/RHYTHM
a metronome

MUSICAL NOTES
G# and C#

DEEP SPACE OBJECT
supernova

June 22

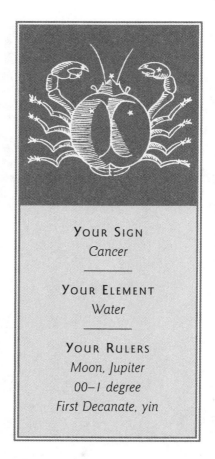

YOUR SIGN
Cancer

YOUR ELEMENT
Water

YOUR RULERS
Moon, Jupiter
00–1 degree
First Decanate, yin

The Astrological Interpretation

You have a deep need to be surrounded by the safe and the familiar in an atmosphere that encourages intimacy, warmth, faith, and trust. You are still unsure of how things are going to come out. In fact, you really want to know the ending at the same time as you create the beginning. As this is impossible, you will be forced to increase your level of courage and bravery and move forward into life. You would do well in a career in which you are helping people find their way, such as a counselor, teacher, or nurse. Shades of blue and violet will appeal to you, and you may find that much of your clothing contains these hues.

Your birthday falls on what astrologers call a "critical degree." This means that experiences in life are rarely neutral. This birthday describes a sympathetic and ambitious person very connected to family and an excellent observer of human nature. To balance your watery nature carry a smooth flat piece of quartz crystal called a tabular crystal. Your house could be a living scrapbook of your family. Photos, artwork from when you were ten, and furniture that may have belonged to your great-grandmother are all objects you will want to have around. Heirloom clocks or a large clock that chimes will be pleasing in your home. Caricatures and comic strip art hanging on the walls or as wallpaper gives you a laugh, while a turtle might be the pet you most enjoy.

Outdoors, you enjoy a flag flying in the breeze. Patriotism and connection to your kin or ethnic group is important to you. Coming right after Gemini, you have an equal love of the water and the breeze. If you don't sail, consider having some pictures of sailboats on the wall. A gliding sailboat is a wonderful meditation image for you.

A Kabbalistic Interpretation

This date is strongly connected to the sephira Netzach on the kabbalistic Tree of Life. As a result you have a very passionate nature. Once you forge a serious relationship with someone you are willing to give them your all and then some! If you want to best communicate and express your emotional fire, opt for some touches of brilliant emerald green in your outfits.

Your intense passion is matched with internal power. The influence of the Emperor card from the tarot makes you extremely strong-minded and self-willed. You are likely to use this faculty most in your working life. Your office is effectively your power base, and you can strengthen yourself by adding a painting or sculpture of a ram to your room's design.

You have quite an abstract mind and are good at thinking in terms of concepts and logic. You may choose a profession with a mathematical or scientific base. In your home, geometric patterns on your walls and in the shapes of your furniture will both intrigue you and help you feel comfortable.

A Numerological Interpretation
YOUR MAGIC NUMBERS: 10 AND 3

The twenty-second day of the sixth month reduces to ten, the number of perfected expression. Ten is the end of the process, and the pause before a new cycle of manifestation begins. Born on this day, yours is a path of detachment. You have the capacity to step back and view the road ahead as if from an aerial perspective. This pattern calls for you to disengage from compulsive or addictive behaviors and dispassionately evaluate and choose your actions and responses.

Take an early morning flight in a small plane, and soar over a patchwork quilt of farmlands. Play chess or solve word puzzles. Cultivate the faculty of abstraction. Onyx will heighten your sense of objectivity and clear vision. Shades of orange will warm your heart. The 174th day of the year reduces to three, which contributes the quality of boundless creative self-expression to support your path.

OBJECTS/IMAGES
a silver pen, a wind chime of shells, a washboard

SHAPES/MATERIALS
bowl shapes, moonstones

COLORS
gray, opaque colors, indigo, orange

ANIMALS
tree frog, sea turtle

PLANTS, HERBS, EDIBLES
violet, ground ivy, dairy products

ESSENCE
grapefruit

SOUNDS/RHYTHMS
Beethoven's Moonlight Sonata, ship's bells, sea chanteys

MUSICAL NOTES
A and D

DEEP SPACE OBJECTS
Nu Gemini, Propus

June 23

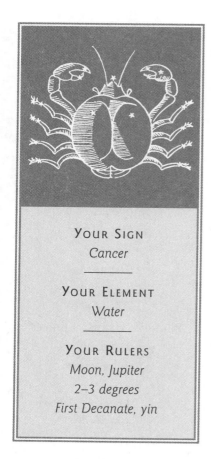

YOUR SIGN
Cancer

YOUR ELEMENT
Water

YOUR RULERS
Moon, Jupiter
2–3 degrees
First Decanate, yin

The Astrological Interpretation

Your birth date points to those experiences in life that take you out of your concern for yourself and your personal welfare. It is important for you to realize that many people in your environment are just as sensitive as you. The more you acknowledge and respect their feelings, the more you will be honored in return. Open yourself to the larger community, take a hand in charitable efforts and humanitarian organizations, and you will see how many kind people may share your life. You do need time alone, as you have moods, thoughts, and feelings that you need to work out. A walk in the park (especially near bodies of water) and a trip to the zoo (especially to see the newborn animals) will always uplift your spirits.

Your birthday has an all-around geniality that makes life flow easily. Controversy arises, but you usually can discern a way out of difficulty. Home and family are important to you. You may like a space with many windows and interior curves. Very angular designs are too sharp for you. Your kitchen and dining room may be the focus of your home. Have wood cabinets and a central wooden dining table. A circular vase where you can float blossoms will encourage harmony and conversation at dinner. Try having a lounging chair in the dining room. You can get restless after dinner and just want to flop somewhere rather than remain at the table. Choose neutral colors for decor. Pale green or gray would be excellent.

Outdoors, June 23 would enjoy having an underground root cellar. An image is an old icehouse. There is something peaceful for you about going into a dark cool space. Gardens around a fish or water lily pond suit you, and you would love a greenhouse. Choose zinnias, tulips, and freesia for your garden.

A Kabbalistic Interpretation

You have a strong lunar influence in your life, and if you wear colors appropriate to the Moon's nature you will feel much more in tune with your own feelings and emotions. An absolute must color combination for you is rich midnight blue and silver. The amount of Moon energy affecting your personality may make you slightly absentminded. If you wear a topaz on a chain or a ring you will find that your powers of concentration are much improved.

Another strong force in your personal makeup is the element of air. The air element is indicated in the importance of the letter *Vau* in your birthday's value, suggesting that you can be a thoughtful, idealistic individual. Burning frankincense in the evening while playing some quiet classical music will help you to focus on the things that are important to you.

Despite your idealistic way with the world you do have a practical side. This manifests itself especially in the garden. The lunar energy of this day will almost definitely bless you with a green thumb, and you have the determination to make your garden look truly wonderful. White flowers and any delicate plants will make particularly good additions to your garden.

A Numerological Interpretation

YOUR MAGIC NUMBERS: 2 AND 4

The twenty-third day of the sixth month reduces to two, the ancient number representing the life force in action. This is a path of carving your individuality out of circumstances different from the norm. Your irrepressible spirit causes you to blaze new trails in whatever circumstances you find yourself. You reject the ordinary limits and boundaries of compartmentalized, rectangular life in the city, and yearn for more open space and fewer restrictions. A century ago you would have blazed a trail across America in a covered wagon.

Volunteer for the Forest Service. Apache flame agate will fire your imagination and give you courage for the journey. Shades of violet are soothing to your inner restlessness. The 175th day of the year reduces to four, adding the influence of ordering, measuring, and classification to this pattern.

OBJECTS/IMAGES
ESP, monocles, pantomimes, piers

SHAPES/MATERIALS
marcasite, opals, plastics, silver

COLORS
sea blue, bittersweet

ANIMAL
river otter

PLANTS, HERBS, EDIBLES
Swiss cheese, milk, mercury plant, shitake mushrooms, narcissus

ESSENCE
hyacinth

SOUNDS/RHYTHMS
melody, music from the 1930s

MUSICAL NOTES
C# and D#

DEEP SPACE OBJECT
Gamma Monoceros

June 24

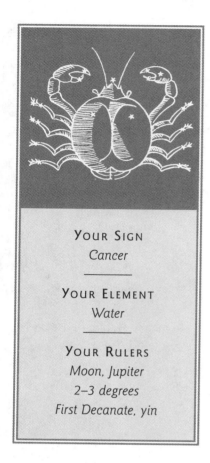

YOUR SIGN
Cancer

YOUR ELEMENT
Water

YOUR RULERS
Moon, Jupiter
2–3 degrees
First Decanate, yin

The Astrological Interpretation

The moon is your ruling planet. As you observe its passage, note how many phases it goes through while it changes its size and shape during the course of a single month. Your emotional life is created very much in the image of our celestial neighbor. As such, you will find that you move in and out of many shapes of feelings and moods. Sometimes you will want to be with a lot of people, sometimes you have to be entirely by yourself. Your birth date is especially connected to this alternation of emotional rhythm. Dance with the differences in beat, and enjoy each song. You will like silver jewelry, moonstones, garnets, and pearls. As a very sensual person, the touch of fine fabrics, especially silk and linen, will give you much delight and pleasure.

The fixed star Tejat is located near some June 24 birthdays. A binary and variable star, Tejat was thought to indicate pride and overconfidence. Your birthday is adventuresome, so overconfidence may come from ill-conceived projects. You enjoy moving from what is known to what is unknown. An image for you is a pith helmet. In your imagination you are always on safari and pursuing adventure. Antique nautical instruments such as a compass or telescope may interest you. Consider having a ship's bell to call the family to dinner. Mount photographs of your travels. Investing in good photographic equipment would be worthwhile. A calendar that clearly shows the phases of the moon should be on your kitchen cabinets or refrigerator. If you keep track of its waxing and waning you will understand something of your own rhythm.

Outdoors, June 24 might enjoy a "scholar's" garden. Study Chinese gardens that were created as places where scholars could rest their brains after thinking. Arch shapes and paths lined with white pebbles and low-lying shrubs are all soothing to you. A pond with water lilies and a frog would be the perfect place to dream up your next adventure.

A Kabbalistic Interpretation

The driving energy of the letter *Lamed* makes you a person of considerable vision and determination. It would take an express train to slow you down when you are really motivated to get something done. Wearing something with a mix of deep blue and green will enhance and increase this quality. On the other hand when you need to slow down, an infusion of chamomile will have a relaxing, soothing effect.

The tarot card the Lovers is important to this day, pointing mainly to indecision in relationship matters. You are more than likely an extremely attractive person who gets more than their fair share of positive attention from others. Unfortunately you can find it very difficult to resist temptation, and that can cause problems in a serious relationship. Try getting yourself a sapphire ring and wearing it on your index finger—it should help you focus on what is important to you when it comes to love.

A Numerological Interpretation
YOUR MAGIC NUMBERS: 3 AND 5

The twenty-fourth day of the sixth month reduces to three, the number of imagination and creative self-expression. This day's path is one of creating the appropriate frame of mind before moving into action. You enjoy planning a trip, buying maps, and scheduling itineraries more than the actual travel. If you build a house, you almost prefer the blueprints, floor plans, and design phase more than living in the completed structure.

This pattern is one of desiring to confirm your own motives and values. Plan less and do more. Cultivate spontaneity. Wear orange socks and yellow shorts for the sake of outrageousness. Work as a planner, whether you plan buildings, weddings, or parties. Hang schematic drawings of ocean liners over your desk. Rainbow jasper will aid your sense of looking at the spectrum of all the options. The 176th day of the year reduces to five, contributing the electric quality of change to the equation of this day. You are always willing to change your plan.

OBJECTS/IMAGES
shepherds, silver baby cup, taprooms, sleighs

SHAPES/MATERIALS
soft stones, canoe shape, elenite, mother of pearl

COLORS
pearly white, ginger

ANIMAL
sheep

PLANTS, HERBS, EDIBLES
toast, mineral water, coquille St. Jacques, alfalfa sprouts

ESSENCE
lavender

SOUNDS/RHYTHMS
musical scale of F, prophetic words

MUSICAL NOTES
D and E

DEEP SPACE OBJECTS
Mu Gemini, Tejat Posterior, the Heel

June 25

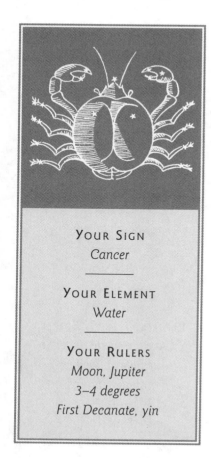

YOUR SIGN
Cancer

YOUR ELEMENT
Water

YOUR RULERS
Moon, Jupiter
3–4 degrees
First Decanate, yin

The Astrological Interpretation

You are soft and vulnerable no matter what your exterior projection may be. You know that you can be reached, touched, and caressed if you allow it to happen. Life is asking you to develop the strength that comes from trusting yourself. It is important to realize when you are creating an internal situation that pulls you in so deep that others cannot reach you. It is your responsibility to come out of hiding so that you may be loved the way you wish to be.

Your sensitivities mean that your challenge will be to find a workable compromise with life as it is. Sharing your feelings through artistic expression is a positive use of your talents. You may particularly enjoy journal writing. Bring earplugs or listen to a Walkman whenever you might be in a noisy situation. At home, you would be very comfortable on a lounge chair with a gray or blue throw. You take great comfort in soft and fluffy blankets and pillows, they make you feel safe and warm. Make sure that your room is filled with objects that give you this sensation.

Lilies and white roses are for you; have a crystal bud vase to hold them. Consider lighting a candle at the new moon as a meditation for each month's projects. As you soak in a tub with jasmine bath salts you may want to imagine the lunar tides ebbing and flowing.

Outdoors a river or lake with willow trees is a perfect place for you to walk, dream, or ponder. You may want to keep a pet turtle at home for luck, but just finding one basking in the sun is enough.

A Kabbalistic Interpretation

Energetic and vigorous, you approach life with considerable intensity. You don't like to wait for results and are more than happy to rattle a few people if that is what it takes to get the job done. The influence of the letter *Shin* is at work this day and it is *Shin*'s association with fire and its character as "the biting one" that gives you this striking nature. In the evenings you might try burning some jasmine incense or a few drops of jasmine oil. This will help to relax you without taking away any of your natural vitality.

The number eight also exerts a strong influence over this day. This number is connected to the sephira Hod, the seat of our intellectual and rational self. Your mind is extremely active, and you have excellent problem-solving skills. A careful use of blue and orange in your study or office will help bring out these qualities.

The full value of this day is a prime number—it can only be divided by itself and one. This indicates an individualistic person who likes to set her own standards and is happiest living a unique lifestyle. You can express this positive trait by seeking out unusual clothing or ornaments with which to decorate your home.

A Numerological Interpretation

YOUR MAGIC NUMBERS: 4 AND 6

The twenty-fifth day of the sixth month reduces to four, the ordering, naming, and structuring principle of the universe. Four contains the blueprint that maps the outcome in any situation. This is a path of recognizing the forces at work or in motion in any set of circumstances. The pattern calls for the cultivation of will to change the course of those forces midstream and thus alter the outcome of events. This path requires that you be brutally true to yourself.

Topaz is an ancient stone that will strengthen your sense of self. Build a model village for your train set. What happens when it derails? Play billiards or pool, and observe the actions and reactions of the balls in motion. Contemplate the action of a snowball down a mountain or a train rushing out of control. The 177th day of the year reduces to six, contributing the influence of beauty and perfect symmetry. This supports your path by adding a need for harmony and balance.

OBJECTS/IMAGES
A water slide, a high diver

SHAPES/MATERIALS
selenite, silver

COLORS
yellowish white, chartreuse, apricot

ANIMALS
oyster, night owl

PLANTS, HERBS, EDIBLES
cheese, smoked fish, colewort

ESSENCE
clary sage

SOUNDS/RHYTHMS
the beat of a different drum, silence broken only by a rippling brook

---

MUSICAL NOTES
D# and F

DEEP SPACE OBJECT
black hole

June 26

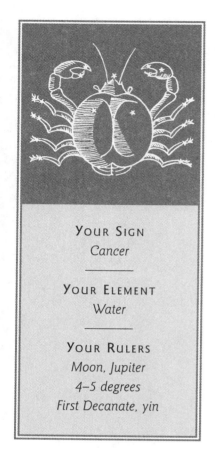

YOUR SIGN
Cancer

YOUR ELEMENT
Water

YOUR RULERS
Moon, Jupiter
4–5 degrees
First Decanate, yin

The Astrological Interpretation

People born on this day take great pains in cultivating those close to them. Although you may know a lot of people, your intimate friends are few and made to be kept for life. Family is uppermost in your mind and heart, and if you had a difficult childhood you will spend time trying to heal those wounds. Make sure that injuries from the past are not interfering with the possibilities for happiness in the present.

You are very attracted by good food and may find that you are most at home either in the kitchen preparing for others or in a fine restaurant being served. Your joy is in providing comfort and caring. You tend to be especially fond of dairy products and sweets plus lots and lots of pasta!

Some June 26 birthdays will fall on the fixed star Dirah, a yellow and blue star that the ancients considered protective and powerful. Let your intuition safeguard your trusting nature. Your sense of hearing is acute, and you may be disturbed by sounds that other people do not hear. At home, surround yourself with pleasant sounds: a fountain gurgling, tapes of bird calls, soothing music, and a chime or gong. When traveling, carry earplugs and a portable white noise machine. These will help you sleep in foreign environments. The bathtub is the place to retreat and clean off any unwanted vibrations. Soak in the tub with rosemary essential oil. Keep the tap running, as the sound of rushing water will be an extra attraction.

Outdoors, June 26 likes a patio with furniture for outdoor entertainment and gatherings. Lightweight aluminum furniture is a good choice. Your own pool would be a luxury, but a nearby brook or river does just as well. Growing plants such as night-blooming cereus may be a particular hobby or interest.

A Kabbalistic Interpretation

This date has many associations with earth and generates more than its share of people who like to work with their hands. You are especially skilled in the technical aspects of home decorating and probably feel comfortable with a drill or a hammer. A good item for you to keep in your garage is a large metal case in which to keep all your tools.

When you are done with a hard day's work, consider massage as a great way to unwind and enjoy time with your partner. You are a deeply sensual person, and the application of hands on body will do as much for your soul as working with your hands in wood or metal does for your home. Try olibanum or other musk-based oil and you will find the massage will do more than just relax you.

Your day's value has connections with the sephira Tiphareth. This is a key position on the Tree of Life for occultists, as it represents the achievement of considerable understanding and self-knowledge. It also indicates that you have the potential to be a high achiever. Using plenty of warm yellows in your office environment will enhance that potential.

A Numerological Interpretation
YOUR MAGIC NUMBERS: 5 AND 7

The twenty-sixth day of the sixth month reduces to five, the number meaning adaptation, means, and agency of accomplishment. Born on this day, yours is a path of conscious participation in the destiny of a group through cultivation of your natural gifts. This pattern calls for you to flourish, as you bloom where you are planted. Show scrupulous attention to detail in everything you tackle. Your home is very important to you, and you enjoy the nesting process. Make your abode as comfortable and secure as you can, nurturing your spirit. Have a cage of brightly colored and musical finches. Contemplate whether they are better off safe inside or cageless and fending for themselves in the wild.

Be comfortable but not obsessive about security. Take calculated risks to widen your comfort zone. Topaz and citrine will heighten your awareness of ordinary things. Wear yellow for cheerfulness. The 178th day of the year reduces to seven, adding the influence of peace, rest, and safety. This aids your pattern with the understanding of how important rejuvenation is to the spirit and mitigates the sense of constant change.

OBJECTS/IMAGES
steam baths, silverware, breasts

SHAPES/MATERIALS
soft white stones, marcasite

COLORS
iridescent blue, spring green

ANIMALS
tadpole, crab

PLANTS, HERBS, EDIBLES
soup, squashes, trefoil

ESSENCE
cucumber

SOUNDS/RHYTHMS
silence, tinkling Tibetan bells, the sound of a canoe paddle entering the water, sound of a washing machine

MUSICAL NOTES
E and F#

DEEP SPACE OBJECTS
Zeta Canis Major, Furud, Single One

June 27

YOUR SIGN
Cancer

YOUR ELEMENT
Water

YOUR RULERS
Moon, Jupiter
5–6 degrees
First Decanate, yang

The Astrological Interpretation

You are gifted with a wonderful sense of humor and a very special laugh. As a person who is in touch with your own and other people's foibles and weaknesses, it is easy for you to see the little jokes that life plays on us. You seek to have people around you who feel the same as you do, and one of the most wonderful common denominators is laughter. Yet there is a side to your nature that is quite serious. You do not take human suffering lightly and are quick to respond when people are suffering, whether they are members of your family or strangers.

June 27 is quite fortunate in attracting material well-being through his own efforts. The challenge will become finding an easy relationship with your good fortune. There can be a tendency toward hoarding and stinginess. Encourage generosity in yourself by conscious charitable giving. You may be a collector of antiques or other objects not only for their worth but also for the intrinsic pleasure you derive from old objects. A coin collection would be particularly pleasing. Your personal wardrobe is an area of creativity for you. It does not have to be elaborate but expressive of your individuality. Men may want to carry handkerchiefs and wear cuff links with dress shirts; women will be partial to sweater dresses and coat/dress ensembles. Your color scheme is basic and muted: gray, white, black, and blue.

Outdoors, June 27 loves a palatial feel to gardens and grounds. A home by the sea would be ideal. You could import some water into your yard with a portable pool or a sprinkler system. Your garden should feature hydrangeas. When you feel troubled, find some willow trees and sit under them. You may find the tree has done your weeping for you.

A Kabbalistic Interpretation

One meaning of today's value when converted into Hebrew is "spring," as in a fountain or source of natural water. It is probable that you like the idea of living near water. This is more likely to be a river or a lake than by the ocean. If you happen to live a long way from a natural source of water then make some kind of water feature a central focus of your home.

The tarot card Fortune is influential in this day, and its effect is to make you very flexible and adaptable. Your ability to accept change with the resilience of flowing water rather than solid steel is Taoist in its nature. You might find a great deal of interest in reading a translation of the classic the *Tao Te Ching*.

Another tarot card that has a positive effect on your life is the Star card. This card suggests that you will always be able to find your way out of seemingly problematic situations as long as you remain confident in your ability to do so. You might like to wear some form of silver jewelry, which will help you to feel the protective energy of this card.

A Numerological Interpretation

YOUR MAGIC NUMBERS: 6 AND 8

The twenty-seventh day of the sixth month reduces to six, the number of beauty and love. Six balances and harmonizes opposites. Born on this day, yours is a path of healing the stresses of everyday life by building bridges into the land of imagination for yourself and others. Your service is creating a space where beleaguered and battle-weary hearts can heal and ready themselves for the next onslaught. You are capable of creating an island of magic in an ocean of madness.

Watch fairies dance in the moonlight. Sail away with Peter Pan to Never-Never Land. Make believe; read or write children's stories, making young eyes wide with wonder and young-at-hearts thrill to the magic of believing. Fluorite and tourmaline will open your heart and fire your imagination. Collect hardbound editions of your favorite children's tales. The 179th of the year reduces to eight, contributing the instinctive awareness that as soon as the pendulum swings to one extreme, it will move in the opposite direction.

OBJECTS/IMAGES
thermos bottles, dressmakers, ferryboats

SHAPES/MATERIALS
china, canal shapes, paua shell

COLORS
pale green, forest green

ANIMALS
eel, hen

PLANTS, HERBS, EDIBLES
bouvardia, pygmy water lily, cottage cheese

ESSENCE
clary sage

SOUNDS/RHYTHMS
a brook's ripple, "The Star-Spangled Banner"

MUSICAL NOTES
F and G

DEEP SPACE OBJECT
Rosette Nebula

June 28

YOUR SIGN
Cancer

YOUR ELEMENT
Water

YOUR RULERS
Moon, Jupiter
6–7 degrees
First Decanate, yin

The Astrological Interpretation

No matter how busy your life may be on the outside, it cannot compare with your inner life. Feelings and emotions filter through you like water rushing through a sieve. Sometimes you have all you can do to keep up with the intensity of this "in-pouring" of sensation. You need to find an externalization for this rich subjective life. This could come through art, especially watercolors, or music. You would enjoy singing in a chorus and might wish to investigate this possibility at your local place of worship. Theater could be another excellent arena for you to express your "extra" emotions with other creative people. Try telling stories to children or reading to older people.

The nighttime is a great comfort to you, as you are able to enter a trancelike concentration in which you can solve or escape the problems of the day. Your home, however crowded with people or things, should have a cozy corner for you with books, perhaps a journal, water in a favorite glass, and a mirror. If the mirror reflects the moonlight, so much the better.

Personal mementos from the past are comforting to you and pleasing to your imagination. Midnight blue, silver, white, black-and-white combinations, and aquamarine are all important colors for you. Moonstone and pearls are the most beneficial materials for you to wear.

The ideal outdoor environment features plenty of shade and perhaps a small greenhouse or special spot devoted to nurturing plants. Flowing water aids your thoughts. An old apple tree or other familiar trees (perhaps the same as you had in your childhood home) can bring back pleasant memories. These memories are a powerful source of solace and inspiration.

A Kabbalistic Interpretation

The total value of your birthday reduces to ten, which is associated with the tarot card the Hermit, a symbol of wisdom and understanding. Surround yourself with bright yellows, as this color represents the element of air, the element most conducive to thought.

Like many Cancers you are a highly emotional person, and are in fact more inclined than most to melancholy and bouts of anxiety or even depression. In order to combat these feelings, surround yourself with things that make you feel cheery and bright. Include some primary colors in your wardrobe, as strong vibrant hues may counter your tendency to feel somewhat lethargic at times.

You will always be drawn to the emotional side of life. Playing with different combinations of music and art is a good way for you to explore your emotions. You could listen to your favorite composer, sit with some watercolors or finger paints while burning some jasmine incense. The scent of jasmine is soft and romantic and aids the clarity of your mind.

If you know someone born on this day and you want to feed them when out on a date be extra attentive to the food. The value of this date suggests an affinity for light and delicately flavored offerings— nothing heavy, hot, or spicy will do.

A Numerological Interpretation
YOUR MAGIC NUMBERS: 7 AND 9

The twenty-eighth day of the sixth month reduces to seven, the number signifying victory and success. Implicit in seven is the promise of eventual victory, no matter how far off the goal may seem. This pattern calls for a projection of your imagination upward into the highest spiritual realms you can envision. This is a walk of undaunted idealism and utopian dreams. Visit Disney World, and stretch your mind at EPCOT and Tomorrowland. Let your imagination soar as you record your visions in a secret journal.

Learn the technique of the shamanic journey, and visit other dimensions and the beings who reside there. Amethysts and green quartz will open the inner doorway of your mind to other realms. Green is a color to stimulate your flights of fancy. The 180th day of the year reduces to nine, adding the confidence of successful completion to your path. You inherently know that where you venture you will prevail.

OBJECTS/IMAGES
boats, water bottles, glassware

SHAPES/MATERIALS
glass, mirrors

COLORS
silver, green, kelly green, royal blue

ANIMALS
hamster, crustaceans

PLANTS, HERBS, EDIBLES
almonds, melon, sweet marjoram

ESSENCES
juniper, elder

SOUNDS/RHYTHMS
waves, light thoughtful music

MUSICAL NOTES
F# and G#

DEEP SPACE OBJECTS
Gamma Gemini, Ahena (mark on the back of a camel)

June 29

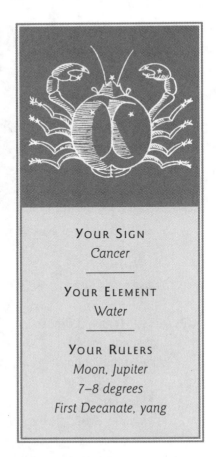

YOUR SIGN
Cancer

YOUR ELEMENT
Water

YOUR RULERS
Moon, Jupiter
7–8 degrees
First Decanate, yang

The Astrological Interpretation

Your energy is that of a flower waiting for spring rain in order to bloom. The potential inside you requires just the right stimulus to explode into color. Your job is to place yourself in the best environment so that just the right amount and quality of moisture may fall upon your head. This will require that you move outside your routine and open yourself to new experiences. You may be reluctant to do this, especially if such shifts alter the relationships you have with friends and family. You definitely do not like being an outsider but may have to risk some sense of alienation in order to become more of an individual.

June 29 has a free-flowing imagination given to building castles in the air. Your feelings are refined and you sometimes wish for a world less encumbered by earthly necessities. Your challenge is to be open without feeling threatened. An image for you is a competitive diver before the plunge. At the moment of liftoff everything is possible; after the plunge, we rank the experience and gather the points. In your spare time, try swimming, water-skiing, or lounging in a hot, foaming bath. At home encourage your imagination with scents in an aromatherapy atomizer: neroli, orange, and rose may be particularly evocative. To keep mindful of practicalities place a rock in each of the four corners (north, south, east, and west) in your home. You may have cooking abilities and be expert at creating a masterpiece from leftovers. Soufflés and dairy dishes are also part of your repertoire.

Outdoors a well and water pump would please you. Even if your home has town or city water consider building an old-fashioned pump for yourself. A vegetable garden with cucumbers and squash would be a great focus for you

A Kabbalistic Interpretation

This day has a value that corresponds to a kabbalistic notaquarion. A notaquarion is a way of expressing a phrase in a single word, similar to the idea of an acronym. The notaquarion that applies to this date refers to the strength and power of the divine. It is likely that you have an exceptionally strong character and a strong sense of moral duty. The furniture in your home should be of dark wood with a deep green covering, as this will suit your strong moral temperament.

You have a great deal of positive energy and are happy to use it to help others. Your energy and vitality are experienced by those around you as a palpable force. You can actually give others energy through your infectious enthusiasm! Grow a mass of sunflowers in your garden to reflect the warmth and enthusiasm that you emanate, and to resonate with your energy.

Family ties are important to you, so you will want to keep some reminders of your closest relations around you at home. Paint or buy some frames with a gray and pink marbled effect to display your photos on the wall. The photos will keep your family ever in your thoughts and the colors will actively encourage a sense of unity.

A Numerological Interpretation
YOUR MAGIC NUMBERS: 8 AND 10

The twenty-ninth day of the sixth month reduces to eight, a number signifying rhythm, vibration, and the undulating of matter in motion. Born on this day, you have a path of unbridled curiosity. This pattern calls forth an inclination to experience events without inhibition. Your ability to express yourself with abandon is an example and inspiration to those who are more reserved and self-controlled. At your best, you have the innocent and powerful curiosity of a child.

Turquoise and moonstone will purify your intentions and focus your curiosity. Live near water, or keep a tank of fish. Wear lots of blue to remind you of the ocean and sky. The 181st day of the year reduces to ten and one, adding the enjoyment of the completed process and the urge to start again. This supports your path with confidence.

OBJECTS/IMAGES
landscapes, rafts, swimming pools

SHAPES/MATERIALS
mother of pearl, selenite, curved pipes

COLORS
green watered silk, cream color, aquamarine

ANIMALS
Galapagos turtle, garden snail

PLANTS, HERBS, EDIBLES
moonwort, porcini mushrooms, sandwiches

ESSENCE
rose de mai

SOUNDS/RHYTHMS
rain on a roof, rushing water, the shuffle

MUSICAL NOTES
G and A

DEEP SPACE OBJECT
Monoceros Nebula

June 30

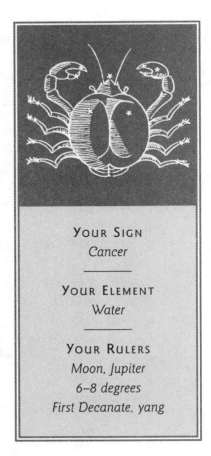

YOUR SIGN
Cancer

———

YOUR ELEMENT
Water

———

YOUR RULERS
Moon, Jupiter
6–8 degrees
First Decanate, yang

The Astrological Interpretation

No matter what your age, you feel like a child on the verge of its next growth spurt. Yet you sometimes hold yourself back out of fear of the unknown. Will your next phase of development force you out of a protective womb? Do you dare to advance further than your partner? You can become entrenched because your attachments are strong. Work to cultivate "loving detachment" and do what is best for yourself. Know that you are neither selfish nor uncaring. Whatever you earn in knowledge or finance, you share with those around you. It is their responsibility to accept your gifts and your responsibility to gift yourself. Speaking of gifts, dried flowers, seashells, and crystals are some of your favorites.

Some June 30 birthdays will be close to the fixed star Alhena, a brilliant white star said to be the wound in Achilles' heel. Each person has personality traits where they are vulnerable. For you it is excessive sentimentality and a tendency to blame. Calm your tides by wearing gray. The color is soothing and includes black, which helps protect your boundaries. Make your bedroom a retreat with light blue drapes and moon-shaped pillows in muted colors. Cozy slipper socks will rest your feet. The kitchen is a focus for you. If you did not grow up cooking, take a few lessons. You will be surprised how naturally blending ingredients comes to you. Share your abilities with others.

You have a wonderful imagination and may want to create a fanciful landscape outside. Consider a teepee or geodesic dome where you can camp out in the summer months. An outdoor table for eating and a sprinkler, pool, or fishpond complete your home in nature. A greenhouse is a wonderful luxury. Visit public ones or construct your own.

A Kabbalistic Interpretation

The tarot card the Hermit depicts a hooded figure carrying a lantern in an outstretched hand. This is an excellent symbol for your inner nature. While you do not like to show off or overwhelm people with your personality, you have a great deal of natural wisdom and are always willing to offer advice to others when you can. If you grow some garlic in a little herb garden or keep a sprig of hawthorn in your home you will enhance your ability to offer a light to others.

The full value of this date gives us the Hebrew word for "fisher." This has biblical connotations, and like the Hermit card, it suggests that you enjoy a certain amount of seclusion in your life. You might literally take up fishing or simply meditate on the image of fish and fishermen. The motion of fly casting and the quiet stillness of a lake or slowly moving river is meditative for you.

Yours is an extremely sensitive nature. You feel deeply for those who come to you for help. As a result you may be subject to melancholy. When you feel this way, taking a walk in the country can restore your equilibrium and help you feel more upbeat.

A Numerological Interpretation
YOUR MAGIC NUMBERS: 9 AND 2

The thirtieth day of the sixth month reduces to nine, the number meaning completion and the accomplished goal of an endeavor. Born on this day, you have a path of assessing potential outcomes and applying your skills to bring matters to successful conclusion. This pattern is one of transforming diamonds in the rough, or partially cut, into priceless gems.

You have the capacity to see the finished statue latent in the block of marble, and your walk requires carefully sculpting away the excess stone. Study sculpture, or work with clay. Enjoy the works of Michelangelo and other great artists. See the potential masterpiece of your life, and cut away everything nonessential. Apache flame agate and garnet are stones to fire your enthusiasm. Wear red to increase your energy. The 182nd day of the year reduces to two, adding the vital quality of reflection and replication, helping you reproduce your successes.

OBJECTS/IMAGES
sculpture, bas relief, pomegranates, funny hats

SHAPES/MATERIALS
hexagons, diamond shapes, cut glass, crystal

COLORS
burnt sienna, fiery orange, crimson

ANIMALS
redheaded woodpecker, red fox

ESSENCES
myrrh

PLANTS, HERBS, EDIBLES
rose petals, snapdragons, persimmons

SOUNDS/RHYTHMS
waltz tempo, violions

MUSICAL NOTES
G# and C#

DEEP SPACE OBJECT
Gemini, Alzirr

July 1

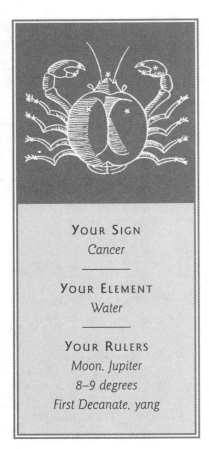

YOUR SIGN
Cancer

YOUR ELEMENT
Water

YOUR RULERS
Moon, Jupiter
8–9 degrees
First Decanate, yang

The Astrological Interpretation

You birth date is symbolic of a swimmer in a deep lake holding his head above the water and seeing all the homes, boats, and people on the shore. You tend to lose yourself in your own emotions (the deep lake). It is important for you to stay objective to the larger world in which you live. You bring to your environment all of the nutrients that are found in your lake but must work at structuring your mind so that your feelings have a balance in clear logic.

This birthday's ingenious quality allows you to be versatile and bold. Your enthusiasm predominates and possible consequences just don't occur to you. You retain the child part of your nature throughout life. A simple fishbowl with a goldfish will be a prized object. Curved shapes and comfortable objects should surround you. Curtains made from a great-great-grandmother's wedding dress would be the kind of heirloom you might like. Any artwork that combines a mythic feeling with scenes from childhood will be especially pleasing. Aquamarine and blue topaz are two stones that will give you a lot of pleasure to wear. Avoid eating when you are nervous, drink a glass of pure water instead.

For personal style emphasize darker colors, especially blues. Black is also very flattering and helps keep your sensitivities contained. Pearls are the perfect accessory; you might consider carrying a mother-of-pearl shell.

Outdoors, have a built in fishpond or a small pool of water. You like lawns, and the garden might feature some night-blooming water lilies. If you can't sleep at night, going into the garden in the moonlight is a perfect restorative. City dwellers should go up to the roof or to a balcony and look at a book of photographs or drawings of flowers.

A Kabbalistic Interpretation

Today is definitely a day for lovers. You are physical in all your relationships and enjoy hugging, touching, and embracing friends and family as well as being deeply intimate with your partner. In your personal life you are driven by attraction. Wearing a ring of lapis lazuli will help you express your sensual nature in a positive way.

The letter *Nun* has a powerful influence on this day. As a result you can be more strongly affected than most by emotional loss. In order to avoid excessive grief or emotional upheaval when a relationship is going through a difficult period, wear some jewelry or clothing with a yellow and azure pattern.

The long value of this day is numerically equivalent to a phrase meaning "great dragon." In most cultures the dragon is a creature of great dignity and power. In ancient Celtic culture as well as in China the dragon is considered very lucky. In order to encourage luck in your home, have a dragon sculpture in your entrance hall. Study dragons and collect books and images of these fascinating mythical creatures.

A Numerological Interpretation
YOUR MAGIC NUMBERS: 8 AND 3

The first day of the seventh month reduces to eight, the number of rhythm and vibration. Eight expresses the truth that opposite and varied forms of expressions always stem from a single originating source. Born on this day, you carry a path of accentuating uniqueness. You love to be one of a kind, and your tastes require that you possess originals, not copies. Although you innately understand that all forms of expression can be traced back to a common origin, this pattern drives you to make the most of inventiveness and originality. You strive to create a style that can't be copied.

Clowns, mimes, and mimics fascinate you. Go to the circus, and enjoy the panorama. Teal and orange are colors to enliven your creativity. Try weaving fabric on a loom, creating your own blend of colors and textures. Rutilated quartz and African picture stone are gems to harmonize with your sense of the unusual. The 183rd day of the year reduces to three, adding a lively creativity to your quest for individuality.

OBJECTS/IMAGES
*a chef's toque,
a lighted country inn,
a fairy castle*

SHAPES/MATERIALS
*angel hair, iridescent materials,
milk glass dishes, selenite*

COLORS
*pale green, silver,
opalescent white, teal, russet*

ANIMALS
*frog, kissing grammies
(tropical fish)*

PLANTS, HERBS, EDIBLES
*freshly baked bread, crayfish,
Queen Anne's lace (wildflower)*

ESSENCE
cucumber

SOUNDS/RHYTHMS
*mambo, indoor fountains,
an ocean liner leaving port*

MUSICAL NOTES
G and D

DEEP SPACE OBJECT
spiral galaxy

July 2

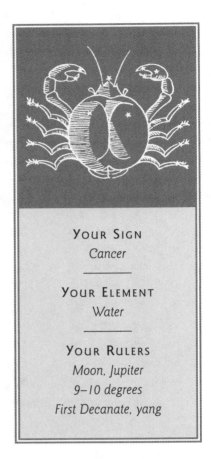

YOUR SIGN
Cancer

YOUR ELEMENT
Water

YOUR RULERS
Moon, Jupiter
9–10 degrees
First Decanate, yang

The Astrological Interpretation

You have a prodigious memory and rarely forget anything. When you are in a difficult mood, you can sum up all the injustices and hurts that have occurred in your life and add to the depth of your emotions. In the same way, you can recall any of the situations that have occurred in your life that were wonderfully joyous, laughing out loud to no one in particular at these thoughts. Surround yourself with mementos and objects from your childhood, especially photographs and small trinkets that have only pure, sentimental value. You will like the "oldies but goodies" from your youth and most likely have quite the collection of tapes, LPs and even eight-tracks from the past.

July 2 has a tender sensitive nature; your life principle is strong, and you may not be able to stomach ego battles. Your imagination is well developed and your greatest joy comes from artistic pursuits for their own pleasure. An image for you is an ever-fruitful farm.

No matter what kind of work you do your home is your cottage industry. A corner in the kitchen may be the place to gather your arts and crafts materials. Cooking may be of interest to you, and having restaurant quality cookware would be a plus. Creating imaginative soups could be your specialty. The bathroom is a home workshop of another kind. Here in the tub with bath salts of lavender and jasmine, you dream up your projects. A scrapbook and photo album of your creations is a good way to record your successes.

Outdoors a greenhouse is a luxurious addition to your home. If you do not have room for a greenhouse, visit nurseries to see which plants and bulbs are in stock. Iris and the vine moonseed resonate with your fruitful nature.

A Kabbalistic Interpretation

Although born in summer, the energies of spring are most vital for filling you with inspiration and optimism. You can create the feeling of spring year-round by keeping a vase of corn flowers or a brightly painted spring scene in the eastern part of your home. Consider a Japanese lithograph or print depicting cherry blossom season.

The tarot card Temperance has a considerable impact on this day. It represents the calming influences in your life. You are certainly happy to socialize, but you also like to have your own quiet space where you can be alone with yourself. Create such a space in your home, whether a study, your bedroom, or the privacy of the bath, and decorate it with shades of mauve and violet.

One meaning of this date is the name "David." Other influences this day indicate an abiding concern for justice and a tendency to favor the underdog. Think of the biblical David and his struggle against Goliath. To remind yourself of the beauty and importance of what may seem small and timid, keep a vase of fresh daisies on your desk. Read the *Te of Piglet*.

A Numerological Interpretation

YOUR MAGIC NUMBERS: 9 AND 4

The second day of the seventh month reduces to nine, the number of attainment and fulfillment. This day's path carries within it the need to complete and express yourself on a universal level. You have the capacity to integrate the achievements of all the cultures of humanity within your own field of endeavor. We all advance to the degree that all of humanity can benefit from the achievements of individual cultures. Traveling to foreign lands is essential for you. Immerse yourself in the philosophies and cultural traditions of the entire human family. At your best, you can offer your broad scope of vision to your own community, enlarging the provincial view of your local area.

Howlite and green quartz are gems to help you spread your wings. Fill your home with art and artifacts from around the world. The 184th day of the year reduces to four, adding the influence of ordering and classification to your aerial view of reality. This enables you to easily gain the lay of the land when you venture far from home.

OBJECTS/IMAGES
sea grass rugs, steam baths, a sketch pad, camera lenses

SHAPES/MATERIALS
rainbow moonstone, a periscope shape, claw shapes, pearls

COLORS
pale yellowish white, azure, persimmon

ANIMALS
crane, turtle

PLANTS, HERBS, EDIBLES
turnips, wallflowers (plant), cloud ear mushrooms

ESSENCE
narcissus

SOUNDS/RHYTHMS
splashing sounds, nostalgic song

MUSICAL NOTES
G# and D#

DEEP SPACE OBJECTS
Alpha Canis Major, Sirius, the Shining One

July 3

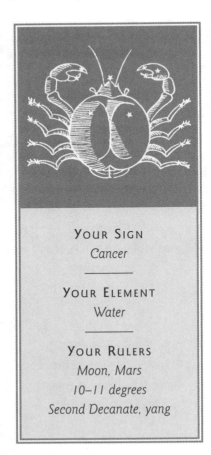

YOUR SIGN
Cancer

YOUR ELEMENT
Water

YOUR RULERS
Moon, Mars
10–11 degrees
Second Decanate, yang

The Astrological Interpretation

Your dreams are very significant to you. You are impressionable, and many of the events that occur during the day reappear in your sleep. Take the time that you need upon awakening to recall these dreams, so that you can have a deeper understanding of events that have already occurred. You are also good at seeing the meaning in events that take place in the lives of your friends and associates. You are far more objective about others than you are about yourself, and people will find you a natural confidante and counselor. Deep purples, midnight blue, and silver are colors that will attract you, and you may also like to wear amethyst jewelry.

Your mind has total sense recall for pleasures and slights. First impressions, if negative, are hard to undo. Coupled with these strong feelings is a great sense of humor and the ridiculous, which allows you to laugh at yourself and others. Home is your castle. You are a very good cook and will enjoy restaurant-quality appliances to aid your culinary efforts. Power for you is in gathering and collecting objects that evoke the past. Colored glass bowls and plates might be pleasing. Men sometimes are fond of pocketknives, especially with mother-of-pearl cases. Women may enjoy jewelry that has been passed down through the family.

Decorate with indoor bulb plants as well as annuals in the garden. You enjoy watching the sprouts shoot up from the earth. Keep flowers blooming even in the winter months in a greenhouse or potting shed. Try to have a source of water in your yard. With Mars coruling this Cancerian birthday you might install a place to practice your golf swing or a batting cage. You can work off aggressive energy through sports.

A Kabbalistic Interpretation

The primal spark of divine fire represented by the letter *Yod* is a great influence on your nature. You are possessed of incredible drive and will, and this is obvious to people within hours of meeting you. Have your bedroom decorated with brilliant white walls and white bed-clothes, as this will direct energy to you while you sleep.

It may appear that you are driven mainly by material desire. In reality, a sense of achievement is more important to you than monetary gain. Decorate your home in a manner that suggests a certain degree of success. Oak furniture is an excellent choice for you, as its solidity implies certainty and worth.

In spite of what is likely to be a heavy and hectic workload, it is critical for you to make time for leisure activities. A connection in the full value of this date between the Hebrew words for *hand* and *eye* suggests that an artistic hobby is the best way to spend your leisure hours. Try painting landscapes. You will enjoy the hours spent in the outdoors, as well as seeing and re-creating details from the world.

A Numerological Interpretation

YOUR MAGIC NUMBERS: 10 AND 5

The third day of the seventh month reduces to ten, the number of completed processes and the perfect embodiment of the cycle. Ten also reduces to one, automatically seeding the next cycle of expression. This day's path is one of moving ahead with confidence. You have a quality of determination that can seem at times like the irresistible force blasting through the immovable object. You are practical and responsible, and at your best zero in on your target and accomplish your objective steady as she goes. Take care that you don't plow under every perceived obstacle in your path. Blue chalcedony will temper some of your latent aggressiveness. Citrine will focus your mind as you move along your path.

The 185th day of the year reduces to five, adding the important element of versatility to your path. Wear shades of blue to calm your sense of urgency. Work in a garden with growing things, and cultivate a green thumb. Can some of your own fruits and vegetables to enjoy during winter.

OBJECTS/IMAGES
water tanks, a sailboat on the distant horizon, antique snuff boxes

SHAPES/MATERIALS
Venetian windows, marcasite, silver lamé

COLORS
opalescent hues, silver, sea blue, indigo, pale yellow

ANIMALS
rabbit, pollywog

PLANTS, HERBS, EDIBLES
iris, dandelion root, turtle soup

ESSENCES
balsam, white lily

SOUNDS/RHYTHMS
beguine, the sound of splashing, Renaissance instruments

MUSICAL NOTES
A and E

DEEP SPACE OBJECTS
Zeta Gemini, Mekbuda, the Lion's Paw

July 4

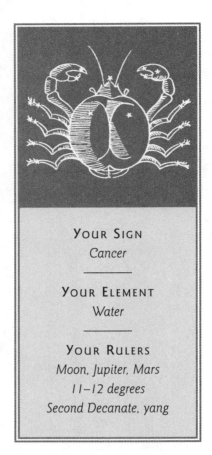

YOUR SIGN
Cancer

YOUR ELEMENT
Water

YOUR RULERS
Moon, Jupiter, Mars
11–12 degrees
Second Decanate, yang

The Astrological Interpretation

You are a sentimental and empathetic individual. Your heart is very inclusive, and you feel other people's troubles deeply. Yet it is essential that you do not involve yourself to such an extent that you forget to keep your own feet on the ground. Exaggerated concern on your part will lead to feelings of being taken advantage of emotionally. You will then suddenly withdraw into yourself, leaving your friends and loved ones to wonder why you have seemingly abandoned them after having given so much of yourself. Make sure that you state your needs as distinctly as possible so that you do not find yourself feeling overlooked and unnurtured. When in distress, you tend to like "comfort foods" such as cereal or cookies with milk, puddings, soups, and ice cream.

You love the concept of home and family yet believe in the individual to such an extent that home and family may suffer. Your birthday has naive faith in patriotism and belief in the rewards of hard work. You are a self-made person whatever work or path you follow. In your home you will enjoy a large space and reminders from different historical periods. French antiques may particularly appeal. Tissue paper blue is a color for you to use on your walls. You may be fond of labor- and waste-saving gadgets in the kitchen. A special toothpaste squeezer that gets out the last drop would be a prized item.

Outdoors, a garden based on historical gardens such as those at Williamsburg would please you. Zinnias, hydrangeas, and dogwood are all flowers for July 4.

A Kabbalistic Interpretation

There are a number of influences in your birthday's value that point to a spiritualized view of the world. This manifests itself in you not as a strong religious commitment but as an interest in the supernatural. Read about the paranormal, ghosts, and other supernatural phenomena. A traditional Victorian book of ghost stories would make a great present for you.

The Tower card can be a forbidding card, as it represents a shattering of the status quo. In your case it is likely to be your core beliefs and values that are radically altered at a key developmental point in life. When this happens, frightening though it may be at first, it will come as a prelude to a much more satisfying time. Symbolize accepting the changes in your life by wearing a tie or neck brooch in Venetian red.

You can expect to be a genuinely singular person, especially as one of the Hebrew equivalents for this day is "the first." You love to express your individuality, and some unusual jewelry especially with stone settings is an ideal way to do this.

A Numerological Interpretation
YOUR MAGIC NUMBERS: 2 AND 6

The fourth day of the seventh month reduces to two, the number of reflection and receptivity. Two is the principle of duplication and replication and carries the energy of the first expression onward into manifestation. This day's path is one of reaching into the deep well of collective experience and memory to strengthen your immediate destiny. You have an intrinsic sense of how the future flows from the past and present. At your best, you can access deeper and hidden aspects of consciousness and draw upon wisdom that seems inaccessible to most. Amber is a gem formed by the forces of nature over vast amounts of time. Often small creatures are captured within the solidified resin, bringing a moment from antiquity into the present. Wear a pendant of amber set in sterling silver to remind you of this mystery.

Indigo is a color to deepen your introspection. Study hypnotic regression, and pay attention to your dreams. The 186th day of the year reduces to six, which contributes the principle of balance to your path. Ponder the principle of reciprocity, and always return something to nature as a symbol of what you have received.

OBJECTS/IMAGES
lunch, breasts, pantries, oceans

SHAPES/MATERIALS
fens, bottle shapes, lighting oils, marcasite

COLORS
silvery gray, vermilion, chartreuse

ANIMAL
crab

PLANTS, HERBS, EDIBLES
sandwiches, moonwort, pearlwort, pumpkins

ESSENCE
wintergreen

SOUNDS/RHYTHMS
Louis Armstrong's trumpet playing

MUSICAL NOTES
C# and F

DEEP SPACE OBJECT
pulsar

July 5

YOUR SIGN
Cancer

YOUR ELEMENT
Water

YOUR RULERS
Moon, Mars
12–13 degrees
Second Decanate, yang

The Astrological Interpretation

Your birth date speaks of a person who has looked long and hard for truth. Your life takes you on many emotional and physical voyages, forcing you at times to leave the familiar in search of life's meaning. This exploration leads you to many spiritual doors, and although it may be frightening at times to go through them, you have little choice. Going back into your shell is definitely not an alternative. Continue to strive for spiritual significance, as many treasures of understanding await you. Reading is a great source of inspiration for you, especially books about history, philosophy, and the biographies of people you admire.

You are interested in delving into life's details and mastering them. You like to exert control over your environment and implement your vision for a home. No detail is too small. Your favored decor tends toward elegance with antiques and family heirlooms. Images of ancient warriors are a reminder of the power and supremacy of the individual. The public rooms of the house will be decorated in an elegant way, but down in the basement or a special corner, you may want to keep some article from childhood that means comfort and security. It could be a stool, a favorite rug, or records or CDs that hold memories.

Outdoors, the space will reflect your desire to create monuments. Perhaps there is a stream through the yard. You may build banks of flagstone to contain the water. A set of carved doorposts announces the driveway or entryway. In the yard the perfect furnishing is a hammock. With all that building, July 5 has to rest!

A Kabbalistic Interpretation

Dedication is your key word in life. The influence of the Hanged Man card from the tarot indicates you are willing to endure periods of unpleasantness in order to achieve an ultimate goal. If you keep some sage and basil in a pouch or growing in a window box you will find that the difficult periods in life pass much more easily.

Another card connected to this day is the Star card. As a sign of external protection this card shows that any sacrifices you make early in life are bound to pay off. Keeping a full-length mirror in the east of your home will encourage successful energies, especially if you make a point of looking into it early each morning.

Hebrew words that correspond to the value of this day have a definite theme of construction and building running through them. This might point toward a possible career direction for you. At the very least it suggests that you would enjoy making models as a hobby. Build ships in bottles. Re-create famous cathedrals and bridges. Create miniature airplanes that fly.

A Numerological Interpretation

YOUR MAGIC NUMBERS: 3 AND 7

The fifth day of the seventh month reduces to three, the number of multiplication, growth, and unfoldment. Three gives birth to the combined energies of one and two. This day's path is one of giving birth to the avenues of your creativity. You have the capacity to enjoy yourself fully whenever you involve yourself. Take care not to overdo it. This day's pattern carries the risk of overindulgence as a reward for accomplishment, or because you feel lacking in another area. At your center, you understand the innate richness of life and wish to feel full to overflowing with life's gifts. This is the essence of the creative process.

You love cafeterias and buffets where you can sample a wide variety of items and have as much as you like. Try surfing the Internet for the ultimate potpourri of selections. The 187th day of the year reduces to seven, adding the sense that you should rest between each cycle of your activities. Seven also inspires you with a sense of confidence that you will emerge victorious from each encounter. Purple and yellow pansies will always lift your spirits. Dark purple amethyst will connect you with your highest ideals.

OBJECTS/IMAGES
circular armchairs, fountains, labor saving gadgets, inherited objects, a silver thumb ring

SHAPES/MATERIALS
circles within circles, silver, citrine

COLORS
pale green, tissue paper blue, black, burnished gray, orange, grass green

ANIMALS
collie dog, tree frog, hermit crab

PLANTS, HERBS, EDIBLES
charlotte russe pastry, salami, butterscotch, oregano, crab apples

ESSENCE
wintergreen

SOUNDS/RHYTHMS
maracas, folk tunes, songs with catchy lyrics

MUSICAL NOTES
D and F#

DEEP SPACE OBJECT
NGC 2324, galactic cluster

July 6

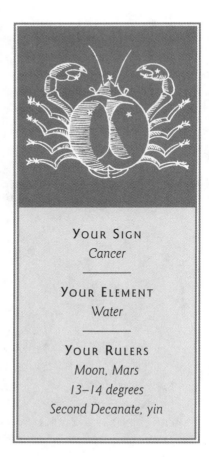

YOUR SIGN
Cancer

YOUR ELEMENT
Water

YOUR RULERS
Moon, Mars
13–14 degrees
Second Decanate, yin

The Astrological Interpretation

You take a great deal of comfort and pleasure from surrounding yourself with plenty. You like to amass things and may have a number of collections. But there is a great difference between collecting and cluttering. You may find that your closets, drawers, attic, basement, and especially your refrigerator are just too full! Take a good look around you and then get rid of the excess—and do this on a yearly basis. This applies as well to your habit of "emotional collecting." There are many feelings that are just not worth holding on to, so do your best to transform them through forgiving, releasing, and letting go. Physical exercise will help you circulate your energies, so joining a gym and doing aerobics will be very much to your advantage.

July 6 can be both the location of the fixed star Sirius and a critical degree. Sirius, known as the Dog Star, was said to confer great dignity; however, there could be a chance of dog bites! You are an emotional person and have a strong religious sense. Tibetan religious symbolism and sand drawings could be of particular interest to you. The natural world, particularly astronomy and botany, are fascinating and you may enjoy tinkering with and repairing clocks. The intricacy and beauty of a clock's works engage your mind and relax your emotional disposition. Home is important to you. Research your family's roots, as it may give you valuable information for your own character. Historical books could be prized possessions. Cream colors are perfect for your home and wardrobe.

Outdoors, July 6 prefers a shady yard and a garden of subtle flowers and vegetables. Starflower, bunchberry, and turtlehead may intrigue you. Mark out curved pathways in your garden with white pebbles. Aluminum lawn furniture is a perfect addition to your yard. On the full moon sit awhile and meditate on your garden bathed in moonlight.

A Kabbalistic Interpretation

There are energies in this day that indicate you are someone who is not that fond of change. However, the Death card, which represents major changes in life, is also critical this day. You need not be bothered by these inevitable upheavals, as they will always have a good outcome for you. Keeping a miniature palm or other flexible plant in your bedroom will help you adjust positively to the idea of adapting.

You have a wonderful imagination and should allow it full rein in your free time. There is a strong possibility that you have talent as a writer. A small mirror with a red painted iron border will give you the initiative to make the most of your talents.

When dealing with crises you are able to keep your head and stay practical while others hit the panic button. This is a wonderful and useful quality. You can enhance your ability to be calm and decisive by burning some cedar wood incense or cedar oil in the evenings.

A Numerological Interpretation

YOUR MAGIC NUMBERS: 4 AND 8

The sixth day of the seventh month reduces to four, the number of order and abstract reason. Four is the logical, orderly outcome of the principles unfolded in three. This day's path is one of becoming hypersensitive to everything in your environment that can potentially concern you. This pattern is like a pilot or ship's captain continually making adjustments and refinements based on weather and wind to assure their craft remains on course. Your path urges you to examine the events in your life logically and judiciously, and alter your course settings and responses to keep you on the beam. Learn to sail; feel the wind and water and your response to the elements as you tack your vessel across a body of water. The set of the sail, not the force of the wind, determines the direction. The 188th day of the year reduces to eight, contributing the quality of rhythm and vibration, flux and reflux, thus assisting your capacity for responsiveness. Black opal is a gem that will deepen your sensitivities.

OBJECTS/IMAGES
classic diners, cupboards, flasks, nursery furniture

SHAPES/MATERIALS
all containers, china, uncut emeralds

COLORS
iridescent gray, tangerine, turquoise

ANIMAL
whooping crane

PLANTS, HERBS, EDIBLES
dogtooth (violet), duckweed, endive, cottage cheese

ESSENCES
all cooking smells

SOUNDS/RHYTHMS
mating calls, the click of a camera

MUSICAL NOTES
D# and G

DEEP SPACE OBJECTS
Delta Gemini, Wasat, the Middle

July 7

YOUR SIGN
Cancer

YOUR ELEMENT
Water

YOUR RULERS
Moon, Mars, Jupiter
14–15 degrees
Second Decanate, yin

The Astrological Interpretation

You are a builder and your primary project is yourself. You periodically add or subtract a room in your inner house and reshape your psychological floor plan. You will find that in the material world as well, you change your furniture and household possessions in accordance with your moods and feelings. At times, you even change houses and move when you are going through deep, emotional crises and transformations. Have a room as a place of special retreat or at least a corner and chair where you go for comfort. You are good with your hands and enjoy making things and decorating. Many people born on this day are known to give their friends and loved ones special sweets baked at home.

July 7 is versatile with talents in business, music, writing, fine arts, and mathematics. Carefully evaluate what you need and what is excess. You can be emotionally retentive and hold on to feelings, habits, and objects for the sake of sentiment. A basement space would do very well for your at-home retreat. Old floppy furniture and an old record player could create a clubhouse feel. Consider playing recordings of big band and swing music. Blue is a favorite color for you. Black-and-white clothes may appeal to you; or you could go through an all-black and then an all-white phase.

Outdoors, you like a sunporch and sliding glass doors between home and yard. A hammock under an apple tree is a perfect spot for a summer nap. If you live near a pool or have one of your own, buy a floating raft with a holder for beverages. Floating on the water, sipping lemonade or ice tea, is a perfect way to spend a summer afternoon. Note the pictures that come into your mind; they may lead you in surprising directions.

A Kabbalistic Interpretation

The letter Zayin means "sword" in Hebrew. Its two occurrences in this date suggest that you have the capacity to respond aggressively when roused to anger. There is nothing wrong with sticking up for what you believe in, but there are times when you could soften your temper.

Sleeping with an amethyst under your pillow will help you to achieve a calm perspective.

You have a brilliant mind that is at its best when faced with issues that need a quick and a creative solution. A consultancy role would suit your personality well. The Sun card from the tarot highlights your mental abilities. You can draw on the positive effect of this card's influence by keeping a small laurel bush in your garden's east corner.

The letter *Samech,* which means "prop" or "support," is also important to your day. When people need a reliable pair of hands to insure that a job gets done you are an ideal choice. In your relationships you are a supportive partner and will do your best to help loved ones achieve all the things they hope for. Yellow in your bedroom will help bring out this side of your nature.

A Numerological Interpretation
YOUR MAGIC NUMBERS: 5 AND 9

The seventh day of the seventh month reduces to five, a number signifying adaptation, transition, and agency. Five is midway between one and ten and mediates the process of unfoldment on the way to completion. Born on this day, your path is one of continual refinement of the secrets of your soul. This pattern requires that you pursue every possible avenue of expression for your talents and gifts toward their ultimate perfection. Your life is a quest for the holy grail of your unique contributions.

Blue agate and labradorite are stones to connect you with your true worth and potential. Collect statues of wizards, and study the true meaning of the philosopher's stone, the goal of the ancient alchemists. What is the lead in your life that must be transformed into gold? What do you need to release? The 189th day of the year reduces to nine, contributing the promise of attainment, which fires your confidence and zeal to attain the promised flower within the seed of your desire.

OBJECTS/IMAGES
a daguerreotype, a water pipe, cooking pans

SHAPES/MATERIALS
deep bowl shapes, moonstones, pearls

COLORS
opalescent colors, mushroom color, yellow, sky blue

ANIMALS
otter, shrimp

PLANTS, HERBS, EDIBLES
honeydew melon, dogtooth violet, ice cream

ESSENCE
jasmine

SOUNDS/RHYTHMS
sound of poured liquid, swing rhythms

MUSICAL NOTES
E and G#

DEEP SPACE OBJECTS
Gamma Canis Major, Muliphen

July 8

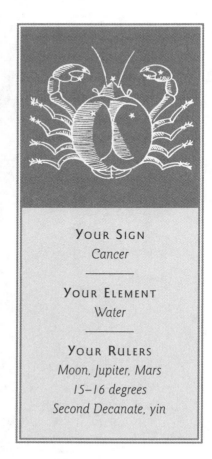

YOUR SIGN
Cancer

YOUR ELEMENT
Water

YOUR RULERS
Moon, Jupiter, Mars
15–16 degrees
Second Decanate, yin

The Astrological Interpretation

Your birth date is symbolized by a small tree connected to huge roots. What appears on the surface of your life does not at all reflect your true potential. If you feel that your creative possibilities are greater than the events in your life reveal, it is your responsibility to find the means to develop yourself. We all need to be supported by people and events in our surroundings. You may rely too much on this kind of backing before you give yourself the chance to show what you can do. Once you have harnessed your will and focused your ambitions, once you have stepped outside of your protective coating and opened yourself to new experiences, you will find that the support you are asking for will be right at hand.

Banking, finance, creative marketing, advertising, and real estate are all career areas that are good for you. You may not necessarily be rich but you understand principles concerning money and are handy with numbers and finance. Your talent comes because life for you is a process of continually considering the ideal potentials of practical realities. Home is where you can explore and perhaps indulge your feelings. A large quartz crystal could figure prominently in your living or dining room. If there are many facets and one happens to break off, carry it with you. It will be a connection between you and your home that will help you stay centered. A comfortable sofa where you can lounge is an essential piece of furniture. If you have a formal living room try to also have a family room where comfort is the rule. July 8 may be quite athletic. Consider becoming a member of a gym with a pool or having one of your own.

Outdoors, July 8 wants a yard and garden in which he/she can putter. A greenhouse would be perfect. Consider planting some vegetables such as cucumber and zucchini as well as flowers. Flowers that July 8 might particularly enjoy are the water plants, marsh marigold, water lettuce, and fragrant water lily.

A Kabbalistic Interpretation

You are always at your happiest when you are close to nature. The Devil card indicates that the material side of life has a heavy impact on your day. The emphasis is on material in its literal sense—a relationship with the earth itself. The ideal leisure activity for you would be gardening, especially cultivating a host of colorful and vibrant flowers.

At times you have a tendency to let your job rule your life, so rather than working to live, you end up living simply to work. This is not a healthy approach for your life, but it can be easily turned around. If you keep some personal photos on your desk in a frame that is gold and emerald in color, or wear some jewelry in those colors, you will find that you become more relaxed about your career.

A Numerological Interpretation
YOUR MAGIC NUMBERS: 6 AND 1

The eighth day of the seventh month reduces to six, the number of beauty and the harmony of opposites. Six balances polarities and neutralizes antagonism. This path is one of reciprocity. The pattern calls for you to gain a deep understanding of the relationship between what you put into life and what you receive in return. You inherently comprehend that there's no such thing as something for nothing, but you must refine this awareness to the point of seeing which stimulus generates which response. The effort you expend will bear fruit in a complementary result and reward. If you plant corn, you won't reap wheat. Have a garden, and learn the direct relationship between the soil and the gardener.

The 190th day of the year reduces to one, which impels you to initiate new efforts so that you can enjoy ever greater rewards. Ruby is a stone to mobilize your energies. Pale green colors will clear your mind of distractions.

OBJECTS/IMAGES
bakers, cameras, the masses, motherhood

SHAPES/MATERIALS
shape of a maple leaf, nozzle shapes, selenite, phosphorescence

---

COLORS
white, lime green, cardinal red

ANIMALS
pollywog, mountain beaver

PLANTS, HERBS, EDIBLES
adder's-tongue, coralworts (plant), croissants, spire lily

ESSENCE
cassia

SOUNDS/RHYTHMS
a motorboat splashing, boogie-woogie

MUSICAL NOTES
F and C

DEEP SPACE OBJECTS
Alpha Gemini, Castor

July 9

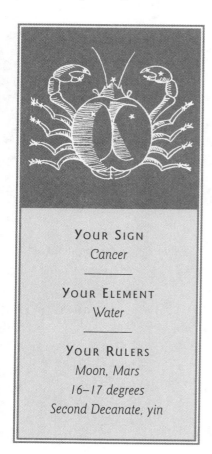

YOUR SIGN
Cancer

YOUR ELEMENT
Water

YOUR RULERS
Moon, Mars
16–17 degrees
Second Decanate, yin

The Astrological Interpretation

This birth date is especially connected with family, children, and the act of being a mother. No matter what your gender, you will find that you have an urge to take care of others and to bring a nurturing presence to your daily life. This may take the actual form of a family, in which case you are a protective and concerned parent. If children are not your orientation, you will find that you treat your partners, friends, and loved ones with a sincere interest and active involvement in their well-being. You would do well in any of the helping professions, including that of teacher, medical worker, diet or nutritional counselor. You are particularly sensitive to scents and will avoid harsh detergents, cleansers, or even strong perfumes and incense.

July 9 has great energy and determination in exploring self-knowledge. Sometimes creative energy becomes nervous energy and it is hard to know what to do with yourself. Deep-breathing exercises are the best way to keep a smooth flow. An image for you is the philosopher's stone, the alchemical material that could transmute base metal into gold. Your home is a retreat and sanctuary. Decorate with shapes of the various phases of the moon: crescent, half full, full, and waning. Water imagery is important to July 9. Fill some clear old bottles with blue-and-green colored water and place them where they will catch the light. An antique water pipe may be a curiosity that you could display. You like to hold on to mementos from your past. Have a keepsake box and mark your own psychological growth by what you decide to throw away.

Outdoors, July 9 would be very happy with a garden and greenhouse. Whatever your profession is you will enjoy puttering around a garden. Consider raising white roses as well as water lilies in a pond.

A Kabbalistic Interpretation

This day is an exciting combination of fire and air energy in equal measure. This makes you a stimulating person to know, as you are always full of vigor and enthusiasm for your latest ideas. In order to make sure that your ideas have a likelihood of becoming realities you need to add some earth energy to your life. A long stroll in the country at least once a month is just what you need to keep in touch with the earth.

In your workplace you make time for coworkers and are therefore a popular individual. You work hard to facilitate the development of others as well as yourself. Increase the nurturing aspect of your personality by using some blue and mauve glass ornaments in your bedroom and bathroom.

The long value of this day has the same value as the word *primordial*. This indicates a fascination with prehistory. You might like to investigate archaeological matters or the origins of life. Pick up a book on dinosaurs or visit a natural history museum.

A Numerological Interpretation

YOUR MAGIC NUMBERS: 7 AND 2

The ninth day of the seventh month reduces to seven, a number that means victory. Seven has the connotation of an oath or a sworn compact like a vow. Seven is the number of victory, which contains within it the promise of the ultimate mastery at the end of the cycle. Born on this day, you have a path of honoring and serving the everyday institutions of human life. In service to established rituals, you will find a deep and abiding fulfillment. Opal is a gem that is formed of iridescent spheres, each tiny portion contributing to the luminescence of the whole. Ponder your own contribution.

The 191st day of the year reduces to two, contributing the influence of reflection and replication. This assists you to compare, contrast, and evaluate the worth of forms you surround yourself with. The danger of this path is a blind obedience to authority, or a mindless allegiance to ritual or forms that have outlived their usefulness. Strive to be conscious of where you pledge your troth.

OBJECTS/IMAGES
chandeliers, brooks, cafés, china

SHAPES/MATERIALS
loaf shapes, a baptismal fount, selenite, moonstone

COLORS
silvery gray, emerald green, burnt sienna

ANIMALS
mackerel, ruddy duck

PLANTS, HERBS, EDIBLES
beer, betony stonecrop, butter, water arrowhead

ESSENCE
hyssop

SOUNDS/RHYTHMS
frog calls, hens clucking

MUSICAL NOTES
F# and C#

DEEP SPACE OBJECTS
Epsilon Canis Major, Adhara, the Virgins

July 10

YOUR SIGN
Cancer

YOUR ELEMENT
Water

YOUR RULERS
Moon, Mars, Jupiter
18 degrees
Second Decanate, yin

The Astrological Interpretation

You are a natural-born peacemaker. It is difficult for you to stand by passively watching friends, family, or coworkers in conflict with one other. It is easy for you to see each person's point of view, so you try to find solutions that are inclusive and helpful to all parties. You know that wounds take time to heal; you hold the people you care about in your heart and wait until the right moment to confront them. This talent can be applied professionally, as you would make a great mediator and diplomat. When you are not busy with your relationships, you enjoy spending as much time alone as possible. You definitely have your "own thing" in life and try to apportion a part of each day to explore and investigate what interests you. Films, art, cultural events, dance, and music are all activities that resound with you.

Very close to the fixed star Propus, July 10 birthdays register with extremes of temperament. Your home is a retreat from the bustle of the world and should be cool and orderly. Noise is particularly distracting to July 10 people and choosing a quiet neighborhood is essential. You might particularly enjoy a basement lined in wood panels or cork.

You have very strong protective feelings and prefer a space that feels cozy and enclosed. Curtains of midnight blue could surround the bedroom. Keep a full refrigerator and create a kitchen where people can gather and linger. A breakfast nook would be a nice touch; in the early morning people will feel tucked in and chummy.

Outdoors smooth green lawns with a brook or other small source of water is important. A screened-in porch gives the feeling of protection with the pleasure of outdoors. Mementos from family members are cherished objects. Musical instruments or a collection of records is an important part of your home.

A Kabbalistic Interpretation

We all have dreams, but many of us never really believe that our wildest ones will come true. In many ways all any of us need to succeed is to believe that we can. You have the capacity to believe in yourself deeply and have the idealism to pursue your dreams. You can increase that energy by keeping some valerian or vervain in a little pouch.

While you have all the energy you need to achieve your dreams, you lack some of the more grounding benefits of earth energy. This will be important to you when you need to attend to the organization of your life. Use autumnal tones in decorating your main working area in the home and you will draw some of the stability of earth to you.

Your quick-wittedness and ability to think on your feet often encourage your bosses to consider you for promotion. A ruby ring worn on your little finger will help keep your mind razor sharp.

A Numerological Interpretation
YOUR MAGIC NUMBERS: 8 AND 3

The tenth day of the seventh month reduces to eight, the number meaning involution and evolution. The energy of eight ebbs and flows in ever repeating equal and opposite cycles. Born on this day, you have a path of exalting in the moment and making life a symphony. You have the innate capacity to understand the interplay and exquisite possibilities that each individual can offer to the music of life. Imagine life as a stage musical, where at any moment someone will burst into song and uplift everyone's spirits. You have such capacity. You have deep and strong feelings that when stirred and shared can move the emotions of everyone around you.

The 192nd day of the year reduces to three, adding the ebullient energy of creative self-expression to this path. Don't hold back. Step out on the balcony of your life and serenade the stars. Love songs need to be shared. Aquamarine is a gem to open your heart to the myriad emotions of humanity.

OBJECTS/IMAGES
heirlooms, military medals, insignias, dewdrops in the dawn

SHAPES/MATERIALS
silver, enclosed circles, lagoons, marcasite

COLORS
sea green, shimmering silver, iridescent hues, aquamarine, salmon

ANIMALS
turtle, goose, hen

PLANTS, HERBS, EDIBLES
jade plant, water lilies, melons, brandy, cucumbers, gourds

ESSENCES
honeysuckle, calla lilies, petunia

SOUNDS/RHYTHMS
steady rain showers, military marches, sound of footsteps

MUSICAL NOTES
G and D

DEEP SPACE OBJECTS
Beta Canis Minor, Gomeisa, Little One

July 11

YOUR SIGN
Cancer

YOUR ELEMENT
Water

YOUR RULERS
Moon, Mars
18–19 degrees
Second Decanate, yin

The Astrological Interpretation

You have a way of seeing the best in people and the potential that each individual gains from working harmoniously in groups. You are able to achieve a particularly strong sense of personal satisfaction when you organize a group of people around your creative inspirations. Your organizational skills are not confined just to business. You like to produce a festive mood whenever and wherever possible. Catering is your forte, as a full table of delicious treats and delicacies is a pleasure to your eyes. Although your home is your real base of operations, you do enjoy traveling to interesting places, preferably with friends or that special someone in your life.

Contrary to the dreamy image of many Cancerians, the Mars rulership of the second decanate gives real grit and will to this day. There is also a tradition of military service and interest in music associated with July 11. Consider including some insignias or coats of arms in your home. If you or a relative served in the military, display any medals or honors. In your wardrobe a snappy blazer or shirt with epaulets can be the touch of Mars that you need to remind you of your strength. For your musical inclinations perhaps stenciling musical notes around the top of one of your rooms would be fun. Combine music and the military with a few rousing marches in the morning! You like labor saving gadgets. Perhaps get yourself a salad spinner or a gadget to open tightly closed jars.

July 11 is a receptive sign and capable of in-depth research for spiritual concerns. Keep track of the phases of the moon and try to spend some time each month outdoors gazing at the moon. Your lunar ruler will influence your dreams.

A Kabbalistic Interpretation

It is highly likely at some point in your life you will find yourself in a senior role at your workplace. You have an excellent way with your fellow workers, especially when acting as an arbiter in disputes. You can ensure the fairness of your decisions at work by keeping a red five-pointed star in one of your desk drawers.

The influence of the Hierophant card this day emphasizes your role as an authority in some aspect of your life. It also points to very high moral standards, which from time to time result in real moral crises for you. When you experience this you should sit facing east on a cushion or chair with a red and yellow pattern, as this will help you to reach a decision that squares with your ethics.

When the date is fully spelled out in Hebrew, the value of this day has an association with the sephira Malkuth. Malkuth represents the normal day-to-day world, to which you are deeply connected. At times it would be good for you to raise your sights to higher things. A pendant of amber may help you do this.

A Numerological Interpretation
YOUR MAGIC NUMBERS: 9 AND 4

The eleventh day of the seventh month reduces to nine, the number that connotes the principle of attainment and successful completion of an endeavor. Nine is the culmination of the process begun in the number one. Born on this day, you have a path of excellence in whatever field or activity you pursue. This pattern calls for you to discover yourself and your soul's gifts through the intrinsically spiritual human value of doing your best and striving to excel. Your voice is a potentially powerful tool for healing. Sing or chant to exercise your vocal chords. Take speech lessons and join a group like Toastmasters. Blue zircon and yellow garnet are stones to intensify your aspirations. The 193rd day of the year reduces to four, adding the quality of planning and ordered measurement to your path. This will aid you in mapping out your strategies for achievement. Shades of blue will focus your intentions and bring out nobility of purpose.

OBJECTS/IMAGES
tinsel on a Christmas tree, a key chain

SHAPES/MATERIALS
aluminum, nubby sweaters

COLORS
pearly colors, China blue, peach

ANIMALS
frog, tunny, night owl

PLANTS, HERBS, EDIBLES
dogtooth violet, honeysuckle

ESSENCE
neroli

SOUNDS/RHYTHMS
lullabies, rocking rhythms

MUSICAL NOTES
G# and D#

DEEP SPACE OBJECTS
Beta Gemini, Pollux

July 12

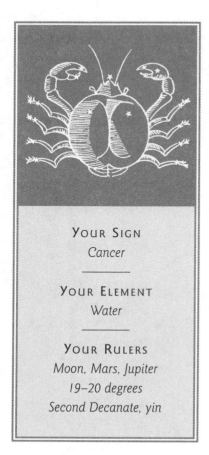

YOUR SIGN
Cancer

YOUR ELEMENT
Water

YOUR RULERS
Moon, Mars, Jupiter
19–20 degrees
Second Decanate, yin

The Astrological Interpretation

You have a deep lunar rhythm that is connected to the variations in your moods. Sometimes you feel you are at high tide. During these times, you are expressive and eagerly rush forward into the experiences of life. At other times, you move quietly back into yourself, seeking peace and solitude. It is hard to predict which of these two sides you will present in any encounter. You may even suddenly shift from one to the other. People close to you have learned that it is best to leave you alone during your emotional low tides, as nothing and no one can change this mood but yourself.

The fixed star Castor is located on some July 12 birthdays. Castor was the mortal twin of the heavenly pair Castor and Pollux, associated with Apollo. The ancients believed this position gave sudden honors followed by disgrace. Perhaps the ancients were familiar with Andy Warhol's claim that "in the future everyone will be famous for fifteen minutes"! Regardless of any honors attained in life, you have a serious, studious nature and the ability to share your talents and create cooperative relationships among people. Books, particularly finely bound leather volumes, will be important to you. Books that have been in your family for years are especially meaningful. Music is also important. An image for you is a boat on calm waters where the person rowing is singing. You might enjoy a reproduction of Apollo's instrument, the lyre, as a decorative object. At home have a variety of china. You might have some heirloom pieces and then some white porcelain plates that are just for fun.

Outdoors, the crescent moon is a shape to guide you. Initiate projects at the new moon and work steadily until the full moon. From the full moon through the dark of the moon, let your projects grow. Take it easy during the dark of the moon, your energy is usually low at this time.

A Kabbalistic Interpretation

The planet Mars exerts quite an influence on your day, making you someone with great leadership potential. The more confrontational aspects of Mars are dampened down by other influences, but with Mars energy, you always need to be on guard against a lack of humility. Tending a small vegetable patch or growing some plants in a window box will ensure that your pride doesn't overcome you.

This is a day blessed with good financial fortune, and you can maximize its benefits. Buy a gold seven-pointed star and wear it at all times as a pendant. You are lucky not only when it comes to finances, but you are also likely to have an easy time as far as relationships are concerned. People who attract you are likely to pick up on your intense sexual energy and creativity. Keeping some soft fruits like peaches or plums on your kitchen table will enhance this side of your personality.

A Numerological Interpretation

YOUR MAGIC NUMBERS: 1 AND 5

The twelfth day of the seventh month reduces to one, the number signifying beginnings, initiative, and originality. One carries a singleness of purpose and a sense of unity. Born on this day, you have a path of sensing and responding to the potential in what seem to be chance events. This pattern evokes the intriguing phenomenon of serendipity. You have the capacity to create what appears like magic to others. At your best, you grasp the ramifications present in any set of circumstances. Visit a busy marina and watch the sailboats come and go, contemplating their chance encounters.

This is a path of action rather than an accumulation of facts and data. You must seize the opportunities you perceive and act on their potential. The paradox of this pattern is that you must maintain an outward calm and an inner poise in order to be receptive to the signals. Ruby and fire opal are gems to ignite your sense of initiative. The 194th day of the year reduces to five, adding the important quality of adaptation and versatility to this path.

OBJECTS/IMAGES
old sheet music, mirages, moats

SHAPES/MATERIALS
freshwater pearls, irregular curves, tortoise shells

COLORS
dark blue, cherry red, bright yellow

ANIMALS
owl, oyster

PLANTS, HERBS, EDIBLES
prickly lettuce, meadow lilies, lobsters

ESSENCE
wintergreen

SOUNDS/RHYTHMS
Italian boat songs, "Old Man River," barcaroles

MUSICAL NOTES
C and E

DEEP SPACE OBJECT
pulsar

July 13

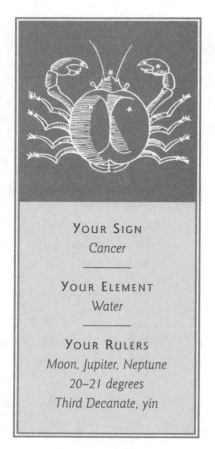

YOUR SIGN
Cancer

YOUR ELEMENT
Water

YOUR RULERS
Moon, Jupiter, Neptune
20–21 degrees
Third Decanate, yin

The Astrological Interpretation

You are not the kind of person who likes to get stuck in highly complex emotional issues. You prefer to be like an ice skater, gliding over a smooth surface, whirling and twirling with the music. Sometimes this is just not possible, and you find yourself in the tight and burdensome situations you seek to avoid. You are then forced to put on a heavy mantle of responsibility even though you would rather wear the lightest of silk. Accept the fact that life moves in cycles. Some allow you to be a carefree child, but other cycles force you to become an adult. As you integrate these two sides of your nature, you will find greater success.

An image for July 13 is of a person standing on a dock waiting for a sailboat; your ship will come in. At home, furnish a retreat space with a special cup for coffee or tea. If you have china from your grandparents, use that in your retreat. Candlelight is peaceful for you; a small votive candle in a blue glass container might be particularly pleasing. July 13 favors nighttime colors such as midnight blue or black, but avoid wearing black all the time. Books are important to you. You may collect a variety of bookmarks to keep track of your various studies. In the kitchen have a small stool where you can sit as a rest from cooking or while a spouse or friend cooks.

Outdoors, July 13 wants shade and comfort. A screened-in porch is probably the ideal environment. A walk in a shady forest next to a small river or creek is a perfect outdoor activity. Walking, even from room to room in your home, is a way to solve problems and burn off excess energy. A small birdhouse or a goldfish pond would each be a source of endless pleasure.

A Kabbalistic Interpretation

The tarot cards the Hierophant and the Wheel of Fortune play an important part in the makeup of your personality. While the Hierophant suggests a definite interest in the world of spirituality and religion, the Wheel of Fortune card indicates that you retain a healthy skepticism, as chance seems to determine much in your life. Wear some dark blue Tibetan prayer beads and meditate with them from time to time.

The short version of the value of this day equals the value of the Hebrew word meaning "brotherhood." Along with other energies, moss green in this date indicates a love of group activity. Play an active role within some organization, whether it is a sports club or a sewing circle. A bronze ring worn on your third finger will encourage your social activities to bear fruit.

Another meaning for this day is "valley," a word representing wealth and abundance in the hermetic tradition. In order to encourage more wealth in your life, try filling your favorite room in the house with lush green potted plants.

A Numerological Interpretation

YOUR MAGIC NUMBERS: 2 AND 6

The thirteenth day of the seventh month reduces to two, the number of duplication and polarity. Two is the twin of one by duplication, its polar opposite by division. Yours is a path of comparing and contrasting the events of your life in search of an ever-widening horizon. This pattern is one of rigorous examination of your efforts so that your results may reach exacting levels of performance. Join a literary society or book discussion club. Read reviews written by film and theater critics.

This day's path requires you to understand and develop the positive aspects of constructive criticism as a mechanism for improvement, not a discounting of someone's performance. Sodalite is a stone on which you can grind and hone your mental processes. Warm tones of yellows and orange will take the edge off potential sarcasm. The 195th day of the year reduces to six, contributing the essential ingredient of beauty and the harmony of opposites to this path. Strive for synthesis, not just dissection.

OBJECTS/IMAGES
water fountains, canals, a book holder

SHAPES/MATERIALS
womb shapes, black onyx, silver

COLORS
Blue-green, green and purple together, rust, moss green

ANIMALS
stuffed animals, a dog baying at the moon

PLANTS, HERBS, EDIBLES
mushrooms, valerian, crab cakes

ESSENCE
petitgrain oil

SOUNDS/RHYTHMS
ballads, lullabies

MUSICAL NOTES
C# and F

DEEP SPACE OBJECTS
Alpha Canis Minor, Procyon, Before the Dog

July 14

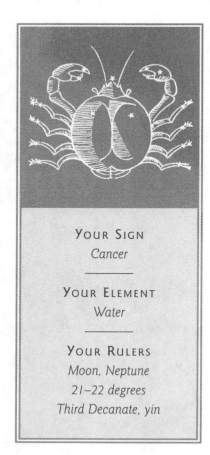

YOUR SIGN
Cancer

YOUR ELEMENT
Water

YOUR RULERS
Moon, Neptune
21–22 degrees
Third Decanate, yin

The Astrological Interpretation

Your immediate environment is like a second layer of clothing. Your personal sensitivity is not confined merely to sensory stimuli. You are also aware of the emotional and psychological content of your surroundings. If this sensitivity is not objectified and contained, it can make you overly skittish and thin-skinned, even to the point of only feeling comfortable in very controlled circumstances. Yet this same part of your nature, coupled with the right education and training, can be your greatest gift. It may be the basis of a great talent as a counselor, teacher, or psychologist and can also be applied to establish a close relationship to animals and plants.

July 14 has poise and patience. Chance events give you indications of the tides of your life, and you wait for your ship to come. The challenge will be to use chance to pursue your goals and dreams, rather than relying on accidents of fortune to steer your ship. Men and women born on July 14 may like to wear suspenders. Photography intrigues you; have some disposable cameras handy in case you want to capture a special shot. Keep books of poetry in your living room or bedroom and take a poetry break every once in a while. Emphasize water in your environment with a fountain or humidifier. Your bedroom should include round mirrors. An old-fashioned vanity with a mirror top would be a perfect piece for you.

Outdoors, July 14 likes to putter in the garden or lawn. Mowing the lawn, weeding, and creating order in nature are restful activities for you. Vegetables, such as cucumbers and zucchini, and fruit such as watermelon would interest you. If you live in the country consider having a roadside stand. You might also sell baked goods.

A Kabbalistic Interpretation

The World card from the tarot, symbolizing completion, influences this day. To complete your living environment you need to achieve a balance of elements. You can do this literally, drawing from the elements in your decorating scheme, or symbolically with color—blue for water, yellow for air, red for fire, and green for earth.

You should experience very little difficulty achieving the top of your chosen profession, as you have the ability to persuade and manipulate others to great effect. You tend to be very ethical and would never advance yourself beyond your merits. The influence of Mercury gives you this trait, and you can enhance it by keeping a large picture of an Egyptian ibis or a swallow on your office wall.

One Hebrew equivalent to the value of this day is "firstborn." Traditionally this refers to the expected heir of the family. In modern terms the word implies that you have the capacity to take on great responsibility. Keeping a fire burning in your home or using a flame-colored scarf or necktie will assist you in coping with the burdens of responsibility.

A Numerological Interpretation

YOUR MAGIC NUMBERS: 3 AND 7

The fourteenth day of the seventh month reduces to three, the number meaning multiplication, development, and unfoldment. Three is the number of growth and expression. Born on this day, you have a path characterized by the lesson of distinguishing between the transient needs of day-to-day life and the more universal requirements of your soul's growth. This pattern calls for you to swear your primary allegiance to the goal of higher order. This requires the discipline of mediating the competing demands of ordinary needs and the inner urging of spirit.

The 196th day of the year reduces to seven, adding the influence of the ancient significance of a sworn oath to your path. Contemplate the difference between a small garden patch versus a family farm, which will feed many mouths. What is the contribution to society between sleeping under a tree in the forest versus a walled town that safely houses hundreds? Heliodor, golden beryl, is a stone that will stimulate your sense of noblesse oblige. Wear something purple to make you feel regal.

OBJECTS/IMAGES
bartenders, blushing, chefs, cradles

SHAPES/MATERIALS
aluminum, Tahitian pearls, all container shapes, moonstone

COLORS
moonbeam silver, sunshine yellow, cobalt blue

ANIMAL
clam

PLANTS, HERBS, EDIBLES
arrowhead (water plant), caltrops, heavy cream, blue cheese

ESSENCE
clary sage

SOUNDS/RHYTHMS
lambs bleating, frogs croaking

MUSICAL NOTES
E and G#

DEEP SPACE OBJECTS
Alpha Carina, Canopus

July 15

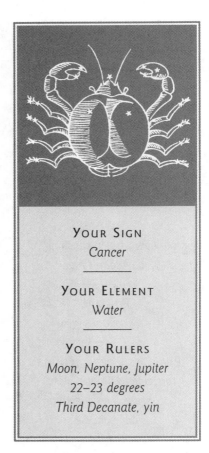

YOUR SIGN
Cancer

YOUR ELEMENT
Water

YOUR RULERS
Moon, Neptune, Jupiter
22–23 degrees
Third Decanate, yin

The Astrological Interpretation

You have a tendency to feel responsible for the people close to you. This characteristic is based on a sense of emotional insecurity and the urge to control your environment and the people with whom you are sharing your life. Although your intentions are good, you have to check your motivations to see if fear of loss is the activating force. Intimacy is an important factor in your relationships, but you must also allow people to set their own boundaries. Once these feelings have matured and you are acting independently, you will be happy and content to support the individual growth of those you love.

You will hold on to any object that has sentimental meaning for you, so have lots of closet space. A locket with a picture of a favorite relative might be a valued piece of jewelry. Scrapbooks and old diaries help you keep a record of your past. Your bed should be near a window so you can catch the moon when it is shining. Keep the color scheme restful and place a glass of water by your bed or have a bowl of water somewhere in the room. Moonstone is a mineral that smoothes your energies.

Your garden might have a lily pond with special night-blooming lilies. A telescope will let you stargaze at night or spy out to sea. Go to an old whaling village and visit houses with a widow's walk. Here, in days past, women waited for word of their men at sea.

A Kabbalistic Interpretation

You have a great desire for success, though not material success in the common sense of financial gain. You long for a personal sense of achievement, which in the context of other factors affecting your day, you largely relate to pleasure seeking. In order to help focus your energy to achieve the things in life that are important to you, wear a tie or brooch in rich purple.

Although you are generally driven by a desire to enjoy life rather than to learn from it you are nonetheless a wise individual. The tarot card the Hermit affecting this day refers to emotional wisdom and understanding. There is a definite connection to the Empress card as well. A lead sculpture of an eagle, representative of this card, or similar bird on your bedside table will enhance your natural emotional insight.

Your day has the same value as the name Eve. Like Eve in the Garden of Eden, you have a natural inclination to take risks. This can be a very positive approach to life—if it hadn't been for Prometheus, the Greeks would never have discovered the secret of fire. What could be a better inspiration for an Eve than to keep a bowl of fresh apples on your kitchen table.

A Numerological Interpretation

YOUR MAGIC NUMBERS: 4 AND 8

The fifteenth day of the seventh month reduces to four, the number that connotes order, abstract reason, and measurement. Born on this day, you have a path of leadership and stewardship of the general welfare. This is a pattern of involvement and not isolation. The degree to which you develop your capacity to lead is the degree to which you will experience personal fulfillment as well as gratification that you have served people. At your best, you can make a dramatic contribution to society by bringing out the best in others. The danger of this path is an inflated sense of your own importance. Maintain your sense of humor and perspective, and don't take yourself too seriously.

Turquoise set in gold will maintain a sense of equanimity. Cover a chair in green brocade to remind you of your destiny. The 197th day of the year reduces to eight, adding the innate awareness of the ebb and flow of all things. This helps you to not cling too tightly to your creations. Volunteer for Scouting; your natural leadership will be an example for young people.

OBJECTS/IMAGES
walking boots, a glass milk bottle, a ship's bell

SHAPES/MATERIALS
watered silk, crescents, selenite

COLORS
iridescent shades, silver color, navy blue, tangerine, turquoise blue

ANIMALS
turtle, otter, oyster

PLANTS, HERBS, EDIBLES
cloves, oregano, hydrangeas

ESSENCES
cucumber, narcissus

SOUNDS/RHYTHMS
sound of waves lapping against a boat, swing rhythms, 1940s big-band sound.

MUSICAL NOTES
D# and G

DEEP SPACE OBJECT
NGC 3147, spiral galaxy

July 16

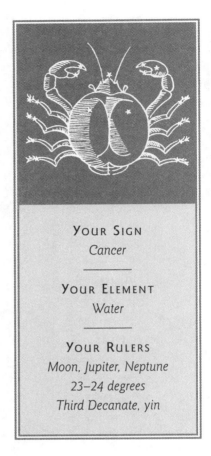

YOUR SIGN
Cancer

YOUR ELEMENT
Water

YOUR RULERS
Moon, Jupiter, Neptune
23–24 degrees
Third Decanate, yin

The Astrological Interpretation

Your birth date is associated with the science of genealogy and the complex interconnections of characteristics that travel from one generation to another. You can extend this natural proclivity into a wider view of history and the ways human beings have built and destroyed their societies. Sociology, psychology, economics, and the history of art are all subjects that will appeal to and benefit you. It is important for you to see what you have inherited from your parents. You have the power and responsibility to keep the strong and good that has been given to you and to release what you no longer wish to maintain. Work at establishing your own firm sense of yourself as your foundation for the future.

Your birthday brings a heightened imagination and a sense of daring, which will bring panache to your life. You have great charm and may be interested in performing as well as mysticism. Writing is a perfect outlet for your creativity. An image for you is a castle on a high promontory with a flag flying in the wind. This symbolizes the heights of your imagination and the strength of the fortress you must build to support your vision. In your home have a small refuge place where you can retreat among your keepsakes. An aquarium in this corner would aid your thoughts. Minerals such as quartz crystal and colemanite would be perfect decorations for your imaginative retreat.

Outdoors, July 16 would like a sense of privacy. High privet hedges or a wooden fence that defines the yard is essential. Himalayan indigo growing against your fence would be a perfect way to insulate your outdoor space. Flowers for July 16 could be moonwort, magnolia, and all night blooming flowers.

A Kabbalistic Interpretation

This is a day with a strong connection to the Hierophant card, which indicates intense spiritual leanings and a high regard for authority. In your case the Hierophant interacts with the Moon card and suggests that you have a very individual and somewhat mystical approach to your religious beliefs. Keeping a silver framed mirror in your bedroom will help you to develop your personal belief system.

The stereotypical view of a mystical-minded person is of someone who finds it difficult to function in the world of business and industry. You, on the other hand, have a dynamic nature when it comes to the world of work. The influence of the letter *Lamed* in your day indicates that you can be quite driven when you are set an important task. Keeping some cloves on your desk or in your pocket will help you to maintain high energy.

Your colleagues and friends will recognize a generous streak to your personality. You may not always have the solution to people's problems but you will always do whatever you can to help. One way to encourage your ability to provide a sympathetic ear would be to grow an ash or an elder tree in your garden.

A Numerological Interpretation
YOUR MAGIC NUMBERS: 5 AND 9

The sixteenth day of the seventh month reduces to five, the number of change and adaptation. Yours is a path of finding a seemingly impossible still point in the center of a chaotic world. Seek the eye of the storm and let chaos swirl around you while you repose in the middle. This pattern calls for a razor's edge sort of awareness. You must cultivate the ability to restore and regenerate your energies, without succumbing to self-indulgence or laziness. This stillness is the refueling of your spirit that prepares you for the conquest of the next adventure.

The 198th day of the year reduces to nine, adding the critical qualities of completion, attainment, and goal orientation to your path. This aids you in experiencing a sense of culmination during your moments of utter stillness. Aquamarine is a gem to remind you of the ocean, which can be calm as glass one moment and turbulent and dangerous the next. Study storms, volunteer to be a storm spotter, and learn about their violent and transformative nature.

OBJECTS/IMAGES
beach clubs, water bottles, babies, barges, fairy-tale illustrations

SHAPES/MATERIALS
aluminum, white Arabian (stone), silver-colored pyrites, bowl shapes

COLORS
iridescent green, lemon, royal blue

ANIMALS
firefly; Harvey, the six-foot rabbit

PLANTS, HERB, EDIBLES
cabbage, chickweed, crabs

ESSENCE
neroli

SOUNDS/RHYTHMS
unfurling a sail, arpeggios

MUSICAL NOTES
E and G#

DEEP SPACE OBJECT
quasar

July 17

YOUR SIGN
Cancer

YOUR ELEMENT
Water

YOUR RULERS
Moon, Neptune
24–25 degrees
Third Decanate, yin

The Astrological Interpretation

You have a rebellious streak that has served you well in your attempts to individualize yourself. Any form of physical or psychological constriction is against your nature, but you should not confuse the process of maturing with the need to relinquish individuality. You worked hard to become who you are and may now contribute to making the world a better place in which to live. You may already recognize this process from your experience and are already involved in helping others to grow. Teaching is a natural outlet for you and you will be attracted to those subjects that give people practical tools for living. Your focus is on how to make a better living and you would do well in commerce, business, money management, and techniques for financial growth.

July 17 works hard to make a unique mark on the world. An image for you is the turtle, who carries his home on his back. You like to move around and be "at home" wherever you find yourself. Carry a favorite pillowcase or pictures of family with you on your travels. At home, aquariums and terrariums are restful objects for you. Your personal style is somewhat dashing; dark colors such as navy blue and gray are preferable. Your friends and family will always be cheered by your lunar humor. Encourage yourself and them with tapes of classic comedies and sitcoms.

Outdoors, July 17 enjoys a lofty pine tree near some source of water. Shade is important to you, and a collection of white adirondack chairs under the pines is the place to plan your next campaign. Wildflowers that grow well in shady woods are pink lady's slipper and wild bergamot.

A Kabbalistic Interpretation

The world really is your oyster. The influence of the Star card from the tarot ensures that life has a tendency to look after you rather than present challenges to your success. In addition the Chariot card indicates an ability to stick to your goals. A pack of playing cards kept in the south of your home will encourage you to take more risks in life.

Life with you is always a lot of fun, although at times it can seem a bit like a roller-coaster ride in the dark—exhilarating but slightly unnerving! You do have a tendency to spring surprises on people. These can be local, such as arranging surprise parties for your close friends, or global surprises, such as a sudden decision about changing home or career. Wearing jewelry with arrow images encourage you to be even swifter in your decision-making processes.

The lightning speed of your mind is matched by your manual dexterity, but how this manifests itself will vary from person to person. There is a connection in this day to mythical figures representing the arts, in particular music. You might like to consider trying your hand at the piano and see where it takes you.

A Numerological Interpretation

YOUR MAGIC NUMBERS: 6 AND 1

The seventeenth day of the seventh month reduces to six, a number that connotes beauty, harmony, and the balancing of polarities. Six carries the ability to reconcile adversaries and volatile situations. Yours is a path of aligning with the powers of nature. The water of a gentle rain can quench the dry earth and bring new life. The raging waters of a flood can destroy everything in its path. This pattern requires that you come to terms with the potential power that can be unleashed through your own personality. By channeling these forces of your nature, you can accomplish miracles.

Volunteer for the Red Cross and assist victims of natural disasters. Immerse yourself in the consequences of untamed force. Fire opal and obsidian are gems to remind you of the often volatile nature of creation. The 199th day of the year reduces to one, adding the singleness of purpose necessary to harness these forces at will and do so with beneficence. Wear red to energize your will.

OBJECTS/IMAGES
motels, calm seas, taprooms, shopkeepers

SHAPES/MATERIALS
silver lamé, chalk, crystals, emeralds

COLORS
iridescent white, spring green, scarlet

ANIMALS
hamster, crawdaddy, buffle duck

PLANTS, HERBS, EDIBLES
zucchini, white truffles, bur cucumber vine, water lilies

ESSENCES
mimosa

SOUND/RHYTHM
jug bands

MUSICAL NOTES
F and C

DEEP SPACE OBJECTS
Eta Canis Major, Aludra, the Maiden

July 18

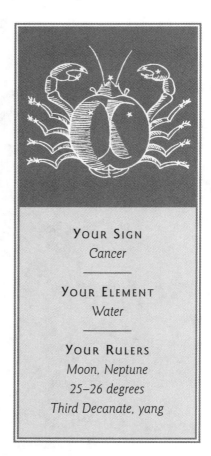

YOUR SIGN
Cancer

———

YOUR ELEMENT
Water

———

YOUR RULERS
Moon, Neptune
25–26 degrees
Third Decanate, yang

The Astrological Interpretation

A romantic person at heart, you like to create the perfect settings for intimate encounters. White flowers are especially connected to your birth date, including lilies, roses, and irises. Health should not be of particular concern, but you do have to watch out for your emotional state, as it is through your feelings that you develop any weaknesses in your body. You are at your most robust and creative when feeling emotionally secure. This means that you need to be with people who can accept the ways that you love them. If you are meeting too much resistance and thus lowering your physical vitality, leave the situation and look elsewhere.

July 18 falls near the fixed star Procyon in the constellation Canis Minor. Your birthday indicates that you may well achieve honors in life. Your nature is poetic and you do not enjoy routines. An image for you is a meteor that follows an eccentric path as it falls to earth. You are sensitive to noise and should protect your ears from mechanical sounds and high screeches. A white noise machine or background music is essential for city dwellers. At home surround yourself with a sectional sofa that curves around and enfolds you. There should be a feeling of luxury in your home no matter what your finances are. You may prefer an old-fashioned way of doing things, like having a percolator coffeepot or a glass juicer. In your bedroom consider bent willow wood furniture. If you could find a willow headboard it would add a special resonance to your home.

Outdoors, July 18 wants a clear space to catch sight of any falling stars or meteors. A garden with a fishpond in an odd shape, such as an anchor, would please you. Emphasize water flowers such as water hyacinth, and lotus in your pond and zinnias and gladiolas in your garden.

A Kabbalistic Interpretation

Nobody could be more concerned about personal appearance and image than you. You are a natural for fields where appearance is all-important such as the media or fashion industries. This concern stems from the influence of the sun and the Empress card on your day. Try wearing gold jewelry and especially some hair ornaments and you will find that you look even better than you usually do.

Passion should really be your middle name. This doesn't mean that you are an unusually physically passionate person. It is your deepest emotions that you feel intensely, partly due to the effect of the Hebrew letter *Shin*. Personal souvenirs of relationships hold a very special appeal for you; try keeping them in a vermillion box made of almond wood.

A sense of harmony in your life is extremely important for you, especially given your deeply passionate nature. Employing the strength of the planet Mars through the use of objects in your home can help keep you emotionally grounded. Keeping a set of cast-iron, old-fashioned weighing scales in the kitchen will help.

A Numerological Interpretation

YOUR MAGIC NUMBERS: 7 AND 2

The eighteenth day of the seventh month reduces to seven, the number of victory and safety. Seven is the period of rest after creation. Yours is a path of bridging and blending older ways of knowing with more modern views. This pattern demands a spirit of cooperation between diverse elements within yourself and the culture. You have the capacity to act as a mediator or a translator of sorts among cultures and generations.

The danger of this path can be a tendency to be too conservative, to hold on to the past for fear of change. Orange is a color that will open your mind to new possibilities. Wear rainbow jasper and agate to aid your acceptance of diversity. The 200th day of the year reduces to two, providing the element of receptivity and reflection to assist you in your process. Study history and observe the constants of civilization. Study native peoples around the world and internalize what they have held as ageless values. Endeavor to combine the best of both in your life.

OBJECTS/IMAGES
*ship in a bottle,
washing machines,
a lava lamp, markets*

SHAPES/MATERIALS
*canvas, soft white stones,
teardrop shapes*

COLORS
*iridescent blue, forest green,
vermilion*

ANIMALS
*Rhode Island red hen,
long-eared owl*

PLANTS, HERBS, EDIBLES
*woodbine, yellow flag iris,
water lettuce, snails*

ESSENCE
lovage

SOUNDS/RHYTHMS
*Handel's Water Music,
an E-flat chord, poetry*

MUSICAL NOTES
F# and C#

DEEP SPACE OBJECT
NGC 2681, spiral galaxy

July 19

YOUR SIGN
Cancer

YOUR ELEMENT
Water

YOUR RULERS
Moon, Neptune, Jupiter
26–27 degrees
Third Decanate, yang

The Astrological Interpretation

You need a strong financial foundation not only to prove your self-worth but also to show your family that you have the ability to make it in the world. At times this drive is all pervasive and you find that you are tense and sensitive. You may cry or become angry or be harsh with yourself without good reason. Perhaps you have neglected our common and deepest roots in favor of material ambitions. Your birth date is symbolic of a need to return to the comfort and security of the oceans, forests, and lakes. Take every opportunity to hike, stroll, and camp in natural surroundings. This will bring balance and give you even greater strength to climb your mountain of personal achievement.

Some July 19 birthdays will fall on a critical degree, which tends to bring strong reactions to the highs and lows in life. You enjoy the vibrant feeling and heightened awareness that intensity can bring. Your challenge will be to create with the full force of your feelings rather than entertaining yourself with turmoil. You feel comfortable in a home with lots of house plants, such as dieffenbachia and jade trees. Preparing food is calming; egg dishes such as quiche lorraine or a soufflé may be a specialty. Decorate with watery blues and greens. Seascapes and pictures of surfers remind you of the beauty and power of water. A library corner with rare or antique volumes suits your sentimental nature. You may have a strong feeling for other historical times; having books or prints from those times is a way of maintaining a connection.

Outdoors, July 19 wants a place to raise vegetables. Visits to a farm would be restorative and interesting for you. If your own yard is small consider planting cauliflower, squash, carrots, and peas. Flowers for June 19 are all night bloomers and water lilies

A Kabbalistic Interpretation

The influence of the sephira Hod is strong this day, explaining a tendency to high intellectual achievement. To enhance your already sharp mind, keep a fire opal gem in your pocket or on your desk. When you want to relax in the evening listen to some books on tape or on a CD rather than music.

The number thirty-one is highly significant this day. This particular number is extremely important in the Western mystery tradition, as it means both "God" and "nothing." As all words of the same value are said to have a relationship with one another this combination is deeply significant. In terms of your personality it suggests that you have the capacity to achieve great things but need to be vigilant to avoid the danger of putting too much energy into a dead end. Growing sage in a window box will help you to make long-term decisions from a wise place.

The letter *Peh*, meaning "mouth," has an influence on this day in conjunction with the letter *Tau*, which represents an altruistic approach to life. It is likely that you will find yourself involved in some form of socially beneficial volunteer group, especially if some form of communication skill is needed.

A Numerological Interpretation

YOUR MAGIC NUMBERS: 8 AND 3

The nineteenth day of the seventh month reduces to eight, the number that means rhythm, vibration, and evolution. Eight contains the knowledge that opposite forms of expression stem from a single cause. Born on this day, yours is a path of developing your faculty of discernment so you can perceive true worth and value. This pattern requires that you discern what is universal and similar behind the mirage of appearance and apparent contradiction. This is how you come to understand your own true worth and express your uniqueness.

Turquoise and citrine are stones to steady your mental processes. Shades of blue and green will enhance your serenity. The 201st day of the year reduces to three, adding the quality of growth and natural unfoldment to this path. At your best, you can follow the root cause of a certain manifestation back to its source. Be an amateur detective to exercise these skills.

OBJECTS/IMAGES
kitchenware, lakeside cottages, aquariums, bathhouses

SHAPES/MATERIALS
basinlike containers, marcasite, moonstone

COLORS
silvery gray, aquamarine, ginger

ANIMALS
boreal owl, frog

PLANTS, HERBS, EDIBLES
evening lychnis, a pear tree, hyssop, whipped cream

ESSENCE
clary sage

SOUNDS/RHYTHMS
water gushing from a hydrant, sipping soup

MUSICAL NOTES
G and D

DEEP SPACE OBJECTS
Zeta Cancer, Tegmine, the Shell

July 20

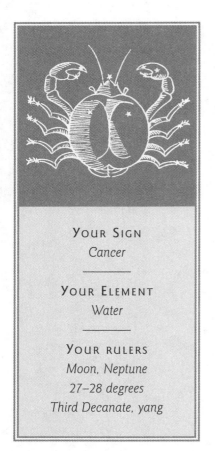

YOUR SIGN
Cancer

YOUR ELEMENT
Water

YOUR RULERS
Moon, Neptune
27–28 degrees
Third Decanate, yang

The Astrological Interpretation

Your life is deeply connected to strong and intimate relationships with others. You search for partners with whom you can share mutual support for your many plans and projects. Yet the quality of your relationships is a reflection of your own strengths and personal characteristics. You bring a sense of wholeness and caring to each of your friendships and do not need to wait for another person to express these fine qualities. Indeed it is your responsibility to make sure that you fulfill your own needs without waiting for someone to supply the missing part. Nothing is missing! Things can only be added.

You have something of a frontier spirit and feel attached to the land of your birth. No matter what your cultural background, consider hanging some mementos from that culture on your walls. Blending your ancestry with your current family and friends is always of interest to you.

July 20 also has a deep connection to the fruits of the earth. A pear tree with large ripe fruit is a symbol of fruition in your life. The soft cream color of a ripe pear is an excellent color to wear. At home focus on comfy furniture that you have had a long time. Reupholstering your grandmother's sofa is preferable to buying something new. You have two favorite rooms in your house, the kitchen and the bathroom. Body oils, fragrant soaps, and luxurious creams and ointments will strongly call out to your sensual nature. An old-fashioned, deep bathtub is where you will get some of your best ideas.

Outdoors, July 20 wants the sea or a large body of water nearby. If you don't live near the water take frequent trips or create your own home "beach" with colorful beach towels and a pool. City dwellers should consider a circular home fountain or at least play a tape of a gurgling brook.

A Kabbalistic Interpretation

One of the Hebrew equivalents to the value of this day is "quenched." You do like to drain as much interest and enjoyment from life as possible. Just make sure you don't drain yourself while you are at it. Keep a good supply of healthy food, especially fresh fruit, in your kitchen—it will encourage your eager approach to life while keeping you fit.

You do sometimes reach points when your enthusiasm wanes. At these times, thanks to the influence of the planet Saturn, you can become quite melancholic. A good way to fend off those feelings would be to draw on the much more positive solar energies of your day by wearing yellow or sitting toward the south whenever possible.

The tarot card Death indicates that change is going to be a major factor in your life. It is unlikely that you will settle in one location or career path until relatively late in life. If you want to introduce a greater feeling of stability into your life, try putting some pictures of autumn landscapes in your main living room.

A Numerological Interpretation
YOUR MAGIC NUMBERS: 9 AND 4

The twentieth day of the seventh month reduces to nine, the number of fulfillment and attainment. Nine is the completion of the process begun in one. Yours is a path of conscious connection to your roots. At your best, you exemplify all the finest aspects of your personal and cultural inheritance. This pattern requires a steadfast conviction in your tenets and ideals. The danger of this path is a mind closed to change and new ways of looking at the world. Study revolutionary wars and the influences of tradition versus the forces for change. One generation's revolutionaries are another generation's conservationists.

Be clear on what is of value and do not retain beliefs or possessions merely because they have been around a long time. Star sapphire will widen your vision. Emerald will connect you to enduring beauty. The 202nd day of the year reduces to four, which contributes the quality of solidity to support your belief that certain realities are eternal and unchangeable. Focus your respect on lofty principles, not ephemeral forms. Wear green to connect you to the earth.

OBJECTS/IMAGES
blue glass bottles, a hidden lagoon, candles

SHAPES/MATERIALS
pearls, silver-colored pyrites, anything curved and covered

COLORS
pearl gray, midnight blue, loden green, bright blue, taffy

ANIMALS
beaver, owl

PLANTS, HERBS, EDIBLES
beer, cuckoo flowers, daisies

ESSENCES
smell of apple pie, maple syrup, light colognes

SOUNDS/RHYTHMS
beguine rhythm, ethnic dances

MUSICAL NOTES
G# and D#

DEEP SPACE OBJECTS
Iota Ursa Major, Talitha

July 21

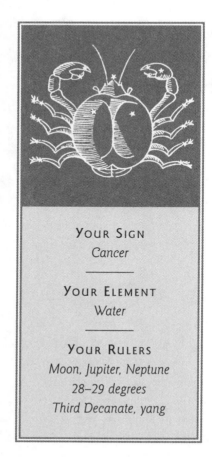

YOUR SIGN
Cancer

YOUR ELEMENT
Water

YOUR RULERS
Moon, Jupiter, Neptune
28–29 degrees
Third Decanate, yang

The Astrological Interpretation

Your birth date is symbolized by a romantic drama projected onto a large movie screen. You have a vivid imagination and a strong emotional life. It is important for you to stand outside the "film" so you can watch things unfold with a careful and critical eye. Work on becoming more objectively detached. You like clothing and may have quite the collection of different outfits for all sorts of occasions. Parties, plays, dances, and other forms of festive social occasions appeal to your outgoing side. Yet there are times when you withdraw deeply into yourself and prefer to remain at home surrounded by the safe and familiar. It is not uncommon for you to keep souvenirs from childhood in plain sight.

Your birthday at the very end of Cancer lives life based on inspiration and impulse. While your approach can create a life in tune with your inner nature you could benefit from sticking to plans and practicing a certainty that you may not always feel. At home you like to keep books, records, CDs, papers from your past, and then may decide one day to throw them all out. Heirloom china, glasses, and photographs of relatives will also appeal to you and you will treasure things from your family's past more than personal items. Decorate your home with subdued colors. Your bedroom could have a canopy bed with curtains that you can close to create your own special space.

Outdoors July 21 loves gardens and forests. Living by the water would be the ideal. If you do live inland have a pond or pool you can visit. An old tire hanging from a tree is a perfect swing for you. Swing over a flower garden of milky bellflower, columbine, and blanket flower.

A Kabbalistic Interpretation

The Hebrew word that means "lament" and other words expressing sorrow are directly linked to the value of your day. Other indications show you to be a well-balanced individual generally, suggesting that you enjoy indulging in sentimentality rather than being subject to any deep unhappiness. You are probably someone who loves to rent all the old weepies—even though they really get to you and you need to sit with a big box of tissues! On the rare occasions when you do feel seriously down, try drinking an infusion of burdock or mint tea.

Another association of this day is with the sephira Netzach. Each sephira is connected to a range of different human attributes, and other pointers indicate that it is Netzach's connection to the world of creativity that affects you. The fact that one of the values of your day is equivalent to the Hebrew word for "clay" may point you specifically toward pottery or even sculpture as a hobby.

A Numerological Interpretation

YOUR MAGIC NUMBERS: 1 AND 5

The twenty-first day of the seventh month reduces to ten and one, perfecting the cycle and urging you forward to a new beginning. Born on this day, you are filled with a sense of unlimited potential and complete confidence in your abilities to accomplish whatever you set out to do. There is a sense of irresistible energy and movement about this path that propels you forward without inhibition or resistance. You expect to get what you want; the danger of this path is that any thwarting of your desires can result in a blocking or damming up of your energies. This pattern requires that you learn to temper your strong will and modulate your emotions to allow for the needs and desires of others.

Red jasper is a stone to maintain your confident sense of self. Moonstone will connect you to others. The 203rd day of the year reduces to five, adding the quality of adaptation and versatility to this path, which will help you become more flexible.

OBJECTS/IMAGES
dew, mothers, periscopes, showers

SHAPES/MATERIALS
opals, kerosene, palm fronds, all white stones

COLORS
milky white, rose, butter yellow

ANIMALS
crab, shrimp

PLANTS, HERBS, EDIBLES
cream cheese, egg whites, chickweed, cauliflower

ESSENCE
jonquil

SOUND/RHYTHMS
a baby's cry, Cat Stevens's "Peace Train"

MUSICAL NOTES
C and E

DEEP SPACE OBJECTS
Kappa Ursa Major, Al Kaprah, Front Toes of the Bear

July 22

YOUR SIGNS
Cancer/Leo

———

YOUR ELEMENTS
Water/Fire

———

YOUR RULERS
Moon, Neptune, Jupiter, Sun
29 degrees Cancer–
00 degrees Leo
Third Decanate, yin
First Decanate, yang

The Astrological Interpretation

You have worked hard to build a foundation for your life, an internal home that is a source of strength and inner refuge. You take this dwelling with you wherever you go, making it easy for you to travel and be among different kinds of people. You are constantly experimenting with creative possibilities as you endeavor to build beautiful additions to your "house." Working with children and young people comes naturally to you. You are yourself a child at heart who looks forward to enjoying free time and playing with your friends. You are especially fond of water sports, beaches, and seafood. A cruise to a romantic island with a special loved one is your idea of a perfect vacation—staying there endlessly, your concept of a perfect life!

Our two major lights, the moon (Cancer) and the sun (Leo) rule July 22. The watery, emotional nature of Cancer is brightened by the fiery Leo nature, and Cancer sensitizes Leo. However, water puts the fire out and the challenge for July 22 will be to balance introverted and extroverted sides. Those born with a Cancerian influence may have reputations for being avid collectors. Colored glass and bottles may be particularly appealing. You may also collect something unusual, such as antique watering cans or water jugs. Cancer prefers silver and Leo gold. Consider placing silver picture frames and gold-plated mirrors around your home.

Outdoors, you are comfortable in both day and night environments. A cupola or rooftop where you can go and see the dawn and also be close to the full moon is an asset for you. If there is a large body of water in the distance the picture is complete. In your garden have a lily pond and a section for sunflowers. By surrounding yourself with objects, flowers, and materials from both signs you'll never rain on your own parade.

A Kabbalistic Interpretation

The Wheel of Fortune card combines with other influences this day to create a situation ideal for all forms of travel. It may even be that your career involves traveling. For recreation it is likely that you will enjoy any fast-moving form of transportation, whether that's a powerboat, go-cart, or rollerblades. You should give some thought to making a vacation of driving across the country or at least travel where you are free to cover a fairly large area.

One word that is equivalent to the value of this day is the Hebrew word that means "calamity." This indicates that you may be accident-prone or awkward. You can help yourself by buying a seven-pointed star to wear as a pendant, which will give you more luck in life than you are used to experiencing.

Most of us have one or more of the four basic elements missing or underrepresented in our makeup. In your case that element is air. Air relates mainly to thought processes and ideas and is very useful when it comes to getting new projects off the ground or tackling a puzzling problem. You can encourage the air element in yourself by burning frankincense and keeping some yellow ornaments around the house.

A Numerological Interpretation
YOUR MAGIC NUMBERS: 2 AND 6

The twenty-second day of the seventh month reduces to two, the number that means duplication and replication. Born on this day, you have a path of susceptibility to suggestion. This pattern asks that you master your ability to act on your hunches and learn to discern the practical applications. Your enthusiasm can be contagious. In fact, you can be a bit like the pied piper, luring others off on a fantastic voyage that hasn't been thought through. Don't lose your passion for life, just add the ingredient of logic.

Carnelian and sodalite will ground you and fuel your logical mind. Indigo is a color to maintain your equilibrium. The 204th day of the year reduces to six, contributing the important element of balance and symmetry. This will help you keep things in perspective. Remember to look at all sides of a situation before you march off into the sunset, playing your flute.

OBJECTS/IMAGES
votive candles that float, gold and silver charms

SHAPES/MATERIALS
glitter, canvas

COLORS
silver, burnished gold, carmine, chartreuse

ANIMALS
lion cub, hermit crab

PLANTS, HERBS, EDIBLES
goldenseal, raisins

ESSENCES
balm perfumes

SOUNDS/RHYTHMS
a cackling laugh, island hot night rhythms

MUSICAL NOTES
C# and F

DEEP SPACE OBJECT
Beta Cancer

July 23

YOUR SIGN
Leo

YOUR ELEMENT
Fire

YOUR RULER
Sun
00 degrees
First Decanate, yang

The Astrological Interpretation

Your birthday is definitely influenced by Cancer—we might even say that you are symbolized by a mythological creature with the head of a lion and the body of a crab. Not a pretty sight, you might say! But look at the possibilities. You have the potential for the lion's courage and masterfulness, its passion and its poise. Yet you also possess the sensitivity of the sea creature, mindful of its intimate connection to the mother of all life, the ocean. Properly balanced, you have the grace and strength of the land animal as well as the compassion and understanding associated with water. That is quite a collection of cosmic gifts.

July 23 is often very attractive to the opposite sex. You tend to dramatize many life situations and can get so caught up in your own theater that you vacillate from "show" to "show." Express your ideas rather than imitating others and you will feel more rooted. Use your dramatic skills to decorate your home. Putting furniture on different levels in a room will appeal to you. Place a medallion of the sun and your family name over the fireplace. You might also find a ceramic clock with a sun face. Consider long dresses and double-breasted suit jackets for flair in your personal wardrobe. A large topcoat for men gives the impression of royal robes. You like shining trinkets of all kinds: crystals, gemstones, hair ornaments, and especially the glint of gold. Men should indulge in brightly colored ties and women in scarves. In your bedroom have a large bed and heart-shaped pillows. Leo rules the heart, and July 23rd needs to "fall in love" with himself to build confidence.

Outdoors a garden with large showy flowers will delight you. Dahlias, asters, bougainvillea, oleander, and hibiscus are all good candidates.

A Kabbalistic Interpretation

The energies of this day are strongly masculine. What that means is that you are likely to have the qualities, both positive and negative, that were traditionally associated with men, such as leadership potential, physical courage, and a natural capacity to defend your beliefs fiercely. It would certainly be worthwhile to cultivate some traits that are historically seen as feminine such as warmth, compassion, and receptivity to others. You can remind yourself of this by wearing some blue and green in your outfits.

Fairness is extremely important to you and this is indicated by the influence of the Justice card. In your dealings with others you always try to see their side of the situation. It is likely that you have a lot of respect from your colleagues for this approach. An emerald ring, especially worn on your little finger, will help to enhance this quality.

At work as well as at home you are an excellent facilitator of other people's self-development. You have a sense of openness in your dealings with people and like to reflect that sense in your physical environment. If at all possible you should find a home with an open plan or large airy rooms with sliding rather than hinged doors.

A Numerological Interpretation
YOUR MAGIC NUMBERS: 3 AND 7

The twenty-third day of the seventh month reduces to three, the number of multiplication and imagination. This pattern calls for you to be open to every possible circumstance in order to glean priceless knowledge. At your best, you realize that no experience is too small or insignificant to contain a great lesson. This path is like the princess who was willing to kiss the toad and was rewarded when the curse fell away; the humble and unattractive toad was restored to being a handsome prince. Immerse yourself in even the silliest of society's activities, for yours is a path of drawing out archetypal significance, and applying what you learn to your own growth and unfoldment.

Yellow jasper is a gem to help you appreciate the beauty in simple things. Amethyst will bind you to your higher self. Decorate in shades of yellow to clarify and intensify your mind. The 205th day of the year reduces to seven, providing a deep sense of peace and satisfaction with your journey.

OBJECTS/IMAGES
dawn, deserts, firstborn children, royal couches

SHAPES/MATERIALS
satin brocade, hyacinth, precious metals, igneous rocks

COLORS
yellow, bittersweet, kelly green

ANIMAL
salamander

PLANTS, HERBS, EDIBLES
St. Peter's wort, brown rice, yellow pimpernel, marigolds

ESSENCE
myrrh

SOUNDS/RHYTHMS
rolling dice, shuffling cards

MUSICAL NOTES
D and F#

DEEP SPACE OBJECT
NGC 2623, peculiar galaxy

July 24

YOUR SIGN
Leo

YOUR ELEMENT
Fire

YOUR RULER
Sun
00–1 degrees
First Decanate, yang

The Astrological Interpretation

Your birth date reveals an individual who bursts forth into his or her surroundings like a powerful ray of sunshine. As the first degree of Leo, you may be a little naive about the potency of the creative force within you. At times, you shine too brightly and obscure other people's presence with too much self-importance. At other times, you do not shine brightly enough and tend to feel that it is you who are standing in someone else's shadow. Life calls to you to understand how to regulate your "creative frequency" so that you may contribute to and be accepted by the social circumstances you encounter in your environment. You are careful about your hair, as it is your favorite adornment. Like the lion's mane, you want it to state that you are virile as well as beautiful.

Work to emphasize and enhance your innate kindness. Without kindness and consideration your talents could lean toward pomposity and authoritarianism. You need a public forum in which to express yourself. Consider inviting the neighbors over for a discussion of ideas. You will feel comfortable in a home that is a beehive of activity. In your living room have a collection of chairs with a distinct style: a peacock chair, a wing chair, a Bank of England chair. Each "throne" has a mood, and you and your guests can take turns trying them out. Your symbol, the lion, should be present in a photo, collage, statue, or painting. If you draw, consider creating a painting of a lion looking toward a rising sun. Colors for you are burnt orange and crimson . . . though perhaps not together.

Outdoors, July 24 may have a special relationship with trees. From ancient times trees have been associated with different gods and goddesses and were said to have different emotional qualities. July 24 resonates well with sequoias, walnut trees, and baobab trees.

A Kabbalistic Interpretation

This is a day full of energies and influences that are typical of a Leo personality. There is a definite association with ideas of kingship or royalty. When it comes to furnishing your home you should opt for heavy traditional furniture. Try to find a large oak chair epecially for your own use.

Chesed, one of the second triad of sephira, is also important this day. Chesed is connected to the god Jupiter in its benevolent but judicial nature. One of the associations of Chesed is with mercy and forgiveness. You can help to generate and maintain such feelings by keeping two rich blue bowls by your bedside.

An important zodiacal influence is the sign Aries. Aries's fire acts to increase your already energetic nature. You are likely to enjoy a range of physical sports, the more demanding the better. Try sports with a sense of ruggedness and challenge such as rock climbing.

A Numerological Interpretation

YOUR MAGIC NUMBERS: 4 AND 8

The twenty-fourth day of the seventh month reduces to four, a number representing the principles of order, classification, and tabulation. Born on this day, you have a path of utilizing the principle of ordering the routine aspects of your world in order to free up the latent talents and gifts that beg to be developed. You feel at home with military precision and understand the underlying reason beneath discipline and formality. When details are ordered automatically, there is much more time to pursue avenues of new exploration.

Pursue trophies and medals as evidence of your accomplishments. Put on your dress blues, and attend a formal occasion. At your best, you are capable of earning the esteem of others and exercising a gift for leadership. Your troops would follow you into the gates of hell. Labradorite is a gem to connect you to your emotional nature. The 206th day of the year reduces to eight, adding a sense of rhythm and flow to this process. Enjoy parades, especially the marching bands.

OBJECTS/IMAGES
rituals, full-spectrum lamps, an obelisk, males

SHAPES/MATERIALS
alectoria (stone), reception halls, shape of a racing track, amber

COLORS
poppy red, tawny yellow, teal

ANIMAL
jaguar

PLANTS, HERBS, EDIBLES
sun tea, safflower oil, walnuts, turnsoles

ESSENCE
musk

SOUNDS/RHYTHMS
parade music, theme songs

MUSICAL NOTES
D# and G

DEEP SPACE OBJECTS
Xi Puppis, Asmidiske, the Stern

July 25

YOUR SIGN
Leo

YOUR ELEMENT
Fire

YOUR RULER
Sun
1–2 degrees
First Decanate, yang

The Astrological Interpretation

Your orientation to life is based on expressing your unique personality. You may thus consciously acquire certain quirks, traits, and characteristics of dress and demeanor that work to set you apart from others. Sometimes you feel that you would just like to blend into your surroundings, finding peace in anonymity. But this mood lasts only a short time, and then you once again project your special image into life.

You are restless and may not feel sure of your work or profession. Rest assured that you have abilities and talents; seeking how to best apply them is a worthwhile endeavor. Amber is a stone you may enjoy wearing or keeping on your desk. Have lots of mirrors in your home and workplace and hang a prism above the mirror to create rainbows. A library or book-lined room is a restful place for you. You will enjoy decorating your home with unusual fabrics and are especially fond of orange, gold, and bright pastels. Your metal is gold, so if you feel down in midwinter due to lack of sunlight, wear gold jewelry.

Outdoors, July 25 wants a yard that has an entryway. If you can grow olive trees in your climate, do so, as they are very supportive of your energy. Or try walnut or citrus trees. Include a lion's head fountain in your garden. If you place a bird feeder where you can see cardinals and scarlet tanagers your retreat will be complete. No matter where you wander you'll always have company to come home to.

A Kabbalistic Interpretation

Your day is deeply influenced by the number three, a number linked to ideas of creativity. Other aspects of this day make it likely that you will express this aspect of your nature through some sort of visual art. A good gift for you would be a set of watercolors and fine sable brushes.

The element of air is very strong this day. Linked with other influences—particularly the Fool card—this can give you something of a dreamy personality. When it comes to the purely pragmatic side of life you may find that you have difficulty keeping organized. A really good set of steel kitchen knives hanging in your kitchen should help you increase your efficiency overall.

It is a common idea that a fool is incredibly close to wisdom, and this is certainly true of your own personality. At one level you seem to live only for the enjoyment of the moment. However, you have a deep level of understanding that assists you as you negotiate the complexities of human relationships. When you feel the need to be particularly joyous in your life wear something with a red and yellow pattern, and your cares will drop away.

A Numerological Interpretation
YOUR MAGIC NUMBERS: 5 AND 9

The twenty-fifth day of the seventh month reduces to five, a number signifying change, adaptation, and uncertainty. The path of those born on this day is one of being pushed to the limit in order to evolve or change into someone larger than they presently are. Imagine yourself poised at the edge of a precipice, pursued by a dangerous foe. You can fight or leap into the void, but you cannot remain on the edge. Either choice will change you forever and enlarge your sense of who you are.

This pattern is one of continual thresholds you are required to cross and new horizons of conquest you are offered. Try parachuting or mountain climbing to stretch your limits. At your best, you excel in a crisis. The danger of this path is one of charging ahead without thinking, or jumping off a cliff unnecessarily. Howlite and lapis are gems to keep you centered. The 207th day of the year reduces to nine, adding the element of attainment, completion, and goal achievement. This influence keeps you motivated.

OBJECTS/IMAGES
halos, Christmas ornaments, playrooms

SHAPES/MATERIALS
gold ore, fur

COLORS
yellow-brown, bright yellow, lemon yellow, China blue

ANIMALS
racehorse, sea lion

PLANTS, HERBS, EDIBLES
blueberries, celandine, eyebright

ESSENCE
orange water

SOUNDS/RHYTHMS
a rhythmic heartbeat, a mummer's parade

MUSICAL NOTES
E and G#

DEEP SPACE OBJECTS
Gamma Cancer, Asellus Borealis, the Northern Donkey

July 26

YOUR SIGN
Leo

YOUR ELEMENT
Fire

YOUR RULER
Sun
2–3 degrees
First Decanate, yang

The Astrological Interpretation

There is no such thing as growing old in your astrological forecast! You have the fire of eternal youth within you, and as you progress through middle age and beyond, you cultivate the company of younger friends and admirers. You like to keep up with what is new and dress in the latest fashions and styles. In fact, you tend to spend a good portion of your income on personal adornments and ornamentation. Watching your budget is definitely not one of your favorite things, and you have to take care that you do not spend above your means. Friends mean a great deal to you and you tend to play favorites, sometimes choosing one as your special "consort" and sometimes another. Loyalty is an essential quality in those few people you allow to be close to you.

July 26 is always on the move. An image for you is a carrier wagon with a tarpaulin cover. Such wagons used to be associated with traveling road shows. Your panache and abilities enable you to be your own road show. At home you may enjoy having a special relaxation costume: pipe and slippers is a good image for a man, or if you are a woman you may enjoy the luxurious simplicity of a flowing kaftan. Deep reds and oranges are for you. July 26 may have an interest in mythology, and images of the various sun gods would be perfect decorative objects. Wear plenty of gold in the winter months when there is less sunlight.

Outdoors, July 26 likes to use nature as a backdrop for schemes and plans. Why not a small amphitheater in your backyard? You could do free shows for the neighborhood. Consider a garden space filled with sunflowers, dahlias, and orange gladiolas. Grow grapefruit trees if your climate allows.

A Kabbalistic Interpretation

Success, success, and more success—this is what drives you above all else. In today's competitive world, having such determination is extremely useful and may even be essential in some careers. You do need to keep an eye on your emotional life though, as the word *lament* is also indicated in this day. Keeping a vase of pink roses on your desk should help you to give attention to your loved ones.

The Strength card from the tarot is a strong influence on your day, once again connected to ambition and drive. In order to maximize your chances of staying the course and achieving your goals, consider keeping a small statue of a lion in the south of your home. In addition wearing emerald green on critical days will help.

Another important factor in your personality is the effect of the letter *Zayin*. It means "sword" in Hebrew and is again an influence related to drive and a willingness to fight for one's aims. In leisure terms it may well be that you would enjoy some form of martial art, especially one that involves more thought than physical strength. Equally you might like to try your hand at war games.

A Numerological Interpretation
YOUR MAGIC NUMBERS: 6 AND 10

The twenty-sixth day of the seventh month reduces to six, the number of balanced polarities and the harmony of opposites. Six equalizes the teeter-totter of seemingly opposing forces through the healing power of love. Born on this day, you have a path of understanding and honoring the contributions of the past, while also looking ahead with optimism to the promise of the future. This is a path of cooperating with forces and influences that on the surface seem to compete with one another. This is a pattern of examining contrasting values and synthesizing the worth inherent in each.

Adventurine is a gem to harmonize your mental and emotional natures. Blue violet is a color to deepen your insights. The 208th day of the year reduces to ten, adding ease of transition from endings to beginnings. This aids your awareness of the hidden connection between the old and the new.

OBJECTS/IMAGES
a carnival barker, picnics, hairbrush

SHAPES/MATERIALS
rubies, stadium shapes, amber

COLORS
magenta, apple green, fire engine red

ANIMALS
peacock, Arabian horse

PLANTS, HERBS, EDIBLES
eglantine, mistletoe, dill

ESSENCE
bergamot

SOUNDS/RHYTHMS
a lion's roar, a sun dance

MUSICAL NOTES
F and C

DEEP SPACE OBJECTS
Delta Cancer, Asellus Australis, the Southern Donkey

July 27

YOUR SIGN
Leo

YOUR ELEMENT
Fire

YOUR RULER
Sun
3–4 degrees
First Decanate, yang

The Astrological Interpretation

You are proud of your achievements and don't mind that other people know it. Whether it is a new suit or dress you have purchased, or a new lover that you have conquered, you will let other people know that you have achieved the object of your desires. Generous to a fault, you tend to reward people who have been kind to you with gifts and other tokens of affection. Yet your mood can change radically if you feel you have been betrayed, and someone who was at the center of your heart will find himself totally outside of your immediate circle. You like personal communication toys such as cell phones, handheld computers, and fax machines. You might enjoy sending highly personalized messages at odd times of the day or night.

You can easily rise to a quarrel but also attach your temper to a cause for justice. Learning how to rule your anger is a lifelong challenge. At home exercise your leadership abilities in your domain. A work area with a large swivel chair on wheels facilitates moving to wherever you need to be. Emphasize your loyalty by keeping pictures of a pride of lions on the veld. You might even have jungle noises on tape or on your computer. It will give you a laugh. Another image for you is the circus ringmaster. He keeps it all going no matter if the dog act goes awry. In your bedroom have an old-fashioned set of combs and brushes. If you are bald it doesn't mean you are less a Leo; caress your head and use a musk scent to stir your nature.

Outdoors, July 27 enjoys the sun and may want to mount a punching bag or basketball hoop. This is the place to shake off your cares. If your "sports center" is in sight of large yellow and red flowers such as gladiolus and rose mallows you'll get an aesthetic charge as well as a workout.

A Kabbalistic Interpretation

One of the meanings of the value for your day is "uneducated." It is always important when engaging in a kabbalistic interpretation to avoid being too literal and to look underneath the obvious to what is really being indicated. Taking all the other factors of this day into account what is suggested here is that you have a preference for physical rather than mental exertion. You are extremely well-suited to most sports and outdoor activities. In particular you should really enjoy riding horses.

The Fortune card tells us that travel is a very good experience for you. Seek an occupation that requires you to spend at least part of your time on the road. You can maintain energy and enthusiasm for all this coming and going by keeping something richly purple in your car or travel bag.

Another word that matches the value of this day is "willing," which reflects a genuinely giving nature. Your friends and neighbors know that if they need a hand you are available. Growing sage and rosemary together on a windowsill in your kitchen will encourage your helpful spirit.

A Numerological Interpretation
YOUR MAGIC NUMBERS: 7 AND 2

The twenty-seventh day of the year reduces to seven, the number of victory and satisfaction. Seven is the period of temporary cessation after a period of activity or creation. Born on this day, you have a path of developing your own sense of the eternal. This pattern asks that you examine what it is you can really be sure of in life. Gaze at the night sky and ponder the mystery that the light we see may be from a star that burned out countless millennia ago, and yet the star is a luminous presence in our night sky.

Watermelon tourmaline is a stone to inspire your admiration of nature's creativity and diversity. Study astronomy and physics, especially Einstein's theory of relativity. Things are not always as they seem. The 209th day of the year reduces to two, adding the quality of reflection, assisting you to integrate the lessons you've learned during your cycles of rest between periods of activity.

OBJECTS/IMAGES
a roulette wheel, the spotlight, eyes

SHAPES/MATERIALS
vine shapes, rubies, spirals, cat's-eye

COLORS
gold, grass green, apricot

ANIMAL
lynx

PLANTS, HERBS, EDIBLES
honey bell, oranges, heliotrope, palm trees

ESSENCE
lime

SOUNDS/RHYTHMS
theater music, opera

MUSICAL NOTES
F# and C#

DEEP SPACE OBJECTS
Gamma Draco, Giansar

July 28

YOUR SIGN
Leo

YOUR ELEMENT
Fire

YOUR RULER
Sun
4–5 degrees
First Decanate, yang

The Astrological Interpretation

You have a great deal of creative equipment with which to succeed in life, but at times you can take things too personally. You wear your vulnerability on your sleeve and can feel rejected by a person who really means nothing to you in the long term. The truth is that you cannot be accepted, admired, or appreciated by everyone. Cultivate the quality of impersonality so that you do not run such highly charged emotional risks. The highs and lows are just not worth it and a more impersonal attitude to life will free up your time to become even more successful.

You have a natural taste for the finer things and would do well helping to create beautiful environments both for yourself and others. You have a deep respect for learning and talent in research. On the island of Delos in Greece there is an avenue of ancient lions carved in pure white marble. Delos was the island of Apollo, the sun god, and you would enjoy looking at pictures of these sculptures. A trip to Delos could be a highlight. Closer to home, you want a living space with a circular feel and a centrally placed chair, good for thinking and researching. In your wardrobe emphasize clothes with a dramatic flair such as capes or long coats. This birthday has a strong affinity with the sense of smell. Oils and essences such as orange, neroli, and lemon grass are particularly evocative.

Outdoors, you enjoy a combination of dry hot weather and the sea. A trip on an outrigger sailboat such as those that sail the Mediterranean is a perfect vacation for you. Spend some time watching sailboats glide on a river or a lake. For landlubbers, a hay wagon would be an interesting addition to your yard.

A Kabbalistic Interpretation

You are someone who tends to like a fairly private life, as indicated by some of the words associated with this day. You are very comfortable with the idea that "a man's home is his castle." In other words your home is your own wholly private domain free from intrusion by others. You should consider building a hedge, ideally of hawthorn, around your home for added seclusion.

The number eleven, highly significant this day, is long associated with magic and the occult. It may be that you already have a passing interest in the unknown and the mysterious. Buy yourself a pack of tarot cards or some basic books on practical occultism, as you may well find that you are a natural.

The letter *Teth* has a number of associations, but important to this day is the meaning "serpent." Other aspects of your day indicate an interest in the exotic, and you could find that getting yourself an unusual pet such as a lizard or snake may spark your imagination.

A Numerological Interpretation

YOUR MAGIC NUMBERS: 8 AND 3

The twenty-eighth day of the seventh month reduces to eight, the number of involution and evolution, the rhythmic ebb and flow of all the events and manifestations of the universe. Born on this day, you have a path of connecting to this vibratory rhythm, and internalizing the meaning of revolution and evolution. The great wheels of manifestation revolve in vast cycles. At the beginning of each new turning point, new ideas are seen as revolutionary. They are in fact the lubrication that turns the wheel.

Study famous revolutionary movements from history, including the American Revolution. What begin as radical thoughts act as leaven, transforming the societal recipe, and later form the basic architecture of a society. Chrysocolla and yellow jasper are stones to clarify your mental processes. The 210th day of the year reduces to three, adding to this path an intrinsic awareness of how the creative process unfolds. Each cycle should build on the foundations of the one before and benefit from the lessons and experience of that epoch.

OBJECTS/IMAGES
*large buildings,
gold leaf frames*

SHAPES/MATERIALS
brocades, carbuncles, circles

COLORS
*grapefruit yellow, vibrant reds,
turquoise, sunset orange*

ANIMALS
crocodile, glowworm

PLANTS, HERBS, EDIBLES
*blueberries, angelica,
St. John's wort*

ESSENCE
bitter orange

SOUNDS/RHYTHMS
*a peacock's cry, Elgar's
"Pomp and Circumstance"*

MUSICAL NOTES
G and D

DEEP SPACE OBJECT
black hole

July 29

YOUR SIGN
Leo

YOUR ELEMENT
Fire

YOUR RULER
Sun
5–6 degrees
First Decanate, yin

The Astrological Interpretation

You are a person who is shaped by the prevailing social trends in your environment. It is important that you fit in and do what is expected of you, not so much so that you may be considered a "good boy or girl," but so that you may anchor a position in society. You have firm values that you stick to no matter what forces oppose you. As a friend, lover, or parent you are steadfast and determined to be supportive of those close to you. It is important for you to know that you have contributed to their lives and you do not mind at all if they reward you through gifts and compliments.

The fixed star Presaepe will be located on some July 29 birthdays. The ancients considered this star to give a tendency for adventure and wantonness as well as great prowess and leadership abilities. You have respect for tradition and the formality of the past but want to bring all activities and personal style up-to-date. At home vary your decor and change paintings and photographs on the wall frequently. An image for you is the fire-eater. He seems to do the impossible and make it look exciting and easy. The carnival atmosphere that surrounds the fire-eater is just as important as the show itself. Your belongings such as wallet, key chain, checkbook, or purse, should be ornate and individual. If you are a cook consider using saffron as a seasoning.

Outdoors, the direction for you is east. When beginning a new project you may want to get up at dawn on the day of the new moon and pray toward the east. At home a sundeck would be a wonderful addition to your home. Vines growing around your home and bright sunflowers complete your world.

A Kabbalistic Interpretation

One equivalent of the value of this day is the Hebrew word that means "shine," and that is exactly what you try to do in life. Other energies in this day suggest that you possess a number of qualities that will draw you to other people's notice. If you want to give those qualities a helping hand keep a mixture of fresh basil and laurel in a little pouch in your pocket.

Having a desire to be noticed and appreciated for your abilities does not mean that you are in any way selfish or try to blot out other people's light in trying to reveal your own. The Justice card's influence this day indicates that you are a deeply fair person. If you want to remain fair and just in your dealings with others keep a turquoise elephant statuette in the west of your main living space as a reminder.

You are an enormously energetic individual, mainly revealed in your ability to generate new ideas with enormous speed. At work this can be a useful talent as well and it also provides an interesting home life. Maintain your mental energy by keeping a single white candle burning beside you in the evenings.

A Numerological Interpretation

YOUR MAGIC NUMBERS: 9 AND 4

The twenty-ninth day of the seventh month reduces to nine, the number signifying attainment, fulfillment, and the achievement of the ultimate goal. Born on this day, you have a path of idealistic self-expression and the pursuit of excellence through personal handicrafts and cultural artifacts of your own design. This pattern is one of uniting with the principle of creative fire and of literally breathing life into your creations. Study unique crafts such as glassblowing, tatting, and cloisonné. Collect and display one of-a-kind artifacts from cultures around the world; their diversity will inspire you. Serpentine is a gem that responds to carving and designing into beautiful shapes and settings. Use blues and greens to stimulate your creativity. The 211th day of the year reduces to four, adding the important quality of measuring, surveying, and the principle of naming to your artistic endeavors.

OBJECTS/IMAGES
a scepter, a parade, jewel cases

SHAPES/MATERIALS
a proscenium shape, teardrop shapes, diamonds

COLORS
saffron, delph blue, butterscotch yellow

ANIMALS
peacock, panther

PLANTS, HERBS, EDIBLES
cinnamon, oranges, gin

ESSENCE
bergamot

SOUNDS/RHYTHMS
triumphant music, shuffling cards

MUSICAL NOTES
G# and D#

DEEP SPACE OBJECT
supernova

July 30

YOUR SIGN
Leo

YOUR ELEMENT
Fire

YOUR RULER
Sun
6–7 degrees
First Decanate, yin

The Astrological Interpretation

Your birth date is concerned with the cultivation and use of willpower. Once you conceive a project, you martial inner and outer resources and proceed, not resting until you have completed your task. Sometimes the opposition you encounter is not so much a test of your determination and talents as it is life asking you to halt, reexamine your motives, and take another direction. It is up to you to know when adversity is a friend in disguise. This can be especially true in relationships when the other person's heart may not be conquerable, no matter how much you love and how hard you try.

Two fixed stars, Asellus Borealis and Asellus Australis, lie within the province of July 30 birthdays. The Aselli are the donkeys ridden by Vulcan and Bacchus in the war between the gods and the titans, and they bring courage, patience, adventure, and wantonness. Your fire element needs to be moderated by cooling herbs like eucalyptus, hyssop, and lemon. Gold with a slightly rosy tint is powerful for you. At home, have a special oversize chair where you gather your thoughts. If the chair is near a sunny window all the better. A canopy bed completes your bedroom. Stuffed lions, paintings, or miniature china lions will all keep you tuned into the generosity and magnificence of your abilities. History should interest you, especially the lives of monarchs, and you will enjoy picture books of castles and palaces.

A telescope for stargazing is a wonderful toy for July 30. You might even be able to see the Aselli and feel your stellar roots. A colorful garden with cedar, ash, or palm trees is a playground for you. For summer parties, have some flaming torchlights. The effect will be dramatic and in keeping with your favorite element.

A Kabbalistic Interpretation

We live in a world where the ability to act as a team player is increasingly important. You are particularly adept at keeping the unity of a group going, especially when the odds are stacked against you. Books about explorers beating all the obstacles raised against them would make interesting additions to your shelf.

Luck is important in your life, and many of your important life changes come as the result of chance meetings or opportunities. You can maximize the luck in your life by using circular shapes in laying out your home and office arrangements.

One of the words that shares a value with your day is the Hebrew word that means "knot." In the sense of tying things together, this increases the image of you as someone happiest in a team. At the same time knots represent complexity and intricacy, and the weaving together of different elements. Look for jewelry and art objects for your home with traditional Celtic and Anglo-Saxon patterns. The intricate interlace will inspire you.

A Numerological Interpretation

YOUR MAGIC NUMBERS: 1 AND 5

The thirtieth day of the seventh month reduces to one, the number of new beginnings, originality, and singleness of purpose. This day's path contains the mission of refining your receptivity and intuition. This is a pattern of feeling pushed to the limits of your tolerance only to receive guidance and miraculous solutions if you take the time to pray. Born on this day, you are asked to develop patience and faith, which will be rewarded handsomely. Your blessings will come unbidden and unexpected. Wake before dawn on a summer morning, and walk at sunrise with bare feet in the dew-covered grass. Thrill as the damp flowers, closed for the night, open their hearts to the warmth of the sun. Wear yellow to enhance your cheerfulness and optimism. Rhodonite and citrine will strengthen your will. The 212th day of the year reduces to five, adding the critical element of flexibility and versatility to this path. Strive always to adapt.

OBJECTS/IMAGES
a sundial, spotlights, showboats

SHAPES/MATERIALS
fusilli, spirals

COLORS
tangerine, blood red, golden yellow

ANIMAL
sea lion

PLANTS, HERBS, EDIBLES
sun tea, eyebright, marigold

ESSENCES
lemon, rosemary

SOUND/RHYTHM
applause

MUSICAL NOTES
C and E

DEEP SPACE OBJECT
supernova

July 31

YOUR SIGN
Leo

YOUR ELEMENT
Fire

YOUR RULER
Sun
7–8 degrees
First Decanate, yin

The Astrological Interpretation

You are an ambitious person who definitely wants to reach a place of secured success in life. You have a strong need to provide for your family or, if not married, to supply yourself with the necessities, and luxuries, of life. Your pride might stand in the way of asking for help from people in positions of authority, but this characteristic must be overcome to get the training and experience that will support you. You are especially fond of leisure and enjoy sensual pleasures. Rich and fancy foods, large and exotic buffets, and fine wines tempt your palate. But make sure to exert the extra effort life requires in order to get the education and knowledge it takes to move up your personal ladder.

Some July 31 birthdays will be located on the fixed star called the South Asellus. The South Asellus was rumored to be a position of fevers and potential slander. July 31 may very well burn, but it is due to the strength of idealism and ardor that shines within. An image for you is a glassblower; watching the deftness with which glass is blown one can easily forget the heat and the consequences of a mistake. At home have some items of handblown glass as decorative objects. Red frill dishes piped in yellow would perfectly suit Leo's love of color. At home a sunroom with large white peacock chairs would be the perfect environment for you to get through the winter or enjoy summer.

Outdoors, you enjoy pyramid shapes. The pyramid with an eye in the center, which appears on one-dollar bills, is an occult symbol for July 31. Building your garden around this symbol might be interesting and profitable. Plant tickseed, dahlias, and marigold.

A Kabbalistic Interpretation

The number nine is important to this day, carrying a sense of duty and obligation. Your sense of loyalty to others is high and you can be trusted by all around you. Any decoration with a chain pattern, which is symbolic of connection and ties to others, will help you in your intentions to be dutiful and loyal.

Loyalty is indeed a wonderful quality, but be sure to temper it with a full understanding of the motivations of those around you. The

Hebrew words for *innocent* and *green* both have an equivalent value to this day. This suggests that you can be somewhat naive in your dealings with others. Keeping a lead figurine in the west of your bedroom will help you to develop a little healthy cynicism.

The letters *Teth* and *Gimel* both have an influence in the energies of your personality. The serpent Teth and the camel Gimel are both extremely resilient animals. Other signs in this day also indicate that you have a strong determined streak in your nature. Growing sunflowers in your garden will enhance that aspect of your nature.

A Numerological Interpretation
YOUR MAGIC NUBMERS: 2 AND 8

The thirty-first day of the seventh month reduces to two, the number connoting reflection and receptivity. Born on this day, you have a path of understanding your particular place in the scheme of things by how you are mirrored and reflected in the world around you. Pay close attention to the people in your life and any event that seems to recur. The world reflects the Divine to us, and your connection to a higher order should be cultivated through a deep communion with nature. Spend time outside; this will nurture your spirit. Open your windows and drink in the sound of an early morning rain shower. Take a deep breath of moist, fresh air.

Rainbow jasper will connect you to the earth and remind you of the pot of spiritual gold at the rainbow's end. The 213th day of the year reduces to six, adding the element of beauty and symmetry. It is vital for you to have a shrine to beauty, whether an altar in your home or a well-tended garden. Water your flowers at sunset; you'll see the fairies and fireflies dance out of the corner of your eye.

OBJECTS/IMAGES
a flaming triangle, towers, stadiums

SHAPES/MATERIALS
satin, white sand, straight columns

COLORS
magenta, lime green, russet

ANIMAL
bobcat

PLANTS, HERBS, EDIBLES
bay leaves, olives, passionflowers

ESSENCE
neroli

SOUNDS/RHYTHMS
the musical scale of C, vaudeville songs

MUSICAL NOTES
F and C#

DEEP SPACE OBJECTS
Beta Ursa Minor, Kochab

August 1

YOUR SIGN
Leo

YOUR ELEMENT
Fire

YOUR RULER
Sun
8–9 degrees
First Decanate, yin

The Astrological Interpretation

This birth date is symbolized by a lion coiled up and ready to pounce on its prey, and yet he holds himself back from the expression of his full power. The meaning refers less to personal inhibition and more to wise restraint in the wild release of passion. You are a highly sensual, romantic person, yet if you project your intentions too strongly, you just might frighten away the object of your desires. Diplomatic and careful courting of an intended partner is a much better way to go about things than the intensity of a full frontal attack. This same discretion should be used in your business and professional dealings. There is no lack of determination in your advances, but you will obtain better results with a more subtle approach.

The objects you surround yourself with should be chosen to calm and moderate your intense energy. The answer is creative activity. You will enjoy many forms of games, especially cards, interactive videos, and charades. Think about taking up glassblowing or surrounding yourself with handblown glass. Your collection will require care, and watching the light through the various pieces of glass will focus your mind and help channel your energy. Crafts that require manual dexterity are excellent pursuits. Cooling herbs like mint and basil are very good for August 1. Also sleep with light-colored sheets, no reds, blacks, or purples; yellow or white will help balance you while you sleep.

Outdoors, August 1 wants a garden to wander in. Pacing is calming and gets the creative juices going. A maze or path through the grass would be perfect. Evergreen trees and low green bushes are excellent plants to inspire you and to keep your energies flowing in a balanced way.

A Kabbalistic Interpretation

One of the words with a strong connection to the value of this day is the Hebrew that means "sorcerer." This same Hebrew word, *Aub*, can mean a necromancer or a powerful ghost. With such associations you may be drawn to read about or involve yourself in the mystery traditions of the world. An item for your living room is a low cedar wood coffee table. Cedar has associations with magic going back to very early traditions.

You are most influenced by the Temperance tarot card, giving you a gentle and understanding nature. The effect of Temperance is to create an awareness of balance and harmony in all our relationships. A water feature of some sort in your garden, especially in its center, will bring out your milder side. Water is a powerful influence in your life, as the letter *Mem* is also represented in the kabbalistic analysis of this date. *Mem* is a positive emotional symbol dealing mainly with the creation or beginning of emotional relationships. By keeping a mixture of roses and tulips in your home you will be able to prolong the excitement that you find in the early stages of your relationships.

A Numerological Interpretation
YOUR MAGIC NUMBERS: 9 AND 7

The first day of the eighth month reduces to nine, the number of fulfillment and completion. Nine carries a need for culmination in whatever you set out to do. You don't like to rest until things are finished. Born on this day, you have a path of recapturing the spirit of delight that is possible with a childlike approach to life. The magic inherent in this pattern is enrichment of your personal life when you align with your larger sense of the world. Reclaim your sense of wonder.

Take a friend to the park, and push as high as you can on the big swings. Play in the sandbox, and climb the jungle gym. You possess a refinement of spirit that complements your innocence. Sugilite, a purple gem from South Africa, will enhance your openness of mind. The 214th day of the year reduces to seven, a number meaning victory and rest after labors. This facilitates innocent, childlike sleep after your healing periods of play.

OBJECTS/IMAGES
*thick mane of hair,
gold charms on a bracelet,
a showboat*

SHAPES/MATERIALS
*hyacinth (stone), amber,
gold lamé*

COLORS
*sunshine yellow, rusty orange,
Christmas red, sky blue,
grass green*

ANIMALS
ocelot, crocodile

PLANTS, HERBS, EDIBLES
*laurel, marigold, lemon trees,
fennel*

ESSENCES
mandarin, lemon verbena

SOUNDS/RHYTHMS
*saxophone jazz, the crackle of
a fire, a bugle blowing reveille*

MUSICAL NOTES
G# and F#

DEEP SPACE OBJECTS
*Alpha Cancer, Acubens,
the Claw*

August 2

YOUR SIGN
Leo

YOUR ELEMENT
Fire

YOUR RULERS
Sun, Mars
9–10 degrees
First Decanate, yin

The Astrological Interpretation

Your birth date brings with it a number of crises of transformation that will test your ability to reorient your life. The purpose of such situations is to allow you to release those people, places, and values that no longer have any essential meaning to your creative potential. You do not have to find yourself at the edge of the precipice before deciding to leave a situation and look elsewhere for success. Make your move before you are too exhausted to do so. If you examine your life, you will see that each time you have released and moved on, you have qualitatively improved your career, relationships, and financial prospects— not to mention your self-confidence.

Some August 2 birthdays fall on a critical degree. Whatever highs and lows come to you as a result, your gift for finding gold in rocks that look ordinary and useless will carry you through. Pleasurable and opulent surroundings suit you. Have a few columns on the front facade of your home with circular steps leading up to the front door. A doorknob in the center of the door would please you. Inside, decorative touches from the French court at Versailles may interest you. The fleur-de-lis is a shape for you, and sunburst designs could grace your furniture or drawer pulls. Colors for your personal wardrobe should stay in the red/orange/yellow spectrum, especially during gray winter days.

Outdoors, a terraced garden highlights your sense of pride. Sunflowers, golden daisies, peonies, and poppies are flowers that will brighten your spirits. Arrange your yard so that you have room for a garden and some free grass for games. Croquet may be particularly appealing. Urban dwellers should visit gardens where they can take photos or sketch. Keeping a beautiful environment in mind helps you when the sun isn't shining.

A Kabbalistic Interpretation

It is not very easy for other people to get close to you or to feel that they know you in any significant way. One of the words associated with this day is the Hebrew word that means "wolf," and while wolves run in packs, you are the image of the lone wolf, preferring to lead a private life. When roused to anger you can become quite fierce. A home that is decorated in a traditional style, with plenty of wood, will help you feel more mild and relaxed.

The Devil card from the tarot often suggests a great deal of sexual energy in an individual. In other cases it represents a concern with the material and worldly ambition. In your case, it suggests a degree of cynicism and world weariness. When you bathe try adding a few drops of rosemary and jasmine oil and you will begin to a find a much more joyful approach to life.

A Numerological Interpretation
YOUR MAGIC NUMBERS: 10 AND 8

The second day of the eighth month reduces to ten, the number of embodiment and final completion of the process begun in the number one. Yours is a path of celebrating your achievements and accomplishments in the context of your social self. This pattern evokes the understanding that nothing humans do occurs in a vacuum. What we accomplish is given meaning by the acknowledgment and recognition of our family, friends, and community. Our deeds flow out to others. Involve yourself in organizations that give awards and recognition. Work where you can give and receive medals and plaques. It's not the trophy that is important, but sharing your achievements with others.

Jade, an ancient gem prized by many cultures, will anchor you to the earth and inspire your admiration. Study the history and lives of great achievers. The 215th day of the year reduces to eight, adding the important realization that even the most celebrated accomplishments are fleeting.

OBJECTS/IMAGES
casinos, desert sun, kings and queens

SHAPES/MATERIALS
circles, diamonds, amber, rhinestones

COLORS
orange, indigo, teal

ANIMALS
firefly, lioness, peacock

PLANTS, HERBS, EDIBLES
golden alexanders, knapweed, rose hips

ESSENCE
musk

SOUNDS/RHYTHMS
jazz, a school bell

MUSICAL NOTES
A and G

DEEP SPACE OBJECT
nova

August 3

YOUR SIGN
Leo

YOUR ELEMENT
Fire

YOUR RULERS
Sun, Jupiter
10–11 degrees
Second Decanate, yin

The Astrological Interpretation

If you examine your family background—its spiritual and ethnic traditions and roots—you will find much depth, meaning, and strength that can be incorporated into your own way of life. This is true even if you had problems with your family growing up. You do not like being told what to do and are much better at giving than taking orders. There is a natural tendency for you to take charge and be in control of the people closest to you. Although you may do this from a deeply protective place, you still have to be careful not to cut people off from the right to make their own decisions (and mistakes!).

August 3 brings childlike delight and great versatility to life. Your instincts are highly developed, and you have great skills in getting the spotlight on you. Theater and films, especially musicals and comedies, are excellent for you. As August 3 evolves, spiritual interests and sharing your generosity become more important. The solid oak tree is an image for you. In ancient mythology, the oak tree was the symbol of Zeus, king of the gods. Whenever you feel dispirited or angry go tell your troubles to an oak tree. You may find surprising relief. At home, you want space and furniture that is large and somewhat imposing. Southern exposures with wide windows are good. In the winter use full-spectrum lighting instead of fluorescents, as these will help you maintain your energy. Take a brief walk in the morning so that you get some sun. Amber jewelry is a talisman for you.

Consider hanging a swing from your trusty oak tree in the yard. Swing with the sun in your face and your eyes closed, and see all the colors of the rainbow. Lacking an oak, any tree will do—the important element is to have a playground for yourself.

A Kabbalistic Interpretation

Influences around your day suggest a strong interest in the past. You may well love history or genealogy. Particularly suggested is a love of cultures that have retained a strong connection with the natural world. You can bring this passion into your home by using decorations and ornaments form these cultures. Hang an authentic dream catcher above your bed.

Catastrophes occur from time to time in all of our lives. The presence of the Tower card in your date suggests that you will go through a number of life changes that will be extremely difficult for you. However, the link to the Tower card comes from the union of the letters *Heh* and *Mem*, indicating that these changes when they come will be for the best. Keeping a vase of lilies by your bedside will help you accept changes when they come to you.

A Numerological Interpretation
YOUR MAGIC NUMBERS: 2 AND 9

The third day of the eighth month reduces to two, the number of reflection. Two is the mirror in which one sees oneself. Born on this day, you have a path of applying all the lessons of the past, yours and those of humanity, to the problems of the present and future. This pattern calls for you to develop your powers of looking backward. At your best, your mind is like a legal library, locating exactly which case to refer to when seeking to apply a principle. Visit senior citizens centers, and listen to the stories of your elders. Volunteer at a nursing home, and keep your mind open to the marvelous stories and memories. Tell your own stories to your children, grandchildren, nephews, or nieces. Write your memoirs.

The danger of this path is a tendency to live in the past because it is a known entity. Orange sapphire is a gem to awaken your memories. The 216th day of the year reduces to nine, adding the wonderful element of endings to your frame of reference. You instinctively know that nothing lasts forever.

OBJECTS/IMAGES
crown jewels, lion tamers, charm bracelets

SHAPES/MATERIALS
circles with rays, brass, brocades

COLORS
mandarin red, gold, royal purple, rust, midnight blue

ANIMALS
ocelot, racehorse

PLANTS, HERBS, EDIBLES
sunflower seeds, goldenseal, green olives

ESSENCES
orange water, hibiscus

SOUNDS/RHYTHMS
limbo, island rhythms

MUSICAL NOTES
C# and G#

DEEP SPACE OBJECT
quasar

August 4

YOUR SIGN
Leo

———

YOUR ELEMENT
Fire

———

YOUR RULERS
Sun, Jupiter
11–12 degrees
Second Decanate, yin

The Astrological Interpretation

Money and financial success are important to people born on this day. You like to drive a new car, wear expensive clothing, and eat at the finest restaurants. It is important for you to impress people and you feel very complimented when brief acquaintances remember your name and the circumstances surrounding your meeting. You are also concerned that your partner take pride in his or her looks. You can balance your intensity by learning how to relax: literally let your hair down, put on some sloppy jeans, and just hang out every now and then.

August 4 is generous and easily leads by persuasion. You have a talent for seeing what is advantageous to you and following through to obtain it. Many times these experiences will be about self-growth. Part of your generosity is sharing his/her development with family, friends, and perhaps a wider circle. Your home is open and hospitable, and you like to entertain. Stock your pantry with two of each item, as you never know when you'll need an extra bottle of salsa and bag of chips. Mirrors are wonderful decorative items for you. Gilt or gold-plated ones are especially pleasing. In your bedroom have a few robes to lounge in.

Outdoors if your home has a deck that leads into a garden area you have the perfect setup for summer lawn parties. Hang a badminton net between two oak trees. Flowers for August 4 are dahlias, hibiscus, trumpet honeysuckle, and the shrub pineapple guava.

A Kabbalistic Interpretation

You approach each day with a sense of optimism and anticipation. This is in part the result of the influence of the Star card from the tarot, whose protective energy means that you tend to meet little in the way of obstacles in life. The element of water has a positive effect on your personality. You can increase your general happiness by keeping some gleaming goldfish in a bowl in your living room.

One meaning of this day is to "seize" or "lock up." In work terms this could mean that you might be suited to a career in law enforcement or as a museum curator. In your personal life it indicates a need to keep your personal thoughts very close to your chest. You might like to buy yourself an attractive diary that you can lock or a bureau with hidden drawers where you keep all your most personal things and thoughts.

When it comes to your emotional life you have a tendency to feel a little insecure. You can be very possessive and worry whether your loved one is being faithful to you. The sapphire is a gem associated with fidelity; giving a sapphire ring to your partner may help to settle your internal fears.

A Numerological Interpretation

YOUR MAGIC NUMBERS: 3 AND 1

The fourth day of the eighth month reduces to three, the number of unfoldment and creative expression. Three needs to grow and is in constant motion. Born on this day, you have a path of carefree and innocent involvement in every creative opportunity your life presents. This pattern provides the opportunity to heighten your sensitivity to rare opportunities and momentary or serendipitous chances to explore your aspirations. Keep your antennae up and moving. Your open mind and eagerness to explore are great assets.

Play games such as bridge or chess, which require you to focus your attention, memory, and intuition. Apache flame agate and fire opal are gems to fire your imagination. The 217th day of the year reduces to one, which helps keep you on your toes, always ready for the next signal that's right around the corner.

OBJECTS/IMAGES
rulers, mansions, dawn, gold coins, Superman and Superwoman logos

---

SHAPES/MATERIALS
rare woods, hyacinth, palm shapes, gold

COLORS
yellows, coral, crimson

ANIMAL
lion cub

PLANTS, HERBS, EDIBLES
sunflowers, Rice Krispies, viper's bugloss (herb), walnuts

ESSENCE
tangerine

SOUNDS/RHYTHMS
the buzz of a casino, brass bands

MUSICAL NOTES
D and C

DEEP SPACE OBJECTS
Alpha Ursa Major, Dubhe, back of the Bear

August 5

YOUR SIGN
Leo

YOUR ELEMENT
Fire

YOUR RULERS
Sun, Jupiter
12–13 degrees
Second Decanate, yin

The Astrological Interpretation

You delight in accumulating experiences that you can turn into anecdotes to amuse your friends. You have no problem dramatizing or slightly changing a situation in order to prove a point or give your audience greater amusement. Children will love for you to read them stories or, even better, to make up a game in which you fully participate. Kind and sincere, generous and well-meaning, you can nevertheless take yourself too seriously and have to be careful that you do not mutate your concept of reality into the world of fantasy. You enjoy reading travel adventures, romantic novels, and children's books. Travel is a number one priority on your list, and you will take every opportunity you can to book an airplane ticket and be off to some exotic locale.

In addition to great energy and passion, your goal is to achieve mastery of all situations. Your home should feature a rocking chair, and if it is placed on a front porch with a view of the sea, you will be supremely content. A combination living/reception hall gives you a sense of importance and pride. Near the bedroom, a separate dressing area with a dressing table and gold-plated brushes, combs, and hand mirrors suits your taste and delight in personal grooming.

Although yours is a fire sign, there is a fondness for sailboats and nautical themes. Old maps of sea voyages or antique schooners remind you of places to explore, with you as ship's captain of course! An elevated area in the garden where you can survey the land gives you a feeling of satisfaction. Flowers like dahlias and marigolds are especially pleasing.

A Kabbalistic Interpretation

Your mind is your greatest asset in life. You have a good memory and can use it creatively. If you have children you will be able to tell them wonderfully detailed stories of your own childhood. Buy a scrapbook and start jotting down all sorts of personal anecdotes, as you never know what they might become.

You are decidedly a night person and always feel much more alive once the sun sets. One of your greatest enjoyments is basking in the sense of peace that the nighttime brings. Make sure you have heavy curtains of a dark material and use candles to light your rooms when you curl up on your sofa to relax at night.

Friendships are extremely important in your life—you probably have a wide circle of people to whom you feel a close and special bond. To help yourself fully express your affection for people use blue and violet in your outfits. When socializing find some earrings or a tie with a rabbit pattern on them, as these will enhance your feelings of friendship and closeness with others.

A Numerological Interpretation

YOUR MAGIC NUMBERS: 4 AND 2

The fifth day of the eighth month reduces to four, a number signifying order, classification, and measurement. Born on this day, you have a path of pageantry. Your pattern asks that you involve yourself in the exhibition of your own and your community's accomplishments. This is not the arrogant strutting of a rooster, but rather a genuine and proud sharing. Attend a county fair where the contributions of many people are on display to be enjoyed and appreciated. Volunteer for children's theater. Make costumes. Organize a parade with marching bands from regional schools and floats constructed by local citizens.

Peridot and moss agate are stones to feed your creativity. The 218th day of the year reduces to two, contributing the influence of duplication and replication, making it easier for you to repeat your successes. Repetition is the mother of retention.

OBJECTS/IMAGES
a telescope, brass buttons

SHAPES/MATERIALS
the horizon, cat's-eye, gold coins

COLORS
tangerine, red-purple, royal blue, butterscotch, rust

ANIMALS
sea lion, ermine

PLANTS, HERBS, EDIBLES
turmeric, primroses, angelica,

ESSENCES
orange water

SOUNDS/RHYTHMS
ships' bells, polka beat, ragtime music

MUSICAL NOTES
D# and C#

DEEP SPACE OBJECT
external galaxy in Hydra cluster

August 6

YOUR SIGN
Leo

YOUR ELEMENT
Fire

YOUR RULERS
Sun, Jupiter
13–14 degrees
Second Decanate, yin

The Astrological Interpretation

Your birth date embodies the urge for self-development and the actualization of your creative urges. You will find that you have quite the dose of "divine discontent," as your surrounding circumstances may inhibit the fuller expression of your talents and abilities. This can be a blessing in disguise, as you will never see the end to your willingness to explore the many avenues open to you. No matter how passionate you feel about your ideas, there is an important difference between your creative impulse and the disciplined effort over time that it takes to get things done right. The key word is commitment. If you are involved in a project or relationship, take it through to its next step, or if need be, to its conclusion. Watch how things unfold naturally, without you having to push them all of the time. Be more concerned with your path and less obsessed with your goals.

August 6 may attract publicity in whatever field of endeavor he/she chooses. A thought for August 6 to keep in mind is: "true creativity comes with the death of ambition." Your home should be a creative workshop with numerous "toys" and art supplies. A video camera might be a way of studying life for you. You easily see the dramatic possibilities in everyday situations. Decorate your walls with bold colors and murals. Octagon shapes may be particularly appealing to you. A pool table would be a perfect relaxation toy. The colored balls rolling around will also stimulate your creativity. Children, your own or other people's, interest you, and you have a natural talent for teaching and communicating with them.

Outdoors, August 6 likes hilly ground that commands a view. If your climate permits, consider a series of terraced gardens with citrus trees.

A Kabbalistic Interpretation

You have a special talent for connecting with people and helping them see the good side of life. The Sun card and the Temperance card come together this day, indicating a personality full of warmth and benevolent feelings. To keep these feelings at their height, hang some brightly painted sun images in your bathroom.

The letter *Tzaddi* has a significant impact on the way in which you approach your life. *Tzaddi* means "fish hook," symbolizing an ability to be extremely tenacious in getting what you want or need from life. To do this you must maintain the right focus and will. Keeping a clear quartz crystal in the northeast corner of your living room will help you develop your ability to positively focus on your goals.

There is a real need for a genuine sense of belonging expressed in the value of this day. If you live in a large city you may feel somewhat alienated and at times lost and alone. Consider moving to a small town, but if this is not possible, keeping reminders of your past in all your rooms will help you to feel more secure.

A Numerological Interpretation

YOUR MAGIC NUMBERS: 5 AND 3

The sixth day of the eighth month reduces to five, the number signifying change, transition, and uncertainty. Five is unpredictable. Born on this day, yours is a path of learning to rebound from whatever life presents. This pattern asks that you rise the morning after a terrible storm and see the crystal clarity that the storm's cleansing vehemence has wrought. You are charged with learning the significance of the healing and purification processes of life. Nothing remains the same, and just like spring cleaning, the process of change can be messy and uncomfortable. Have a predictable grandfather clock in your foyer for a soothing sense of stability. Topaz and golden beryl are gems to open your mind and heart to the possibilities of rainbows. The 219th day of the year reduces to three, which provides the innate awareness of nature's growth and unfoldment.

OBJECTS/IMAGES
stockbrokers, rituals, pride, masterpieces

SHAPES/MATERIALS
rare woods, tigereye, concentric circles

COLORS
ruby red, lemon yellow, orange

ANIMALS
salamander, firefly

PLANTS, HERBS, EDIBLES
fine wines, viper's bugloss, heart trefoil, sundew

ESSENCE
Rosmarinus pyramidalis

SOUNDS/RHYTHMS
Richard Wagner's "Ride of the Valkyries"

MUSICAL NOTES
E and D

DEEP SPACE OBJECTS
Lambda Leo, Alterf

August 7

YOUR SIGN
Leo

———

YOUR ELEMENT
Fire

———

YOUR RULERS
Sun, Jupiter
14–15 degrees
Second Decanate, yin

The Astrological Interpretation

You are born at the exact midpoint of your sign, Leo, the most "fixed" degree of this segment of the zodiac. You carry all of the pride, passion, and potency of this sign to its fullest extent. It is important for you to be recognized as an expert in your field, a success in your enterprise, and a winner in your relationships. You are not a particularly humble person and do not take career losses or romantic failures lightly. In fact, you take everything about yourself with great seriousness, even if you are the first one to laugh at your own foibles—as long as no one else laughs at them! You can be generous to a fault but should not expect others to give back measure for measure.

Your showmanship is a talent, especially when it is used to share your abilities with others. Your home and personal style should reflect your flair. A sunporch or solarium is a place to recharge. Glass balls that resemble bubbles are good decorative objects. You may want to have some bubble liquid and blowers handy. Watching the colors reflected in the bubbles keeps you in touch with the sublime. Decorate indoors with yellow and red flowers. Around your sunporch you might plant vines such as ivy or bougainvillea.

August 7 likes to create a dramatic outdoor space. A shape for you is the arch. Investigate photographs of the lion's gate of ancient Mycenae. This ancient structure was the entry to Agamemnon's palace. You might want to create your own lion's arch as an entry to your garden. Fill your garden with sunflowers and hibiscus flowers. They celebrate the sun and make you feel your kingdom is rich.

A Kabbalistic Interpretation

The energies of this day make you very attractive to others. Even when many of us are past the time when we can turn heads you still attract a fair share of admirers. In addition the influence of the Devil card from the tarot means that you have a powerful sexual appetite. Include some dark purple in your outfit whenever you really want to make an entrance.

In the workplace you cut a very different figure and are likely to be the image of responsibility. It would be unusual for someone born on this day to not be in a managerial position. You need to be careful that you are not too judgmental in your treatment of your staff. Try decorating your office with cream and pale blue ornaments and you will find that you become a more understanding boss.

The influence of the Moon card from the tarot is slightly negative this day. This is largely because of the solar nature of all the other energies that affect your personality. As a result you may feel tense or depressed around the time of the full moon. You can combat this by carrying a yellow jasper stone with you at these times.

A Numerological Interpretation
YOUR MAGIC NUMBERS: 6 AND 4

The seventh day of the eighth month reduces to six, the number connoting beauty, symmetry, and the balancing of polarities. Born on this day, you have a path of living the true essence of community. This pattern calls for you to immerse yourself in group efforts, preferably creating something beautiful and harmonious as a result. A vocal group or chorale is an excellent expression of this principle. The whole is greater than the sum of its parts. When the efforts of the individuals come together in a blended result where single voices aren't heard, the overall sound is triumphant.

Involve yourself in some kind of team effort. Tourmaline and fluorite are gems whose colors blend to make a more beautiful whole. The 220th day of the year reduces to four, contributing the influence of order and measurement. This aids your innate appreciation of the mathematical and geometric underpinnings of beauty.

OBJECTS/IMAGES
a castle on a hill, emblems, a casino

SHAPES/MATERIALS
shield shapes, diamonds, spirals

COLORS
lemon yellow, royal purple, apple green, honey

ANIMALS
Great Dane, starfish

PLANTS, HERBS, EDIBLES
pimpernel, aromatic saffron, grapefruit

ESSENCE
tuberose

SOUNDS/RHYTHMS
trumpet flourishes, a marching band

MUSICAL NOTES
F and D#

DEEP SPACE OBJECTS
Zeta Puppis, Naos

August 8

YOUR SIGN
Leo

YOUR ELEMENT
Fire

YOUR RULERS
Sun, Jupiter
15–16 degrees
Second Decanate, yin

The Astrological Interpretation

You can awaken suddenly from a sleepy period in your life and spring forward with enormous, passionate vitality. On the other hand, you can move seemingly effortlessly from an extremely charged battle with life into a passive and very laid back state, as if nothing of importance had taken place. Your powers of recuperation are excellent, and you should maintain a healthy vigor throughout life. If there is any weak spot, it is your heart. It tends to get broken. You put so much of yourself into your relationships that you can become easily disappointed when those closest to you do not live up to your expectations. But take note: these are your expectations, and they may have little to do with the other people's abilities or interests.

You have a talent for forgiveness and have come to the realization that it is only when we can forgive the people and understand the situations plaguing us that we can begin to recuperate and heal. An image for August 8 is the sunshine that comes after a storm. At home surround yourself with pictures of your goals and desires. You may want to draw sun rays around images or objects that particularly interest you. Your personal wardrobe should include a very comfortable terry cloth robe or a robe similar to those that prizefighters wear. Decorative objects or a walking stick or cane from olivewood resonates strongly with your nature. The Mediterranean area in general is restorative for you because of its sunshine. A trip to Italy, Spain, or Greece would be very special.

Outdoors, if you can grow citrus trees and create a clearing where you and guests can sit and pluck an orange or tangerine, then you are in your element. Large yellow, red, and pink flowers are the best choices for your garden. Anemone, pink rockrose, and yellow horned poppy are a few possibilities.

A Kabbalistic Interpretation

The planet Saturn has a major influence on your personality. On the positive side you have a very wise head on your shoulders and will be able to take on roles of considerable responsibility. Paired with this is a tendency toward melancholy. Soften this tendency by decorating your main living room in autumnal colors such as russet and olive.

The World card from the tarot indicates that you are someone who can always be relied on to get a job done. You will be in great demand at work to ensure that all projects are completed on time. At home for relaxation you may find that you enjoy pastimes that demand completion such as mental puzzles or computer strategy games.

The letter *Kaph*, which is connected to the hand, is important to this day. Taking into account other factors in your personality this suggests that some form of manual work would be a good way for you to relax. The connection with Saturn points in the direction of gardening as a hobby, possibly growing your own vegetables.

A Numerological Interpretation
YOUR MAGIC NUMBERS: 7 AND 5

The eighth day of the eighth month reduces to seven, the number of victory and promise. Seven connotes a temporary period of cessation after an interlude of activity. Born on this day, you have a path of mastering the processes of nature. You have a powerful and penetrating mind, and you desire to learn the principles and reasons behind why things work. This pattern asks that you keep probing the mysteries; your ultimate success is assured. Purify your motives. The danger of this path is sticking too much to the rule book. Remember, sometimes it is better to color outside the lines.

Have a chemistry set that you can tinker with to exercise your scientific muscles. Work in research and development if you can. Keep pansies and violets on your windowsill. Amethyst and citrine are gems to intensify your powers of concentration. The 221st day of the year reduces to five, providing the quality of adaptation to your process. You always search for the means to the end.

OBJECTS/IMAGES
the stage, emblems, castles, therapeutic lamps

SHAPES/MATERIALS
rare woods, pyrite, tigereye, the shape of a scepter

COLORS
lime, forest green, golden yellow

ANIMALS
salamander, lion cub

PLANTS, HERBS, EDIBLES
calendula, almonds, chamomile, key lime pie

ESSENCE
amyris

SOUNDS/RHYTHMS
Greek dulcimer music

MUSICAL NOTES
F and D#

DEEP SPACE OBJECTS
Beta Ursa Major, Merak, Ñloinâ

August 9

YOUR SIGN
Leo

YOUR ELEMENT
Fire

YOUR RULERS
Sun, Jupiter
16–17 degrees
Second Decanate, yang

The Astrological Interpretation

You have a way of looking into people's hearts and acting upon their inner needs and wishes. You therefore like nothing better than to bring joy into people's lives through special gifts and favors—especially if they have not asked you for them. You only wish that you had limitless financial resources so that you could make everyone's dreams come true. But what of your own dreams? Do you expect people to have this same sensitivity and orientation toward your secret desires? Too often you do, and that is when you can become disappointed. Give when and as you wish to, but give freely, without attachment.

August 9 goes to a beat of a different drummer. If you feel misunderstood try not to bear a grudge toward those who can't follow. Flexibility and compassion are the best ways for you to reach success and contentment. Sun medallions in your home remind you of your ruling planet. Consider yellow for your kitchen with sun imagery on towels and even stenciled on cabinets and drawers. With Jupiter ruling your decanate you may like a spacious home with lots of room. Frequently, those born on your birthday have an interest in aviation. August 9 might like large model airplanes as decorative objects. Your artistic abilities tend toward visual or performance. If you like to paint, have a large roll of paper that you can pull down and paint right on the wall. Finger painting might be a way of beginning to enjoy swirling colors on paper.

Outdoors, you like to entertain, and a barbecue in the yard is a perfect way. A stainless steel outdoor fireplace would also be good. Flowers for you are hardy orange, poppy anemone, and coreopsis.

A Kabbalistic Interpretation

Your day's value tells us that on the whole your life is going to run pretty smoothly. Planting a nut tree in your garden such as a walnut tree could significantly enhance your luck. Using some almond essence in an oil burner will also have a positive impact.

One of the words that is equivalent to the value of this day is the Hebrew word that means "joy." You are aware of your fortunate situation in life and you intend to make the most of it. You are excellent company to be around, as your enthusiasm tends to be infectious. If you really want to spread your positive energy, make sure to wear either fresh lemon yellow or grass green in your outfit.

This day has a lot of fire energy coursing through it, and at times you do need to dampen this intensity with some water energy. One approach to energize the water element within yourself is to make a ritual out of a regular bath time. Take time over your bathing and consider lighting some scented candles to illuminate the bathroom while you are in the tub.

A Numerological Interpretation
YOUR MAGIC NUMBERS: 8 AND 6

The ninth day of the eighth month reduces to eight, the number of rhythm, vibration, and evolution. Born on this day, you have a path of getting into the flow of your relationships. This pattern is one that generates social intercourse and provides the ability to master working with others in more informal settings. You have a naturally pleasant disposition and can positively influence others with your sunny charm. Volunteer for the PTA, or coach a children's soccer team. You can make a tremendous difference in others lives if you are willing to get involved. The danger of this path is a tendency to self-indulgence, or the belief that you can charm your way out of anything without consequence. Moss agate and green quartz will connect you to your optimism and integrity. The 222nd day of the year reduces to six, adding the influence of balancing polarities and harmonizing opposites. This comes in very handy when you are looking for a fourth for bridge.

OBJECTS/IMAGES
athletes, castles, circuses, minarets

SHAPES/MATERIALS
gilt, round shapes, hyacinth (stone), felt

COLORS
royal purple, turquoise, chartreuse

ANIMALS
kingfisher, Lipizzaner stallion

PLANTS, HERBS, EDIBLES
centaury, chamomile, clementines, eucalyptus trees

ESSENCE
lime

SOUND/RHYTHM
Edward Elgar's "Pomp and Circumstance," a tambourine

MUSICAL NOTES
G and F

DEEP SPACE OBJECTS
Lambda Ursa Major, Tania Borealis

August 10

YOUR SIGN
Leo

YOUR ELEMENT
Fire

YOUR RULERS
Sun, Jupiter
17–18 degrees
Second Decanate, yang

The Astrological Interpretation

The special magic in your relationships with others is your ability to add vitality to social situations. Your natural optimism is very encouraging, and you have a highly developed sense of humor, allowing you to see the ridiculous in the somber, the pretentious in the pompous, and the silly in the serious. You have many friends and admirers as a result of your buoyant attitude. Perhaps you have learned the art of seeing what is important in life but not taking yourself too seriously. Physical exercise, especially when it comes to keeping the spine supple, is advised, as you may not be too excited about getting your hands dirty and you like to relax as much as possible.

The word for this day is *shining*. August 10 has considerable mental abilities and reverence for community activities, which blend this day's individual "shine" with group harmony. You like to be surrounded by glittery materials—gold, of course, but sequins or costume jewelry are also good. Your home should be spacious with perhaps an arch leading into the living room to give a suggestion of a stage or performance space. A convenient ballroom would be nice! Bright, sunny windows are essential, and venetian blinds rather than curtains are preferred. A den with a large prominent chair is a power spot for you. A profusion of furniture, art, and props abound in your interiors, as you are more interested in the exuberance of sharing life than in keeping order. Gold-framed mirrors that reflect the sun keep you cheery even in the midst of winter.

Outdoors you like wide expanses of forest or parkland usually with some hills or elevated areas. Hills of daffodils leading into a forest are energizing. If there were a thronelike chair at the top of a daffodil hill, you could sit and contemplate how to get people working together on various inventions and projects.

A Kabbalistic Interpretation

The two elements of earth and water are well represented in the energies of this day. This means that you are likely to be at your happiest when constantly surrounded by nature. Make sure that at home and work you keep plenty of lush plants. If you do this and keep a vase of water in the west of your home you will feel centered and secure in your life.

A lack of fire and air energy in your personality can make you feel lethargic at times and also prevent you from making the changes necessary in life to set you off in new and exciting directions. Keep a picture of some sunflowers on your desk at work and eat more spiced foods such as apple with nutmeg, as these will help energize the fire and air elements.

One of the values of this day has the same value as a Hebrew word meaning "earthenware pot" or "jar," which were traditionally used to collect water. If you buy some clay jars you should paint them red and leave them empty. This will provide an appropriate means of uniting all the elements.

A Numerological Interpretation

YOUR MAGIC NUMBERS: 9 AND 7

The tenth day of the eighth month reduces to nine, the number of attainment and completion. Born on this day, you have a path of ceremony. This day's pattern calls forth your awareness that your life and very existence stem from a higher order of being. At your best, your life itself is a sacred ritual. You love to develop practices and customs to honor the things you hold dear. This is not idle superstition but a way to be true to enduring values. Celebrate your rituals, and share them with others. This will strengthen your faith in the Divine. Blue zircon and carved hematite are stones to maintain your abiding sense of tradition. Live where you can watch the seasonal movements of the sun. Watch the sun rise on the equinoxes and solstices, and burn sacred sage to purify your heart. The 223rd day of the year reduces to seven, contributing a sense of commitment and a promised oath to your ceremonies.

OBJECTS/IMAGES
crowns, scepters, picture windows, resorts, sunporches

SHAPES/MATERIALS
minarets, balcony, spotlight, olive wood, hairbrushes, hyacinth (stone)

COLORS
vibrant yellow/gold, bright orange, carmine red, royal blue, kelly green

ANIMALS
starfish, sea lion

PLANTS, HERBS, EDIBLES
sunflowers, chamomile, marigolds, dill, lemon trees

ESSENCES
sandalwood incense, spicy smells

SOUNDS/RHYTHMS
processionals, brass groups, cicadas whirring

MUSICAL NOTES
G# and F#

DEEP SPACE OBJECTS
Epsilon Leo, Ras Elased Australis

August 11

YOUR SIGN
Leo

YOUR ELEMENT
Fire

YOUR RULERS
Sun, Jupiter
18–19 degrees
Second Decanate, yang

The Astrological Interpretation

This is a Leo birth date that is deeply connected with the art of conversation and communication. There is a fountain of creative ideas bubbling inside of you, and your natural orientation is to project these concepts into life with such enthusiasm that you immediately gain loyal support for your plans and goals. You definitely want others to benefit from your ideas so that all may prosper, yet you have to make sure that you are consistent in the way you nurture people with your creative vitality. Be careful not to involve friends or coworkers in projects, only to shift your attention away from them once they have agreed to participate. Work to develop a true sense of equality in all that you do and avoid taking the "lion's share."

There is a rebellious streak in you and a desire to change existing conditions, which connects you to your spiritual nature. This side of your personality will sustain you if the party lets you down. An image for you is a star surrounded by many rings. Your job is to keep your star sparkling through good health, generosity, and moderate activity. At home have a large wing chair where you can face the sun and think. Put your furniture on casters so you can easily change the design of your rooms. Mirrors that catch the sun particularly please you. In addition to a few large ones, position smaller mirrors in strategic places throughout your home. It is good to carry a small gold-plated compact with you. It is not vanity for you to check yourself out; looking in the mirror gives you a centered feeling.

Outdoors, you need the sun and large oak trees. A tree house for children and adults is a perfect place for a party or a retreat. In the sunny part of the yard a colorful garden with sunflowers and marigolds reminds you of your own shining life.

A Kabbalistic Interpretation

One of the values for this day is equivalent to the value of the Hebrew name Eve. In Kabbalistic terms this connection reveals you to be a person of great passion and self-belief. On those rare occasions when you begin to doubt your sense of direction, visit an art gallery and look at some impressionistic landscapes. These visits can help you find any lost confidence in your chosen goals.

The feminine nature of the Eve association is balanced by the masculine influence of your key planet, Mars. Mars acts to increase your passionate nature and may lead you to be temperamental in emotional matters. On those days when you feel agitated try wearing a mixture of blue and orange.

You are a very self-motivated businessperson. It is likely that your role in the office will involve making deals with other individuals, and you may even be an entrepreneur. Your dynamic martial nature urges you to close each deal as swiftly as possible. Wearing a lily of the valley in your buttonhole may help you to take the slower but more successful route in negotiations.

A Numerological Interpretation
YOUR MAGIC NUMBERS: 1 AND 8

The eleventh day of the eighth month reduces to one, the number of singleness and unity, representing the conscious mind. Born on this day, you have a path of ferreting out your perceived inadequacies, and overcoming them. In fact, this pattern requires that you turn deficiencies into strengths. This is like the heroic path of Helen Keller, or the accomplished orator who began life with a speech impediment. Identify the areas of your life that you perceive to be weaknesses, and then settle for nothing less than triumphant success in overcoming them. Wear red to increase your energy level. Ruby is a gem to light the fire of your ambition. The 224th day of the year reduces to eight, adding the influence of rhythmic cycles to your experiences. Contained within eight is the sense of the real power hidden beneath outward appearance.

OBJECTS/IMAGES
a citrus grove, smiley faces, a magic wand

SHAPES/MATERIALS
charcoal briquettes, gold sequins, fusilli pasta

COLORS
magenta, bright yellow, rose, sea foam green

ANIMALS
tiger, tomcat, a party animal

PLANTS, HERBS, EDIBLES
St. John's Wort, mistletoe

ESSENCE
bergamot

SOUNDS/RHYTHMS
reggae music

MUSICAL NOTES
C and G

DEEP SPACE OBJECTS
Mu Ursa Major, Tania Australis

August 12

The Astrological Interpretation

Take care that you are not seduced by flattery and compliments. If you grow beyond such narcissism, you come into the higher nature and greater potential for this degree of Leo. You are capable of devoting yourself to causes and issues that can be of great benefit to others. The generosity of spirit that is so strong within you has an opportunity to reveal itself. You will feel most at home working for the rights of children and the advancement of education. Yours is also a fun-loving spirit, and you will be entirely in your own element in amusement and theme parks, cruise ships, and sporting arenas.

The fixed star Algenib, or Al Gambi, will be located on some August 12 birthdays. The ancients considered that this star brought many changes into the life, gave a slightly bombastic tendency, and facilitated artistic perceptions and expression. Keep contact with your inner light so that what you present will be in keeping with your inner self. An image for August 12 is a circus that must constantly be put up and taken down. The enjoyment of life exists whether the show is open or closed. Star shapes are very pleasing to you. Give yourself your own star dressing room! Include a playroom for yourself and your children at home. Look for southern exposures and maximum sunlight. Your color scheme should be in the red, yellow, and orange spectrum. A poster or painting of a sunrise is a wonderful decorative object.

Outdoors, August 12 wants sun and space. An effortless slightly wild garden is for you. Feature foxglove and delphiniums. You have a sacred sense of the continuity between older values and modern ones. You might consider some symbols or objects from the Zuni people, who worshipped the sun, in your garden or outdoor space.

A Kabbalistic Interpretation

You are someone with a strong character, and your significant drive and vitality are obvious to all your friends and acquaintances. The solar nature of your personality puts all other aspects quite literally in the shadow. If you want to celebrate your fiery Sun-driven dynamism consider putting a gorse bush in your garden.

One of the words connected to this day means "plasterer." Like a plasterer filling holes and cracks in a wall to be painted, you also spend your time fixing cracks. But these cracks are in relationships rather than in walls. You can assist your talent at encouraging good relationships among people by wearing a midnight blue tie or scarf when speaking to people where a relationship problem exists.

The number twenty-four has an important effect on this date and on your personality. Its energy indicates the ability to hold considerable responsibility in life and to wield your authority carefully and fairly. A chair or table in your office made from the wood of an ash will help you meet the challenges of your office.

A Numerological Interpretation
YOUR MAGIC NUMBERS: 2 AND 9

The twelfth day of the eighth month reduces to two, the number of receptivity and reflection. Born on this day, you may develop the complementary aspects of your consciousness to the point of drawing all things necessary from your environment in every situation. This pattern calls for you to hone your mental processes to a fine point of receptivity. What is the influence or mechanism that draws a lost animal across a continent to find its family? Study the behavior patterns of carrier pigeons or beekeepers.

The answers to every question already exist. Yours is a path of precision in asking the question, and patience and alertness in listening for the answer. Carnelian and blue agate are gems to amplify both hemispheres of your brain. The 225th day of the year reduces to nine, adding the quality of the pure, clear expression of a seed idea. This aids your process as it unfolds.

OBJECTS/IMAGES
sunscreen, stained glass, party favors

SHAPES/MATERIALS
a throne shape, sun-bleached cloth, burnished gold

COLORS
mandarin yellow, russet, bright blue

ANIMALS
cheetah, wildcat

PLANTS, HERBS, EDIBLES
French tarragon, St. John's wort, curry

ESSENCE
lemon verbena

SOUNDS/RHYTHMS
cheers, the sound of billiard balls breaking

MUSICAL NOTES
C# and G#

DEEP SPACE OBJECTS
Mu Leo, Ras Elased Borealis

August 13

YOUR SIGN
Leo

YOUR ELEMENT
Fire

YOUR RULERS
Sun, Jupiter, Mars
19–21 degrees
Third Decanate, yang

The Astrological Interpretation

Your sense of personal security is often uppermost in your mind. You need to know your pantry is full and that there is something stored away for tomorrow. Like a squirrel, you tend to hide special little treasures in nooks and crannies. Sometimes, you are amazed when you lift up a pile of socks and discover a small catch of misplaced dollars underneath. You often worry about things that have not happened yet. In terms of investment, you should go for the safe and secure. It is more natural for you to have long-term growth in a small-risk annuity than to leap into a high-risk venture, even though it may promise you much greater rewards.

August 13 has a vibrant nature that commands attention. You have leadership abilities and can be fierce if you feel thwarted. There is a touch of absolutism here! Shift your will to understanding and you'll be better able to moderate your life. At home calm your exuberance with azurite. You may find it helpful to have different "uniforms" for your activities: a martial arts suit for yoga and sports, an apron for kitchen activities; a floppy red dress or sweater for creative projects, and absolutely nothing for sleeping. August 13 needs a little drama and changing costumes helps you get in the mood. Sleep with white sheets; you don't need any nighttime stimulation.

An outdoor image for August 13 is an ancient magus in prayer on a mountain plateau. Greet the day with an exercise routine and mediation on the color red. If you can do your morning routine outdoors it would be great for your health. Flowers such as bleeding heart and marigold are perfect companions to your outdoor meditations.

A Kabbalistic Interpretation

A number of wise people have declared that love is all that matters. You are one of those rare people who can find within you the ability to be kind to almost everyone you meet. You never seem to bear a grudge and have a natural talent for forgiveness. Decorate your bedroom in a range of cream and pink tones to encourage your goodwill toward others.

The letters *Kaph* and *Cheth,* which influence this day, suggest that you act as something of a protector to those in your care. It is likely that your work involves dealing with children or other vulnerable individuals. A shepherd's crook would make a wonderful object for you: keep it in pride of place in your living room, as it represents the caring way in which you approach those who depend on you.

One quality you admire above all else is honesty. You have the highest regard for the truth and encourage the same in others. If you want to increase the positive effect of truth, try hanging a mirror with a white and gold frame somewhere in your home.

A Numerological Interpretation

YOUR MAGIC NUMBERS: 3 AND 1

The thirteenth day of the eighth month reduces to three, a number signifying growth, development, and unfoldment. Born on this day, you have a path characterized by childlike courage and optimism. Picture the force of curiosity and drive for self- mastery that drives a young child to conquer the environment and learn to walk or manipulate a spoon. This is a pattern that requires you to maximize any potential you find in your environment. Those around you may accuse you of rushing in where angels fear to tread, but your courage can be an example to others.

The danger of this path is that you may become like a two-year-old petty tyrant, always expecting to have your way. Try learning to write with the opposite hand. Amber and red jasper are stones to keep matters in perspective. Wear an amber pendant to open your heart to the feelings of others. The 226th day of the year reduces to one, contributing the need for new beginnings. This aids you in this path of self-discovery.

OBJECTS/IMAGES
a scepter, gold epaulets, a three-ring circus

SHAPES/MATERIALS
ruby, a crown shape, atomic molecules

COLORS
fuchsia, grapefruit yellow, burnt orange, scarlet

ANIMALS
shaggy dogs, mountain lion

PLANTS, HERBS, EDIBLES
walnut trees, rue, olives

ESSENCE
rosemary

SOUNDS/RHYTHMS
John Philip Sousa's marches, a sizzling fire

MUSICAL NOTES
D and C

DEEP SPACE OBJECTS
Gamma Ursa Minor, Pherkad

August 14

YOUR SIGN
Leo

YOUR ELEMENT
Fire

YOUR RULERS
Sun, Mars
20–21 degrees
Third Decanate, yang

The Astrological Interpretation

You sometimes express the simplicity and open faith of a child. You are definitely not a schemer. It is much easier and far more natural for you to be up front with your feelings and opinions than to try to mask them behind some false face. It is hard for you to tell when someone is not telling the truth, and all falsity surprises and distresses you. You need to cultivate subtlety, as it is hard for you to contain yourself, and at times you can overdramatize your enthusiasm and eagerness to be seen and heard. You are a natural-born actor and will be attracted to theater, opera, and film. You will enjoy people and countries that embody the flair and panache that are so much a part of your nature.

Some August 14 birthdays will be located on a critical degree. This means that you feel highs and lows in life intensely. Your intuitive mind is highly developed and you seem to find out just the right piece of information that you need. This same intuition allows you to understand how to lead and manage people. An image for you is an orchestra conductor tapping for attention and then giving the downbeat to begin. At home you might want to keep a conductor's baton on your desk. Spices in your food are appealing. If you like to cook, study Indian or Thai cuisine. Frequent changes in your daily patterns will keep your energy fresh. In your kitchen keep a wreath of laurel or bay leaves. In ancient times these were given to winning athletes. You might appreciate seeing that symbol of victory.

Outdoors, August 14 likes a dramatic environment set for entertaining and convivial gatherings. Potted geraniums and begonias may be more interesting to you than a whole garden. An interesting hobby could be raising carrier pigeons. They may carry a message to your true love!

A Kabbalistic Interpretation

The Fool card from the tarot has a considerable influence over this day. You have a lively manner that tends to be highly infectious. Whenever you are at a social gathering it is certain that everyone is going to have a great time. You should make sure that you have a good store of comedy videos on hand for nights when you are at home on your own.

In tandem with your love of great social occasions is your delight in good food. It is unusual for you to sit down to a prepackaged or take-out dinner, as you take a pride in preparing your own meals. You like to create a sumptuous spread if you have company. If you want to treat yourself well, make sure you have plenty of desserts available, especially premium ice cream.

Despite your outward good humor you may harbor certain negative or cynical ideas. One of your greatest fears is that the pleasure you have in life will somehow disappear. An excellent good luck charm for you that can help keep your optimism intact would be an Egyptian-style scarab beetle.

A Numerological Interpretation

YOUR MAGIC NUMBERS: 4 AND 2

The fourteenth day of the eighth month reduces to four, the number of the four-square physical world, and the stability of matter. Four is steady and predictable, but also mysterious. Born on this day, you have a path of gleaning the secrets and maximizing the interrelationships among inner realities and the material accoutrements humanity amasses. This path is similar to the biblical allegory of the talents. Resources, both material and those of our talents and gifts, are meant to be developed and shared with the larger community. To the degree that you develop and exalt these resources in your life, to that degree will you move yourself forward. That is how we contribute as individuals in moving the universe ahead toward higher forms of expression. Tigereye is a gem to heighten and intensify your aspirations. The 227th day of the year reduces to two, giving added impetus to introspection.

OBJECTS/IMAGES
a proscenium, an amphitheater, managers, emperors

SHAPES/MATERIALS
ruby, sun ray shapes, vine shapes, red gold

COLORS
saffron, salmon, vermilion

ANIMALS
ocelot, lynx

PLANTS, HERBS, EDIBLES
cinnamon, mahlepi, walnut oil, sun tea

ESSENCE
myrrh

SOUNDS/RHYTHMS
jingle of charm bracelets, official music

MUSICAL NOTES
F and D#

DEEP SPACE OBJECTS
M97, the Owl Nebula

August 15

YOUR SIGN
Leo

YOUR ELEMENT
Fire

YOUR RULERS
Sun, Mars
21–22 degrees
Third Decanate, yang

The Astrological Interpretation

When you step back and look at life, you sometimes feel that you are in a circus. You are very aware of the little dramas that take place and can be amused by the comedies as well as distressed by the tragedies. Many people admire your sense of bravado and the courage you have to be so open about yourself and your feelings. Yet others experience this self-projection as "too much personality" and can turn away from you, interpreting your urge to bring a smile as a need to dominate the environment. It is important for you to know your own boundaries so that you do not infringe on other people's space.

This birthday is meant to serve as well as to rule. Your spiritual nature leads you to explore and expand your knowledge and share that knowledge with others. To help you on your way keep a variety of aromatics, like sage and rosemary, around your home. Incense is a good idea. A magic wand or wand with a glass globe at the end inspires visions and dreams. Lighting is important to you, and you will use lamps and shades to their best decorating advantage in your home or office. A fireplace and mantel are wonderful points of focus in the living room. You may derive power from books of poetry. Keep some on the mantel with gold-colored book ends. Or why not write your own?

High mountains stir your poetic nature. In your backyard try to have a raised area where you can view the neighborhood. A raised deck will do if your yard is flat. A southern exposure so you receive maximum sun is ideal. The garden can be a bit of a jungle with no clear definitions among flower beds. Surround yourself with flowers that are tall and lively and reach for the sun, such as sunflowers, dahlias, and gladiolas.

A Kabbalistic Interpretation

This day is ruled by the tarot card the Hanged Man. This card indicates an ability to put your own desires on hold in order to help others to achieve their goals and ambitions. There are of course times when you will feel drained by the needs of those around you. If you keep four blue glass goblets with a yellow border in your bedroom you will find that you have much more energy in your life.

The letter *Lamed* affects this day, indicating that you have a strong sense of urgency. At times you may be working much harder and faster than is actually necessary in order to succeed. If you want to slow down a little, buy an old-fashioned oil lamp with an emerald-colored glass casing. If you keep this lamp on your desk at work then you will be less likely to burn the midnight oil when it is not necessary.

One of the values of this date is connected to a Hebrew word meaning "fearless." This connects with the energy of *Lamed*. You enjoy sports that have a built-in danger factor. Try bungee jumping or hang gliding. You'll no doubt find them exhilarating

A Numerological Interpretation
YOUR MAGIC NUMBERS: 5 AND 3

The fifteenth day of the eighth month reduces to five, the number of change, uncertainty, and adaptation. Born on this day, you have a path of responding to the challenges and opportunities life presents, and adapting. This pattern requires that you dig deep into the recesses of your creative process, and develop inventive ways to overcome what might, at first glance, look like obstacles. This is a pattern of turning stumbling blocks into stepping-stones. Study the lives of great inventors. Ride a camel across desert sands, and imagine the mechanism of evolution enabling the creature to store its own water supply during arid journeys. Yellow jasper and moonstone are gems to enhance your sense of self-sufficiency. The 228th day of the year reduces to three, adding the element of creativity to the novel solutions you envision.

OBJECTS/IMAGES
crowns, jewelry boxes, a snow globe with a castle inside

SHAPES/MATERIALS
diamonds, sunbeams, hyacinth (stone)

COLORS
yellow, red, gold, taffy, apricot

ANIMALS
panther, palomino horse

PLANTS, HERBS, EDIBLES
aloe vera, ash trees, chamomile flowers

ESSENCES
grapefruit, heliotrope

SOUNDS/RHYTHMS
humming, Indian ragas, a crackling fire

MUSICAL NOTES
E and D

DEEP SPACE OBJECT
supernova

August 16

YOUR SIGN
Leo

YOUR ELEMENT
Fire

YOUR RULERS
Sun, Mars
22–23 degrees
Third Decanate, yang

The Astrological Interpretation

The symbol for your birth date is a "concentrated heart." A cat easily leaps from rooftop to rooftop when it gathers in its forces before it springs. You can make use of your creative energies in the same way. This requires that you take the time to carefully prioritize your goals and pull in your strength before making your move. When you scatter yourself in many directions at the same time you can weaken yourself both energetically and creatively. The same is true in your personal relationships. You like the flattery of several people's attention, but monogamy is your best path. To gain a better sense of energy balance, you might wish to work with tai chi or hatha yoga. Even modern jazz dancing or aerobics will be helpful to you.

Some August 16 birthdays may fall on a critical degree, which brings strong reactions to the highs and lows of life. You have an audacious attitude that gives you the wherewithal to deal with whatever life brings. The military and the performing arts may attract you. In whatever profession you choose you will try to innovate and make your mark. An image for you is a bright blue star shining over a clear lake. At home you may like to pace while thinking things over. You may have an interest in military matters and favor brass buttons or insignias that have a military feeling. Combat boots, khakis, and camouflage caps may also appeal as an occasional fashion statement.

Outdoors, August 16 may have a fascination for waterwheels. Visit an old-fashioned mill. If you can construct a miniature wheel on a brook in your yard you may feel a special kinship with your creation. Flowers for your garden could include corydalis, heliotrope, and sunflowers.

A Kabbalistic Interpretation

When you need to you can approach life with the unstoppable force of an express train at full speed. The two tarot cards the Tower and Strength both interact in the value of this date. While the Tower card indicates a number of significant obstacles in your life, the Strength card suggests that you will overcome them through sheer force of will.

A small statuette of a chariot or an eagle on your desk at work will help you find the required level of determination to succeed.

One of the Hebrew names of God is reflected in the value of this day, suggesting a strong system of values and morals. The surrounding context of your personality points to a need to avoid being rigid in those beliefs, especially when dealing with other people. Fresh sage in your cooking or growing in a small window box should encourage you to be more tolerant.

A word meaning "power" is equivalent to this day's value. As long as it is used in a carefully directed way your ability to exercise influence over others can be very positive. A replica of a Roman javelin or similar artifact can help keep you single-minded and clear about what you are trying to achieve in life.

A Numerological Interpretation
YOUR MAGIC NUMBERS: 6 AND 4

The sixteenth day of the eighth month reduces to six, the number signifying beauty, symmetry, and the equilibrium of balanced polarities. Born on this day, you have a path of resonating with the inherent order of nature. Your pattern asks that you see beyond the mundane manifestations of life to the beauty within. Scientifically, a rainbow is merely a refraction of moisture in the sky from sunlight passing through water drops, but it is a thing of exquisite beauty and a profound symbol of God's grace. Live your life from that perspective, not a narrow definition of scientific explanations.

Indigo and green are colors to widen your horizons. Take photographs of the faces of children and the beautiful things you see in nature. Wear fluorite to harmonize your energy field. The 229th day of the year reduces to four, making it easier for you to sense the inherent order of the material world.

OBJECTS/IMAGES
emblems, furriers, the stage, vacation resorts

SHAPES/MATERIALS
helium, amber, gold leaf

COLORS
bright yellow, lime green, honey yellow

ANIMALS
mountain lion, lioness

PLANTS, HERB, EDIBLES
cowslips, eyebright, blood oranges, clementines

ESSENCE
mandarin

SOUNDS/RHYTHMS
film music, "You Are My Sunshine"

MUSICAL NOTES
F and D#

DEEP SPACE OBJECT
Alpha Pisces

August 17

YOUR SIGN
Leo

YOUR ELEMENT
Fire

YOUR RULERS
Sun, Mars
23–24 degrees
Third Decanate, yang

The Astrological Interpretation

It would be difficult for you to follow a path set down by others, no matter how generous and loving the offer. Your task is to find the inner source of your own strength, generate your own sunlight, and create your own reality. It is common for people born this day to leave home at an early age and make their mark without the support of family. As you move forward in life, you meet men and women who become a new family to you. The great gift of your birth is the chance to instigate new opportunities to fulfill your goals and ambitions as a result of such relationships. You are not a selfish person and are sincerely grateful for what others give you. You reward your friends with shared pleasures: tickets to concerts, invitations to parties, and spontaneous trips and outings.

August 17 energetically pursues whatever gives meaning to life. There is a proclivity for a rustic life, and you may enjoy having or visiting a farm. Decorate your home with the color white and have splashes of other color for accents. Ceiling medallions would be an elegant addition to the living or dining room. You might enjoy carrying a brass or gold money clip. Cuff links for both men and women are particularly suited to your love of decorum. Ancient coins or engraved gold are perfect materials for you.

Outdoors, August 17 should have a white gate around the house and/or yard. A view of mountains would keep everything in perspective for you. The southwest may be a direction of power. Planting white flowers such as dahlias and asters will add to August 17's luster.

A Kabbalistic Interpretation

You come across as an exceptionally delicate individual with a somewhat fragile demeanor. You do tend to dislike activities that require intense physical exertion, yet despite outward appearances, you possess an inner core of steel. People realize this when they see you tackle difficult problems and crises at work. A painting of a swan would be a good image for you, as it reflects both the delicate and strong aspects of your personality.

Your day's value connects directly to the sephira Malkuth, representing the everyday world and the planet Earth itself. It is likely that you feel a very strong connection to the Earth and have a great deal of interest in environmental movements across the globe. A good way for you to make your home more personal is to reflect this connection to the Earth in your decorating. Recycle furniture and decorate with found objects. Use natural fabrics and undyed materials.

Although you have an Earth-based nature, you are also influenced by the energy of the moon. It is this influence that gives you your emotional sensitivity and ability to express yourself. To enhance the lunar influence, try burning some ambergris incense.

A Numerological Interpretation

YOUR MAGIC NUMBERS: 7 AND 5

The seventeenth day of the eighth month reduces to seven, the number of rest, security, and perceived safety. Born on this day, you have a pattern of discerning cycles and knowing when it is time to pause between periods of creation to rest. The sun comes up each morning, and although it is in constant motion, that movement is predictable. This constant return and rebirth is comforting. This cyclic pattern of change can teach you about larger cycles and patterns in the universe itself. As above, so below.

Tourmaline wands will clarify your mind and calm your emotions. The 230th day of the year reduces to five, contributing the influence of change, transition, and mediation, making it easier for you to flow with the cycles. Cycles of change give you a sense of continuity. No matter how dark the night, dawn always comes.

OBJECTS/IMAGES
palaces, athletes, gift shops

SHAPES/MATERIALS
sunburst shapes, chrysolite, brass

COLORS
mango, pea green, saffron

ANIMALS
desert animals, thoroughbred horses

PLANTS, HERBS, EDIBLES
pineapples, rue, rice, hibiscus flower

ESSENCE
lemon verbena

SOUNDS/RHYTHMS
triumphant marches, musical chairs

MUSICAL NOTES
F# and E

DEEP SPACE OBJECTS
Omicron Leo, Subra

August 18

YOUR SIGN
Leo

YOUR ELEMENT
Fire

YOUR RULERS
Sun, Jupiter
24–25 degrees
Third Decanate, yang

The Astrological Interpretation

Your life embodies the search for the anchoring and creative expression of your true values. You will go through many "incarnations" in this lifetime, inventing and then reinventing yourself as you work to project your real nature. Do not be too discouraged if a number of your tests, trial runs, and experiments fail. This is all part of the process of elimination that will lead you eventually to the correct focus for the richness of your life force. Try to be more circumspect and objective in your efforts, as you tend to give too much of yourself to each project and risk being disappointed. A symbol for this date is the rainbow, and these bright, celestial colors can only come after the rain. In this respect, you will enjoy the rainbow of colors found in gemstones and take great pleasure in wearing a great mixture and assortment of these beautiful gifts of nature.

An image for you is a camel slowly but surely crossing the desert. One of your tools as you move toward your goals is humor. You may have a talent for creating jokes or seeing the silly side of everyday situations. Jot down your funny thoughts, they may come in handy. A bulletin board with cartoons, humorous pictures, or your own creations would be a focal point for your home. Consider creating a "joke of the day" and keeping track of them in a binder. Large red, yellow, and orange pillows are perfect decorating accents for your home. If you have a fireplace, put the pillows nearby, look up at a skylight, and concoct your next adventure or joke.

Outdoors, you may be fond of citrus trees. Oranges and lemons growing in your backyard would suit you. A garden of dahlias, asters, and hibiscus is also pleasing. Consider placing humorous garden statues such as pink flamingos or a quizzical rabbit in your garden. Whatever makes you laugh is worthwhile.

A Kabbalistic Interpretation

In your nature all the elements are balanced against one another in harmony. As a result, you are extremely adaptable and not easily flustered. Try having a circular table in your kitchen with four square table mats placed on it. This harmonic setup in the hearth of your home reflects and resonates with your sense of balance.

The word *drops* has the same value as one of the ways in which we can kabbalistically represent this date. Other associations with that which is very small can also be found. You have the ability to see the value in all things and people wherever they may be in life. Keeping a vase of daisies or snowdrops on your desk will encourage this positive, healing way of viewing the world.

Another connected phrase means an "empty brook." This is a complex reference in terms of a personality, suggesting that you may have difficulty expressing your emotions easily to others. Wearing a ruby ring on your little finger will help you to speak much more freely about how you feel.

A Numerological Interpretation
YOUR MAGIC NUMBERS: 8 AND 6

The eighteenth day of the eighth month reduces to eight, the number of involution and evolution, the back-and-forth movements of the energies of the universe. Born on this day, you have a path of uniting with the transcendence of the ordinary miracles of life. This pattern calls for joy in simple birdsong and the fragrance of your garden. You have the capacity to align with everything that is simple, beautiful, and good and thereby enrich the world. There is profound magic in what we might mistakenly call ordinary things.

Turquoise and amethyst are gems to intensify your sense of the miraculous. Walk in the forest and acquaint yourself with the sounds and wild voices. Have bird feeders, and revel in the movements of your feathered companions as they feast from your bounty. The 231st day of the year reduces to six, adding the important element of beauty to this path, amplifying your sense of magic.

OBJECTS/IMAGES
actors, deserts, grandeur, the heart

SHAPES/MATERIALS
the shape of atoms, red-gold, lyncurius (gem stone), garnet

COLORS
pineapple yellow, aquamarine, lime

ANIMALS
bantam rooster, bobcat

PLANTS, HERBS, EDIBLES
jasmine rice, blueweed, red grapes, sweet goldenrod

ESSENCE
rosemary

SOUNDS/RHYTHMS
joyous laughter, "God Save the King"

MUSICAL NOTES
G and F

DEEP SPACE OBJECTS
Alpha Hyades, Alphard Solitary One

August 19

YOUR SIGN
Leo

YOUR ELEMENT
Fire

YOUR RULERS
Sun, Mars
25–26 degrees
Third Decanate, yin

The Astrological Interpretation

Your heart beats strongly with compassion especially toward children and people less fortunate than yourself. It is highly likely that at some point in your life you will be involved in working with young people who need help. You have an affectionate attitude and enjoy stroking, touching, and being caressed in return. This should not be misconstrued as sexual in nature, as giving hugs and kisses, warm pats, and snuggles are a part of who you are. Yet when your heart turns to romance, there is no mistaking your intentions. You are then the personification of the infatuated romantic lover: poetic, ardent, adoring, and relentlessly passionate. You love all of the things that make for the right atmosphere for Eros: candles, easy listening music, chocolate, and a bright bottle of bubbly!

August 19 reaches for understanding in all forms of endeavor. You may succeed at making a living in a unique and perhaps unlikely profession. Whatever you do if you strive for goals with a spiritual dimension your innate generosity will flourish. A symbol for you is the rainbow. At home, August 19 enjoys humor in her surroundings. You have a great sense of festivities and occasion. You may also enjoy simple magic tricks or learning how to make balloon animals. Choose bright colors such as yellow and orange for your home; sun images will keep things cheery. Rainbow shower curtains, a rainbow calendar, or photos of rainbows are all good ways of keeping you in tune with your highest self.

Outdoors, August 19 enjoys country life and stables. Horse shows and races might be great entertainment for you, even if you don't ride. An exuberant garden is a way that you could express yourself. Forsythia, trumpet creeper, clematis, and all large yellow flowers are resonant for you.

A Kabbalistic Interpretation

One of the words that is equivalent to the value of this day is the Hebrew word meaning "enigma," which can be a riddle or a puzzle. Much of kabbalistic analysis is like solving such a riddle. It may well be that you would enjoy experimenting with kabbala yourself, especially with the twisting and turning nature of gematric interpretation. Try playing with logic problems and word puzzles in your spare time, as this will enhance your problem-solving prowess.

Many of those who know you find you to be an intriguing individual. You have a chameleonlike personality, and it is never fully possible to pin down exactly what you are like. In some relationships this can be extremely useful. However, there are times when you want to be quite clear about exactly who you are. A small piece of iron pyrite kept in your pocket will help you to be true to yourself when you want to.

A Numerological Interpretation
YOUR MAGIC NUMBERS: 9 AND 7

The nineteenth day of the eighth month reduces to nine, the number that represents completion and attainment. Nine fulfills the ultimate expression of the idea that started the cycle in one. Born on this day, you have a path of responding to the creative aspect of life itself. You have a deep sense of integrity and are unwilling to compromise your principles to have temporary satisfaction in your life. This pattern evokes your sense of what is possible, even beyond the bounds of reason. Let your imagination soar. Read fantasy and science fiction. Pay attention to your hunches, and learn to trust your intuition.

In retrospect, you see that your best advice came unbidden. Aquamarine is a gem to link you to your subconscious. The 232nd day of the year reduces to seven, contributing a sense of security and safety in your ability to follow your mental messages.

OBJECTS/IMAGES
moneychangers, mansions, fame, children

———

SHAPES/MATERIALS
satin, alectorie (gemstone), shape of a nucleus, vine shapes

———

COLORS
yellow-brown, azure, emerald green

———

ANIMALS
pedigreed horses

———

PLANTS, HERBS, EDIBLES
Jerusalem sage, African marigold, peony, risotto

———

ESSENCE
neroli

———

SOUNDS/RHYTHMS
theme songs, racing bugle

———

MUSICAL NOTES
G# and F#

———

DEEP SPACE OBJECTS
Gamma Vela, Suhail a Muhlif

August 20

YOUR SIGN
Leo

YOUR ELEMENT
Fire

YOUR RULERS
Sun, Mars
26–27 degrees
Third Decanate, yin

The Astrological Interpretation

Passion is a continuing theme in your life, but take care that it is not all-consuming. You demand that your love be returned with the same fervor, devotion, and loyalty that you bring to your special relationships. You can consider it the worst sort of treason when the object of your affections even contemplates an intimate friendship with another person that could take his or her attentions away from you. Give yourself and your partner a chance to explore your individual identities. Possessiveness will definitely lead to loss, but when love is real, everyone is a winner. Build your sense of personal security through the expression of your own creativity. You are good with your hands; making of jewelry, clothing, and beautiful artifacts will come naturally to you—what you don't sell or give away, you can wear.

This energetic birthday has a happy lightness and lives life at full tilt. There is a great desire for material wealth as well as knowledge. Your home should be high up; sleep at the highest part of the house. For apartment dwellers make sure that the bed is elevated. The bed itself is central. Let it be big with a metal frame and perhaps a sun medallion. You should definitely have many pillows and comforters in vibrant colors but without busy designs. This is your throne, and you may conduct a lot of your life from your bed. It worked for Louis XIV!

When you emerge from the bedroom, consider carrying a piece of golden beryl with you. No matter what the weather, you will have a little piece of sunshine. Outdoors, a sundial is a wonderful addition to your garden. Arrange flowers in a circular fashion, and you will be able to promenade through your garden and gather your thoughts and feelings.

A Kabbalistic Interpretation

The letter *Tzaddi* has an influence on this day, creating a tendency toward possessiveness. You like to make sure that anyone you are in a relationship with understands that you expect absolute loyalty. One very good way to avoid being too clingy with your partner would be to add a few drops of lavender oil to your bathwater.

All forms of manual work are extremely well aspected this day. This is especially true of things that you do for enjoyment rather than to earn a living. A great hobby for you would be do-it-yourself projects around the home. Anything you can make out of wood—from cabinets, to tables, to shelving—will probably turn out well.

The planet Saturn has an influence in your makeup. In your particular case it is the planet's association with farming that most affects you. Fill your home with some wonderful traditional ornaments such as quilts, horse brasses, or even hang a dried flower wreath on your front door.

A Numerological Interpretation
YOUR MAGIC NUMBERS: 10 AND 8

The twentieth day of the eighth month reduces to ten, the number that represents embodiment and perfected process. Born on this day, you have a path of learning discernment. This pattern is one of building trust in your fellow human beings, even in the face of betrayal and disillusionment on the part of some individuals. You are asked to develop not only confidence in others but also a healthy sense of skepticism where appropriate. You have the capacity to win the respect and trust of others. Examine your own criteria for trusting another.

Sodalite is a gem to strengthen your integrity and discernment. Volunteer for jury duty, or visit courtrooms. Practice the discipline of presuming someone innocent until proven guilty. The 233rd day of the year reduces to eight, adding the instinctive awareness that even opposite forms of expression ultimately stem from a single cause.

OBJECTS/IMAGES
lion tamers, Christmas ornaments, emblems

SHAPES/MATERIALS
pink-gold, rainbow arc, brocades

COLORS
royal blue, ruby red, orange, midnight blue, turquoise

ANIMALS
panther, racehorse, rooster

PLANTS, HERBS, EDIBLES
marigolds, truffles, juniper

ESSENCES
orange water, lemon cologne

SOUNDS/RHYTHMS
marching bands, jazz trombone

MUSICAL NOTES
A and G

DEEP SPACE OBJECTS
Zeta Leo, Aldhafera

August 21

YOUR SIGN
Leo

YOUR ELEMENT
Fire

YOUR RULER
Sun, Mars
27–28 degrees
Third Decanate, yin

The Astrological Interpretation

You are a person who relies a great deal upon your instincts. This birth date indicates a life that can benefit from developing instinct into objective and conscious thought. Do not get so caught up with the drama of your life that you forget that you are in the theater! Observe your mind and feelings at work, and learn to control and direct your instinctual nature so that you are not limited by uncontrollable emotional responses or unclear and illogical thoughts. Your mind should be the tool, and you are the toolmaker. Professionally, you are well suited to the expression and circulation of information. Writing and working with communication devices are natural extensions of your talents and abilities. You like sharing your ideas and are friendly, sociable, and enjoy vivid and animated conversations with your friends.

Your birthday, toward the end of Leo, is a steadily glowing fire rather than a conflagration. You have a strong will and may be known for mature and wise judgments. Mathematics may attract you. Compasses, protractors, T squares, rulers, and slide rules all have resonance for you. You may enjoy seeing stacked reams of white paper ready and waiting for whatever use you decide for them. Decorate your kitchen in shades of yellow with pocketbook plants and perhaps a pineapple plant on your windowsill. Star cacti and other succulents may appeal to you. In the bedroom, curtains or lighting that cast a yellowish light similar to those in Renaissance paintings would create a fertile atmosphere for your ideas and dreams.

Outdoors August 21 likes to entertain and share conversation around a picnic table. Torchlights and an outdoor barbecue or campfire add to a festive atmosphere. Outdoor flowers for you are bird-of-paradise, false dragonhead, and Jerusalem sage.

A Kabbalistic Interpretation

One meaning of this day is "overturn." You have the ability to see completely new ways of approaching problems or organizing life. Rather than gradually evolving a new idea or plan you tend to make swift, effective changes in your life. An image or statuette of any horned animal will help you to find success with this approach.

You have an easy manner with people and are able to communicate quite effectively at all levels of society. In the kabbalistic analysis of this day a positive relationship with all signs of the zodiac is revealed, indicating your social mobility. In your kitchen you should opt for a circular table for everyone to sit around. Look for one with three concentric rings etched into its surface.

We all have one issue in life that tends to function as our Achilles heel. In your case, you can sometimes become worried that your plans are going to fail just when you are on the brink of success. This can be explained as a fairly common fear of success, which helps you to avoid disappointment if things fail. By keeping a bloodstone in your pocket you will be able to maintain a positive approach.

A Numerological Interpretation
YOUR MAGIC NUMBERS: 2 AND 9

The twenty-first day of the eighth month reduces to two, the number of polarity, division, and the ancient emblem of the life force. Born on this day, you have a path of building strength of character through fulfillment of your ambitions. This pattern asks that you devote your energies to accomplishing high ideals. As a result, you will carve out for yourself a place of dignity and respect. You will enjoy both tangible and intangible rewards for your efforts.

Orange and blue sapphires are gems to elevate your sense of destiny and increase your drive. Involve yourself with large service organizations to allow yourself plenty of room to grow. The 234th day of the year reduces to nine, adding the crucial element of attainment and goal achievement to this path. You will be supported by the inner knowledge that you can finish anything you begin.

OBJECTS/IMAGES
proud people, fathers, solariums, roulette wheels

SHAPES/MATERIALS
fan shapes, petrified and rare woods, ray shapes

COLORS
magenta, carmine, royal blue

ANIMALS
circus lion and tiger

PLANTS, HERBS, EDIBLES
sunflower seeds, pineapple, guava, St. John's wort

ESSENCE
neroli

SOUNDS/RHYTHMS
a rooster's crow, Tarzan's yell

MUSICAL NOTES:
C#, G#

DEEP SPACE OBJECTS
Eta Leo, Al Jabhah

August 22

The Astrological Interpretation

Your birth occurs at the very tail of the celestial lion as you turn from the more instinctual nature of this animal toward the mental and logical domain of Virgo. Sometimes this leads to confusion, as your heart speaks with one voice while your mind speaks with another. You have your own way of dressing and speaking, and have consciously made an effort to be unique. Many people will admire you for your steadfast and determined attitude, while others think you are merely stubborn. The fact is, you are a railroad that runs on its own tracks, and you are proud to be able to take care of your own responsibilities in life.

August 22 likes to have fingers in many pots at once. The motivation is the joy found in creativity and seeing how many opportunities there are for self-fulfillment. Sometimes this exuberance makes you unable to compromise with the pesky demands of everyday living. To support your efforts, a thick gold band, whether you are married or not, is a symbol of unity for you. Wear it either on your ring or pointer finger. At home, you like a shipshape environment with flair. An open room with a large fireplace is the center of the home. The fireplace may be traditional brick or a hooded hearth with a wide circle of bricks on which people may sit. A stained glass window or pieces of stained glass where the sun can shine through is a perfect addition to your home. Choose pieces that emphasize reds and purples.

You like the outdoors and may be fond of a garden or yard with a wall around it. The idea is not to keep people out but to have a view of the surrounding countryside. If you live in a city try to live up high for the full 360-degree panorama.

A Kabbalistic Interpretation

This day is influenced by two tarot cards, the Fool and Strength. This combination suggests that you have an essentially innocent approach to the world around you and may indeed seem somewhat naive. However, when you really need to get something done or have your point of view heard you have the strength of will to make it happen. An ideal color scheme for your office partakes of both cards: white with little touches of crimson.

The value of your day is equivalent to the Hebrew word meaning "strength."

While this partly connects to the Strength card, this association has more to do with physical strength than strength of will. You are likely to be a very physically active person, especially in areas that rely on power rather than agility. If you have room in your home create a small weight-training area to develop your physical prowess.

Emotionally you tend to be a fairly stable individual. You are likely to have a wide circle of acquaintances rather than a few extremely close friends. There are times when you will need to decide between your friends and a commitment to your partner. Keeping some roses in your bedroom will help you to make the right decision.

A Numerological Interpretation
YOUR MAGIC NUMBERS: 3 AND 1

The twenty-second day of the eighth month reduces to three, the number of growth and unfoldment. Born on this day, you have a path of developing and strengthening your deepest devotions and cultivating moral courage. This pattern requires that you cultivate your sense of belonging spiritually and engage in some sort of service to humanity. A dramatic example is the path of Joan of Arc. You must heed the call to contribute where you are beckoned, and the result will be tremendous satisfaction and richness of spirit.

Be a missionary for a cause that fires your heart. Volunteer or contribute to organizations like the International Red Cross, or Save the Children. Amber and ruby are gems to strengthen your will and heart. The 235th day of the year reduces to one, adding the singleness of purpose that this path requires.

OBJECTS/IMAGES
rhinestone jewelry, jungle prints, lighters, mermaids

SHAPES/MATERIALS
vine shapes, diamonds, circular shapes

COLORS
orange, yellow, sunset orange, ruby red

ANIMALS
peacock, crocodile

PLANTS, HERBS, EDIBLES
walnuts, eyebright, olive oil, poppies

ESSENCE
chamomile

SOUNDS/RHYTHMS
Claude Debussy's "Claire de Lune," musicals, morning music

MUSICAL NOTES
D and C

DEEP SPACE OBJECTS
Alpha Leo, Regulus, the Little King

August 23

YOUR SIGNS
Leo/Virgo

—

YOUR ELEMENTS
Fire/Earth

—

YOUR RULERS
Sun/Mercury
29 degrees Leo–
00 degrees Virgo
First Decanate, yang
Third Decanate, yin

The Astrological Interpretation

Your birthday is on the cusp between Leo and Virgo. The symbol for this date is the sphinx, a powerful creature with the body of a lion and the head of a monarch looking out to the horizon. The meaning is clear: human logic and reason have come to dominate passion and instinct. You have the vital power of the lion's energy, but it is used with clarity, direction, and wisdom. The horizon of the world awaits your participation, yet you hold back, not moving forward unless the right opportunity presents itself. Although you are eager to succeed in life, you want your actions to be correct. You are attracted to the practical and know that you will be financially and professionally rewarded when you make the right choices. You may sit and wait for a while, but will definitely make your move.

Some August 23 birthdays fall on the fixed star Regulus, which is located at the very end of Leo. Regulus was called the Lion's Heart and was one of the Royal Persian stars, known as the Watcher of the North. The star indicated magnanimity, destructiveness, military honors, and independence. Those whose birthdays fall in the beginning of Virgo get a fiery boost from Leo and have a sociable and poetic character. At home think in terms of fire and earth. You might feature bricks in your kitchen or have an outdoor oven. Handmade pottery would be a plus for your home. You could be very fond of kittens and cats. Keep one room cat free, as you like the pets but hate the mess. In the bedroom keep an arrangement of dried flowers in muted reds and purples.

Outdoors, August 23 would enjoy space to entertain and a sandbox . . . for children and adults. For summer evening dinners have a bunch of Chinese lantern and torchlights. A garden space with white flowers will suit both Leo and Virgo.

A Kabbalistic Interpretation

The letter *Shin* dominates the way in which you approach both work and personal life. The path of *Shin* in the Tree of Life is sometimes referred to as the "biting one." Everything is done at a blistering pace and with total concentration. You can enhance this tendency by wearing a scarf or tie in scarlet with flashes of gold running through it.

Your day is associated with ideas of kingship but also with the Hebrew word that means "ruin." You need to take great care when it comes to your material position. You may have a tendency to spend without thinking, or to take excessive risks with capital. Keeping some basil on your window ledge will encourage wealth to approach you. In addition, try keeping a small square of tin in your pocket or purse.

When it comes to matters of the heart there are few who possess as deep an understanding of people as you do. Your relationships should progress very well, as your partners always know that if they have a problem they can talk about it completely frankly. Keep a small angelica plant in a blue-green painted pot and you will find that your emotional life goes from strength to strength.

A Numerological Interpretation
YOUR MAGIC NUMBERS: 4 AND 2

The twenty-third day of the eighth month reduces to four, the number of order, reason, and the solid, four-square reality of the physical world. Born on this day, you have a path of setting your sites on a heavenly star and never veering from your course. You have the capacity to dialogue with the angels and often reach out to those realms for guidance and comfort. Listen to their replies. There is always guidance and support available for the faithful heart. Display paintings of angels in your home. Decorate with shades of white, gold, and a sprinkling of stars and fairy dust. Citrine and emerald are gems to anchor your soul to the earth and stars.

The 236th day of the year reduces to two, adding the element of reflection and receptivity. Watch the twinkling stars in the still of the night, and know that you are loved.

OBJECTS/IMAGES
train conductors,
large walnut desks,
celebrity autographs

SHAPES/MATERIALS
amber, reddish agates,
cinnabar

COLORS
rose beige, butterscotch,
maroon

ANIMALS
peacock, cat

PLANTS, HERBS, EDIBLES
brick-oven pizza,
aperitifs and digestivos,
goldenrod, hornwort

ESSENCE
lemon verbena

SOUNDS/RHYTHMS
Edgar Lee Masters's
Spoon River Anthology

MUSICAL NOTES
D# and C#

DEEP SPACE OBJECT
Gamma Ursa Major, Phad,
the thigh

August 24

YOUR SIGN
Virgo

YOUR ELEMENT
Earth

YOUR RULER
Mercury
00–1 degree
First Decanate, yin

The Astrological Interpretation

You have acquired and developed a number of practical tools and talents with which to be successful in life. But you also have a discriminating nature. It is important for you to make a place for yourself that fits into the larger scheme of things. In this respect, you do very well working with other people in large corporations, provided that your own particular position is well defined. You need to be the head of your own department, and although you appreciate being given a general sense of direction, you like being left in control of your particular jobs or tasks. You will enjoy office supply stores where there are large assortments of stationery, pens, clips, and other things that make your job easier and more fun.

Your birthday has firmness of character and excellent strategy skills. Your mind can think on several levels and juggle many thoughts at once. An image for you is an air traffic control tower with all the planes stacked up and waiting to land. You will guide all your ideas safely by bringing them down to earth rather than hanging in the air. At home concentrate on your element, earth, by having minerals such as brown hornblende, rose quartz, or agate displayed. Houseplants are a miniature way to garden. Consider maidenhair fern and climbing philodendron. Your bedroom could also serve as a study. A bedstead with bookshelves built in would suit your love of knowledge and serve as a hiding place for a journal and other writings or sketches you may do.

Outdoors, indulge yourself with a garden. Plant herbs, wildflowers, lily of the valley, tulips, thrift, and begonias. You like cats and dogs, and a doghouse would go well in your yard.

A Kabbalistic Interpretation

You would never be described as someone who likes to let the grass grow under your feet. Your life tends to be extremely active, and it is often hard to keep up with you. Even in your leisure time you enjoy sports that focus on speed. One meaning of your day is the name of a swift sailing boat, so give it a try!

Another word connected to your date is the Hebrew for "needy." This does not refer to your own personal state, as you are likely to be fairly comfortable in terms of your material position. Rather it suggests that you are likely to be quite seriously involved in charity work. This commendable activity will be very rewarding for you, although it will also be very tiring. Try burning some myrrh incense or oil to help revitalize your charitable energies.

The tarot card the Chariot is a significant influence on this day. On the one hand it emphasizes your enjoyment of speed when traveling. In addition it also points to a determination and a confidence that you are going in the right direction. With all your concern for others it is important that you keep this element of yourself energized. You can do this by hanging pictures of horses or possibly Roman charioteers in your main living room.

A Numerological Interpretation
YOUR MAGIC NUMBERS: 5 AND 3

The twenty-fourth day of the eighth month reduces to five, the number of change and uncertainty. Born on this day, you have a path of gaining comfort with constant change. This pattern requires that you develop flexibility in your responses to the events in your life. You have the capacity to be in the forefront of social change, and your versatile approach to dealing with cultural diversity can be an example and an inspiration to others.

Work or volunteer for organizations that seek to topple social barriers and break glass ceilings. Teach remedial English at evening classes. Orange and yellow are colors to cheer your spirit. Topaz is a gem to widen your horizons. The 237th day of the year reduces to three, adding the influence of creative self-expression to your path.

OBJECTS/IMAGES
hallways, handwriting analysis, novels, servants

SHAPES/MATERIALS
mercury, fingerprints, spool shapes, chrysoprase

COLORS
neutral, lemon, rust

ANIMALS
hare, kit fox

PLANTS, HERBS, EDIBLES
morning honeysuckle, Plains bee balm, lavender, grits

ESSENCE
jasmine

SOUNDS/RHYTHMS
oratory, sarcasm

MUSICAL NOTES
E and D

DEEP SPACE OBJECTS
Delta Ursa Major, Megrez, Root of the Tail

August 25

YOUR SIGN
Virgo

YOUR ELEMENT
Earth

YOUR RULER
Mercury
1–2 degrees
First Decanate, yin

The Astrological Interpretation

Your birth date is associated with the symbol of a basket full of ripe vegetables and fruit. Your own inner harvest of talents and abilities is replete with abundance. The raw materials are there in plenitude; it is up to you to find the right methods, techniques, and processes to make the best of what you have. You are dedicated to making your life a success and have no trouble putting in the extra hours to make this a reality. You are naturally attracted by tools and objects that have practical uses. You like the latest gadgets for both home and office. Catalogs are some of your favorite "magazines," and you are as keen to get the newest can opener as you are to acquire the most recent software for your computer.

Your orderly and penetrating mind excels at strategy. A chess game is an excellent image for you. Fundamentally, you seek a sense of spiritual belonging but may not be interested in orthodox religion. Your home could have a certain artistic clutter, and you may feel best surrounded by your stuff. Darker colors, such as plum or slate blue, appeal for the bedroom. Place a few old-fashioned lamps with lace shades that give a Victorian feel to your space. Novelties such as pens with liquid glitter are useful for you; play with them before you tackle your next project. Have a crystal glass filled with water on your desk. Water is the element of feelings, and keeping a glass around will remind you to unite mind and heart.

August 25 enjoys working and gardening in the earth. Gardening can be a therapeutic as well as an aesthetic activity. Have some verdigris wind chimes in your garden. You might also consider planting flowers by color: one corner for white, another for yellow, and another for blue.

A Kabbalistic Interpretation

The letter *Ayin,* meaning "eye," has a strong influence on your personality. With your excellent skills of observation and eye for detail, consider taking up some form of painting as a hobby. Landscapes, especially inhospitable and rocky ones, are good subjects for you.

Your creativity goes beyond the ability to create good visual art. You are equally creative with products of the mind. The number three combines with the energy of the Strength card from the tarot, meaning you are excellent at taking an idea and making it happen. Upward pointed triangle patterns incorporated in the design of your office will help you in this area of your life.

One meaning of the value of this date is "garment" and another is "splendor." This combination suggests that the best way to exercise your creative talents is in the fashion world. It certainly means that you know how to dress to impress. This is a very useful skill to have in terms of getting through your next interview and for that first date with a new partner. In terms of color you will never go wrong with indigo.

A Numerological Interpretation

YOUR MAGIC NUMBERS: 6 AND 4

The twenty-fifth day of the eighth month reduces to six, the number of symmetry, beauty, and balance. Born on this day, you have a path of seeking beauty in the inner realms of your experience, and carrying your visions forward into outer reality. This pattern connects you to the archetypal plane of existence where legends and fairy tales live. These stories form a critical body of information that acts as a common mythology for the human race. Some of our greatest heroes and teachers come from this collective landscape.

Sodalite and jade are gems to open the door of your mind and maintain your connection to the earth. Keep your outlook sunny, and always expect the best. The 238th day of the year reduces to four, contributing the instinctive awareness that there is a profound, unchanging reality beneath the myriad shifting shapes and forms we call the material world.

OBJECTS/IMAGES
postage stamps, hat pins

SHAPES/MATERIALS
box shapes, beehive shapes

COLORS
tan, dusty rose, chartreuse, amber

ANIMALS
cat, ground dove

PLANTS, HERBS, EDIBLES
lemon curd, jade trees, parsnips

ESSENCE
oakmoss

SOUNDS/RHYTHMS
limericks

MUSICAL NOTES
F and D#

DEEP SPACE OBJECT
NGC 3344, spiral galaxy

August 26

YOUR SIGN
Virgo

YOUR ELEMENT
Earth

YOUR RULER
Mercury
2–3 degrees
First Decanate, yin

The Astrological Interpretation

Your birth date speaks of a maiden waiting for the right knight to come along so that she may be transformed into a woman. This symbolism indicates the hidden potential that only needs the perfect stimulation to burst forth into form. There is always more to you than what appears on the surface, more potential than what is on your résumé, more talent than the task in front of you requires. Although you sincerely do your best at whatever you undertake, there is the gnawing sensation that you could do better if only the right circumstances would appear. Take each moment as its own perfection; you are creating your future in the present moment. Gardening, especially the cultivation of cooking or healing herbs, will give you a great deal of relaxation and satisfaction.

August 26 is a tireless worker. Giving kind service to others is part of your nature. You may be particularly attracted to angels. Investigate some of the great artworks, such as Jan van Eyck's *Annunciation* that include angels, and hang reproductions in your home. On a more earthly plane, August 26 has skill with drawing and measuring tools such as a ruler, protractor, compass, and X-Acto knife. A small set of wooden stacking drawers near your work area will keep all your tools in place. In the dining area include a bowl full of unshelled mixed nuts. The texture, taste, and colors all remind you of a bountiful harvest.

Outdoors, August 26 wants an artistic garden that may include pieces of sculpture. White flowers such as hostas, white tulips, and chrysanthemums would complement whatever art pieces you have. During the winter don't miss the opportunity to make snow angels!

A Kabbalistic Interpretation

One of the possible values of this day connects directly with the title "God the father" in Hebrew. This suggests that you are in a position of high regard and considerable authority and that you take a benevolent approach to those who are dependent on you. You can encourage this attitude by investing in a solid oak chair for yourself.

The view of you as someone who deserves a degree of respect from others is confirmed by the tarot card that has the most influence on this day: the Hermit is primarily associated with learned wisdom. It is highly likely that you will accumulate much of that quality as you go through life. Keeping a lamp, especially a yellow one, beside you at your desk will help you put your experience to good use.

The value of this day is also connected to the Hebrew word that means "lead." Lead is the metal of the planet Saturn, and his influence over your personality creates a danger of making you too dour. You can lighten your general temperament by opening yourself up to a more Mercurial energy. Wearing a fire opal ring on your little finger will help you to do this.

A Numerological Interpretation
YOUR MAGIC NUMBERS: 7 AND 5

The twenty-sixth day of the eighth month reduces to seven, the number signifying victory, peace, and satisfaction. Seven connotes the pause between cycles of expression and creation, which allows for refueling to continue the journey. Born on this day, you have a path of childlike and joyful participation in the wheel of life. At your best, you approach life like a child at a carnival, full of excitement and anticipation. This pattern asks that you remain alert and aware of how you can fill the lessons and experiences of your life with fun, enhancing the quality of learning.

Work in children's education, and observe how much easier it is to learn when the process is experiential and fun. Enroll in an outdoor learning course for yourself. Take your best friend to an amusement park, and ride the roller coaster. Amethyst and emerald are gems to enhance your sense of magic. The 239th day of the year reduces to five, providing the additional influence of adaptation, versatility, and flexibility to this path.

OBJECTS/IMAGES
closet organizer, paper penny rolls, a hutch cabinet

SHAPES/MATERIALS
pink jasper, zircon, scrolls of paper

COLORS
wheat color, bright green, pale yellow

ANIMAL
cat

PLANTS, HERBS, EDIBLES
bachelor's buttons, crab apple (Bach remedy), succory

ESSENCE
angelica

SOUNDS/RHYTHMS
arpeggios, a nutcracker cracking nuts

MUSICAL NOTES
F and E

DEEP SPACE OBJECTS
Chi Ursa Major, El Koprah, Seat of the Bear

August 27

YOUR SIGN
Virgo

YOUR ELEMENT
Earth

YOUR RULER
Mercury
3–4 degrees
First Decanate, yin

The Astrological Interpretation

A symbol closely connected to this date is a pregnant woman waiting to give birth. Her unborn child is healthy as is she, but still the pregnancy does not come to term. You know that you are filled with a tremendous, unrealized potential. You feel you are ready for a great task and are impatient with the arrival of what may be the most fulfilling moment of your life. And yet you have to wait. No outside event will quicken the arrival of your inner child. Your task is to awaken the unborn infant yourself. How you go about this is your path. Once this internal birth occurs, the outer form of the perfect job or relationship will appear, but not until them.

August 27 emphasizes the service nature of Virgo. You may be the power behind the throne or someone who is willing to work quietly and effectively behind the scenes. You are a hard worker and strive for perfection in whatever you do. Calm your mind with lots of houseplants and natural objects in your environment. Pieces of driftwood or wood that you whittle or rub smooth could grace your desk or hall table. Houseplants for you are maidenhair ferns and climbing philodendron. August 27 is very sensitive to scents and skin products. Use natural-based products: anything with lavender scent will appeal to you. Landscape paintings and intricate macramé hangings on your walls would perfectly blend your natural and artistic interests.

Outdoors, August 27 has a green thumb for flowers as well as vegetables. Where ever you live try to raise a few herbs such as mint, oregano, and basil. Virgo's symbol is the goddess of the harvest, and August 27 will find continuity by tilling the soil . . . no matter if it is only in a window box.

A Kabbalistic Interpretation

This day contains a value that is enormously significant in the tradition of kabbala and ceremonial magic. The number seventy-two is associated with the so-called *schemhamphorasch.* This strange word is used to refer to the seventy-two spirits found in the Torah. Its presence indicates that you have a wealth of hidden talents. To really help bring out these talents get a simple gold pendant and have the number seventy-two engraved, perhaps in Hebrew, on its front.

Another number associated with this day is eleven, a number that has strong connections with magic. It also connects to the tarot card the Wheel of Fortune. The Fortune card is associated with travel and in your case points to travel overseas. A good addition for your living room would be an antique globe to remind you of your travels.

In your work it is probable that you supervise others. You are certainly capable of motivating others to work efficiently and effectively. However, you also tend to drive people too hard. You can soften that tendency by keeping a vase of daisies on your desk.

A Numerological Interpretation

YOUR MAGIC NUMBERS: 8 AND 6

The twenty-seventh day of the eighth month reduces to eight, signifying the continuing ebb and flow of experience. Eight is concerned with the issues of material security and the overriding issues of the physical plane. Yours is a path of examining all of the compromises and trade-offs you make in your quest to feel comfortable. This pattern will ultimately require you to probe the depths of your motivations. Where have you lost a battle, or even surrendered, because you thought you might win the war? This path allows you to see the consequences of your compromises. Ultimately, you will be forced to forsake ease and comfort and move toward freedom and independence. Comfort and a sense of security can at times be your worst enemy.

Take calculated risks to exercise your speculative muscles. Turquoise and sodalite are stones to enhance your confidence and inner security. The 240th day of the year reduces to six, assisting your process through an inner compass or gyroscope, aiding your equilibrium.

OBJECTS/IMAGES
librarians, envelopes, fables, barns, a roadside vegetable stand

SHAPES/MATERIALS
origami paper, jasper, stalk shapes (corn, wheat, etc.)

COLORS
Della Robbia blue, sea foam green, lime

ANIMAL
greyhound

PLANTS, HERBS, EDIBLES
licorice, parsley, pomegranates

ESSENCE
lavender

SOUNDS/RHYTHMS
proverbs

MUSICAL NOTES
G and F

DEEP SPACE OBJECTS
Alpha Sextans

August 28

YOUR SIGN
Virgo

———

YOUR ELEMENT
Earth

———

YOUR RULER
Mercury
4–5 degrees
First Decanate, yin

The Astrological Interpretation

You like to design and develop your own systems, methods, and techniques for getting things done in life. You can potentially turn this personal characteristic into a great career. Look to the creation of business or computer programs in which people may structure and use their talents and resources more efficiently. You do not like waste and can be very careful with money. But Virgo is the sign of the harvest, and your birthday gives you courage and self-motivation. There will always be more than enough. Train yourself not to worry about potential lacks but to acknowledge the abundance that surrounds you. You will enjoy taking care of small animals and may have a special affinity with birds. Sing along with them.

August 28 can fall on a "critical degree," which means that you feel highs and lows keenly. You have great mental agility and are likely to dream clearly and be able to translate visions from a dream state to everyday reality. Poetry and all rhythmic spoken words are particularly appealing to you. At home, wear a long flowing gown.

A Kabbalistic Interpretation

The key word for this day is *surrender*. The foundation of your success lies in the realization that true accomplishment rests on the help and support of others and a reliance on a power greater than your personality. Surrendering does not mean losing or giving up but understanding the power in partnership.

The Tarot card of the Hermit can act as a visual guide to remind you of the lessons of this day. The Hermit began his journey as the Fool and has regained the mountaintop after mastering life's lessons. Remember to listen to the counsel of those wiser than you. Experience is often the best teacher. Listening to the voice of experience can prevent painful mistakes. Focus your heart's desire on the eternal lamp of wisdom rather than on an accumulation of worldly possessions.

The Hebrew letter *Yod*, the first letter in the Tetragrammaton, is related to this day. *Yod* represents the creative hand that fashions the universe. The theme of service permeates your life. Be mindful of opportunities to accept the hands extended to you in friendship or need.

A Numerological Interpretation
YOUR MAGIC NUMBERS: 9 AND 7

The twenty-eighth day of the eighth month reduces to nine, the number signifying fulfillment, achievement, and attainment. Born on this day, yours is a path of willingness to enter the stream of a particular endeavor, and extend yourself to learn, knowing that inherent in the risk and the involvement is the ultimate crowning achievement. You love the diversity of the parade of life, and the infinite contributions to the pageantry. Your pattern requires that you engage in activities and work that takes you from unskilled apprentice to master craftsman. You must take the initial awkward steps in order to move along the spectrum of competency. Take dance lessons, gourmet cooking classes, or study carpentry. Diamonds are gems to remind you of this process. What ends up as a cut and polished stone began as a worthless lump of coal. Wear a blue diamond ring as a constant reminder.

The 241st day of the year reduces to seven, providing the instinctive expectation of victory in every effort you undertake.

OBJECTS/IMAGES
grandfather clock, metronome, copper cookware

SHAPES/MATERIALS
seven petaled flowers, prisms, layers of fabric

COLORS
Royal blue, grass green, smoky gray

ANIMAL
raven

PLANTS, HERBS, EDIBLES
violets, chive, pansies, arugula

ESSENCE
Iris

SOUNDS/RHYTHMS
African drubms, marching bands

MUSICAL NOTES
G# and F#

DEEP SPACE OBJECT
Upsilon Ursa Major, Alula Borealis

August 29

YOUR SIGN
Virgo

YOUR ELEMENT
Earth

YOUR RULER
Mercury
5–6 degrees
First Decanate, yang

The Astrological Interpretation

The key to your success in life is synthesis. It is very important for you to pay attention to how parts fit into larger wholes, and keep greater goals always in mind. Beware of clutter of all kinds—physical, mental, and emotional. Eliminate what is no longer necessary in your life and do not be afraid to leave an empty space. When the time is right, you will find what is required to fill the vacancy. Concentrate on what is present and work to refine what you have. Your actions and efforts toward the positive construction of your life will attract what is correct for you. Do not be afraid to destroy what needs to be reborn. You will find yourself attracted by ecology and the conservation of nature, as you are yourself in the constant process of recycling.

You have a youthful, pleasure-seeking nature. You may always look younger than your years, and your buoyancy insures that you develop your talents and skills throughout your life. A challenge for you is to remain persistent when obstacles occur. An image to consider is Switzerland: the chocolate is delicious and the clocks never stop! At home, the dining room is a focal point for you. The table is for eating, doing creative projects, and organizing. Laying out a whole plan on a wooden dining table will help organize it for you. You may be interested in collecting china cups and displaying them in your dining room or kitchen, using cupboards with painted or stenciled designs. Keep some reminders of the harvest in your home. A cornucopia with nuts and fruits could be a centerpiece year-round.

Outdoors a garden is an area for creativity and summer meals. Place a picnic table and chairs in the middle of your space and plan on eating outdoors whenever you can. Gloxinia is a perfect flower for you and lilac bushes around a gazebo complete your pleasure environment.

A Kabbalistic Interpretation

The key word for this day is the Hebrew word meaning "strength." This does not refer to physical strength but the strength that lies in your inner self and will. It is likely that you are already aware of your great powers of focus and concentration. If you would like to increase those powers you might consider taking up some form of regular meditation practice.

The Death card from the tarot has an important role to play in the makeup of your personality. As always it points toward changes that have a major impact on your life. It is likely that most of these upheavals relate to moving to a new location. Keep some mugwort in a small pouch in the east of your hallway and you will find it easier to make important changes and decisions.

One of the words that is equivalent to the value of your day is a Hebrew word meaning "berries." This is more likely to refer to associations with berries, such as sweetness or summertime, than to berries themselves. Yet keeping a big bowl of cherries or other berry fruit in your kitchen will evoke long summer afternoons in your heart.

A Numerological Interpretation

YOUR MAGIC NUMBERS: 1 AND 8

The twenty-ninth day of the eighth month reduces to one, the number of originality, inception, and initiative. Born on this day, you have a path of cultivating distinctiveness. This pattern requires that you carve out your uniqueness among your fellows. The danger of this path is that you take this to extremes. Strive for balance so that your distinct expression of personality is an asset, not a distraction or an undermining influence. You should be attracting others, not polarizing and sending them away because you are too different. You are following a path of self-discovery into the misty arena of the future.

Study acting and involve yourself in fiction or theater. Have fun playing roles and wearing costumes. Ruby and fire opal are gems to galvanize your imagination and enthusiasm. The 242nd day of the year reduces to eight, adding the easy knowledge that disparate forms of expression always stem from a single source of creation. This aids your quest for originality.

OBJECTS/IMAGES
thin, tall glasses, newspapers, pencils

SHAPES/MATERIALS
beehive shapes, papyrus, looms, cross-stitched samplers

COLORS
slate gray, royal blue, grass green

ANIMALS
groundhog, rabbit

PLANTS, HERBS, EDIBLES
hazel trees, cow parsnip, brazil nuts

ESSENCE
myrtle

SOUNDS/RHYTHMS
rhymed couplets, a cadenza

MUSICAL NOTES
C and G

DEEP SPACE OBJECTS
Alpha Draco, Thuban

August 30

The Astrological Interpretation

You have a tremendous need for things to be "right." But if you attach yourself to the concept of absolute purity and perfection, you will make yourself frustrated trying to live up to impossible standards. Work to accept yourself as you are rather than criticize yourself for not living up to ideals. We all need to grow and develop and make the most out of who we are, but you cannot do this by tearing yourself down or by measuring yourself against someone else. Open yourself to the wider world through travel, documentary films, and the study of human psychology. Learn to listen less to the little voice that says: "You are not," and pay more attention to the greater voice that says: "You are!"

Your sense of style is often noteworthy. Classical fashions predominate, and good value is important. At home, encourage your sly sense of humor with cartoons on the refrigerator. As your ruler, Mercury, rules communications, you may enjoy having a variety of telephones in your home, including an old-fashioned black dial phone. Keep fresh flowers such as freesia and yellow tulips in a low cut-glass bowl on your dining table. Quality of sound is important to you. If you live near heavy traffic, invest in a white noise machine to muffle the beeping horns. Keep a variety of nature tapes handy. Birdsong, babbling brooks, and gentle rain are all good ideas for you.

Your nervous system needs to be soothed, and a walk outside is a perfect tonic. Your garden can be simple, with grapevines and perhaps a small arbor where you can sit and have summer meals. If you visit the country, you may enjoy learning about beekeeping.

A Kabbalistic Interpretation

This date has associations with both the Hebrew word meaning "love" and meaning "innocent." There are few things more romantically appealing than unconditional or innocent love. At the same time it is important to have some worldly wisdom about you. You can encourage some worldliness by drinking an infusion of nettle tea.

As this day also has connections to ideas of wealth, an awareness of the potential for bad motives on the part of others would be extremely useful to you. You are likely to do well for yourself financially, but there is certainly no harm in giving fate a little nudge. Try hanging a metallic six-pointed star above your front door or above your desk in your office.

You prefer to socialize after the sun has gone down, and ideally you like to entertain in your own home with just a few friends. As you like animals, an ideal pet for you to buy would be a black cat. Contrary to popular belief, she will bring you luck.

A Numerological Interpretation
YOUR MAGIC NUMBERS: 2 AND 9

The thirtieth day of the eighth month reduces to two, the number representing duplication, reflection, and replication. Two is the realm of the subconscious mind. Born on this day, you have a path of cultivating transcendental ways of knowing. You have the capacity to tap into a higher order of knowing. You can engage both hemispheres of your brain at will, and can access memory and intuition. This pattern calls for you to integrate the various aspects of how your mental processes operate, and offer a further development of intelligence. Join Mensa or a group that emphasizes the enhancement of the mind. Study individuals such as Albert Einstein, whose manner of accessing his most brilliant insights was different from that of ordinary individuals.

This path calls for exploring the mind and expressing new frontiers of mental awareness. The 243rd day of the year reduces to nine, contributing the quality of clear, pure expression of seminal ideas to your quest. All colors of quartz crystals will aid your communication abilities with alternate ways of knowing.

OBJECTS/IMAGES
a silo, beehives, sewing machines

SHAPES/MATERIALS
tissue paper, mercury, secret compartments

COLORS
slate, copper, China blue

ANIMALS
all small felines

PLANTS, HERBS, EDIBLES
popcorn, mandrake

ESSENCE
carrot oil

SOUNDS/RHYTHMS
a metronome, Union songs, theme songs

MUSICAL NOTES
C# and G#

DEEP SPACE OBJECTS
Epsilon Ursa Major, Alioth

August 31

YOUR SIGN
Virgo

YOUR ELEMENT
Earth

YOUR RULERS
Mercury
7–8 degrees
First Decanate, yang

The Astrological Interpretation

At times you pay more attention to the minute details of a situation and lose sight of the whole. It is important to notice that a screw is missing from a picture frame—you do not want the whole thing to collapse. But the screw is not the picture or even the frame. You will find that your life contains many tests of priorities, and learning to assess correctly the relative importance of events is an essential component of your success mechanism. You do have the ability to make the most out of the least and to be quite resourceful. Affirm the abundance of life through walks in nature, where you can gather berries and other wild edibles, and quiet times of contemplation in the outdoors.

You may find deep satisfaction in solo contemplation yet will want to share your thoughts with others. August 31 has writing and storytelling abilities, as well as practical abilities. The facets of a many-sided crystal are a good image for August 31. You may have a penchant for collecting rocks from your various travels. Set these in your home as reminders of the earth. August 31 may also enjoy miniature china pieces or Limoges collectibles. Arrange these in artful displays in curio cabinets or on shelves. Nutrition is a subject that should be of interest to you, as your digestion can be delicate. Meals accompanied with mint tea or fennel will help you absorb your food. Keep a pantry filled with dry goods so you are never short of ingredients.

Outdoors, the northwest is a direction for you. August 31 likes to divide space into clear patches. A small garden or clearing is all you really need. Border plants such as moss verbena are perfect to outline your garden.

A Kabbalistic Interpretation

August 31 is an exceptionally tranquil day. The tarot card Temperance instills in you a love of harmony with others and in your home. You are attracted to delicate things; an ideal form of decoration for your living room would be a number of crystal vases all with a hint of balanced but differing color.

The word *spoiled* in the sense of dirtied or polluted is also connected to this day. Taken with your concern for harmony and positive connection to the world of nature this indicates a desire to actively do something to clean up the world and make it purer. Wear white with a touch of emerald green or gold, as these clothes will put you in touch with these positive energies.

A final touch of tranquillity in your personality is added by your profound desire for peace. One word connected to the value of your day is *dove*, which has obvious associations with peace. Try to encourage peace in others, beginning with those closest to you, by giving them a small piece of amethyst to carry as a symbol of peace.

A Numerological Interpretation
YOUR MAGIC NUMBERS: 3 AND 10

The thirty-first day of the eighth month reduces to three, the number signifying the archetypal principles of growth, unfoldment, and upward expansion. Born on this day, you have a path of heightened perceptiveness. You are required to hone your already well-developed eye for detail to a razor sharpness. This is a pattern of specialization through a multiplicity of expressions. You are charged with exploration of all the possibilities within the sphere of a given endeavor or situation.

Work in a think tank or brain trust where speculation and mental exercise of "what ifs" are rewarded. This is the path of a research scientist. Orange zircon will open your mind to endless possibilities. The 244th day of the year reduces to ten, aiding your process with an innate confidence in your ultimate success. The last day of the month also contains the impulse to move ahead to the next horizon.

OBJECTS/IMAGES
*dining rooms,
textile designers, silos*

SHAPES/MATERIALS
*woven grasses,
woven materials, sardonyx*

COLORS
*maize color, carrot orange,
navy blue*

ANIMALS
*woodchuck, golden-mantled
ground squirrel*

PLANTS, HERBS, EDIBLES
*valerian, poultry, oats,
Michaelmas daisy*

ESSENCE
spike lavender

SOUNDS/RHYTHMS
*sound of a piano being tuned,
ships' bells*

MUSICAL NOTES
D and A

DEEP SPACE OBJECT
quasar

September 1

YOUR SIGN
Virgo

YOUR ELEMENT
Earth

YOUR RULER
Mercury
8–9 degrees
First Decanate, yang

The Astrological Interpretation

Your birth date is strongly aligned with the powers of Mercury, the messenger. You are most suited to creating connections between ideas and the forms they take in the practical world. You have a need to examine every side of a situation, every possibility before taking action. Sometimes you see too many potential flaws and then you stop in your tracks, unable to move. You are at your best when your vision allows you to perceive how a given situation can be improved, and then you take action to improve it. There is a big difference between constructive criticism and negative thinking. Many of your life experiences will serve to make this distinction very well known to you. You can be most assertive about what you believe and are quick to defend those in need. In this respect, you can be most helpful in collecting funds for charities and good causes.

September 1 enjoys architectural clarity in all surroundings. This birthday has an innate feel for structure and has a number of talents. At home, right angles and sharp corners make you feel rooted. Decorate each corner of the room with something special, like a dried flower arrangement, so that the space is defined as well as beautiful. Colors should be muted and restful. On the wall, line drawings that show futurist environments are stimulating to your mind. Experiment with all forms that highlight your unique abilities. Seek softness in your wardrobe. Consider cashmere sweaters and jersey materials.

Outdoors, you like defined space. A French garden with clear paths and blocks of flowers keeps you oriented. Consider an herb garden with a small wooden bench on the side. Here you can discover new ways to use plants or contemplate your next adventure. You like to travel, and you usually feel at home anywhere in the world.

A Kabbalistic Interpretation

The Hebrew letter *Yod* has a strong influence over your personality. In the context of the other aspects of this day the effect of *Yod* is to add weight to your feelings of family loyalty and obligation. A good present for you would be a leather-bound photo album in which to keep treasured pictures of all your family.

You possess considerable sexual energy, although this may not be immediately obvious to those around you. The tarot card the Devil is responsible for providing the energy behind this aspect of your personality, while other elements in this day point to your sexuality being very much confined to your thoughts. Keeping a vase of purple tulips in your bedroom will help you to express your true nature.

This is a very physical day, and you are likely to be an extremely fit individual. All sports should be attractive to you. The influence of the letter *Zayin* suggests that you would enjoy activities that require a practiced agility and grace. Kendo or fencing may well appeal to you.

A Numerological Interpretation
YOUR MAGIC NUMBERS: 10 AND 2

The first day of the ninth month reduces to ten, the number of embodiment and the completion of the process begun in one. Ten holds dominion over, and perfect expression of, the seeds sown at the onset of the cycle. Born on this day, you have a paradoxical path of giving expression to your inherited tendencies and gifts, which have been supplied by genetics, while at the same time responding to the soul's more universal inner stirrings for growth and unfoldment. The soul is a matrix for its own expression and physical manifestation. You may find the experiences of your life centered around issues that have been a source of conflict for numerous generations.

Plot your genealogy on both sides of your family tree, and study the historical patterns of your ancestors. Adventurine and citrine are gems to open your mind and heart to transcendental possibilities. The 245th day of the year reduces to two, contributing the element of reflection and receptivity to your journey.

OBJECTS/IMAGES
suitcases on rollers, notebooks, Etch-A-Sketch

SHAPES/MATERIALS
Doric columns, hematite

COLORS
muted blue, cinnamon, wheat color, indigo, burnt orange

ANIMALS
hen, field cat, squirrel

PLANTS, HERBS, EDIBLES
chicory, bay leaves, popcorn

ESSENCES
rosemary, celery tonic

SOUNDS/RHYTHMS
square dance rhythms, a metronome

MUSICAL NOTES
A and C#

DEEP SPACE OBJECTS
Epsilon Antlia, Al Suhail

September 2

YOUR SIGN
Virgo

———

YOUR ELEMENT
Earth

———

YOUR RULER
Mercury
9–10 degrees
First Decanate, yin

The Astrological Interpretation

Your hands reach out in service to others, as you feel most at ease when you are performing helpful tasks. You have a great desire to be accepted and will most easily find a place for yourself in the larger social context through being of support. But there is a great difference between being a server and being a servant. Check out your boundaries and make sure that you do not cross over your own lines! You appreciate polite people and are very much at home when men and women are acting like gentlemen and ladies. You are entitled to your own standards, providing that you live up to them yourself.

September 2 has innate curiosity and interest in nature's mysteries. Your fields of inquiry may include both psychic and religious areas. Your interests may lead you to be an explorer or adventurer. Maps, topographical charts, and blueprints intrigue you. Whether you are contemplating a journey or not, hang maps or charts on your walls. A drawing compass and a navigational compass are both objects you would enjoy having on your desk. Bookcases in a variety of sizes fit in with the wide range of your interests. Large bookcases are like your warehouse, and you need small portable bookcases to house your revolving interests. You will enjoy collecting dried flowers, unusual matchbook covers, souvenir menus, and small, pretty stones. You may want to devise some organizational system for your kitchen ingredients, home files, and clothes, books, and music.

Outdoors September 2 wants an environment that is interesting as well as natural. Visits to nearby parks, nature preserves, and areas that feature interesting geological formations spur your imagination. In your own yard consider a garden of medicinal herbs such as mandrake, fennel, and marjoram and decorate it with pieces of marble.

A Kabbalistic Interpretation

Various important numbers in your day point to a mystically minded personality. The number eleven, key number for all things magical, is significant to you. In the evenings, when you are settling down for some quiet time, try lighting a pair of purple candles. This will enhance your understanding of the world of the unknown.

Life tends to go very well for you, and this is in part related to the protective energy of the Star card from the tarot. To encourage this positive influence on your life and achieve more success for yourself, consider wearing a pendant with a seven-pointed star made of bronze.

The number seventy-eight is important this day. To occultists and kabbalists alike the number seventy-eight is significant, as it equals the total number of cards in a tarot deck. Your connection to this number suggests that you have a wide range of possibilities open to you. An original and thought-provoking way to decorate your living room would be to use some blown-up pictures from a traditional tarot set as artwork. They may inspire you to find the path aligned with your true nature.

A Numerological Interpretation
YOUR MAGIC NUMBERS: 2 AND 3 .

The second day of the ninth month reduces to two, the number of receptivity, duplication, and the polarizing alternation as one divides into two. Two is the quintessential number of subconsciousness and the pristine potential aspect of the mind. Born on this day, you have a path of unconditional willingness to be like a white canvas upon which the universe paints the masterpiece of your life. Inherent in this pattern must be a purity of motive and intention and an unspoken sense of faith and confidence in the outcomes. You carry the energy and archetype of Isis unveiled. At your best, your life is a witness to and a microcosm of pulling away the veil of mystery that shrouds the act of creation itself.

Fire opal is a stone to fuel your aspirations. Keep a barite rose rock on your altar as a symbol of your dedication. Wear orange to enhance your courage. The 246th day of the year reduces to three. This supports your path with the pregnant developmental powers of three—a sure sign you will carry all the creations of your mind to full term.

OBJECTS/IMAGES
butter churn, cafés, cereal canisters

SHAPES/MATERIALS
pink jasper, bee shape, marble

COLORS
indigo, crimson, cantaloupe

ANIMALS
kitten, chickadee

PLANTS, HERBS, EDIBLES
malt, white clover, nodding ladies' tresses

ESSENCE
blue mallee

SOUNDS/RHYTHMS
threshing sounds, oboe music

MUSICAL NOTES
C# and D

DEEP SPACE OBJECTS
Delta Leo, Zosma, the Girdle

September 3

YOUR SIGN
Virgo

YOUR ELEMENT
Earth

YOUR RULERS
Mercury, Saturn
10–11 degrees
Second Decanate, yang

The Astrological Interpretation

"There is a place for everything and everything has its place" could be your motto, as you enjoy neatness, order, right timing, and ritual. You are aware of spatial relationships and believe in quality not quantity. You like being treated well and can become quite upset if you feel that you are not being appreciated or that your small wishes are not being met. This can be especially true when you have gone out of your way to be particularly generous. Yet you are often reluctant to tell a person what would please you, and you may expect sensitivity from one who is incapable of giving it.

The fixed star Zosma is located quite close to some September 3 birthdays. Some ancient texts say this position makes the native fearful of poisoning. While unlikely, you do need to be careful about what you eat. The intestines, ruled by Virgo, need good healthful food to operate efficiently. You worry easily, and mental agitation affects the body. The best de-stressor is to drink lots of water, have a massage with sesame oil, and cleanse with oatmeal soap. An image for you is a red pyramid. You might even sleep under a pyramid structure. Photography is a favorite pastime for you. Have a good camera for serious work and carry a disposable one for sudden inspiration.

Outdoors you will enjoy a plot of grass with carefully tended border flowers. Nut-bearing trees remind you of the harvest symbolism of your sign. Consider a basket of nuts for your dining room table. You may enjoy visiting greenhouses, rose gardens, and zoos where the animals live in relatively natural habitats.

A Kabbalistic Interpretation

The number six appears in a number of places in the value of your birthday. This number refers to the letter *Vau,* which represents the element of air. You will find that the element of air dominating your birthday works to encourage your mental processes. You can maximize air energies in your life by placing a yellow fan in the east of your home.

Relationships take priority over work for you, and you try your best to be a good partner. While many of us find it difficult to fully talk about the really important aspects of a relationship, you are genuinely communicative with your partner. You can strengthen this quality by keeping a piece of rose quartz under your pillow at night.

One of the words equivalent to the value of this day is *die*. In this context, this word refers to an internal emotional process of letting go and making room for new experience that can be quite positive. Many of us get trapped in a particular way of viewing the world, but this word suggests that you are able to continually reinvent yourself. Keeping a cactus plant in your house will help you to activate these changes in your life.

A Numerological Interpretation

YOUR MAGIC NUMBERS: 3 AND 4

The third day of the ninth month reduces to three, the number of growth, unfoldment, and multiplication. Born on this day, you have a path of imagining and seizing the opportunities your life presents for rising to any occasion. This is a pattern of grasping lessons present in crises and challenges. You have the innate capacity to assume leadership in such situations and thereby gain tremendous experience, and you can then be an example to those around you. You seem to consistently find yourself in situations where you intervene on behalf of others to avert or solve a critical situation.

Don't submit to timidity; dive in and help. Wear a ring of imperial jade to remind you of the spectrum of quality and value that exists within the third-dimensional world. Become certified to do CPR and first aid; you'll have cause to apply these skills. The 247th day of the year reduces to four, aiding this path with an innately ordered mental process. You are always able to see the big picture, and take a long-range view, even in the midst of a crisis.

OBJECTS/IMAGES
a tea cart, crystal paperweight, a sheaf of dried flowers

SHAPES/MATERIALS
pink jasper, chalcedony, muslin

COLORS
beige, white, dark blue, orange, eggshell

ANIMALS
kitten, bee

PLANTS, HERBS, EDIBLES
bluebells, barley, avocado

ESSENCES
pine, laurel

SOUNDS/RHYTHMS
reading aloud, folk songs

MUSICAL NOTES
D and D#

DEEP SPACE OBJECT
quasar

September 4

YOUR SIGN
Virgo

———

YOUR ELEMENT
Earth

———

YOUR RULERS
Mercury, Saturn
11–12 degrees
Second Decanate, yang

The Astrological Interpretation

This birth date is connected with an image of a huge potluck dinner to which many happy friends have brought exactly the right things. It is easy for you to understand the inner virtues and special talents of friends and coworkers, and you take great pleasure in bringing such gifts out into the open. You know what each person may contribute to a party or project and are careful to organize things in such a way that every individual's offering fits together into a beautifully organized whole. You tend to be precise and meticulous but can also laugh at the natural gaffes and faux pas that are part of every social occasion. Take care not to attempt too many things at once; when you have exceeded your mental storage capacity, things become loose and chaotic.

September 4 likes mystery and looking behind the veil of seemingly simple experiences. You may be drawn to study astrology or mystical disciplines. Figure eights are good images for you to meditate on. Mentally trace a figure eight pattern on your body with the center point at the navel. A large vase of bamboo plant branches near the entryway of your home would be a healthful decorative touch. Decorate your home in earth tones and touches of white. Chenille throws or crocheted afghans over your sofa invite lazy day dreaming. September 4 should take every opportunity to still the mind. An ornate birdcage could be a decorative item as well as a palace for a parakeet.

Outdoors, an herb garden with dill fennel and valerian would support your mystical experiments. Flowers for September 4 include white tulips, Queen Anne's lace, and wild oats.

A Kabbalistic Interpretation

Change is very much the order of the day. The Death card from the tarot indicates that your life is likely to be dominated by a small number of highly significant changes in direction. The accompanying influence of the moon this day suggests that you can find these changes rather unsettling. Try keeping some fresh red chili peppers on your kitchen windowsill, and you will find the confidence to have a more positive attitude toward change.

The lunar influence also has a number of positive effects. The association of the day's value with the Hebrew word meaning "poverty" indicates the moon's effect in giving you a sensitivity to the plight of those less fortunate than yourself. Wear a pearl brooch or a pearl-decorated tiepin, and you will find your naturally charitable feelings enhanced.

It may be that you possess some clairvoyance or extrasensory ability. Your day is connected to the sephira Yesod, which represents the astral level of the universe and the kabbalistic Tree of Life. Even if you don't wish to experiment, a crystal ball would make an interesting addition to your home.

A Numerological Interpretation
YOUR MAGIC NUMBERS: 4 AND 5

The fourth day of the ninth month reduces to four, the number signifying order, measurement, and classification. This is a path of breaking with tradition and exploring your own destiny. The forces of tradition can take on an inertial force of their own, propagating values and actions that can continue to be unexamined. This pattern calls for your apples to fall far from the tree, and not to succumb to a provincial view of life. In a sense, this is like the path of the prodigal son. It is not so much an antagonism with family values as much as a search at a soul level to grow completely new branches on the ancestral tree. The danger of this path is having a false sense of heritage, rather than faith in yourself to express a distinct aspect of self.

Travel to distant lands, either literally or through books and videos. Malachite will give you a sense of comfort with what has gone before, and lapis will aid you in maintaining a mind open to change. The 248th day of the year reduces to five, supporting your path of comfort with change. This facilitates your personal process of evolution.

OBJECTS/IMAGES
atlases, catalogs, beekeepers, purity

SHAPES/MATERIALS
hyacinth, chintzes, cinnabar, agate

COLORS
navy blue, sandy yellow, ivory

ANIMAL
white cats

PLANTS, HERBS, EDIBLES
chicory, endive, hay, lilacs

ESSENCES
petitgrain

SOUNDS/RHYTHMS
music by Anton Bruckner

MUSICAL NOTES
D# and E

DEEP SPACE OBJECTS
Theta Leo, Coxa

September 5

The Astrological Interpretation

Your family has been very important to you. You have had to work hard to root out any inherited traits and characteristics that inhibit your best interests. Yet there is much from your background that is worth conserving. Your job has been to successfully separate the genetic wheat from its chaff. You do not wish to feel limited by past concepts of who you are and what you can do in order to be successful in life. You want to be free to experiment with the limits of your talents and resources and enjoy surpassing yesterday's limits. You will be attracted by adventurous sports such as rock climbing and skiing, as well as traveling to exotic and unusual spots.

This birthday has unseen protection throughout life. Skills in politics and the art of compromise are innate. Figure eights are good images to contemplate or casually draw. You are comfortable in a spare space without many distractions. Wood furniture with classic lines is preferred. Ingenious cabinets with divisions for paper, pencils, paper clips, CDs, etc., are useful and decorative. The bedroom is the place where you could indulge your more romantic side. A white dust ruffle and matched bed linens help calm your busy mental life.

Outdoors, you like an open lawn with brick paths and a small Zen-like garden. A bench facing east to catch the sunrise enhances a feeling of well-being. Carry a pad and sketch your environment or jot down some ideas. If confusion threatens, retreat to the outdoors, calm the mind, and then the "answer" will come.

A Kabbalistic Interpretation

You tend to be an extremely social person, a characteristic pointed to by the importance of the Empress card this day. You like to make your home an inviting place for visitors. Try putting a birdbath in your garden, and paint it vibrant green. Your guests will mimic the birds and flock to you!

Though you have a very open personality when it comes to dealing with people, you can be somewhat close-minded in other ways. The influence of the Devil card from the tarot has the effect of making you suspicious of anything that can't be explained by logic. A good present for you would be a book that seriously examines some of the underlying scientific potential in the world of the unknown.

The planet Venus wields a significant power over your physical appearance. Combined with the Empress card, this planet ensures that you are possessed of a natural beauty. When you want to make the most of your physique you should take this planetary impact into account. The ideal colors for you to wear would be gold and green. In addition soft but heavy fabrics suit you particularly well.

A Numerological Interpretation
YOUR MAGIC NUMBERS: 5 AND 6

The fifth day of the ninth month reduces to five, the number characterized by change, uncertainty, and adaptation. Five connotes a sense of flexibility and versatility. Born on this day, you have a path of continually searching for the finer things in life as they are expressed as humanity's search to align with a higher reality. You are possessed of considerable charm, and you desire to be the means or agency whereby more civilized behavior exists in the world. If you had lived in the Middle Ages, you would have been a knight and a troubadour.

You have a highly developed sense of beauty and the aesthetically pleasing things of life, and your taste is refined where decorating is concerned. Your passion may be to restore and decorate a Victorian mansion in period furniture. The danger of this pattern is that you could seem pretentious to others. Each facet of the Divine expression has its own justification for exploration. Precious opal is a gem to inspire your sense of the beautiful and transcendent. The 249th day of the year reduces to six, enhancing your appreciation for beauty, symmetry, and harmony of opposites.

OBJECTS/IMAGES
a set of encyclopedias, an organized pantry, bud vase

SHAPES/MATERIALS
stretch jersey, flowing materials, origami paper

COLORS
cranberry, spruce, charcoal, lemon yellow, lime green

ANIMALS
prairie dog, rabbit, hamster

PLANTS, HERBS, EDIBLES
peppermint, dill, endive, barley

ESSENCE
jasmine

SOUNDS/RHYTHMS
rhymed couplets, sound of wheat being threshed

MUSICAL NOTES
E and F

DEEP SPACE OBJECT
NGC 3227, external galaxy

September 6

YOUR SIGN
Virgo

YOUR ELEMENT
Earth

YOUR RULERS
Mercury, Saturn
13–14 degrees
Second Decanate, yang

The Astrological Interpretation

This is a birthday that is especially connected to the artistic and the beautiful. It will be very difficult for you to be in a room that is painted in colors that clash or offend you. You like to set a table just so and make sure that every detail is in harmony. This extends to the right background music and, if you are so inclined, the correct wine to serve with each course. Your home has to be an example of the physical perfection that you seek. You need not only a peaceful retreat but also an emotionally uplifting sanctuary in which to entertain your friends or raise your family. You will love antiques but will be especially selective, for not only do they have to match and perfectly blend in with what you already own, but they also have to "feel" right.

September 6 enjoys gentility and harmony in personal relationships at home as well as at work. You have a talent for peace. If you feel fussy then something is out of balance in your life and you can calmly adjust it. Your own family lineage is of interest to you. Consider hanging a large family tree on a wall in the kitchen or family room and filling it in with your ancestors. With Saturn ruling your decanate, September 6 finds value in heirlooms and old crystal glasses. You may want to display the crystal rather than use it. Your home should have a quiet order about it with many different boxes and drawers to keep everything straight. If you work at home try to keep your work area separate, as it is easy for work to spill over into family time.

Outdoors, September 6 loves gardening and composting. You could develop a hobby of raising organic herbs and salad greens. A rock garden as well as a place for vegetables would delight you. Consider planting rock alyssum, red valerian, and edelweiss.

A Kabbalistic Interpretation

Your personality is a rich balance of earth and air energy. You tend to take a rationalistic view of the world. It may well be that you work in the sciences or research, as the idea of probing the physical world is appealing to you. Try using square patterns in the design of your office to encourage a scientific approach.

The influence of the letter *Kaph* suggests that you enjoy working with your hands. At the same time it is unlikely that this enjoyment stems from any artistic endeavor. Rather, you get more pleasure from making something functional for use in your home.

You are a very talkative individual and are able to hold forth at length on a number of different subjects. This is often very interesting for those around you, as you are knowledgeable as well as loquacious. However, it is important to be able to listen to others. Drinking an infusion of mint and nettle tea will help you to learn when to keep your silence.

A Numerological Interpretation
YOUR MAGIC NUMBERS: 6 AND 7

The sixth day of the ninth month reduces to six, the number meaning balance, equilibration, and reconciled polarities. Born on this day, you have a path of identifying sources of power within the primal aspects of your nature that can be mobilized to deal with events or challenges in your life. This pattern endows you with an instinctive ability to get down to basics and peel away superficial layers. At your best, you are in conscious control of the divergent aspects of your personality and can marshal these forces to address the situation at hand. You don't deny the more primitive urges of humanity, in fact, you can use them to your advantage.

Go camping in the wilderness and carry in all your supplies. Sodalite and hematite are minerals to enhance your intrinsic common sense. The 250th day of the year reduces to seven, contributing the ability to step back and examine the significance of your lessons.

OBJECTS/IMAGES
harvests, coupons, atlases, butlers

SHAPES/MATERIALS
polka dots, hematite, cinnabar, Arabic calligraphy

COLORS
beige, olive, grass green

ANIMALS
ant, baby chick

PLANTS, HERBS, EDIBLES
parsnips, privet, birch beer, oats

ESSENCE
oregano

SOUNDS/RHYTHMS
oratory, throaty laughter

MUSICAL NOTES
F and F#

DEEP SPACE OBJECTS
Zeta Ursa Major, Mizar, the Apron

September 7

YOUR SIGN
Virgo

YOUR ELEMENT
Earth

YOUR RULERS
Mercury, Saturn
14–15 degrees
Second Decanate, yang

The Astrological Interpretation

The condition of your physical body is of extreme importance to you. Your stomach and lower intestinal tract tend to be very sensitive, and whenever you become emotionally upset, your digestive system immediately reacts. To reduce any complications in this area, you should always eat wisely and never be self-indulgent when under either mental or emotional duress. If you know this about yourself, you have reached an inner balance that will insure a long and healthy life. Many people born on this date shop exclusively at health food stores, prefer organic foods, and keep quite a storehouse of vitamins, minerals, and other nutritional supplements.

September 7 greets the world with grace and intrinsic elegance. You are interested in your better impulses and associating with others who are on an upward, spiritual path. An image for September 7 is a knight of the Round Table. Purity is your quest. In more material terms, you may enjoy fine napkins, towels, tea towels, and handkerchiefs. Virgo, in general, is very handy with crafts, and you might enjoy making a bedcover from antique hand towels. There is great tenderness in your nature, and cats and puppies gravitate to you. Your mind is strong and assertive, as Saturn, ruler of your decanate, can ground the darting fussy quality you may have. To keep your mind grounded and void Saturn's occasional gloom, carry a small bottle of eucalyptus with you. If you feel overwhelmed, take a whiff.

Outdoors, September 7 enjoys working in a garden or visiting one. Lilacs are particularly pleasing. If you don't have any in your neighborhood, make a trip to an arboretum or park each spring when the lilacs are in bloom. Keeping lilacs in your home can be your own spring celebration and ritual.

A Kabbalistic Interpretation

Privacy is extremely important to you, and you are a wonderful confidant, as you can be trusted implicitly never to reveal anything told to you in confidence. If you want to enhance your ability to keep the secrets of your close friends you should wear an onyx ring on your little finger.

The major tarot influence on this day is the World card. In conjunction with other kabbalistic evidence it appears that this card acts to underline your ability to develop a deep understanding of the way the world operates. Your wisdom about the political world can be enhanced by keeping an ash tree in your garden.

The Hebrew word meaning "dedicated" is equivalent to the value of your birthday. You will never leave a task half finished, but will cut a way through whatever obstacles you find in order to reach a satisfactory conclusion. Keeping some reddish amber ornaments around your work space will help you to keep focused on the task at hand.

A Numerological Interpretation

YOUR MAGIC NUMBERS: 7 AND 8

The seventh day of the ninth month reduces to seven, the number signifying victory and the satisfaction that comes with success. Born on this day, you have a path of constant expansion and searching for new barriers to break through. You are always looking for the next conquest or challenge, and you need to recognize the value of a good rest in between campaigns.

This pattern is similar to the sheer passion and creative force that drove van Gogh to slice off his own ear. Strive for patience and tolerance. Try rock or mountain climbing to test your skill and endurance. Practice yoga or tai chi to gain control of your energy and focus its use. Amethyst and amazonite are gems to enhance your sense of equilibrium. The 251st day of the year reduces to eight, adding the influence of rhythm and the balance of an even number to this path. The mountain will still be there in the morning.

OBJECTS/IMAGES
grain barns, sewing machines

SHAPES/MATERIALS
hematite, straight lines

COLORS
cream, navy blue, pine, sea foam green

ANIMALS
cat, chicken

PLANTS, HERBS, EDIBLES
marshmallow, mandrake, baby's breath

ESSENCE
cerato

SOUNDS/RHYTHMS
precise beat, brush strokes, rap music

MUSICAL NOTES
F# and G

DEEP SPACE OBJECTS
80 Ursa Major, Alcor, The Rider

September 8

YOUR SIGN
Virgo

YOUR ELEMENT
Earth

YOUR RULERS
Mercury, Saturn
15–16 degrees
Second Decanate, yin

The Astrological Interpretation

Although you appear modest and demure, you have a deeply passionate facet of which few are aware. In general, you are not emotionally demonstrative. Many people these days customarily exchange friendly hugs and kisses upon meeting and departing. You prefer a sincere smile and a warm handshake. When you do open yourself to an intimate experience, it is with someone for whom you have a very clear and profound attraction. Either you are really turned on or completely turned off by someone—there is very little middle ground. It may take a while for you to open yourself to the object of your affections, but when you do, there is little doubt that your gentle exterior hides a molten core.

September 8 has considerable intellectual abilities and is able to make connections among people and ideas that can bring about much needed change. Your organizational skills are often in the service of social reform, and you effortlessly seem to meet or know the right people to move projects forward. An image for you is a group of people seated around a large wood conference table eagerly discussing plans. Keep your mind and health sharp through good nutrition and supplements. What your body can absorb is often more important than what you eat. You may find the herbs ginkgo biloba and royal bee jelly helpful. At home keep notepads in handy places so you can jot down thoughts. You may want to have a variety of desks to use for different projects. A desk where you could stand when writing or thinking may be very useful to you.

Outdoors is where September 8 renews energies. A garden would be a way for you to order your thoughts as well as think up new projects. Weeding, watering, pruning, and planting are meditative activities. Plants herbs such as chicory, valerian, and succory and the flowers bachelor's button, and light pink cosmos.

A Kabbalistic Interpretation

One of the words that is equivalent to the value of this day is the Herbrew word meaning "joy." This word points to not only your general attitude to the outside world but also indicates that the world has a tendency to work with you rather than against you. You can bring some of this joy to your friends by keeping your kitchen decorated in bright colors, especially oranges and yellows.

Another word associated with this day is the word meaning "alas." It is unlikely that this word relates to your own feelings, but it may indicate your concern for those who have less happy lives. It may be that you are involved in some sort of socially beneficial work. Counseling would be an ideal career for you, as you can combine your genuine concern for others with your excellent communication skills. Your chief aim is to empower those people who come to you for help. You can encourage this by keeping a reddish orange pyramid on your desk. By drinking an infusion of burdock each morning you will protect yourself from being overly affected by others' negative emotions.

A Numerological Interpretation

YOUR MAGIC NUMBERS: 8 AND 9

The eighth day of the ninth month reduces to eight, the number that carries the meaning of vibration, involution, and evolution. Born on this day, you have a path of cultivating comprehension of true inner guidance. This pattern requires that you sharpen your inner hearing and develop the acumen to dismiss idle mental chatter. Experiment with a pendulum for divination. Have your own set of tarot cards, and keep them wrapped in a blue silk cloth.

The danger of this path is superstition or bondage to a superficial form of fortune telling. Your requests for guidance should not be frivolous. Labradorite is a gem to open a channel to the unseen realms. The 252nd day of the year reduces to nine, adding the quality of the clear expression of the idea that began the cycle. This aids the comprehension and clarity of your inner voices.

OBJECTS/IMAGES
streetcars, tennis courts, governesses, closets

SHAPES/MATERIALS
kernel shapes, chintzes, stacks of paper, zircon

COLORS
slate blue, turquoise, sky blue

ANIMALS
meadow vole, tabby cat

PLANTS, HERBS, EDIBLES
large-flowered trillium, azaleas, calomel, whole grain bread

ESSENCE
palmarosa oil

SOUNDS/RHYTHMS
trombone alarms, Antonin Dvorak's New World Symphony

MUSICAL NOTES
G and G#

DEEP SPACE OBJECTS
Beta Canes Venatici, Asterion

September 9

YOUR SIGN
Virgo

YOUR ELEMENT
Earth

YOUR RULERS
Mercury, Saturn
16–17 degrees
Second Decanate, yin

The Astrological Interpretation

You have a special code of behavior and a very definite set of personal boundaries. Should a person cross over or trip on one of your invisible lines, that individual will not be particularly welcomed in your life. One complication in this is that you often do not tell others what is on your mind. Your expectations are silent, and people may not know that they are being offensive to you. You will find that the more patient and tolerant you are of yourself, the easier it will be to accept weaknesses in others.

Generally, you are prudent and hardworking, but you are also creative, which must find an outlet. However you choose to express yourself keep persistent and wait for inspiration, which will come. At home have a variety of "idling" projects such as sharpening your pencils, rolling change in wrappers, and labeling spices. Mundane routines will divert your mind and then you'll have a good idea and be off. You tend to collect small boxes, chests, baskets, and other places of storage that are both decorative and functional. A decorative object for your home could be Russian dolls or globes that fit inside one another. On your walls you may enjoy macramé tapestries or large pieces of woven cloth. The color scheme should be in earth tones with a hint of pink or red. A portrait of a ruler or wealthy person in a sedan chair may be an image that stirs your imagination.

Outdoors, September 9 would be very happy where you can raise crops or vegetables. A farm vacation could renew your energies. If your yard is small consider planting carrots, beans, corn, and flowers such as buddleia and bouvardia. Wildflower such as Dutchman's-breeches, cowwheat, and prairie mimosa also appeal.

A Kabbalistic Interpretation

You have an exceptionally powerful and impressive character. Your charismatic nature is immediately apparent to those who come into contact with you. This aspect of your character is suggested by the influence of the serpent on this day. The serpent is a very important character in kabbala, as it represents both personal desire and a

Promethean drive to better one's self. Keeping a gold-colored statuette of a snake on your desk will help you maintain your drive in life.

The Promethean aspect of the serpent is enhanced by a connection to the planet Mercury. This planet also boosts your intellectual abilities. When you need to have a particularly clear mind, wear a touch of bright orange, the color of Mercury, in your outfit.

The Hebrew word meaning "flower" is equivalent to one of the values of this day. In the context of the other influences, this association refers to your ability to create a blossoming of the potential of those around you. A large spray of flowers on your desk will encourage this positive effect of your personality.

A Numerological Interpretation
YOUR MAGIC NUMBERS: 9 AND 10

The ninth day of the ninth month reduces to nine. This string of nines emphasizes that this day's path is one of completion. It's as if you live with the constant impression that your life is a contest, and you're always striving to outdistance your competition and be first at the finish line. This pattern is one in which self-mastery comes through a positive comparison with others in which you strive to improve. Healthy competition is one of the best ways we can perfect our skills. If we have no yardstick by which to measure our progress, it is difficult to know if we are advancing in performance.

Regardless of the arena in your life, you will always feel as if you are engaged in a game of skill. Learn to relax, not everything is a contest. A string of pearls will remind you of the sacrifices often made to beauty. Adventurine is a stone to temper your burning sense of conquest. The 253rd day of the year reduces to ten, the number of perfection and dominion. This only adds to your sense that you have to reach the top of the mountain first. Take care, it's lonely at the top.

OBJECTS/IMAGES
birdcages, beekeepers, sewing notions, filing cabinets

SHAPES/MATERIALS
jasper, mercury, haystacks, beehive shapes

COLORS
indigo blue, royal blue, deep purple

ANIMALS
red squirrel, black-tailed prairie dog

PLANTS, HERBS, EDIBLES
fontina cheese, Cornish game hen, endive, Queen Anne's lace

ESSENCE
cilantro

SOUNDS/RHYTHMS
a scythe cutting hay, Otis Redding's "(Sittin' on) the Dock of the Bay"

MUSICAL NOTES
G# and A

DEEP SPACE OBJECT
pulsar

September 10

YOUR SIGN
Virgo

YOUR ELEMENT
Earth

YOUR RULERS
Mercury, Saturn
17 degrees
Second Decanate, yin

The Astrological Interpretation

A symbol for this birth date is a beam of laser light. You can spot a hole in someone's logic as easily as you can see a hole in their sock. Nothing escapes your eye for detail. Sometimes you wish you could turn this honing device off, as it is sometimes annoying to catch the little mistakes in the world around you. Nevertheless, your ability to spot that tiny glitch often leads to the prevention of more severe errors. One of your major lessons in life is the development of mental discrimination. This involves knowing when leaving well enough alone is the right course of action. You need feel no guilt over your own or especially other people's imperfections.

This birthday is signified by what astrologers call "critical degrees," which means that highs and lows register strongly throughout life. The fundamental nature of the birthday is tremendous energy. September 10 strives to use the analytic qualities of Virgo for self-examination. At home you surround yourself with either creative clutter and the accoutrements of your latest project or keep the space bare and immaculate so the mind can roam free. You can be happy in a small or large home. Your style tends toward the angular, with an emphasis on dark comfortable furnishings. Mission furniture may be a particular favorite. Your work space is the center of your home and should include some kind of "shop" where you can fix, putter, and create.

Outdoors a garden is relaxing with white geraniums and a weather vane. Chipmunks seem particularly attracted to you; watching them scamper is a relaxing break. You might enjoy keeping a compost pile, and you definitely want to include vegetables and herbs in the garden. In the country, an old-fashioned root cellar will keep fruits and preserves ready for use.

A Kabbalistic Interpretation

The earth energies that influence people born under your sign of Virgo are given some vitality and drive by the influence of the planet Mars this day. The planet Mars is well known as a planet of war, but it also represents a pioneering spirit in individuals. You can encourage your initiative and bravery by wearing some jewelry with an arrow design.

Not only do you have the ability to initiate new ideas and projects, but you are also good at bringing those ideas and plans to fruition. The phrase "a bushel of wheat" in Hebrew is connected to this day and it refers to the bringing in of a harvest. A corn husk doll kept in the north of your main living room will assist you in achieving your chosen goals.

The Fortune card from the tarot is also important this day. It is in its aspect as a champion of risk that the Fortune card influences this day. This is an essential part of being a pioneer in any field. However in order to balance this energy with some necessary caution, keep a little pouch of sage in your pocket at all times.

A Numerological Interpretation

YOUR MAGIC NUMBERS: 1 AND 2

The tenth day of the ninth month reduces to one, the number of beginnings, initiative, and originality. Born on this day, you are likely to be the leader of the pack. This pattern thrusts you into a variety of experiences where you can test your flair for maximizing the dividends in any situation. You have a gift for bringing the world to your doorstep, but you are not unwilling to go out after it too.

You love variety. Given the resources, you would have more than one car, a vacation home in France, and a condo on the ocean. The danger of this path is having a constant sense of restlessness. Cultivate patience. Learn to meditate when you get itchy to be on the move for no reason. Cinnabar and wulfenite are minerals to enhance your zest for diversity. The 254th of the year reduces to two, assisting your path with the capacity to still your mind and reflect.

OBJECTS/IMAGES
embroidery thread, postmen, proverbs, a scribe working on papyrus, dominoes

SHAPES/MATERIALS
right angles, triangles, feathery materials, window boxes, shutters, abalone, light agates, mother-of-pearl.

COLORS
crimson, geranium orange

ANIMALS
parrot, bee, hyena

PLANTS, HERBS, EDIBLES
papaya, woodbine, clover, beans, avocado, Queen Anne's lace

ESSENCES
classic perfumes, the smell of freshly mown hay

SOUNDS/RHYTHMS
steady even tempi, scales, poetic verse

MUSICAL NOTES
C and C#

DEEP SPACE OBJECT
supernova

September 11

Your Sign
Virgo

Your Element
Earth

Your Rulers
Mercury, Saturn
18–19 degrees
Second Decanate, yin

The Astrological Interpretation

You have a restless and adventurous nature and enjoy traveling and seeing the world. But you prefer to leave nothing to chance. You pack all the little medicines, cosmetics, toiletries, and sundries you could ever need. All your clothing and accessories have to match, and there has to be an outfit for every occasion. You make sure that you have traveler's insurance, and before you go anywhere, it is vital that you are totally confident about pet and plant care. Once everything is in place, then you feel free to give yourself over to pure pleasure. You are attracted to resorts where every little whim is catered to with ease and graciousness. After all, you definitely deserve it.

September 11 brings literary talent and the desire to express feelings on paper. This is good practice for you, as the Mercury rulership of your sign can encourage mental whirls disconnected from the emotions. Let whatever you have to say pour out. Your writing or work space may have a pleasant clutter to it, but do clear a space on your desk every time you write something. Even in the age of the computer, sharpening pencils may be a ritual that will get you in an expressive mood. Little boxes to hold supplies or keepsakes are good decorative objects for you. In the kitchen you will feel well organized if you have a correct utensil for every need. Put all cooking spoons, spatulas, etc., on a hanging rack in front of the stove. Everything should be convenient.

You may not be involved with farming per se, but you enjoy escaping to wide open fields. Bring some reminders of the earth indoors. An urn filled with sheaves of grain or dried flowers could grace your front hall. Fresh wildflowers are always a good idea. You may want to dry some and press them in a collage.

A Kabbalistic Interpretation

The rat race holds little appeal for you, as you have a very artistic temperament. While it is an enormous risk you have significant talent, and it may well prove worthwhile to forgo a regular job to work on your creative projects. As there are connections in this day to the Hebrew word for "clay" and the letter *Kaph,* meaning "palm," sculpture may be the medium for you.

Another word that connects to your day is the Hebrew word for "vision." In one sense this refers again to your artistic abilities and eye for detail. At the same time it refers to the need for long-term planning, which is so important to keeping yourself organized. Buy some good filing boxes and paint them yellow to encourage a clearer approach to planning in your life.

The moon has a far-reaching effect on your personality. You may find that you are more creative when there is a full moon. Lunar energies will act as a boost to your imagination. You can encourage the moon's effect by burning some frankincense.

A Numerological Interpretation

YOUR MAGIC NUMBERS: 2 AND 3

The eleventh day of the ninth month reduces to two, the number of replication, dependence, and polarized expression. Because one divides to create two, the number can carry the energy of antagonism born of separation. Born on this day, you have a path of gaining an intimate understanding of the principle of division of labor. This pattern calls for pursuit of specialization and your own personal refinement.

The paradox of this path is that your ultimate expression is tied to outstanding cooperation with other people. Satisfaction occurs when others are as rewarded as you. Play in a softball or volleyball league for fun. Discover which position you fill best, and enjoy the results when the whole team excels. Citrine is a gem to highlight your specialties. The 255th day of the year reduces to three, adding the helpful influence of creative self-expression and unfoldment. This helps keep you on the move to improve.

OBJECTS/IMAGES
a quill pen, a cornucopia, multicolored paper clips

SHAPES/MATERIALS
slender curves, bamboo

COLORS
gray/green, beige, dark blue, carmine, peach

ANIMALS
kitten, beetle

PLANTS, HERBS, EDIBLES
blue flag, marshmallow, popcorn

ESSENCES
fennel, sandalwood

SOUNDS/RHYTHMS
tapping of fingernails, bees buzzing

MUSICAL NOTES
C# and D

DEEP SPACE OBJECTS
Beta Leo, Denebola, the Lion's Tail

September 12

YOUR SIGN
Virgo

YOUR ELEMENT
Earth

YOUR RULERS
Mercury, Saturn
18–19 degrees
Second Decanate, yin

The Astrological Interpretation

You have the ability to turn your thoughts into pictures. Once you envision your goals, and take the necessary time to connect with your inner power, there is no stopping you. It is easy for you to gather the necessary resources to achieve your objectives. You know where everything and everyone fits, as you have an inner game plan thoroughly structured and outlined prior to setting off. You like maps, charts, and graphs. You like to see where you are going and will investigate who went there before you. If you can profit from the mistakes of others, or learn from their successes, you feel better equipped. Business and commerce are definitely your areas, and you will be especially attracted to the retail trade. You like exotic objects from many countries not only for your of business but also to adorn your personal space.

For you, winning and how you play the game are important. Your imagination—being able to visualize wishes and hopes very concretely—is a great asset. You may have a fondness for country life and agricultural pursuits. At home, have a variety of seed and flower catalogs. Rotate flowers in your home according to the seasons. Poinsettias for winter, lilacs for spring, azaleas for summer, and chrysanthemums for fall. Decorative planters may also be a way to express your creativity. Around your desk area keep decorative wooden or metal organizers for pencils, pens, and paper clips. September 12 doesn't want to waste time searching for tools. A thorough dictionary should also be by your desk. Even in the times of spell check, you will want to consult a dictionary to explore words and their etymologies.

Outdoors, continue the agricultural theme with a garden, and if you have a lot of space, a field of corn or grain. Running a farm stand or growing vegetables would be great hobbies for you. Investigate medicinal herbs and organic farming.

A Kabbalistic Interpretation

The word *meditation* has the same value as this day, and it has enormous influence over your whole personality. You are more concerned with your self-development than you are with financial success. A wonderful gift for you would be a Tibetan mandala to help you achieve deeper insights through meditation.

Another word connected to this day is *purity*. This again emphasizes your emotional or spiritual state. A sense of moral well-being is important to you, and you like to make your home environment reflect your relationship with the world. A number of pictures of birds around your home would make an appropriate decorative addition.

It may seem that this day is full of spiritual concerns but is lacking fire energy to keep you going in your day-to-day life. In actual fact you have a vital personality and are bursting with positive energy. If you can find a gold ring inlaid with ruby to wear on your index finger you will be even more energetic and motivated.

A Numerological Interpretation
YOUR MAGIC NUMBERS: 3 AND 4

The twelfth day of the ninth month reduces to three, the number of development, growth, and multiplication. Born on this day, you have a path of pursuing the unfolding values of the culture. You have a strong sense of right and wrong, and this translates into a staunch moral code that drives your actions and beliefs. You possess a belief in stewardship of the tenets and values you cherish, and do not dismiss the ideals of others easily. Study the U.S. Constitution or the Magna Carta. At your best, you can motivate others to support a noble and common cause.

Create a personal coat of arms that embodies personal symbols and values, and hang your design where you will be reminded of them. Amber is a gem to inspire your sense of the molding forces of nature and culture. The 256th day of the year reduces to four, contributing the ordering influence of the physical world to your process.

OBJECTS/IMAGES
a nib fountain pen,
a tailor sewing,
a commemorative plaque

SHAPES/MATERIALS
porcelain, bamboo, rice paper

COLORS
tan, orange, golden yellow

ANIMALS
prairie dog, fox

PLANTS, HERBS, EDIBLES
lovage, hay, chia seed

ESSENCE
elecampane

SOUNDS/RHYTHMS
clear speech,
Maurice Chevalier's singing

MUSICAL NOTES
D and D#

DEEP SPACE OBJECT
Alpha Antlia

September 13

YOUR SIGN
Virgo

YOUR ELEMENT
Earth

YOUR RULERS
Mercury, Saturn, Venus
19–20 degrees
Second/Third Decante, yin

The Astrological Interpretation

You live in a world of enormous potentials and possibilities. Your challenge in life is picking the right ones. You expect to be entirely fulfilled by the object of your devotion. This is true whether it is a relationship or a career. One problem is that even with the best of intentions, your loyalty can waver. There is the sense that a better opportunity is just around the corner but you are stuck away somewhere, missing the boat. The point is—you are the boat! Life is indeed like an ocean with currents that pull us one way and then another. But you are responsible for the oars and the rudder. It is your clarity of insight and precision of discrimination that will bring your ship ashore.

Some September 13 birthdays fall on the fixed star Denebola, located in the Lion's tail. The ancients claimed this star brought honors and wealth along with regrets. You have a strong mind and dislike being challenged. An image for you is a fencer parrying and thrusting. Your mind is a fencer's foil that elegantly and effortlessly defends your views. A variety of notebooks will keep all your thoughts and projects organized. At home, have a fountain somewhere in your living space. If you can find one built around a rotating wheel then the motion and the sound of the water will calm you. An eye pillow filled with lavender is a perfect relaxer for you. In your work area have elegant cream-colored vellum stationery. When you write your letters to the editor, your stationery needs to be as elegant as your ideas.

Outdoors, you find inspiration in wildflowers. Queen Anne's lace and oregano blossoms are particularly appealing. Have azaleas bordering your yard; you like clear distinctions between areas. Pomegranate trees are also in tune with September 13.

A Kabbalistic Interpretation

You approach each day with an enormous sense of enthusiasm and optimism. The influence of the Fool card from the tarot means that you are always open to new experiences in life. Burning chalcedony incense in the evening will encourage this openness to life.

The Fool refers to an attitude we take to life, but as it is connected to the element of air, it lacks any influence over action. This is compensated for by a connection to the sephira of Netzach. This sephira is associated with the element of fire and represents the seat of emotional passions. In order to energize the effect of this sephira in your life, burn a green candle in the south of your living room.

Your day has quite a significant amount of fire energy, although much of it is directed at your thoughts rather than your emotions. This can have the effect of making your thoughts somewhat muddled and confused. By adding water energy you will gain some clarity about what you really want to do. This can be achieved by keeping some fresh water in a yellow-colored bowl.

A Numerological Interpretation

YOUR MAGIC NUMBERS: 4 AND 5

The thirteenth day of the ninth month reduces to four, the number signifying order, reason, and tabulation. The character of four is to give everything a place and make sure things stay put. Born on this day, you have a path of overcoming your tendency to order your world so well that you respond habitually. This pattern calls for you to take inventory of your own potentials and exercise the will and self-discipline to bring these talents to fruition. Engage all of yourself in this quest; you will be amazed at the results. Go to the zoo and see what you can learn from the instinctive and habitual behavior of animals. Automatic behavior can save time and energy if tasks require no thought or change.

Don't surrender your power of reason or choice for the sake of convenience. Amazonite is a stone to open your mind. The 257th day of the year reduces to five, providing a stimulus to change and adapt. This will help you look at other options.

OBJECTS/IMAGES
weather forecasters, dresser valet, Filofax

SHAPES/MATERIALS
flint, hyacinth, sheaf shapes

COLORS
the color of driftwood, honey, pale yellow

ANIMAL
dachshund dog

PLANTS, HERBS, EDIBLES
avocado, bee jelly, malt

ESSENCE
citronella

SOUNDS/RHYTHMS
whispering, the sound of typing

MUSICAL NOTES
D# and E

DEEP SPACE OBJECTS
Epsilon Carina, Avior

September 14

YOUR SIGN
Virgo

YOUR ELEMENT
Earth

YOUR RULERS
Mercury, Venus
20–21 degrees
Third Decanate, yin

The Astrological Interpretation

It is necessary for you to develop a kind of internal glue, a type of personal magnetism that allows you to hold the many bits and pieces of your diverse energies together. When you are upset and unduly worried, you lose this magnetic center, and like a dandelion in the wind, you burst into segments that fly away. If you are born on this day and haven't yet found your center, this should be your objective. Work on achieving a knowledge of correct breathing techniques. Your breath will calm the emotions and center your mind. You already know the benefits that fresh fruit and vegetable juices bring into your life. Add to this a regular regimen of slow and deep breathing, especially before you undertake any major effort or have an important confrontation.

September 14 has an innate sense of nobility and refinement. You may dedicate yourself to a cause or study the laws of nature. In your quest to let people know "the way things are," you may be a bit imperious. Your challenge is to back up your sense of right with knowledge and humility. At home you might enjoy ordering your kitchen cabinets according to colors. A file box of recipes should be updated frequently. Consider subscribing to a newsletter of interesting health tips. Rattan is a material for you, and kitchen implements hung on a lattice type rack will help keep you organized. In your work space—at home or at an office—have an assortment of boxes that are colorful as well as practical. With Venus ruling your decanate you want beauty as well as order.

Outdoors, September 14 should invent a coat of arms to display over the garden gate. You might want to include some family symbolism such as a sheaf of grain, or a special flower, like lilacs.

A Kabbalistic Interpretation

Everyone who knows you will have the greatest respect for your very clear and firmly held sense of ethics. The influence of the Hierophant card from the tarot, with its emphasis on morality and social stability, is at work here. You can encourage a sense of stability in your life by hanging a picture of a bull or oxen on the north side of your bedroom.

The full value of this day is a prime number, indicating a strong sense of individuality. It is good to be unique, especially with pressures today that encourage conformity. Celebrate your own particular nature by keeping some unusual objects in your home. A collection of air plants would be an ideal addition to your home.

The letter *Tzaddi* is connected to this day, and its main influence relates to this letter's connection to the sign Aquarius. This is one of the air signs of the zodiac and also refers to a strong sense of individuality. To keep your thoughts clear, try placing some yellow painted water jars around the outside of your house.

A Numerological Interpretation
YOUR MAGIC NUMBERS: 5 AND 6

The fourteenth day of the ninth month reduces to five, the number of change and uncertainty. Five is in constant motion. Born on this day, you have a path of wide-eyed exploration of the world around you. You possess a thirst for discovery and always yearn to find adventure. This pattern requires that you couple your ingenuous approach to life with an adult sense of responsibility.

At your best, you can convert your native charm into something constructive. Volunteer at a library and read stories to children. Try your hand at writing a children's fairy tale. The danger of this path is a temptation to be a Pollyanna or Peter Pan. Blue lace agate and sodalite are gems to keep you grounded. The 258th day of the year reduces to six, adding the important influence of balanced polarities and complementary activities to this path.

OBJECTS/IMAGES
luggage, forgery, business forms, clear glassware

SHAPES/MATERIALS
needle shapes, oscillating shapes, chrysolite

COLORS
dusty blue, daffodil yellow, apple green

ANIMAL
chihuahua

PLANTS, HERBS, EDIBLES
thimbleweed, oconee bells, star chickweed, and nail-wort

ESSENCE
carrot seed

SOUNDS/RHYTHMS
talking birds, dialects

MUSICAL NOTES
E and F

DEEP SPACE OBJECTS
Alpha Crater, Alkes

September 15

YOUR SIGN
Virgo

YOUR ELEMENT
Earth

YOUR RULERS
Mercury, Venus
21–22 degrees
Third Decanate, yin

The Astrological Interpretation

It is up to you to use the power of your mind and the strength of a love-centered will to transform your raw animal vitality into a force for positive, creative self-expression. The animal trainer has to be courageous and learn techniques that transmute fear into strength. This is done through education and its application in daily life. You may have to be patient with yourself, and be willing to unlearn those habits that distract you from your success. You are a perpetual student and should be involved in taking those courses, seminars, and workshops that give you the ability to learn new "tricks."

Your ideas and intelligence often bubble over. Sometimes the mind gets going faster than the body can support. September 15 needs to take good care of nutritional needs. Taking vitamin and mineral supplements is a good idea, as is eating in a quiet environment. There is a natural aristocracy in September 15, and you might enjoy having insignias or coats of arms displayed somewhere in your home. You could research if your family has its own coat of arms, but any herald that appeals will do. Monogrammed silverware, towels, and sheets give you a personal feeling of pride and heritage.

Solid colors in muted shades are best for you to wear and to decorate with. Think of the colors of a wheat field and arrange your palette around it.

Outdoors September 15 derives power from the earth. Lying on the grass or sitting on a bench in your garden is just the cure for too many thoughts. You might find a copy of Rodin's statue *The Thinker* and place it in your garden for company. A sandy beach is also a great pick me up. You may enjoy the beach more on cloudy days.

A Kabbalistic Interpretation

You are demanding of yourself and others, and this can make you seem quite a forbidding individual. The combined energy of the Devil card and the letter *Teth*, meaning "serpent," mean that you can be extremely aggressive in pursuit of your goals. While ambition and drive are good facets of your personality you need to offset them with a little forgiveness. Keep some rowan and rue leaves in your pocket in a blue pouch and see if it softens your character.

You have unusual reserves of energy and an ability to keep going when others need rest. It is important that you not make unrealistic demands on yourself. No one can keep working flat out forever. You can encourage yourself to relax more by adding a few drops of ylang-ylang oil to your bathwater.

If you can lighten your workload, you will discover that you have hidden talents. This day has energies that suggest a particularly artistic nature. Set a room aside for you to practice artistic pursuits; for exceptional inspiration, use triangular patterns in the design of this room.

A Numerological Interpretation
YOUR MAGIC NUMBERS: 6 AND 7

The fifteenth day of the ninth month reduces to six, the number that represents love, balance, and complementary activities. Yours is a path of building a sterling reputation. This is a pattern of pursing worthwhile endeavors for the sake of your soul. This path can confer a sort of immortality in the sense that your achievements are recorded in the annals of history. Respect is important to you, and you believe this admiration should be earned. But this not a shallow desire to have power. Visit the Vietnam Memorial or the Holocaust Museum. What are the actions or contributions that merit a place in history? How do you wish to be remembered? Strive always to reach your ideal.

Star sapphire is a noble gem to remind you of worthiness and strengthen your resolve. The 259th day of the year reduces to seven, providing the instinctive confidence that victory is assured.

OBJECTS/IMAGES
*snow angels,
dried flower arrangements
or collages*

SHAPES/MATERIALS
kohl, marble, star shapes

COLORS
*cream white, slate blue,
moss green, kelly green*

ANIMALS
*chipmunk, tabby cat,
guinea pig*

PLANTS, HERBS, EDIBLES
cumin, valerian, bonsai trees

ESSENCE
lily of the valley

SOUNDS/RHYTHMS
*Chinese cymbals, mild wind
through leaves,
exhalation of breath*

MUSICAL NOTES
F and F#

DEEP SPACE OBJECTS
*Alpha Corvus,
binary star system*

September 16

YOUR SIGN
Virgo

YOUR ELEMENT
Earth

YOUR RULERS
Mercury, Venus
22–23 degrees
Third Decanate, yin

The Astrological Interpretation

You are a fertile field upon which an abundance of trees, bushes, shrubs, vegetables, and flowers happily flourish. Yet it is very difficult for you to find time for cultivating the many forms of flora that take root in your "garden." You go through periods of extremely careful attention, leveling each blade of grass to the correct height. At other times your plants are growing so fast that they are literally taking over the house while you lie on the couch thinking about job possibilities. You then leap back into action, scissors and scythe in hand, and bring order once again into your life. Use a day planner to keep track of things, making sure it has plenty of room for all the little notes and personal reminders that you tend to write to yourself.

September 16 is an enthusiastic birthday with a roving eye and thirst for romance. The quest for purity that underscores all Virgo birthdays is here expressed in having adventures and telling stories. You may have a special love of pets and of cats in particular. If you can't keep pets do have some paintings or drawings of kittens on your walls. With Venus ruling your decanate, beauty in your surroundings is important. Crystal paperweights, or small carved pieces of glass are perfect decorative objects. If you are a traveler you may want to collect matchbooks or wrapped sugars from the various places you stay and display them in a bowl or under a coffee table glass.

Outdoors, September 16 would enjoy a garden with stepping-stones. Tiles, flat pieces of polished wood, or slate would all be possible materials. A white garden gate and fence would set off your space perfectly. Flowers for you are dogtooth violet, and globe flower.

A Kabbalistic Interpretation

Few people have such strongly held views as you. You are one of those rare people who will actually take action to back up your beliefs. This attitude about those issues that are dear to your heart is indicated by the combined energies of the Chariot and the Hebrew word *Al* in your day. When you need to temper this crusading energy, burning a blue candle on a white holder will create a sense of peace.

You will probably be regarded by your friends as something of a bon vivant, as this date has very strong associations with the enjoyment of good food. Everything we eat affects our mood and elemental balance to some degree. As this day lacks sufficient air energy, try to eat foods that will encourage this element. Anything that is light and airy in consistency will help.

Family is very important to you, and the letter *Beth*, which means "house" and refers to our emotional loyalties, has a strong influence this day. This letter combines with *Tzaddi*, which means "fishhook" and indicates that you like to keep your family close by. A good present for you would be a photo album with a cream-and-pink marbled cover.

A Numerological Interpretation
YOUR MAGIC NUMBERS: 7 AND 8

The sixteenth day of the ninth month reduces to seven, the number of victorious achievement, security, and temporary cessation between cycles. Seven pauses to admire the accomplished work before resuming the quest for the summit. Born on this day, you have a path of joyous appreciation for your gifts, and a transcendent dedication to building a better world, and sharing the bounty with those around you. The danger of this path is temporarily losing sight of your ideal and building for the sake of being busy.

Volunteer to coach a children's athletic activity. Being around young people will help maintain your perspective. Rhodochrosite is a gem to galvanize your highest motivations. The 260th day of the year reduces to eight, which provides the quality of rhythm and vibration to your path. This aids your ability to take stock and, when necessary, make adjustments to your course.

OBJECTS/IMAGES
vouchers, signs, patterns, looms

SHAPES/MATERIALS
hegolite (stone), emerald, pearls, sheaves of grain

COLORS
creamy beige, willow green, teal

ANIMALS
thirteen-lined squirrel, kitten

PLANTS, HERBS, EDIBLES
lilacs, colicroot, shepherd's needle, wheat berries

ESSENCE
bergamot

SOUNDS/RHYTHMS
whistling, trombone music

MUSICAL NOTES
F# and G

DEEP SPACE OBJECTS
Delta Crater, Labrum

September 17

YOUR SIGN:
Virgo

YOUR ELEMENT
Earth

YOUR RULERS
Mercury, Venus
23–24 degrees
Third Decanate, yin

The Astrological Interpretation

You are possessed of a special gift that can only be called the "simplicity of innocence." No matter how busy and complex your life may be, there is a fundamental core within you that remains pure. You simply do not understand and refuse to accept that there are elements of cruelty in life. At times, you close your eyes, preferring not to see. Yet many people born on this day work with people in distress. Some of you are called to the medical professions, while others prefer social services. It is important for you to be of use, knowing that your life counts as you reach out across the pain of ignorance and selfishness into the lives of others. You find it natural to wear simple clothes, preferably in lighter colors. You would enjoy wearing white but have a definite problem with stains, specks, and spots.

You are a hard worker and can certainly be mature and adult when it matters, but your true nature is to explore your own creativity with a sense of play. Criticism of yourself or others is anathema to play. If you catch yourself overanalyzing, hum the nursery rhyme "Mary Had a Little Lamb." At home your decor should be simple and elegant. Bookshelves set into the walls with fluted columns please you. You may read a good deal and want to keep many volumes. Some September 17 birthdays favor clutter, while others are scrupulous purgers. Colorful stamps are pleasing to you, and even if you don't collect stamps you would prefer to use a new issue that looks beautiful. Cooking is another creative opportunity for you. Devise your own recipe filing system so you can keep track of dishes that work particularly well.

Outdoors, September 17 likes to garden and enjoys white flowers, especially white lilac. All wildflowers are ruled by Virgo. September 17 may particularly enjoy wild madder, sweet cicely, and featherbells.

A Kabbalistic Interpretation

The cards the Hermit and the Star wield a great and wholly positive influence over your personality. The Star represents protection and bodes well for your progress. The Hermit refers to the wisdom that activates the energy of the Star. Hanging an old-fashioned lantern over your front door optimizes the protective and positive effect of these two cards.

You are very much an outdoor person, and one of your favorite hobbies will be gardening. The energy of the planet Saturn suggests that you enjoy growing your own vegetables. You will get the best results from your garden if you use tools with green-painted wooden handles.

The full value of this day comes to ninety-three. This is a highly significant number in occultism, as it represents the will. You can draw on the energy of this number by wearing a pendant with a sun image or a traditional Egyptian eye of Horus design

A Numerological Interpretation
YOUR MAGIC NUMBERS: 8 AND 9

The seventeenth day of the ninth month reduces to eight, the number signifying the ebbing and flowing motion of everything in creation. Eight is a number of material success and comfort at manipulating the physical world. Born on this day, you have a path of maximizing the legacies of earlier generations. This pattern requires that you develop your capacity to distill and internalize the noblest virtues and values from preceding generations. Implicit in the pattern is your own responsibility to pass along the pearls of wisdom and strength of character you have achieved. Each breed of animal, such as domestic dogs or cats, possesses certain qualities that have been cultivated.

Indulge in high tea, sipping from the finest porcelain china. Moonstone is a gem to link you to ancestral memories. Celestite is a stone to elevate your ideals. The 261st day of the year reduces to nine, contributing a sense of fulfillment and comfort with endings.

OBJECTS/IMAGES
bee-shaped night-lights, monocles, grocers

SHAPES/MATERIALS
pink rhodochrosite, papyrus, satchel shapes

COLORS
navy blue, aquamarine, royal blue

ANIMALS
white cats, white-breasted nuthatch

PLANTS, HERBS, EDIBLES
lavender, avocado, tread-softly

ESSENCE
jasmine

SOUNDS/RHYTHMS
the sound of tennis balls bouncing back and forth, jazz trumpet

---

MUSICAL NOTES
F# and G

DEEP SPACE OBJECTS
Eta Ursa Major, Alkaid, Leader of the Mourners

September 18

Your Sign
Virgo

Your Element
Earth

Your Rulers
Mercury, Saturn
24–25 degrees
Third Decanate, yang

The Astrological Interpretation

When you are expressing your talents and abilities to their highest degree, you are like a dedicated researcher, always seeking to improve the status quo. Your job is to perfect, polish, and refine all undertakings. You have a way with rough edges, knowing how to smooth them to a sharp, gleaming blade. Although you like working with a team of like-minded men and women, you have a special need to have your own particular tasks well-defined. You do not mind being alone, in fact you appreciate not having anyone make undo demands upon your time and energy. It is difficult for you to say no to someone who asks you for help, so it is far easier for you just to concentrate on your work in comfortable solitude.

The fixed star Labrum is located near some September 18 birthdays. This star has been associated with the Holy Grail, spiritual intelligence, and a search for perfection. You have a fascinating charm that intrigues people. An image for you is a golden ball twirling in space. This is a good meditation whenever you feel confused or become overly critical of yourself or others. At home keep some woven materials of natural fabrics around you. These could be shawls, afghan throws, or table linens. Learning to weave would be an excellent hobby. You might enjoy wearing handwoven cotton sweaters. In the bedroom a wicker bed frame would be excellent for you. Consider having a whole bedroom set of white wicker. The feeling of a summer seashore home pleases you.

Outdoors, in addition to a simple colorful garden, you would enjoy hanging a lattice piece against a wall where you could train flowers into a variety of shapes. Virgin's bower, clematis, and morning glory are all excellent choices for you.

A Kabbalistic Interpretation

The energies of your day all point toward the possibility of achievement, promising a full successful life. You may have a tendency, however, to give up on your goals at the last minute. Wearing an item of jewelry made of iron or colored in crimson will help you to keep going right up to the completion of your projects.

Other people's needs are as important to you as your own desires in life. People around you will be very appreciative of your willingness to assist them in their own lives. Your altruistic nature is indicated by the Hanged Man card from the tarot. If you want to enhance your benevolent and principled personality, grow an ash or cypress tree in your garden.

Water is the primary element on this day and is concerned with emotional states. Of the other elements, fire energy is underrepresented, and this may adversely affect your motivation and drive in life. If you buy a statuette of a lion, especially one colored emerald green, you will find that you have greater vitality in your approach to life.

A Numerological Interpretation

YOUR MAGIC NUMBERS: 9 AND 1

The eighteenth day of the ninth month reduces to nine, the number signifying attainment and the end of a cycle. Nine embodies the fulfillment of a goal. Born on this day, you have a path of seeking satisfaction through your inner life. This pattern is one of mastering your interior landscape and, as a result, finding complete wholeness. This is not a journey of isolation but rather of intense self-control. You are uniquely suited to perform solitary tasks and don't require the constant stimulation of others to feel complete.

The danger of this path is that no one can measure up to your expectations. Belong to some sort of group. You may not think you need people, but in fact we are all related. Azurite is a gem to ground your energies and open you to others. Wear rose quartz to warm your heart. The 262nd day of the year reduces to one, adding the crucial element of unity and singleness of purpose to support this path.

OBJECTS/IMAGES
slander, colored pencils, magazines, learning

SHAPES/MATERIALS
wicker, bamboo, marble, rolled shapes

COLORS
dusty blue, cobalt blue, cherry

ANIMALS
greyhound, gerbil

PLANTS, HERBS, EDIBLES
prairie mimosa, Greek valerian, wood sage, peanut butter

ESSENCE
spikenard

SOUNDS/RHYTHMS
soliloquies, simultaneous translation

MUSICAL NOTES
G# and C

DEEP SPACE OBJECTS
Beta Virgo, Zavijava

September 19

YOUR SIGN
Virgo

YOUR ELEMENT
Earth

YOUR RULERS
Mercury, Venus
25–26 degrees,
Third Decanate, yang

The Astrological Interpretation

This birth date is especially connected to the quality of calm self-reliance. Never one to panic or to crumble under pressure, you know that even the most complicated of life situations can be solved with time and the right approach. You carry within yourself an inner first aid kit, the complete contents of which are not known to you. You just know that whenever a challenge comes up, you manage to handle it with confidence and efficiency. Yet this ability is available not only when things are rough. You can also put together a great party with a moment's notice, and you have the ability to know just who should sit next to whom at dinner.

You have a deep respect for accumulated knowledge and will want to add your own insights. Consider writing or researching a family history with references to the historical events of the period. You may also be the family record keeper with copies of birth certificates, Bibles, and papers and scrapbooks. You may prefer to write in pencil and a supply of good number 2s will delight you. In your home Venus, your coruler, reigns. A curio cabinet to display decorative objects would be a wonderful addition to your living room. Built-in bookshelves with columns or decorative wooden moldings please your sense of order and aesthetics.

Outdoors, September 19 likes a garden with a touch of confusion. The mix of colors and shapes are so pleasing that your usual sense of order is suspended. Think about having wildflowers such as pyxie, starflower, and beetleweed together with lilac bushes, tulips, and morning glories. Having a series of low stools that you can easily move throughout your garden would be a good way to take in the whole space.

A Kabbalistic Interpretation

The Fortune card from the tarot has a double effect on your day. On the one hand it indicates a willingness to take risks, especially when connected with a business venture or career prospects. Additionally it suggests that if you decide to set up your own business you will do well in an area connected to travel of some kind. Hanging a traditional ship's wheel on your wall will give you the impetus you need to strike out on your own.

The planet Jupiter is also connected with good fortune and favors those who attempt to make their own way in the world. It is likely that you will be able to derive positive energy from the influence of this planet. You can encourage its influence by keeping a small square of tin with an upright triangle engraved upon it in your pocket.

Emotionally you are likely to have quite a turbulent series of relationships. Indeed this day's value suggests that there will be many times when you are faced with a choice between your work commitments and your love life. Wearing a sapphire ring on your middle finger will help you to make the right decisions.

A Numerological Interpretation
YOUR MAGIC NUMBERS: 1 AND 2

The nineteenth day of the ninth month reduces to one, representing beginnings, initiative, and singleness. One is symbolic of the conscious mind. Yours is a path of moving into new areas of human expression. This pattern calls for you to discover the potential that exists in seed form in the embryonic stage. Humanity isn't finished yet. We are baby godlings who have not yet left our playpens. This path asks that you are reasonable about our status and yet stretch your mind to see and understand the ultimate possibility.

The mystery of Isis veiled is contained in this journey, for although we can glimpse the end product, we cannot yet grasp the measure of our full potential. Banded Brazilian agate is a stone to connect you with your inner fire. Wear a pendant of amber to awaken ancient memories. The 263rd day of the year reduces to two, accentuating the hidden nature of your quest. Two adds the capacity to go within and reflect on your experiences.

OBJECTS/IMAGES
craftsmen, doctors' offices, meadows, notebooks, Hummel statues

SHAPES/MATERIALS
sardonyx, emerald, colander shapes

COLORS
delft blue, scarlet, rust

ANIMAL
blue-eyed cats

PLANTS, HERBS, EDIBLES
obedient plant, Plains bee balm, Darjeeling tea, millet cakes

ESSENCE
ylang-ylang

SOUNDS/RHYTHMS
whir of a sewing machine, fingernails tapping on a keyboard

MUSICAL NOTES
C and C#

DEEP SPACE OBJECTS
Kappa Vela, Markab

September 20

YOUR SIGN
Virgo

YOUR ELEMENT
Earth

YOUR RULERS
Mercury, Venus
26–27 degrees
Third Decanate, yang

The Astrological Interpretation

You wonder at times just how much of yourself you are willing to give up for professional goals and harmony in relationships. You can be satisfied with relatively little but are often tempted to go beyond the intimate and protective circle you create for yourself, as the wider world and all of its beauty beckons. You are very reliable, highly organized, and structured. You prefer to live within your means and avoid the excess pressures of debt. Yet you dream of more excitement and spontaneity and wonder how you can integrate a wider realm of personal freedom with still wanting to hold on to the safe and secure. This duality can be resolved by going "up" rather than "out." Seek a philosophy or spiritual path that focuses on inner freedom and you will be less bothered by outer restraints.

September 20 blends a sense of beauty with a quest for purity in everything they do and have. Blond wood furniture is especially pleasing to you, and a beautiful and useful desk is a prized possession. To avoid fussiness at the lack of perfection in the world, you should surround yourself with smooth curved shapes. A window seat in a bay window is the spot in which to dream, organize, and create. A single natural-color beeswax candle in the window will provide focus and clarity.

Outdoors, September 20 likes wide rolling lawns with clumps of trees. A golf course is an ideal picture, even though you may not play. In your own backyard, plant small flowers along the borders of your property. If you have a garden keep your flowers and herbs in separate areas. You will enjoy walking from the wildflowers, through the herb garden, to the rhododendron bushes.

A Kabbalistic Interpretation

Community holds a very special place in your heart. You would be well suited to living in a small town where you can make a genuine contribution. One possible path for your involvement is some form of construction enterprise. Wearing a yellow topaz on a pendant will help your concentration and focus when you are involved in this work.

You have an exceptionally strong mind, both analytically acute and swift thinking, thanks to the influence of Mercury and the sephira Hod. It is highly probable that reading will be one of your favorite hobbies. If you can, you should have a metallic chair painted in orange and blue in which to sit when you want to really concentrate on your current book.

The words *where* and *how* in Hebrew are connected to the value of your day. This connection relates to the communicative element of the planet Mercury and a desire within you to explain new concepts to others. Teaching will be a key element of your chosen career. Keep a silver-framed mirror in your study or reading room to encourage this ability within yourself.

A Numerological Interpretation
YOUR MAGIC NUMBERS: 2 AND 3

The twentieth day of the ninth month reduces to two, signifying polarity, duplication, and the principle of the life force in action. Two is the replication of one by division. Born on this day, you have a path of exceptional receptivity and alertness to inner prompting. Your life seems charmed to others. An extreme and amusing example is the cartoon character Mr. Magoo. Nearly blind, he blithely makes his way through life, protected and unaware of his many narrow escapes. Another image is children being protected by a guardian angel. Your way of life and attitude toward spirit is your constant safeguard. Because of this orientation, the universe seems to shape and affect circumstances in a miraculous way.

Citrine and rutilated quartz are stones to harmonize your mental energies and keep the communications pathways clear. The 264th day of the year reduces to three, adding the natural unfoldment of creative expression to this path, supporting the seemingly miraculous way the events of your life unfold. Even your challenges seem ordained.

OBJECTS/IMAGES
*calligraphy pen,
well-worn leather briefcase,
harvesting wheat*

SHAPES/MATERIALS
*straight lines,
mixed agate stones, whirlwinds*

COLORS
*slate gray, beige, rich brown,
burnt sienna*

ANIMALS
squirrel, kitten

PLANTS, HERBS, EDIBLES
*avocado, pomegranates,
myrtle trees*

ESSENCES
eucalyptus, smell of clover

SOUNDS/RHYTHMS
*children's nursery rhymes,
steady heartbeat,
the crinkle of tissue paper*

MUSICAL NOTES
C# and D

DEEP SPACE OBJECT
Alpha Centauri

September 21

YOUR SIGN
Virgo

YOUR ELEMENT
Earth

YOUR RULERS
Mercury, Venus
27–28 degrees
Third Decanate, yang

The Astrological Interpretation

Although you are a very independent person, you are seeking those rules and patterns in life upon which you can place your trust. Your question (and your quest) is: What works? You are not satisfied with most religious doctrines or teachings and certainly have moved away from those that were embodied by your parents. You are a practical person, with a strong need to be professionally and financially secure. A symbol for your birth date is a coiled spring. It indicates that you think in many intricate and convoluted ways that can result in a great deal of inner tension. Yet when the spring springs, you are charged with a sense of purpose and mission that takes you to your goals. You are mechanical by nature and seem to be able to fix anything. You appreciate all kinds of tools, from needles to wrenches, pencils to computers.

The fixed star Markeb will be located on some September 21 birthdays. The ancients thought this placement indicated piety, educational work, and voyages. In whatever way you explore life, September 21 actively seeks knowledge. Your imagination feeds on details and facts. Reading or writing mystery stories is excellent food for your brain. You enjoy word games, crossword puzzles, and card games. You may have an excellent memory for card sequences. Keep a diary of thoughts and activities. If you like to cook you may keep a special diary of successful recipes. In your home hand-loomed fabrics such as flax or spun cotton are pleasing to you. Consider having a loom yourself and see what you can create.

Outdoors your garden and environment may be a naturalist's laboratory. You enjoy researching medicinal herbs and cultivating them. Organic gardening or farming may be one of your interests. Herbs for you are dill, fennel, and parsley. Medicinal flowers such as arnica, hollyhock, and lavender also appeal.

A Kabbalistic Interpretation

Fairness and justice are all-important to you in life. Everyone around you, especially in your workplace, will recognize your ability to act in a genuinely independent way when it comes to resolving a dispute. You could try putting a black-and-white tiled floor in your kitchen to enhance this admirable aspect of your personality.

The moon also exerts a positive influence on this day. Its main effect is to create a sensitivity to the needs of others, which may even result in some natural healing ability. A pearl brooch or tiepin will encourage your ability to develop a healthy optimism in others, and your potential to act as a solid rock of support to those in need.

For all your generous and kindly attributes there is a core of steel running through your character. It takes major opposition to stop you from pursuing and achieving your goals in life. This inner resilience will be a great source of strength to you. It can be maximized by keeping a five-pointed star of metal in your pocket or purse.

A Numerological Interpretation

YOUR MAGIC NUMBERS: 3 AND 4

The twenty-first day of the ninth month reduces to three, the number signifying growth, development, and creative expression. Three develops and multiplies the principles of one and two. Born on this day, yours is a path of continually projecting yourself into experiences. This pattern propels you into life unconditionally. Your path is a blend of a never-ending quest for perfection and a desire to capture something of beauty forever.

A dragonfly captured in amber is an emblem of this pattern. It is as if the creature is perfectly captured in suspended animation to be viewed and examined. Visit a natural history museum, and reflect on the captured beauty of exotic butterflies in acrylic cases. At your best you are able to articulate these feelings to yourself and others. Wear amber and malachite to intensify your imagination. The 265th day of the year reduces to four, contributing the element of order, classification, and tabulation.

OBJECTS/IMAGES
stamps, masseurs, locks, magazines

SHAPES/MATERIALS
square trunk shapes, rattan, quicksilver, turquoise

COLORS
wheat color, taffy, ginger

ANIMALS
chipmunk, gray squirrel

PLANTS, HERBS, EDIBLES
wood sage, valerian, savory, dill, fennel, parsley, peanut butter and jelly sandwiches

---

ESSENCE
fennel

SOUNDS/RHYTHMS
lyrics, chantlike melodies

MUSICAL NOTES
D and D#

DEEP SPACE OBJECTS
Kappa Boötes, Asellus Tertius, the Third Little Donkey

September 22

YOUR SIGN
Virgo

YOUR ELEMENT
Earth

YOUR RULERS
Mercury, Venus
28–29 degrees
Third Decanate, yang

The Astrological Interpretation

You are born on the last day of the sign Virgo and may feel the pull of the next segment of the zodiac, Libra. The combination of these two signs gives rise to a person who takes great pride in completing very complicated tasks. You have an anchored system of how to approach most problems and challenges in life. You have an eagerness to project yourself outward and explore who you are through your personal relationships. There is a tendency to alternate between deep personal commitments and a desire for total independence. Yet you are more flirtatious than promiscuous. You like to play much more than perform, enchant much more than capture. Your need for personal freedom to investigate additional possibilities for creative self-expression is very strong.

Your analytical nature is directed toward creating beauty in yourself, your environment, and others. Communication and friendship is part of your job. Your home, work space, and car should be as orderly and beautiful as possible. If you have the clutter urge, keep it organized and clean or your mind may be confused with too much stuff. Fresh scents like peppermint, lavender, and camphor keep confusion at bay. At home, wallpapering with images of grain and wildflowers will remind September 22 of the fruits of the earth. You have a lot of curiosity, and you may want to have a series of small bookshelves throughout your home. This way you can pull out an interesting book for a quick read here and there. Telephones are interesting to you. An old-fashioned princess phone might be just the right touch. Make sure the ring is a pleasant sound rather than a harsh beep.

Outdoors, a garden is a real source of pride and beauty for you. An herb as well as flower garden will give you a feeling of well-being and luxury. Fennel may be a particular herb for you and Queen Anne's lace a beautiful flower. Urban dwellers could have window boxes or an indoor herb garden.

A Kabbalistic Interpretation

The letter *Shin* has a significant effect on your personality. Its meaning is "tooth," and it is connected to the element of fire. In terms of your personality this letter indicates that you have a great deal of drive and determination. You can increase the level of your inner focus by keeping a real fire in your living room, ideally in the south side of the room.

One meaning of this day's value is "to grow great." This day is connected to eating and could mean physical changes, but it is much more likely to refer to your personal development. You have the capacity to grow great in your career and can enhance this by wearing scarlet in your outfit on important days.

The word *white* is also connected to this day, suggesting a particularly virtuous approach to life. You have a great desire to influence others to follow your own example in the way they deal with people. Burning a simple white candle in the evening will help you to achieve this.

A Numerological Interpretation
YOUR MAGIC NUMBERS: 4 AND 5

The twenty-second day of the ninth month reduces to four, the number that embodies the physical world. Four is the number of concrete reality and stability. Born on this day, you have a path of learning to transmute your familiarity and comfort with the physical world into a new awareness of ways of being beyond the physical. This pattern constantly moves you out of your comfort zone and into the unknown. You feel as if you live your life on the verge of something. There is a sense of anticipation. Relax, you are giving birth to your divine self.

Aquamarine is a gem that will open your mind beyond the physical realm of the third dimension. The 266th day of the year reduces to five, adding a familiarity with change. Five is a number of transition and helps offset feelings of uncertainty.

OBJECTS/IMAGES
stacks of paper, a bowl of nuts, a map room

SHAPES/MATERIALS
beehive shapes, origami paper

COLORS
dusty blue, light brown, ecru, salmon

ANIMALS
prairie dog, gopher

PLANTS, HERBS, EDIBLES
endive, toasted marshmallows, root beer

ESSENCE
elemi

SOUNDS/RHYTHMS
repetitive chant, smooth rhythms

MUSICAL NOTES
D and D#

DEEP SPACE OBJECTS
Kappa Boötes, Asellus Secundus, the Second Little Donkey

September 23

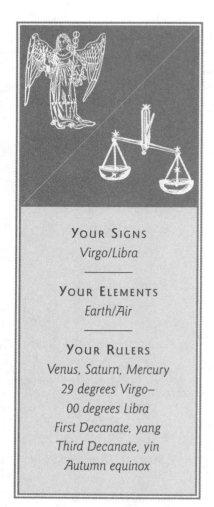

YOUR SIGNS
Virgo/Libra

YOUR ELEMENTS
Earth/Air

YOUR RULERS
Venus, Saturn, Mercury
29 degrees Virgo–
00 degrees Libra
First Decanate, yang
Third Decanate, yin
Autumn equinox

The Astrological Interpretation

Welcome to the realm of Libra and the autumn equinox. Touch me, feel me, see me, you seem to say as you move vivaciously out into life. You love the excitement of interchanging with others. The key to your happiness is more than just a one-on-one intimate relationship, it is being accepted by the many people that you meet. Although still unsure of yourself, you test your attractiveness at every opportunity. You have to be careful of a certain degree of naïveté in all of this interpersonal interplay. Where others are concerned, you often lose sight of the need to be discerning and discriminating. Always one to make a good appearance, you have an inner sense of color coordination and love the texture and feel of fine fabrics.

Libra is the only sign of the zodiac whose symbol is inanimate. The scales of justice need human mercy and experience to keep them balanced. Your birthday is the very beginning of Libra but may have a memory of the preceding sign, Virgo. You have a fastidious nature and are scrupulously honest. An image for you is a perfect cube. Pieces of marble sculpture or marble tabletops would be welcome additions to your home. A copy of a Greek statue such as one of the caryatids combines Aphrodite (goddess of Love) and Ceres (goddess of the harvest.) The overall feel of your home should be beautiful and orderly. In the bedroom have a padded silk headboard. September 23 likes to feel like royalty.

Outdoors a garden with white pebbled paths and flowers requiring little extra care suits your nature. You may enjoy dancing, and having an outside area where you could practice a pirouette would please you. Flowers for September 23 are forget-me-nots, tulips, and rose acacia.

A Kabbalistic Interpretation

Everyone has a good time when you are around, as you have a great sense of humor and know how to lighten the atmosphere in difficult situations. You like to laugh as much as you enjoy raising the spirits of those around you, and a great gift would be a collection of comedy tapes or books.

Although you know how to have fun you are also a very hard worker. Not only do you put in the hours, but you also tend to work at a much quicker pace than your colleagues. Your alacrity comes courtesy of the association of the Chariot tarot card with this day. Any artwork with images of speed, especially any representing horses, will inspire you to be your dynamic best.

One word that shares its value with this date is *beginning*. You have a definite knack for coming up with new ideas. However, you can sometimes find it hard to maintain your enthusiasm long enough to see the results. Try growing a sizeable hawthorn hedge around your house, as it generates a positive energy conducive to success.

A Numerological Interpretation

YOUR MAGIC NUMBERS: 5 AND 6

The twenty-third day of the ninth month reduces to five, the number that connotes mediation, adaptation, and transition. The number five mediates and shifts processes into their next phase. Born on this day, you have a path of an insatiable appetite for the new. Your pattern makes you a herald for what is to come. You always want to be in the forefront of what is new and unusual. You love to try the latest gadgets and adore anything innovative, like phoning a friend from an airplane. You will be among the first to have a video phone and call your partner from the space shuttle.

Positive application for the betterment of humanity is the key. Alexandrite is a gem to enhance your mental frequencies. The 267th day of the year reduces to six, contributing the element of beauty and balance to this path of the future.

OBJECTS/IMAGES
perfume, sachets, sororities, fraternities, sonnets

SHAPES/MATERIALS
ovals, sodium phosphate, white coral, copper

COLORS
pastel blue, bright yellow, chartreuse

ANIMAL
ring-necked pheasant

PLANTS, HERBS, EDIBLES
calypso wildflower, rose moss, kidneywort, butterscotch

ESSENCE
citronella

SOUNDS/RHYTHMS
serenades, old British music hall songs

MUSICAL NOTES
E and F

DEEP SPACE OBJECT
super galactic center

September 24

The Astrological Interpretation

You are constantly testing the limits of your attractiveness through strong and direct interchanges with others. Although you prefer, really insist upon, creating harmony with all and everyone, you surprise yourself with how many oppositions there are in your life. It seems that for every action you take, there is another, opposite reaction to your movements and desires. You then find yourself reacting to the reaction, and this can go on and on, like kids playing on a seesaw. Yet you are very uncomfortable with any form of argument or discordance and do all you can, even to the point of self-compromise, to "make everything okay."

Your birthday brings an excellent imagination and a refined mind. Yours is a personality searching for wisdom and life experiences that will help you grow. Surround yourself with beauty, colors that resonate with your personality, and objects that you like. An image for you is a collection of brightly colored butterflies. You will enjoy earrings of all kinds and probably have quite the collection of jeweled accessories. Small painted boxes for special jewelry or paper clips will appeal to you. Using aesthetic objects for practical purposes is fun for you. Consider having a crystal dish for your keys and spare change. Have wood furniture of a variety of fruitwoods in your home. Carved wood with vines and scroll shapes particularly appeal.

Outdoors September 24 loves gardens that are organized and well planned. Grass surrounded by shrubs such as buddleia and bouvardia, accompanying urn-shaped planters with godetia and creeping jenny and flower beds of white roses create a feeling of harmony akin to the inner balance you seek.

A Kabbalistic Interpretation

People who know you well know that there are some days when it is best to keep a low profile, as you have a tendency to be irritable from time to time. It may not happen often, but when you do get into a bad mood everybody feels it. Your tendency to become angry easily is related to the enormous amount of fire energy in your personality. You can help control your temper by keeping a sprig of angelica in your pocket at all times.

The Strength card from the tarot also connects to this date. The main thrust of this card indicates that you have great strength of will and considerable courage when faced with difficult situations. You can increase your bravery in the face of opposition by wearing an emerald ring on your index finger.

Equally important to this day is the Justice card from the tarot. This card indicates that you have a strong sense of right and wrong, and that you are as rigorous in your demands on yourself as you are on others. It is important to remember that justice involves mercy and clemency as well as judgment. A pair of bronze weighing scales in the western quarter of your kitchen will help you feel more compassionate toward those who disappoint you.

A Numerological Interpretation
YOUR MAGIC NUMBERS: 6 AND 7

The twenty-fourth day of the ninth month reduces to six, the number signifying beauty, equilibrium, and harmony of opposites. Six naturally harmonizes polarities. Born on this day, you have a path of social involvement. This pattern draws you out of personal concerns into the broader arena of group fellowship. This path provides opportunities to practice nonjudgment and unconditional acceptance of others. You are also invited to widen your risk-taking quotient, and express yourself without inhibitions. Organize group functions that include the widest diversity of people, ages, and cultures. Sing songs around a campfire.

Green quartz and rainbow jasper are stones to extend the limits of your circle. The 268th day of the year reduces to seven, providing the healing influence of peace, security, and satisfaction. This supports your feeling of confidence as you step out.

OBJECTS/IMAGES
architecture, bridal chambers, butlers, cabarets

SHAPES/MATERIALS
opals, white beryl, college quads, clown ruffs

COLORS
pastel pink, spring green, spinach green

ANIMALS
dolphin, Hungarian partridge

PLANTS, HERBS, EDIBLES
strawberry tree, rose of Sharon, toffee, apple butter

ESSENCE
mandarin

SOUNDS/RHYTHMS
aeolian harp, giggles

MUSICAL NOTES
F and F#

DEEP SPACE OBJECT
NGC 4261 supermassive black hole

September 25

YOUR SIGN
Libra

YOUR ELEMENT
Air

YOUR RULER
Venus
1–2 degrees
First Decanate, yang

The Astrological Interpretation

The Navajo Indians of the American Southwest have a saying: "I walk in beauty." It is the affirmation of the splendor of creation of which we are all a part. You have a great need not only to walk in beauty but also to be a vehicle that brings beauty into other people's lives. You cannot tolerate disharmony, whether that is in the colors or furnishings in your work or living space, or between yourself and other people. Art is a great friend to you, as you can find tremendous strength and personal integration when surrounded by examples of great masters of painting and sculpture.

September 25, ruled by the planet Venus, is deeply connected to beauty and a refined aesthetic. Experiment with the many ways you can beautify yourself, your environment, and share your experiments with friends. Furniture with brocade upholstery and in pastel colors would be a lovely decorating touch. A window seat in a bay window, overlooking a garden, is a wonderful place to sit and think, particularly if you decorate it yourself. You spend a lot of time smoothing and balancing problems, so staring out the window is the perfect way to work it out. In the rest of your home have lamps that create a rosy dawn. Pink lamp sconces may be a perfect touch. A fire opal is a mineral for you. Wear it in a ring or carry an uncut piece in your pocket. The flashing colors remind you of internal and external beauty.

Outdoors, September 25 would enjoy a formal French garden with a rose arbor and grass cut in geometric shapes. Pansies bordering the grassy area complete the picture. In your own yard you might consider planting a center circle of grass, then four curved wedge shapes around the circle with white pebbles dividing the shapes. The overall feeling should be balance and symmetry.

A Kabbalistic Interpretation

You have a pioneering spirit and are eager to explore new ideas and experiences. The impetuosity that is needed by anyone who wants to be inventive in their life is tempered in your case by the influence of the Hermit card from the tarot. Encourage the Hermit's wisdom in the way you approach the world by painting a wooden chair grayish purple; keep it as your own personal chair in your living room.

A connection to the sephira Malkuth along with other influences this day suggest a desire to do well financially. As you are inventive and determined there is no reason you shouldn't achieve this goal. Your one obstacle is getting a handle on organization. Invest in a decent set of file boxes to help you keep your affairs in order. If these boxes are russet and olive, so much the better.

The letter *Mem*, which means "water" and is associated with positive and deeply felt emotions, is important this day. It refers to a connection with your family and in particular to a desire to keep a very close connection to your parents. Keeping a dark blue vase in the west of your living room will help ensure that you maintain your close familial links.

A Numerological Interpretation
YOUR MAGIC NUMBERS: 7 AND 8

The twenty-fifth day of the ninth month reduces to seven, the number that represents victory, rest, and temporary cessation between periods of activity. Yours is a path of seeking to understand hidden mysteries. Your pattern beckons you inward to contemplate the great secrets of life. At your best, you are able to draw profound realizations from a deep well of universal knowledge and communicate this to others. Have a discussion group in your home with like-minded seekers.

Banded agate is a gem to heighten your sense of inspiration. Collect stones of varying color combinations. The 269th day of the year reduces to eight, adding the comforting awareness that nothing in this world lasts forever. All things have their season.

OBJECTS/IMAGES
flowing fabric,
luxury furniture

SHAPES/MATERIALS
cameos, brass, Thai silk

COLORS
pastel blues and greens,
aquamarine

ANIMAL
ladybug

PLANTS, HERBS, EDIBLES
ficus trees, oleander, burdock

ESSENCE
ylang-ylang

SOUNDS/RHYTHMS
minuet,
"The Blue Danube" waltz

MUSICAL NOTES
F and F#

DEEP SPACE OBJECTS
Theta Boötes, Asellus Primus,
the First Little Donkey

September 26

YOUR SIGN
Libra

YOUR ELEMENT
Air

YOUR RULERS
Venus, Saturn
2–3 degrees,
First Decanate, yang

The Astrological Interpretation

Aside from being with your chosen partner, you like most to share with friends moments of social pleasure. You make definite alliances with others and strive to blend the people in your life so that everyone you love eventually comes to love one another. Sometimes this is impossible, and you can suffer a great deal of grief if you discover that two of your best friends, or your best friend and your lover, do not get along. You must learn to accept that not everything in life can be harmonious. You may need to learn to integrate the reality of the moment with your profound idealism and come to realize that there are situations you just cannot fix.

September 26 combines steadfastness with the ability to see both sides of a question fairly. Once you make a decision on any matter you stick with your convictions. Make your home comfortable for entertaining and gatherings. A pair of love seats, perhaps in light green, placed opposite each other with a low coffee table in front and two armchairs at each end of the table is a good design for your living space. Everyone can be comfortable and see one another. Your bedroom is private space and should include a vanity with a mirror and a chaise longue. Tapestries on the wall are perfectly in keeping with your aesthetic sense.

Outdoors your yard should have a lot of space and a socializing area around a campfire. September 26 may prefer cut flowers to gardening. Roses and dogwood would all be perfect decorations for your outdoor patio or pavilion.

A Kabbalistic Interpretation

This is a day for a vigorous character; the number of the date—twenty-six—can be reduced to the number eight, which corresponds to the tarot card the Chariot. The Chariot is concerned with victory and suggests a confident, somewhat strident approach to life. If we add the month to the date we get thirty-five, which again reduces to eight—so this day really does produce winners and fighters.

In all of us there are certain strong traits that can be positive. Yet it is often those same characteristics that need balancing if we are to achieve a healthy life. You can offset your natural fighting nature and access your calmer, gentler side by carrying a small piece of rose quartz in your pocket. The Chariot is symbolically opposite to the tarot card the Moon, whose associated colors are buff and silver. Wearing these colors when you are feeling particularly intense will have a calming effect. Yet you will not want to do away with your drive and ambition altogether, and there will be days when you want to accentuate that side of your nature. Pointed jewelry or arrow-shaped pendants will help focus your martial spirit.

People born on this day are drawn to powerful sensory experiences. If you want to attract someone born this day try a musky perfume rather than a flowery scent. The value of this day has certain correspondences with the Sphinx, so any images of this mystical creature will be very attractive.

A Numerological Interpretation
YOUR MAGIC NUMBERS: 8 AND 9

The twenty-sixth day of the ninth month reduces to eight, the number of rhythm, involution, and evolution. Born on this day, you have a path of gaining a penetrating insight into the true significance of your ideals. You have a highly developed imagination, and your own perfected mental landscape is your favorite abode.

Your pattern requires that you translate your high-mindedness into practical applications in your daily life. Work where great visions and true teamwork are rewarded. You cannot tolerate hypocrisy in others, so your own life should personify your values and ideals. Turquoise is a gem to help ground your idealistic visions in a practical way. The 270th day of the year reduces to nine, giving you a strong sense of confidence that you can accomplish your task. Reach up and catch a star.

OBJECTS/IMAGES
*witty repartee,
crystal perfume bottles,
leather driving gloves, art deco*

SHAPES/MATERIALS
*balanced shapes, taffeta,
diamond*

COLORS
*pink, pastel peach, teal,
royal blue*

ANIMALS
polo pony, dolphin

PLANTS, HERBS, EDIBLES
tea, sorrel, grapevines

ESSENCE
chamomile

SOUNDS/RHYTHMS
*nocturnes, Gershwin's
Rhapsody in Blue*

MUSICAL NOTES
G and G#

DEEP SPACE OBJECTS
Zeta Draconis, Nodus

September 27

YOUR SIGN
Libra

YOUR ELEMENT
Air

YOUR RULERS
Venus, Saturn
3–4 degrees
First Decanate, yang

The Astrological Interpretation

A symbol for this birth date is a mountain climber preparing to reach a new plateau. Although it is through relationships that you experience many of the important experiences of your life, it is the quality of these encounters that is essential to your well-being. You are deeply connected to the concept of balance. This means that you tend to meet people only on your level. But if you want to rise in life, if you want your relationships to be with people who help you to advance, you have to make the effort to advance yourself. You cannot rely on another mountain climber to toss a rope to you. You have to anchor your own feet on the next upward level of life's experiences.

September 27 combines boldness with great need for human fellowship. The challenge here is to remain yourself in a group and to rest content when alone. There is a dreamy quality to some September 27 people, and expressing yourself in the arts is quite likely.

At home you may want to decorate with touches from whatever art appeals to you. A painter's palette or ballet shoes could hang on the wall. A collection of theater tickets and programs under your coffee table glass would bring back pleasant memories. Symmetry is important for September 27. An image for you is a cornice and pedestal over a perfectly centered front door. Noticing balanced geometric figures and imagining yourself right in the middle will help keep you centered.

Outdoors, September 27 enjoys white roses, wild cherry trees, and almond trees. Plan a white circular bench in the center of your garden and serve tea to your friends. If you feel you are living in a Jane Austen novel you have created the right environment.

A Kabbalistic Interpretation

You enjoy making other people feel at ease. You have a wide circle of friends and like nothing more than to have a bunch of them over to your home for a get-together. The best place to center your evening is in your kitchen. Arrange things in groups of three to really get your party off with a kick.

Although you like to make your house open to others you are scrupulous about its cleanliness and order. The connection of *Beth*, meaning "house," and the hygiene-conscious aspect of Virgo confirm this attitude. A very house-proud individual, you prefer modern sleek lines in your home's layout to emphasize a sense of structure. A collection of white bone china mugs would be a very appropriate addition to your home.

The Temperance card from the tarot also affects this day's energy. Its emphasis on a sense of balance and harmony can relate to your enjoyment of a carefully organized home. Equally it refers to a desire for peaceful and calm emotional relationships. As your own sign of Libra is connected to balance, you might like to buy a pair of traditional scales with one of the pans painted red and the other blue.

A Numerological Interpretation
YOUR MAGIC NUMBERS: 9 AND 1

The twenty-seventh day of the ninth month reduces to nine, the number that represents completion, attainment, and the end of a cycle. Born on this day, you are very goal oriented, and because of your shrewdness and focused attention, you have a gift for accomplishing everything in your life with apparent ease. Your innate ability to keep things in balance, and not waste any effort, creates a flow to your experiences that amazes others. Your challenge is to see past the surface organization and assure that you are tending to matters of the soul.

Nature has an inherent ordering system within the mineral, plant, and animal kingdoms. Contemplate how humanity fits into the complete picture of the cosmos. What might exist beyond Homo sapiens? All colors of jasper will be a soothing influence. Keep a quartz crystal in your pocket for good luck. The 271st day of the year reduces to one, providing the impetus to move onward and upward to new horizons of experience.

OBJECTS/IMAGES
sachets, rings, drawstring purses, statues

SHAPES/MATERIALS
ribbon shapes, organza, sapphires, voile material

COLORS
pale nectarine, sapphire blue, blood red

ANIMAL
snowshoe hare

PLANTS, HERBS, EDIBLES
ivy-leaf morning glory, green tea, scones, date nut bread

ESSENCE
orris

SOUNDS/RHYTHMS
lullabies, zither music

MUSICAL NOTES
G# and C

DEEP SPACE OBJECTS
NGC 4826, the Black Eye Galaxy

September 28

YOUR SIGN
Libra

YOUR ELEMENT
Air

YOUR RULERS
Venus, Saturn
4–5 degrees
First Decanate, yang

The Astrological Interpretation

You are an idealistic person, one who tends to project dreams, hopes, and wishes into the life around you. Your aspirations may be very beautiful, but they cannot crystallize into solid form unless you work at committing yourself to them. You may have the tendency to avoid doing this, thinking that if you pledge yourself to someone or something in the present, you may miss a better opportunity tomorrow. But today *is* tomorrow and the future is now! Right and wrong are never absolute for you, and you learn through trial and error. You are attracted by all that is beautiful and have a natural affinity to opals, marble, and quartz.

Your birthday is ruled by Venus. Venus makes us mad with or for love and rules over the arts and design. Finding the middle path in love matters is your great challenge. To keep balance in mind, consider having a replica of Venus in your home. A picture or copy of the *Venus de Milo*, or Botticelli's *The Birth of Venus* will inspire and delight you. A shape for September 28 is interlocking circles. The two circles represent the comingling of partnership with the preservation of self. At home, have pale green or peach on the walls. You might also enjoy stenciling an ivy vine down one side of your walls.

Your senses come alive in nature. A cricket singing is a soothing and romantic sound for you. A wide green lawn, one that you do not have to tend, is the place to picnic and stretch out. A park with a tea-house or café in the center is a perfect place for you to enjoy nature and be with friends.

A Kabbalistic Interpretation

This day has an altruistic aspect to it indicated by its connection to the Hanged Man card from the tarot. You may well work in a caretaking profession, and you can encourage your kindly and caring side overall by using aquamarine in your office and keeping some lotuses or other water-based plants near your desk.

When you have time to yourself you love to travel. Even if it is just a drive out in the country you still get pleasure out of simply seeing the world beyond your doorstep. It is probable that you tend to leave any traveling arrangements to the last minute, as you lead a very busy life. You can avoid any difficulties in your arrangements by keeping a sprig of mugwort next to your telephone or in your pocket.

Although you have a lot of time for others, especially those who are in need, you are good at making sure that you also make time for yourself. The Devil card from the tarot suggests that you have a highly sensual nature, and you should make sure that you explore that side of yourself. An excellent way for you to unwind would be to have a massage with patchouli or sandalwood oil.

A Numerological Interpretation
YOUR MAGIC NUMBERS: 10 AND 2

The twenty-eighth day of the ninth month reduces to ten, the number that represents dominion, embodiment, and the finalization of the process. Ten is the ultimate mastery of what was set in motion in one. Born on this day, you have a path of mastering the concept of inertia and understanding how you can use this law to advantage in your life. Both objects in motion and at rest must be acted upon by a greater outside force to overcome their steady state. Sometimes it is better to leave well enough alone.

Your pattern requires discerning where to act, then summoning enough will and energy to accomplish your objective. Sit in front of a blazing fire and contemplate the necessary actions to keep the fire alive. Rose and amethyst quartz are gems to heighten your powers of perception. The 272nd day of the year reduces to two, providing the principle of duplication and replication. This aids your forward motion.

OBJECTS/IMAGES
sachets, a smile lit up from the inside, a shawl

SHAPES/MATERIALS
white stones, curlicues, talcum powder

COLORS
lemon chiffon, natural linen, navy blue, vermilion

ANIMALS
bunny rabbit, orchard oriole

PLANTS, HERBS, EDIBLES
beauty bush, violets, sycamore trees

ESSENCE
centaury (Bach Remedy)

SOUNDS/RHYTHMS
Gershwin's Rhapsody in Blue, a balletic pas de deux

MUSICAL NOTES
A and C#

DEEP SPACE OBJECTS
Nu Virgo, Zanish

September 29

YOUR SIGN
Libra

YOUR ELEMENT
Air

YOUR RULERS
Venus, Saturn
5–6 degrees
First Decanate, yin

The Astrological Interpretation

You try to be a very fair and equitable person, one who sees both sides of every situation and who avoids making distinct preferences. This quality allows you to be friends with many different kinds of people and frees your heart from undue prejudice. But this same characteristic does not lead to decisiveness, and you can waste a great deal of time and effort making up your mind about the smallest of details. As you are so agreeable, it is easier for you to let someone else order for you at dinner, for example. You can get lost at a buffet, as you will be mentally balancing one dish (and its colors!) against the others. You not only want to create a meal but you also want it to look beautiful on your plate.

Imaginative possibilities spur your creativity, but it is your hard work that prevents you from whiling away the time in pure escapism. You may be involved with social justice, public policy, or the arts. Quartz crystal is very good for you to carry or have in your home. Clear quartz has a steady vibration that helps focus your ideals. On the way to your ideal world, pamper yourself at home. Pastel colors are best for decorating, and a thick carpet with a symmetrical design is very soothing. You may enjoy an Oriental rug in light colors rather than traditional reds and blues. White marble is an excellent material for you to use. Perhaps you could have an old-fashioned sink or tub made of white marble. In a more modern home consider a countertop, tray, or cheese plate.

You may enjoy visiting old inns and taverns and having a sign from one in your backyard. Antiques you can use as planters remind you of days gone by. Flowers you enjoy are begonias and anemone.

A Kabbalistic Interpretation

Seven has been considered a number of exceptional good fortune in a range of mystical and cultural traditions. The strong presence of this number on this day suggests that you will lead a successful and enjoyable life. You can increase the positive benefits of this number's connection to your birthday by wearing a silver seven-pointed star on a pendant necklace.

The word *innocent* is connected to this day through its numerical value. It is highly likely that your innocent nature finds expression in an unchanging optimism toward life. This attitude alone will prove effective in attracting good fortune. You can help to maintain your bright-eyed outlook by growing snowdrops in your garden or using a daisy pattern when decorating your kitchen.

The tarot card the Sun has an influence on your personality, granting you sufficient fire energy to make sure that you have drive and ambition to go with your optimism. The Sun card also indicates a high degree of mental agility. In the context of other energies it is likely that you will use your well-honed mind to work in a field of technological innovation. Hanging a gold-painted sun image in the south or northeast of your home will increase the Sun's influence in your life.

A Numerological Interpretation
YOUR MAGIC NUMBERS: 2 AND 3

The twenty-ninth day of the ninth month reduces to two, the number of replication, dependence, and an ancient emblem of the life force in action. The number two moves one forward into more experience through duplication. Born on this day, you have a path of coming to terms with time, and how the past and present are related. You do not exist in a vacuum or an independent moment in the space-time continuum.

In order to move ahead and realize your dreams, you must make a critical inventory of your heritage. What are the talents and characteristics you possess by virtue of biology and culture? How do these assets provide a foundation for all your future expression? Study your genealogy as well as history. Heliodor is a stone to open your mind to both memories and possibilities. The 273rd day of the year reduces to three, contributing the important quality of natural unfoldment and multiplication to this path.

OBJECTS/IMAGES
brides, bouquets, draftsmen

SHAPES/MATERIALS
brooch shapes, linens, pink zircon, triangle

COLORS
copper color, bright red, russet, ivory

ANIMAL
Australian lyrebird

PLANTS, HERBS, EDIBLES
strawberry begonia, macaroons, bouncing bet, allspice

ESSENCE
peppermint

SOUNDS/RHYTHMS
crickets, recorder music

MUSICAL NOTES
C# and D

DEEP SPACE OBJECTS
Iota Carina, Aspidiske

September 30

YOUR SIGN
Libra

YOUR ELEMENT
Air

YOUR RULERS
Venus, Saturn
6–7 degrees
First Decanate, yin

The Astrological Interpretation

The truth is very important to you. You have a difficult time with people who are not straightforward. Although you really want to know what has taken place, you sometimes do not want to know things that may disillusion you about someone you care about. You can thus create confusion for yourself by going back and forth between your urge to act on the reality of a situation, and your wish to avoid disappointment. You can always leave your cares behind you through music. You like to have some playing in the background, whether at work or at home. Dancing is an especial treat for you, especially when it involves the opportunity for romance.

You are interested in the ideal, and you are devoted to harmonizing your relations with others. The challenge for you is to find the middle ground between theory and practice. A seer has offered the image of an angel standing in midair with a long scroll covered with writing in his hand. See who will listen to your ideas of a gentle world, but avoid despairing over those who won't. Create a harmonious, peaceful environment for yourself. Pale colors such as aqua, peach, and lavender are great for decorating. Silk flower arrangements could be in every nook and cranny. You may also want to place sachets in your drawers: lavender is a perfect choice. Avoid heavy perfumes; your preference is for light florals or fruity smells such as ylang-ylang.

Outdoors, those born on September 30 may enjoy antiques in their yard. A butter churn or old wheelbarrow would make a beautiful planter. Find an antique knocker for the front door. You like gardens but are not very interested in tending them. Best choice is an old inn with gardens where you and a friend can stroll and think.

A Kabbalistic Interpretation

A phrase with the same value as this day is "Jehovah Achad," referring to the divine as a perfect unity containing all things. Other complementary influences in this day make it likely that you will have a strong connection to the earth and nature, and a spirituality bound up in the idea of all things being part of the Divine. Combining your love of music and the natural world, a tape or CD of whale songs would make a wonderful present for you.

The two cards, the Chariot and Strength, both have an influence on your personality. These cards bring great determination and energy. You may choose to use all this surplus vitality to actively involve yourself in environmental campaigns. Whatever path you choose in life you will have the determination to see it through. If you keep a piece of turquoise in your pocket you can increase your chances of having luck on your side.

The word meaning "serpent" in Hebrew has an influence on this date, suggestive of a tendency to strike with some ferocity when you feel thwarted or threatened. The ability to stand up for yourself is positive, but you will need to leaven your potential for anger. Burning some ylang-ylang oil will lower your stress levels while the scent of rosemary can keep you mentally sharp and alert.

A Numerological Interpretation

YOUR MAGIC NUMBERS: 3 AND 4

The thirtieth day of the ninth month reduces to three, the number signifying unfoldment, growth, and development. Born on this day, yours is a path of searching for adventure and new experience. This pattern carries an inborn willingness to risk in order that you can learn and develop competence. You desire to master whatever circumstances you are involved in. You are no armchair quarterback. Try kayaking down a white-water river, or parachuting. You are driven to stretch your limits so you can feel a sense of power when you achieve. Your successes benefit all of us.

Shades of green and yellow jade will inspire your sense of what is possible. The 274th day of the year reduces to four, contributing the element of planning, surveying, and gaining the lay of land. This is very helpful before you strike out alone on an adventure. Don't forget your map.

OBJECTS/IMAGES
brass candlesticks, symmetrical architecture

SHAPES/MATERIALS
white marble, trailing vine shapes

COLORS
pale pink, carrot orange, coral

ANIMAL
French poodle

PLANTS, HERBS, EDIBLES
archangel, chamomile, kiwi fruit

ESSENCE
jonquil

SOUNDS/RHYTHMS
major thirds, chimes echoing across a mountain

MUSICAL NOTES
D and D#

DEEP SPACE OBJECTS
NGC 5383, bright diffuse nebula

October 1

YOUR SIGN
Libra

YOUR ELEMENT
Air

YOUR RULERS
Venus, Saturn
7–8 degrees
First Decanate, yin

The Astrological Interpretation

You have a keen interest in being with other people and enjoy nothing better than going to parties or sporting events with friends. Yet you do not always know if your actions are correct. Like a nervous debutante at her debut ball, you constantly question yourself about what the right thing to do might be in a given social context. It is hard for you just to be yourself, as you feel the presence of others judging your behavior or commenting upon your actions. Try to relax; you can't be anyone else but yourself, and it is useless to try to pretend. The more you enjoy yourself, the more other people will enjoy being with you.

October 1 looks at the world and sees its ideal potential, then may be disappointed with the reality that seems to prevail. Rose-colored glasses would shield you so you can maintain your optimistic vision, but do take the glasses off and look around. At home, you want a big bed with lots of flouncy material. This is your retreat. Place the bed so that you can see the sun. A symbol for this birthday is the true lover's knot. Your affectionate nature is in love with love. Gold jewelry, ribbons, strings that are woven together in a seamless knot are excellent talismans for you.

In nature you renew your energies. A park with a little hill is as good as a stretch of wilderness. A walk on paths through the woods where there is a teahouse or café at the end of the trail is the ideal way for you to relax. Another outdoor possibility is sitting around a burning fire and telling stories. You are a great raconteur and enjoy company.

A Kabbalistic Interpretation

This day is strongly influenced by the energy of the number eleven. This number is associated with the occult and is known as the number of magic. You might begin an exploration of the unknown and discover a side of yourself of which you are unaware. A good starting point would be a tarot deck and an introductory book on how to work with it.

The presence of the Devil card from the tarot deck indicates a temptation to encounter the darker side of human nature. This may simply materialize as an interest in psychology or some similar avenue of study. If you incorporate figure eight patterns into the design of your bedroom you can protect yourself from any negative connections that might otherwise occur.

The full value of this day is a large prime number. This suggests that you are a person with a strong sense of your own individuality and unique identity. You are very happy being different, but at times you feel a need for acceptance and stability. Keeping some lead figurines in the north side of your home will help generate stability within yourself.

A Numerological Interpretation

YOUR MAGIC NUMBERS: 2 AND 5

The first day of the tenth month reduces to two, the number of division, receptivity, and alternation. Born on this day, yours is a path of refinement and specialization. This pattern requires that you recognize and accept without reservation your particular area of focus, and then dedicate yourself utterly to the goal of perfection. Your path demands a measure of sacrifice, as your single-minded determination must be keen.

This day's course might be symbolized by an operatic diva or a college professor, each spending a lifetime building knowledge and skill. The danger of this path is pride. The gifts must be shared; they are not individual possessions of the ego. The applause you receive is well deserved, but know that your accomplishments are on behalf of humanity. Carnelian and lapis are gems to widen your vision to the larger scheme of things. The 275th day of the year reduces to five, adding the helpful influences of adaptability and flexibility to your path.

OBJECTS/IMAGES
crocheted purses, trailing vines, brass keepsake box

SHAPES/MATERIALS
equilateral triangle, pink coral, washed silk

COLORS
lime green, aquamarine, rosy pink, geranium, gold

ANIMALS
swan, dolphin, hart

PLANTS, HERBS, EDIBLES:
bonbons, almonds, Irish moss

ESSENCES
sweet smells, honey

SOUNDS/RHYTHMS
bang of a gavel, buzz of parties, iambic pentameter verse

MUSICAL NOTES
C# and E

DEEP SPACE OBJECT
NGC 4038, Ringtail Galaxy

October 2

Your Sign
Libra

Your Element
Air

Your Rulers
Venus, Saturn
8–9 degrees
First Decanate, yang

The Astrological Interpretation

At times you are like the calm freshness of an early autumn morning after a tremendous rainstorm. At other times you are more like the storm. When you have too many decisions to make at the same time, your mind moves with gale force winds, stirring up all sorts of possibilities that may never come to pass. Yet you also have within you a place of deep repose that emerges when the mental winds die down. It is then that you do some of your favorite things. You pick up a hot cup of tea or coffee, settle in with some fashion or entertainment magazines, and find some time when you can be totally and peacefully alone. It is then that, seemingly on their own, the right answers and the correct course of action arise within you.

Your birthday's genial Venusian nature is strengthened by Saturn. Saturn is considered well placed in Libra because it steadies the tendency of vacillation present in some Librans. Additionally, the fixed star Vindemiatrix, said to give charisma, will be located on some October 2 birthdays. You have the ability to see the wider implications of your own experience and share this universal reality with others. At home, you may enjoy a white marble tabletop. It is important for you to be around things that have meaning. Consider symbols from world religions such as a mandala or a Christian icon as part of your decor. Flowers at home are always a good idea. White tulips, freesia, and Thai orchids may be particular favorites. Paintings that have the feeling of old masters resonate with your nature. Though you do not wish for times gone by, you do appreciate the fullness of the past.

Outdoors October 2 enjoys an enclosed but tidy yard or garden. Wildflowers such as pink lady's slippers and Queen Anne's lace may flourish in your space. Place a statue of Venus, your ruler, somewhere in your yard, and it will inspire you.

A Kabbalistic Interpretation

Air is the key element in your personality. The letter *Vau*, which represents air in the kabbala, has a specific effect on your communication skills. You are a great talker and may also have a talent for writing. Wearing a yellow tiepin or brooch will help to enhance this skill.

The Tower card from the tarot is significant this day, representing major upheavals. In your case it is likely that any significant challenges will revolve around important journeys, especially if a move is involved. You can counter some of this energy by keeping garlic cloves in your pocket when you are traveling or planning to travel.

When you are interested in a subject you will pursue it doggedly until you have found out all that you want to know. The letter *Tzaddi* meaning "fishhook," indicates that you can find the slightest clue to whatever you are searching for and follow it until it yields results. With your writing skills you could have a career as a journalist. Keeping a tigereye stone on your desk will encourage this determined streak.

A Numerological Interpretation

YOUR MAGIC NUMBERS: 3 AND 6

The second day of the tenth month reduces to three, the number representing growth, unfoldment, and development. Yours is a path of developing the strength of your personality through curiosity and self-expression. The pattern entails engaging your self-confidence in day-to-day affairs, and thus developing your broader potentials. Through dedication and involvement in what might mistakenly be called the mundane circumstances of life, you are building a better world one day at a time with your unfolding strength of character and integrity.

Topaz and turquoise are gems to instill confidence and courage. Wear a turquoise ring to ground your emotions. The 276th day of the year reduces to six, contributing the quality of love and reciprocity to the relationships you forge on your quest.

OBJECTS/IMAGES
Tibetan monks' robes, wigs, a firm handshake

SHAPES/MATERIALS
oblong shape, spar, black opals

COLORS
crimson, orange, olive green

ANIMALS
white-crowned pigeon, orchard oriole

PLANTS, HERBS, EDIBLES
slender bush clover, queen of the prairie, peanut brittle

ESSENCE
champac

SOUNDS/RHYTHMS
viola music, the mandolin

MUSICAL NOTES
D and F

DEEP SPACE OBJECTS
Alpha Coma Berenices, Diadem

October 3

YOUR SIGN
Libra

———

YOUR ELEMENT
Air

———

YOUR RULERS
Venus, Saturn
9–10 degrees
First Decanate, yin

The Astrological Interpretation

You have a deep desire to accumulate knowledge. You love to have interesting conversations with fascinating people and always want to have something to say that will hold the attention of the people with whom you are involved. If you cannot create mental rapport with others, no matter how beautiful they may be, you will simply lose interest. Travel is a wonderful teacher for you, and you will take as many opportunities as you can to see the world and converse with men and women who are very different from yourself. You are open, friendly, and very curious about the ways other people live.

October 3 waivers between love of refinement and love of risk. Surround yourself in equal measure with objects and materials that represent both urges and you'll find a happy medium. Perhaps you could have a pink canoe for white-water rapids! At home your love of refinement wins. White walls and furniture with brightly colored silk pillows are a way to keep your environment flexible. You could have different color accents as each season changes. An hourglass is an object to feature in your living space. The motion of the sand running through the glass is mesmerizing and relaxing.

Outdoors, October 3 wants a natural environment that is controllable. A small rippling brook is more desirable than a huge roaring waterfall. A garden with lovely flowers with a definite perimeter is more pleasing than acres of tulips. A large outdoor compass is an object that reminds October 3 that adventures depend on planning rather than on happenstance.

A Kabbalistic Interpretation

You have a definite creative side to your nature that has been apparent from a very young age. You are particularly adept at any of the plastic crafts such as sculpture or tapestry. One way to help to bring out your imaginative energies is to wear a triangular pendant or earrings in bright green.

Your life tends to proceed very smoothly as a rule with little in the way of major challenges to be faced and defeated. The reason for this seemingly untouchable status is a very strong protective influence from the tarot card the Star. You can enhance the benevolent influence of this card by keeping a statuette or painting of a peacock in your living room.

As you have a generous nature, you are keen for other people to do well in their lives. Rather than gloating over your unusually lucky life you will try to use your own successes as a means to assist others. This is particularly the case in the workplace, and you should keep a pouch of garlic and parsley in your desk drawer to assist your ability to be an empowering friend to your coworkers.

A Numerological Interpretation

YOUR MAGIC NUMBERS: 4 AND 7

The third day of the tenth month reduces to four, the number of classification, recording, and naming. Four brings order to the explosive multiplication of three. Born on this day, you have a path exercising your ability for reason and logic. This is a paradoxical pattern, since you are called to a life of responsibility without losing your childlike sense of wonder. Imagine that it is your job to inventory all the toys created by the elves in Santa's workshop. Your life is like that; you run a tight ship but without losing sight of the magic inherent in everything you classify and tabulate. Read the story of Peter Pan, and ponder the significance of maturity.

Malachite will aid your focus. Watermelon tourmaline will enhance your sense of the miraculous in ordinary things. Blow bubbles with children at twilight, and marvel at the iridescent spheres of liquid, dancing like crystals in the fading light. The 277th day of the year reduces to seven, providing a natural sense of peace and assuredness of ultimate victory.

OBJECTS/IMAGES
curved vases, brightly colored gloves, an old-fashioned scale

---

SHAPES/MATERIALS
lapis lazuli, copper, hexagon

COLORS
saffron, malachite green

ANIMALS
swan, turtledove

PLANTS, HERBS, EDIBLES
forget-me-nots, marzipan, cranberry

ESSENCES
lavender, lilac, camellia

SOUNDS/RHYTHMS
viola music, waltz, paso doble rhythm

MUSICAL NOTES
D# and F#

DEEP SPACE OBJECTS
Epsilon Virgo, Vindemiatrix

October 4

YOUR SIGN
Libra

YOUR ELEMENT
Air

YOUR RULERS
Venus, Saturn, Uranus
10–11 degrees
Second Decanate, yin

The Astrological Interpretation

You need to work at a career that gives you ample space to express your highly individualistic personality. The worst thing for you is to be stuck behind a desk all day. You need the freedom to mingle with people and a certain flexibility in your work schedule. It is also important that through your work you bring pleasure into other people's lives and that they can give you their sincere thanks for your help in making their day a little brighter. Your needs are not complex, and the accumulation of luxuries is not your goal. Your needs are very normal: a strong relationship, a comfortable home, and a job that brings you some inner satisfaction. Because you do not ask for much from life, you will receive a great deal.

You have a naive self-confidence that life will go your way. Some experiences may prove otherwise, but you will maintain your optimistic joy and keep trying. You have both artistic abilities and leadership abilities. Beauty is important to you. In your home have touches of elegance such as an Oriental carpet or a marble pedestal. Your taste is refined, and you are very sensitive to color. Pale green and purple may be a combination you particularly like. Consider placing clusters of quartz crystal in the four corners of your home. If you imagine a canopy of crystalline energy it will protect you even when your faith in life is dimmed.

Outdoors, October 4 loves gardens with variety. A colonnade encircling flower beds of gladiolas, tulips, and pansies is a perfect environment for you. Place a statue of Aphrodite or Venus in the center of your garden and you will have a reminder of your ancient Greek ancestor.

A Kabbalistic Interpretation

The energies framing this day are quite intense, suggesting that you are an emotionally driven person with deeply rooted and passionate ways of viewing the world. It is likely that your more powerful feelings are buried in your unconscious. To assist in bringing these emotions to the surface you should try hanging some rich violet and mauve drapes in your bedroom. There is very little in your life that you feel simply okay about—you tend to either love or hate things and experiences. One area of your life about which you feel passionately is food. Your culinary taste is affected by the influence of the Moon card in your day. Its effect is to give you a taste for seafood, especially shellfish, and an ideal treat for you would be fresh lobster.

The full value of this day is associated with the Hebrew letter *Mem.* This letter is connected to the sphere of the emotions and the element of water. You have a very open and friendly manner with your work colleagues and may well enjoy inviting them around for a chat and a laugh. An excellent addition for your kitchen would be a large Russian samovar, or if you drink coffee a king-size coffeepot.

A Numerological Interpretation
YOUR MAGIC NUMBERS: 5 AND 8

The fourth day of the tenth month reduces to five, the number that connotes change, adaptation, and transition. Yours is a path of gaining discernment of how you expend your resources. This pattern asks that you become keenly aware of the choices you make. You must budget your time and energy and learn to reserve time for going within, as a way of orienting yourself to the unseen realms. Meditate daily, and drink from an inner spring of healing and inspiration. This path cultivates powerful, conscious choice.

Amazonite is a stone that will aid your powers of rejuvenation. Take a holiday in a tropical climate, and enjoy the soothing midday siesta. Sway in a cotton hammock under the shade of a palm tree while the blistering sun moves across the sky. The 278th day of the year reduces to eight, which adds the awareness of rhythm and cycles to your path, aiding your awareness of energy conservation.

OBJECTS/IMAGES
love potions, keepsakes, honeymoons, clowns

SHAPES/MATERIALS
opal, swirling shapes, purple jade, pearls

COLORS
lavender, lemon yellow, teal

ANIMALS
collie dog, goldfinch

PLANTS, HERBS, EDIBLES
kiwi fruit, marzipan, pomegranates, cherries

ESSENCE
lemon verbena

SOUNDS/RHYTHMS
piano music, three-part harmony

MUSICAL NOTES
E and G

DEEP SPACE OBJECTS
Gamma Virgo, Porrima

October 5

YOUR SIGN
Libra

YOUR ELEMENT
Air

YOUR RULERS
Venus, Uranus
11–12 degrees
Second Decanate, yin

The Astrological Interpretation

Your birth date evokes the symbol of a deep mine that only reveals its riches the more profoundly you dig. It is natural for you to enjoy activities that allow you to glide quickly over the surface of things such as skiing, rollerblading, and ice-skating Your life will carry you to many enjoyable places and put you in contact with a number of beautiful and interesting people. Yet you will not feel that you are living up to your creative or spiritual potential unless you investigate some of the more profound issues of life. There are many social events on your calendar, yet you cannot seem to evade a calling from within you that is trying to reveal life's deeper realities. Open yourself to this call, it contains something of enormous value for you.

This Libra birthday finds great joy in a country environment where there are mountains and brisk air. If you are a city dweller plan rural escapes to restore your balance. A shepherd's crook could be a favorite antique and remind you of traipsing over the mountains with your flock. This birthday also gives the ability to reason clearly, and you will be sought out for your wise counsel. Your home could feature a brass scale of justice placed behind your desk.

Design is important to you. Geometric shapes, especially circles, ovals, and pentagons stir your imagination. In placing your furniture avoid right angles. October 5 needs a place high up from which to think. An attic corner by a window, a bench on a hill, or part of a rooftop will give you the perspective you need to keep your balance and share with others.

A Kabbalistic Interpretation

It is unlikely that you will spend all your working life as someone else's employee. You have a strong streak of independence coupled with an entrepreneurial mind, which will be a great advantage to you when you decide to go it alone. In order to encourage the financial success of your business, try growing a money tree in your office in a crimson pot.

You like to play as hard as you work, which is very hard indeed. Certain energies in this day suggest that you have a natural rapport with children, and when it comes time to play, you can get a lot of satisfaction from coaching a local Little League or peewee athletic club. To stay in touch with a sense of your own inner child, keep a few board games around the house.

Energy positively shoots from you, and those around you will tend to feel enervated by spending a few minutes with you, though they may be equally worn out after an hour or so! This abundance of vitality is largely due to the solar nature of the value of your day. A few orange-red cone- or pyramid-shaped ornaments around the home will help you to keep your energetic approach to life permanently activated.

A Numerological Interpretation

YOUR MAGIC NUMBERS: 6 AND 9

The fifth day of the tenth month reduces to six, the number signifying balance, symmetry, and the harmony of opposites. Six acts always to establish equilibrium. Born on this day, you have a path of learning to understand the significance of the patterns and directions in your life. Whether or not you are consciously aware of it, your life has a defined orbit, a circular path around the central sun of your soul. This day's path requires that you make continual adjustments and modifications to keep your soul's course true.

Study the movements of the planets. Monitor the annual journey of the sun, and reflect on the monthly cycle of the moon. Sodalite and peridot are gems to aid you on your journey by grounding and centering your mental energies. The 279th day of the year reduces to nine, the number of fulfillment. Nine carries the reassuring knowledge that you will accomplish your goals, and gain a chance to try again.

OBJECTS/IMAGES
*a small brass treasure chest,
a rainbow-colored slinky,
cold air while in a warm bed*

SHAPES/MATERIALS
*silk pajamas,
asymmetrical placement,
pink zircon*

COLORS
*pink, turquoise, bright purple,
peacock green, cerulean*

ANIMALS
*griffin, Samoyed dog,
goldfinch*

PLANTS, HERBS, EDIBLES
*nonpareils, chamomile, curry,
apple cider vinegar*

ESSENCE
lemon verbena

SOUNDS/RHYTHMS
*piano scales, classical guitar,
boogie-woogie beats, ships' bells*

MUSICAL NOTES
F and G#

DEEP SPACE OBJECTS
Gamma Corvus, Gienah

October 6

YOUR SIGN
Libra

YOUR ELEMENT
Air

YOUR RULERS
Venus, Uranus
12–13 degrees
Second Decanate, yin

The Astrological Interpretation

You are very good at following directions. Once given a task you respond by doing more than your share to improve the situation. Yet you may hold yourself back from expressing yourself individually. You need to create the time and place to allow your imagination full sway. Engage in painting, writing poetry, and traveling someplace you wouldn't ordinarily go. You respond exceedingly well to aesthetically pleasing surroundings, so see how you can effectively place yourself in such environments. You sometimes avoid going to places or events by yourself. But this could be the best thing for you. You are naturally attractive, and there soon will be another person happy to share the enjoyments of life with you.

Part of beauty for you is harmonious personal relationships. If you try to live with people as they are and not how you would like them to be romance and marriage will be easier. At home have some images of cherubs. You may put a few peeking out of a curtain or decorating a mirror. Glass bricks are materials for you to use in a variety of creative ways. Uranus is the ruler of your decanate, and modern, sleek lines may be your favorite style. Even though most of your home may be modern, do have a few homey touches in the kitchen such as an old-fashioned cookie jar. In the bedroom cozy floppy slippers for men and mules with feathers for women would be just the right touch.

Outdoors, October 6 likes unusual plants. Birds-of-paradise appeal. If you do not live in a tropical climate or lack a handy greenhouse, consider spider lilies, blood lilies, and fluttermills.

A Kabbalistic Interpretation

The Tower card from the tarot has a strong influence on this date. This card represents unexpected life changes or even traumas and catastrophes. In your case these relate to a tendency to allow your plans and hopes to become muddled. You can help offset any lack of mental clarity by keeping a clear quartz crystal with you and sleeping with it under your pillow at night.

Another card that affects your personality is Judgment. The effect of this card can reduce the negative effect of the Tower card, as it enhances your ability to make decisions. If you have a job that involves a lot of judgment calls keep a small iron statuette of a lion on your desk.

Mars is a key planet with influence over your emotions. Mars holds a dominant and powerful energy and may drive you to take charge in your emotional relationships. You need to temper this inclination with an inclusive approach when it comes to important decisions affecting both you and your partner. Try putting a large circular table in the kitchen, and use this as a base for all your discussions.

A Numerological Interpretation
YOUR MAGIC NUMBERS: 7 AND 10

The sixth day of the tenth month reduces to seven, the number signifying victory and rest between labors. Yours is a path of learning to draw motivation for new and higher accomplishments from the disappointments in your life. The challenge of this day's pattern is to understand that you are not a helpless victim of events. The violent forces of nature can seem as if their only purpose is to destroy what humanity has built. The paradox is that we always build again, hopefully better, stronger, wiser. Stretch your mind to see the larger scheme of things, and to know that if something seems to be taken away, you can create something better.

Talc, or soapstone, cleaves perfectly in one direction, and is widely used by humanity. Talc's metamorphic creation process is a symbol of your path. Smooth talcum power on your skin, and ponder the close relationship between destruction and creation. The 280th day of the year reduces to ten, bringing a sense of dominion and mastery to the closing of each cycle.

OBJECTS/IMAGES
dressing tables, clown costumes, dimples

SHAPES/MATERIALS
tulle, ramie, blossom shapes, black opals

COLORS
light blue, grass green, midnight blue

ANIMALS
turtledove, white cottontail rabbit

PLANTS, HERBS, EDIBLES
dried apricots, ash trees, cranebill (plant), jujubes

ESSENCE
amyris

SOUNDS/RHYTHMS
chimes, harmony

MUSICAL NOTES
F# and A

DEEP SPACE OBJECTS
Alpha Corvus, Alchiba

October 7

YOUR SIGN
Libra

YOUR ELEMENT
Air

YOUR RULERS
Venus, Uranus, Saturn
13–14 degrees
Second Decanate, yin

The Astrological Interpretation

The place where your Libran balance is most revealed is in the realm of social activity. Things sometimes get out of hand when you commit to too many activities and responsibilities and then do not know how you are going to handle them all. *Yes* is a much easier word for you to say than *no*. It is essential that you balance yourself with a more perfect understanding of the scope of your own limitations. Your other alternative is to close yourself down and hide away. Find the middle ground upon which you may walk and then stick to this path.

October 7 birthdays will sometimes fall on a "critical degree," which gives greater highs and lows to your life experience. More fuel for Libra's balancing act! A good image for you is the Theory of Complementarity from physics, which states that, depending on one's perspective, light can be both a wave or a particle. October 7 should look for the *and* rather than the *but*

You have a great deal of energy and need mental, physical, and aesthetic activities to keep your flow. The Egyptian god Anubis, who weighed souls on their way to the underworld is an interesting image for you. At home, old-fashioned postal scales could be a decorative object. With Uranus ruling your decanate, there is a streak of eccentricity. Why not wear blue and green nail polish or mismatched cuff links?

Outdoors, you like humor in your environment. A rock garden with little gnomes or statues of flamingos might be just the right touch. White roses are special flowers for you, and growing or seeing unique violet-tinged roses would be a thrill.

A Kabbalistic Interpretation

The Hebrew phrase for "make joyful" is equivalent to a value of this day. This phrase aptly describes your typical effect on people who are close to you. You can enhance your gift for bringing happiness to others by wearing a square-shaped ring on your index finger.

One of the most intriguing cards in the tarot deck, the World card, relates to this day. One of its aspects is an idea of universal unity. You can encourage greater unity in yourself and those around you by keeping a traditional mortar and pestle, especially if the bowl is blue and the pestle deep red.

You have a creative imagination, and rather than sit in front of a television, you will probably opt to spend your leisure hours reading or listening to music. One word associated with the value of this day is the Hebrew meaning "dream." While this points to your imaginative potential it also suggests that you might give your actual dreams special attention and consideration. A good addition for your bedroom would be a traditional dream catcher. Keep a notebook by your bed to collect your early morning thoughts.

A Numerological Interpretation
YOUR MAGIC NUMBERS: 8 AND 2

The seventh day of the tenth month reduces to eight, the number that represents the cyclic ebb and flow of the cycles and energies of life. Born on this day, you have a path of entering the flow of the cycles of your own life, and perceiving their patterns. You are asked to probe deeply into your experiences in order to understand their lessons. Enter into a place of stillness, and contemplate the significance of your many achievements. Don't succumb to the temptation of resting on your laurels.

Spend time at the ocean, and reflect on the spectrum of manifestations of power of the sea, from gentle tides to tsunamis. Contemplate the back-and-forth movement of tides and their relationship to the moon. Drift in a small craft and watch moonlight dance on the waves. Aquamarine is a stone to connect your spirit with the shifting tides of the physical world. Amber is a gem to remind you how enduring life is. The 281st day of the year reduces to two, adding the ability to be receptive.

OBJECTS/IMAGES
a heart-shaped box, embroidered handkerchiefs, dolls

SHAPES/MATERIALS
opals, pink zircon, bow shapes

COLORS
light peach, cloudy colors, turquoise, pomegranate

ANIMALS
stuffed animals, dolphin

PLANTS, HERBS, EDIBLES
marzipan, scleranthus, burdock

ESSENCE
Bulgarian rose oil

SOUNDS/RHYTHMS
duets, promenades, love songs

MUSICAL NOTES
G and C#

DEEP SPACE OBJECT
Delta Corvus, Alograb

October 8

YOUR SIGN
Libra

YOUR ELEMENT
Air

YOUR RULERS
Venus, Uranus
14–15 degrees
Second Decanate, yin

The Astrological Interpretation

This birthday is connected to the image of the calm both before and after the storm. It is easy for you to be a refuge when your friends and loved ones are distressed. You walk with a natural calm and serenity that is much appreciated by people in emotional turmoil. But do not let this virtue turn into a weakness when it comes to standing up for yourself. Loving a person also means bringing certain challenges into their lives so that they may grow and you may truthfully represent yourself. Express rather than suppress your real thoughts and feelings.

October 8 is a sociable and socially acute birthday. The lure of superficiality exists but will ultimately prove hollow. An image for you is circular paths leading to a center point. No matter how far you roam, inevitably life falls into place. Round shapes in your environment will help you keep focus. Have a round or oval dining room table and chairs that have circular backs. In the bedroom, an art deco dresser with a large round mirror would be appealing. Your color scheme should include pastel colors to create a light rainbow effect. At work keep a vase of flowers on your desk. Glancing at color in the midst of the workday will aid your concentration. Also decorate your work space with posters of impressionist painters that you enjoy. Herbal teas, especially those made from fruits and flowers, are right for you.

Outdoors, perhaps you can build a maze or mark out a circular "tour" through your garden. Flowers lining these paths and leading to a center area of grass would be an excellent way to help you sort out what is enduring. All flowers are ruled by your sign, Venus. October 8 may particularly enjoy the autumn zephyr lily and blue false plumbago.

A Kabbalistic Interpretation

This day is linked to the sephira Hod, the sephira most concerned with matters of the intellect. Your interest in the abstract and rational connects to an equal concern with the physical world, which results from the power the sephira Malkuth has over this day. You might like to get yourself some office toys such as a minigyroscope. They will spark your intellectual curiosity and satisfy your mechanical interests.

The Emperor card's influence on this day indicates leadership abilities and may well point to the possibility of considerable wealth accumulated later in life. In order to optimize the effect of this card, decorate your office in bright red and green. If this is not possible wear a red-and-green-striped tie or scarf to work whenever you are working on a crucial project.

The word in Hebrew meaning "circle" has the same value as the value of this day. In kabbalistic thought all geometric figures are hugely significant, none more so than the circle. Mystically the circle implies eternity and the nature of the universe as a single unity. At the practical level it refers to a need for continuity and stability. To help you feel more secure in your life use plenty of circular designs in decorating your home.

A Numerological Interpretation
YOUR MAGIC NUMBERS: 9 AND 3

The eighth day of the tenth month reduces to nine, the number that represents the end of a cycle and the goal of an endeavor. Nine manifests the seed planted in one. Yours is a path of dealing with the principle of consequence. This pattern calls forth your innate ability to recognize the relationship of cause and effect in any set of circumstances. You have the opportunity to see the highest potential in a situation and therefore understand the potential outcomes from the menu of choices available. At your best, you choose the most noble course of action and move your own growth forward. The danger of this path is impulsiveness.

Turquoise and jade are gems to clarify your vision and strengthen your patience. The 282nd day of the year reduces to three, contributing the quality of imagination and creativity.

OBJECTS/IMAGES
courtships, easels, embroidered place mats, harlequins

SHAPES/MATERIALS
garland shapes, gilt, enamels, curves

COLORS
pink, azure, apricot

ANIMALS
pronghorn, ladybug

PLANTS, HERBS, EDIBLES
foxglove, red grapes, raisin bread, floribunda rose

ESSENCE
clove

SOUNDS/RHYTHMS
duets, guitars

MUSICAL NOTES
G# and D

DEEP SPACE OBJECTS
NGC 4594, the Sombrero Galaxy

October 9

YOUR SIGN
Libra

———

YOUR ELEMENT
Air

———

YOUR RULERS
Venus, Uranus
15–16 degrees
Second Decanate, yang

The Astrological Interpretation

There is nothing you like better than to be an agent for peace and happiness for the people you know and love. You are good at resolving disputes and have a natural talent for mediating between conflicting ideas, feelings, and opinions. In your own life, it is very difficult for you to let an argument or disagreement with a friend remain unresolved. Even if it was a problem that occurred long ago, the fact that it is still not settled will weigh on you for many years. You like to blend and match, unify and unite. You are good with color coordination and are known to dress well for any occasion. You are also attracted to the decorative arts and enjoy the sight of beautiful furniture correctly placed in a room. You will certainly notice if anything in the room is out of balance!

The fixed star Seginus will be located on some October 9 birthdays. Seginus was reputed to indicate a subtle mind. At home keep a variety of chimes to "clear the air" between projects. Movable screens would be handy items for your home. You could move them to divide your space in different ways. You can become overstimulated with socializing. Set some time aside to sit and stare at the corner without talking. If you prefer not to sit on the floor, plain wooden chairs would be best for you. An image for October 9 is the aurora borealis. These northern lights have Libra colors and an electrical intensity that may resonate with you.

Outdoors, October 9 likes a clear path through a garden and a small wall or fence around the garden. Flowers that grow along the wall such as morning glories and jasmine will calm your mind and delight your eyes.

A Kabbalistic Interpretation

This day is connected to Hebrew words and phrases related to the mind and to the head. You are likely to be a very thoughtful individual and you may well be interested in the nature of thought itself. Psychiatry is a good career choice for you. A great gift for you would be an old-fashioned pottery head like the ones used by Victorian phrenologists.

Also connected with things of the mind is the Hermit card from the tarot. This card deals with wisdom rather than knowledge, and in your case it refers to an ability to have a deep and intuitive understanding of complex and abstract concepts. When it comes to choosing artwork for your home the influence of the Hermit may lead you to opt for abstract twentieth-century art such as Kandinsky or Mondrian prints.

The Hebrew meaning "water pot" is also connected to the value of this day. This association suggests that you need to hold on to your emotional energy. You need to maximize water energy wherever possible. A series of large earthenware pots positioned around the outside of your house containing water plants such as lilies or bulrushes will help to develop your emotional side.

A Numerological Interpretation
YOUR MAGIC NUMBERS: 1 AND 4

The ninth day of the tenth month reduces to one, the number signifying originality, singleness, and isolation. Born on this day, you have a path of divergence. Your pattern drives you toward an expression of diversity for the sake of being different. You possess a passionate freedom of spirit, and at times you can feel like exercising a bit of rebellion for its own sake. You have such an intense need to be original that you can border on oppositional behavior. Channel this capacity into a constructive application of the devil's advocate principle. Volunteer for a legal organization that fights for positive social change.

Apache flame agate and rainbow jasper are stones to complement your strong sense of independence and diversity. The 283rd day of the year reduces to four, which contributes the important element of reason and order to your path. Sometimes flaunting convention is appropriate, but anarchy is not.

OBJECTS/IMAGES
women's underwear, upholsterers, valentines, tips

SHAPES/MATERIALS
bronze, brass, cameo shapes, beryl

COLORS
blue-green, claret, golden yellow

ANIMALS
show cat, white-winged dove

PLANTS, HERBS, EDIBLES
peach trees, tussock bellflower, blazing star

ESSENCE
jonquil

SOUNDS/RHYTHMS
the bossa nova, John Lennon's music

MUSICAL NOTES
C and D#

DEEP SPACE OBJECTS
Nu Draco, Aldhibain

October 10

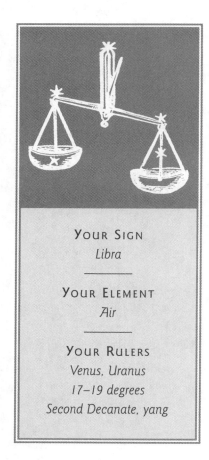

The Astrological Interpretation

You are a very attractive person and are possessed of a natural social magnetism. You will never lack the opportunity for partnership—you just have to make the right choices! What is important for people born this day is the mastery of maintaining personal integrity. This is especially true when you find yourself overly bound up in the life of your lover or spouse. There is a distinct tendency for you to lose the power of decision making once you are involved with someone. You may give so much power away to the other person that you come to feel restricted and restrained by the very love you thought would free and liberate you. Do not seek to get lost in love. Find yourself through painting, floral arrangement, jewelry making, and poetry.

Your energies overflow sometimes, and you can become quarrelsome and argumentative. The Libra balancing mechanism can transmute in you into your taking an opposing point of view just for the sake of expressing yourself and causing controversy. A better idea is to write, sing, compose, or paint. Melodies are important to you, and even if you are not a trained musician you may make up songs. At home, have a window seat where you can curl up and dream. If you find that argumentative energy bubbling up, then give yourself some time in the window seat. You may enjoy playing string games like cat's cradle or playing with a yo-yo. Decorative objects for you are an alabaster bird or an ornate brass scale.

Outdoors, October 10 wants flowering fruit trees and benches to gaze up at the branches. Japanese dogwood, crab apple blossoms, and almond blossoms all resonate with your nature.

A Kabbalistic Interpretation

There is a kabbalistic saying that "Kether is in Malkuth and Malkuth is in Kether but after another fashion." While whole books could be written on the deep meanings of this short phrase, at a very basic level this is saying that the divine can be found in the material and vice versa. As both the highest and the lowest sephira are represented this day, it is likely that you will have a strong spiritual side to your personality and that you will be able to see spirit in even the simplest aspects of nature. A vase of daisies kept on your desk will help to maintain this very wise insight.

Having a very spiritual nature does not mean that you are incapable of functioning successfully in the workplace. The influence of the planet Mars gives you considerable ambition and a will to achieve your goals. Any object made of iron in your office will help to focus this energy. Ideally you should find an iron ring to wear on your index finger.

The Moon card from the tarot reemphasizes the importance of the nonmaterial aspects of your life. It is also likely that the moon's influence will result in a tendency to be overanxious about relationships. If you keep a bloodstone with you it should help to reduce your propensity to worry too much.

A Numerological Interpretation
YOUR MAGIC NUMBERS: 2 AND 5

The tenth day of the tenth month reduces to two, the number connoting reflection, duplication, and replication. Born on this day, you have a path of increasing receptivity to a higher order of knowing, thereby developing penetrating insight into the mysteries of life. This pattern also requires that you share your knowledge and wisdom in a loving way. Your life should be an increasing testimony to the heritage of eternal values that have been handed down through millennia by dedicated souls. Study the ancient texts from various traditions and apply their principles in your life. But always remember: knowledge without love is empty.

Precious opal is a gem to open your heart and inspire your mind. The 284th day of the year reduces to five, providing the crucial component of versatility and adaptability to this path.

OBJECTS/IMAGES
napkins, cosmetics, lithographs, parasols

SHAPES/MATERIALS
locket shapes, lacquers, stalactite (mineral), polished substances

---

COLORS
pale orange, chestnut, ivory

ANIMAL
fluffy cats

PLANTS, HERBS, EDIBLES
mint, pennyroyal, mallows, pecan trees, Chinese wisteria

ESSENCE
lemon

SOUNDS/RHYTHMS
Verdi's operas

MUSICAL NOTES
C# and E

DEEP SPACE OBJECTS
Beta Corvus, Kraz

October 11

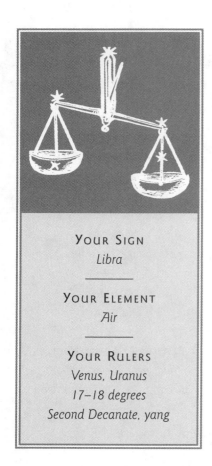

YOUR SIGN
Libra

YOUR ELEMENT
Air

YOUR RULERS
Venus, Uranus
17–18 degrees
Second Decanate, yang

The Astrological Interpretation

You are a person of high ideals and a distinct social conscience. It is difficult for you to stand by and watch as some segments of society are treated well while others are put down and oppressed. One of your natural talents is social organization. You will find that at some point in your life you will want to combine your sense of equality with your ability to join people in a common purpose. You are naturally attracted to law and will be interested in politics, government, and large social issues. In your personal relationships, you are constantly making emotional as well as material contracts with people and get very upset when these agreements are broken.

This birthday is particularly talented in hospitality and often is well known for an open home filled with guests. The home space needs a large living and dining room that is well lit. French doors opening onto a deck or patio would be nice. Unique lamps that cast a variety of pale colors are a welcome addition. A loft space where the living configuration can be changed suits October 11's nature. Home is a busy place, so the area for retreat and renewal might be a high attic corner or a window seat. You prefer white backgrounds on which you can add a few pastel colors. Light gray, lavender, and pearly white are good colors for you. Hardwood floors in light woods complete a sense of airy order.

Outdoors, October 11 revels in gardens with defined paths and a deck where people can sit, chat, and watch the sunset. Little Chinese lanterns complete the environment. Have a number of sets of dishes . . . just for change.

A Kabbalistic Interpretation

Honesty is the most significant quality in your way of viewing life. You may feel dismayed as you walk through the world at the seeming lack of truthfulness you see around you. At least one room in your house should be painted in pure white with minimal furnishing in the palest of shades. This room will provide you with a calm haven of purity in which to retreat and renew your dedication to truth.

The value of this day is connected to the Hebrew letters *Yod Heh Vau Heh*. These four letters make up the Hebrew spelling of *Jehovah*. This association adds additional weight to your strong sense of morality and personal honor. You are determined to set a positive example among your peers, and you can help yourself do this by wearing a diamond ring on your middle finger.

Although you are more concerned than most with issues of morality and truth you are also a highly practical individual. You should get a lot of pleasure out of activities that require manual work. Indeed you may be a whiz at home improvement. A good present for you would be a large square steel cabinet in which you can keep your various do-it-yourself tools in pristine condition.

A Numerological Interpretation
YOUR MAGIC NUMBERS: 3 AND 6

The eleventh day of the tenth month reduces to three, the number meaning growth, unfoldment, and multiplication. Yours is a path of learning to develop your own sense of self-sufficiency. You are a very social creature, loving parties, games, and situations where people have a good time. This pattern requires that you learn to entertain yourself and become your own best friend. Yours is not a solitary path, but you must develop comfort in solitude. Though you can be the life of the party, and the one to arrange all the social outings for your circle of friends, also schedule alone time. Sit in the silence and still the chatter of your mind.

Citrine is a gem that will enhance your optimism. Sodalite will calm your emotions. The 285th day of the year reduces to six, the number of balanced polarities. This will aid your efforts to feel complete within yourself.

OBJECTS/IMAGES
west wall of a room, a boutique filled with silk scarves, a musical jewelry box, Fiestaware

SHAPES/MATERIALS
white marble, oval shapes, carnelian, organza

COLORS
cherry blossom pink, chrysanthemum yellow, pale green, bittersweet, lime green

ANIMALS
dove, swan, apricot toy poodle

PLANTS, HERBS, EDIBLES
spice drops, lemon thyme, columbine, foxglove

ESSENCES
sandalwood, light cologne, violet essence

SOUNDS/RHYTHMS
oriental music, fox-trot, vocal melodies, leaves rustling in the wind

MUSICAL NOTES
D and F

DEEP SPACE OBJECTS
Gamma Boötes, Seginus

October 12

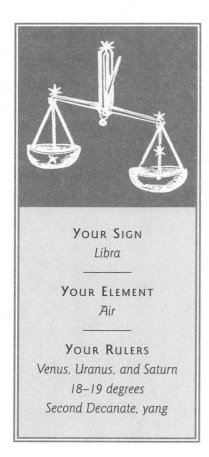

YOUR SIGN
Libra

YOUR ELEMENT
Air

YOUR RULERS
Venus, Uranus, and Saturn
18–19 degrees
Second Decanate, yang

The Astrological Interpretation

You are very attracted to order. The coronation of a monarch, the wedding of a prince, the beauty of an ancient religious ceremony, all appeal to your inner sense of elegance and aesthetics. You may neither be particularly pretentious nor attend a place of worship regularly, but you just enjoy the beauty and sense of mystery that come with rites and practices. You likely take charge of all your family's ceremonies: weddings, anniversary parties, communions, bar mitzvahs, or even funerals can benefit from your special touch. On the other hand, you try to avoid the ugly and the less than perfect. Yet this is also part of life and has to be accepted in order for you to achieve true balance.

October 12 strives to balance the expression of natural talents with an erratic streak that can sabotage those abilities. Uranus, ruler of your decanate, is the planet of revolution and sudden impulse. You may have inspirations that illuminate your art or profession and then go off on a tangent that is less than creative. At home indulge your love of luxury with nice scents. Violet, narcissus, and bitter orange would all suit your nature. You might also want to carry a small bottle of an essential oil . . . a discreet sniff will immediately relax and center you. Lamps in circular shapes and pastel colors catch your eye. In the bathroom, you would enjoy a tub with a view. Stepping from the bath into a warmed towel is a sensual experience. On your refrigerator have a rotating gallery of cartoons. Part of October 12's nature is an easy sense of humor.

Outdoors, let a circular shape filled with flowers focus your garden. Columbine, candytuft, and bougainvillea are all Libra flowers sure to keep you creative.

A Kabbalistic Interpretation

The key tarot card in determining your personality is the Fool. The Tree of Life used by most modern kabbalists associates the Fool with the first path from the highest sephira of existence. The Fool has two distinct identities—one is the wise fool, but the other is simply the jester figure who lacks foresight and wisdom.

The influence of the Strength card tempers the potentially negative effect of the Fool. The fact that you have a very strong sense of purpose in life and an iron will means that you avoid simply being an irresponsible joker. You are perfectly capable of focusing on your chosen goals and making sure that you achieve them. You can help to develop your will by keeping a clear crystal in the south corner of your office or living room.

The number 120 is important this day. This number is very significant to those occultists who follow the famous Golden System of kabbala and hermetic philosophy. The number is connected to the image of the hexagram and ideas of universal balance. In life the ideal position is that of the reconciler holding the balance between two opposing views in any situation. A golden star of David, or more properly the Seal of Solomon, will assist you in achieving that level of balance in your own life.

A Numerological Interpretation

YOUR MAGIC NUMBERS: 4 AND 7

The twelfth day of the tenth month reduces to four, the number signifying order, measurement, and classification. Four always acts to minimize the effort required. Yours is a path of seeking optimum ways to take advantage of life's opportunities. You have a strong sense of community and wish to provide efficiently for the needs of the greatest number of people. You derive great satisfaction by pleasing others and have an instinctive ability to sense just what people want.

Work in public service, or volunteer for a charitable organization that dispenses food or clothing to needy citizens. Tourmaline wands will widen the scope of your philanthropy. The 286th day of the year reduces to seven, providing a natural sense of security and satisfaction to this path. This helps you know when to pause and admire your handiwork.

OBJECTS/IMAGES
*a banquet,
a modern art museum,
limousines*

SHAPES/MATERIALS
opals, copper, kidney shapes

COLORS
apricot, salmon, forest green

ANIMALS
queen bee, partridge

PLANTS, HERBS, EDIBLES
*heartsease, blossoms,
almond trees*

ESSENCE
rosewood

SOUNDS/RHYTHMS
banjos, clarinets

MUSICAL NOTES
D# and F#

DEEP SPACE OBJECTS
Nu Boötes, Muphrid

October 13

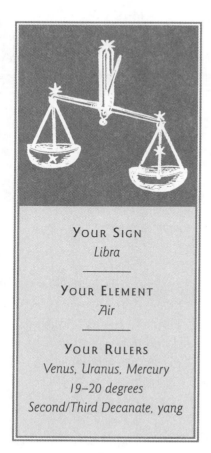

The Astrological Interpretation

It is easy for you to connect with others, as you are open, easygoing, graceful, and very pleasant to be with socially. You have a natural charm and charisma and find it simple to blend in with any group of people. You always want to see the good in others and may have a blind spot when it comes to identifying other people's weaknesses. You would do well as a managerial consultant. You see the positive possibilities that come about through working harmoniously together. If business is not your calling, you will want to be in a position to make people healthier or more beautiful. Cosmetics, clothing, and health food products are other industries that can work out very well for you.

October 13 is a powerful birthday. You may be skilled in politics and have an intrinsic understanding of power dynamics. Your birthday blends masculine eternal values with feminine receptivity. An image for you is Athena, goddess of handicrafts and protector of the great center of ancient civilization, Athens. In your home include some art or reminders of your ethnic heritage. Researching your roots may be of interest to you. All communication tools—such as computers, fax, telephone, and beepers—will be important to you. Don't settle for standard black! Try and find these items in a variety of colors but allow some time every day when you are incommunicado. During those times visualize pink silk and hold a piece of clear quartz. For real lounging try pink silk pajamas.

Outdoors, October 13 would enjoy a Mediterranean home with an interior courtyard. This is the perfect blend of interior and exterior. The courtyard might have potted plants and be designed for restful walks. Have a center fountain with some blue-green tiles or mosaics or a circular plot of flowers. Petunias and pansies would be excellent choices.

A Kabbalistic Interpretation

Some of us want to be loved, others want to have fantastic careers. More than anything, you want to be intrigued. The Hebrew word that means "astonishment" has the same value as this day, and in conjunction with other influences it indicates that you love to have your curiosity challenged. The Hebrew words for "riddle" and "enigma" are also connected to this day. These relate to your intellectual interests. Do the crossword on the train in the morning and try all sorts of logic puzzles. A great gift for you would be a three-dimensional jigsaw puzzle.

Your interest in what is unusual and out of the ordinary often extends to your choice of friends and even partners. The influence of the Hanged Man refers to an altruistic concern for others. For you, it indicates a concern for those people that the rest of the world tends to shy away from. Wearing any gold jewelry will help you to find that special person for you.

A Numerological Interpretation
YOUR MAGIC NUMBERS: 5 AND 8

The thirteenth day of the tenth month reduces to five, the number signifying activity, means, and the agency of accomplishment. Yours is a path of self-realization. Your pattern evokes a response to the role you choose to play in life and to the caliber of your performance. You are asked to deliver nothing short of a true virtuoso performance, and to accept the resulting rewards and accolades with grace and humility. You will not be content to perform as an amateur but will strive for mastery of your chosen endeavor. Remember to enjoy the great masters from all walks of life to counteract the potential narrowness of specialization.

The danger of this path is a hollow expectation that rank has privilege apart from any contribution. Labradorite is a gem to enlarge your scope and help set your sites high. The 287th day of the year reduces to eight, helping you to keep things in perspective. Success is ephemeral, but no failure is permanent.

OBJECTS/IMAGES
an electronic scale, a copper bracelet, a statue of Athena

SHAPES/MATERIALS
lapis lazuli, gentle curves, fire opal

COLORS
celadon, lilac, yellow, aquamarine

ANIMALS
French poodle, mink

PLANTS, HERBS, EDIBLES
strawberries, penny candy, alfalfa

ESSENCE
clary sage

SOUNDS/RHYTHMS
hurdy-gurdies, harp music

MUSICAL NOTES
E and G

DEEP SPACE OBJECTS
Zeta Virgo, Heze

October 14

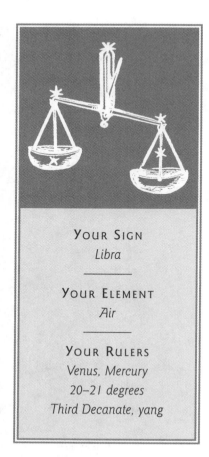

YOUR SIGN
Libra

———

YOUR ELEMENT
Air

———

YOUR RULERS
Venus, Mercury
20–21 degrees
Third Decanate, yang

The Astrological Interpretation

The underlying gift of this birthday quickens your awareness to the creative possibilities in your environment. You are like an explorer who finds himself each day in a new land of miracles and marvels. You are a keen observer of how people interact and exhange ideas with one another. These observations stimulate and inspire you to creative ideas of your own. You tend to avoid prioritizing your life and have a difficult time with creating clear preferences and making definitive choices. Everything looks so good, why do you have to pick just one thing or one way to succeed? You do not. The key is to learn how to select and properly coordinate what you have chosen. Like the Chinese acrobat who can spin many plates at the same time, your sense of balanced timing had better be good.

October 14 has a wealth of charm that makes all social aspects of life flow smoothly. Your interests are both scientific and entertaining. You can employ your social skills to bring about the most unlikely cooperation between people. Sports and travel are activities for you. Your birthday has a religious side, so you might be comfortable in a medieval cloister. A home designed around an interior courtyard would be very harmonious for you. Windows with diamond-shape latticework are aesthetically pleasing. Hang a prism in any window that catches the light and watch where the rainbow spectrum falls.

Outdoors, October 14 likes a planned garden. The shape of a square bordered by planters facing north, south, east, and west will be a centering outdoor space for you. Consider begonias, canterbury bell, and the wildflower called Venus's looking-glass.

A Kabbalistic Interpretation

The Lovers card has a significant effect on this day. This card relates to making choices in life, especially about your emotional relationships. You are likely to have difficulty deciding between relationships that are good for you in the long term and those that are short-lived but have strong physical appeal. You will find it easier to make your decisions if you keep two orange-framed mirrors in your bedroom facing each other on opposite walls.

The energies of this day make it unlikely that in business you will strike out on your own. However, you do have a range of innovative ideas and are likely to be a very valuable member of a team or group. The connection of this day to the Hebrew word meaning "overturn" indicates that many of your thoughts can really result in effective change. If you want to increase the chances of your revolutionary ideas being put into effect, use some wheel images in decorating your office.

The other significant influence this day is the Death card from the tarot. This card serves to reemphasize the aspect of your personality that is associated with change and development. All things pass away to make room for the innovative and new. There are occasions when the pace of change can be rather worrying. If you burn some myrrh incense in the evenings you will find that you feel much calmer about the rhythms of your life.

A Numerological Interpretation
YOUR MAGIC NUMBERS: 6 AND 9

The fourteenth day of the tenth month reduces to six, the number that signifies balance, symmetry, and beauty. Born on this day, you have a path of striving for uniqueness and originality in your personal expression of beauty. You have an innate ability to see beauty where a more superficial or jaded eye might see ugliness. At your best, you quickly detect innovative ways to solve a problem by focusing on what is possible. You are ever on the lookout for just the right opportunity to develop your special destiny in a totally distinctive manner. Listen to talented musicians improvise, and hear the way the notes weave a pattern around one another.

Peridot and adventurine are gems to enlarge your vision of what's possible. The 288th day of the year reduces to nine, providing you with the inner confidence that you can ultimately attain a perfect and beautiful result in whatever you seek.

OBJECTS/IMAGES
bouquets, brushes, crowns and tiaras, cartoonists, frescoes

SHAPES/MATERIALS
cornelian, curves, enameled woods, valuable fur

COLORS
crystal blue, chartreuse, rust

ANIMALS
queen bee, warbler

PLANTS, HERBS, EDIBLES
bouncing bet, brambles, pound cake, honey butter

ESSENCE
vanilla

SOUNDS/RHYTHMS
e. e. cummings's poetry, torch songs

MUSICAL NOTES
G and C#

DEEP SPACE OBJECTS
Nu Carina, Foraman

October 15

The Astrological Interpretation

You have a generous and kind nature, one that offers friendship and companionship to all. People are like gemstones to you, objects that you value and find precious. You see the shining facets of other people's personalities and respect each one's individuality, knowing that no two crystals are alike and yet each has its particular beauty. Air is your element, and it is natural for you to want to get out and "circulate." You certainly look forward to the pleasures of the weekend. Yet you have to take care not to dissipate your energy with too many parties, relationships, and social gatherings. The daffodil is your flower, peppermint your herb, and pomegranate your fruit.

Those born at twenty-first degrees of Libra on October 15 are traditionally thought to have an affinity with the stage and comedy in particular. Having a pair of old-fashioned weights and scales in your home will remind you to find the balance between pleasing yourself and pleasing others. Your home environment should be elegant and unique. October 15 might like to have pieces of colored sea glass on the coffee table or a blue ribbon hung over the doorknob. The idea is to have color and beauty wherever you turn. Drawstring purses are objects that will give you pleasure and hopefully remind you to keep the purse strings tight.

Outdoors, October 15 wants an overflowing garden that retains a sense of symmetry. A circular, elevated birdbath at the center of the garden is a wonderful focal point. Place some wooden chaise longues near the birdbath and you and your friends can all watch the different colored birds as they come to drink or bathe. City dwellers should plan to spend some time in a park and be sure they get some sunlight every day.

A Kabbalistic Interpretation

The planet Mars has a powerful effect on your personality, making you an individual with considerable ambition and determination to succeed. Your ability to maintain this drive and vitality is likely to be noticed by your employers and will certainly help your promotion prospects. You can enhance this ability by keeping a picture of a ram in your office.

When you are at home it is important that you are able to unwind and relax. The fact that your day is also affected by the letter *Lamed,* meaning "ox goad," suggests that you may find this difficult to achieve. Playing soothing classical music should help you relax. Try some Chopin etudes in the evening. Also keep some mallow in a little pouch in the south of your living room.

Leisure activities are important in your life as another means of relieving the pressure of work. While it is likely that you will be drawn to physical pursuits you also have an artistic side. If you have a den or personal space, try decorating with triangular patterns, as this will encourage you to explore your creative side.

A Numerological Interpretation

YOUR MAGIC NUMBERS: 7 AND 10

The fifteenth day of the tenth month reduces to seven, the number that connotes victory, peace, and a pause between cycles of expression. Born on this day, you have a path of developing spontaneous adaptability. This day's pattern endows you with an innate resourcefulness in dealing with the exigencies of life. You are required to cultivate sensitivity to the information and clues in every experience, and to see how certain responses benefit all, while other actions are not constructive. At your best, you can see the interrelatedness of all things and discern potential mutual benefit.

Volunteer for the United Nations or other large global organization. Amethyst crystals will elevate your motivations. The 289th day of the year reduces to ten, providing faith in the outcome of your ultimate goals and a capacity to look at the big picture.

OBJECTS/IMAGES
mask of comedy, colored glass vases in unusual shapes, statue of blind justice

SHAPES/MATERIALS
brass, pastel drawing pencils, pink coral

COLORS
iris, Wedgwood blue, pale yellow, grass green, indigo

ANIMALS
Siamese cat, miniature collie

PLANTS, HERBS, EDIBLES
nasturtium, ambrosia, bluebells

ESSENCES
caramelized sugar, almond

SOUNDS/RHYTHMS
iambic pentameter poetry, waltzes

MUSICAL NOTES
F# and A

DEEP SPACE OBJECTS
Alpha Virgo, Spica, Ear of Wheat

October 16

YOUR SIGN
Libra

YOUR ELEMENT
Air

YOUR RULERS
Venus, Saturn, Mercury
22–23 degrees
Third Decanate, yang

The Astrological Interpretation

Your birth date is the epitome of Aphrodite Pandemos, Greek for "Venus, goddess of all the people." This beautiful name has a double meaning. You can be a bit flirtatious and indiscriminate in your choice of intimate relationships and rather oriented to the pleasures of the senses. Yet Aphrodite Pandemos also means that you can be a loving and helpful friend to all, regardless of social background, gender, or age. Your heart is filled with an impersonal loving nature. But should it be pierced by the arrow of Eros, god of the more erotic side of your nature, this passion is expressed within a loving and balanced context.

October 16 retains an idealistic originality throughout life. Your challenge will be to participate in life as you find it and not as you would like it to be. Meditate on the image of a clear blue sky dotted with stars. Consider pasting glow stars on your bathroom ceiling so you can enjoy the patterns while taking a bath. At home, you will enjoy symmetrical placement of furniture. Pictures hanging crooked on the wall drive you wild. You might like dried or pressed flowers mounted as a wall hanging. Any awards or honors you have received should be beautifully framed and prominently displayed. If you paint or draw consider having a "gallery" of your works. Your bedroom could be painted pale green with some seascapes. Libra is a mental air sign and needs to be reminded of earth and water.

Outdoors, a yard with well-kept green grass may be more interesting to you than a garden. October 16 likes flowers but enjoying a table and chairs, and badminton on the lawn is the perfect way to spend a summer's evening. Flowers for you include pansies, impatiens, and sweet william.

A Kabbalistic Interpretation

You have a much greater concern for the emotional and spiritual aspects of life than for your material situation. This characteristic tends to make you a very responsible person when it comes to human relationships. At times you may be overdemanding when it comes to personal morality. You can encourage a less harsh approach by burning some musk essence or aromatherapy oil in the evenings.

The Tower card from the tarot has considerable impact on this day, pointing to potential dangers in not keeping a proper eye on your financial position. If you grow some basil on your kitchen window ledge and keep a statuette of a lion next to your front entrance hall you should find that you are able to attract more wealth into your life and manage it well once it arrives.

The letter *Lamed* combines with the Emperor card from the tarot to give you a great deal of energy and commitment to your chosen goals. Although your main motivation is never likely to be financial your determination to get a job done, and done well, will certainly improve your chances of financial reward. Wearing a red-and-green striped tie or scarf will enable you to maintain an impressive level of drive and vitality.

A Numerological Interpretation
YOUR MAGIC NUMBERS: 8 AND 2

The sixteenth day of the tenth month reduces to eight, the number of rhythm, vibration, involution, and evolution. Yours is a path of self-discipline. This is a pattern of gaining personal mastery over the circumstances of your life. This day carries the inherent paradox that the measure of your successes in manifesting this destiny is determined by your alignment with your soul's own best interest. The degree to which you aspire to your highest unique contribution is the degree to which the material circumstances of your life appear to bend to your will and thought. Stated another way, seek first the kingdom of heaven and all other things will be added.

Mother-of-pearl and amber are gems to open your heart and soul. The 290th day of the year reduces to two, contributing the quality of reflection and replication to your path.

OBJECTS/IMAGES
grace, lofts, and fine arts

SHAPES/MATERIALS
chrysolite, pink zircon, alcove shapes, and white marble

COLORS
crimson, turquoise blue, sunset orange

ANIMALS
chinchilla, vicuña

PLANTS, HERB, EDIBLES
heartsease, Chinese-star jasmine, sweet pea, and black cherry preserves

ESSENCE
lemon verbena

SOUNDS/RHYTHMS
puns, double entendres

MUSICAL NOTES
G and C#

DEEP SPACE OBJECTS
Alpha Boötes, Arcturus, Guardian of the Bear

October 17

YOUR SIGN
Libra

YOUR ELEMENT
Air

YOUR RULERS
Venus, Saturn, Mercury
22–23 degrees
Third Decanate, yang

The Astrological Interpretation

Your birth date opens you up to a great deal of social experimentation. Even though you appreciate and find beauty in the traditions of love, marriage, and family, you may stand outside of these established patterns. You need to be free to interact with many different kinds of people, creating all sorts of relationships as you go through life. You enjoy the development of intellectual, action-oriented friendships and are highly selective about the men or women with whom you choose to share yourself more intimately. You will enjoy social clubs and traveling. You will especially like to go on cruises or to resorts.

Some October 17 birthdays will have either the fixed star Spica or the fixed star Arcturus located on their birthdays. Spica is thought to give a very sweet nature, and Arcturus is the brightest star in the Northern Hemisphere, dubbed "the star of the artists." Perhaps the strongest characteristic of October 17 birthdays is the belief in the potential of the individual to improve the world. An image for you is a chemist mixing potions to find the ones that will bring out caring and consideration in people. On a more practical level, October 17 likes well-decorated surroundings and may have a particular fondness for fashion. Both men and women would enjoy cashmere turtleneck sweaters. In the boudoir, silk is the material for you. A robe or lounging pajamas insulate you from the harshness of the world.

Outdoors, October 17 enjoys adventure and a touch of danger. If you are working in an artistic field consider building a special cabin for your creations. A garden would be pleasant, especially one entered through a wooden gate and enclosed by a fence. Morning glories entwined on the fence give you the assurance that beauty will survive.

A Kabbalistic Interpretation

The Buddha famously said that the cause of all sorrow is desire. The influence of the Fool card from the tarot suggests that you are likely to have the innate wisdom of being beyond desires. In order to encourage the supremely wise innocent in you, keep a white porcelain bowl with lotus flowers on the center of your kitchen table.

Among the words and phrases that have a gematric relationship with this day is the Hebrew word meaning "purity." To best create the feeling of universal harmony and peace in your personal living space, opt for open room plans and very large windows to let in as much light as possible. In addition, keep some sizable pieces of uncut crystal around your home.

There is an indication in this day's value that you have a scientific turn of mind. It is also suggested that you have an interest in what we might call the first causes of life. Great strides are being made in the fields of astrophysics and cosmology. A great present for you is a refractor telescope so that you can gaze back toward the origins of the universe yourself.

A Numerological Interpretation

YOUR MAGIC NUMBERS: 9 AND 3

The seventeenth day of the tenth month reduces to nine, the number meaning completion, attainment, and fulfillment. Nine contains the clear, pure expression of the idea that started the cycle. Born on this day, you have a path of striving to see the big picture. Sometimes you feel as if you contain within yourself every potential of the human race. If you stretch your mind just a little, you can imagine the individual and collective possibilities of humanity and reflect that back to those around you. At your best, you are talented at responding and adjusting to all situations.

The danger of this path is you may escape idealistically into fantasy. Involve yourself in strategic planning and story-boarding techniques where the sky's the limit. Moonstone will deepen your idealistic visions, and fire opal will fire your aspiration to achieve your dreams. The 291st day of the year reduces to three, providing the influence of growth and unfoldment and supporting you with courage.

OBJECTS/IMAGES
weddings, leather-bound books, a porcelain dinner bell

SHAPES/MATERIALS
white coral, taffeta, S-curve shapes

COLORS
yellow-orange, cobalt blue, tangerine

ANIMALS
miniature collie, purple martin

PLANTS, HERBS, EDIBLES
strawberries, white roses, lemon thyme, pansies

ESSENCE
Moroccan thyme

SOUNDS/RHYTHMS
a harmonium, promenade music

MUSICAL NOTES
G# and D

DEEP SPACE OBJECTS
Beta Boötes, Nekkar, Ox Driver

October 18

YOUR SIGN
Libra

———

YOUR ELEMENT
Air

———

YOUR RULERS
Venus, Mercury
24–25 degrees
Third Decanate, yang

The Astrological Interpretation

Your symbol is a golden triangle with a diamond at its center. There are three elements in life that when properly blended give rise to the way of human perfection. These are will, love, and intelligence. You will find that one of these three elements is underdeveloped within you and creating an imbalance in your life. You have the opportunity to possess the diamond if you make the necessary effort to formulate this essential triangle. Take up a martial art for will; study psychology, history, or sociology for intelligence; and work with children to develop love.

October 18 has a number of talents and must focus creativity on one path at a time. If you go in too many directions, you will be pulled into trifles and superficialities that can create indecision. With Mercury ruling your decanate, you might profit from writing down your thoughts and keeping a journal. It will help you organize and separate what is important from what is a vogue of the moment. An image for you is the yellow brick road. There are adventures on either side of the road, but Emerald City is the destination. At home, you may want to keep replicas of ancient Greek statues. Looking at carved white marble is intrinsically aesthetic and may help you focus. In the bedroom have a blond wood bedstead and a quilt bedspread with a center medallion. Colors for October 18 are pastels with deep purple and blue for accents.

Outdoors, flowers are pleasing and restorative. Keep cut flowers in your home. In the garden have a birdbath or garden table and benches. Flowers for you are yellow horned poppies, fairy's thimble, and pink rockrose.

A Kabbalistic Interpretation

There's a song that says what a difference a day makes. While yesterday's focus was the eternal and the great mysteries of life, your primary concern is with the here and now. In particular you have a great ambition to make a career success of yourself. By wearing a seven-pointed star pendant, especially in red with a thin green border, you will give yourself the best chance of success.

Although you are very definitely a career-motivated person you are also emotionally sensitive, although people may not often see this side of your personality. There will definitely be times in life when you will benefit from not letting your emotions get the better of you. On such occasions a tigereye stone carried in your pocket will help you to steel yourself against feeling downhearted.

You aim high in life, however, and money alone is not much of a motivator for you. The influence of the sephira Kether in this day suggests that winning the respect of your peers is as important as any financial gain. In order to maintain your high standards you should keep an almond tree in your garden or add some almond essence to your bathwater.

A Numerological Interpretation

YOUR MAGIC NUMBERS: 1 AND 4

The eighteenth day of the tenth month reduces to one, the number signifying beginning, initiative, and self-consciousness. One is characterized by singleness of purpose. Yours is a path of continual forward progress into the unknown. This pattern requires strength of purpose and courage. At times, your life may feel like the darkest hour before the dawn, but you possess the intrinsic knowledge that the light will always reappear. There is a quality of receptivity that draws the things you desire to you if you keep the faith. Volunteer for Scouting, and take young Scouts on overnight camping trips. Learn basic survival skills.

Garnet and moss agate are stones to fuel your courage and feed your unflagging will to continue your quest. The 292nd day of the year reduces to four, contributing the ability to easily gain the lay of the land. This supports your forward movement out of the darkness into the dawn.

OBJECTS/IMAGES
statues, sofas, trinkets, thimbles

SHAPES/MATERIALS
stretch lace, filament silk, emerald, ribbon shapes

COLORS
purple, blush, cream

ANIMAL
whistling swan

PLANTS, HERBS, EDIBLES
self-heal (herb), rye, Italian bellflower, bleeding heart

ESSENCE
clary sage

SOUNDS/RHYTHMS
musical solos, a Welsh harp

MUSICAL NOTES
C and D#

DEEP SPACE OBJECTS
Epsilon Boötes, Izar

October 19

The Astrological Interpretation

With will, love, and intelligence already balanced on this birthday, a new challenge emerges—the task of creating an orientation to relationships so that the individual's inner spiritual potential may emerge victorious. This does not mean abandoning personal intimacy. It does mean that such relationships need to be geared toward a focus in which the love and joy between you and your partner may be offered to some larger humanitarian cause or ideal. Your interpersonal love will be sustained by the generosity of your hearts. Troubles come about in relationships when you and your partner do not share the same sense of idealism or altruism. To keep the outer structure strong, make sure to build your inner temple.

October 19 has a refined mind and great tenacity. Your sensitivities are highly developed, making maintaining detachment from annoying everyday realities difficult. Indulge your sensitivities at home and try and keep cool when encountering an environment that rubs you the wrong way. An image for you is an eagle and a dove alternately turning toward each other. At home decorate with swirling, colorful abstract paintings or designs. You may be adept at making designs yourself. In the kitchen, copper cookware could stimulate your cooking abilities. Brass candlesticks in the window are another homey touch you would enjoy. If you have a tendency to overspend, exercise some discipline and keep a piggy bank in plain sight. It will increase your resolve to save.

Outdoors, October 19 would enjoy visiting an expansive and complicated garden. You want maximum beauty and minimal upkeep. Flowering shrubs and bushes are perfect for your own yard. Rose acacia and Japanese snowballs are two possibilities.

A Kabbalistic Interpretation

In days gone by you would probably have entered the warrior class of society, as you have an extremely courageous nature. It is unlikely, however, that your independent personality would be well suited to the discipline of life in the modern armed forces. There is a connection between your bravery and the animal kingdom, which suggests a fascination with wild animals. Take a trip to Africa and go on a safari expedition.

The planet Jupiter exerts a benevolent influence on this day, in particular as a source of luck and good fortune for you. You can maximize the good luck that this planet can bring you by keeping a square of tin in your pocket or inside your desk drawer. Ideally you should have an upright pointed triangle engraved on this little square.

You are a resolutely independent and individualistic person. This side of your personality can be very attractive to those around you. Wearing a ring mounted with lapis lazuli on your third finger will enhance your charismatic attraction.

A Numerological Interpretation
YOUR MAGIC NUMBERS: 2 AND 5

The nineteenth day of the tenth month reduces to two, the number of polarity, alternation, and the ancient symbol of the life force in action. Born on this day, you have a path of connectivity. You love to perceive the interconnectedness of things, and your mind always works to connect the dots in mental pictures that others are not able to conceptualize. This talent enables you to expand the imaginations of those with whom you share your visions. You would thrive working where you could create new worlds like those in the TV series *Star Trek* or the *Star Wars* movies. You would love to be on the team for first contact with visitors from other worlds.

Carnelian will accelerate your mental processes. White turquoise acts as a grounding influence to keep your circuits clear. The 293rd day of the year reduces to five, which provides a facility with transitions and a constantly changing frame of reference.

OBJECTS/IMAGES
jugglers, keepsakes

SHAPES/MATERIALS
pale jade, heart shapes, hippodrome shapes, linen

COLORS
Wedgwood blue, bright yellow, copper

ANIMALS
purple finch, heron

PLANTS, HERBS, EDIBLES
honey, indigo plant, magnolia, flowering peach

ESSENCE
mandarin

SOUNDS/RHYTHMS
limericks, harmonica music

MUSICAL NOTES
C# and E

DEEP SPACE OBJECT
supernova

October 20

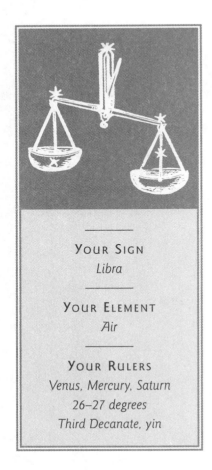

YOUR SIGN
Libra

YOUR ELEMENT
Air

YOUR RULERS
Venus, Mercury, Saturn
26–27 degrees
Third Decanate, yin

The Astrological Interpretation

You are a born matchmaker, and marriage comes much more easily than divorce. Whether it is a romantic connection or a simple friendship, you find it hard to part from an individual even when it is obvious that the time has come for you to go your separate ways. You can make things rough on yourself when you force the other person to break up with you or just wait until they "disappear." At times, when you can no longer wait, instead of coming right out and making a clean exit, you create such confusion that the other party has little choice but to say good-bye to you. Examine your reluctance and learn how to release the lever before you're the one who gets hung!

October 20, astrologically, is considered a "critical degree." This means that all experiences register strongly throughout life. October 20 will rarely be in the shadows. Perhaps because life often creates dramatic situations for you, you may personify the saying: "when the going gets tough, the tough go shopping." Choose objects that enhance your life rather than clutter it. Heart shapes are always pleasing. Consider a few well-chosen candy dishes. Your living room should be large enough to entertain. Pale green on the walls or pale green carpeting calms your nerves. Carry quartz crystal in your pocket and, during October, matching opal jewelry will remind you of the delicacy and fire October 20 brings to life.

Your garden might include gladiolas in a variety of colors. Placing a large vase of these dramatic flowers by a mirror in an entry hall will create a focal point as you move inside from outdoors. You like moderate heights with a vista. A small rustic cottage under a cedar tree is a perfect hideaway and symbol for your hospitable nature.

A Kabbalistic Interpretation

As indicated by the Justice card, a sense of fairness in life is important to your well-being. Your friends and work colleagues will most likely turn to you for advice whenever they are experiencing some kind of conflict. You are always happy to offer assistance in such matters, but you also need to maintain some mental space for yourself. A good solid wooden chair with a blue and red cushion positioned in a quiet corner of your home is the ideal place for you to sit and think quietly about your own life and direction.

Another card with a significant effect on this day is the Sun card. This card represents your infectious enthusiasm for life. One way in which you can spread that enthusiasm is to opt for a touch of orange or red in your outfits when you go to work. The Sun card is connected to the element of fire, which will be useful to you when it comes to seeing a project through to the end. You can activate the fire within you in a number of ways. One very simple approach is to include some cinnamon in your diet. This spice corresponds to the Sun card and contains fire energy.

A Numerological Interpretation
YOUR MAGIC NUMBERS: 3 AND 6

The twentieth day of the tenth month reduces to three, the number that connotes imagination, growth, and development of the creative process. Yours is a path of mental discovery. Your pattern involves the generation and multiplication of knowledge. Your search should result in guidance and practical application of the information for the benefit of all humanity.

The danger of this path is accumulating facts and data just for the sake of possessing the information. Knowledge is not always power. Not all knowledge is worth having; some information is just clutter. Tigereye will sharpen the focus of your inner vision. Sodalite will enhance the practical application of your mental pictures. The 294th day of the year reduces to six, supporting your path with an intrinsic sense of symmetry and balance.

OBJECTS/IMAGES
satin sachets,
leather driving gloves,
a carved mahogany chest

SHAPES/MATERIALS
concentric circles, linen, opals

COLORS
apricot, crimson, ivory,
flame orange, spring green

ANIMALS
Labrador dog, blue heron

PLANTS, HERBS, EDIBLES
spearmint leaf candy,
maraschino cherries,
sweetbreads

ESSENCES
Shalimar perfume,
lemon verbena

SOUNDS/RHYTHMS
stones skipping on a lake,
whistling, the two-step

MUSICAL NOTES
D and F

DEEP SPACE OBJECT
black hole

October 21

YOUR SIGN
Libra

———

YOUR ELEMENT
Air

———

YOUR RULERS
Venus, Mercury
27–28 degrees
Third Decanate, yin

The Astrological Interpretation

You have an inborn instinct about people. People do not have to say anything for you to spot their inner weaknesses and strengths. But you use this knowledge to help them rather than taking advantage of them. No matter what your age or gender, you are very much like the hostess who takes it upon herself to make sure that everyone is enjoying themselves at the party and that conversation flows easily among guests. You support the differences among people so long as these differences are complementary. You therefore tend to have a mature and executive social orientation and take your responsibilities toward others seriously.

With Gemini ruling your decanate it may be a good idea for you to write your thoughts down rather than try them out verbally. Speaking your thoughts out loud may be confusing and embroil you in decisions before you are ready.

In your home emphasize curves. An oval dining room table and perhaps a circular rug would be soothing to you. A spiral staircase linking floors would be a good structural item. Doodling with colored pencils before you go to sleep may give you Technicolor dreams. In your bedroom hang ribbons and necklaces from hooks. You may even want to create your own gallery of designs. In the kitchen use mason jars as canisters. October 21 likes clear glass and the variety of colors that sugar, coffee, etc., make through the glass.

Outdoors, you would enjoy a garden fit for a tea party. A small garden house or screened-in gazebo would also be perfect. Hang a wind chime on your porch or gazebo and listen to it while admiring your garden of peonies, pansies, and lilies of the valley.

A Kabbalistic Interpretation

Air is the most powerful element in the makeup of this day. Its influence acts to give you a strongly analytical and problem-solving mind. You do have a lack of earth energy, so in order to help you translate your ideas into reality you should wear a fire opal ring on your third finger.

The Emperor card suggests that you will be able to wield authority responsibly and effectively. In addition you have a great ability for bonding people together as a team, so whatever field you work in it is highly likely that you will have a management role. To encourage this ability you ought to keep a sprig of hawthorn on your desk or even a bonsai hawthorn in a ceramic pot.

Always a popular guest, you have the ability to mix with a whole range of different types of people. This is partly due to the energetic spirit you possess. This spirit is suggested by the importance of the letter *Shin* in your day, as that letter is connected to the Ruach, or the enlivening spirit, in kabbalistic thought. Wearing a brilliant orange bracelet or watch strap will increase your ability to liven up any social gathering.

A Numerological Interpretation
YOUR MAGIC NUMBERS: 4 AND 7

The twenty-first day of the tenth month reduces to four, the number of order, surveying, and topography. Yours is a path of wide-ranging discovery. You are filled with a desire to experience all of life, and your passion to venture far and wide knows no bounds. Your nature endows you with understanding and empathy for the vast diversity of expression of the human condition, and you want to experience it first-hand. Work in the travel industry so you can take advantage of exotic journeys to faraway places. Your natural friendliness will ensure your acceptance wherever you roam.

Fluorite is a stone to stabilize the potential extremes of your emotions. Apricot agate from Botswana will temper your longing for faraway lands. Collect minerals from around the world so you can always enjoy a tangible remembrance of your sojourns. The 295th day of the year reduces to seven, providing the essential ingredient of rest between your far-flung adventures.

OBJECTS/IMAGES
corsages, necklaces, gloves, ornaments

SHAPES/MATERIALS
onyx, paint, oxygen, linen

COLORS
pink, tangerine, jade green

ANIMAL
song sparrow

PLANTS, HERBS, EDIBLES
omelettes, nectarines, pastries, poppies

ESSENCES
benzoin

SOUNDS/RHYTHMS
Franz Liszt's Hungarian Rhapsody

MUSICAL NOTES
D# and F#

DEEP SPACE OBJECT
NGC 3918, planetary nebula

October 22

YOUR SIGN
Libra

———

YOUR ELEMENT
Air

———

YOUR RULERS
Venus, Mercury, Saturn
28–29 degrees
Third Decanate, yin

The Astrological Interpretation

You are deeply affected by the cultural context in which you were raised. You are aware of your ancestors and the contributions they made not only to your own family but also to humanity. This means looking at your background from the point of view of the history of nations, races, and religions. Your view of life and society is wider than most people's. It is hard for you to understand prejudice of any kind and impossible for you to accept it. You are likely to be part of a non-denominational religion or philosophical organization. If you are involved in a traditional church, you tend to be more connected to its progressive rather than its conservative wing.

Your birthday, near the end of Libra, has a touch of Scorpio in it. This combination of air and water gives great charm and sex appeal. Sometimes there is too much reliance on insubstantial activities such as trying to please and manipulate people. October 22 should rely on very real talents and abilities; they will take you where you need to go. An ancient serpent is a meditation image for October 22. For both men and women, the serpent is sexual power that fascinates and also heals. Your bed is the place where you can retreat to and dream: alone or with company. Think about having blankets, comforters, and sheets for different seasons: apple green for spring, white for summer, mauve for fall, and dusty rose for winter. The smell of freshly baked cookies is irresistible to you. Bring a plate up to your bedroom and see what creative thoughts come. The sound of cooing doves is pleasing.

Outdoors October 22 wants a space to walk and think. A bridge that you can walk over is focusing and a good image for you. A bridge links one place with another, metaphorically linking people, ideas, and creations together. Flowers for you are deep red chrysanthemums and orchids. You may enjoy having cut flowers more than flowers in a garden.

A Kabbalistic Interpretation

The energies of this day point strongly toward a fearless character with a great desire to explore new places and ways of living. While there are no new continents left to discover you can still apply that energized curiosity to your life by seeking out a range of different activities. Consider decorating your walls with some old-fashioned maps to inspire your adventures.

One of the factors that suggests an interest in the world is the importance of the sephira Malkuth to this date. This association indicates that you are likely to have a love of nature, particularly woodlands and the plants that grow there. Keep a bonsai ash or willow tree in your living room and you will never be far from these energies.

Friendship is an important and serious bond for you. The word in Hebrew meaning "unity" is equivalent to the value of this day, indicating the way you keep a link with all your closest friends. The blue-laced agate stone is associated with deep and unconditional affection; you should try sleeping with one of these stones under your pillow, as it will help to strengthen your friendships.

A Numerological Interpretation
YOUR MAGIC NUMBERS: 5 AND 8

The twenty-second day of the tenth month reduces to five, the number signifying change, uncertainty, and mediation. Five is halfway between one and ten, and seeks for the agency to move the process toward completion. Yours is a path of total immersion in your life. You are utterly involved with both people and events and do not hold back your feelings. There is a quality to this pattern similar to that of the wounded healer in shamanic traditions. You willingly feel both the sorrow and joy of those around you. Strive to cultivate some detachment.

Learn to meditate and take a long-range view of life's struggles. Blue and yellow topaz will brighten your spirits and strengthen your will. The 296th day of the year reduces to eight, adding the awareness that all things in life ebb and flow. Whatever the crisis of the moment, this too shall pass.

OBJECTS/IMAGES
*a black lace fan,
Cleopatra reclining on her barge,
a silk purse*

SHAPES/MATERIALS
oval china, satin, raw silk

COLORS
*pale peach, aqua, rose,
ivory, teal*

ANIMALS
rabbit, praying mantis

PLANTS, HERBS, EDIBLES
*catmint, ginseng, dourian
(fruit from Thailand)*

ESSENCES
musk, bitter orange

SOUNDS/RHYTHMS
triplets, courtship dances

MUSICAL NOTES
E and G

DEEP SPACE OBJECT
Delta Draconis

October 23

YOUR SIGNS
Libra/Scorpio

———

YOUR ELEMENTS
Air/Water

———

YOUR RULERS
Venus, Mars, Pluto
29 degrees Libra–
00 degrees Scorpio
Third Decanate, yin
First Decanate, yin

The Astrological Interpretation

You are born on the cusp of two signs: Libra and Scorpio. This marks a stillness like the calm before a storm. The time and particular year of your birth will determine which of the two is your own sun sign. The symbol for this degree is the inner marriage. It speaks about the potential joining of the male/yang and the female/yin energies within you. This day represents the ultimate blending and balance of Libra and the result of this process: a rebirth through Scorpio into a person capable of abundant creativity. Your ideal partner will not make you whole, for you are that already. Your perfect relationship is with a man or woman who is an independent and total individual; no one less will do.

Suffice it to say this birthday has the power to fascinate. Self-expression and moderation are the keys to mental and emotional balance. When decorating your home try to include both air and water elements for both your signs. For example, a corner of the living room with an open window, wind chimes, and an aquarium is a perfect combination for October 23. The bedroom will be a focal point for you. If at all possible do not work there. The atmosphere should be peaceful and meditative. Choose rich blues and greens for bed linens and lighter versions for curtains and wall colors. A photograph or painting of swans swimming would be a perfect image for your bedroom.

Outdoors, October 23 likes gardens with trees and benches where you can sit in the sun and breathe deeply. October 23 likes to be on the go and to socialize and needs to plan on quiet moments. Flowering crab apples and quince would please you, and an evergreen forest is a perfect retreat.

A Kabbalistic Interpretation

The number three is important to this date. Three is a number symbolizing the process whereby something is made or brought into being. In addition it refers to abundance of those things essential for a happy home such as food and warmth. Use patterns of three and triangles wherever possible in your home to encourage the greatest impact of this positive and warming influence.

In the office you are likely to be highly regarded as an idea person. While you are not so good at methodically working at a given task you are excellent at coming up with new proposals. The Strength card from the tarot gives you the will to stand up for your ideas no matter how strange they may seem to others at first. A statuette or painting of a lion by your desk will assist you in meeting each challenge.

In the kabbala there are four worlds of existence, each one closer to the divine than the last. This day has the same value as the Hebrew meaning "Assiah," which is the first of these four worlds and corresponds to the material plane. You have an affinity for the solidity of the natural world and dislike the abstract in terms of art and design. If you design your kitchen in a very traditional style with lots of dark wood, you will feel right at home.

A Numerological Interpretation
YOUR MAGIC NUMBERS: 6 AND 9

The twenty-third day of the tenth month reduces to six, the number of balance, equilibrium, and the harmony of opposites. Born on this day, you have a path of intense involvement in your family and community, however you define them. This pattern endows you with an innate sense of fulfillment in sharing the lives of others. You would be at the height of your element at an old-fashioned barn raising. Volunteer for United Way or the Salvation Army.

It is essential for you to feel helpful, and casting your bread upon the waters contributes to your natural sense of spiritual reciprocity. Sodalite and peridot are gems to enhance your sense of balance and serenity. The 297th day of the year reduces to nine, contributing a deep sense of accomplishing your goals where you have extended yourself to others. You feel complete when you have given something away.

OBJECTS/IMAGES
parquet floors, leather upholstery, clear glass vases, black towels

SHAPES/MATERIALS
hematite, tigereye, coiled shapes, black opals

COLORS
burgundy, lime green, royal blue

ANIMAL
red-shouldered hawk

PLANTS, HERBS, EDIBLES
passion fruit, red ginseng, Venus flytrap, pepper vodka

ESSENCE
opopanax

SOUNDS/RHYTHMS
altos, vocal tone

MUSICAL NOTES
F and G#

DEEP SPACE OBJECT
NGC 5927, globular cluster

October 24

YOUR SIGN
Scorpio

YOUR ELEMENT
Water

YOUR RULERS
Mars, Pluto
00–1 degree
First Decanate, yin

The Astrological Interpretation

You are born on the very first degree of the sign Scorpio, symbolized by the image of a high flying eagle. This is a bird that is known for its keen sight—its eagle eyes! So too are your eyes bright and piercing. You are at your most free when you can detach from the intensity of your feelings and desires and soar above the chaos and confusion of life. This element of detachment is your greatest gift, for it enables you to see the real strengths and the true weaknesses of people around you. You are a very sociable person and have a great need for passion and faithfulness in your relationships. Yet you often need to stand alone so that you may be free to explore life on your own terms.

Very little escapes your keen mind, and your talent is to size up a situation quickly and work until it yields the best possible outcome. You may "save the day" frequently. Ruled by both Mars and Pluto October 24 enjoys a home that has an underground feel. Secret passages, back alleys, and dumbwaiters that are concealed all appeal to you. Dark wood paneling adds elegance to your surroundings. You may be interested in collecting antique medical instruments. Intricate designs such as a Greek key or Celtic knot appeal. Consider stenciling a design around your ceiling or finding a rug with bold geometric designs.

Outdoors, October 24 loves the feeling of the approaching winter darkness. Burnt auburn chrysanthemums are flowers you may want in a garden or as a house plant. A visit to a colonial garden where there is a box hedge maze would be fun and interesting to you. You are naturally attracted by deep reds and purples and will like blood roses and lilacs.

A Kabbalistic Interpretation

Wisdom is possibly the greatest gift that anyone could have, and because of the influence of the Hermit card this day you are blessed with an abundance of it. The importance of the water element today means you are likely to have a deep understanding of relationships. Grow an apple tree in your garden and you may increase your ability to help people with the emotional aspects of their lives.

The number thirty-four, associated with the planet Jupiter, is highly significant to your birthday's value. It is the aspect of Jupiter as friendly father figure that has the greatest effect on your nature. Burning some cedar incense in the morning will encourage that benevolent but authoritative aspect of your personality.

A sense of balance and harmony is very important to you at home and at work. You like an atmosphere of mutual affection and find any kind of underlying conflict disturbing. Placing a pale blue crystal vase in the east of your office and bedroom will encourage the atmosphere of peace and contentment that you desire.

A Numerological Interpretation
YOUR MAGIC NUMBERS: 7 AND 1

The twenty-fourth day of the tenth month reduces to seven, the number signifying victory, safety, and rest after a period of creation. Born on this day, you have a path of responding to the inner light of your being and carrying that light into the world. This pattern endows you with a strong awareness of realms beyond the physical. As a child you may have had companions from unseen dimensions and conversed with elves and fairies. You comprehend the interconnectedness of all things, and have respect for all the kingdoms of nature. Spend time in the wilderness; this will nourish your soul. Listen to the voices of the wild creatures, and don't be surprised when you understand their messages.

Watermelon tourmaline is a gem to remind you of the many levels and facets of manifestation. The 298th day of the year reduces to ten and one, contributing a satisfying sense of completion to all your endeavors and the inner urging to begin again.

OBJECTS/IMAGES
physicians and healers, swamps, pharmacists

SHAPES/MATERIALS
tourmaline, serpentine shapes, cadmium, palm fronds

COLORS
reddish purple, kelly green, cherry red

ANIMALS
praying mantis, wasp

PLANTS, HERBS, EDIBLES
woad, pulsatilla (herb), heather, turtle soup

ESSENCE
vetiver

SOUNDS/RHYTHMS
keening, a raven's call

MUSICAL NOTES
F# and C

DEEP SPACE OBJECT
Tau Centaurus

October 25

YOUR SIGN
Scorpio

YOUR ELEMENT
Water

YOUR RULER
Mars
1–2 degrees
First Decanate, yin

The Astrological Interpretation

Although you are a trusted friend and confidante, you are quite reluctant to let anyone in on what is going on inside of you. Those whom you do count within your inner circle must continually prove their loyalty. Once betrayed, you never let the offending individual into your heart again. Timing is everything with you, and you can hold yourself back until you nearly burst. When you finally release, a tremendous flood of energy comes forth, allowing you to accomplish a great deal. The important thing is not to allow this tension to become a burden. Physical exercise and competitive sports will do a lot to tone down your emotional intensity. Swimming, sailing, and diving are other natural attractions.

October 25 has penetrating power in whatever he pursues. Your greatest talent is in expressing conflicting feelings and transforming that raw material into a new creation. An image for you is a nomadic warrior searching for battle. Learning when to go into the fray and when to sit out is your challenge. A bloodstone is a perfect mineral for you. You may also want to investigate some materials from alchemy. Two stones called urim and thummin, one black and one white, were used to obtain oracular answers to questions; black meant yes and white meant no. Try this system and see where your intuition leads you. Scent is very important to you. Consider collecting perfume bottles and using scents such as patchouli and myrrh.

Outdoors October 25 enjoys extreme environments. A glacier might be interesting or a journey into the desert. Take nature trips as a way to relax, and you may discover new thoughts according to each environment. Closer to home, October 25 likes to sit under a shady tree by a creek or rivulet. Skipping stones is a perfect low-intensity pastime. You may also want to study medicinal herbs and plants, especially poisonous ones. Materials that many people think of as waste are the seeds of creativity for you.

A Kabbalistic Interpretation

Travel is very well aspected in the value of this day. As much as you like to explore the countryside, it is equally important for you to have a definite home base, as you love to come home in the evening to familiar surroundings. Keep some mugwort in a yellow pouch tied behind your back door to encourage enjoyment on both sides of the threshold.

The Emperor card's energy of confident, earthly power combines with the Mars aspect of Scorpio this day to make you a difficult customer to disagree with! Although it is wonderful to make a success of yourself, make sure that you don't lose your sensitivity along the way. Keeping a pearl inlaid mirror in your bathroom can help you to prevent this.

As the total value of your day generates a prime number, you are likely to be highly idiosyncratic. It may sometimes be necessary to tone down your unique approach to life, though this will not come easily to you. A sprig of angelica in your desk drawer will help you to temper your eccentricities when it is useful to do so.

A Numerological Interpretation
YOUR MAGIC NUMBERS: 8 AND 2

The twenty-fifth day of the tenth month reduces to eight, the number connoting the ebb and flow of the cyclic manifestations of nature. Eight symbolizes the one reality behind differing outward appearances. Yours is a path of learning how to hold to that central reality through all the ups and downs of personal experience. This pattern requires that you find your inner poise and hold that alignment like a gyroscope. You have a naturally strong personality, which helps your quest.

The danger of this path is stubbornness; not everyone has the same mission in life, and each individual should be free to march to their own drummer. Spend time on the water, the movement of waves is soothing to your spirit. Turquoise and amber are gems to steady your emotional nature. The 299th day of the year reduces to two, providing the element of reflection. Center yourself by peering into a still, clear lake.

OBJECTS/IMAGES
the yin/yang symbol, stagnant ponds, a sorcerer's wand

SHAPES/MATERIALS
six-pointed star, malachite, plutonium

COLORS
murky red, charcoal, aquamarine, russet

ANIMALS
snake, merlin (bird)

PLANTS, HERBS, EDIBLES
datura, delphinium, arsenic

ESSENCE
sweat

SOUNDS/RHYTHMS
klezmer music, snake charmer's music

MUSICAL NOTES
G and C#

DEEP SPACE OBJECTS
Beta Carina, Miaplacidus

October 26

YOUR SIGN
Scorpio

YOUR ELEMENT
Water

YOUR RULERS
Mars, Pluto
2–3 degrees
First Decanate, yin

The Astrological Interpretation

You are keen on making a lot of money, so it is important for you to learn how to use your resources wisely. You will find that you are naturally attracted to what others have and that you can be very helpful in supporting people to make the most out of their talents and possessions. In return, you will be invited to share in their enterprises, pleasures, and opportunities. Learning the lessons of unselfish cooperation is the key to your success. Make sure that what you want is a choice and neither an obsession nor a compulsion, so that if you do not get it, you can be free to get on with life. You do well in professions that involve investments in beautiful and valuable objects, such as jewelry, art, and real estate.

October 26 is a thoughtful soul who uses Scorpio's intensity to be genuinely helpful. Don't be surprised if you have a reputation for solving others' problems just by listening. The other person says "thanks a lot, I feel better," while you may think that you didn't do anything. The quality of your listening is enough. To support your energy meditate with a red stone such as a polished garnet or bloodstone. It is not advisable to carry this stone all the time. At home your decor may tend toward the spartan. If you feel at sea on how to arrange things and make a cozy home, consult a friend. Recessed lighting and a lamp with an amber-colored shade would suit your contemplative nature. Your personal wardrobe should be shades of dark green and crimson.

Outdoors, October 26 likes rugged nature in small doses. Nature trips suit you, and a trip to the Grand Canyon may feel like a pilgrimage for you. Your own yard could include pine trees and Oregon holly grape. Orchids are an indoor flower for you.

A Kabbalistic Interpretation

You have an enormous connection to the sephira Hod, which represents the mental level of existence within individuals. Intellectually it would be difficult to find your superior; you have a very powerful mind and may well work in some academic or senior research capacity. A bookcase colored in violet would make a good addition to your study area and will help you to keep your thoughts clear.

The Justice card from the tarot is important to this day. However, the overwhelming influence of the sephira Hod means that it is likely to be the idea of justice as an intellectual concept that interests you. A nice present for you would be a statuette of the classical representation of justice complete with sword and scales.

Not everything in your world is purely abstract though. When it comes to emotional relationships your feelings are as strong as anyone's. In fact the influence of the moon in this day indicates that you may well feel things more intensely than most. By keeping a moonstone in your pocket you can ensure that you stay in touch with your feelings.

A Numerological Interpretation
YOUR MAGIC NUMBERS: 9 AND 3

The twenty-sixth day of the tenth month reduces to nine, the number signifying attaining and accomplishing a goal. Nine is the closing of the cycle. Born on this day, you have a path of ambition. You are endowed with keen instincts where successful projects are concerned, and you have both initiative and determination to see things through. You don't mind investing a proportionate amount of energy, and you enjoy reaping the rewards. The danger of this path can be the illusion that somewhere there really is a free lunch. If you remain practical, then you will realize many benefits from your insights.

Golden beryl and pyrite are stones to aid both your aspirations and your common sense. Don't be deceived by fool's gold. The 300th day of the year reduces to three, providing the added element of growth and unfoldment. This aids the plentiful harvest where you have planted your best seeds.

OBJECTS/IMAGES
apothecary jars, a beer stein, a house-raising

SHAPES/MATERIALS
iron, malachite, geyser shapes

COLORS
dark brown, bright blue, carrot orange

ANIMAL
skunk

PLANTS, HERBS, EDIBLES
blackthorn trees, horehound, wormwood

ESSENCE
hyssop

SOUNDS/RHYTHMS
chants, heavy metal music

MUSICAL NOTES
G# and D

DEEP SPACE OBJECTS
Delta Boötes, Princeps

October 27

Your Sign
Scorpio

Your Element
Water

Your Rulers
Mars, Pluto
3–4 degrees
First Decanate, yin

The Astrological Interpretation

You are a person who is attracted by the emotional intensity of religious and other ceremonial rituals. You love the magic and drama of pageantry, the smell of incense, the veneration of sacred objects, and the power of invisible forces. It is important that you balance these leanings with an equally strong understanding of the philosophy and belief system that stands behind such rites. You are drawn to those who have lost their way in life and who have redeemed themselves through an association with the mystical and the transcendental. You know about compulsion, but you also know about the healing power of love. Your life is not led on superficial levels. You have a penetrating insight into the real meaning of human existence and can be counted on to give advice and counsel from this depth.

You have a tenacious mind that excels at structure and planning, but these abilities may lead you to become a trifle adamant about execution. If you find that the plan becomes more important than the people involved or the goal, rethink your ideas. At home, you enjoy a lot of space and decorative objects from nature. Old prints and botanicals and Audubon plates of birds and mammals all appeal to you. Candles may be favorites of yours. Have them in a variety of shapes and colors and light them frequently. A symbol for October 27 is a double triangle. This may have been a symbol of the magician in times gone by, and you would enjoy learning a few feats of illusion.

Outdoors, you have a rough and ready attitude. Spending time in an awe-inspiring natural environment is a religious experience for you. You have a soft spot for animals and may feed strays that come around the garden. A plant that might interest you is monkshood.

A Kabbalistic Interpretation

The Hanged Man card has an important role in your approach to the world. It confirms your strong desire to help others and in particular it points to a concern for the underdog. Altruism is one of your finest character attributes. Growing an ash tree in your garden will encourage your more charitable side.

You have a campaigning spirit and you will fight tooth and nail for a cause you believe in. The world needs people like you to make sure that we don't all become the prey of enormous multinational corporations. From time to time though even you feel yourself flagging. On those days you should make sure you wear something with a touch of the deepest crimson.

Family and the domestic environments have a great effect on your sense of stability and security. Your connection to the sephira Binah means that you have a deep attachment to family members, and if you have children you will see your parental role as primary. Have some deep-piled rugs on the floor, as your home should be a cosy and comforting place.

A Numerological Interpretation
YOUR MAGIC NUMBERS: 10 AND 4

The twenty-seventh day of the tenth month reduces to ten, the number that signifies embodiment and the perfection of the cycle. If nine is the end of the pregnancy, ten represents the perfect child the moment before birth. Born on this day, you have a path of taking everything to the limit. Your pattern asks that you explore deeply, probing and penetrating each experience for every facet and detail of significance.

Yours is a mission to go to the core of the human experience, and mine the depths of passion and feeling. This path is like peering into a microscope not a telescope. Learn to scuba dive and discover the magnificence of the underwater world. Aquamarine and pearl are gems to deepen your resolve and open your mind to the vastness of inner space. The 301st day of the year reduces to four, supporting your path with the important quality of order and classification.

OBJECTS/IMAGES
bawdiness, dice, divining rods, beer kegs

SHAPES/MATERIALS
natural domes, mazes, red jasper

COLORS
mottled gray, midnight blue, butterscotch

ANIMALS
ferret, glowworm

PLANTS, HERBS, EDIBLES
hemlock spruce, thistle tea, swamp milkweed

ESSENCE
ambergris

SOUNDS/RHYTHMS
bubbling potions, gypsy folk dances

MUSICAL NOTES
A and D#

DEEP SPACE OBJECTS
Iota Virgo, Syrma

October 28

YOUR SIGN
Scorpio

YOUR ELEMENT
Water

YOUR RULERS
Mars, Pluto
4–5 degrees
First Decanate, yin

The Astrological Interpretation

No matter what the external pressures of life may be, you have a definite "never say die" attitude. You are determined not only to survive but also to prosper from the challenges that life brings. You have tremendous recuperative powers. This does not mean that your life is always problematic for you. You have your just share of joy and happiness. But unlike many people, you seem to function at your best in times of trouble and chaos. You do well leading your friends out of any morass of emotional confusion and internal perplexities. You seem to be able to find the light shining at the end of the proverbial tunnel, pulling yourself and your loved ones behind you. It is from such battles that you emerge victorious.

October 28 has a poised spirit that balances many talents and practical necessities. As long as you keep expressing yourself, you will avoid turning your energies in on yourself. Sports or yoga are good ways to keep the body tuned up and energized. At home, you enjoy a muted color scheme and dark wood. An old carved trunk of teak or mahogany is a perfect symbol for your mysterious and self-possessed character. Keep the chest in the entryway so anyone coming in or out will pass by it. Stretchy smooth fabrics that fit you like a second skin are made for October 28. If you've got it, flaunt it! Scent in the bedroom is a definite asset; patchouli and mimosa could be two favorites.

Your outdoor environment could include a pond and a field of clover. The three-leaf clover represents faith, hope, and charity. Nature's raw grandeur gives you peace and perspective. Visit large rocky cliffs by the sea.

A Kabbalistic Interpretation

The value of this day is associated with the Hebrew word meaning "innocent." You are likely to have a strongly idealistic view of the world, with boundless optimism and hope for the future. However, it is also important that you are able to cope with the sometimes harsh realities of day-to-day life. A mirror in an iron frame hung above your bed will help you to develop a useful level of resilience.

The Death card from the tarot indicates that you will face a number of life-altering changes. These are most likely to relate to your emotional relationships and they will be hard for you to handle, although they will prove beneficial in the long run. Burning some jasmine-scented candles will help you to accept these changes when they occur.

Another word that is equivalent to the value of this day is the word meaning "foundation." This suggests that you are proficient as a generator of ideas. In order to make the most of your ability in this area you need to be able to turn your plans into actualities. You should try keeping notes of your ideas in an olive- or russet-colored box file, as this will keep them in mind for you when the opportunity arises to do something with them.

A Numerological Interpretation
YOUR MAGIC NUMBERS: 2 AND 5

The twenty-eighth day of the tenth month reduces to two, the number that represents reflection, polarity, and the subconscious mind. Two is a very fluid energy, and like water, it responds by conforming itself to the shape of a container or the nature of its surroundings or relationships. Your path is the pursuit of magic present in ordinary things. This pattern contains a natural recognition of the potential attraction and connection possible between two twin souls. At the deepest level of your soul, you hunger for such a union. This sort of idealistic joining lifts ordinary human beings out of their habitual responses to something more transcendent.

Take a moonlight sail on the ocean and watch the moonlight ripple and sparkle across the surface of the dark water. Moonstone and jasper are gems to highlight your reflectivity. The 302nd day of the year reduces to five, enhancing your path with a supple responsiveness to change.

OBJECTS/IMAGES
a pirate ship, prongs, scrimshaw

SHAPES/MATERIALS
alexandrite, lead

COLORS
dark green, ochre, persimmon, egg yolk yellow

ANIMALS
cormorant, saber-toothed tiger

PLANTS, HERBS, EDIBLES
arnica, asafetida (Indian spice), bayberry trees

ESSENCE
cherry plum

SOUNDS/RHYTHMS
rock music, requiem masses

MUSICAL NOTES
C# and E

DEEP SPACE OBJECTS
Lambda Centarus, diffuse nebula

October 29

YOUR SIGN
Scorpio

YOUR ELEMENT
Water

YOUR RULERS
Mars, Pluto
5–6 degrees
First Decanate, yang

The Astrological Interpretation

The symbol most closely associated with your birth date is an ancient alchemist. Yours is the gift of transformation; your challenge is how to use it selflessly. You are a magnetic person who has a way of changing any environment in which you find yourself. You sense what is invisible in the feelings and emotions of people around you. You know when a smiling person is actually crying on the inside, and with a simple word or two, you can evoke those tears. You also can transform a situation that is just the reverse and bring a smile to a weeping face. Many people born on this day are attracted to the physical and psychological healing professions where such a gift can be put to the best possible use.

There is great strength in October 29 birthdays and the ability to keep a poker face no matter what situation arises. The ancient Stoics are an interesting image for you. Their philosophy emphasized reason and virtue and shunned emotions. October 29 is emotional but prefers to reveal feelings in private. At home have a leopard print pillow. You can strangle, cuddle, throw it, or balance it on your head. The bedroom is the place to indulge yourself. Consider listening to a tape of heartbeats or meditation music before you sleep. You may have a vogue for a water bed. In the bathroom keep some geranium bath salts on hand and decorate the walls with seashell prints and pieces of sea glass. In your living space you may collect valuable antiques. Ancient Greek vases would be an expensive but valued possession.

Outdoors a garden on low marshy land appeals to you. The heath country of England is worth a visit. Cattails may be a plant that appeals to you.

A Kabbalistic Interpretation

The Hebrew phrase meaning to "dwell" or "abide" is equivalent to the kabbalistic value of this day. With these phrases comes an idea of continuity and stability within a home setting. It is likely that your sense of contentment is highly dependent on exactly where you are living. In order to boost a sense of stability place some lead figurines or lead colored vases around your home, especially in the north.

Your day has a lot of fire energy rushing through it, and while this is beneficial in terms of your ability to get things done quickly it also can have a fairly unsettling effect on you. The Temperance card from the tarot encourages balance in your personality. A fountain or other water feature in the garden would be a good way of counteracting the excess of fire and invoking the calming influence of the Temperance card.

The sinister and shadowy side of life attracts you. While you would never involve yourself in any malevolent organization, you get a thrill from reading about such things. You enjoy old mysteries and sophisticated presentations of horror. Try getting hold of some Dennis Wheatley novels, as they should be right up your street.

A Numerological Interpretation
YOUR MAGIC NUMBERS: 3 AND 6

The twenty-ninth day of the tenth month reduces to three, the number that means growth, development, and multiplication. Three expresses the outworking of the principles begun in one and two. Born on this day, you have a path of self-renewal through stewardship. Your pattern requires that you tend equally to all levels of your being. You must remain in touch with all of your needs and responsibilities, both spiritual and material. Within the context of this path, body, soul, and spirit are seen as possessions or vehicles that must be kept in peak running order.

Exercise and meditate regularly to stay connected to your inner world. Remember to change the oil in your car and have an annual physical. Rhodochrosite and moss agate are minerals to support your path with open-mindedness and grounded discipline. The 303rd day of the year reduces to six, adding the element of balance and complementary activities. This helps you maintain your perspective and manage your priorities.

OBJECTS/IMAGES
incense burners, humorous war cartoons, a butcher's shop

SHAPES/MATERIALS
alexandrite, khaki cloth, tigereye

COLORS
bloodred, taffy, sea foam green

ANIMALS
locust, hawk

PLANTS, HERBS, EDIBLES
rhododendron, flaxweed, elephant garlic

ESSENCE
mastic

SOUNDS/RHYTHMS
magic spells, cries of seagulls

MUSICAL NOTES
D and F

DEEP SPACE OBJECTS
Gamma Crux, Gacrux, top of the Southern Cross

October 30

YOUR SIGN
Scorpio

YOUR ELEMENT
Water

YOUR RULERS
Mars/Pluto
6–7 degrees
First Decanate, yang

The Astrological Interpretation

Your birth date is connected to the passing of ideas, objects, people, and time. Observe nature in its yearly round. Watch how the leaves from the autumnal trees make a bed of rich fodder for the buds of spring. Look how new life grows out of the destruction of a volcano. You will be asked by life to allow the lesser within you to die—lesser desires, lesser emotions, lesser life objectives. If you follow this process and confront your natural fears and resistance, you will find that after a time of seeming emptiness, you will reemerge with renewed vitality and vigor.

You are a hard, tireless worker interested in plumbing the depths of your interests. An excellent image is a deep-sea diver who gets to the bottom of things. Colors that especially appeal to you are white, black, brown, and deep burgundy. Black leather looks good on you and protects your feelings. At home, a workbench is a good piece of furniture even if your work is painting or writing. A painting of a medieval alchemist working in the laboratory is a powerful image; all Scorpios seek to transmute lead into gold. On a less abstract level, you might work transformative wizardry in the kitchen. Chinese star anise and Middle Eastern spices are exotic tastes around which you can create new dishes. The bedroom is a place for deep-sea experiences. Sheets and towels can be white or dark colors like green or brown. Think retreat and you will come up with the perfect realm for your dream life.

Outdoors, October 30 will enjoy blue spruce trees and pine. If there is a cave nearby it is a perfect place for you to explore. Minerals such as mica, lodestone, and vermilion are in tune with your nature. Looking at a fountain with a central waterspout will clear your mind.

A Kabbalistic Interpretation

Emotions tend to rule the way you see the world, reflecting the significant impact of the letter *Mem* this day. It is most important for you to feel loved, though at times this may lead you to relationships that are not ideal. In order to boost your self-confidence and self-love, try bathing in water to which you have added some witch hazel oil.

The number eight in its connection with the sephira Hod and the intellect is important to this day. Your thoughts tend to focus on your own life direction. You can use the energy of this sephira to give you greater clarity of thought by burning an orange candle on a white pedestal when trying to make important decisions.

The letters *Ayin* and *Shin* both wield an influence over the artistic side of your life. The former gives you an excellent eye for detail while the latter provides the energy you need to be creative. A good outlet for artistic expression would be in the field of drama. Consider joining a local theater group.

A Numerological Interpretation
YOUR MAGIC NUMBERS: 4 AND 7

The thirtieth day of the tenth month reduces to four, the number of reason, order, and measurement. The number four is equated with the quality of mercy on the Kabbalistic Tree of Life. Born on this day, you have a path of responding to the basic human need for fellowship. This pattern moves you into constant group interaction and asks that you elevate this relationship for the common good. Through your participation in groups, you can discover how to best contribute as an individual. This path is one of coming into alignment with your personal aspirations and the knowledge of how to fulfill your dreams within the context of community.

Fluorite is a gem to increase your tolerance. A string of pearls is a beautiful reminder that the whole is something greater than the sum of individual units. The 304th day of the year reduces to seven, the number of victory and sworn compact. This provides a sense of inner peace where your life path is concerned.

OBJECTS/IMAGES
glass figurines, the flower that grows through a quagmire

SHAPES/MATERIALS
topaz, plutonium, sperm shapes

COLORS
bloodred, caramel, kelly green

ANIMALS
hornet, scorpion, hawk

PLANTS, HERBS, EDIBLES
horseradish, sarsaparilla, alligator meat

ESSENCE
patchouli

SOUNDS/RHYTHMS
hypnotic rhythms, snake charmer music

MUSICAL NOTES
D# and F#

DEEP SPACE OBJECTS
NGC 5128, black hole

October 31

YOUR SIGN
Scorpio

YOUR ELEMENT
Water

YOUR RULERS
Mars, Pluto
7–8 degrees
First Decanate, yang

The Astrological Interpretation

There is a silence within each of us that holds a deep voice of understanding. This voice is your gift, but it is one you will have to work very hard to obtain. You are a passionate person with a very set agenda. You want what you want when you want it! The potency of your will is commendable. Many waver where you are certain; many hesitate while you move ever forward. But to what end? Take time each day to still the outer, louder songs of your desires. Open yourself to the more subtle sounds that seek to echo forth from within. Do not move until you know that it is the heart that is commanding your actions. Therein lies your success.

October 31 may have a deeply religious streak and is very capable of handling practical details of life. There is executive ability and frequently great bodily strength. You need to pay attention to details to keep your entire being in smooth working order. At home you may enjoy preparing tonics, potions, and health-oriented concoctions. Studying herbs and their properties is a special talent to explore. You are a restless person and need downtime to curb overstimulation. A comfortable black leather reclining chair with a footstool and a solitary light could be the place for you to zone out and recoup your energies. An indoor plant such as flamingo flower (anthurium) could sit on your windowsill to provide a splash of red.

Outdoors October 31 enjoys stargazing. Keep watch for comets, as they have special resonance for you. In your garden, plants needing minimal maintenance plants such as shrubs and bushes would work out best. Holly, Oregon holly grape, and oleander are all possibilities.

A Kabbalistic Interpretation

As this is Halloween, or more correctly Samhain, it is not surprising to find that the Tower, the card of catastrophe, is represented this day. At one level it suggests that in order to achieve your goals you will have to face a number of traumatic challenges. Given the significance of this day the Tower also points to the need for a day when all our fears are made manifest in order that we can defeat them. A nice present for you would be a beautifully bound collection of Victorian ghost stories.

You have a great love of gardens, and if you do not have one you will definitely want a variety of plants growing inside your home. You are chiefly attracted to the simplicity and beauty of plant life. Try growing an almond tree or keeping some daisies in a little vase on your kitchen table.

One trait you possess in abundance is charity. It is likely that you are already a member of a voluntary group and that you are active in serving your community in some way. If not, you should definitely give it some thought, as you have a real desire to do good in the world. In general carrying some parsley and rosemary in a cream pouch will encourage you to help others whenever you can.

A Numerological Interpretation
YOUR MAGIC NUMBERS: 5 AND 8

The thirty-first day of the tenth month reduces to five, the number signifying mediation, adaptation, and the agency of accomplishment. Yours is a path of striving always to come to the center. You experience phase changes in your life, like water changing from ice to liquid to steam. You have an innate ability to understand the extremes of a situation, and you can be a natural mediator. You naturally gravitate toward circumstances where you can comprehend every facet and emotion held by group members, and then distill a workable consensus.

Observe the dynamic process of a Quaker meeting. Members sit together in silence and speak when they feel moved to do so; their sharing is organic. Celestite and topaz are gems to galvanize your mind to hold accelerated energy fields. The 305th day of the year reduces to eight, supporting this path with the ability to reside at the still point where the back and forth movements of manifestation meet.

OBJECTS/IMAGES
canals, cuspidors, garter belts, barbells

SHAPES/MATERIALS
rutile (mineral), gushing shapes, topaz

COLORS
murky red, cream, turquoise

ANIMALS
gecko, ant

PLANTS, HERBS, EDIBLES
Armenian cherry trees, coconut palms, espresso coffee

ESSENCE
myrrh

SOUNDS/RHYTHMS
old music hall tunes, G scales

MUSICAL NOTES
E and G

DEEP SPACE OBJECTS
Zeta Centarus

November 1

YOUR SIGN
Scorpio

———

YOUR ELEMENT
Water

———

YOUR RULER
Mars
8–9 degrees
First Decanate, yang

The Astrological Interpretation

There are computer games such as Dungeons and Dragons, word games such as Scrabble, card games such as poker, and all the life games found within the nature of relationships. You can win at such efforts, as you are a very subtle strategist. You are quiet and unassuming but an astute judge of character. Your gift is that you do not say what you see and do not let on to others what you know. You have a sensitivity that penetrates through the emotional blocks and walls that others put up as they attempt to mask themselves. But these masks cannot withstand the persistent bombardment of your silent probing. You do well sitting in at business meetings seeing everything and only saying the very essential, and even that with great diplomacy and care.

This birthday gives a restless energy with a considerable amount of will. Since the amount of power is considerable, November 1 would be advised to turn toward creativity and light. To help you on your journey, keep a double terminated quartz crystal in your pocket. You may also want to keep some larger quartz crystals at home and take them into the bathtub with you. Mirrors framed in metal are perfect objects to have around your home. Consider having them in every room. Mirrors should be high enough so that the tallest person in the house can see him or herself fully.

Outdoors, November 1 likes the feel of the heath or a wide expanse of field with a stream close by. In your backyard consider clearing away brush and bushes so that you have as much uninterrupted space as possible. A small garden with fall colored chrysanthemums (gold and auburn) will help keep November 1 from dissipating energy.

A Kabbalistic Interpretation

This day is full of references to occultism. It may be that you already have some interest in the area of the mysterious and unknown. If you decide to pursue this interest, a good starting point would be to invest in a set of tarot cards or an introductory aromatherapy kit. It may be that you end up making a career out of it.

The Star card from the tarot has a powerful influence this day. It exerts a protective power that should ensure that you avoid any truly awful experiences in life. There are a number of ways you can enhance this effect, all of which involve items sympathetic to the energy of this card. In your case the best method is through food. If you use more coconut flavoring you will increase your natural good fortune.

Another important card this day is the Hierophant. This card indicates that you have a high sense of personal morality and ethics. It is likely that this strong personal code of behavior stems from a deeply held religious belief. An attractive and appropriate addition to your home would be a religious icon, especially one in white marble.

A Numerological Interpretation

YOUR MAGIC NUMBERS: 3 AND 9

The first day of the eleventh month reduces to three, the number of development and unfoldment. Born on this day, you have a path of serendipity. This pattern urges you to seize the significance of seemingly chance or random events in your life. If you make a wrong turn at your regular intersection, keep driving. If someone other than the person you meant to call answers the phone, don't hang up. Learn to trust the flow and release your ideas of how it should be. Your innate enthusiasm for the unpredictability in your life assures that all will be well.

Visit Las Vegas, and play the slots for fun. Cat's-eye chrysoberyl will remind you of your nine-plus lives, so go ahead and take the plunge. Follow the yellow brick road. The 306th day of the year reduces to nine, contributing a sense of foregone conclusion to your success.

OBJECTS/IMAGES
a geyser erupting,
clear glass paperweight,
the phoenix bird

SHAPES/MATERIALS
magnets, topaz,
fine worsted wool, arrow shapes

COLORS
mottled red, clove, black,
carmine, azure

ANIMALS
eagle, cormorant, wolf

PLANTS, HERBS, EDIBLES
charlock, dong quai,
hot lemon water

ESSENCE
musk

SOUNDS/RHYTHMS
tango, serpent dances
(Middle Eastern rhythms),
rustle of dried leaves

MUSICAL NOTES
D and G#

DEEP SPACE OBJECTS
Beta Corona Borealis,
Nusakan, two lines of stars

November 2

YOUR SIGN
Scorpio

YOUR ELEMENT
Water

YOUR RULERS
Mars, Pluto
9–10 degrees,
First Decanate, yin

The Astrological Interpretation

Your birth date is connected to the concept of the conservation and recirculation of energy. You are not a person who wastes anything. In fact, it can be difficult for you to throw anything away. This applies as much to old newspapers and magazines as it does to old thoughts and memories. Your greatest gift is your ability to reuse what seems useless. You do very well helping people to find their hidden talents and resources, aiding them in establishing their self-esteem and giving them the needed boost to get on their way. Your greatest challenge is a result of your holding on to your own inner (and outer) refuse, watching your own garbage decay. Get rid of those old clothes! Throw out those eight-tracks! Pack up those useless hurt feelings and bring them to the recycling center.

November 2 can fall on a critical degree, which means a person feels highs and lows in life very keenly. November 2 has a great deal of creative energy, but it must be channeled to be effective. There is a touch of the recluse in your character. You may enjoy a rugged decor at home like a log cabin or ski chalet. Surround yourself with natural woods and fabrics. Spiral designs on your rug or upholstery may be meditative for you. Masks from primitive cultures, the theater, or a carnival in Venice are decorative items to hang on your walls. You enjoy sensual experiences, and a hot tub under some large pine trees outside your home would be a perfect way to relax.

Outdoors, November 2 likes wild terrain and strong weather conditions. Keep some snowshoes around if you live in the north, as you enjoy being out in a blizzard. When spring and summer come you may be content with whatever wildflowers pop up. Fringed gentian is a bloom worth looking for.

A Kabbalistic Interpretation

You are primarily an emotionally driven person. The way you feel at a given time affects not only how you behave with a particular person but also how you work and how you approach your life overall. You may have a tendency to stop yourself from fully expressing emotions, as you are aware of how powerful they can be. By keeping next to your bed a blue bowl that contains green glass pebbles you can help yourself be more effectively expressive.

The Moon card is significant this day, and its effect is also mainly on your emotions, thanks to your overwhelmingly water-based personality. The lunar influence of this day suggests that you have a tendency to become anxious about many parts of life. One way to counter this aspect of the moon is to drink an infusion of burdock, especially around the time of a full moon.

In Hebrew the name Solomon has the same value as the numerical equivalent of this date. Solomon was renowned for his great wisdom and ability to adjudicate in the most difficult of circumstances. You can maximize your own sagacity by wearing a "seal of Solomon," or six-pointed star, around your neck.

A Numerological Interpretation
YOUR MAGIC NUMBERS: 4 AND 10

The second day of the eleventh month reduces to four, the number of order, reason, and classification. Four demands to know how everything fits. Born on this day, you have a path of learning politics. Your pattern thrusts you into dramatic, and sometimes flamboyant, social situations where you can experience the interplay firsthand. Keep your cocktail party attire at the ready. Attend a black tie dinner and observe the intrigue and jockeying for position.

Jasper and onyx are stones to deepen your perceptiveness. Probe beneath the surface. You will be among the first to notice that the emperor isn't wearing any clothes. The 307th day of the year reduces to ten, which adds the element of attainment, fulfillment, and confidence about reaching the top of the ladder.

OBJECTS/IMAGES
archaeologists, bridges, a G string

SHAPES/MATERIALS
swirling shapes, cloisonné enamel, alexandrite

COLORS
mottled red, russet, navy blue

ANIMALS
salamander, iguana

PLANTS, HERBS, EDIBLES
swamp honeysuckle, rattlesnake plantain, Venus flytrap

ESSENCE
patchouli

SOUNDS/RHYTHMS
hypnotic music, Alcaic strophe

MUSICAL NOTES
D# and A

DEEP SPACE OBJECTS
Beta Crux, Mimosa

November 3

YOUR SIGN
Scorpio

YOUR ELEMENT
Water

YOUR RULERS
Mars, Neptune
10–11 degrees
Second Decanate, yang

The Astrological Interpretation

The spider is an insect that falls under the rulership of your birth date. Like yourself, this small creature is resilient and resourceful. She is capable of weaving a shiny and perfectly formed web out of the substance of her own body. You can weave very intriguing emotional webs, as you are a most seductive person. But when your objective is caught, do you remove its life energy or do you drain it of its negativity and poisons so that it may leave the web and fly free? You have the power to do both. During your life, you will have to choose until you realize the joy that the freedom and healing you offer others is the source of your own growth and abundance. Then your web will be spun of pure gold.

The waters of life flow abundantly for November 3; it is up to you how you swim in them. The birthday gives creative gifts, and the most important aspect of life is to express your feelings so they do not remain internal and stagnate. On the journey, carry clear quartz crystal or tourmaline. At home, seascapes and shells will be powerful reminders of the water. You might invest in an aquarium with tropical fish. The sound of the motor and watching the bubbles float upward provide a meditative climate. You may be surprised at the creative thoughts that occur to you. Your personal wardrobe will tend toward dark colors, but with Mars as ruler of Scorpio, consider a flash of brilliant red. Perhaps red silk thermals are just the thing to keep November 3 warm and vital.

Outdoors, November 3 may enjoy a modest yard. You may have a great fondness for pets and some success in bringing feral cats indoors. Rhododendron bushes are a beautiful addition to your landscape.

A Kabbalistic Interpretation

The combination of the Hebrew words meaning "hand" and "gold" this day indicate that you are someone who is prepared to put in a lot of work as long as the reward at the end is sufficient. Still, even you have moments when you would be happy to throw in the towel. A large block of granite on your desk will give you the motivation and determination you need to keep going.

The Sun card connects this day to the image of gold. It also suggests a strong intellect and implies that you will achieve your aims through brain work rather than physical exertion. It is important that you keep your mind finely honed and sharp. You can help to achieve this by keeping a painting of a bird of prey above your desk or on the southern wall of your office.

The two Hebrew words meaning "bird" and "peace" also figure in the value of your birthday. Whatever personal ambitions you may have, you are also a beneficent and harmonious individual. Use lots of white and glass in the decoration of your bedroom to encourage a feeling of peace and contentment in your life.

A Numerological Interpretation

YOUR MAGIC NUMBERS: 5 AND 2

The third day of the eleventh month reduces to five, the number of agency, adaptation, and change. Born on this day, you have a path of inventiveness. This pattern confers the capacity to express true creative genius. You must draw on your resources and act; you must not retreat into self-indulgent daydreams. Your flights of imagination may be lofty, but the true joy of this path comes from realization of your dreams and making the transition to practical application. Create something with your hands. Refinish an antique. Azurite and Chalcedony are gems to widen the vistas of your mental landscape and crystallize your thoughts. The 308th day of the year reduces to two, supporting your path with the ability to constantly compare and contrast the effectiveness of your endeavors.

OBJECTS, IMAGES
marsh lands, grave rubbings, a detective

SHAPES, MATERIALS
bloodstone, agate, squiggle shapes

COLORS
lemon and maroon

ANIMALS
scorpion, possum, lobster

PLANTS, HERBS, EDIBLES
Angel's trumpets, dong quai, oysters

ESSENCES
musk, strong scents

SOUNDS/RHYTHMS
wolf whistles, incantatory music, Native American rhythms

MUSICAL NOTES
E and C#

DEEP SPACE OBJECTS
Alpha Crux, Acrux

November 4

YOUR SIGN
Scorpio

YOUR ELEMENT
Water

YOUR RULERS
Mars, Pluto, Neptune
11–12 degrees
Second Decanate, yang

The Astrological Interpretation

The symbol for this birth date is an atom smasher. You are capable of breaking up the energy of harmful habits both in yourself and others. You can then rechannel the energy that was blocked and locked up in these negative behavior patterns into some wonderfully creative expressions. You are therefore a natural-born therapist. Massage therapy, aerobic exercises, and dancing are some of the ways in which you can open yourself to your inner potency. If you insist on holding on to what is harmful, if you do not stretch your body, mind, and emotions, you will find that you are constantly coming up against brick walls within yourself that will stop you from going further in life. Many people born this day enjoy studying physics and chemistry. You may also fancy deep-sea fishing, diving, and exploring caves.

The fixed star Alphecca will be located on some November 4 birthdays. The ancients deemed this star as giving gifts in the direction of poetry and artistic sensibilities. You like to get your own way. You also enjoy secret storage places. An antique desk with many cubicles and perhaps a hidden drawer would be useful and fire your imagination. Mystery stories may entertain and fascinate you. If you follow the arts have a special workroom where you can decide who can see your works in progress. A fountain in your home would be a pleasant addition to either your work or living space.

Outdoors, November 4 would enjoy very high privet bushes or bulky rhododendrons to ensure privacy. Evergreen trees are also pleasing to you. If you have an old tree with a knothole in it you may consider writing down secret messages and wishes. Put them in the tree knot and see what happens!

A Kabbalistic Interpretation

It is a fact, albeit a difficult one to accept at times, that in order to create we must destroy. The influence of the sephira Geburah in this day means that you have an intrinsic appreciation of this truth. In order to ensure that you can act with the necessary detachment this implies, you should have a small statuette of a phoenix somewhere in your place of work.

You have vast reserves of energy and can keep going long after your coworkers are ready to go home and sleep. This is indicated by the importance of the letter *Shin* in this day. As your career is very important to your sense of self-esteem you should encourage this side of your nature. One good way to boost your vitality is to have a vase of red poppies by your side.

The Chariot card is associated with drive, determination, and victory at any cost. Other energies in this day have already shown you to be a deeply goal-oriented person with a powerful drive to succeed. It might be a good idea to temper that urge on occasion. A vase of roses in your main living room or a large bunch of lavender in your bathroom will help you to bring out your softer side.

A Numerological Interpretation
YOUR MAGIC NUMBERS: 6 AND 3

The fourth day of the eleventh month reduces to six, the number of balance, equilibrium, and the harmony of opposites. Born on this day, you have a path of making connections. You have a gift for making links and serve well as an instinctive networker. The World Wide Web is a natural playground for you. Visit on-line chat rooms, and make new interfaces around the globe. Read Native American stories about spider woman, who spun the world into existence. Quartz crystals are natural conductors. Carry a rose quartz crystal in your pocket to keep your circuits clear. Amber is a gem to help anchor you to the physical realm. The 309th day of the year reduces to three, adding the element of creative imagination to your spontaneous manner of connecting people, places, and things.

OBJECTS/IMAGES
catacombs, chemistry, dice, monsters

SHAPES/MATERIALS
alexandrite, nickel, obsidian, pyramids

COLORS
dark red, lime green, coral

ANIMALS
bat, falcon

PLANTS, HERBS, EDIBLES
aloes, box trees, Armenian cherry trees, maidenhair

ESSENCE
musk

SOUNDS/RHYTHMS
riddles, magic spells

MUSICAL NOTES
F and D

DEEP SPACE OBJECTS
Alpha Corona Borealis, Menkent

November 5

The Astrological Interpretation

In your personal relationships, you will be tested to see if you know the difference between love and lust. At times you will be attracted more by the senses and will deny your highest good. Your life path teaches you how to value the heart above all else. Once this is accomplished, sex, desire, and passion will cease to be a focus of frustration and turmoil, but instead they will become vehicles for growth and even for the cultivation of a certain degree of wisdom. If you have already accomplished this personal transformation, you are now sitting in a place of real power and compassion. People are already seeking you out for advice and comfort.

This birthday usually gives great cleverness and a powerful, independent nature. You are an inventor and innovator and need a solitary corner that you can call your own. If there are glass shelves where you can keep a variety of your projects it will help keep ideas flowing. The basement would be a good place for your "workshop," but the kitchen would also do. Pictures of medieval towers remind you of the alchemist who labored in the laboratory to transform lead into gold. When you are pursuing your creative activities put on a special "costume" of a white robe or white shirt; it will keep you in the zone of creativity. In general, you prefer to look elegant but understated. Silver and onyx jewelry, black lace, and expensively tailored suits strongly appeal to you.

Outdoors, November 5 likes a deck or balcony overlooking the woods. A group of shade trees and a lawn chair provide a focus for thoughts and plans. If your yard has a little stream of water you will enjoy the sound. If not, thoughts come best when you are watering the lawn with the hose or watching a sprinkler move back and forth.

A Kabbalistic Interpretation

Anyone who engages in a relationship with you will have an experience that they will remember forever. The Devil card from the tarot has a powerful influence over your personality, giving you intense sexual energy and charisma. The sexual connotations of tulips and orchids make these the ideal flowers for anyone to give to you as a token of their affection.

When you are not busy seducing the neighborhood you are an efficient and reliable worker. Despite your initial enthusiasm, you can often tire of a project before it is finished. An onyx ring worn on your index finger will help you to maintain your commitment to the task at hand, and may even have an impact on your fidelity in relationships.

In spite of your exciting lifestyle you yearn for a degree of calm and tranquillity in your life. This is suggested by the correspondence of the phrase "in peace" to this date's value. To increase the sense of calm and stability in your home, try growing some water lilies in urns around the outside of your home.

A Numerological Interpretation
YOUR MAGIC NUMBERS: 7 AND 4

The fifth day of the eleventh month reduces to seven, the number of peace, safety, and satisfaction. Born on this day, you have a path of appreciating joy in simple and spontaneous pleasures. This pattern endows you with a quality of innocence and simplicity. Spend time with children, and internalize their approach to life and growth. Buy yourself a coloring book and a giant new box of crayons. Play in a sandbox.

Don't spend too much time on busy freeways. Instead, take a leisurely drive down a country road. Milk a cow and pick ripe apples from a tree. The 310th day of the year reduces to four, providing the added quality of stability to your path. Fluorite tetrahedrons will remind you of the ordered nature of reality.

OBJECTS/IMAGES
underground water passages, coil bracelets, jackknife,

SHAPES/MATERIALS
spirals, snake skin, decorative glass, mud baths

COLORS
winter white, auburn, murky red, pine green, tawny yellow

ANIMALS
adder, black cat

PLANTS, HERBS, EDIBLES
coffee, blackthorn trees, marsh grass, brewer's yeast

ESSENCES
holly, cointreau

SHAPES/RHYTHMS
folk circle dances, repetitive trancelike music, Tai Chi hand movements

---

MUSICAL NOTES
F# and D#

DEEP SPACE OBJECTS
Alpha Libra, Zubenelgenubi, Southern Claw

November 6

YOUR SIGN
Scorpio

YOUR ELEMENT
Water

YOUR RULERS
Mars, Pluto, Neptune
13–14 degrees
Second Decanate, yang

The Astrological Interpretation

You are capable of turning the wildest dog into a meek puppy. You are neither frightened by anger and emotional outbursts nor intimidated by people's darker moods. In fact, you have a way of soothing and calming even the most frightened of people. You know how to hold your own center steady while a torrent rages around you. You are therefore free to act clearly in emergencies and help others out of the deepest confusion. You also know how to create confusion consciously. It is one of the many tactics you employ to obtain your goals. While other people are ranting and raving, you spot the advantage in the moment and grab it! You will enjoy observing normal people in unusual life situations. This is why certain television game and talk shows appeal to you. You like the human interest stories on the news, especially sexual and political scandals.

November 6 has a special understanding of the interconnection that links all people. You can be a true friend. At home a wine cellar would be a prized possession; however, November 6 should avoid self-indulgence. Appreciate the wine slowly. Your home should include furniture that facilitates conversation among people. Circular arrangements are best and a casual style is in keeping with your nature. Glass-topped tables may particularly appeal to you, and terrariums or eco-spheres are both interesting and decorative. Magnets may fascinate you. You could investigate current research on magnets and health or find a way to display magnetic properties in your home.

Outdoors, November 6 would enjoy a garden of flowering bushes and flowers. Hydrangeas, calico pipes, oriental poppies, and geraniums are all possibilities for your yard. Place a pyramid structure in your yard and experiment with how you feel lying or sitting there. You may conduct some of your magnetic experiments under the pyramid.

A Kabbalistic Interpretation

The value of your day is equivalent to the Hebrew word meaning "to dream" and this may well indicate a certain visionary capacity. A common trait among people born under the sign of Scorpio is a latent ability as psychics, especially clairvoyance. Whether this potential ever manifests itself or not, an interesting addition to your living room might be a crystal ball.

Another, far less spooky, equivalent word for this day is the Hebrew word meaning "joy." All of your friends, and you have many, notice the wonderfully optimistic way in which you approach life. As you want to spread your sense of joy at the simple business of living, try wearing some circular jewelry. A tie or scarf with a series of spiral patterns in silver would have a similar effect.

The only danger in taking such an optimistic view of the world is that you may fail to notice problems when they are approaching over the horizon. If you only realize you are in trouble when the trouble starts to bite then life can be far less enjoyable than it has to be. A tetrahedron of topaz on a pendant will help you to sense when difficulty is on its way.

A Numerological Interpretation

YOUR MAGIC NUMBERS: 8 AND 5

The sixth day of the eleventh month reduces to eight, the number representing rhythm, vibration, and the cyclic flow of life. Born on this day, you have a path of discerning and utilizing the power of mind-set. This pattern teaches that you can go as far and as high as you believe you can. You have an ability to change the chemistry of any situation when you share a heartfelt smile. Become conscious of the magic of personality and its constructive use. You are capable of acting as a positive agent of change in volatile situations to diffuse the potentially explosive energy.

Observe the behavior of negotiators in tense hostage situations. Turquoise and amber are gems to magnify the influence of your personal energy field. The 311th day of the year reduces to five, adding the crucial element of adaptability.

OBJECTS/IMAGES
bacchanals, sulfur matches, rockets, quicksand

SHAPES/MATERIALS
white jade, healing muds, nickel

COLORS
pirate red, teal, honey

ANIMALS
white-footed mouse, red-backed vole

PLANTS, HERBS, EDIBLES
bittersweet nightshade, water plantain, locust tree, sweetbreads

ESSENCE
tonka

SOUNDS/RHYTHMS
riddles, a sousaphone playing Sousa marches

MUSICAL NOTES
G and E

DEEP SPACE OBJECTS
Delta Libra, Zubenelakrab

November 7

YOUR SIGN
Scorpio

YOUR ELEMENT
Water

YOUR RULERS
Mars, Neptune, Pluto
14–15 degrees
Second Decanate, yang

The Astrological Interpretation

You are familiar with the deepest passions and the most profound emotional obsessions. Nothing about people shocks or surprises you; you have definitely "been there and done that." You are attracted by nightlife and enjoy clubs and discos, more because of the human dramas that take place than for the music. Your lovers are important to you, so much so that you have found yourself in periods of great emotional upset and chaos. After the storm passes, there is a welcomed peace that comes into your life. This, however, is soon quite boring, as you feel the need rise up within you to explore your desires once again. If you have passed through this stage of life and have come out on the other side, you are quick to offer your advice to those still on the sensual carousel.

In ancient times, this degree was called "the center of regeneration" and "the eagle point." The eagle, a bird that soars above mankind and swoops down to capture its prey, is an excellent image for you. Your creative passions can go in many directions. As long as you keep experimenting with different ways to express yourself, you will feel content. But when energy dams up inside, you can become your own worst enemy. Choose objects that speak to your work or interests. A musician might want the collected works of a favorite composer. The bedroom is a central area for November 7. Make sure you have drapes or blinds in a subdued color. You usually prefer to sleep in total darkness. Deep burgundy and brown are restful colors for you. Your element is water, and a small metal fountain with water flowing lightly would be a great addition to your bedroom.

The beach is a perfect environment for you. Hunt for beach glass and driftwood and start a collection. Building sand castles is a way for you to use your creative powers. You may find old navigational charts and maps of interest. If you place them in your living room then you will feel connected to the sea.

A Kabbalistic Interpretation

The tarot card the Star is important for you, as it protects against a range of possible trials. It is particularly effective this day against financial difficulty. To make the most of this beneficial influence burn some galbanum incense in the evenings, as this will increase your financial security.

The presence of the symbols of the planet Mercury and the element of air in the value of your birthday mean communication is highly important in your life. It may be that your profession relies upon your ability to communicate, and you may even be a writer by trade. A great addition for your desk would be a traditional feathered quill pen.

Although the Star card protects you in terms of your financial stability, the word meaning "difficulty" indicates that you may suffer from time to time from a lack of mental clarity. You can ensure that your thought processes are as focused as possible by keeping a clear quartz crystal under your pillow at night.

A Numerological Interpretation
YOUR MAGIC NUMBERS: 9 AND 6

The seventh day of the eleventh month reduces to nine, the number representing completion, fulfillment, and attainment. Yours is a path of giving birth to the children of your creative imagination. This path requires that you cultivate discernment between ephemeral and eternal values in terms of what you give life. Resolve internal conflicts by bringing the opposing forces of your own nature into balance. You are goal oriented and desire to see physical outcomes from your creative endeavors.

Monitor a complete creative cycle. Keep a garden, or let your cat have a litter of kittens. The birthing process is the same for all creations. Plant a seed, tend the emerging creation, and give birth according to what was sown. Sodalite and blue onyx are gems to keep you focused and clear. The 312th day of the year reduces to six, contributing a keen sense of beauty and the ability to bring diverse energies and points of view into harmonious balance.

OBJECTS/IMAGES
an old-fashioned apothecary, mud baths, a butcher's cleaver

SHAPES/MATERIALS
smoky topaz, garnets, spurting shapes

COLORS
molasses color, soft black, cerulean, apple green

ANIMALS
scorpion, bat

PLANTS, HERBS, EDIBLES
arugula, sea anemone, sea urchins

ESSENCE
holly

SOUNDS/RHYTHMS
tango, mating calls

MUSICAL NOTES
G# and F

DEEP SPACE OBJECTS
dark nebula, the Coal Sack

November 8

YOUR SIGN
Scorpio

YOUR ELEMENT
Water

YOUR RULERS
Mars, Pluto
15–16 degrees
Second Decanate, yin

The Astrological Interpretation

You seem to have a built-in radar that tells you immediately about a person's sexual nature. It is easy for you to know if someone is truly as passionate as he wants you to believe. You can also use this inner guidance system to let you know who has the real power in a business or social situation. You can focus your laser beam, and the truth within another person just pops up on your screen. You are not an extrovert by any means and much prefer sitting off in a corner enjoying an intimate conversation with an attractive person than being center stage holding court. Your taste in vacations runs to secluded beaches rather than large resorts, islands much more than cities.

November 8 is an ardent character and belies Scorpio's deceptive reputation. You are truly interested in contributing to humanity through the use of your skills. The arts and medicine may be fields where you feel your contributions will best serve. Although Scorpio is a water sign, fiery Mars is its ruler. A fitting image for November 8 is a red flame ascending. Meditating on this image will help you manage your power. You may enjoy art and want to fill your home with paintings and pieces of sculpture that appeal to you. Painting would also be a wonderful pastime for you.

Your bathroom is an area of retreat for you. A sleek modern tub with whirlpool jets is the best place for you to relax. You may be partial to a black motif for the bathroom, but do include some red in your color scheme. Decorative objects from Russia such as tea glass holders or copies of Fabergé decorated eggs may be interesting accents for your home.

Outdoors, November 8 would feel very special if there were an underground cave nearby. Topiary trees or bushes are an excellent way for you to be outdoors and express creativity. Consider a garden of medicinal herbs such as arnica, birthwort, and nightshade.

A Kabbalistic Interpretation

The only thing that you really lack in your life is self-confidence. Although you have a wealth of personal skills and talents you have a tendency to be nervous about putting yourself or your ideas forward for consideration. Carry a bloodstone in your pocket or your purse and you will find that you have much greater self-belief.

The influence of the planet Mars indicates that you have the capacity to be a great pioneer or innovator. It is also likely that you have an interest in the activities of historical pioneering figures. An attractive and inspiring addition to your living room would be a painting of pioneers or an early wagon train heading west.

A correspondence between the value of your birthday and the word in Hebrew meaning "prayer" indicates that there is a considerable religious influence in your life. You might like to try taking up some form of meditation to get in touch with your inner spirituality. If you do attempt this a white-scented candle at each corner of the room will help you to get into the appropriate frame of mind.

A Numerological Interpretation

YOUR MAGIC NUMBERS: 10 AND 7

The eighth day of the eleventh month reduces to ten, the number of finished embodiment and the completion of the process. Born on this day, you have a path of consummation. This pattern requires that you exalt every potential you have been given, and that you do so with élan. Your personal fulfillment depends on the degree of excellence you exhibit, and you have no tolerance for mediocrity.

Walk in the woods at the peak of autumn color and contemplate the majesty of the conclusion of the annual cycle. Amethyst and adventurine are gems to galvanize your ambition and strength of will. The 313th day of the year reduces to seven, providing the impetus to rest between periods of intense activity and enjoy the fruits of your labors.

OBJECTS/IMAGES
sleep, puzzles, the FBI, places of pilgrimage

SHAPES/MATERIALS
serpentine, sphalerite, tar, steel, rushes of upward energy

COLORS
royal purple, navy blue, grass green

ANIMAL
masked shrew

PLANTS, HERBS, EDIBLES
swamp lily, water hemlock, aeonium, conch chowder

ESSENCE
vetiver

SOUNDS/RHYTHMS
slang, tarantella music

MUSICAL NOTES
A and F#

DEEP SPACE OBJECT
globular cluster

November 9

YOUR SIGN
Scorpio

YOUR ELEMENT
Water

YOUR RULERS
Mars, Pluto, Neptune
16–17 degrees
Second Decanate, yin

The Astrological Interpretation

The symbol for your birth date is a released arrow made out of gel. You always have a target in mind, for you are a very goal-oriented person. You also have the power of the arrow in flight, propelled by the bow of your desires and the intensity of your will. But the substance of your arrow has some unusual properties. The gel allows you to gently but firmly ooze your way into the bull's-eye, hardly making a ripple as you do so. Before a person knows what has happened, you are already inside! The victory is yours. The test is the quality of your gel. Is it sticky so that you may grab the other person's resources and capture her strength? Or is it a cool and healing balm, soothing the other person's pain?

It is possible for you to get stuck in a cycle of passion that is destructive. Creativity is the way to best use your powers. At home surround yourself with symbols of renewal such as pussy willow branches in the spring, a picture of a phoenix, or glass figurines of baby chicks, kittens, or puppies. Your home would benefit from a large quartz crystal cluster or single point. Keep the crystal on a table by the front door so that everyone who passes by will benefit. Red candles on your dining room table are good for decoration. You might also want to have some red table linens in winter. The color for the dining room in the warmer months is white.

Outdoors November 9 would enjoy a landscape with a low-lying garden and some marshes or wetlands. Visiting a nature preserve where there are swamplands will be peaceful for you. In your own yard emphasize subdued autumn/winter flowers such as cockscomb, blue spirea, and spider chrysanthemums.

A Kabbalistic Interpretation

The Magician card is important in this day, suggesting that you have the capacity to make an excellent entrepreneur. If you are currently employed by someone else you should give serious consideration to starting your own business. A staff of hazel wood kept in the eastern corner of your living room will help you to make the break and run with your own ideas.

This day is also connected to the sephira Hod. This sephira on the Tree of Life is associated with the mind and rational thought. In cosmic terms it refers to the stage of development where the possibility of material form emanates. It has a similar meaning for the individual's ideas and thoughts. A statuette of the god Hanuman in the east of your home will bring good fortune to the activation of your plans.

The Death card from the tarot tells us that your life is going to be subject to a number of major changes. These will relate to work and are likely to include a significant relocation, possibly to another country. No matter where you go, bringing a personal chair made of oak with leather upholstery will help to give you a sense of stability.

A Numerological Interpretation

YOUR MAGIC NUMBERS: 2 AND 8

The ninth day of the eleventh month reduces to two, the number of repetition, duplication, and mirroring. Yours is a path of shaping conscious existence according to your desires, constantly comparing and contrasting what you want to replicate. Your pattern can make you feel as if you are at war with some force outside yourself as you forge your individuality. It is often difficult for those close to you to understand you, so your success is easier away from home ground.

Have a parrot and marvel at the tonal accuracy of its repetitions. How does the parrot choose which sound to replicate? Is it merely a hollow echo of the original, or does the animal have intention? Carnelian and hematite are stones to keep you grounded. The 314th day of the year reduces to eight, providing a rhythm and flow to your experiences. This tends to keep you moving from one replication to the next.

OBJECTS/IMAGES
pirates, plumbers, reincarnation, first aid kits

SHAPES/MATERIALS
pyramids, rubellite, sardonyx, peat

COLORS
scarlet, coral, teal

ANIMALS
rattlesnake, mouse

PLANTS, HERBS, EDIBLES
saffron, coconut palms, maidenhair (plant), seaside gentian

ESSENCE
elemi

SOUNDS/RHYTHMS
rushing floodwaters, buzzing insects

MUSICAL NOTES
C# and G

DEEP SPACE OBJECT
pulsar

November 10

YOUR SIGN
Scorpio

YOUR ELEMENT
Water

YOUR RULERS
Mars, Pluto, Neptune
17–18 degrees
Second Decanate, yin

The Astrological Interpretation

You often experience yourself as a tightrope walker; the excitement of the tension involved is so very stimulating to you. Even when the situations in your environment are calm and serene, you add a certain spice and create an edge that heightens the emotional content in the air. You need other people's energy for the stimulation that it brings to you. Even though they scared you (or perhaps because they scared you), you enjoyed horror films as a child. As an adult you are attracted to action movies, especially those based on science fiction. You like to wear clothing that reveals your body, enjoy being admired, and have no difficulty accepting your sexuality.

Your birthday has a brave character and heightened sensitivities to your own and other people's feelings You may sometimes feel jealous because you can catch subtle vibes and then blow them out of proportion. Concentrate on your own development and leave others to theirs. You have artistic abilities and are very sensitive to color. An image for you is the snake charmer. If he pauses in his music there is a chance he'll get bit! At home, keep polished geodes of minerals as decorations. Any rock with a reddish hue suits you. In the bedroom have a large brass bed with tiger or leopard print bed linens. If you find a clothes hamper that reminds you of a snake charmer's basket you might want to keep it around. A photograph of the African savanna may encourage interesting dreams.

Your outdoor environment should be colorful with flowers and garden statuary. Place pink flamingos in your garden or perhaps a miniature teepee among beautiful autumn flowers such as cockscomb, China asters, and "naked boys."

A Kabbalistic Interpretation

The tarot card Judgment suggests that you will be called upon to use your abundant analytical skills to make frequent decisions about individuals. The influence of the water element in this day means that when it comes to judging people you may be too soft. To help you be more objective you should buy an old-fashioned oil lamp and put red-colored glass in the casing.

The Hebrew word meaning "puzzle" is equivalent to the value of your day. You might enjoy applying your mental dexterity to quizzes and logic problems. This exercise will help to keep your brain operating at the peak of its ability. A great present for you would be an up-to-the-minute three-dimensional jigsaw, especially one with an abstract pattern.

It is likely that your ability to speak persuasively is your route to career success. The letter *Shin* gives you considerable reserves of energy that you can use to achieve your chosen career goals. To maximize your potential wear a tie or scarf with bright red and azure stripes on it whenever you are expecting a critical day at the office.

A Numerological Interpretation
YOUR MAGIC NUMBERS: 3 AND 9

The tenth day of the eleventh month reduces to three, the number representing growth, unfoldment, and imagination. Born on this day, you have a path of bravely crossing thresholds. This pattern compels you to probe beneath surface appearances and penetrate the inner realities of what you see. You are consumed with a sense of mystery about life, and refuse to accept superficial answers to your questions. Watch *The Wizard of Oz*; you are Dorothy confronting the wizard.

You have a great deal of courage and are willing to leap into the void, risking everything for the sake of what might be. Tigereye is a stone to fuel your courage. Moonstone will clarify your vision. The 315th day of the year reduces to nine, adding the assurance of attainment at the end of your quest. You cannot fail, you can only learn and grow.

OBJECTS/IMAGES
horror films, hobos, nudists, universal love

SHAPES/MATERIALS
tourmaline, grottoes, mineral springs, peat

COLORS
pirate red, butterscotch, blueberry

ANIMALS
terrapin, gnat

PLANTS, HERBS, EDIBLES
cedar trees, hemlock spruce, ay-ah-e-yah (plant), alligator meat

ESSENCE
cypress

SOUNDS/RHYTHMS
riddles, volcanoes erupting

MUSICAL NOTES
D and G#

DEEP SPACE OBJECT
quasar

November 11

The Astrological Interpretation

People with this birth date are natural communicators but prefer to connect with others indirectly. The Internet could play an important role in your life, as you will be attracted by a profession that allows you to reach people either through images or the written word. It also gives free reign to your imagination and allows you to be flirtatious as well as to participate vicariously in many people's lives. You are a person of many moods and deep emotional needs. You like costumes and enjoy changing your clothes frequently. You may find that the Internet is a good and relatively safe way to express your hidden self.

November 11 is a birthday of mastery; your talents are many. Surround yourself with those things that bring out the child in you, as this will go a long way toward realizing your potential. The home should have enough room for your creative pursuits with a special emphasis on the kitchen table. Be sure to have lots of ingredients on hand for meals and other endeavors. You might feel particularly at home in an old leather chair in the basement. There is a lot to think about, and having someplace removed from daily activities is welcomed. The color scheme tends toward monochromatic and stylish. November 11 dislikes mismatched objects and would prefer to have fewer things but of excellent quality.

The staircase is a perfect place for a gallery of family pictures and black-and-white prints. The bedroom is a sexy place for November 11. Why not some leopard sheets or at least a scent of musk to keep you in touch with your instincts. A northerly view is in keeping with your thoughtful nature. Also a bedside humor book is good for a laugh before sleep.

Outdoors a rock garden would fulfill November 11's connection to the earth. A small fishpond with glinting red fish soothes your water nature and leads your thoughts in the direction of creative projects.

A Kabbalistic Interpretation

The number eleven is traditionally associated with the sphere of occult or magical activity. As other influences in this day indicate a deep affinity with nature, consider studying the world of paganism. One way into this world is to buy a book about Wicca or other magical arts.

Your day is connected to the sephira Netzach, associated with the passionate emotions within us. You tend to feel your emotions intensely, and it is important for you to express those emotions creatively. You possess a natural talent for artistic pursuits. Wearing anything in a rich emerald green will help you to express your emotions in all their intensity and to get results if you are engaging in any artistic activity.

The tarot card the Lovers connects to the value of this day, suggesting that you can have difficulty in making emotional or moral choices. This indecision can cause an unwanted feeling of melancholy and anxiety. Keeping a piece of amber by your bedside and meditating with it when you are faced with a difficult decision will help you to make the right choice.

A Numerological Interpretation

YOUR MAGIC NUMBERS: 4 AND 1

The eleventh day of the eleventh month reduces to four, the number signifying the ordering and regulating principle of life. Born on this day, you have a path of discerning what constitutes duty. What is yours to regulate and oversee? This pattern causes you to confront the dilemma of your obligations, versus your heart's desires, and bring those into alignment. You possess the willingness to follow the course of your own integrity and honor in the face of formidable opposition or sweeping public opinion.

This is a pattern of a conscientious objector to war, or one who would revolt against tyranny. You have a quality of restlessness. When you are at home, you want to travel. When you are abroad, you wish to be home. Fire agate and obsidian are stones to enhance your courage and help with patience. The 316th day of the year reduces to one, contributing a singleness of purpose and a natural isolation. You feel solitary even in the midst of others.

OBJECTS/IMAGES
cut glass, swamp grass, mechanical toys, jukebox

SHAPES/MATERIALS
serpent shape, potter's clay, lumber, malachite, brimstone

COLORS
scarlet, magenta, bloodstone, caramel, crimson

ANIMALS
hawk, panther, phoenix

PLANTS, HERBS, EDIBLES
cattails, brambles, aloes, senna tea

ESSENCES
passion perfume, witch hazel

SOUNDS/RHYTHMS
Indian ragas, tango, bubbling oil

MUSICAL NOTES
D# and C

DEEP SPACE OBJECTS
Beta Libra, Zubeneschemali, Northern Claw

November 12

The Astrological Interpretation

Like a scientist at work in a laboratory trying to unlock the hidden secrets and mysteries of creation, you use your X-ray vision to probe underneath the surface of things. You know that there is always more than meets the eye at first glance. You are a patient person, with an excellent sense of timing. If something does not work out for you in the present moment, you will just wait and watch until it is appropriate for you to act. You are a skillful manipulator of circumstances but have to take care that what you set in motion is as good for the other person as it is for you. You enjoy playing with forms and may find that working with clay, using a potter's wheel, and even blowing glass are hobbies that attract you.

The fixed star Serpentis may be located close to some November 12 birthdays. This star has a sexy reputation in astrological circles. Your life is about transformation. Consider using objects from chemistry such as beakers and Bunsen burners in your kitchen. November 12 likes the feeling of experimentation even while cooking. You may be particularly fond of marble and metal sculpture. Smooth shapes that feel cool are particularly soothing. A toy for you is a Slinky. In moments of stress watching that Slinky go down the stairs will improve your mood. November 12 has a great sense of humor, and you may be able to create your own jokes and riddles. Write them down and be sure to share them with friends

Outdoors November 12 may have a fascination with tar pits. You probably wouldn't want one in your backyard but a visit to one could be very interesting. Bushy trees and hedges are all the garden you need.

A Kabbalistic Interpretation

It is likely that you tend to be up with the sun every day, even when you are on vacation. The connection of your day with the Hebrew word meaning "life" and other influences tells us that you like to get the most out of every day. You like to surround yourself with living things, so be sure to have plenty of potted plants in your home.

YOUR SIGN
Scorpio

YOUR ELEMENT
Water

YOUR RULERS
Mars, Pluto, and Neptune
19–20 degrees
Second Decanate, yin

Another word that connects to this day is the Hebrew meaning "overturn." Pointers within the kabbalistic analysis of this day suggest that this relates mainly to your career. It is probable that you would excel in any role that involves the generation of new ideas. In order to give you the impetus to get your evolutionary views heard, keep a small figurine of a chariot in your office.

This day is equivalent in value to the Hebrew word *Assiah*. This word refers to the lowest of the four worlds of the kabbala. This world of *Assiah* is associated with the material plane of existence and as such it is likely that you feel a strong connection to the earth. Consider adding your energy and enthusiasm for life to the cause of environmentalism. Perhaps you can set up a neighborhood recycling program.

A Numerological Interpretation

YOUR MAGIC NUMBERS: 5 AND 2

The twelfth day of the eleventh month reduces to five, the number of change, adaptation, and means of accomplishment. Yours is a path of exploration and discovery. This pattern sends you on hunting expeditions for information and possessions. You are filled with aspiration, and take pride in your successes along the way. Because you are adept at taking what you need from any situation and making the most of things, you are generally fortunate from a material standpoint.

The danger of this path is an unconscious exploitation of resources. The end doesn't always justify the means. Spend time in the country, and observe the circle of life. Unlike humans, animals take only what they need. Moss agate and green quartz are stones to complement your sense of simplicity and practicality. The 317th day of the year reduces to two, contributing the element of polarity. Try to see how things are alike as well as how they differ.

OBJECTS/IMAGES
mysteries, running a gauntlet, a Byzantine icon

SHAPES/MATERIALS
plutonium, igneous rocks, lodestones

COLORS
scarlet, bisque, titian

ANIMALS
bat, serpent

PLANTS, HERBS, EDIBLES
rhubarb, coconuts, cactus juice

ESSENCE
coriander

SOUNDS/RHYTHMS
football songs, the hula

MUSICAL NOTES
E and C#

DEEP SPACE OBJECTS
Delta Libra, Zubenalgubi

November 13

YOUR SIGN
Scorpio

YOUR ELEMENT
Water

YOUR RULERS
Mars, Pluto, Moon
20–21 degrees
Third Decanate, yin

The Astrological Interpretation

There is great loyalty and steadfastness in your attitude toward friends and loved ones. You prefer to create relationships that will last and will choose to know fewer people intimately than many superficially. It takes a long time for you to develop faith and trust in another, but once you know a person is as real to you as you are to them, you cement a bond that lasts for life. The other extreme of this tendency is possessiveness and jealousy. You are a passionate person who does not reveal the extent of your feelings easily. You may seem rather calm and collected, but this is just the surface layer. Underneath this poker-faced exterior is a seething volcano. When you feel betrayed, this hot lava will erupt from its fiery and highly pressurized core. You then can be a devastating adversary.

The fixed star Unakalhai, is located on some November 13 birthdays. The ancients thought this star connoted impulsive activity and possible accidents. The birthday does have a tenacious nature with little respect for rules and conventions. If you feel hemmed in or cramped, an image for you is a buffalo pawing the ground and snorting. Imagine how the buffalo might solve your problem—or at least let him run and blow off steam. At home you want a simple environment. Your basic decorating equation could be black, white, glass, and water. Use all these elements to create a sleek space. Mars, your ruler, was the ancient god of war; a decorative object for you could be an ancient Roman or Greek helmet. The helmet reminds you to choose your battles wisely. To relax, consider aromatherapy with the scents geranium and hyssop.

Outdoors, November 13 wants space and an environment that comes alive at night. Imagine the sounds of a jungle in the dark and you will feel stimulated and comforted. Night owls and bats may interest you. For urban dwellers the most interesting nighttime environment could be under a jungle print comforter in dreamland.

A Kabbalistic Interpretation

The letter *Vau* is the representative of the element of air in the kabbalistic tetragrammaton, or four-letter name of God. The impact of the element of air in your particular case is that it makes you excellent at all forms of planning and organization. You can enhance this natural ability by working at a yellow-colored desk.

Another letter that has a significant influence this day is *Lamed*. The presence of this letter indicates that you have a tendency to drive yourself too hard. It is important to remember that life is not just about achievement. Keep a small amount of the skullcap and wormwood plants in a red-colored leather pouch. Carrying this with you will help you learn to relax and enjoy yourself.

The Hebrew word meaning "tongues" is equivalent to the value of your day. When combined with air it is likely that this correspondence points to a facility with foreign languages. It might be that you have a job where the ability to speak more than one language is a requirement. At any rate, enjoy learning as many languages as you have the time for.

A Numerological Interpretation

YOUR MAGIC NUMBERS: 6 AND 3

The thirteenth day of the eleventh month reduces to six, the number signifying love, complementary activities, and reciprocity. Yours is a path of transformation. This pattern moves you through various forms and stages of manifestation of your life's journey. Your individuality is in a constant state of metamorphosis, like the phases of an emerging butterfly. Humanity itself is in a chrysalis state of unfoldment. We are caterpillars longing for brightly colored wings. Most of the potential linkages of our DNA strands remain unconnected. Contemplate what might be possible for you as a fully realized human. Peridot and orange sapphire are gems to ignite your imagination. The 318th day of the year reduces to three, providing a natural sense of creative unfoldment to your path of becoming.

OBJECTS/IMAGES
a hookah pipe, tombstones, reincarnation

SHAPES/MATERIALS
golden topaz, the shape of an eagle's wings, coco mats

COLORS
mottled red, lime green, salmon

ANIMALS
python, peregrine falcon

PLANTS, HERBS, EDIBLES
coconuts, stinging nettles, leeks

ESSENCE
patchouli

SOUNDS/RHYTHMS
the bell of a prize fight, jungle drums

MUSICAL NOTES
F and D

DEEP SPACE OBJECTS
Alpha Serpens, Unakalhai, Neck of the Snake

November 14

YOUR SIGN
Scorpio

YOUR ELEMENT
Water

YOUR RULERS
Mars, Pluto, Moon
21–22 degrees
Third Decanate, yin

The Astrological Interpretation

You always know what is going on under the surface of things. If someone is keeping back information that is important for you or others to know, you make sure to press the right buttons and apply the necessary pressure to bring such knowledge to light. You are quite sensitive to social injustice and may find yourself very interested in the law, politics, and government. You like to dress for success and are quite determined to go as far as you can in your chosen field.

Some November 14 birthdays will fall on a critical degree, which indicates that you will react strongly to both highs and lows in life. Your life's path is one of transition and transformation. You may spend some time trying to find appropriate outlets for your restlessness. An image for you is a waterfall flowing from rocky ledge to rocky ledge. November 14 has a great interest in the occult, astrology, and alternative medicine. You may benefit from using Bach flower remedies. At home keep symbols of occult knowledge such as a crystal ball, runes, or Native American shaman rattles. You may use these tools or just like to have them around. Night dreams may figure strongly in your life, and you would enjoy a whimsical night-light such as a lighted fairy or a Tinkerbell lamp.

Outdoors, November 14 is strongly influenced by water. Perhaps you could create a water sculpture on your own property. If not, investigate waterfalls in the surrounding areas. Aquatic plants and bushes are the best type of plants for you. When given the opportunity, you will take long, contemplative walks by yourself, especially in woodlands and deep forests.

A Kabbalistic Interpretation

You have an extremely strong character and a noticeably powerful presence about you. This is thanks to the influence of the planet Mars in this day. You can add to your naturally high levels of energy and courage by wearing any kind of iron jewelry. Additionally you can increase your likely good fortune by keeping a painting of a magpie in your home.

The value of your day is equivalent to Al, which is one of the Hebrew names of God. This connection suggests that you have a highly developed moral sense, while other influences ensure that you are ethical without being overbearing. Burning a white candle on a white pedestal in the western corner of your bedroom will help to preserve your ethical stance toward life.

The association of the Hermit card with this date creates recognizable wisdom. People will undoubtedly come to you for advice on a variety of issues. One way to increase your natural wisdom is to keep a statuette of an elephant or the elephant-headed Hindu god Ganesh in your living room.

A Numerological Interpretation
YOUR MAGIC NUMBERS: 7 AND 4

The fourteenth day of the eleventh month reduces to seven, the number of victory, security, and rest after fruitful labor. Born on this day, you have a path of intellectual attainment. This pattern endows you with the capacity to be a great teacher. You have a gift for speaking as an authority and drawing in an audience when you give voice to your inner understanding. You possess a quality of assurance, as if you were Moses returning from the mountaintop clutching the clay tablets with the still fiery letters of the Ten Commandments.

You are like a magnet for power; take care not to abuse this asset. You are the instrument, not the music, and the level of your attunement will determine the sweetness of the melody. Emerald and amethyst are gems to inspire your vision and ground your understanding. The 319th day of the year reduces to four, contributing the element of order and classification to the knowledge you transmit.

OBJECTS/IMAGES
bandits, new beginnings, enigmas, Pippi Longstocking, erasers

SHAPES/MATERIALS
mushroom cloud shape, suspension bridges, curative earth or springs

COLORS
luminous white, forest green, gold

ANIMALS
stingray, marmot

PLANTS, HERBS, EDIBLES
asafetida, bloodwort, black snakeroot, wild geranium

ESSENCE
cedar wood

SOUNDS/RHYTHMS
*"La Habanera"
(from Bizet's* Carmen*), scurrying mice*

MUSICAL NOTES
F# and D

DEEP SPACE OBJECTS
Beta Centarus, Hadar

November 15

YOUR SIGN
Scorpio

———

YOUR ELEMENT
Water

———

YOUR RULERS
Mars, Pluto, Moon
22–23 degrees
Third Decanate, yin

The Astrological Interpretation

You will find that you undergo a series of intense transformations during the course of your life. At times you feel like a caterpillar, crawling along munching leaves for survival. This phase of relative inactivity allows you to build up strength. You then tend to create a strong shell around yourself and cannot be reached or touched even by the people who mean you the most good. You are then in a stage of letting go and releasing some deep emotional pain that is holding you back from your next step forward. Once you have yielded, once you have detached from the desire that is causing so much frustration, once you "die" to your old self, your beautiful wings emerge and you are free to fly! Trust in this process, as it will lead you eventually to your highest good.

November 15 is near the fixed star Agena, which from ancient times was considered a degree of respect and good health. Some people born on this birthday will channel their formidable energy into the arts and others into healing fields. Although not traditionally associated with Scorpio, quartz crystal is good to carry in your pocket. Quartz balances feelings, and November 15 has many that need balancing. The home needs a nook or cranny where you can be alone. A special lamp with an amber glass shade or even Tiffany lamps give you a circle of solitude. This is very important, both to recharge your batteries and to know your feelings. The world often mistakes your silence for coldness. Not true! All Scorpios need quiet so they can safely locate their feelings. Jewelry such as a coiled necklace or bracelet reminds you of the amount of hidden power you have. Men born on this day might enjoy snakeskin wallets or boots.

Outdoors, you particularly enjoy waterfalls. If it is possible to construct one in your yard then it will provide hours of entertainment and encourage creative daydreams. Rushing water is a good metaphor for you: water is light, constant, and powerful.

A Kabbalistic Interpretation

Possibly your best quality is your capacity for unselfish behavior. This altruistic side to your nature is indicated by the presence of the letter *Tau* this day. This letter means "cross," a symbol long associated with self-sacrifice in many cultures. You can maximize this personality trait by keeping a rose quartz in your pocket or purse.

The sephira Hod gives a tendency to take a rational view of the world. Other energies indicate a concern with the material world and a possible interest in physics. A great office toy for you would be a minigyroscope, as this would keep you intrigued for hours.

A phrase that shares its value with this day is "search out diligently." This suggests that you have an investigative turn of mind. It may well be that you are employed in some capacity where an element of detective thinking is required. Whatever your career, it is highly likely that you will enjoy a well-composed thriller. When you want to while away an hour or two try Agatha Christie or maybe John Grisham.

A Numerological Interpretation
YOUR MAGIC NUMBERS: 8 AND 5

The fifteenth day of the eleventh month reduces to eight, the number that signifies rhythm, vibration, and the mystery that opposite forms of expression stem from a single cause. Born on this day, you have a path of revelation. This pattern impels you to uncover the secrets of nature and make that knowledge available to the masses. Investigate all clues. You have the capacity for penetrating insight akin to Superman's X-ray vision. On a search for answers, you would enter the gates of hell without regard for your personal danger.

Read all the episodes of Sherlock Holmes for fun and inspiration. Celestite and topaz are gems to intensify your powers of concentration and your focus of attention. The 320th day of the year reduces to five, adding the ability to adapt and be versatile in any set of circumstances. Take the role of devil's advocate now and then.

OBJECTS/IMAGES
jets of water, circle bracelets, an upward spiral with rays coming out of the top

---

SHAPES/MATERIALS
a pool of light, bloodstone, magnets

COLORS
black, deep red, warm brown, turquoise, ecru

ANIMALS
crawfish, snake, eagle

PLANTS, HERBS, EDIBLES
brambles, celery tonic, anchovies

ESSENCES
patchouli, dead sea minerals

SOUNDS/RHYTHMS
tambourines, maracas, castanets, flamenco dancers

MUSICAL NOTES
G and E

DEEP SPACE OBJECTS
Mu Draconis, Arrakis, the dancer

November 16

YOUR SIGN
Scorpio

YOUR ELEMENT
Water

YOUR RULERS
Mars, Pluto, Moon
23–24 degrees
Third Decanate, yin

The Astrological Interpretation

You have a tendency to be overly self-protective. To you, most people seem to have hidden agendas and secrets that they are not telling. Could it be that this is your own self-projection at work? You want to be released from the burden of suspiciousness and open yourself to a more fluid interchange with life. Take seminars, workshops, and courses in self-development that can help you to unveil yourself. You know that underneath your guarded shell, there is a soft and nurturing core. Psychology, sociology, and the history of art are all subjects that can benefit you in your search to gain the knowledge that leads you to a more abundant life.

Some November 16 birthdays will fall on the fixed star Agena, a position thought to bring good health and universal respect. November 16 is a politician, in the best sense of the word. You can compromise and see the other person's point of view. At home, November 16 may enjoy having a collection of books or documents from a favorite author or notable person. Record your own thoughts on tape, as they will be fuel for future projects; people will also want to listen to your ideas. Your decor at home will tend toward simplicity. Decorate in shades of white, black, and sage green. You may find copies of Christian icons to be beautiful decorative objects as well as religious symbols. Books on Near Eastern archaeological tablets and remains could fascinate you. A glass tabletop covering artfully arranged seashells would be a prized possession.

Outdoors, November 16 is partial to mountain climates and vistas. You prefer shade to sun and enjoy nature by hiking and walking. The Everglades in Florida may be an environment that attracts you also. Flowers at home for you are black tulips and narrow-leafed gentian.

A Kabbalistic Interpretation

This day is connected to the sephira Yesod and to the moon. This combination of influences is likely to make you a sensitive person when it comes to emotional relationships. In addition these two factors give you a natural affinity for psychic phenomena. Practice meditation. Get a book about astral projection and see how you fare.

Creativity is clearly suggested by the influences that make up this day. Your inspiration may lead you to take up painting. You are more likely to paint ideas and scenes from your mind's eye than to record an image that already exists in nature. You can encourage your creative energies by growing some vervain in the eastern kitchen of your main living room.

You enjoy a varied social life and have something of a reputation as someone who knows how to throw a good party. You like to make sure that all your guests feel at home and enjoy themselves. You are no pushover, and the letter *Teth,* meaning "serpent," tells us that if anyone tries to take advantage of you, you will be quick to strike. A ring with a snake design worn on your index finger will give you even greater confidence.

A Numerological Interpretation
YOUR MAGIC NUMBERS: 9 AND 6

The sixteenth day of the eleventh month reduces to nine, the number meaning completion, attainment, and achieving the goal of an endeavor. Yours is a path of increasing alertness to the potential rewards in your life. This pattern keeps you on the lookout, ready to respond at the spur of the moment. Your life experiences seem to thrust you into circumstances where your native resourcefulness mines gems from the most unpromising situations. Take a survival course, camp in the wilderness, and attempt to find all you need in your immediate surroundings. Pan for gold in a mountain stream.

Alexandrite, whose color appears to change with atmospheric and lighting conditions, is a gem to heighten your sensibilities. The 321st day of the year reduces to six, providing the quality of balance and complementary activities to this pattern.

OBJECTS/IMAGES
clairvoyance, enigmas, imps, lizard skin boots

SHAPES/MATERIALS
shape of onion domes, clay, tar, red spinel

COLORS
crimson, black, China blue, chartreuse

ANIMALS
firefly, blowfly

PLANTS, HERB, EDIBLES
stinging nettle, enchanter's nightshade, stiff gentian, fish roe

---

ESSENCE
basil

SOUNDS/RHYTHMS
sleep talking, obscenities, trance music

MUSICAL NOTES
G# and F

DEEP SPACE OBJECT
Beta Lupis

November 17

YOUR SIGN
Scorpio

YOUR ELEMENT
Water

YOUR RULERS
Mars, Pluto, and Moon
24–25 degrees
Third Decanate, yin

The Astrological Interpretation

It is often frustrating for you to continue with the tasks and events of everyday life when you know that there is something far more glorious waiting for you beyond the boundaries of ordinary perception. Like Alice, you have glimpsed through the looking glass and seen the promise of your own wonderland. The question is how to get there? If you wait for someone else to come along and take you, you may have to wait quite a while. At best another person can only transport you to his or her special place, not your own. No, it is your responsibility to find your own way. You have the determination, so keep on walking. The passion of romance and the call of possessions are your biggest tests. They are also your best teachers.

November 17's mind is as penetrating as an X ray. With such a potent intellect the danger is that you will develop a habit of skepticism that can limit your enjoyment of life. Suspend your doubts and take life on faith; it will still be intense and interesting. An image for you is the Red Cross flag. Consider yourself neutral territory aiding in healing yourself and others. At home, November 17 is mindful of the creative use of what others may consider waste. A simple example is to line the walls of a practice room with empty egg cartons to absorb the sound. You may have a particular fondness for occult objects such as crystal balls or runes. Magic tricks and illusion interest you. Smoky quartz crystal would be a good mineral for you to meditate with or carry.

Outdoors your recycling ability may find unusual uses. A compost heap would provide your garden with rich soil. Gardens set in low ground where heather can easily grow are a resonate environment for November 17.

A Kabbalistic Interpretation

A combination of the Hebrew meaning "hand" and "defense" tells us that you are very protective toward your closest friends and family. A nice addition to your home would be a collection of heraldic shields or some other decoration reminiscent of the age of chivalry.

The planet Jupiter is connected to the value of this day. In particular it is its paternal aspect that is represented in your personality. This paternalistic benevolence extends beyond your close family to your colleagues and staff at your place of work. You can increase your ability to act in a protective role at work by wearing a sapphire ring on your index finger or by keeping an image of the Norse god Wotan on your desk.

The two words meaning "oil" and "heaven" point to an ability to act as a mediator. You are capable of pouring oil on troubled waters and coming up with the best possible outcome. It is likely that you get a great deal of satisfaction from encouraging harmonious relationships among people. You should keep a blue candle on a gold-colored pedestal at the side of your bed and light it for a short time each night before you go to sleep.

A Numerological Interpretation

The seventeenth day of the eleventh month reduces to one, the number signifying beginnings, initiation, and singleness of purpose. Yours is a path of discerning your cosmic marching orders. Your pattern demands that you marshal your talents and resources in a focused contribution to society. At your best, your energy is akin to the channeling force of rushing water that carved the Grand Canyon. Intrepid mobilization of energy will enable you to surmount any apparent obstacle. Blow your own horn, but do so as a member of the band, not as a solo instrumentalist.

Listen to the music of John Philip Sousa at maximum volume. Apache flame agate and fire opal are gems to fuel your aspirations. The 332nd day of the year reduces to seven, providing the helpful influence of shore leave between your active campaigns.

OBJECTS/IMAGES
wizards, temples, puzzles, surgeons

SHAPES/MATERIALS
zinc, tungsten, green tourmaline

COLORS
royal purple, scarlet, emerald green

ANIMALS
turtle, mouse

PLANTS, HERBS, EDIBLES
skunk cabbage, lizard's-tail (wildflower), purple trillium

ESSENCE
tonka oil

SOUNDS/RHYTHMS
New Orleans jazz dirges, healing tones

MUSICAL NOTES
C and F#

DEEP SPACE OBJECT
quasar

November 18

YOUR SIGN
Scorpio

YOUR ELEMENT
Water

YOUR RULERS
Mars, Pluto, and Moon
25–26 degrees
Third Decanate, yang

The Astrological Interpretation

The magnetism of your personality is one of the greatest gifts of this birth date. This is not an issue of physical beauty, although you do tend to have piercing and hypnotic eyes. You exude an air of mystery, something that tells others that there is more to you than your surface appearance lets on. You can and do test this magnetism by quietly focusing on a person until he or she comes up to you, asking you to enter his or her life. Life is usually kind to you and gives you what you want. Be discriminating in your wishes, for you may get too much and then be at a loss as to what to do with it. Although you have a tendency to enjoy such emotional dramas and complications, you will find that life requires you to refine your choices.

November has keen and sophisticated powers of analysis. Your ideas and character are unusual, and you will pursue your plans without regard to personal danger. This is not foolhardiness but an almost naive faith in your indestructibility. You may find birth and death images from nature fascinating. The image of the snake swallowing its tail is meditative for you. You may feel a kinship with Native American culture and want to have baskets, rugs, or medicine wheels in your home. You might also enjoy turquoise jewelry. The bedroom is an important room for you. Create a retreat for yourself and have a pine wooden bed with thick bedposts at both the head and feet. Dark colors for sheets, comforters, and blankets suit your intense nature.

Outside, November 18 likes an organized environment that stimulates thoughts. Pets may be important to you, and walking the dog is a way to air out your brain. Indoors, cacti such as rattail cactus and echeveria would interest you. If your climate permits cacti outdoors, create a cactus garden alongside a place for more temperate plants such as celosia and marsh marigold.

A Kabbalistic Interpretation

This is a day overwhelmed with water energy. In addition to the water sign of Scorpio, this day is connected to the energies of the sign Pisces. In order to counteract any excessive water energy increase the amount of fire within yourself. You can do this in a range of ways, from wearing more red or crimson to using more pepper in your cooking.

Agla, a Hebrew name for God that refers to his ineffable strength, corresponds to the value of this day. The implication of this connection is that you have a strong character and are likely to find yourself in a position of authority. You can enhance the respect with which you are regarded by using an oak leaf pattern in the decoration of your office.

The day's value also accords with one of the mystic titles of the sephira Kether. Kether is the highest sephira on the Tree of Life and is related to the aspect of the divine that we as humans are capable of conceiving. In personal terms this indicates that you have very high ideals and aspirations. To help you focus on your worthy goals burn frankincense in a room lit only with white candles.

A Numerological Interpretation
YOUR MAGIC NUMBERS: 2 AND 8

The eighteenth day of the eleventh month reduces to two, the number signifying reflection, duplication, and receptivity. Born on this day you have a path of promise through genuine, inner self-realization. This pattern demands that you experience your true nature independent of the world of outer form and time and space. You must choose where you pledge allegiance in your life, as circumstances will continually test your resolve and integrity. Temporal hierarchies are ephemeral; your true loyalty must be aligned with everlasting values.

Orange and blue zircon will strengthen your will. The 323rd day of the year reduces to eight, which provides the understanding that all diverse forms of expression have a common origin and source. The energy of eight moves in constant ebbing and flowing cycles, assuring you that no form is eternal.

OBJECTS/IMAGES
catacombs, nudist camps, laser beams, lava

SHAPES/MATERIALS
canal shapes, alexandrite, obsidian

COLORS
deep crimson, russet, aquamarine

ANIMALS
little brown myotis, osprey

PLANTS, HERBS, EDIBLES
willow gentian, blue spruce trees, cypress trees, wild coffee

ESSENCE
myrrh

SOUNDS/RHYTHMS
dice shaking, funeral bells

MUSICAL NOTES
C# and G

DEEP SPACE OBJECT
planetary nebula

November 19

YOUR SIGN
Scorpio

YOUR ELEMENT
Water

YOUR RULERS
Mars, Pluto, and Moon
26–27 degrees
Third Decanate, yang

The Astrological Interpretation

You invite people into your life with tremendous intensity. It is as if you swing a door open and draw the other person in with promises of the pleasures they will have from knowing you. Often you are truthful in this invitation, but should you find out that the other person does not live up to your expectations, then that same door can suddenly slam right in their face. Is it any wonder that at times you find yourself rejected by the person you desire the most? This is a birth date that teaches patience and compassion in dealing with others. Its lesson is that you are indeed the center of the universe—but so is everyone else! Once this is learned, you will find yourself surrounded by loyal friends and the most attentive of lovers. Velvet, silk, soft wool, and other fine textiles complement your sensual nature.

November 19 has a brave spirit and the ability, through persuasion, to rouse others to action. An image for you is a general directing traffic and vigorously making sure everyone moves along. At home support your energies with natural objects such as fossils, arrowheads, or petrified wood. November 19 is fond of the long perspective. You may also enjoy woven baskets or masks from primitive cultures. Your color scheme tends to be monochromatic and subtle. A flash of military red here and there might be all the color you need. November 19 has an interest in martial arts, and learning something about the samurai culture could be fascinating for you. A touch of softness in your environment would be large plump bed pillows. Have some for sleeping and some for lounging.

Outdoors, November 19 likes society and action. If you are leading the trail ride, nature is interesting in small doses. In your own yard you may want to outline a path with black and white pebbles. All evergreen trees and box hedges evoke your ruler Mars.

A Kabbalistic Interpretation

In your dealings with other people you try to be as fair as you possibly can. The Justice card from the tarot reinforces the importance of fairness to this day. This particular trait can be cultivated by growing a poplar tree in your garden.

The sephira Hod has a significant connection with the value of this day that is specifically related to your career. In particular it bodes well if you intend to set up your own company or business venture. If you want to optimize your chances of making a success of any business or career, use plenty of orange in your office and wear a fire opal ring on your little finger.

You tend to have a lot of respect for authority, as suggested by the importance of the Hierophant card from the tarot. You also have a need to be in charge in your own relationships. As you have the ability to impress others with an air of worldly wisdom you will likely be able to take the reins in your relationships without much opposition. A small statuette or figurine of a griffin, especially in bronze, will help you to maintain your position.

A Numerological Interpretation
YOUR MAGIC NUMBERS: 3 AND 9

The nineteenth day of the eleventh month reduces to three, the number that represents the principle of unfoldment, understanding, and development. Yours is a path of first things first. This pattern forces you to come to conscious terms with the trade-offs you make. Life is a series of choices; some we make consciously, others occur by habitual response. Your personal effectiveness is a result of a balanced awareness of the contribution you make on behalf of the common good and your own self-fulfillment. At your best, you bring these into perfect alignment.

Chrysoberyl is a stone to heighten your power of discernment and personal volition. The 324th day of the year reduces to nine, providing confidence in your ultimate attainment. This takes the edge off the perception of being victimized when you believe you paid too high a price for the sake of others.

OBJECTS/IMAGES
bridges, holy places on mountaintops, laser beams

SHAPES/MATERIALS
the abyss, helium, smoky quartz crystal, labradorite

COLORS
pumice color, apricot, azure

ANIMALS
meadow jumping mouse, mosquito

PLANTS, HERBS, EDIBLES
flaming sword, Italian arum (flower), swamp honeysuckle

ESSENCE
sage

SOUNDS/RHYTHMS
magic words, military band

MUSICAL NOTES
D and G#

DEEP SPACE OBJECTS
Alpha Centauri, Rigel Kentaurus, Foot of the Centaur

November 20

YOUR SIGN
Scorpio

YOUR ELEMENT
Water

YOUR RULERS
Mars, Pluto, Moon
27–28 degrees
Third Decanate, yin

The Astrological Interpretation

This birth date is symbolized by a person with a telescope in hand, standing on the prow of a boat searching for a distant shore. Your boat carries within its hold an enormous cargo of experiences and a great inner wealth that is waiting to be unloaded. Although you feel its presence, you may not know what is actually contained within the many boxes. You seek to find the shore where you can unpack all of what you carry and build a new life that reflects your inner abundance. Your answer may be found in one of the helping professions. Look to an area in which you may be of service to others in their own crossing from one stage of life to the next. Teaching, massage, or other forms of physical therapy are natural areas of expression for you.

Your inner vision is an important and powerful tool and can take you far. November 20 loves solitude and prefers a simple uncluttered environment. You like to see everything rather than tucking things away in closets. Keep mementos and family pictures in glass cases or on glass tabletops. A prized possession could be a clear glass paperweight with engraved initials. The lighting in your home should be soft and shadowy. November 20 likes to burrow on the couch under a comforter with a good book. Your personal style is tailored and classical. Business suits in auburn colors are perfect, and stickpins are a wonderful way of dressing up your work wardrobe.

You are so busy pursuing your personal vision that you may not spend very much time outdoors. Water is the ideal place to relax, but November 20 would rather look at the view than swim or body surf. A walk out to a dock on a lake at the full moon is enough nature for you. If your home has a deck facing some trees then this is also a good place to quiet your very passionate nature.

A Kabbalistic Interpretation

Curiosity, though proverbially a great killer of cats, is your best friend. Your main interest in life is to understand how things work in the world. It may be that you have a job in engineering. Consider investing in a remote-controlled boat or airplane, which will keep you interested for hours.

The Hebrew word meaning "flame" is equivalent to the value of this day. The fire energy within you is a constant and steady force. It is particularly useful as a way to keep going when a task begins to wear you down. A gold-framed mirror in your office drawer or on your wall will help you to benefit from this internal flame.

Your fire energy is balanced by some counteracting forces. The influence of the moon in this day ensures that you don't lose any of the sensitivity and emotional understanding that comes through water energy into our lives. The lunar influence in your day also gives potential for psychic energy to manifest. You can encourage this possibility by keeping an Egyptian scarab beetle amulet with you.

A Numerological Interpretation
YOUR MAGIC NUMBERS: 4 AND 1

The twentieth day of the eleventh month reduces to four, the number of four-square reality, tabulating, and classification. Born on this day, you have a path of healing through humor. This pattern spurs you to see the irony and melodrama inherent in everyday life when we don't take ourselves too seriously. There is the potential for high humor when people poke well-meaning fun at human and cultural foibles. Laughter is a good medicine, releases natural endorphins into the bloodstream, and is more fun than a good cry.

Watch videos of comedians and collect an inventory of one-liners for appropriate timing and delivery. Send funny cards to your friends for no reason at all. Rainbow jasper is a stone to widen your spectrum of awareness. The 325th day of the year reduces to one, adding the element of originality to your comic quest. Your sense of humor is unique.

OBJECTS/IMAGES
*leather date books,
jungle pattern votive candles*

SHAPES/MATERIALS
*pointed objects, bowl shapes,
topaz*

COLORS
*chocolate brown,
gray pinstripes, ivory, honey,
cerise*

ANIMALS
turtle, phoenix, eagle

PLANTS, HERBS, EDIBLES
*hot water and lemon,
white poinsettias, rare orchids*

ESSENCES
juniper berries, witch hazel

SOUNDS/RHYTHMS
*Chinese finger cymbals,
footsteps in a marshy area*

MUSICAL NOTES
D# and C

DEEP SPACE OBJECT
Alpha Chamaeleon

November 21

YOUR SIGN
Scorpio

YOUR ELEMENT
Water

YOUR RULERS
Mars, Pluto
28–29 degrees
Third Decanate, yang

The Astrological Interpretation

You come to life with a tremendous need to reorient your values and redirect the nature of your desires. These are major tasks and require a great deal of inner understanding. By now, you have already discovered that emotional selfishness and passionate obsession do not work for you. You have bumped your head against enough walls and would prefer to be able to leap over them. This requires finding a philosophy or teaching that will act as a guide through life. You may find this in a traditional religion, or in a newer, more humanistic approach. The choice is yours, all paths lead to the same place. You will find yourself interested in people of different ethnic backgrounds as well as individuals who lead alternative lifestyles that invite your exploration.

The fixed star Toliman (Bungula) in the constellation of Alpha Centauri will be located near some November 21 birthdays. The star is considered to give a refined nature and many friends. The very end of Scorpio has often been associated with fatalism. You have a great many interests and may be influenced by fateful coincidences in your life. This leads to thoughts of the intangible world. Symbols from Native American traditions such as a medicine wheel or Tibetan prayer wheels may be sacred objects that interest you. You may enjoy carved incense burners as well as incense. Keep minerals such as garnet crystals or amethyst in your home. Consider creating a fountain around a large amethyst geode.

Gardens that can maintain themselves appeal to November 21. Houseplants like cacti that require minimal care appeal to you. You like to be around plants but have more interesting things to do with your time. An evergreen forest adjoining your yard would be ideal. In your own yard consider creating a self-renewing rock garden. Perennials such as geraniums and hollyhocks are possibilities.

A Kabbalistic Interpretation

Life is a wonderful adventure and you find it hard to see why anyone should take anything but an optimistic view. The Fool card in the tarot suggests that you have a somewhat innocent or naive outlook on the world. This can be positive, as it grants enormous enthusiasm for anything life throws at you. If you opt for a black-and-white-checked kitchen floor, you will gain a useful edge of caution to your personality.

The Hebrew word meaning "innocent" itself appears in the value of your day, which may affect your attitude toward relationships. You will tend to run the biggest risk in terms of losing your partner if you fail to let them know in a mature way that you deeply care for them. Keeping some witch hazel and sage in a bag will help you to express yourself with understanding.

Other values in this day indicate that you have a great love of food. This is especially true of social events, as you love to host large dinner parties for your friends and colleagues. A good investment for you would be a large circular pine table to keep in your kitchen for when they come visiting.

A Numerological Interpretation
YOUR MAGIC NUMBERS: 5 AND 2

The twenty-first day of the eleventh month reduces to five, the number of transition and process. Five is the principle of law, which proceeds for the order of four. Yours is a retrospective pattern. You have high principles and ideals by which you live, and you are vigilant about measuring up to your own standards. This path causes you to look at your past experiences in order to gauge your performance in life. You possess a thirst for knowledge, but its value is measured by how you have applied the information in your earlier experiences.

You are endowed with a great inner strength that sustains you in challenging times. Buy a telescope and look at the stars; you have a keen eye. Lapis and fire opal are gems to widen your inner lens and ignite your zeal. The 326th day of the year reduces to two, supporting this path with the ability to reflect.

OBJECTS/IMAGES
a doctor's bag, breweries, bogs, bathrooms

SHAPES/MATERIALS
snakeskin, S curves, malachite, garnets

COLORS
bloodred, cream, chestnut

ANIMALS
scorpion, red-tailed hawk

PLANTS, HERBS, EDIBLES
belladonna, woad, wormwood, horehound

ESSENCE
cajeput

SOUNDS/RHYTHMS
meditation music

MUSICAL NOTES
E and C#

DEEP SPACE OBJECTS
Beta Hercules, Kornephoros

November 22

YOUR SIGNS
Scorpio/Sagittarius

YOUR ELEMENTS
Water/Fire

YOUR RULERS
Mars/Jupiter
29 degrees Scorpio–
00 degrees Sagittarius
Third Decanate, yin
First Decanate, yang

The Astrological Interpretation

You were born on the cusp of two signs: Scorpio and Sagittarius. Your nature contains the deep emotional depth of the scorpion, with its passionate interest in sexuality and the many complexities of intimate, human relationships. Yet you reach upward into the idealistic fires of the archer, aiming your arrows at a potential life that expands your horizons and opens you to new experiences. You struggle between your emotional attachments and your great need for personal freedom at all costs. Be truthful in what you say to others and in what you really feel within yourself. It is easy for you to paint a picture of what is possible, but it may not be so simple to fulfill these promises. You always have a favorite book near at hand from which you like to quote meaningful passages to friends. Try your own hand at writing, as this may be a very fruitful outlet for you.

In general, Scorpio deepens Sagittarius's joviality, and Sagittarius buoys Scorpio's intensity. It is a favorable combination. The image of a toastmaster at a gathering of friends is a good one for November 22. There is talent for humor, entertainment, and leadership here. Humor plays a large role in your life; if you feel down in the dumps, get a pile of humor books and a selection of comedies, and laugh yourself back into good spirits. At home, you prefer an austere environment—just enough for comfort without too much fuss. S shapes are calming to you. Those who lean toward Scorpio may find the image of the serpent swallowing its tail a powerful meditation image. A circular metal disc is a good image for Sagittarius-inspired November 22.

Outdoors, you can be happy with one large tree. A pine or blue spruce would be an excellent choice. A more elaborate garden could include a fishpond. Room for bow and arrow target practice would appeal to Scorpio's Mars energy and Sagittarius's symbol, the archer.

A Kabbalistic Interpretation

The cry "alas!" in Hebrew is equivalent to the kabbalistic value of your day. This association tells us that you are an emotionally sensitive individual with a slight tendency to become melancholic when things go against you. When things go well you have no trouble maintaining a cheerful attitude, but try keeping some thyme on the window ledge of your kitchen for those times when life gets you down.

You have a very individualistic approach to the world. The Magician card from the tarot indicates your strong individuality and also suggests that you have a charming nature. You can increase your attractiveness to others by wearing a ring with an agate setting on your third finger.

Teaching may well appear to you as a career, since the Hebrew word meaning "guide" points to an ability to train or assist others. The Mercury connection to this day shown by the presence of the Magician also suggests that this guidance you can offer is related to your formidable communication skills. A number of silver or silver-colored objects in your living room will encourage this aspect of your personality.

A Numerological Interpretation
YOUR MAGIC NUMBERS: 6 AND 3

The twenty-second day of the eleventh month reduces to six, the number of love, beauty, and complementary activities. Six acts to harmonize polarities. You live in a sea of potential, and this pattern requires that you crystallize your desires into clearly formed ideas. You have everything you need within reach of your inner creative abilities. Live near the ocean if you can. The fluid, and sometimes violent, movements of the sea will soothe your soul.

Keep a bowl of lemons, limes, and oranges on your kitchen table to brighten your spirit when a squall blows in. Amber is a gem to remind you of the process of creation and the preservation of the past within the present. The 327th day of the year reduces to three, contributing a natural sense of creative unfoldment to your path.

OBJECTS/IMAGES
loving cup, punch bowl, an altar

SHAPES/MATERIALS
firm lines, tin, fur

COLORS
apricot, deep purple, apple green, ginger

ANIMALS
seahorse, mink

PLANTS, HERBS, EDIBLES
rockrose, agrimony, liverwurst

ESSENCE
rosewood

SOUNDS/RHYTHMS
contagious laughter, applause

MUSICAL NOTES
F and D

DEEP SPACE OBJECTS
Omega Hercules, Kajam

November 23

YOUR SIGN
Sagittarius

YOUR ELEMENT
Fire

YOUR RULER
Jupiter
00–1 degree
First Decanate, yang

The Astrological Interpretation

You are a perpetual student, always seeking to widen your horizons through some new course you are taking at school or a specialized weekend workshop that has grabbed your interest. Life is a place of tremendous possibilities, and you do not want to miss any of them. Your challenge is one of choice, as so many things attract you simultaneously. The same can be said in terms of your relationships, which can lead to interpersonal complications with friends and lovers. It will benefit you to keep lists of your current responsibilities and priorities. One of your best friends is your day planner. It is important for you to keep track of your time or else you will definitely find yourself overcommitted.

Your birthday has a flavor of the end of Scorpio as well as the burgeoning fire consciousness of Sagittarius. Your mind is subtle, sensitive, and wise, and you address life with humor and knowledge . . . a powerful combination. An image for you is the letter *S* and all S curves. You may have very precise drawing and drafting skills. Watchmaking could be a hobby or profession. In your home have a number of mechanical toys around to play with at odd moments. Your home should be spacious with no clutter. Colors for you are rich blues and purples. The mineral lapis lazuli could be good luck. You also might want to read up on where this mineral is mined. You like to thoroughly know the background of everything you like.

Outdoors, November 23 likes space to run and jump. A basketball hoop is a good fixture for your yard and a bicycle is a great way for you to get around. If you live in an urban area, skateboarding and rollerblading are also good modes of transportation. Large oaks, birch trees, and lime trees support your energy.

A Kabbalistic Interpretation

You are an extremely loyal friend, particularly when people are in trouble. If your friends are being attacked in any way, you are the first to come to their aid. The Hebrew word meaning "to avenge" is equivalent to the value of this day, and it suggests that you will fiercely defend your loved ones under any circumstances. A good addition for your living room wall would be an antique iron sword.

The number eleven is significant this day. This particular number is strongly associated with all matters of a magical or occult nature. It is highly likely that you are interested in the supernatural, especially in ghost stories. You may find that you develop a serious interest in new developments in the area of parapsychology.

The air element is strong in your personality, making you an excellent thinker. It is possible, given your interest in magic, that you will use your finely honed mind to write on this subject. You will almost certainly have a career that requires you to engage in significant planning and organization. You can help yourself be more organized by keeping a yellow fan in the east of your office.

A Numerological Interpretation

YOUR MAGIC NUMBERS: 7 AND 4

The twenty-third day of the eleventh month reduces to seven, the number of victory, security, and satisfaction. Born on this day, you have a path of mastering every potential that presents itself. Your pattern prods you to excel wherever you extend yourself, and to do so in the widest possible manner. You strive to be a jack-of-all-trades. You are endowed with intense powers of concentration that, at your best, you utilize for constructive purposes. Play chess or bridge competitively, something that challenges your mind.

Green quartz will amplify your ability to focus and concentrate. Amethyst will aid your higher aspirations. The 328th day of the year reduces to four, contributing the quality of reason to your mental mastery.

OBJECTS/IMAGES
vows, courtroom wigs, gamblers

SHAPES/MATERIALS
black velvet, topaz, cashmere, alpaca wool

COLORS
wine, jade green, saffron

ANIMAL
whale

PLANTS, HERBS, EDIBLES
blackberries, banana bushes, date palms, figs

ESSENCE
oakmoss

SOUNDS/RHYTHMS
church hymns, a Moslem mullah's call

MUSICAL NOTES
F# and D#

DEEP SPACE OBJECTS
Delta Scorpio, Dschubba (forehead)

November 24

The Astrological Interpretation

You have a strong need to bring harmony and unity into your life and into the lives of those close to you. Yet your challenge consists in unifying the dual nature of Sagittarius, which is so strongly rooted in your personality. With your higher nature you aspire to bring out the best in yourself. You are generous with your possessions and open in the ways you share and give of yourself. There is always some noble target toward which you have aimed your arrow. Yet your lower nature is totally pleasure seeking and self-indulgent. You have to take care not to sabotage your best interests through a wanton disregard of personal responsibilities. You are attracted to all competitive sports but are more attracted by playing than by the need to win.

There are two fixed stars that may be located on some November 24 birthdays. The first is Yed Prior, which was thought to bring revolutionary tendencies and immorality. The second is Isidis, which was thought to bring sudden assaults and immorality. Further research has not corroborated these ancient findings. Instead, November 24 seems to be visionary and practical. You take an irrepressible delight in everyday matters and can imbue mundane chores with excitement. Imagining a suspense drama while doing the dishes or taking out the garbage is an example of your buoyant imagination. Keep your home slightly rustic and comfortable. Even if you live in the city you might enjoy exposed wooden beams and a log cabin feel to your space. Large windows let you track weather fronts as they move through. You may want a telescope to keep your eyes on the stars.

Outdoors, November 24 is fond of the wild. A large waterfall is a place you will want to visit. For your own yard consider an exuberant garden with lots of color. Tall flowers such as gladiolus, sunflowers, hibiscus, and iris will suit your nature.

A Kabbalistic Interpretation

The Justice card indicates that you have a very high regard for ideas of morality and fairness. You make many demands on yourself and can often make the same demands on others. While personal ethics and morality are good in themselves, there is a danger that you can be excessively repressive. Listen to rock music or watch comedy shows to help you learn to relax your somewhat stern outlook on life.

The Hebrew word meaning "multiply" is connected to this day, as is the idea of travel. As other energies in this date also suggest that you are likely to do very well in your career, it may be that you will multiply your wealth through some business connected with travel. You should keep some mugwort and some basil in your travel bag, as this will encourage both money and rewarding travel.

Another word that corresponds to this day means "weeping." This suggests that although you have a driven side to your nature, you are also deeply sentimental. This aspect of your character balances and softens your personality. Treat yourself to an afternoon in front of some weepy pictures or read a sentimental historical novel.

A Numerological Interpretation
YOUR MAGIC NUMBERS: 8 AND 5

The twenty-fourth day of the eleventh month reduces to eight, the number that represents the entering and reentering of energy into matter in an eternal cyclic flow. Yours is a path of enthusiastically leaping into new experiences. This pattern creates a life experience that is always new and always changing. You eagerly accept these changes, and engage in your new lessons with all the courage and tenacity of an infant learning to walk. Take dance lessons to stay nimble on your feet, and trip the light fantastic with your favorite partner.

Turquoise is a stone to give you a sense of permanent reality behind myriad changing forms. Sapphire will deepen your insight into the meaning of your escapades. The 329th day of the year reduces to five, supporting your path with an innate comfort with change.

OBJECTS/IMAGES
voyages, textbooks, western saddles, star guides

SHAPES/MATERIALS
tin, ore mines, squares, the papal seal

COLORS
royal blue, teal, lemon yellow

ANIMAL
Tennessee walking horse

PLANTS, HERBS, EDIBLES
blueberries, lingonberries, thorn apple plant, nodding thistle

ESSENCE
clove

SOUNDS/RHYTHMS
ocean surf, waterfalls, waltzes

MUSICAL NOTES
G and E

DEEP SPACE OBJECTS
Beta Scorpius, Graffias, Crab

November 25

YOUR SIGN
Sagittarius

YOUR ELEMENT
Fire

YOUR RULER
Jupiter
2–3 degrees
First Decanate, yang

The Astrological Interpretation

Your quiver is full of more arrows than you know what to do with! The fiery, self-expressive urge within you is often greater than the discipline required to guide your projectiles successfully to their targets. Although your strategy is often one of hit or miss, your cheerful optimism allows you to go through life without getting too upset about temporary defeats. You are simply not a person who stays down for long. Your natural enthusiasm is your saving grace, and you carry within yourself the sense that you are basically a fortunate person, one who consistently manages to land on your feet. Anyway, you are right—this birth date does get a little extra "boost" from the zodiac. Take care not to take this too far as you have a tendency to gamble, especially on lotteries and horses.

November 25 has business, draftsmanship, and sports ability. An image for you is the statue of justice; included in this symbol is mercy. Your ability to temper justice with mercy is the basis for your life's wisdom. At home, indulge your sense of luxury with velvet. In the bedroom consider velvet drapes or a comforter cover in deep blue velvet. What about a velvet robe with an ermine collar? You could pretend you were a judge dispensing the wisdom of Solomon. An adjustable drafting table might be the ideal workspace for you, even if you are not an architect. November 25 has a lot of energy, and it might be more productive for you to work standing up at a desk rather than be seated.

Outdoors November 25 wants room for sports and walking. A batting cage would be a great place to practice and blow off steam. Fencing is a sport that you might pursue. In your garden or yard ash trees and sunflowers support your magnanimous character. You might have a section of your yard where your friends and neighbors can hang out. Urban dwellers might try to preside over a portion of the park.

A Kabbalistic Interpretation

Socializing is quite possibly your favorite pastime. You love to spend time with your friends and should try to arrange your chairs in sets of three when you have visitors. This will encourage an atmosphere for stimulating conversation. Spread your extroverted energy to others by wearing some bold primary colors when you have people over.

An altruistic, selfless attitude to life is indicated by the presence of the Hanged Man card from the tarot. You can use the water element in your home environment to enhance your altruistic side. Have a house near a stream or add water features such as a pond, an aquarium, or miniwaterfall.

The number 120 is significant this date. The number's symbolic significance is that it represents the idea of perfect balance between moral extremes. You can replicate the symbolism of this number in your home by having one of your floors covered with a black-and-white-check floor. If you could work out 120 tiles, it would be ideal.

A Numerological Interpretation
YOUR MAGIC NUMBERS: 9 AND 6

The twenty-fifth day of the eleventh month reduces to nine, the number representing attainment, fulfillment, and the end of the cycle. Yours is a path of steadfastness in holding true to common values and societal ideals. Your pattern requires that you uphold your commitments and be a paragon of wisdom for your family and the collective conscience. You are cast in the role of matriarch or patriarch of the clan.

The danger of this path is a narrow provincialism. Read the works of great philosophers and ponder the distinction between knowledge and wisdom. Sodalite and marcasite are stones to strengthen your insight and will. The 330th day of the year reduces to six, complementing your pattern with the energy of balance and equilibration. This helps you weigh and balance the answers you give to those who seek your counsel.

OBJECTS/IMAGES
expansive gestures, medals, holy objects

SHAPES/MATERIALS
chinchilla, iris (stone), plumes

COLORS
hunter green, purple, cerulean, chartreuse

ANIMALS
shark, caribou

PLANTS, HERBS, EDIBLES
polypody, pinks, nail-wort (plant)

ESSENCE
clove

SOUNDS/RHYTHMS
laughter, spirited religious songs

MUSICAL NOTES
G# and F

DEEP SPACE OBJECTS
Nu Scorpio, Jabbah

November 26

The Astrological Interpretation

There is always something in your life about which you are particularly enthusiastic. You are a convincing person and like nothing better than to share your latest discovery with those around you—even if they do not want to hear about it! You sometimes talk too much and too loudly for your own good, alienating the people you most wish to impress.

Try to slow down a little in order to be more receptive to your audience. Does the person really want to hear what you have to say now? Would he or she be more receptive at another time? Some of these rebuffs are there to teach you to cultivate a better balance in the give-and-take of social intercourse. Nevertheless, you do well in the areas of public relations, advertising, broadcasting, and publishing.

Your birthday combines prudence and daring. There is at the same time a love of home and a desire to see the world. A good image for you is an explorer fully equipped for any emergency and yet knowing there is an element of danger in all adventures. Pictures of high mountains and rugged natural terrain might quiet your restlessness when you can't roam. Equipment catalogs are also of interest to you. Adventures can also be of the mind and imagination. November 26 likes to do things differently. How about going to work in safari clothes? At home you may decide to eat off wooden plates or roast your dinner in the fireplace. Engage your imagination in everyday tasks and you will encourage your creativity. Keep a lot of space around you. Your bed should be as big as you can manage.

A garden is tame for November 26. Outdoors, have trees such as oak, maple, and birch where you can sit and rub saddle soap into your boots or repair other equipment. Large bushes also provide a hideaway for you. Take a blue blanket and sit in the bushes and dream up your next adventure.

A Kabbalistic Interpretation

Your career is certainly central to your sense of self. The Hebrew word meaning *professional* is numerically equivalent to the kabbalistic value of this day. You can help to ensure that you reach the best professional standard possible by wearing jewelry or a tie with an arrow pattern; ideally the arrows should be colored in red.

Job changes are likely to be quite a common affair for you. The Death card from the tarot has an impact on your day, and its significance is to indicate that your life will be punctuated with a number of major life changes. To ensure that these changes are positive moves for you, buy a briefcase with a greenish blue lining.

In addition to being an achiever you have a well-developed wit. You have a very mercurial nature, which makes you wily when you need to be. A good figurine to keep on your desk would be a silver or pewter fox. This will help you to exploit your ability to be sly and clever.

A Numerological Interpretation
YOUR MAGIC NUMBERS: 10 AND 7

The twenty-sixth day of the eleventh month reduces to ten, the number that represents dominion, perfection, and embodiment of the seed planted in one. Yours is a path of mastering the details of what you set out to accomplish so that you can respond in a crisis. This pattern demands that you commit to memory the rules of engagement for any contest of skill or arena you enter, and that you play your part strictly according to the rules. At your best, you are the player that hits a home run with the bases loaded. Proper preparation assures that you rise to the occasion when it counts the most.

Go out to the ballpark and enjoy a game. Adventurine and fluorite are gems to help you keep your eye on the ball. The 331st day of the year reduces to seven, assisting your path with an assured sense of final victory.

OBJECTS/IMAGES
bridles, combat boots, velvet leg warmers

SHAPES/MATERIALS
the horizon, arrow shapes, stones with mixed red and green colors

COLORS
hunter green, indigo, emerald green

ANIMALS
elk, bison

PLANTS, HERBS, EDIBLES
lobelia, beets, wild game

ESSENCE
nutmeg

SOUNDS/RHYTHMS
harp music, hunt calls

MUSICAL NOTES
A and F#

DEEP SPACE OBJECTS
Lambda Ophiuchus, Marfik

November 27

YOUR SIGN
Sagittarius

YOUR ELEMENT
Fire

YOUR RULER
Jupiter
4–5 degrees
First Decanate, yang

The Astrological Interpretation

You have a sense about life that goes beyond the ordinary affairs of daily experience. You really want to know the meaning of existence and take it upon yourself to study and learn things of a metaphysical, occult, or spiritual nature. At one time, you may have even seriously thought about becoming a minister, priest, or rabbi—perhaps you are! Yet the pleasures of the flesh and the stimulation of the senses will probably keep you far from a convent or monastery. If anything, you are a lay preacher, doing your best to help people find a better way of life. You are a person with a definite sense of mission. If this is applied to the world of commerce and industry, you will work hard but happily to achieve a high position of economic and social success.

Some November 27 birthdays may fall on a critical degree, which means that experiences, both high and low, are felt keenly. But you have such an expansive character that whatever life brings, it will not stop you. Your enthusiasm is a talent and easily shared. At home have an open corner for your cherished objects. These could be first editions of a favorite author, an autograph of someone you admire, or copies of a painter's work. It is your own sacred space, and you may want to change the objects you place there as your interests change. A crossbow may be a symbol or an object that will have meaning for you. November 27's essential metaphor is being ready and eager for the battle of life, and anything that makes you feel equipped should be part of your household. A bicycle could be part of your cavalry.

Outdoors, November 27 would like a playground in the yard with a seesaw and a swing set. Your garden may be simple but include the flower rose of Sharon.

A Kabbalistic Interpretation

The Hebrew word meaning "innocent" is equivalent to the value of this day. In the context of this day this word refers mainly to a rather naive approach to emotional relationships. You have a tendency to allow people to pull the wool over your eyes from time to time. If you keep a piece of iron pyrite in your purse or pocket, then it will help you to see the reality of situations more clearly.

In the workplace you always try to create harmonious working relationships. The effect of the Temperance card this day is to give you a desire for balance and peace among people. An image or painting of the goddess Diana will help you to create the atmosphere that you want within the office.

This day has a strong influence from the element of air. Its impact on your personality is to make you philosophical in your outlook. You like to have some time for yourself each day, and you should create a space for yourself within your home. Color this personal area yellow, as this will activate your mental processes.

A Numerological Interpretation
YOUR MAGIC NUMBERS: 2 AND 8

The twenty-seventh day of the eleventh month reduces to two, the number signifying duplication, polarity of opposites, and receptivity. You are an incurable romantic. This pattern thrusts you into relationships in order to learn about yourself. At your best, you see yourself reflected by those you relate to and grow stronger and more sensitive to others as a result. Send candy and valentines to that special someone. Read romance or adventure novels, and examine the true dynamic in storybook love affairs. We are always seeking to complete ourselves. Learn also to cultivate a relationship with yourself.

The danger of this path is indiscriminate desire. Citrine and turquoise are gems to deepen your devotion and ground your romantic energies. The 332nd day of the year reduces to eight, providing the ability to see that all forms ultimately stem from the same source.

OBJECTS/IMAGES
coats, convents, a gavel, a fur-trimmed crown

SHAPES/MATERIALS
newly mown hay, hyacinth (stone), plume shapes

COLORS
deep blue, claret, sea foam green

ANIMALS
mink, Irish setter

PLANTS, HERBS, EDIBLES
chervil, aniseed, raspberries, blueberries

ESSENCE
myrrh

SOUNDS/RHYTHMS
galloping horses

MUSICAL NOTES
C# and G

DEEP SPACE OBJECT
Alpha Apus

November 28

YOUR SIGN
Sagittarius

YOUR ELEMENT
Fire

YOUR RULER
Jupiter
5–6 degrees
First Decanate, yin

The Astrological Interpretation

No matter your gender, you tend to act as a knight in shining armor, always ready to slay dragons and save damsels in distress. In your personal relationships, you are most attracted by men or women in need of help. You are at your best and most passionate when you can lift a person out of the muddy moat, and carry him or her off to your castle tower. But then what happens after they are safe and dry? More likely than not, you accept their affections and go off in search of another soul to save. The high drama of romance is at the center of your being. As you mature emotionally, you will find that this orientation will change from the personal to situations that involve many people who may be helped by your courage and bravado.

November 28 is a jovial birthday interested in changing circumstances. "Let's take a gamble" may be your phrase. When you feel connected to your speech the effect is startling and meaningful. If you are just chatting for chat's sake, however, the communication can be superficial and tactless. Demosthenes, the ancient Greek orator who practiced speeches with marbles in his mouth, is an excellent image for you. You might even want to keep a bowl of marbles around. At home, November 28 would enjoy an Oriental rug in red and blue. The size doesn't matter; the appeal is in the color and geometric design. In your living room or family room keep available a deck of cards, some small puzzle games, or games that require eye-hand coordination. November 28 may find having fun brings new ideas.

Outdoors an image for November 28 is a mill wheel driven by the wind. Lacking a convenient mill, your own yard should be simple and spacious. Oak trees and especially red oak enhance your energy. Visiting a nearby playing field would be good. You might jog around the track or jump a few hurdles just for the fun of it.

A Kabbalistic Interpretation

Abundance is a key word for this day. It is connected directly to the Empress card, associated with fortune and fecundity. It is likely that you will always be comfortable materially and that you enjoy sharing what you have with your friends. A good addition for your kitchen would be a painting of a traditional cornucopia horn, which can encourage continuing good fortune.

While the Empress tells us that you will have plenty of material things, the Devil card indicates that you will also have many exciting relationships. You have an extremely sexual nature and gain great satisfaction from intimate relationships. You enjoy the whole process of seduction as much as you do the relationship that follows. To maximize the sensual atmosphere of your home, fit out your bedroom with deep violet velvet drapes.

The Hebrew word meaning "pleasure," which has the same numerical value as this day, indicates a personality geared toward enjoyment and fun. It is important that you find a balance for your fun-loving energy. Burning cedar oil in the evening will help you to accept responsibility and handle it well.

A Numerological Interpretation
YOUR MAGIC NUMBERS: 3 AND 9

The twenty-eighth day of the eleventh month reduces to three, the number signifying growth, unfoldment, and creative expression. Yours is a path of constructing life from the matrix of your desires. The materials at hand are the experiences in which you find yourself, but the urging itself flows upward from the deepest levels of your being. This pattern demands that you waken your own becoming from a gestating slumber. Visit a steel mill and observe the metamorphic and alchemical process that smelts this modern metal. Ponder the titanic action of an erupting volcano and the potential for change it represents.

Fire opal and amazonite are gems to fuel your personal transformation. The 333rd day of the year reduces to nine, contributing the sense of a foregone conclusion to your ultimate attainment.

OBJECTS/IMAGES
diadems, a parade float, a jewel hanging on the forehead

SHAPES/MATERIALS
nubby wool, church steeples

COLORS
royal blue, magenta, salmon, sapphire blue

ANIMALS
ostrich, dragon

PLANTS, HERBS, EDIBLES
wild celery, blue flag, carnations

ESSENCE
nutmeg

SOUNDS/RHYTHMS
wooden ceremonial drums, bagpipes

MUSICAL NOTES
D and G#

DEEP SPACE OBJECTS
Delta Scorpion, Al Niyat, the Shield

November 29

YOUR SIGN
Sagittarius

———

YOUR ELEMENT
Fire

———

YOUR RULER
Jupiter
6–7 degrees
First Decanate, yin

The Astrological Interpretation

You like giving yourself physical tests of endurance and will enjoy long distance running, rowing, and hiking. Although you tend to be a physically healthy person, you do suffer from one malady—foot-in-mouth disease! It can be difficult for you to hold your tongue or say your say with diplomacy and subtlety. You recognize the truth in every situation and you feel that it is your job to announce your perception to the world. You are basically a person who wants to have a quick solution to every problem. However, sometimes it just is not your job, especially where your children or your boss are involved.

Your birthday celebrates romance and intelligence. November 29 is a romantic with a fondness for reading. You have literary talent yourself and are a very persuasive talker. A challenge in your life will be moderating your desire to be involved in all-consuming relationships. Save some of your romantic notions for literature and appraise your situation in life coolly. At home have a prominent divan where you can look out the window and receive guests. You should create a living space where you can hold court and provide entertainment for a number of people. Velvet throw pillows would be particularly suitable for your decor. Decorative images of cupids, either of wood or plaster, are in tune with November 29's nature; they may also remind you of the sting of Cupid's arrows.

A garden space bursting with blossoms is an apt realization of your relationship to the outdoors. An arbor of grapevines is the perfect place for a romantic stroll. Oleander trees, Japanese maples, apricot trees, and ash trees would also provide shade and beauty for your outdoor space.

A Kabbalistic Interpretation

Family connections are highly significant in your life. This is partly indicated by the presence of the letter *Mem* this day. The older you get the more you will want to be in touch with your relatives. You should keep photos of loved ones in an album with a cream-and-pink marbled cover.

One phrase equal to the value of this day is "make joyful." This is a very good description of your general attitude to the world. Your friends are very fond of your determination to see the silver lining in the darkest of clouds. To help you maintain your cheerful manner, keep a collection of figurines or paintings of a variety of small woodland animals.

Along with your good humor, you have a significant degree of understanding. Your wisdom is recognized by those around you, which is very rewarding for you. To boost your level of wisdom keep an oak tree in your garden. Alternatively you could get yourself a desk with an oak leaf pattern engraved upon it.

A Numerological Interpretation
YOUR MAGIC NUMBERS: 4 AND 10

The twenty-ninth day of the eleventh month reduces to four, the number of reason, order, and gaining the lay of the land. Yours is a path of service to humanity. This pattern contains a responsibility to teach and shepherd those members of society who are either less able or too young. Inherent in this pattern is the awareness that society is an evolved or developed agreement by a large number of people to abide by a certain set of rules. Teach school, or volunteer for an organization such as the United Way. Your own sense of compensation will come as a result of educating those who do not yet know the way of things.

Jasper and alexandrite will provide a grounded understanding and a more stable thought process. The 334th day of the year reduces to ten, supporting your path with a sense of consummation and perfection when you finish a project.

OBJECTS/IMAGES
horse trainers, a jury box, a passport

SHAPES/MATERIALS
fleecy clouds, iris, ash-colored pyrites

COLORS
violet, caramel, midnight blue

ANIMALS
Saint Bernard dog, chinchilla

PLANTS, HERBS, EDIBLES
chestnuts, chicory, carnations

ESSENCE
amyris

SOUNDS/RHYTHMS
paeans, advertising jingles

MUSICAL NOTES
D# and A

DEEP SPACE OBJECTS
Zeta Ophiuchus, Han

November 30

YOUR SIGN
Sagittarius

———

YOUR ELEMENT
Fire

———

YOUR RULER
Jupiter
7–8 degrees
First Decanate, yin

The Astrological Interpretation

You dream of faraway places and distant shores. The sense of life as adventure came to you early, and even in your youth, you spent as much time away from the house as possible. You are fond of international food, and depending on your finances, you will make every effort to eat in many ethnically diverse restaurants, preferably in their native countries. Cooking and entertaining are a great delight for you—but definitely not the cleaning up! You take pleasure in being generous and spontaneous with your friends and are known for your open and carefree nature. No matter what your actual physical stature, you are a big person in terms of your attitude toward life.

November 30 is an interesting Sagittarian blend of strategy and chance. The trick is to know when to trust luck and when to apply practical action. In any case, your nature is jovial and attracts friends. At home, have space and a corner divan where you can lounge and survey all the traffic coming and going in the room. A carved Moroccan table or other articles of furniture you bring back from your travels will keep your imagination fresh during more sedentary times. Goblets in the shape of chalices may be your favorite way to drink any beverage. The chalice shape reminds you of the Holy Grail you seek in your more philosophical moments. Suede clothes, especially vests, are particularly appealing for you. Blunt speech is the birthright of Sagittarius though sometimes November 30 may take this too far. To encourage thinking before speaking, carry a smooth, purple stone.

The open range is November 30's territory. Even if you live in a city find a wide street where there are few people so you can stride without interruption. Large rock formations such as Mount Rushmore, the Grand Canyon, or Arizona mesas, stir the fibers of your soul. Spend some time in deep natural environments. Riding a horse and opening yourself up to nature's vibrations will fuel your system for work projects and more confining times.

A Kabbalistic Interpretation

You have a great love of children, indicated by the equivalence of the Hebrew for "mother" to the value of this day. It is likely that you will have children of your own and, whatever your gender, that they will be the central focus of your life. If you don't have children, consider working with them. A good addition to your living room would be a number of Norman Rockwell-style paintings of young children.

The Star card from the tarot tells us that you are very lucky. This card's influence acts as a strong protective force around you. To encourage this protective force in your life, buy yourself a seven-pointed star pendant. Wear a touch of emerald green in your outfits to further enhance the positive effect of this card.

Family is important to you, and you tend to structure your life around your loved ones. If you have a partner and a family to raise, then you will tend to see your main reason for working as supporting that family. If you want to create the best fortune possible, burn a white candle on a violet and blue pedestal in the evening.

A Numerological Interpretation

YOUR MAGIC NUMBERS: 5 AND 2

The thirtieth day of the eleventh month reduces to five, the number representing change, means, agency, and adaptation. Yours is a path of achieving crowning success for the sake of society. Your immediate motivation may be the rewards and accolades you receive for your efforts, but at your best, you retain a noble awareness of the big picture. This pattern endows you with a hearty dose of self-confidence, and you are not reluctant to seize the bull of opportunity by the horns, because you are confident of your good fortune.

Blue lace agate and carnelian are gems to enhance your natural optimism. The 335th day of the year reduces to two, allowing you to easily replicate your successes and double your money.

OBJECTS/IMAGES
dreams, yardsticks, vows

SHAPES/MATERIALS
wide S curves, poles, zinc

COLORS
rich blue, butter yellow, persimmon

ANIMALS
elk, Irish wolfhound

PLANTS, HERBS, EDIBLES
rockrose, chicory

ESSENCE
sage

SOUNDS/RHYTHMS
church vespers and matins, the click of a roulette wheel

MUSICAL NOTES
E and C#

DEEP SPACE OBJECTS
Alpha Scorpio, Antares, Rival of Mars

December 1

The Astrological Interpretation

This is a birth date that calls forth the urge to be a teacher. Even if you do not work as an educator, your attitude to those around you is one of a person who likes to explain things to others. You seem to have an extra insight into the most complex life situations and find it totally natural to be the one who can inform, uplift, and clarify. It is important for you to realize that just because a person doesn't say anything doesn't necessarily mean that he or she is ignorant of a subject. Perhaps it would be better for you to ask before you plunge headlong into a complex discourse about a theme that is thoroughly known to the people around you. You love books, libraries, and bookstores, but you sometimes make the mistake of reading a volume and then thinking that you are its author!

The fixed star Antares is very close to December 1. Antares has been called Mars's deputy, or "the watcher of the West." It is considered a powerful placement that can encourage headstrong behavior and rash actions. However, December 1 believes in playing the cards as they fall, and your famous zeal will find the joke and goodness in any situation. Keep circular objects such as cymbals or decorative plates around you. Anything with a theme of chance, such as a wheel of fortune, pleases you. Games of chance attract you, but don't bet the farm.

In your home and outdoors, stairways are structures to pay attention to. Let the stairs be made of wood with wide steps. If you live in an apartment building consider taking the stairs for exercise. If you have a backyard, keep it uncluttered and spacious. Lawn games and a swing under a mulberry tree give December 1 a feeling of freedom.

A Kabbalistic Interpretation

This day has the same numerical value as the Hebrew spelling of the word *love*. This suggests that you see life in a primarily emotional way with an outlook that tends to be both cheerful and romantic. Try and keep a vase of wild roses on your desk to keep you in an optimal frame of mind.

Although you have an extremely positive frame of mind on the whole, your personality is affected by the influence of the Moon card from the tarot. This influence means that you can be overly anxious at times, especially in work situations. If you want to feel more confident at the office, then you ought to keep a bloodstone in your pocket or purse.

You are likely to have at least a few pets as you tend to have a real soft spot for animals. Consider getting involved in an animal action group or charity. One word that has an equivalent value to this day is the Hebrew meaning "horse," and so it may be that you will have a particular love of horseback riding above all others.

A Numerological Interpretation

YOUR MAGIC NUMBERS: 4 AND 3

The first day of the twelfth month reduces to four, the number signifying order, measurement, and four-square physical reality. Born on this day, you have a path of aligning with the order inherent in the physical universe. This pattern requires that you get in touch with your body and its natural wisdom. Learn to listen to the needs of your physical vehicle. This is a pattern of cultivating more intuition and less intellect. Join an exercise club or take regular, long walks. Talk less, and listen more.

Jade and citrine are gems to ground your mental processes and connect you to the earth. The 336th day of the year reduces to three, providing a natural growth and unfoldment to this process. Surrender to your senses and let your body talk.

OBJECTS/IMAGES
playgrounds, racetrack, scepters, a rabbit's foot

SHAPES/MATERIALS
altar shapes, iris (stone), wool

COLORS
purple, wine red, amber, tangerine

ANIMALS
Loch Ness monster, ox, stork

PLANTS, HERBS, EDIBLES
dandelion root, wild yam, fig trees,

ESSENCE
ecclesiastical incense

SOUNDS/ RHYTHMS
sound of a roulette wheel, Latin chants, galloping horses

MUSICAL NOTES
D# and D

DEEP SPACE OBJECTS
Beta Draconis, Rastaban

December 2

YOUR SIGN
Sagittarius

YOUR ELEMENT
Fire

YOUR RULER
Jupiter
9–10 degrees
First Decanate, yin

The Astrological Interpretation

Your special gift from the zodiac is a prophetic quality that pushes your insights beyond the boundaries of today's limiting horizons. You seem to be able to see the seeming coincidences and intimate connections between people and events. You are helpful in expanding people's attitudes and opinions. Your are very open-minded, free of prejudices, and find it irritating when people display any narrow pettiness in their orientation. "Live and let live" is your motto, and live you do! You are especially fond of large, spectacular public events such as the circus, concerts, and major sporting events. You love the Olympics, for example, as this is a gathering that combines your love of athletics with your interest in international cooperation among all the world's people.

December 2 is located close to the fixed star Antares, which the ancients believed signified impulsive actions. You are eminently capable of choosing to direct your energy into inspiration and enthusiasm rather than impulse. December 2 has a freewheeling artistic sense that may result in unusual design and color combinations. Use your home as your palette. You may want to paint your rooms frequently, and murals on the walls would be a good outlet for self-expression. Lucky charms such as a rabbit's foot or a small blue "eye" to ward off evil spirits would be good for you to carry in your pocket. At home furniture made of fruitwoods such as cherry and black walnut will be attractive to you.

The outdoors is a tonic for you; you feel you have enough room to breathe. A hilly yard with an outdoor standing barbecue or campfire would please you. A volleyball net between two trees presents an opportunity to use up some of your energy. If you live in a city try to take hikes in the country. Walking and looking at a clear sky revitalizes your fiery nature.

A Kabbalistic Interpretation

One Hebrew word that is equivalent to the value of this day is the name David. This connection to your day suggests that, like David, you have great faith in the ability of the weak to stand up to powerful

Goliaths and win. You can encourage this approach by keeping some daisies in a gray vase on your desk.

You are happy to stand alone against uneven odds, yet you also belong to a wide social circle. The word meaning "brotherhood" is equivalent to the full value of this day, suggesting that you have a close relationship with a number of your friends. If you invest in a sizable round pine table for your kitchen you will enhance that closeness.

The Fortune card has a significant effect on your personality. It is likely that you enjoy traveling, and it may even be that your job is connected to the travel industry in some way. Your car is your pride and joy and is no doubt kept in pristine condition. To get the most from your journeys you should keep a small wheel charm in the glove compartment.

A Numerological Interpretation
YOUR MAGIC NUMBERS: 5 AND 4

The second day of the twelfth month reduces to five, the number of change, transition, and adaptation. Born on this day, you have a path of rising to the challenge of manifesting your highest ideals, and thereby acting as a precursor or herald to the next step of what is possible for humanity. You are like an advance scout sent ahead to examine the terrain and report back. You are charged with the mission of undergoing a personal transformation, attempting to express the next transition in humanity's unfoldment on behalf of the race, and giving tangible birth to idealistic symbols.

You are gifted with the power to rise, and altitude determines our overall perception. Adventurine and malachite are gems to heighten your aspiration and courage. The 337th day of the year reduces to four, providing the ability to gain the lay of land through surveying and outlining the psychological topography.

OBJECTS/IMAGES
pulpits, racing stables, mascots, extravagance

SHAPES/MATERIALS
tweed, topaz, ermine, curly shapes

COLORS
wine color, ivory, taffy

ANIMALS
stag, wildebeest

PLANTS, HERBS, EDIBLES
red roses, spearmint, sugarcane, swallowwort

ESSENCE
myrrh

SOUNDS/RHYTHMS
religious music, laughter

MUSICAL NOTES
E and D#

DEEP SPACE OBJECT
M10, globular cluster

December 3

YOUR SIGN
Sagittarius

YOUR ELEMENT
Fire

YOUR RULERS
Jupiter, Mars
10–11 degrees
Second Decanate, yin

The Astrological Interpretation

You like to work with those communication tools that allow you to reach as many people as possible. You are quick to take action and do not like to mess around with unessential details. You see your goal, achieve it, and immediately create another focus for your abundant life energy. It is difficult for you to feel that you are without a purpose. Thus at times you may invent aspirations that take you away from your essential life path. You need to respect those periods in your life that seem empty and not fill up the space with a project or a relationship based on your inability to withstand your own restlessness.

Jupiter, planet of generosity and expansion, rules your sign, and Mars, planet of assertion, your decanate. These two fiery planets complement each other and give December 3 an upright character that is not afraid to leap into the fray. The lamps that you have in your home are important objects for you. Have a variety of them: desktop, torchère, wall sconces, whatever suits your imagination. Lamps remind you of the light of wisdom and the many possible forms of self-expression. You might also invest in dimmer switches so you can control the amount of light that comes into a room. Your home space is best when spacious and uncluttered. A mahogany desk might be the only major piece of furniture that you really need. A sculptured panther or a print that features a jungle scene with a full moon may stir feelings from a distant past. You admire big animals such as elephants and horses and enjoy the company of large breeds of dogs.

Outside you want plenty of room to play. Horseback riding or cross-country skiing might be favorite activities. Large pines and balsam trees give you an image of nature's grandeur that spurs your imagination.

A Kabbalistic Interpretation

Though you were born in a winter month your favorite time of year is likely to be spring. This is in part suggested by the correspondence of the Hebrew word meaning "spring" with the value of this day. In order to feel your most cheerful during the colder months keep a corn doll on the northern wall of your living room.

Your day is connected with the sephira Tiphareth on the Tree of Life. This is the central sephira and has a host of mystical and occult meanings. In terms of your personality, Tiphareth is seen by many occultists as the highest point humans can achieve in this incarnation. This sephira is also associated with the energy of the sun. To help you achieve your highest goals in life you should keep a gold-framed mirror in the southern corner of your main living room.

The sign of Aquarius is significant this day. Although its title is "the water carrier," Aquarius is an air sign. This sign makes you creatively inclined, with the source of your creativity springing from your emotional relationships. Keep some yellow-painted water jars around your home to encourage that constant well of imagination.

A Numerological Interpretation
YOUR MAGIC NUMBERS: 6 AND 5

The third day of the twelfth month reduces to six, the number that connotes bringing things into balance. Six equilibrates opposites, harmonizes conflicts, and engenders a sense of reciprocity. Born on this day, you have a path of tending to unfinished business. This pattern demands that you clear the karmic slate at each juncture before moving on to new experiences and the possibility of new karma. There is a quality about this path of dealing with past pain in a manner that is an inspiration. Your example encourages others to face their own hidden wounds so that healing is possible.

The emphasis of this pattern is on a bright future through retribution to the past. Volunteer at inner-city schools. Deliver meals to shut-ins. Amazonite will strengthen your will, and quartz crystals will enhance clarity of vision. The 338th day of the year reduces to five, contributing the comforting awareness that all things are in a constant state of change. However dim or glorious the present moment, this too shall pass.

OBJECTS/IMAGES
red candles, crystal in the shape of a chalice, a roulette wheel

SHAPES/MATERIALS
velvet, iris (stone), chelonite (gem)

COLORS
pale green, dark grape, royal blue, apple green, sunshine yellow

ANIMALS
elk, reindeer, sleigh dogs

PLANTS, HERBS, EDIBLES
ginseng, hearts of palm, lime flowers

ESSENCE
sandalwood

SOUNDS/RHYTHMS
symphonies, organ music, music hall songs

MUSICAL NOTES
F and E

DEEP SPACE OBJECTS
Delta Hercules, Sarin

December 4

YOUR SIGN
Sagittarius

———

YOUR ELEMENT
Fire

———

YOUR RULERS
Jupiter, Mars
12 degrees
Second Decanate, yin

The Astrological Interpretation

This is a birth date particularly gifted by the energy of Jupiter. From the Latin name of this planetary deity we get the word *jovial,* an adjective that aptly describes your nature and character. You are expansive both in mind and body and will want to take care that your tendency to self-indulgence doesn't result in the accumulation of unwanted pounds. You also tend to spend money freely and are challenged by having to stay within a budget. Although you respect and appreciate all people's beliefs and religions, you go your own way spiritually. You will study and experiment with various philosophical orientations and may even be attracted for a while to a particular church or dogma, but you tend to move ever forward on your search for your own brand of truth.

Balance between your happy-go-lucky character and philosophical quests is important to all people born on this day. While thinking out your philosophy, recline on a couch or chaise longue of a deep royal blue, and let your mind relax. Space in your living situation is all-important, even if you lack enough furniture to fill it. You'll get there.

December 4 enjoys being surrounded by deep colored fruitwoods. Having a handy dartboard is a good idea to channel aggressions and keep your archery skills in shape. Outdoors, hiking and rugged scenery are the antidote to too much interior living. Your bedroom should be on a top floor with the bed elevated. Have a special place for stretching and exercising. Velvets in deep rich colors are especially pleasing to you. A mandala helps keep you focused.

A Kabbalistic Interpretation

In order for you to progress well in life you need to find ways to adapt to sudden and major changes. The Tower card from the tarot affects your life and indicates that you will have to face a number of catastrophic changes. These will all turn out to be beneficial in the long run, but you will need to be able to handle them as they occur. Buy an iron figurine of a lion or a sphinx to remind you of life's transformative power.

You don't let anything hamper your relationships, no matter what. This is partly due to the powerful passion that runs through your personality. One word that is equivalent to the value of your day is "to desire." You have an enormous capacity for sexuality, which is often the main energy driving your relationships. You should keep a vase of tulips on your desk at work to ensure that you don't allow that energy to overrun your way of approaching the world.

The idea of sensual enjoyment is also indicated by the correspondence of the Hebrew words meaning "delight" and "pleasure" to the values within this date. These words do not refer to sexual pleasures but can refer to any kind of physical stimulation. Keep a range of musky fragrances that you can bathe with or burn as incense oil in the evening to indulge your hedonistic nature.

A Numerological Interpretation

YOUR MAGIC NUMBERS: 7 AND 6

The fourth day of the twelfth month reduces to seven, the number signifying victory, peace, and a sense of satisfaction. Seven has an ancient meaning of "sworn oath." Born on this day, you have a path of pursuing humanity's spiritual ancestry. This pattern impels you to explore the legacy of our enduring symbols and archetypal memories. This knowledge allows you to make your own mark on the face of collective unconsciousness. Study the ancient traditions of Egypt and the universal nature of anthropological archetypes. Travel to ancient sites, and feel the emotional power these temples invoke. Tigereye and Kalahari picture stone will greatly expand your scope of vision. The 339th day of the year reduces to six, adding the element of beauty and harmony to this quest.

OBJECTS/IMAGES
fireplaces in upper rooms, wheel of fortune, saddles

SHAPES/MATERIALS
tin, turquoise, sapphire, shooting stars, streams of light

COLORS
rich hues, olive green, pale green, royal purple, carmine red, kelly green, chartreuse

---

ANIMALS
horse, mink, ermine, sable

PLANTS, HERBS, EDIBLES
chestnuts, betony, lime flowers, nutmeg, thorn apple

ESSENCES
clove, lapsang souchong tea

SOUNDS/RHYTHMS
military music, steady beat, trumpet music, a crackling fire

MUSICAL NOTES
F# and F

DEEP SPACE OBJECTS
Alpha Hercules, Ras Algethi, Head of the Kneeler

December 5

The Astrological Interpretation

The past is a living reality to you. You are attracted to history and to stored bodies of knowledge. You will have great pleasure pouring over the pages of an encyclopedia, almanac, or historical dictionary. Historical movies, plays, novels, and documentaries are also high up on your list of enjoyments. No trip abroad for you is complete without a visit to an ancient tomb, castle, or a city's major museums. You have the ability to see how history repeats itself and are fascinated by the cycles of human behavior. A career in archaeology or anthropology certainly holds an appeal. At the very least you will enjoy flea markets and antique shops so that you can touch the past with your own hands. You need to be in a relationship with a person whose intellectual interests are similar to your own, a person to whom romance means more than having dinner by candlelight (unless that dinner is in a pyramid).

December 5 is a more adamant birthday than others in Sagittarius. Sometimes you must protect yourself from your own risky schemes. You might have a habit of isolating yourself, and keeping company is a good way to check if your ideas are doable. Home should be open and without a lot of furniture. A circular room or couch that curves around is an excellent place for you to ground your active imagination. A fireplace focuses the mind, and rearranging logs with a cast iron poker is a pleasurable activity that may bring surprising thoughts.

Outdoors, you want room to walk, ride a bike, and exercise. Swinging on a handmade swing is energizing, and resting on redwood lawn furniture is especially pleasing to you. Stock your yard with games: badminton, croquet, horseshoes, lawn boules, etc. A view of a church steeple will be a point of reference for you, as Mars rulership of this birthday needs focus and an upward vision.

A Kabbalistic Interpretation

This date has the same value as the word meaning "dream" in Hebrew. You are well known as something of a dreamer by your friends, and it might be a good idea to keep some rosemary or peppermint on your desk in order to keep your attention on your work. At night it is wonderful to be a creative dreamer, and you might wish to invest in an authentic dream catcher to hang over your bed.

You are a very ambitious individual. The Emperor card from the tarot tells us that you have the ambition and the capacity to take on considerable positions of authority. If you want to increase your chances of getting that promotion you ought to grow basil on your kitchen window ledge.

The materialism that is indicated by the Emperor is also suggested by the connection of this date to the letter *Ayin*. The letter *Ayin* is associated with the goat—the zodiac sign of Capricorn—especially as a symbol of material desire and accumulation. On a physical level the connection to the goat indicates that you have a physical resilience and stamina. You might put your surefootedness to the test by taking up rock climbing.

A Numerological Interpretation
YOUR MAGIC NUMBERS: 8 AND 7

The fifth day of the twelfth month reduces to eight, the number of rhythm, vibration, flux. and reflux. Born on this day, you have a path of placing your finger in the air, feeling which ways the winds of change blow. This pattern casts you in the forefront of change, and you have the capacity to sense a change in the weather. You are a skilled planner, and you have the radar to perceive when the winds shift, sensing when your plan needs to be tailored to meet the new conditions. Learn to sail, and spend time on the water.

Take road trips, and enjoy plotting the journey on maps, always staying open to a surprising and magical change. Turquoise and aquamarine are gems to keep your spirits up and your mind flexible. The 340th day of the year reduces to seven. This supports your path with a sense of victory and encourages you to plan plenty of rest stops along the highway of life.

OBJECT/IMAGES
a lighted globe, leather bridles, the Holy Grail

SHAPES/MATERIALS
spear shapes, turquoise, royal robes

COLORS
olive green, deep violet, midnight blue, aquamarine, pea green

ANIMALS
thoroughbred horses, whale, turkey

PLANTS, HERBS, EDIBLES
featherfew, mistletoe, nutmeg, mulberry trees

ESSENCE
cinnamon

SOUNDS/RHYTHMS
processionals, horses cantering, a hissing fire

MUSICAL NOTES
G and F#

DEEP SPACE OBJECTS
Nu Ophiuchus, Sabik

December 6

YOUR SIGN
Sagittarius

YOUR ELEMENT
Fire

YOUR RULERS
Jupiter, Mars
13–14 degrees
Second Decanate, yin

The Astrological Interpretation

You are a seeker after eternal truths, nothing less will do. Intellectual boredom is your greatest challenge, but it is also your strongest stimulus toward expanding your horizons. The idea of personal confinement of any sort is hard for you to handle. Thus you may find yourself moving from relationship to relationship and career to career. It may be difficult for you to feel anchored and completed by only one person. You are much more geared to having a number of partners than to marrying forever early in life. Stillness is the same as death to you, as you constantly have to find new worlds to conquer. You are attracted to automobiles, as they symbolize your freedom. Your favorite shop is the travel agency.

You may pursue literary interests and have a talent for invention. Your memory is good, and you enjoy researching magic and rituals to fuel your imagination. An image for you is the sphinx at the great pyramid. The sphinx has the body of an animal, usually a lion or chimera, and the head of a human. This is similar to the centaur, Sagittarius's symbol, who transforms raw animal power into arrows of thought. Symbolism is interesting to December 6 and you bring imagination to the most mundane realities. With such a profusion of ideas, you could have a tendency toward clutter. Invent your own system of organization. Colored stacked milk cartons may be just the thing. In your living area decorate with large murals, paintings, or wall hangings. A tapestry of a Buddha or a Tibetan religious figure could be a spiritual focus for you, regardless of your religious beliefs.

Outdoors, December 6 likes flowers and shrubbery with minimum care. Mulberry trees, birch trees, and chestnut trees all resonate with your energy.

A Kabbalistic Interpretation

In your day's value the letter *Vau* is extremely important. *Vau* is symbolic of the element of air, indicating mental focus concentrated on a very idealistic set of values. You will probably have a great admiration for famous idealists. Invest in some black-and-white prints of Gandhi, Abraham Lincoln, or Martin Luther King Jr.

No one could doubt your intellectual optimism and self-confidence. When it comes to relationships, however, you are no longer quite so sure of yourself. This difference in attitude is the result of the influence of the moon this day. One way to counteract the emotional anxiety that the lunar impact creates is to carry a yellow topaz in your pocket or purse.

Your date's value corresponds with the Hebrew meaning "humility." Unlike many people who profess to hold high-minded principles, you are actually likely to act on your beliefs. Become involved in a local charity or community action group. A large white candle on a golden-edged pedestal holder will keep your principles in your mind and heart.

A Numerological Interpretation
YOUR MAGIC NUMBERS: 9 AND 8

The sixth day of the twelfth month reduces to nine, the number representing fulfillment, attainment, and the end of a cycle. Born on this day, you have a path of gaining a sense of the interdependence of creation, while at the same time understanding that you must do your part to create your own welfare. This pattern allows you to develop a reciprocity with other humans and with the animal kingdom, learning how best to do your part. You are endowed with a keen alertness to clues from the environment. Wild animals that are fed by humans soon lose interest in hunting for their food, becoming dependent on us for survival. Ponder the balance we shift when we interject our values into the operations of nature.

Green quartz and amazonite are gems to heighten your sensibilities. The 341st day of the year reduces to eight, contributing a comforting sense of ebb and flow to the events in your life. You understand that everything on earth has a common source.

OBJECTS/IMAGES
a festive holiday party, a Bible, racing stables, certificates

SHAPES/MATERIALS
worsted wool, velour, globe shapes, bow shapes

COLORS
rich green, cerulean, teal

ANIMALS
golden retriever, white whale

PLANTS, HERBS, EDIBLES
red roses, cloves, cinnamon, daisies

ESSENCE
cloves

SOUNDS/RHYTHMS
tribal music, big belly laughs

MUSICAL NOTES
G# and G

DEEP SPACE OBJECT
black hole

December 7

YOUR SIGN
Sagittarius

YOUR ELEMENT
Fire

YOUR RULERS
Jupiter, Mars
14–15 degrees
Second Decanate, yin

The Astrological Interpretation

Your mind is always abuzz with the contemplation of new opportunities. You consider today the springboard for tomorrow and are usually in a state of unbridled excitement or restless agitation. You may have difficulty sleeping, as you are continually charging yourself with vitality. In the course of all your adventures, you should keep your eye out for a teacher or teaching that can help you to bring structure, order, and cohesion into your life. You will naturally be attracted to rich purple fabrics and love the taste of fine wines. But olive green will have a calming effect on you, as will the drinking of mint and other noncaffeinated green teas.

Your birthday combines the joviality of Jupiter with the assertive quality of Mars. You may have some difficulty deciding among the many possibilities in life. An image that characterizes this mood is an arrow in midair. Use your dreams to see where and how the arrow lands. Dreams for you can be a compass leading you on a path that will be supportive and enriching. The scents cardamom and lavender will aid your dreams. Sagittarius rules religious ritual, and you may enjoy including a few objects from a variety of sacred traditions in your home; Tibetan statues, Christian icons, and Native American artifacts come to mind.

December 7 has great flexibility and the ability to move whichever way the wind blows. The image of the groundhog looking for his shadow may be of particular interest to you. Every year he checks and, depending on the weather, decides whether he will move forward or go back and sleep.

Outdoors, you prefer trees and space to gardens. Fig trees and fir trees may appeal. Practice your creative powers on an archery range. Learn to shoot arrows directly on target with your eyes closed.

A Kabbalistic Interpretation

Through a kabbalistic approach to the early books of the Bible, names are seen as important symbols of a particular character type. The fact that this day has the same value as the Hebrew meaning "Eve" suggests you have the courage to challenge authority when you feel poorly used. You should keep a bronze figurine of a cobra on your desk to encourage this approach to life.

Your bravery in the face of opposition is also indicated by the influence of the planet Mars. The energy of this planet also suggests a desire within you to achieve a degree of power in the world. This may mean standing for your local council or simply becoming office manager. Use arrows in the decoration of your office or in your jewelry to increase your chances of success.

While you have the ability to be ruthless in the workplace, you have a completely different personality when you are home with your family. Your loyalty to your family knows no bounds, and you are willing to sacrifice almost anything for them. Photographs of your family should ideally be kept in an ivory-colored album in order to maintain the strength of your bond.

A Numerological Interpretation
YOUR MAGIC NUMBERS: 1 AND 9

The seventh day of the twelfth month reduces to one, the number of beginnings and rebirth of the cycle. Born on this day, you have a path of celebration. You are keenly tuned to the annual cycle of the seasons. This deep connection to the yearly patterns stirs your spiritual sense and creates a bond between you and your fellow creatures. You love ceremonies and rituals, especially when you can experience pomp and circumstance in a large gathering.

Attend inaugural balls or graduation ceremonies; commencement addresses will always move you to tears. Travel to see fiery autumn leaves, cherry blossoms in the spring, pick roses in summer, and ski in winter. Move with the seasons, and stay in the flow. Apache flame agate and obsidian are stones to intensify your emotions and ideals. The 342nd day of the year reduces to nine, adding the ability to bring all your beginnings to full term.

OBJECTS/IMAGES
a goblet, a judge's robes, a Native American dream catcher

SHAPES/MATERIALS
feathers, streaks of color, velvet

COLORS
olive green, wine red, cherry red, cobalt blue

ANIMALS
moose, elephant

PLANTS, HERBS, EDIBLES
mayapple, plum pudding, vervain

ESSENCE
clove bud

SOUNDS/RHYTHMS
hymns, roar of a crowd at sports events, galloping horses

MUSICAL NOTES
C and G#

DEEP SPACE OBJECTS
Lambda Hercules, Maasym

December 8

YOUR SIGN
Sagittarius

―――――

YOUR ELEMENT
Fire

―――――

YOUR RULERS
Jupiter, Mars
15–16 degrees
Second Decanate, yang

The Astrological Interpretation

Your mind is constantly expanding the possibilities for your many involvements. If it is a career opportunity, you envision its optimal success and put all of your power behind its attainment. If it is a man or a woman that you desire, you martial all of your considerable persuasiveness, and set out for the conquest. Your birth date indicates that you are particularly oriented to achieving financial abundance. Bigger is definitely better where you are concerned. You seek to achieve a high social position but may not have the patience, with all of the responsibilities that such a level in society brings. It would be natural for you to find yourself in the import-export business or any commercial venture involving international trade.

December 8 could be gifted with intuitions that are prophetic, however you may also squander that energy in New Age utopian hype. Your sensibility toward life is essentially good-humored, and you find creative release in drama and music. Cartoons catch your eye. Keep a few of your favorites on the wall of your entryway. You might also want to have stationery that includes a cartoon; paying bills while you give your creditors a laugh contributes to a global good mood. At home, leave some room for dancing and whirling. Your furniture should be low to the ground and movable. December 8 may decide to rearrange things frequently. In your personal wardrobe velvet or suede is a fabric for you. Consider a western rough-and-ready style with suede fringed pants or jacket. Chaps would be fun but perhaps not in an urban environment.

Outdoors, you enjoy whimsical landscape design. Consider a series of jockey statues in different poses on your lawn and garden. A large wooden hobbyhorse would be fun, and a seesaw would provide endless delight. You enjoy animals and could have a number of large dogs or, if space permits, horses. Flowers for December 8 should be large and showy. A bougainvillea vine or trumpet creeper would grace your space.

A Kabbalistic Interpretation

The main tarot influence on this day is the Judgment card. This card can often refer to an ability to effectively decide between conflicting possibilities or viewpoints in an objective and fair way. However in your case there is also a tendency to be excessively stern in your judgments of others. Hang a wind chime with a sun image in your entrance hall to help you to see people in a more positive light.

The number twenty-six also contributes to your judgmental energies. This number is the value of the tetragrammaton of Jehovah—a jealous and vengeful aspect of God. To bring out the more sensitive and tolerant side of this tetragrammaton, sleep with a rose quartz under your pillow.

Despite an outwardly prudish-seeming temperament, you can let yourself relax with your really close friends. The Hebrew word meaning "vine" has the same value as this date and has an association with your nature. Like the fruit of the vine you tend to become more delightful with time. Though it may take months or even years to appreciate your finer points, it is well worth the effort.

A Numerological Interpretation

YOUR MAGIC NUMBERS: 2 AND 1

The eighth day of the twelfth month reduces to two, the number signifying receptivity, duplication, and dependence. Two is an ancient symbol of the life force and is represented as wisdom on the Tree of Life. Born on this day, yours is a path of exploration and a continual pushing of the limits of your known world. This pattern drives you incessantly toward new discoveries and boundaries of the unknown.

Astronauts and deep-sea divers are heroic figures to you. The danger of this path is that your curiosity will cause you to take unnecessary risks in your quest for knowledge. Blue sapphire and ruby are gems to widen the horizons of your mind. The 343rd day of the year reduces to one, keeping you always on the verge of the next adventure. Put on your helmet and fasten your seat belt.

OBJECTS/IMAGES
tabernacles, stores, rabbis, priests, prophets

SHAPES/MATERIALS
tallow, diadem shapes, amethyst, levelness

COLORS
iris, russet, wine

ANIMALS
bison, caribou

PLANTS, HERBS, EDIBLES
red roses, tansy, strawberry tree, plum pudding

ESSENCE
hyssop

SOUNDS/RHYTHMS
sound of the wheel of fortune, marches

MUSICAL NOTES
C# and C

DEEP SPACE OBJECTS
Alpha Triangulum, Atria

December 9

YOUR SIGN
Sagittarius

———

YOUR ELEMENT
Fire

———

YOUR RULERS
Jupiter, Mars
16–17 degrees
Second Decanate, yang

The Astrological Interpretation

You are a self-initiator with plenty of internal fuel to keep your creative engine going. You often find the day insufficiently long to accomplish all of your goals. But take note—the key to your success in life will be one-pointedness. No matter how much enthusiasm you bring to life, the results of your efforts will be diminished without the cultivation of fused intent. It may seem boring for you to have to prioritize your interests, but without some discrimination, your energies will scatter to the winds. In your case, less will lead to more while too much will lead to nothing. Mathematics, bookkeeping, and accounting are subjects that are well worthwhile studying.

If you corral your enthusiasm and use your audacity toward self-expression, education, and satisfying achievement you can avoid feeling up the creek without a paddle. At home, emphasize open space with floppy furniture. Reds, purples, and blues are decorative colors for you. You may even want to hang a hammock in one corner of your living room. Fruitwoods resonate with your warm nature. In the bedroom consider having a cherry wood bed with a high headboard and a very low footboard. December 9 does not like to feel hemmed in.

Outdoors, having sports equipment and the space to use it is important. Driving a horse and carriage would be fun for you. An organized garden is not as important to you as open fields. Redwood lawn furniture is a perfect addition to your outdoor environment. Keep some toys like a paddleball, juggling balls, or a bubble wand and liquid around your yard. Playing is the best way for you to focus your energy.

A Kabbalistic Interpretation

It is likely that you take an extremely active approach to life. You see each new day as an opportunity to gain as many interesting experiences as possible. You can help to maintain your life-affirming practices by always wearing at least one item that is decorated with primary colors.

Your approach to life should not be taken to suggest that you have no appreciation of the deeper issues or that you cannot sit down and be serious. In fact, the equivalence of the Hebrew word meaning "enigma" to the numerical value of this date indicates an interest in life's biggest questions. Consider finding a Tibetan mandala that you can look at while you are meditating on these puzzles.

The Chariot card from the tarot suggests that you are someone who tends to achieve your goals in life. Even when faced with considerable opposition you will keep going. An amber ring worn on your index finger will help you to overcome any obstacles in your path.

A Numerological Interpretation
YOUR MAGIC NUMBERS: 3 AND 2

The ninth day of the twelfth month reduces to three, the number of growth and development. Three is the natural unfoldment of the union of one and two. Born on this day, you have a path of looking at life in a different way. Your pattern causes you to question the destructive by-products of our technological civilization and the price we have paid for progress. The thought process of three enables you to see the direct result of our past choices on the present and the legacy we are leaving to the next generation. Your sense of honor causes you to measure the cost in terms of the planet and wildlife extinction.

Volunteer for Greenpeace or an environmental organization you respect. Amber is a gem to remind you of the powerful molding forces of nature, and how the past can be felt in the present moment. The 344th day of the year reduces to two, contributing the quality of reflection to this path. You have a natural ability to hold up a mirror to others so that they can look deeply into themselves and learn what sacrifices may be required.

OBJECTS/IMAGES
churches, blessings

SHAPES/MATERIALS
cloth, bone marrow, carbuncles, jacinth

COLORS
deep blue, peach, chestnut

ANIMALS
walrus, sheepdog

PLANTS, HERBS, EDIBLES
cloves, betony, gooseberries, bilberry

ESSENCE
nutmeg

SOUNDS/RHYTHMS
eulogies, the racing bell

MUSICAL NOTES
D and C#

DEEP SPACE OBJECTS
B72, dark nebula, the Snake

December 10

YOUR SIGN
Sagittarius

———

YOUR ELEMENT
Fire

———

YOUR RULERS
Jupiter, Mars
17–18 degrees
Second Decanate, yang

The Astrological Interpretation

Your birth date is symbolized by an ambitious young carpenter with a garage full of tools, a mind full of thoughts, and a heart full of hopes. You come to life with all the possible creative equipment a person needs for success. All that is lacking is the cultivation of technique. You are brave and eager, but try to pace yourself through life and do not take on responsibilities for which you are not sufficiently prepared. Until you mature, observe more than act, listen more than speak, serve more than demand service. If you are older, you have already learned the value of this path. You are now a teacher, passing on your wisdom to others. This day is associated with trade schools, technical colleges, and vocational learning centers.

December 10 is located on a "critical degree." This gives you a wide latitude of choices and swings of temperament. Think about having an ornate gong in your environment. When you strike it the musical tones bring you back to your center. A low-maintenance home is essential, with a den or game room where you can play and experience the fullness of your robust character. Trophy cases or interesting display furniture will be attractive to you. Favored objects at home would be suede clothing and nature paintings or photographs. A long table like an altar in a hallway passage is a central place for flowers and artwork. Sharing spiritual thoughts and conversations with people is a lifelong interest. Settle into large blue and green batik decorative pillows around a fireplace and let your mind wander. The fact that they easily convert into a bed for overnight guests is a plus.

Outdoors, the environment for you is the open range. City dwellers should take frequent nature breaks where you can walk without interruption. A hedge maze in your garden would be an ideal spot for walking and centering the mind.

A Kabbalistic Interpretation

The Fool card from the tarot is an extremely complex card, reflecting a paradox of all existence: innocence and great wisdom can exist at the same time. Wear touches of the fool's motley yellow and red in your outfits and keep in touch with the innocent pleasure of simple pastimes.

Netzach, the sephira associated with the passions and emotions that make us human, has a connection to the value of your birthday. You will be greatly appreciated by your partner, as you always make that special person feel that he or she is the whole world to you. Keep an image of a lynx or other wildcat in your bedroom to enhance this quality.

The energy of the sign of Aries acts this day to enhance both the Fool influence and that of the sephira of Netzach. Aries as the lamb of the zodiac adds weight to the innocence of the Fool, while the sexually potent ram connects to the Netzach influence. You can keep these two sides of your personality in balance by wearing a tie or scarf that is red with a green stripe.

A Numerological Interpretation

YOUR MAGIC NUMBERS: 4 AND 3

The tenth day of the twelfth month reduces to four, the number of planning, surveying, and order. Four strengthens the powers of abstract reason. Born on this day, you have a path of establishing a deep connection with physical reality. This pattern places you in a position to learn the secrets of the earth, and coax forth miraculous bounty in return. You have an innate curiosity and wisdom about plants. You love to collect rocks, minerals, pinecones, and seashells. Have a garden and grow both flowers and vegetables.

Visit Findhorn and learn about working with the spirits of nature; you have this gift. Jade and citrine are stones to keep you connected to natural rhythms. The 345th day of the year reduces to three, adding the influence of growth and natural unfoldment to all the seeds you sow.

OBJECTS/IMAGES
cowboy or gaucho hat, treasure chest, Oriental rug with large center medallion

SHAPES/MATERIALS
rawhide, ermine collar, felt, sound waves moving out from the center, green marble

COLORS
royal blue, deep purple, ruby red, saffron, tangerine

ANIMALS
elephant, stag, moose

PLANTS, EDIBLES, HERBS
agrimony, pineapples, oak trees (sacred tree of Zeus)

ESSENCES
bitter cleansing herbs, rubbing alcohol, pine

SOUNDS/RHYTHMS
cymbals, processionals, the sound of a flashing sword

MUSICAL NOTES
D# and D

DEEP SPACE OBJECTS
Alpha Ophiuchus, Ras Alhague, Head of the Snake Charmer

December 11

YOUR SIGN
Sagittarius

YOUR ELEMENT
Fire

YOUR RULERS
Jupiter, Mars
18–19 degrees
Second Decanate, yang

The Astrological Interpretation

You are concerned about the people where you live and work and spend much of your time in service to others. You will most likely choose a career that is connected to public education, with such issues as ecology, energy conservation, and animal protection uppermost in your mind. The negative side of this birth date leads to an individual who thinks that his or her opinions are absolute. This attitude leads to conflicts in committee and group work and inhibits one's good intentions and altruistic ideals from manifesting. Many people born on this day are attracted to metaphysical studies such as astrology, the tarot, and numerology as tools that may be used for their service orientation.

December 11 is tuned to the indomitable originality of the human spirit. The challenge is to pour that spirit into a creative, productive life rather than grandiose ideas that are not realized. Music, poetry, and literature all are attractive to December 11. A set of leather-bound books by your favorite author will add to your surroundings. Your personal style has something regal about it. A cape or long coat in rich blue or purple suits you. At home be selective about the furniture that you need and like and "stuff" that is hanging around making clutter. You need space. A prominent red or blue background rug, some pillow furniture, and one large, elegant wooden chair with an upholstered cushion may be all you need in your living space. The stone for you is amethyst. If you can find a pendant in the shape of a Crusader's cross it will be a powerful symbol for you.

Outdoors, you are content with raw nature and big trees. Redwoods are trees that you should see. If December 11 is forced to live frugally, the power of spirit and ideas can sustain you. Choose nature and contact with all the elements to inspire your vision.

A Kabbalistic Interpretation

The influence of the Hierophant card makes you deeply respectful of authority. Joining the armed services could be ideal for your particular outlook on the world. Equally suitable would be a career in the church as a pastor or priest. These two roles may seem contradictory, but in fact it is the need to defer to a higher authority that makes these two careers ideal for you.

The Hebrew word meaning "overturn" has a kabbalistic relationship to the value of your birthday. This association indicates that you have the capacity for imagining innovative ideas and concepts. Your natural deference means that you may find it difficult to voice these ideas. However, if you bathe in water that has been treated with a few drops of juniper oil then it will help you to speak with more confidence.

Whatever path you ultimately choose in life you are likely to be comfortably prosperous and generally content. This is largely thanks to the influence of the planet Jupiter. You can enhance that planet's benevolent effect by carrying a small square of tin in your purse or your pocket.

A Numerological Interpretation

YOUR MAGIC NUMBERS: 5 AND 4

The eleventh day of the twelfth month reduces to five, the number signifying mediation, adaptation, and the means to the end. Five is the number of change and transition; the number of evolution. Yours is a path of learning through imitation and trial and error. This pattern calls forth your powers of imagination and make-believe. In shamanic traditions, masks, skins, or headdresses are worn to invoke the power of the animal or god. In ancient Egypt, statues of the gods were thought to embody their archetypal energy during ritual. Inherent in this walk is the knowledge that acting as if something is already true accelerates the process of growth. Pretending becomes trying on the powers for size.

Examine shamanic lore from around the world. Collect masks and ponder their tribal power. Azurite and malachite, growing together, are profound reminders of the connection among all living things. The 346th day of the year reduces to four, providing a comfort with the natural order of the physical universe.

OBJECTS/IMAGES
jockey's silks, goblets, stables

SHAPES/MATERIALS
slim pointed shapes, ermine fur, curls

COLORS
yellow, yellow-orange, egg yolk yellow, coral

ANIMALS
dinosaur, mammoth

PLANTS, HERBS, EDIBLES
Solomon's seal, red clover, plum pudding

ESSENCE
cinnamon

SOUNDS/RHYTHMS
gongs, processional trumpets, coronation music

MUSICAL NOTES
E and D#

DEEP SPACE OBJECTS
Nu Scorpio, Lesath, the Sting

December 12

YOUR SIGN
Sagittarius

———

YOUR ELEMENT
Fire

———

YOUR RULERS
Jupiter, Mars
19–20 degrees
Second Decanate, yang

The Astrological Interpretation

Your life is a steeplechase race, and there are many jumps, hurdles, and traps to leap over before you can step into the winner's circle. As you are both the horse and the jockey, you may not take outside directions very well. You may make the mistake of having the goal so much in mind that you lose your footing along the way. You will be more successful if you take each barrier as the goal and let the race unfold itself. This birth date is associated with cheering crowds. You are a person who garners support from the people around you. You are openly friendly, very generous, and keen to give advice to others. You will find yourself attracted to coaching amateur athletics, diving, tennis, rock climbing, and almost all forms of outdoor activities.

Your enthusiasm for life is contagious, and you have the ability to initiate reforms for people's benefit. Your restlessness needs many outlets. At home or work keep a set of three small balls or beanbags for juggling, which is a good break between more head-oriented work. Another possibility is a miniature trampoline. A few jumps and you are ready to roll. Your home should be as large as you can manage. The number of rooms is not important; the amount of open space is. Arches leading from one space to another are pleasing shapes for you. Wood furniture from fruitwoods, such as cherry, that allows you a variety of ways to lounge would be perfect for December 12.

Outdoors, a garden with copies of masonry or stones from old cathedrals would be pleasing additions to your natural landscape. Daisies and black-eyed Susans are excellent garden flowers for December 12; other possibilities are fruit trees and jasmine. You might make a collage from pressed daisies for your home.

A Kabbalistic Interpretation

You are an extremely principled individual, and the Hanged Man card from the tarot indicates your devotion to a set of values and beliefs. You are quite willing to sacrifice your own personal desires in order to further a cause in which you deeply believe. You might like to grow an ash or an elder tree in your garden, as this will enhance your altruistic nature.

The two letters *Lamed* and *Aleph* combine in their influence on your work situation. In the office you are known to put your heart and soul into your work while you encourage a sense of unity among your colleagues. You can help to create a sense of camaraderie in the workplace by decorating in plum and pale green.

Although you are extremely committed to your work and to your friends it is important that you do things in life purely for your own pleasure. The values of this day suggest you have a fondness for food and that specifically you have something of a sweet tooth. At the end of a typically busy week enjoy a tub of your favorite ice cream.

A Numerological Interpretation
YOUR MAGIC NUMBERS: 6 AND 5

The twelfth day of the twelfth month reduces to six, the number meaning balance, poise, and equilibration. Yours is a path of harmonizing the often conflicting situations that occur in life. This pattern causes you to feel like the proverbial stranger in a strange land. You feel alone in a crowd. The influence of six allows you to see beauty where others cannot. You capitalize on your very sense of difference to contribute something completely different to the equation, thereby balancing polarities.

On a street filled with clothing stores, operate a laundry. Open a coffeehouse next to a bakery. Fluorite and topaz are gems to steady your powerful mental currents. The 347th day of the year reduces to five, providing you with agility and flexibility to meet the challenges you face.

OBJECTS/IMAGES
a diadem, the dowager empress, a lottery wheel

SHAPES/MATERIALS
gowns, hip hugger styles, ecclesiastical robes

COLORS
royal blue, spring green, gold

ANIMALS
Asian elephant, brontosaurus

PLANTS, HERBS, EDIBLES
gillyflowers, figs, dahlias

ESSENCE
Spanish sage

SOUNDS/RHYTHMS
Handel's Messiah, a gong

MUSICAL NOTES
F and E

DEEP SPACE OBJECT
Alpha Ara

December 13

YOUR SIGN
Sagittarius

YOUR ELEMENT
Fire

YOUR RULERS
Jupiter, Sun
20–21 degrees
Third Decanate, yang

The Astrological Interpretation

This is a birth date of a person who has the potential to combine two important qualities: practicality and foresight. Like all Sagittarians, you are idealistic. You have great hopes for the future and do not shirk when it comes to doing your share. But you have an additional feature less common in this sign—you have a pragmatic sense and know how to save as well as spend, contract as well as expand, and logically plan ahead for tomorrow. You are a diligent worker, and although you may find yourself juggling more than one career at a time, you have an inner sense of balance that allows you to succeed. No matter what your age, you will always cultivate men and women you consider to be good teachers. Journals, diaries, ledgers, and calendars are associated with this day.

December 13 is quick-witted and mindful of both higher and lower levels of life. The higher level is an awareness of philosophy and spiritual seeking, and the lower, unbridled sensual indulgence. There are many shades between these two poles, and December 13 explores all possible colors. An image for you is a wooden bridge arching over a canyon. At home include some equipment for physical exercise. A bicycle may be your modern-day horse, and weights or stretch bars in your home will come in handy when you are working at home. December 13 needs to physicalize energy. Create a diagram of any project or problem you are working on. You may find a triangle shape particularly useful for you.

Outdoors December 13 wants clear space and big trees. Beech and birch trees are particularly appealing. A visit to a merry-go-round is always a mood booster for you. Aim for the brass ring, you have a good chance of getting it.

A Kabbalistic Interpretation

The influence of the planet Mars this day is focused on the warlike aspects of that planet's energies. It is a very brave or possibly foolish individual who picks an argument with you unless he is absolutely certain of his facts. In order to relieve yourself of some of the tension a day generates, take some form of martial art such as karate or fencing.

While you have certain militaristic tendencies you certainly don't enjoy a spartan lifestyle. You will use your aggressive energies in your career to ensure that you have the highest possible standard of living for you and your loved ones. The Empress card from the tarot indicates that you will be successful in achieving this goal, as she is connected to all forms of material abundance. A figure of an eagle in the northern corner of your office will help you to achieve the wealth you desire.

Anything that you achieve in life will almost definitely be the result of methodical hard work and commitment rather than any sudden lucky breaks. In deciding exactly what direction to take in life you are often guided by your parents' views. You can help to maintain that strong link by keeping a small photo of them in a bronze-colored circular locket.

A Numerological Interpretation
YOUR MAGIC NUMBERS: 7 AND 6

The thirteenth day of the twelfth month reduces to seven, the number signifying victory and promises kept. Yours is a path of crossing new thresholds of experience. This pattern is one of constantly meeting crossroads and passing bravely into new frontiers. You seem always to be cast as a pioneer, a role that requires a particular mind-set. You must remain conscious of your experiences and be willing to make adjustments to your beliefs and actions to thrive in new conditions. Consciously accepting the conditions of each new way of being requires you to be receptive to new and different opportunities.

Watch the different versions of *Star Trek*, and vicariously explore strange new worlds. Black opal and kunzite are gems to keep your sites set on the horizon. The 348th day of the year reduces to six, contributing the influence of balance and complementary activities. Don't forget to see the beauty of the landscape wherever you may journey.

OBJECTS/IMAGES
ceremonial robes, certificates, Thigh-master

SHAPES/MATERIALS
shape of bison's horns, velvet, wool

COLORS
cobalt blue, malachite green, turquoise

ANIMALS
mustang horse, dragon

PLANTS, HERBS, EDIBLES
beets, wild celery, carnations

ESSENCE
fir

SOUNDS/RHYTHMS
a judge's gavel, the sung Latin mass

MUSICAL NOTES
F# and F

DEEP SPACE OBJECTS
Beta Ophiuchus, Kelb Alrai, Shepherd's Dog

December 14

YOUR SIGN
Sagittarius

YOUR ELEMENT
Fire

YOUR RULERS
Jupiter, Sun
21–22 degrees
Third Decanate, yang

The Astrological Interpretation

An image that is closely associated with your birth date is the United Nations. All the nations' flags fly freely, as you are accepting of all people and their ways of being. Yet one flag tends to fly higher than the others, the flag of your particular racial or ethnic background. You can use the talents, struggles, and strengths of your ancestors to your advantage—call upon them. It would benefit you to study the people or peoples that make up your particular lineage. If possible, visit your land of origin. Once grounded in your own past, you will have a much more secure base from which to launch travels into the wider world. You are an adventurer, ever seeking to expand the possibilities of your life. Stand firmly on your own ground and then go forth.

The fixed star Rasalhague may fall on some December 14 birthdays. This position was reputed to bring misfortunes through women. Further research has not confirmed this. Your mental gifts are strong and you are interested in mental and spiritual conquests. You aim high and are happiest in pursuit of your ideals. An image for you is two triangles entwined with a third superimposed. Drawing such a figure is a good way to collect your thoughts. You may be fond of collecting statues or images of horses in mythology. Prints of Pegasus and ancient horse and chariot races may keep you in touch with your freedom-loving nature. At home keep a horseshoe above your door for good luck. Believe in your hunches and follow them, as you may be surprised at where they lead you.

Outdoors, December 14 is a sports person and enjoys running, jumping, and bicycling. A garden is a little too staid for you. More interesting would be a trip to Hawaii to surf and be adorned with flowered leis.

A Kabbalistic Interpretation

In this day the intellect is king. The affect of the sephira Hod, connected to rational thought and analytical thought processes, means that you may even find yourself in an academic career. Wherever you find yourself working and thinking, try to have a painting of an Egyptian ibis, as this will help you to develop your mental processes.

Being an objective and potentially intellectual person does not mean that you disregard the more spiritual aspect of life. You not only are likely to have some deeply held religious beliefs, but you are also the sort of person who will apply their beliefs in practice. To help you to do some good in the world, keep a pouch of sage and chamomile in your pocket or purse.

On the whole you are a genuinely sociable and friendly person. When people treat you well you are willing to go out of your way to repay the favor. However, the energy of the letter *Teth* this day means that you can bear grudges if you feel hurt or betrayed. An amethyst under your pillow at night will help you to let go of negative feelings about others.

A Numerological Interpretation

YOUR MAGIC NUMBERS: 8 AND 7

The fourteenth day of the twelfth month reduces to eight, the number of rhythm, vibration, and the ebb and flow of the cycles of life. Born on this day, you have a path of heightened attunement to the signals and messages you receive from your surroundings. This pattern endows you with a keen awareness of nature and her creatures—you feel as if you can communicate with the wild ones.

You are asked to maintain a sense of anticipation and alertness, so when nature calls with a precious opportunity, you'll hear. Spend time outside walking in the woods and touching the earth. Turquoise and amethyst are stones to anchor your energies and deepen your emotions. The 349th day of the year reduces to seven, providing a sense of assured victory to everything you set out to do. Be sure to smell the flowers along the way.

OBJECTS/IMAGES
juries, mascots, totem pole, ecclesiastical robes

SHAPES/MATERIALS
mink's fur, sable, iris, the shape of a courtroom

COLORS
hunter green, sea foam, kelly green

ANIMAL
Appaloosa horse

PLANTS, HERBS, EDIBLES
limes, maple trees, Iceland moss, banana cream pie, liverwurst

ESSENCE
balsam of Peru

SOUNDS/RHYTHMS
the sound of a shot arrow, military commands

MUSICAL NOTES
G and F#

DEEP SPACE OBJECTS
Theta Scorpius, Sargas

December 15

YOUR SIGN
Sagittarius

YOUR ELEMENT
Fire

YOUR RULERS
Jupiter, Sun
22–23 degrees
Third Decanate, yin

The Astrological Interpretation

This birth date is associated with very daring sports: hang gliding, parachute jumping, snowboarding, etc. You are not afraid of the challenges of life, in fact you welcome them. You like to test yourself against the odds and enjoy the rush of adrenaline that such contests produce. This tendency is carried forth into the realm of your romantic relationships. You are very keen on capturing but not overly taming the "wild ones." Perhaps this is because you are a bit of a wild one yourself! You would do well working with disturbed children in need of vocational and other forms of life training. Your skills and fearlessness could also be helpful in the rehabilitation of prisoners.

On the high road, December 15 is a birthday of faith and religious interest. The religion may not be an orthodox one but the feeling is still one of spiritual pursuit. An image for you is a covered wagon traveling west. The early settlers took risks but also took precautions. At home, you will enjoy large rooms with doors connecting them. Keeping the doors open so you can peek into the next room gives you a sense of space and possibilities. An Oriental carpet in deep reds and blues with a center medallion is focusing for December 15. You may want to sit right in the center of the carpet and meditate or daydream. An object of power for you would be a large, uncut amethyst cluster. Carry a small amethyst in your pocket or perhaps a piece of jewelry in the shape of a Crusader's cross with amethyst or alexandrite in the center.

Outdoors December 15 would be happy on an archery range. A large pine tree in the corner of the yard is the place to sit and plan your next move. A view of a neighboring church spire keeps your thoughts focused upward.

A Kabbalistic Interpretation

The letter *Kaph*, meaning "palm," is important in the kabbalistic analysis of this date. implying that you are good at any practical task. Other influences suggest that you may be suited to a career in engineering or a similarly technical occupation. A great present for you would be some kind of working model kit such as a remote-control airplane or boat.

As pragmatically minded as you are, there is also a core of water energy in your personality. This element enhances your emotional sensitivity, which is beneficial to your relationships. It also means that you feel any emotional loss deeply, and in fact you can be prone to bouts of melancholy when life goes against you. At these times try drinking an infusion of burdock tea each morning.

We are all faced with a number of difficult emotional choices in our lives, especially as we grow older and our relationships begin to mature and become more committed. You are no exception to this rule, and yet you do find it more difficult than most to make decisions when these situations arise. If you sleep with a clear quartz crystal at the side of your bed you will find it easier to think with the necessary clarity.

A Numerological Interpretation

YOUR MAGIC NUMBERS: 9 AND 8

The fifteenth day of the twelfth month reduces to nine, the number representing fulfillment, attainment, and completion of a cycle. Born on this day, you have a path of exploration and foreshadowing. This pattern is one of trying on new skills and experimenting with attitudes and states of consciousness that humanity has not yet evolved. There is a wonderful childlike quality to this experience, like playing dress up or make-believe; it is safe to pretend and experiment with more advanced states. Wear your clothes like costumes in a play and try out both fad and fashion just for the fun of it.

Celestite and all shades of turquoise will enhance your sense of discovery. The 350th day of the year reduces to eight, providing a natural sense of rhythm to your explorations and a comfort with diversity.

OBJECTS/IMAGES
brocade-covered boxes, wheel of fortune, dice

SHAPES/MATERIALS
velvet, circles within circles, carnelian

COLORS
hunter green, deep blues and reds, China blue, aquamarine

ANIMALS
elk, giraffe, Indian elephant

PLANTS, HERBS, EDIBLES
green olives, marrons glacés, chrysanthemum tea

ESSENCE
lime flowers

SOUNDS/RHYTHMS
Latin plain chant, banjo music, square dance rhythms

MUSICAL NOTES
G# and G

DEEP SPACE OBJECTS
Kappa Scorpius, Girtab

December 16

YOUR SIGN
Sagittarius

—————

YOUR ELEMENT
Fire

—————

YOUR RULERS
Jupiter, Sun
24–25 degrees
Third Decanate, yang

The Astrological Interpretation

Your spiritual beliefs form the core of your life and are a source of great inspiration. They give you strength in adversity and creative will toward the accomplishments of your goals. You are one person who doesn't have to be reminded to count your blessings. You may take your particular church doctrine to an extreme, believing that it and only it is the "true" faith. If this is the case, examine your fear of being wrong. You need to be surrounded by others who believe the way you do. If such groups consist of people who have overcome separatist theological doctrines, then you will find yourself in the midst of your real "soul mates."

Your exuberance is infectious; communicating the expansive potentials of all people is a special talent. You may express yourself through scholarship, the arts, and music. If your "inner child" gets stuck in overindulgence you will fritter your gifts and merely be a playful child instead of an adult with a playful side. An image for you is three cups of wine on a table. The first is for taste, the second for a heightened sense of reality, and the third for wisdom. At home, have your toys where you can reach them. A collection of dolls or miniature trains may give you pleasure. A large carved wooden chest would be the perfect place to store your toys. In the bedroom emphasize large floppy pillows and comforters. Suede is a fabric you might enjoy. Have a vest or soft overshirt that looks stylish and is warm. December 16 likes images from world religions. A statue of Kali, the many-armed Hindu goddess, or Ganesh, the elephant god, would interest you.

Outdoors, December 16 likes field and stables. Everything should be on a grand scale. If you have a garden, spread out the flowers so they cover as much territory as possible. Linden trees and maple trees are perfect border markers for you. Flowers for December 16 are jasmine and iris.

A Kabbalistic Interpretation

Life is an ongoing mystery for you. Although you do try to make plans for yourself, life has a tendency to come along and overturn them. Luckily, the influence of the Fortune card from the tarot ensures that these surprises will be pleasant and beneficial. You can encourage the positive effect of this card by wearing a tie or scarf with a wheel design on it.

The planet Jupiter has a certain effect on this day complementary to the Fortune card, in that they bode well for all forms of travel. The main effect of Jupiter is its role as a paternalistic energy this day. You will make an excellent manager of people thanks to the Jovian influence. Decorate your desk with a vase colored in azure and yellow to capitalize on the influence of the giant planet.

The word meaning "oaken" has an equivalent value to this day. The connection of your date with Jupiter's tree adds weight to your suitability for a position of considerable authority. You can increase the beneficial effects of this connection by either growing an oak in your garden or keeping a bonsai oak in your living room.

A Numerological Interpretation

YOUR MAGIC NUMBERS: 10 AND 9

The sixteenth day of the twelfth month reduces to ten, the number of mastery and dominion. Ten is the consummation of the process, and the final embodiment of the beginning in one. Another new beginning is also promised. Yours is a path of consecration to an ideal. This pattern calls forth your latent willingness to march into hell for a heavenly cause, and nothing short of total perfection will suit you. Each individual has the potential to be a standard bearer for the race, to march in the forefront of human unfoldment. Your path impels you to make this choice.

Volunteer for a cause you feel passionately about. Sodalite and sapphire are gems to grant you courage and strength. The 351st day of the year reduces to nine, assisting your path with a sense of confidence that you will reach your aim.

OBJECTS/IMAGES
places of worship, yardsticks, yearbooks, universities

SHAPES/MATERIALS
zinc, velvet, tallow, shape of a slalom ski course

COLORS
violet, midnight blue, azure

ANIMALS
basenji dog, Clydesdale horse

PLANTS, HERB, EDIBLES
tomatoes, raspberries, tansy, star thistles

ESSENCE
sandalwood

SOUNDS/RHYTHMS
Beethoven's "Ode to Joy," multination choruses

MUSICAL NOTES
A and G#

DEEP SPACE OBJECT
the galactic center

December 17

The Astrological Interpretation

This birth date is symbolized by an arrow that is perfectly aimed to reach its target. Your career orientation is extremely important and your goals are far-reaching. You have a clear set of priorities and a distinct understanding of what is important to you. You can run into social difficulties when you overly project your preferences, as if they were the law of the land. Even though you tend to be inclusive and have the attitude that "what prospers me will also prosper you," others may feel differently. Since your ultimate success depends on the support your ideas receive from partners and coworkers, you would do well to take their feelings into consideration. You have an entrepreneurial spirit and tend to enjoy investing in business, the stock market, and speculation.

You have a special gift for mimicry, which you can use to amuse yourself and others. Masks from around the world may be interesting objects for you. You may develop your own collection of faces that reflect your varying moods. Inspiration and hunches often come to you. Encourage your intuition with a Ouija board, the *I ching*, or dowsing. At home, sandalwood, cedar, and pine are essential oils that accord with your dynamic energy. You may be interested in studying yoga or another physical discipline that has a spiritual component. Your at-home space should have a room for "experiments in life." Here, with a deep wine-colored rug or drapes you may renew your energies and dream about how to advance your ideals. A collection of minerals such as carnelian and amethyst may spark imaginative conclusions.

Outdoors, December 17 enjoys room to run. A nearby track or park would be perfect. Your own yard could include a garden but more important would be an oak tree. If your native enthusiasm is dampened, tell your story to an oak and you will feel better.

A Kabbalistic Interpretation

The number eleven is important to this day. Eleven is the traditional number of magic and all forms of occultism, so it is likely that you have an interest in this area of life. Other influences in the kabbalistic analysis of this day suggest that you have some natural sympathy for the language of symbols. A great present for you would be a set of tattwa symbols or a richly colored print of a hieroglyphic text.

Although you are generally friendly you like to have your own space, especially at work. Your friends are likely to be made outside the work environment and will be a select few rather than a wide circle of acquaintances. Those people you do choose to spend time with are likely to be very close indeed. In your personal space at home, keep a cushion to sit on when you need to be truly alone with yourself. The cushion should be bright red with touches of palest green if possible.

Your personality has an influence from the zodiac sign of Taurus. In particular it is the sensual nature of that sign that affects you. You should keep some sandalwood massage oil in your bathroom cupboard for those moments when you really want to feel sexy!

A Numerological Interpretation
YOUR MAGIC NUMBERS: 2 AND 10

The seventeenth day of the twelfth month reduces to two, the number of replication, reflection, and receptivity. Yours is a path of pursuing the manner in which you will make your mark on posterity. This pattern urges you from deep inside to project your subconscious outward, and mold the material of your life into a lasting impression for others. It is as if you can see the statue contained within the block of marble, and you wish to sculpt away the inessential to reveal an immortal work of art.

Visit art galleries and contemplate the archetypal contributions of the great masters. What are the qualities that endure? Citrine and adventurine are stones to intensify your creative energies. The 352nd day of the year reduces to ten, enhancing your ability to visualize the perfect embodiment of your creative ideas.

OBJECTS/IMAGES
barons/baronesses, costumes, hip hugger pants, heirlooms

SHAPES/MATERIALS
berry shapes, carbuncles, amethyst, hyacinth (stone)

COLORS
indigo blue, carmine blue, navy blue

ANIMALS
woolly mammoth, turkey

PLANTS, HERBS, EDIBLES
anise, apricots, asparagus, slender bush clover

ESSENCE
oakmoss

SOUNDS/RHYTHMS
spoken vows, cheering of sports fans

MUSICAL NOTES
C# and A

DEEP SPACE OBJECTS
Gamma Draco, Eltanin, Dragon's Head

December 18

YOUR SIGN
Sagittarius

YOUR ELEMENT
Fire

YOUR RULERS
Jupiter, Sun
26 degrees
Third Decanate, yin

The Astrological Interpretation

You see yourself taking a place with the knights around King Arthur's Round Table, consecrated to fulfilling a mission with dignity and honor and proving yourself worthy of a sacred trust. A bit romantic perhaps, yet this is the way you conduct your life. "King Arthur" is your own internal creative source, and you are constantly giving yourself missions and quests to perform. You act under a sense of your own morality, a code of conduct that seems to you to be just and fair. Yet this set of laws may not be universal, and your self-righteousness will be challenged, no matter how just and noble you feel. The gift of this birth date is that it eventually bestows an equality of vision and a comprehensive understanding of life. But this is something a knight must struggle to obtain.

You are well grounded enough to support your idealism and must fight against boredom with everyday give-and-take. You may be a travel buff and delight in handy gadgets that make life on the road easier. An indestructible dress or shirt that always looks good is for you, or a pocket translator so you can manage a few words wherever you are. Your home should be spacious and filled with objects from your travels. African art and tribal artifacts may particularly appeal. Rugs with bold geometric designs and symbols would also stimulate your fertile imagination. Physical exercise is important to you. Zen archery, which combines philosophy and discipline, may satisfy you deeply. Your personal wardrobe will tend to be casual and flexible so that even when you are not traveling you are ready for any occasion.

Outdoors, December 18 would enjoy a ranch or forest where there is room to roam. The desert may be an environment that attracts you for a while, and then you will want mountains. Your own yard could be a simple lawn surrounded by trees with room for team sports and a bicycle or unicycle.

A Kabbalistic Interpretation

Binah is the third sephira in the Tree of Life. It is referred to as the great mother and is the archetypal ocean or womb from which all life springs. In more personal terms Binah indicates a deeply protective and creative person. To enhance your connection to this deep energy, keep a mirror in the western corner of your bedroom, ideally in a silver frame encrusted with pearls.

Emotions and relationship issues are far more critical to your sense of well-being and contentment than work-related matters. The planet Mercury tells us that you have highly developed communication skills. If you want to optimize your ability to convey your feelings, wear on your little finger a ring set with an amethyst.

Because you are such an emotionally charged individual it is a good idea to have some means of creating a sense of security and stability. Within your home environment this can be achieved by increasing the amount of water around you. If you have a number of richly painted water urns dotted around your home then you should feel more balanced and at ease.

A Numerological Interpretation
YOUR MAGIC NUMBERS: 3 AND 2

The eighteenth day of the twelfth month reduces to three, the number of growth and creative expression. Yours is a path of taming the wildness in yourself and in nature, building on the principles of natural unfoldment. This pattern requires that you harmonize the seeming opposites of technology and nature. Life is not about choosing between a cave in the forest or a domed technological city cut off from trees and birds. Rather it is your quest to blend those qualities, like the image of a rose-covered cottage by a stream.

Study the works of architects like Frank Lloyd Wright and Buckminster Fuller. If you live in a city, have plants and a tank of brightly colored fish. Topaz and fire opal are gems to keep your senses tuned to the wild. The 353rd day of the year reduces to two, adding the quality of reflection and receptivity to this path. Be passionate about silence.

OBJECTS/IMAGES
jockeys, judges, luck, humor

SHAPES/MATERIALS
velvet, fox fur, peacock feathers, shape of large edifices

COLORS
rose red, cantaloupe orange, copper

ANIMALS
moose, Great Dane

PLANTS, HERBS, EDIBLES
iris, Chinese star jasmine, leek, linden trees, lungwort

ESSENCE
church incense

SOUNDS/RHYTHMS
wind in pine trees, woodpeckers, staccato

MUSICAL NOTES
D and C#

DEEP SPACE OBJECT
Barnard's Star

December 19

YOUR SIGN
Sagittarius

YOUR ELEMENT
Fire

YOUR RULERS
Jupiter, Sun
26–27 degrees
Third Decanate, yin

The Astrological Interpretation

The symbol for your birth date is a labyrinth whose secret pathway has been uncovered. You are bold and straightforward, unafraid to voice your opinions even if it shocks people around you. You do not believe in spending days and weeks trying to untie a knot when all it needs is a swift slice of a blade! You carry a lot on your plate at all times and cannot waste energy dickering over petty and unimportant details. What you may fail to notice is that what may seem small and insignificant to you can be the central focus of another person's creative efforts. You are great at inspiring others and innovating. You may need to learn compassion, empathy, and acceptance of other people's rhythms.

December 19 may find great satisfaction in guiding other people's talents as well as his or her own. This date is associated with maps, charts, graphs, and grids. You are able to give form to ideas because you see far-reaching possibilities. Your home needs a variety of study/discussion areas, as you will attract many friends who want to sit and talk. A round table in the kitchen, a corner of the living room with bookshelves, some comfortable chairs around a low coffee table, and a gathering place outdoors would all provide a forum for you and your buddies to talk over life. Burning incense might add a mystical touch to your home atmosphere. Woody scents such as sandalwood could be favorites. On the walls you enjoy photographs of wild animals such as elephants and hippopotami. Scenery that is wide open appeals to you. Sagittarius's symbol, the centaur, may have special resonance.

Outdoors, your yard should be free and clear. December 19 likes big trees, and if you set your outdoor discussion area under the trees you might feel transported to the ancient Greek agora or Roman forum.

A Kabbalistic Interpretation

Power is the thing in life that most attracts you. The Emperor card from the tarot indicates that you are likely to be successful in achieving great things in your career. If you wear a ruby or a garnet ring on your index finger you will certainly enhance your career prospects. However, it is important that you remember your loved ones as well as your work. You should keep a square-based bronze vase in your office to help you achieve a balance of family and career.

The element of air, which governs mental activity, is strong in your personality. In order for you to achieve your dreams you need to have both the ideas and the mental focus to carry them out. The element of air will help you in both these areas. Try facing east whenever you think about a new venture and, in addition, wear a touch of yellow in your outfits.

A Numerological Interpretation

YOUR MAGIC NUMBERS: 4 AND 3

The nineteenth day of the twelfth month reduces to four, the number signifying order, measurement, and planning. Born on this day, you have a path of giving beautiful form to the growth of natural forces. This pattern demands that you make your life like a well-tended and beautiful garden surrounded by a manicured lawn. You are asked to do your part to make your literal or metaphorical neighborhood a better place to live. Cultivate growing things, both wildflowers and herbs as well as hybrids and bulbs.

Read about Findhorn and Perelandra, and acquaint yourself with your own garden divas. Emerald and yellow zircon are gems to vivify your green thumb. The 354th day of the year reduces to three, providing a natural ease with growth and multiplication. Sow lots of seeds, and treasure the blooms that reward your stewardship.

OBJECTS/IMAGES
gratitude, deacons, encyclopedias, furniture

SHAPES/MATERIALS
chalice shapes, green Arabian (stone), ermine

COLORS
rich blue, tawny yellow, tangerine

ANIMALS
brontosaurus, whale

PLANTS, HERBS, EDIBLES
angel's-trumpet, hams, houseleek, huckleberries

ESSENCE
marjoram

SOUNDS/RHYTHMS
the sound of prayers, pipe organs

MUSICAL NOTES
D# and D

DEEP SPACE OBJECTS
Nu Ophiuchus, Sinistra

December 20

YOUR SIGN
Sagittarius

YOUR ELEMENT
Fire

YOUR RULERS
Jupiter, Sun
28 degrees
Third Decanate, yin

The Astrological Interpretation

You have a natural urge to gather others together so that group projects can be accomplished harmoniously. Yet you are not the most diplomatic of people and often find that you have inadvertently said something inappropriate to the situation at hand. Nevertheless your intentions are just, and people tend to forgive your verbal indiscretions. Unlike most Sagittarians, you prefer to have long-term, committed romantic relationships. Yet it is still important for you to have your personal freedom. You will seek out a lover who is as independent as yourself. Part of your understanding with your partner will be that you can go out alone with your friends or travel by yourself when your natural urge to explore comes upon you.

December 20 greets the world with calm efficiency and buoyant energy. You like to keep your body in shape, and going to a health spa or gym is a natural part of your weekly routine. At home, December 20 wants a central counter or desk that wraps around like a command station. Here is where you plan your campaigns. A lighted world globe will stimulate your love of travel. Decorative objects should be paintings with country scenes and horses. Perhaps some colors from the racetrack decorate the bathroom, and a lucky horseshoe over the door is a must. Have games throughout the house so that at an odd moment, you can sit down and work on a puzzle. This will invigorate the mind for inspiration.

A lawn mower is for meditation. If you have a large property consider a small tractor, but male or female, you will find peace of mind cutting the grass and working outside. Walking on a flat surface with an uninterrupted vista is a power activity. Always have a backpack so that your arms are free to swing.

A Kabbalistic Interpretation

The Fool card has a significant impact on your personality. While this card gives you an enormous sense of hope for the future, it can also indicate a tendency to be excessively naive. When it comes to relationships you may ignore signs that someone may not be right for you. If you carry a piece of iron pyrite in your purse or your pocket you will find that you are considerably more discerning in your dealings with others.

Your day is numerically equivalent to the word meaning "innocent." This association enhances the connection of your personality with the Fool, granting you an almost boundless enthusiasm and optimism. If you wear a scarf or a tie in orange and green you will be able to maintain this attitude even when things are not going your way.

With your positive outlook on life it is likely that you have an enjoyable social life. You certainly enjoy entertaining at home and will be happy to invite a whole host of people. You should buy a long kitchen table ideally made of oak to seat everyone around when you have a gathering of all your best friends.

A Numerological Interpretation

YOUR MAGIC NUMBERS: 5 AND 4

The twentieth day of the twelfth month reduces to five, the number of mediation, agency, and transition. Yours is a path of existing in multiple dimensions simultaneously. This pattern offers the opportunity to live a transpersonal life as a larger symbol to the rest of humanity. This is a collective walk, not an individual one. There is the sense of carrying out a role on behalf of others so that they can see what is possible. You have an innate feeling of connection to invisible realms. Those who have walked this way before remain available to guide from the other side of the veil.

Take on a role of service in whatever groups you participate. Study the lives of figures like Gandhi, Harriet Tubman, Helen Keller, and Beethoven, whose lives affected us all. Azurite and malachite are gems to stabilize your mental processes and enhance your inner communications. The 355th day of the year reduces to four, contributing the quality of reason and ease in gaining the lay of the land.

OBJECTS/IMAGES
a full wallet, outdoor catalogs, a statue of Zeus

SHAPES/MATERIALS
velvet, wool with natural dyes, large forms

COLORS
purple, rich blues, wine red, sunny yellow, ginger

ANIMALS
walrus, packhorses and thoroughbred horses

PLANTS, HERBS, EDIBLES
tormentil (herb), strawberries, sugarcane

ESSENCES
myrrh, nutmeg

SOUNDS/RHYTHMS
the sound of dice, Beethoven's symphonies

MUSICAL NOTES
E and D#

DEEP SPACE OBJECT
supernova

December 21

YOUR SIGNS
Sagittarius/Capricorn

YOUR ELEMENTS
Fire/Earth

YOUR RULERS
Jupiter, Saturn
29 degrees Sagittarius–
00 degrees Capricorn
Third Decanate, yin
First Decanate, yin
Winter solstice

The Astrological Interpretation

The promise of this birth date is the fusion of man and beast, love and desire, mind and heart, to produce an exceptional person with great capabilities. Yet this metamorphosis does not come without dedicated hard work to resolve all of these dualities. Your innermost task is to be able to identify with your own wholeness of being. This requires a great deal of self-awareness so that you can see how you defeat yourself when you veer away from your highest good. This date is associated with shamans, priests, and priestesses, hierophants, prophets, and alchemists. The purpose of life is to be a vehicle for transmutation so that you may turn your own coal into diamonds.

Your birthday falls on the winter solstice. Depending on your birth time and location you may be the very last degree of Sagittarius or the very beginning of Capricorn. The winter solstice marks the nadir of the sun's light, followed by the increase that leads to the summer solstice. Your birthday is inclined to pursue a mission of some sort. You are a person of principle and like to be at the head of whatever you do. At home have a bowl for goldfish with comical underwater mermaids or treasure chests. Watching the fish swim is the perfect way to relax your mind. You may enjoy herbal wreaths and dried flower arrangements on your dining room table. A string of sleigh bells for a doorbell will be a cheery sound, especially if you live in a cold climate. Emphasize classical styles in your personal wardrobe and the colors brown, black, and crimson.

Outdoors, December 21 loves flowers and pine trees. You may be too busy to garden, but at least think of window boxes with tuberous begonias, Italian bellflower, and wallflower.

A Kabbalistic Interpretation

While most of us spend our lives focusing on our own needs and goals, you have a truly charitable nature. It is likely that you only really feel comfortable and complete when you are helping someone else. You can encourage your benevolent streak by burning myrrh incense oil in the evenings.

One word that has the same value as this date is the Hebrew word meaning "abide." This word suggests a desire to remain in one place for a period of time. This desire is partly related to your charitable personality, as it stems from a wish to be an integral part of a community. You can increase your sense of stability and security by keeping some lead figurines in your main living room.

The Magician tarot card also figures prominently in this day. One of its aspects is to give you a vigorous sense of independence, particularly important in balancing your drive to address the needs of others. This card also suggests that you are dexterous by nature. A good hobby for you to try would be juggling—it is great fun and you will probably be adept at it.

A Numerological Interpretation
YOUR MAGIC NUMBERS 6 AND 5

The twenty-first day of the twelfth month reduces to six, the number that represents balance, complementary activities, and equilibrium. Born on this day, you have a path of single-mindedness. This pattern evokes the emergence of authority within your circle of influence. You continually find yourself with opportunities to test your capacity to assume leadership and wield power constructively. Strive for humility.

You are determined and focused by nature. The danger of this path is inflexibility. Stay open to the desires of those you lead and govern whether they be children, employees, or fellow volunteers within an association. Sodalite and turquoise are stones to keep you grounded. The 356th day of the year reduces to five, contributing the influence of versatility to this path, aiding your ability to be flexible.

OBJECTS/IMAGES
dens, bottles, bricklayers, castles

SHAPES/MATERIALS
ebony, ivory, tesseracts, denim

COLORS
auburn, lime green, cream

ANIMAL
chamois goat

PLANTS, HERBS, EDIBLES
boneset, baby's breath, comfrey, elm trees

ESSENCE
sandalwood

SOUNDS/RHYTHMS
music by Frank Zappa

MUSICAL NOTES
F and E

DEEP SPACE OBJECT
globular cluster

December 22

YOUR SIGN
Capricorn

YOUR ELEMENT
Earth

YOUR RULER
Saturn
00–1 degree
First Decanate, yin

The Astrological Interpretation

This birth date falls on one of the most signicant degrees in the zodi-ac—the very beginning of Capricorn. The symbol is a rising sun, its first rays shining brightly from the heart. This is the time of the winter solstice, the shortest day of the year, yet after this darkest day, the sunlight increases day by day. You carry within you the promise of tomorrow, and your personality is filled with the need to manifest a strong and clear destiny. Your life process involves detaching from the shadows of the past and creating a focus for your inner, solar light to radiate into the world. As this day also falls on the cusp of Sagittarius, you carry the condensed energy of this sign of faith and hope along with you. This day is traditionally associated with feasts of celebration and rejoicing.

Some December 22 birthdays fall on a critical degree and the Galactic Center. Ancient astrologers placed the gravitational center around which the sun revolves at 00 degrees of Capricorn. This tradi-tion has been confirmed by astronomical research. Like the steadfast goat, December 22 slowly makes strides toward the goal. Progress is sometimes slow but always sure, and time is December 22's friend. Timepieces, sundials, water clocks, all might find a place in your home. To keep gravity from pulling you down decorate with colored balloons throughout the year, not just on birthdays. Another tip is a parallel bar in a doorway. A few chin-ups and gentle swinging from the bar is a good way to keep strong and loose. You may feel a kinship with Native American imagery. Turquoise jewelry and a chief's feathered headdress may have particular meaning for you.

Outdoors, December 22 feels comfortable in caves with stalactites and stalagmites. Gardening is a way you maintain contact with the earth. Plant according to the moon, and whenever you move to a new home plant a cypress tree. Watch the tree's growth for a clear image of time passing in each place.

A Kabbalistic Interpretation

This date is influenced by the energy of the planet Jupiter. This planet has a benevolent but authoritative power, and in your case it tends to give you a paternalistic nature. If you have children you are likely to have their utmost respect. The same will be true of your work colleagues. You do know how to have fun as well and may have a penchant for old board games. Keep a selection of these at your house.

The influence of the letter *Kaph* this day tells us that you are not afraid to do physically demanding work. You get a lot of enjoyment and relaxation out of getting your hands dirty. You are comfortable in natural surroundings and should definitely maintain a garden. You might like to build yourself a hawthorn hedge to increase your sense of security.

Numerically this day is equivalent to the full spelling of the Hebrew letter *Beth*, which means "house." A Mercury connection indicates a desire for good communication with other family members. Keeping a large piece of agate in your kitchen will help you to improve your connection with your family.

A Numerological Interpretation

YOUR MAGIC NUMBERS: 7 AND 6

The twenty-second day of the twelfth month reduces to seven, the number connoting victory and a pause between cycles of creation. Yours is a path of discerning the true significance of victory. This pattern thrusts you into the fray of competing interests and conflicting views in order to learn the constructive use of collective power. To the victor go the spoils, but the waste of resources in misguided conflict hurts us all. Study the warlords and the peacemakers of history; not everything is worth fighting for.

Tourmaline wands and amethyst are gems to harmonize your emotional energies. The 357th day of the year reduces to six, contributing the energy of love and harmony of opposites to this path. This enhances your abilities of reconciliation.

OBJECTS/IMAGES
pawnshops, a cloister, leather mittens

SHAPES/MATERIALS
white and black garden pebbles, ointments, onyx

COLORS
gray flannel, auburn brown, winter white, emerald green, chartreuse

---

ANIMALS
lynx, bear

PLANTS, HERBS, EDIBLES
horsetail, thyme, parsnips

ESSENCE
vetiver

SOUNDS/RHYTHMS
Puccini arias, sound of a key in a lock, slow tempi

MUSICAL NOTES
F# and F

DEEP SPACE OBJECTS
Gamma Sagittarius, Alnasr, Tip of the Arrow

December 23

YOUR SIGN
Capricorn

YOUR ELEMENT
Earth

YOUR RULER
Saturn
1–2 degrees
First Decanate, yin

The Astrological Interpretation

You have a tremendous urge to build. There is a need to consult your past (education, family, relationships), extract the most important lessons from these experiences, and use them as the bricks and mortar to construct your life. You may have found your childhood somewhat inhibiting and not supportive of who you are and what you want to be. Yet you can use such struggles as fuel for the future. You need to learn the rules of society, not to conform your life completely to them, but so that you understand the nature of the status quo. You will have to integrate your life within larger social structures and cooperate with the forces that be as you build your own individuality and personal career focus. This day is associated with deep trenches used to anchor skyscrapers, large excavating machinery, as well as steel rods and beams.

You have a deep inner sense of the sacred and may feel reverence for the past and traditions. Maintaining flexibility and avoiding "foolish consistency" will be your challenge. Architectural details interest you. You may want to build a home that has outdoor pillars or some other monumental touch. It isn't the status that interests you, just the beauty of the design. Inside your home shapes such as an arched niche between two rooms or a fluted column flanking your bookshelves would be beautiful. Think about recovering old sofas, especially if they have curved wooden feet, rather than buying new furniture. You might also enjoy needlepoint coverings for footstools, piano benches, and side chairs.

Your earthy sign loves to garden and play in the dirt. A garden shed that doubles as a playhouse would be a great retreat for you. Play with your pets, fool around with a yo-yo, or have a Monopoly marathon in your playhouse. Your flower garden should include white foxgloves, poppies, and delphinium.

A Kabbalistic Interpretation

You were born under the zodiac sign of Capricorn, which is associated with material success. Other influences in this day point toward a concern with achievement in terms of finances and your career. In order to maximize your chances you might like to keep a vase of cornflowers in the northern corner of your office.

The importance of the number eleven in this day indicates that you are likely to have an interest in the mysterious. As a starting point, buy yourself an introductory book on Nordic runes and try casting them.

Family ties are important to you, and you like to spend as much time with your loved ones as possible. For you the most important time of the year is summer. Keep some mugwort and sunflower seeds in a pouch in your car's glove compartment when you go on your family vacation and you may have a particularly pleasant trip.

A Numerological Interpretation

YOUR MAGIC NUMBERS: 8 AND 7

The twenty-third day of the twelfth month reduces to eight, the number signifying rhythm, vibration, and the cyclic ebb and flow of all life. Born on this day, you have a path of enthusiastic desire to improve yourself. This pattern draws you into a kaleidoscope of experiences in order that you ascend a ladder of achievement. Central to the lesson of this path is the spectrum of application of energies. The same fire that warms the home can destroy the structure. Rainfall can gently nourish the garden or wash away a town in the form of a flash flood. Seek to purify your intentions and application of the powerful forces you experience.

Jade and alexandrite are stones to cool your ambition and widen your horizons. The 358th day of the year reduces to seven, supporting your path with a sense of satisfaction and the unspoken integrity contained within an oath.

OBJECTS/IMAGES
trappers, thrift, snow, tongs, and solitaire

SHAPES/MATERIALS
tile, tombstone shapes, turquoise, and staurolite

COLORS
holly green, sea foam, forest green

ANIMALS
ringtail, cairn terrier

PLANTS, HERBS, EDIBLES
raspberry vinegar, wintergreen, woad, and lemon curd

ESSENCE
elemi

SOUNDS/RHYTHMS
melancholy melodies, clock alarms

MUSICAL NOTES
G and F#

DEEP SPACE OBJECT
pulsar

December 24

YOUR SIGN
Capricorn

YOUR ELEMENT
Earth

YOUR RULER
Saturn
2–3 degrees
First Decanate, yin

The Astrological Interpretation

You have very high ambitions and a tremendous need to make a name for yourself in the world. You are determined to succeed at all costs and are willing to take the time necessary to prepare for your achievements. No matter what your age, you always have another plateau to reach on your ascent. Your urge is ever upward, even if you have a fear of falling down! This fear may be literal, in which case you are frightened of heights, or figurative, in which case you are afraid of not succeeding. You are constantly planning, and your mind is an intense factory, manufacturing the ways, means, and strategies for obtaining your goals. You must learn to worry less and to trust in the fact that you will be supported in your climb. Life is a strong rope.

The fixed star Polis lies near some December 24 birthdays. Polis was said to grant keen perception, ambition, and horsemanship. Your birthday does have a talent for concentration. You have an innate appreciation for the sublime, both in terms of art and experience. At home you may enjoy small pieces of stained glass or a few stained glass windows that catch the light. Your personal wardrobe tends toward classical styles, tweeds, and cream-colored crepe shirts or blouses. In the kitchen have a variety of earthenware dishes for baking and serving. You may want to study pottery and feature some of your own works.

Outdoors, December 24 is a gardener and will enjoy visiting greenhouses and botanical gardens during the colder months. You may particularly enjoy visiting the tropics or a garden that has tropical flowers. Ginger flowers, bird-of-paradise, and painter's palette may warm you during the winter.

A Kabbalistic Interpretation

The sephira Yesod is strongly associated with your birth date. This sephira represents the world immediately above the purely material plane and is connected to the imagination and dreams. You will gain much insight into your life by reflecting on your dreams. Keep a notebook by your bed to record your waking thoughts. A good addition to your bedroom would be a traditional dream catcher.

The Hanged Man card from the tarot tells us that you have a self-less side to your personality. In the context of all the energies of this day it is likely that this energy manifests as a concern for your family. You have a strong desire to act as a protective force for your loved ones. Keeping a pet, especially a dog, will help to bring out this aspect of your emotional nature.

You have sincerely held beliefs and aspirations to live a good life. The phrase *ain soph aour* is equivalent to this day's value and refers to a position just beyond the highest sephira on the Tree of Life. Burning a gold-colored candle on a white pedestal in the evening can help you connect with high moral aspirations.

A Numerological Interpretation
YOUR MAGIC NUMBERS: 9 AND 8

The twenty-fourth day of the twelfth month reduces to nine, the number of completion, fulfillment, and the accomplishment of a goal. Born on this day, you have a path of achievement in the context of group endeavors. This pattern endows you with the capability to facilitate collective energies and group dynamics to achieve a common goal. You are driven to manifest a concrete result and are skilled at strategy, planning, and ordering the details of an enterprise.

Strive for consensus. The danger of this path is an overabundance of executive decree. Your projects will function better as team efforts. Aquamarine is a gem to soften your intensity and provide a more fluid movement to your thoughts. Garnet will keep you grounded in practicality. The 359th day of the year reduces to eight, assisting your path with a natural rhythm and flow.

OBJECTS/IMAGES
chiropractors, chronometers, government buildings, and agriculture

SHAPES/MATERIALS
white chalk, peat, boulders, and bridge shapes

COLORS
brushed crimson, cerulean, turquoise

ANIMALS
dromedary camel, bongo

PLANTS, HERBS, EDIBLES
goat's milk, cypress trees, elm trees, and citron

ESSENCE
tea tree

SOUNDS/RHYTHMS
goat's bells, preaching

MUSICAL NOTES
G# and G

DEEP SPACE OBJECT
NGC 6567, the Ring Nebula

December 25

YOUR SIGN
Capricorn

YOUR ELEMENT
Earth

YOUR RULER
Saturn
3–4 degrees
First Decanate, yin

The Astrological Interpretation

A prince sits at the feet of his kingly father, observing, learning, and waiting for his opportunity to rule. This birth date gives you a deep need to rule and govern. Yet you may not know the rules of power and the subtleties of social relationships that elicit loyalty. Pay attention to elders, their mistakes are just as valuable as their achievements. In your youth, you will be attracted to older people, and when mature, you will take on younger people as students, trainees, and surrogate children. You have tenacity and patience, loyalty and respect for people in high positions who, in your opinion, really belong at the top. You easily recognize the weaknesses and foibles of human life and have a wry sense of humor. This date is associated with ice: ice skates, ice chests, ice floes, ice cubes, and icicles.

As a child, you may have resented being overshadowed by Christmas. But your birthday has a high calling and participates in the blessings of the season. Your mind is wise and attuned to spiritual study and your intuition is keen. Lighting fixtures in the shapes of torches appeal to December 25. An image for you is a small child standing in the snow and looking in the window of a warm, brightly lit cottage. All you have to do is walk inside! You may enjoy scents and aromatic oils such as frankincense and myrrh. A massage with either of those scents keeps your bones and mind flexible. December 25 enjoys leather goods. A leather vest would be perfect.

Your outdoor environment should include a garden. December 25 is frequently an avid gardener. Quince and poplar trees are well suited to you. You may want to grow vegetables that can be pickled. Consider constructing a small pyramid in your garden. You can sit in it in the good weather and store your gardening supplies there during the winter.

A Kabbalistic Interpretation

The value of this date corresponds to one of the Hebrew names of God. The particular name is associated with an essentially maternal aspect of the divine as a protective and unconditionally loving force. You can help to build such an attitude in yourself by keeping a midnight blue–framed mirror on the western wall of your bedroom.

The Death card from the tarot is represented in this day and indicates significant changes are likely to occur in your life, often without any warning. Thanks to the surrounding framework of energies it is probable that these shifts in your lifestyle will be extremely positive for you. To give yourself the best chance of grasping opportunities when they arise, keep a piece of red jasper on your desk.

The value of this day also corresponds to the Hebrew word meaning "work." Your career is very important to your sense of self-worth. However, it is not healthy to define yourself purely in terms of your job. Keep a vase of roses on your bedside table to ensure that you remember your emotional life.

A Numerological Interpretation
YOUR MAGIC NUMBERS: 1 AND 9

The twenty-fifth day of the twelfth month reduces to one, the number representing initiative, unity, and originality. Born on this day, you have a path of personal conquest. This pattern stirs your inner impulse to action and hurls you into the midst of causes for which resources need to be mobilized. You are naturally skilled at gaining support and leading the charge to a major group achievement. Practice patience, and learn to listen to others. Don't succumb to a tendency to shoot from the hip.

The danger of this path is misapplied aggression and undue forcefulness. Ruby and sapphire are gems to fuel your ambition and universalize your perspective. The 360th day of the year reduces to nine, adding the influence of attainment and an ease with accomplishing goals.

OBJECTS/IMAGES
a ship's harbor, hemp rope, a leather briefcase

SHAPES/MATERIALS
ebony, denim, large flat rocks

COLORS
sage green, crimson, royal blue

ANIMAL
raccoon

PLANTS, HERBS, EDIBLES
iris, rock candy, Christmas rose

ESSENCE
sandalwood

SOUNDS/RHYTHMS
Christmas carols, nursery rhymes

MUSICAL NOTES
C and G#

DEEP SPACE OBJECTS
Eta Sagittarius, Arkab

December 26

YOUR SIGN
Capricorn

YOUR ELEMENT
Earth

YOUR RULERS
Saturn, Mars
4–5 degrees
First Decanate, yin

The Astrological Interpretation

Your birth date is connected to the more practical and pragmatic sides of Capricorn. Even in your romantic life, you will choose a partner on a basis other than physical appearance and the heart. You need to know that your prospective lover or spouse is financially secure and has ambition and drive. You need a person who not only can be supportive of your aims and goals, but who is also driven by the urge for personal achievement. It also helps if your intended comes from a good and established family. You like to drive a beautiful car and wear fine clothes and, in fact, luxury automobiles and haute couture are connected with this day.

As you construct your pathway to success, make sure to include compassion, charity, and generosity. Your success in the world will be a direct result of the time you spend exploring the inner chamber of your heart. Although you may enjoy spending time alone you are not a hermit and enjoy sharing your thoughts and feelings with friends. An image for you is the light that remains lit in both a theater and a church. To keep your energy high December 26 will benefit from the Chinese herb *lu rong* (deer antler). At home enjoy a cozy book-lined study with a fireplace and Oriental rugs. Earth colors should predominate. Crystal clusters with many facets are perfect decorative pieces. You may create a black and white design with crystals and black onyx. Your personal style is classic, and you will want to wear soft leather in the colder months.

Outdoors, December 26 loves gardens and rocks. A granite fountain is a luxurious addition to your yard or garden. Investigate pictures of Chinese scholars' gardens, and note the blend of plants, rocks, and pebbles. Your garden is the place to think and create.

A Kabbalistic Interpretation

The Justice card from the tarot indicates that fairness and honesty are of paramount importance to you. Anyone who wants to have a relationship with you will need to understand this side of your personality. In order to ensure that your concern for justice is tempered with an appropriate degree of understanding, keep a pair of green-colored bronze scales in your kitchen.

Another card that has an influence on this day is Temperance. This itself acts to calm any excessively moralistic tendencies that the Justice card may produce. In addition it creates a fondness for a peaceful and harmonious home environment. You can help generate a sense of balance and tranquillity in your home by keeping a red and a blue candle on either side of your bed.

The Hebrew word meaning "meditation" is equivalent to the value of this day, and it again indicates the need for personal space and repose. It also suggests that you have quite a spiritual nature. Make sure that you set aside a part of your house for your own quiet time. Decorate in tones of cream and white with a black-and-white-tiled floor to get the most benefit out of this space.

A Numerological Interpretation
YOUR MAGIC NUMBERS: 2 AND 10

The twenty-sixth day of the twelfth month reduces to two, the number connoting division, replication, and receptivity. Yours is a path of conscious direction of your own destiny. You are intensely curious by nature and are drawn to many and various experiences, and seek to duplicate those choices that felt positive. There is a sense that you are standing on a threshold, feeling a restless reaching into the next event. Take care to finish what you begin, and allow time to internalize the lessons contained in the experience.

Finish every book you start. Complete a thousand-piece jigsaw puzzle. Build something with your hands. Amber and sodalite are gems to hold your focus of concentration. The 361st day of the year reduces to ten, the number that completes the process. This supports your path by giving you the tenacity to make it to the finish line.

OBJECTS/IMAGES
a war dance, churchyards, clocks

SHAPES/MATERIALS
jet, tiny trapezoids, bark

COLORS
russet, rust, indigo

ANIMALS
eland, goat

PLANTS, HERBS, EDIBLES
old trees, dock, sour salt

ESSENCE
sandalwood

SOUNDS/RHYTHMS
musical scale of D, the sound of a sigh

MUSICAL NOTES
C# and A

DEEP SPACE OBJECTS
Delta Sagittarius, Kaus Media, Middle of the Bow

December 27

The Astrological Interpretation

You tend to keep your feelings to yourself, as your heart is a tender, easily bruised vehicle. You feel responsible for others and easily become attached to their troubles, which you often take upon yourself to heal and mend. Take care that you not train your immediate family and close friends to depend on you to cure all their ills. You often use other people's life situations to hold yourself back. Only when you nurture yourself as much as you do them, will you find that your own dreams can become reality. People who care for or breed animals are associated with this day: it is a good day for cow herders, shepherds, veterinarians.

Your birthday has a talent for thoroughness and maintaining your integrity no matter what comes your way. Arch shapes throughout your home are good structures for you. They are curved, elegant, and very strong. At home you may want to have a variety of paisley coverings or throws in the living room. Needlepoint pillows or chairs covered with needlepoint designs are visually interesting to you. In the kitchen you may enjoy ceramic dishes in a variety of earth colors and large earthenware vases to hold branches of flowering trees, such as pussy willows and forsythia. An antique rolltop desk could be a cherished possession. December 27 may find a variety of uses for small compartments and secret drawers.

Outdoors, December 27 could build a garden around the arch shape. You might have an arch leading into your garden and one leading out. Incorporate rocks into your garden design. Plants for you include the cup-and-saucer plant and sweet alyssum.

A Kabbalistic Interpretation

The two letters *Yod* and *Beth* are important to the nature and energy of this day. Their combined effect suggests that your home is a central source of your sense of identity and that you should fill it with as much positive energy as possible. Use lots of glass and silver ornaments around the home and look for a house with lots of windows to let in plenty of light.

The Devil card from the tarot has an impact on this day, indicating that you are possessed of a great deal of sexual energy. You are very aware of this side of your personality, but it is likely that you find it difficult to fully express your feelings. If you get a ring or pendant of lapis lazuli you will find that you can be your natural sensual self without any anxieties or fears.

Earth energies are deeply connected to this day, and it is highly likely that you love nature and the country. It will help to ground you if you make a habit of taking a walk in the country as often as possible. Consider growing flowers too, as this will keep you in a constant relationship to the earth.

A Numerological Interpretation

YOUR MAGIC NUMBERS: 3 AND 2

The twenty-seventh day of the twelfth month reduces to three, the number of growth, unfoldment, and creative self-expression. Yours is a path of communication. This pattern endows you with a unique capability to peer into the mists of the future and perceive how the unfoldment of events follows a natural sequence from what has gone before. Your mission is to cultivate your insight and develop your ability to share your visions with others. Study the lives and stories of great seers and oracles. Take care not to place too much interpretation on your revelations; just transmit what you see.

Citrine and quartz crystals will aid your inner sight and enhance the quality of the message. The 362nd day of the year reduces to two, supporting your path with a deep receptivity and the ability to reflect. Strive to keep your mental lens clear.

OBJECTS/IMAGES
ashes, cathedrals, natural dyes, doubt

SHAPES/MATERIALS
calcium, hexagon, reddish clay, coal

COLORS
mustard, carrot, brick red

ANIMAL
dromedary camel

PLANTS, HERBS, EDIBLES
bluebottle (plant), sourballs, dill pickles, boneset (plant)

ESSENCE
rosewood

SOUNDS/RHYTHMS
whispers

MUSICAL NOTES
D and C#

DEEP SPACE OBJECT
Alpha Telescopium

December 28

YOUR SIGN
Capricorn

YOUR ELEMENT
Earth

YOUR RULERS
Saturn, Mars
5–6 degrees
First Decanate, yang

The Astrological Interpretation

You like to be in control and wield authority but are most comfortable in this role when you do not have to relate from a personal context. It is easier for you to sit behind a desk, a title, or a level of social attainment from which you draw power. You are not fond of having your intimate life probed and usually keep a low profile, opening yourself to very few, trusted friends. You have resiliency, stamina, and fixed intent. Your goals are mostly connected to being in a position to aid family members and others close to you. You may not be the easiest person to reach emotionally, but you are certainly not selfish. Stone monuments, obelisks, tombstones, masons, and masonry are all associated with your birth date.

You use Capricorn dedication for your own advancement as well as for others. An analogy for you is the body's skeletal structure. The life structure that you build should be strong enough to support your feelings, desires, goals, and wishes but not be rigid. To encourage flexibility, you may particularly enjoy massage with safflower oil scented with wintergreen or chamomile. Pinewood in some of your house is a supportive material for you. Encourage rest from your goals with soft materials such as mohair and cashmere. Antique carved ivory would also be a beautiful object for your home. You might want to go to a museum and examine carved ivory Chinese globes. The globes within globes, all intricately carved from the inside, will reassure you that anything is possible.

Outdoors, poplar trees and a flourishing garden are for you. Consider an arch or trellis leading into your garden space. There is a great deal of hospitality in December 28, and creating a portion of your garden in the shape of a heart is a nice reminder of your open home.

A Kabbalistic Interpretation

You have a water-based personality, meaning you are dominated by your emotional response to situations. In order to feel comfortable in your home environment you should incorporate water into the layout of your house. Install a large aquarium in your living room. Keeping colorful tropical fish will be particularly effective in keeping your spirits up.

The Tower card from the tarot is important to this day. This card is associated with trying and often traumatic circumstances, but remember its effects are always beneficial in the long term. You can help yourself accept catastrophic changes when they occur and fend off the resultant negative feelings by keeping a clove of garlic and a sprig of burdock in a pouch on your bedroom window sill.

This day is connected to the number 418. In certain occult circles this is an extremely important and mystical number. It suggests that you have the capacity to realize those goals that will serve to define your real purpose in life. To keep your focus strong, keep a small statuette of a falcon on your desk or in your living room.

A Numerological Interpretation
YOUR MAGIC NUMBERS: 4 AND 3

The twenty-eighth day of the twelfth month reduces to four, the number signifying order, measurement, and classification. Yours is a path of discerning the value inherent in the limiting principle of nature. That which gives form, and ultimately brings order out of chaos, has often been considered negative because the energy restricts. Your pattern demands that you see the beauty of this expression and use this principle to your advantage.

You are naturally able to concentrate and work within the parameters of a situation. At your best, you do not chafe against your boundaries, rather you blossom within the confines of your garden wall. Green garnet and amber are gems to enliven your sense of the ordered manifestation of life. The 363rd day of the year reduces to three, contributing the quality of creative expression to this path. This enhances the flowering of your endeavors.

OBJECTS/IMAGES
stoneware, tattoos, an ancient urn

SHAPES/MATERIALS
a skull shape, spade shapes, hematite

COLORS
winter white, black with a slight red strip, persimmon, orange

ANIMALS
lapwing, tree toad

PLANTS, HERBS, EDIBLES
sour pickles, sloes (plant), senna

ESSENCE
lavender

SOUNDS/RHYTHMS
clock ticking, marimbas

MUSICAL NOTES
D# and D

DEEP SPACE OBJECTS
Epsilon Sagittarius, Kaus Australis, southern part of the Bow

December 29

YOUR SIGN
Capricorn

YOUR ELEMENT
Earth

YOUR RULERS
Saturn, Mars
7–8 degrees
First Decanate, yang

The Astrological Interpretation

The image of a sculptor molding a lump of clay into a statue of a person of ideal beauty is symbolic of your birth date. Your thoughts are linear and logical, but also three-dimensional. You can see the finished product at the same time as you work out the steps to accomplish the goal. You are not easily swayed by empty promises, no matter how beautifully they may be packaged. Personal relationships may be challenging, as sometimes another person's personality, appeal, and life goals just do not fit into your overall plan. You are then left in a tug-of-war between your heart and mind. Resolve this one and you will really grow.

December 29 has an intrinsic sense of order and form. Sculpture may fascinate you, with Etruscan pieces being of particular interest. At home consider the shapes that you have around you. Venetian windows or pointed arches are forms that encourage your imagination. Be particular about the front and back doors of your home. A mirror framed in metal or wood opposite each door is advisable. The corners of each room are decorating opportunities. You may enjoy corner hutches or a pedestal with a plant or statue on top. As you survey each room the goal is to have as many interesting shapes as you can and maintain an open feeling. Keep your walls white or a warm beige and add color with fabric and throws. Earth tones are the most suitable for December 29.

Outdoors some garden statues are the right touch. Flowers for December 29 are white iris and wisteria. If you are near a thick pine forest spend some time there. The trees will renew your energies.

A Kabbalistic Interpretation

You have a great fondness for young people. Whether or not you have children of your own you will still be connected to the vibrant energy that children possess, giving you a definite creative flair. You can encourage this creativity by keeping a piece of chalcedony under your pillow.

The tarot card the Star acts as a powerful protective influence this day. In your case, the Star is especially effective as a benevolent energy when you travel, particularly if it involves moving to a new home. You can optimize the energy of this card by keeping a silver-framed mirror in the east of your home.

You are enormously energetic and like to lead a physically active life. You excel in almost any sport you take up. The influence of the letter *Teth*, meaning "serpent," along with other energies this day suggest that you may find interest in investigating the practice of kundalini yoga.

A Numerological Interpretation
YOUR MAGIC NUMBERS: 5 AND 4

The twenty-ninth day of the twelfth month reduces to five, the number of mediation, adaptation, and versatility. Yours is a path of discovering your true purpose and playing your part to the hilt. This pattern endows you with the capacity to detect the intrinsic harmony of life in which we each play a unique part. You are asked to hear the song of your own life, and to sing with sweet surrender. You know without doubt that heaven is within. Complete surrender to divine will is a paradox. What really occurs is a fundamental understanding of our true purpose and place in the scheme of things.

Celestite and serpentine are gems to open your eyes to heaven while keeping your feet firmly planted on the ground. The 364th day of the year reduces to four, supporting your path with the ability to gain the lay of the land and thereby easily determining how things fit.

OBJECTS/IMAGES
puppets, underground passages, underwear

SHAPES/MATERIALS
pyramids, black hematite, sapphires

COLORS
charcoal, lemon, butterscotch

ANIMALS
burro, armadillo

PLANTS, HERBS, EDIBLES
vinegar, yams, sweet peas

ESSENCE
hyssop

SOUNDS/RHYTHMS
sound of marble being sculpted, sound of Tibetan prayer wheels spinning

---

MUSICAL NOTES
E and D#

DEEP SPACE OBJECTS
Lambda Sagittarius, Kaus Borealis, northern part of the Bow

December 30

YOUR SIGN
Capricorn

YOUR ELEMENT
Earth

YOUR RULERS
Saturn, Mars
8–9 degrees
First Decanate, yang

The Astrological Interpretation

There are times when the worrying side of your nature gets the better of you. Your ability to assess the reality of a situation is certainly one of your best traits. It serves you when it comes to advising others and helps you to be efficient, practical, and economical in your chosen career. Yet you have to take care not to exaggerate your disappointment when things do not go your way or you will diminish your ability to change the situation. Who is telling the story going through your head? If you are going to tell yourself a story, tell a good one. This birthday bestows the gift of inner power, but you may mask this bounty through self-denial. Take the time to dance, walk through nature, and count the stars in the sky.

December 30's ambitions may not be for worldly or material success. There is a strong religious temperament and a desire to serve. There could be a feeling of aimlessness until you decide your cause. Meanwhile, having a sense of humor is essential. A collar pin in the shape of a guardian angel keeps you mindful of universal help. Angel imagery throughout the home may be appealing. Why not make angel food cake your specialty? Turquoise and smoky quartz are stones for you. Make a habit of picking up minerals on your travels and displaying them at home. December 30 has a knack with tile, and you may want to set some of your mineral collection and line the bathroom walls.

Outdoors, exotic flowers such as birds-of-paradise are appealing, but if your climate only allows daisies, zinnias, and pansies, they will do just fine. A garden with rocks or a rocky slope will suit your sense of ambition. When the task is slightly difficult, you feel fulfilled. Consider having a carved marble statue or marble column in your garden. This may be the centerpiece of the garden and serve as a metaphoric altar.

A Kabbalistic Interpretation

If you have a problem in life, it is that you are far too generous. You are willing to share almost anything with anyone, which can lead to being exploited. You also could be more organized when it comes to your financial affairs. Try keeping your important papers in a violet-colored box, and put a peacock feather in with them. This will help you control your money and use your generous streak wisely.

The influence of the Moon card from the tarot suggests that you have a tendency to get overanxious, particularly when it comes to your career. Drink an infusion of burdock when you are feeling down and keep a tigereye gem on your desk for confidence.

You also have an extremely practical side to your personality. In fact you get a lot of satisfaction out of do-it-yourself projects. People know that they can always turn to you if they need something fixed in their home. A great present for you would be a workbench or some new power tools.

A Numerological Interpretation
YOUR MAGIC NUMBERS: 6 AND 5

The thirtieth day of the twelfth month reduces to six, the number representing love, beauty, and the harmony of opposites. Born on this day, you have a path of overcoming fear. This pattern demands that you develop radical trust in your life. Identify your fears, and work to confront them; the emotional rewards will be great. You are asked to walk the path of harmlessness, and to learn to radiate love and compassion to all creatures. Have a statue of Saint Francis of Assisi in your garden. Feed the wild birds until they feel safe enough to eat from your hand. What a statement of faith.

Sodalite and blue agate are stones to give you courage and strength of will. Rose quartz will open your heart. The 365th day of the year reduces to five. This aids your path with the quality of versatility and flexibility. There are only two states of mind: fear and love. Choose love.

OBJECTS/IMAGES
*an hourglass,
Sisyphus rolling his stone
up the mountain,
a miner's light*

SHAPES/MATERIALS
pewter, bricks

COLORS
*dark brown, apple green,
bisque*

ANIMALS
animals with horns

PLANTS, HERBS, EDIBLES
knotgrass, thyme

ESSENCE
vetiver

SOUNDS/RHYTHMS
ice cracking, church hymns

MUSICAL NOTES
F and E

DEEP SPACE OBJECT
supernova

December 31

YOUR SIGN
Capricorn

YOUR ELEMENT
Earth

YOUR RULER
Saturn
9–10 degrees
First Decanate, yang

The Astrological Interpretation

If you play Monopoly, you will want to be the banker. In blackjack, you are the dealer; in roulette, you are definitely "the house." But you are not a gambler, for in all of these games, the odds favor the backer, not the player. You always plan your moves carefully. You risk as little as possible to gain as much as possible. When your heart is engaged, you do all you can to advance and protect the interests of those close to you. If you are in a subordinate position at work, you are incredibly loyal, as long as you sincerely respect the people in positions higher than yours. But the truth is that CEO are initials you would not mind having monogrammed on your shirt cuff or handbag!

The last day of the calendar year has a feeling of finality about it; however, December 31 can take a broad view and perceive the trend of events. There is wisdom in your birthday and your prudence will ensure that what you put your mind to will bear fruit. The symbol for Capricorn is a mysterious figure that is half-goat and half-fish. The ambitious goat is the more familiar image, but the fish swims in the deep ocean and brings great sensitivity to life. Burning sage throughout your home may be a purification ritual you enjoy. Mosaic tables are excellent objects for December 31. You may want to have one that doubles as a chessboard. In your bathroom a tile design that includes some mosaic pieces would please you. A large tub with whirlpool jets is the place for you when your sensitivities need soothing.

Outdoors, December 31 may be an expert gardener. Pruning trees may be a meditative activity for you; elm, cypress, and buckthorn trees will all respond to your green thumb. A rock garden may be part of your landscape; consider purple rock cress and gold dust plants.

A Kabbalistic Interpretation

One word that has the same value as your birthday is the Hebrew word meaning "rejoice." This is an appropriate start for the day when we look forward to the new year with all its opportunities and challenges. You can help to keep your sense of optimism alive by burning some almond incense oil while you relax in a deep bath.

The influence of the Sun card on this day also connects with optimism. It is indicative of a well-developed mind and it may be that you choose to work in an academic or teaching capacity. If you want to make sure that your ideas flow, hang a painting of a sun image in the eastern corner of your living room.

The full value of this day is a prime number, indicating that you have a unique approach to life. This is likely to be a result of your superior intellect and your overflowing enthusiasm for life. While an excellent trait, there are times when you will need to temper your individuality in order to progress in your chosen career. Keeping an angelica plant on your desk in the office will enable you to soften your eccentricities while maintaining your distinct personality once you get home.

A Numerological Interpretation

YOUR MAGIC NUMBERS: 7 AND 6

The thirty-first day of the twelfth month reduces to seven, the number of victory, rest, and a pause between cycles of expression. Yours is a path of the true knight. You are possessed of nobility of purpose and at your best have a deep and abiding desire to serve. You are capable of delving deeply into the mysteries of life, and can hold your counsel when necessary. At your best, you exercise wisdom, patience, and good judgment. Strive to share your insights whenever possible.

The last day of our modern calendar enhances your ability to look inward and gain a retrospective awareness of events in your life. Violet sapphire and amethyst are gems to deepen your feeling nature and warm your heart. Don't spend too much time alone. The 366th day of the year reduces to six, supporting your path with a love of beauty and harmony, and an instinctive sense that knowledge not used is empty.

OBJECTS/IMAGES
tailors, religious relics, puppets

SHAPES/MATERIALS
stoneware, spade shapes, snowflakes

COLORS
blue-violet, peacock green, chartreuse

ANIMALS
raven, goat

PLANTS, HERBS, EDIBLES
beechdrops, wood rush, sweet potatoes, henna

ESSENCE
jasmine

SOUNDS/RHYTHMS
a door chime, whir of a potter's wheel

MUSICAL NOTES
F# and F

DEEP SPACE OBJECT
Alpha Scutum

Resource Guide

Herbs and Edibles

Buhner, Stephen. *Sacred Plant Medicine.* Boulder, Colo.: Roberts Rinehart Publications, 1996.

Dobelis, Inge (ed.). *Magic and Medicine of Plants.* Pleasantville, N.Y.: Reader's Digest, 1986.

Hausman, P. and Hurley, J. *The Healing Foods.* Emmaus, Pa.: Rodale Press, 1989.

Lucas, Richard M. *Miracle Medicine Herbs.* West Nyack, N.Y.: Parker Publishing, 1991.

Manniche, Lise. *An Ancient Egyptian Herbal.* Austin: University of Texas Press, 1989.

Rodale's Illustrated Encyclopedia of Herbs. Emmaus, Pa.: Rodale Press, 1987.

Stuart, M. (ed.). *The Encyclopedia of Herbs and Herbalism.* London: Orbis Books, 1979.

Weiss, Gaea, and Shandoor. *Growing and Using Healing Herbs.* Emmaus, Pa.: Rodale Press, 1985.

SOURCES

health food stores, naturepath and homeopath physicians

www.themodernherbalist.com

www.yogitea.com

Essences

Bach, Edward. *The Bach Flower Remedies.* New Canaan, Conn.: Keats Publishing, 1952.

Young, Gary. *Aromatherapy, The Essential Beginning.* Corvallis, Ore.: Essential Press, 1996.

SOURCES

health food stores, naturepath and homeopath physicians

www.essences.com

Gems and Minerals

Chesterman, Charles. *National Audubon Society Field Guide to North American Rocks and Minerals.* New York: Chanticleer Press, 1978.

Cipriani, C., and Borelli, A. *Simon and Schuster's Guide to Gems and Precious Stones.* New York: Simon & Schuster, 1986.

Crow, W. B. *Precious Stones, Their Occult Power and Hidden Signs.* London: Garden City Press, 1968.

Cunningham, Scott. *Encyclopedia of Crystal, Gem and Metal Magic.* St. Paul, Minn.: Llewellyn Publications, 1996.

Kunz, George. *The Curious Lore of Precious Stones.* New York: Bell Publishing, 1989.

Schumann, Walter. *Gemstones of the World.* New York: Sterling Publishing, 1976.

SOURCES

rock shops, museum shops

www.crystals-gems.com

www.africa-quartz-crystals.com

www.nature-gallery.com

Amulets and Talismans

Gonzalez-Wippler, M. *The Complete Book of Amulets and Talismans.* St. Paul, Minn.: Llewellyn Publications, 1991.

Gregor, A. S. *Amulets, Talismans and Fetishes.* New York: Scribner, 1975.

SOURCES

Metaphysical gift stores are the place to look for these items.

Kabbala

Case, Paul Foster. *The Book of Tokens.* Los Angeles: Builders of the Adytum, 1989.

Case, Paul Foster. *The Tarot.* Los Angeles: Builders of the Adytum, 1990.

Fortune, Dion. *The Cosmic Doctrine.* London: Aquarian Press, 1966.

Fortune, Dion. *The Mystical Qabalah.* York Beach, Maine: Samuel Weiser, 1984.

Goodwin, David. *Cabalistic Encyclopedia.* St. Paul, Minn.: Llewellyn Publications, 1994.

Halevi, Z'ev ben Shimon. *Kabbalah.* London: Thames & Hudson, 1979.

Regardie, Israel. *The Complete Golden Dawn System of Magic.* Phoenix, Ariz.: New Falcon Publishers, 1984.

Scholem, Gersham. *Kabbalah.* New York: Penguin, 1974.

Townley, Kevin. *The Cube of Space.* Boulder, Colo.: Archive Press, 1993.

Astronomy

Bakich, Michael. *The Cambridge Guide to the Constellations.* Cambridge, England: Cambridge University Press, 1995.

Chartrand, Mark. *National Audubon Society Field Guide to the Night Sky.* New York: Chanticleer Press, 1991.

Dickenson, Terence. *The Universe and Beyond.* Willowdale, Canada: Firefly Books, 1999.

Ferris, Timothy. *The Whole Shebang.* New York: Simon & Schuster, 1997.

Mechler, Gary. *Galaxies and Other Deep-Sky Objects.* New York: National Audubon Society, Chanticleer Press, 1995.

Sky and Telescope magazine

Astronomy magazine

SOURCES

www.skypub.com

www.fourmilab.ch/yoursky/catalogues/starname

www.nasa.gov

www.science.msfc.nasa.gov

Sky Lore

Allen, Richard Hinckley. *Star Names, Their Lore and Meaning.* New York: Dover, 1963.

Brady, Bernadette. *Brady's Book of Fixed Stars.* York Beach, Maine: Samuel Weiser, 1998.

Krupp, E. C. *Beyond the Blue Horizon.* Oxford, England: Oxford University Press, 1991.

Miller-Mignone, Alex. *The Black Hole Book.* Draconic Publishers, 1995.

Rigor, Joseph. *The Power of the Fixed Stars.* Hammond, Ind.: 1979.

Robson, Vivian. *The Fixed Stars and Constellations in Astrology.* London: C. Palmer, 1931.

Sedgwick, Philip. *The Astrology of Deep Space.* Rochester, Mich.: See-It Publishing, 1984.